M000275391

Learn To...

Configure static routes	**Chapter 6**
Configure Routing Information Protocol (RIP)	**Chapter 6**
Configure Interior Gateway Routing Protocol (IGRP)	**Chapter 6**
Configure RIPv2	**Chapter 6**
Configure Open Shortest Path First (OSPF)	**Chapter 7**
Configure NetWare Link Services Protocol (NLSP)	**Chapter 7**
Configure Integrated Intermediate System to Intermediate System (IS-IS)	**Chapter 7**
Configure Enhanced IGRP for IP	**Chapter 8**
Configure Enhanced IGRP for IPX	**Chapter 8**
Configure Enhanced IGRP for AppleTalk	**Chapter 8**
Use Cisco's context-sensitive help	**Chapter 9**
Issue configuration commands to a Cisco router	**Chapter 9**
Upgrade your Internetwork Operating System (IOS)	**Chapter 9**
Design an IP subnet scheme	**Chapter 10**
Configure advanced TCP/IP properties	**Chapter 10**
Use Dynamic Host Configuration Protocol (DHCP) in a routed environment	**Chapter 10**

Cisco® Routers

24seven™

Andrew Hamilton
John Mistichelli
with Bryant G. Tow

SYBEX®

San Francisco Paris Düsseldorf Soest London

Associate Publishers: Guy Hart-Davis, Neil Edde
Contracts and Licensing Manager: Kristine O'Callaghan
Acquisitions & Developmental Editors: Brenda Frink, Maureen Adams
Editors: Linda Good, James A. Compton, Malka Geffen, Tracy Brown
Production Editor: Leslie Higbee Light
Technical Editors: James D. Taylor, Dana Gelinas
Book Designer: Bill Gibson
Graphic Illustrator: Eric Houts, Epic
Electronic Publishing Specialist: Adrian Woolhouse
Proofreaders: Laurie O'Connell, Dave Nash, Nelson Kim, Alison Moncrieff, Laura Schattschneider
Indexer: Matthew Spence
Cover Designer: Ingalls + Associates
Cover Illustrator/Photographer: Ingalls + Associates

Library of Congress Card Number: 00-102895

ISBN: 0-7821-2646-4

Manufactured in the United States of America

10 9 8 7 6 5 4 3 2 1

This book is dedicated to my parents, Gordon and Nancy Hamilton.
Without your love, support, and sacrifices I would not be where I am today.

Love, Andrew

To my wife, Noel, and children, Johnny and Alyssa.

John

Acknowledgments

First I would like to thank all the people at Sybex: Maureen Adams, for giving me the chance to work on this project and helping with the initial outline; Brenda Frink, for being a great development editor, keeping me motivated, and always insisting on case studies; Linda Good, for being a great editor (I still don't understand how you were able to consistently decipher what I was trying to say and turn it into clear, readable text; good luck in your new job). Thanks to Jim Compton for stepping into a difficult situation and doing a great job; you really made the transitions between editors relatively easy. Thanks to my technical editor, Jim Taylor, who always kept me on my toes and whose numerous insights have made this a much better book. Thanks to my coauthor, John Mistichelli—there is no way I could have written this without you. I also need to thank Bryant Tow for stepping in and helping us finish the book on a very aggressive writing schedule. Finally, I would like to thank Leslie Higbee Light and the rest of the people who were instrumental in pulling this book together. I really appreciate it.

I would like to thank my family for their support throughout this project and in life. Thanks Mom, Dad, Nate, Zach, and Ethan. I love you guys. I would also like to thank my two dogs, Roger and Norman, who were always willing to go outside and play fetch whenever I was fed up with writing.

Thanks to Dana Gelinas for your initial help with the outline and for performing a second technical edit, and to Nancy diBenedetto for suggestions early on that made writing this book a lot easier. Special thanks to Chris Brenton, one of the smartest people I have ever met in this business, for all your help along the way. Thanks to Kathy Hickey for being one of the most amazing people I have ever met and a great friend. I would like to thank Matt Wilson for being a great friend and for his willingness to give me an honest opinion, Good luck to you and Kristen. Thanks to Chris, Greg, Ian, Weasel, Charlie, and Tim. Now that the book is done, I hope to see you guys more. I need to thank Jim Dwyer and Maureen Fortier; I never would have gotten here without your help.

I would like to thank some of the people at AlpineCSI for giving input, making suggestions, and just being cool: Steve Walker, a great friend and coworker; David Pinto; Kevin Tessier, for being a great boss and pal; Bob Medieros; Geoff Shaw; Phil Sointu; Charles Ahern; Ron Hallam; Jim Oliver; Kevin Smith; Liam Scanlan; Ted Shea (thanks for being a pal; if you teach me to kite surf, I might forget about the money you owe me); Tom Nee; the guys in the ARMOC; Jim Gallagher; Bob and Mike Sheehan; Paul Feener; Mark Lafleur; and Jay Roaf.

I would like to thanks all the guys at NEES: Linda, Mukasa, John, Kenny, Doug, Jim, Charlie, Rob, Jay, George, Malcolm, and Ed (may the elephants eat your snow). Finally I would like to thank Jessica Esposito for showing me that you have to take advantages of the opportunities life puts in front of you, M.M. for keeping me inspired (even though you don't know it), and Jennifer Hampton for being cool.

—A.G.H.

I sincerely thank my family and friends who were patient with me through this time-consuming process. Their love and patience have made my contribution to this project possible. I want them to understand that the time I have missed in their lives will be rewarded in the assistance this book provides to others in forwarding their careers, as so many have helped me.

I would further like to thank all the people at Sybex, particularly Brenda Frink, for having the patience and stamina to see this project through and for turning out a product we can all be proud of.

—B.G.T.

Contents at a Glance

Introduction . . . . *xviii*

Part 1   Up and Running   1

Chapter 1   A Brief Review of the OSI Model 3
Chapter 2   LAN and WAN Technologies 29
Chapter 3   Routed Protocols 63
Chapter 4   Network Design 89
Chapter 5   The Cisco Router Product Line 121

Part 2   Routing Protocols   143

Chapter 6   Distance-Vector Routing Protocols 145
Chapter 7   Link-State Routing Protocols 169
Chapter 8   EIGRP: A Hybrid Routing Protocol 191

Part 3   Router Configuration   213

Chapter 9   Configuring a Router: An Introduction 215
Chapter 10   Configuring and Troubleshooting TCP/IP 241
Chapter 11   Internet Packet Exchange (IPX) 271
Chapter 12   AppleTalk 295
Chapter 13   Configuring ISDN and Dial-on-Demand Routing (DDR) 317

Part 4   Optimization and Maintenance   339

Chapter 14   Traffic Prioritization and Queuing 341
Chapter 15   Securing the Environment 383
Chapter 16   Router Management 451
Chapter 17   Troubleshooting Tools 485
Chapter 18   Disaster Recovery 523
Chapter 19   Advanced Topics 547

Appendices   579

Appendix A   Password Recovery/Resetting 581
Appendix B   ICMP Types and Codes 585
Appendix C   Common Cable Pinouts 589

Index. *593*

Contents

Introduction . . . . *xviii*

Part 1   **Up and Running**   **1**

Chapter 1   **A Brief Review of the OSI Model** **3**

The Upper Layers 4

    Layer 7: The Application Layer 4

    Layer 6: The Presentation Layer 5

    Layer 5: The Session Layer 7

The Lower Layers 8

    Layer 4: The Transport Layer 8

    Connection-Oriented versus
        Non-Connection-Oriented Protocols 10

    Layer 3: The Network Layer 18

    Layer 2: The Data Link Layer 20

    Layer 1: The Physical Layer 23

Switching versus Routing 25

Chapter 2   **LAN and WAN Technologies** **29**

Local Area Network (LAN) Technologies 30

    Ethernet/IEEE 802.3 30

    Fast Ethernet 41

    Fast EtherChannel 46

    Token Ring 46

    Fiber Distributed Data Interface (FDDI) 52

    Gigabit Ethernet 55

Wide Area Network (WAN) Technologies 55

    Leased Lines 55

    Circuit-Switched Circuits 55

    Packet-Switched Circuits 56

    High-Level Data Link Control (HDLC) 56

    Point-to-Point Protocol (PPP) 57

Integrated Services Digital Network (ISDN) 60

Frame Relay 61

Chapter 3   **Routed Protocols** **63**

The Internet Suite of Protocols 63

Transmission Control Protocol (TCP) 64

User Datagram Protocol 67

Internet Protocol 67

The IP Address 69

Configuring IP 78

Name Resolution 78

Network Address Translation 79

Easy IP 82

Internet Packet eXchange (IPX) 82

IPX Packet Structure 83

IPX Addressing Structure 84

Configuring IPX 85

AppleTalk 86

Configuring AppleTalk 87

Chapter 4   **Network Design** **89**

Scalability 90

The Core Layer 91

The Distribution Layer 93

The Access Layer 93

Manageability 94

Out-of-Band Management 94

Connectivity 95

Route Summarization 95

Route Redistribution 98

Tunneling 101

Sizing 103

Communication Lines 103

Routers 105

24seven Design 112

Chapter 5   The Cisco Router Product Line **121**

High-End Routers 121

    Cisco 12000 GSR Series 122

    Cisco 7000 Series 122

Small/Medium Business Solutions 129

    800/900 ISDN Routers 129

    1400 DSL Routers 130

    1600 Modular Data Routers 131

    1700 Modular Access Routers 131

    2500 Fixed Configuration Data Routers 133

    2600 Modular Voice/Data Routers 134

    3600 Modular Voice/Data Routers 135

    MC3800 Multiservice Router 136

    4000 Modular Data Router 137

When to Use Which Model 139

Part 2   Routing Protocols   143

Chapter 6   Distance-Vector Routing Protocols **145**

Autonomous System 145

Classfull versus Classless 146

    Administrative Distance 148

    Routing Information Protocol (RIP) 148

Configuring RIP 149

    RIPv2 152

    Interior Gateway Routing Protocol (IGRP) 155

    Split Horizon 162

Chapter 7   Link-State Routing Protocols **169**

Open Shortest Path First (OSPF) 170

    OSPF Operation 170

    Maintaining Adjacencies 171

    OSPF Areas 173

    Configuring OSPF 174

    Verifying OSPF Operation 181

NetWare Link Services Protocol (NLSP). 183

  Configuring NLSP 184

  Verifying NLSP operation 186

Integrated Intermediate System to Intermediate System (IS-IS) . . . 187

  Configuring IS-IS 187

Chapter 8   EIGRP: A Hybrid Routing Protocol. **191**

Enhanced IGRP (EIGRP) 191

  EIGRP Operation: The DUAL Algorithm 193

Configuring EIGRP for IP 195

  Verifying IP EIGRP 197

EIGRP for IPX 204

EIGRP for AppleTalk 208

Part 3   Router Configuration   **213**

Chapter 9   Configuring a Router: An Introduction **215**

The Boot Sequence 216

Your Router and Its Many Modes 217

  ROM Monitor Mode 218

  Rxboot Mode 218

  User Exec Mode 218

  Privileged Exec Mode 219

  Config Mode 220

  Context-Sensitive Help in the Modes 221

Tools for Configuring Your Router 223

  Configuring a Router Using the Setup Script 223

  Configuring a Router Using TFTP 223

  Config Maker 225

  Command Line Interface 225

  Boot System Commands 226

Passwords 227

Configuration and the IOS 231

Backing Up the IOS 231

Updating the IOS. 232

Chapter 10   **Configuring and Troubleshooting TCP/IP.** **241**

Drawing Out the Logical Addressing of the Environment 241

If You Must Draw by Hand.... 242

Software Network Drawing Solutions 242

Cheater Chart. 244

Setting Up Your Routers 245

Verify That Everything Is Physically Connected First 245

Interface Descriptions 246

Point-to-Point Connectivity 248

Confirming Your Environment Is Working Properly 248

Useful Tools for Testing IP Connectivity 248

Useful Debug Commands for IP. 255

Debug IP Packet 257

Changing Your IP Addressing Scheme 260

Deciding on IP Addresses 260

Secondary IP Addresses 261

Setting Up a Simple Statically Routed Environment. 262

Why Use Static Routing? 262

Advanced Static Routing for Route Backup. 264

DHCP in a Routed Environment 266

Chapter 11   **Internet Packet Exchange (IPX)** **271**

IPX RIP 271

IPX SAP 272

Get Nearest Server (GNS) 273

Configuring IPX 274

Filtering SAPs 278

Creating a SAP Filter 278

Applying a SAP Filter 279

Verifying IPX Operation 280

The show ipx route Command 280

The show ipx interface Command 281

The show ipx traffic Command 283

The show ipx servers Command 284

The show ipx access-list Command. 285

Other show ipx Command 286

The ping ipx Command 286

The trace ipx Command 287

The debug ipx Commands 288

Chapter 12   AppleTalk **295**

Configuring AppleTalk 295

Required AppleTalk Configuration Activities. 296

Optional Configuration Activities 297

Debugging AppleTalk 312

Chapter 13   Configuring ISDN and Dial-on-Demand Routing (DDR) . . . **317**

ISDN Components 317

ISDN Reference Points 318

Basic Rate Interface (BRI) 319

Configuring BRI 319

Primary Rate Interface (PRI) 320

Configuring PRI 321

Dial-on-Demand Routing (DDR) 321

Configuring DDR 321

Optional DDR Commands 323

Dialer Profiles 326

Verifying DDR 329

Snapshot Routing 333

Configuring Snapshot Routing 333

Dial Backup 335

Configuring Dial Backup 335

| Part 4 | **Optimization and Maintenance** | **339** |

Chapter 14 | **Traffic Prioritization and Queuing** **341**

Traffic Prioritization 342

Types of Queuing 344

    Weighted Fair Queuing 345

    Priority Queuing 347

    Custom Queuing 351

Another Traffic Control Mechanism: Weighted Random
Early Detection (WRED) 356

Traffic Prioritization for Specific Protocols 360

    Frame Relay Traffic Shaping 360

    IPX Traffic Considerations 365

Chapter 15 | **Securing the Environment** **383**

Making Your Router a Bastion Host 384

    Console Port 384

    Telnet Access 385

    TACACS 387

    Other Router Access Methods 390

Access Lists 400

    Standard Access Lists 402

    Extended Access Lists 405

    Creating Security: A Stance with Access Lists 414

Virtual Private Networks 426

    VPN Configuration 429

    Address Translation 440

Chapter 16 | **Router Management** **451**

Syslog 452

    Buffered Logging 452

    Syslog Servers 455

Getting Router Health Information via the Command Line 457

SNMP and Other Network Management Protocols 463

    Looking at SNMP 464

Management Systems 469

    HP OpenView Network Node Manager 471

    CiscoWorks 473

    CiscoWorks 2000 CWSI Campus 475

    RMON 480

Chapter 17　**Troubleshooting Tools** **485**

Troubleshooting Philosophies 486

Basic Troubleshooting Tools 488

    Ping 488

    Traceroute 492

    The Address Resolution Protocol (ARP) 496

    Cisco Discovery Protocol (CDP). 497

Advanced Tools 499

    Debug Commands 499

    Protocol Analyzers 502

Troubleshooting Specific Elements of the Network 505

    Troubleshooting the Physical Layer. 505

    Troubleshooting the Telecommunication Line 510

    CSU/DSUs and Serial Lines 511

    Frame Relay. 513

Chapter 18　**Disaster Recovery** **523**

Planning for the Worst 523

Redundancy in Hardware 525

    Power Supplies 525

    7000 Series Redundancy 525

    12000 Series Redundant Gigabit Route Processor 525

Backing Up the Router Image and Configuration 526

    Backing Up the Router Image 526

    Backing Up the Router Configuration 528

Swapping Out a Router 530

    Replacing the Router Image 530

Catastrophic Software Failure 531

Replacing Router Configuration 533

Contacting Cisco Technical Assistance Center 537

Cisco Web Support 537

E-Mail Cisco TAC 538

Telephone Support 538

How TAC Works 540

Chapter 19 **Advanced Topics** **547**

Hot Standby Router Protocol (HSRP) 547

What Is HSRP? 547

Why Do I Need HSRP? 548

How Does HSRP Work? 548

HSRP Issues 553

ICMP Router Discovery Protocol (IRDP) 556

IRDP Functionality 556

IRDP Application 557

Advanced BGP Topics 559

BGP Communities 559

The Firewall Feature Set 564

Versions and Compatibility 564

Firewall Features 565

Intrusion Detection System (IDS) 574

Appendices   **579**

Appendix A **Password Recovery/Resetting** **581**

2000, 2500, 3000, 4000, 7000 and AGS Series Routers 581

1003, 4500, 3600, and 2600 Series Routers 583

Appendix B **ICMP Types and Codes** **585**

Appendix C **Common Cable Pinouts** **589**

Index *593*

Introduction

Every day that I work with routers and routing, I discover something new. It is a very exciting time to be working with this technology. Things are moving at a very rapid pace—network demands are increasing, more and more applications are chewing up more and more bandwidth, while at the same time the network is become critical to business processes. It is the router engineer who is responsible for making sure the network can keep up with the demands placed on it by growth. This makes the job of maintaining and designing networks both exciting and challenging.

Routers are one of the few areas in computing and IS where the information you learn today will not be outdated tomorrow. Since routing protocols are all standards-based, it does not matter if you are working with 3com, Lucent, or Cisco routers; most of the stuff works the same way. Cisco routers need to be able to work with the routers of other manufacturers. OSPF is still OSPF no matter whose equipment you are using to implement it. This allows you to build a base of skills upon which to develop more advanced knowledge. By contrast, consider how useful those hard-won DOS skills are today. Yes, DOS was important, and it taught you some things you still use today, but most of that knowledge is obsolete now. In routing, things still move fast and change, but you don't see the drastic changes you see with operating systems. Remember, no matter where you go in the computer industry, if you don't work every day to improve and advance your skills, you are not going to last very long.

The 24seven Challenge and the Cost of Downtime

Throughout this book we'll talk about the "24seven network." To understand why a network needs to be available 24 hours a day, seven days a week, we need to look at the cost of downtime.

With the network such an integral part of most businesses, all network downtime has a cost associated with it. The cost may be the result of lost productivity by employees, lost sales, or some other business-related metric. It's certainly true that cost-of-downtime calculations are easy to manipulate and are typically maximized for effect. Moreover, there are too many variables involved to calculate the exact cost accurately.

Nonetheless, what you need to remember is that downtime is expensive because it severely limits the ability of a business to perform. It is your job to protect the corporation as much as possible from experiencing down time. That's where this book comes in.

Since downtime is inherently expensive, as a network engineer you want to minimize your exposure to downtime at all costs. It was estimated that the denial-of-service attacks of February 2000 cost about $50 billion. While I am not a big fan of downtime cost calculations, this event was a vivid illustration of how integrated networks have become into our society and economy. This attack caused stock prices to fall and generated a great deal of revenue for network security experts.

We are living in a time when it is unacceptable for a network to be unavailable for any reason. It used to be that if the network went down, we just said "Oh, well," and things went on. Now it is a major event. This makes the job of network engineers much harder. Certain changes that once would have been made without a second thought now have to be scheduled weeks in advance and done at odd times. In fact, as I write this I have to get ready to go to a client at 2 AM on a Sunday morning to add a new piece of equipment to the network. The change is relatively simple and there should be no problem. However, this change will cause a recalculation of the network topology, which the client has identified as a potential danger. So the client has requested this change be done at a time when the impact of any outage will be minimal.

As more and more environments rely on their networks to be available 24 hours a day, seven days a week, the job of the network engineer becomes more and more challenging. Running a 24seven Cisco environment is not an easy task; but it is a goal you can attain with careful planning, hard work, and a thorough understanding of how your network should operate. We hope this book helps you tackle the immense task of trying to keep your Cisco-routed environment operational 24seven.

Who Should Read This Book

If you are responsible for administering and maintaining a Cisco router environment, this book is for you.

This book is aimed at the working professional who has an intermediate-to-advanced knowledge of Cisco routers. It assumes that you have some familiarity with most of the topics covered in the book. If you have no idea what a router is or does, this is probably not the book for you. In order to cover the material we wanted to cover, we have had to assume that the reader has some routing experience.

Nor is this the right book for someone who is just looking to pass the Cisco certification tests. Much of the information provided in certification guidebooks is of limited value for the day-to-day tasks involved in maintaining a network. Knowing how many subinterfaces a router can support, for example, is not particularly useful in the everyday world; but the question just might be on a test. What John Mistichelli, Bryant Tow, and I have tried to do is bring together the information we believe is needed to develop and maintain a 24seven Cisco environment and put it in this book.

We have aimed at the individual who has some experience working with Cisco routers in a real working environment and now wants to move to the next level of expertise—to become more efficient at their job responsibilities and to streamline the tasks of maintaining the network. If designed and taken care of properly, a Cisco router network needs very little intervention to stay up and running. We have tried to provide the information needed to get your network to a level where you can walk away from it for a few days and be confident that your pager will not go off every five minutes while you are away. Of course, this book provides the basic information about installing, configuring and maintaining Cisco routers. What we really want to do, though, is give you the information necessary to make your job easier so that you can have more time to pursue the pleasurable things in life.

How This Book Is Organized

This book has been designed so that you can either read it straight through from beginning to end or—more likely—pick and choose the chapters that focus on your immediate networking needs. We've divided the essential topics of Cisco router networking into 19 chapters, grouped into four parts.

Part 1: Up and Running

The first five chapters focus on the information needed in planning and growing a network. Most of this information is not Cisco-specific and is not tied to any particular routing software. The aim of Part 1 is to discuss the back-end topologies and design methodologies necessary in creating a 24seven environment.

Chapter 1: A Brief Review of the OSI Model

Although most network administrators should already be familiar with the OSI model, we begin the book with a review of this material in order to shore up a few essential concepts before we move into some more interesting and complicated topics.

Chapter 2: LAN and WAN Technologies

Chapter 2 outlines the various media types involved in carrying both LAN and WAN traffic, including Frame Relay, ATM, FDDI, and Gigabit Ethernet.

Chapter 3: Routed Protocols

Chapter 3 discusses the various protocols that are used to carry data throughout networks. You'll learn what TCP, UDP, IP, IPX, and AppleTalk actually do and how the elements of the TCP/IP protocol suite correspond to the layers of the OSI model.

Chapter 4: Network Design

Chapter 4 focuses on the design process, addressing the three major design considerations of scalability, manageability, and efficiency. You'll see how to design a fault-tolerant environment for 24seven network availability.

Chapter 5: The Cisco Router Product Line

Chapter 5 provides a quick tour of the Cisco router families, so that you can assess which models best meet the needs of your network, balancing cost and functionality.

Part 2: Routing Protocols

Part 2 discusses the various routing protocols used to determine the path that packets take through the network.

Chapter 6: Distance-Vector Protocols

Chapter 6 discusses the classfull IP protocols such as RIP version 1 and IGRP, and the classless IP protocols such as RIP version 2, as well as fundamental concepts such as autonomous systems, administrative distance, and the split horizon technique.

Chapter 7: Link-State Routing Protocols

Chapter 7 discusses the link-state protocols supported by Cisco—OSPF, NLSP, and IS-IS—including how they work and how to configure them.

Chapter 8: EIGRP: a Hybrid Protocol

Chapter 8 discusses the hybrid protocol EIGRP, showing how to configure it in combination with IP, IPX, and AppleTalk.

Part 3: Router Configuration

The chapters in this part of the book show how to configure the most important types of network environments: TCP/IP, IPX, AppleTalk, and ISDN.

Chapter 9: Configuring a Router: An Introduction

Chapter 9 covers the basics of working with the command line interface and the router's boot sequence. The various ways to configure a router are covered, as well as how to upgrade a router's flash memory. Most of this material should be review for the reader.

Chapter 10: Configuring and Troubleshooting TCP/IP

Chapter 10 covers the various aspects of configuring and maintaining a TCP/IP environment. You'll learn how to diagram the logical addressing of your network, set up your routers, and use the most important debugging commands.

Chapter 11: Internet Packet Exchange (IPX)

Chapter 11 discusses some advanced topics related to IPX routing and to verifying IPX activity, including IPX RIP, IPX SAP, and GNS, as well as configuring and debugging IPX.

Chapter 12: AppleTalk

Chapter 12 shows how to configure and maintain an AppleTalk environment. Addressing concerns, the configuration of routing protocols, and various other topics are discussed.

Chapter 13: Configuring ISDN and Dial-on-Demand Routing (DDR)

Chapter 13 discusses the various aspects of configuring ISDN and dial backup routing. Both the new dial-on-demand routing methods and the legacy method are discussed. Among other topics, you'll learn about traffic control across dial lines.

Part 4: Optimization and Maintenance

The last six chapters cover a range of advanced topics related to keeping your network operating efficiently.

Chapter 14: Traffic Prioritization and Queuing

Chapter 14 discusses the various queuing techniques supported by Cisco routers, looking at the advantages and drawbacks of each type. Underlying all of the techniques discussed is the goal of maintaining an acceptable quality of service for network users.

Chapter 15: Securing Your Environment

Chapter 15 discusses the various security concerns related to routing. You'll learn how to make a router a bastion host, use access lists and packet filtering, and implement virtual private networks (VPNs).

Chapter 16: Router Management

Chapter 16 discusses how to manage and maintain a large network effectively. Tools for fault isolation, modeling, and baselining the network are discussed, as well as things you should look for on a day-to-day basis to ensure that your network is running properly.

Chapter 17: Troubleshooting Tools

Chapter 17 discusses the various troubleshooting methodologies as well as the tools necessary to troubleshoot network problems effectively. Both LAN and WAN troubleshooting techniques are discussed.

Chapter 18: Disaster Recovery

Chapter 18 discusses how to prepare for the events we hope will never happen. At some point in your career you will be faced with a network disaster; the goal of this chapter is to help you to be prepared for that eventuality.

Chapter 19: Advanced Topics

Chapter 19 brings together a number of advanced topics that do not necessarily fit nicely into categories—the Hot Standby Router Protocol (HSRP), some advanced Border Gateway Protocol (BGP) issues, and the Firewall feature set.

Appendices

This book's three appendices include some important reference material: how to recover (that is, replace) a lost password, ICMP types and codes, and pinouts for common cable types.

...and Beyond

Be sure to check the Sybex Web site (`www.sybex.com`) for bonus *Cisco Routers 24seven* materials, including tables of well-known port assignments and commonly encountered register SAPs, and possible updates.

—Andrew G. Hamilton

Part 1

Up and Running

Topics Covered

- An overview of the OSI model
- The three primary OSI layers
- LAN and WAN
- IP and IPX
- Network design
- Router basics

1

A Brief Review of the OSI Model

We realize our readers will be familiar with the OSI model. However, different people have defined the various layers differently, and so we would like to present the model here in review. Throughout this book, when we discuss the layers of the OSI model it will be according to the definitions set out in this chapter.

Sending data from one system to another in today's network environments is a very complicated task. It would be almost impossible to describe without some mechanism to break the process down into smaller, more manageable tasks. This is where the OSI model comes in. Developed in 1983 by the International Standard Organization (ISO), the OSI model describes a method for sending data between two systems. The model works on a layered approach, where each layer is responsible for performing certain functions toward the goal of allowing the two systems to communicate.

Without some kind of standard in place, getting two networked devices to talk to each other would be an extremely difficult task. This is because in a typical network you have hardware from many different manufacturers. You have hubs, switches, routers, NIC cards, and computers, just to name a few. All of these devices have to agree on a way to send data in order for them to be able to talk to each other. By defining a standard, the OSI model allows us to use multiple vendors in our environment. Thus, we can have Cisco routers and 3Com hubs connecting Compaq computers. Manufacturers whose products adhere to the OSI model should be able to connect their products to those of any other manufacturer whose products also adhere to the OSI model.

As shown in Figure 1.1, the OSI model is composed of seven distinct layers, each with their own functions. By breaking down the tasks involved in network communications, the model makes writing software much easier. Developers need only interface with the layer in which they are interested; they can assume that if they interface properly with that layer, their data will be transferred properly.

Figure 1.1   The seven layers of the OSI model

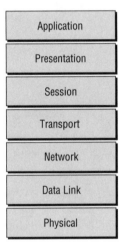

The Upper Layers

Three layers comprise the upper layers of the OSI model:

- The Application layer
- The Presentation layer
- The Session layer

Layer 7: The Application Layer

The Application layer is the highest layer of the OSI model. The Application layer is responsible for supporting the communication components of an application. Programs that use the Application layer are known as *application processes*. It is possible for a user program to interface directly with the Presentation layer; however, to do this, the program must include protocol modules to initialize communication with peer Application Processes, establish appropriate Presentation contexts, and transfer files or messages. Alternately, user-level processes may include available modules which support commonly required application-related services, such as file transfer, e-mail, or Novell file and print services. These modules provide a standard method of passing data to the Presentation layer. User-level processes are actually gateways to the Presentation layer. Using these available modules constitutes using the Application layer of the OSI model. It is typically easier to use these modules than to worry about interfacing properly with the Presentation layer.

NOTE Word processors and other such user-level programs do not reside at the Application level, but instead interface with it when they need network services such as file transfer.

Layer 6: The Presentation Layer

Originally the Presentation layer was conceived to allow ASCII machines to talk to EBCDIC machines. Later it was seen as a way to let visually-oriented programs, such as text editors, work with different terminal types. Today the role of the Presentation layer has been significantly expanded. It is now responsible for handling all issues related to the representation of transmitted data. These issues include compression, encryption, and conversion.

Different machines have different ways of representing data internally, so conversions are required to ensure that different computers can understand each other. The job of the Presentation layer is to take the internally formatted data from the sending machine, convert it into a suitable bit stream for transmission, and then decode it to a format the receiving machine can understand on the other end.

The role of the Presentation layer cannot be overstated. Although one might assume that a computer is a computer is a computer, and that internal data representation would therefore be the same from computer to computer, this is far from the case. IBM mainframes use the EBCDIC character set, while almost all other computers use the ASCII character set. This means that the Presentation layer is responsible for converting ASCII to EBCDIC, or vice-versa. In this case, the Presentation layer can be thought of as an interpreter who understands both character sets and is responsible for making sure both computers get information in a format they can understand.

Little Endian and Big Endian

Another example of differing internal data representations is the difference between *little-endian* and *big-endian*. The terms *little-endian* and *big-endian* refer to which value in a sequence is considered the most significant. A big-endian system will store the most significant chunk of the sequence first, in the lowest storage address. A little-endian system will store the most significant chunk of the sequence last, in the highest storage address.

For example, if you were to store the hexadecimal value 3DF2, which requires 2 bytes of storage, on a big-endian system, it would be stored as 3DF2, with 3D stored at address 1000 and F2 stored at address 1001. On a little-endian computer, exactly the opposite would be true. F2 would be in storage address 1000 and 3D would be at storage address 1001; so the value would effectively be stored as F23D in memory. Obviously, if a little-endian and a big-endian computer were to try to communicate without proper conversion it would not work out too well: One machine would be transmitting 3DF2, and the other would be receiving F23D.

IBM 370s, most RISC-based computers, and Motorola processors all use the big-endian approach, which seems to make more sense for those of us who read from left to right. All Intel processors, such as the Pentium III and DEC Alphas, use the little-endian approach, which at first glance seems to be backward. However, there are merits to each approach: Certain mathematical operations may be simpler to implement on a little-endian system because the most significant bits are stored last. Since we are not talking about processor design, however, we only need to know that the big-endian to little-endian conversion, if needed, occurs at the Presentation layer.

Data Compression and Encryption

All other functions of the Presentation layer are really just extensions of its role as a translator. These functions include data compression and encryption. Both of the functions can be viewed as logical extensions of translation services of the Presentation layer.

Compression   A 32-bit integer can easily be sent as 4 bytes across the network. However, 95 percent of all integers transmitted are between 0 and 250. Because we can represent up to 255 in one byte, it is possible to send these integers as a single unsigned byte and use the code 255 to signify that a true 32-bit integer follows. While this does mean that it will require an expenditure of 5 bytes to send a true 32-bit integer, you are only doing this about 5 percent of the time; the other 95 percent of the time you are *saving* 3 bytes. There are numerous other ways to compress data; the above is just a simple example of what can be done at the Presentation layer to decrease the amount of data that gets put on the network.

Encryption   Encryption is important because, as networks have grown, and with the mass acceptance of the Internet, it is more and more difficult to keep data from prying eyes. There are a lot of utilities out there that will allow packet capture, so it is more important than ever to have data encrypted. With encryption, only those who should rightfully be receiving the data can read it. Encryption will be covered in more detail in the Security section. What is important for now is to realize that encryption occurs at the Presentation level.

Layer 5: The Session Layer

The primary function of the Session layer is to allow users to establish connections or sessions, and to transfer data over those sessions or connections in an orderly manner. There are two types of service provided by the Session layer: administrative and dialog.

The *administrative service* handles the establishment and tear-down of a connection between two Presentation entities. The administrative service also determines the type of connection established. For example, a connection might be duplex or half-duplex. Sessions are established when one Application process requests access to another Application process. After the session is established, dialog services are used to control and supervise the actual data transfer.

Examples of Session-layer protocols are:

- Digital Network Architecture, Session Control Protocol (DNA SCP), which is DECnet's Session-layer protocol
- AppleTalk Session Protocol (ASP), which establishes and maintains sessions between an AppleTalk client and server
- Structured Query Language (SQL), a database language developed by IBM as a way to give users an easier way to specify the information they want on local and remote systems
- Remote Procedure Call (RPC), which allows clients to execute commands on servers
- Network File System (NFS), which allows file systems on remote servers to be mounted as if they were local to clients

Together, the Session, Presentation, and Application layers are often referred to as the upper layers. Their responsibility for the most part is with setting up the interactions for user-level applications; they do not have a lot to do with what we will be discussing for the remainder of the book. Still, it is vitally important to understand how the OSI model is supposed to function as a whole. Now, however, we will turn our attention to the lower four layers, which are much more relevant to how routing and routers work.

The Lower Layers

The Transport, Network, Data Link, and Physical layers make up what are commonly known as the *lower layers* of the OSI model. These are the layers with which we will deal primarily throughout the remainder of the book.

Layer 4: The Transport Layer

The Transport layer is the highest layer that is directly associated with the transport of data through the network. The Transport layer defines end-to-end connectivity between host applications. The basic functions of the Transport layer are as follows:

Establish end-to-end operations   Provides end-to-end transport services, which constitute logical connections between the sending and receiving hosts.

Segment upper-layer applications   Allows multiple applications to use the network simultaneously, as it segments data from multiple upper-layer applications into the same data stream for transport on the network.

Send segments from one host to another   Uses checksum calculations and built-in–flow-control mechanisms to ensure the integrity of segmented data.

Ensure data reliability   Can request that the receiving host acknowledge that it is actually receiving the data (this is optional, depending on whether a connection-oriented or connection-less protocol is in use).

There are five Transport-layer protocol classes that define how robust and complex a protocol is. These classes are shown in Table 1.1. The three network types that go with the protocol classes are shown in Table 1.2.

Table 1.1   The Transport-Layer Protocol Classes

Protocol Class	Network Type	Name
0	A	Simple Class
1	B	Basic Error-Recovery Class
2	A	Multiplexing Class
3	B	Error-Recovery and Multiplexing Class
4	C	Error-Detection and Recovery Class

Table 1.2   The Three Network Types Associated with the Transport- Layer Protocol Classes

Network type	Description
A	Flawless error-free service; no N-RESETS
B	Perfect packet delivery, but N-RESETS
C	Unreliable service, lost and duplicate packets, and N-RESETS

N-RESETS are transport layer elements used to report catastrophic network failures, such as the loss of the medium, or the crash of the sending or receiving host.

Now, let's take a look at the information in these two tables.

Protocol Class 0

Protocol class 0 (zero) is the simplest class, because it assumes a flawless type-A network. Therefore, it does not have to worry about any type of sequencing or error correction.

Protocol Class 1

Protocol class 1 (one) is the same as class 0, except it adds the ability to recover from N-RESETS. This means the two transport entities communicating need to be able to resynchronize the connection should they lose contact with each other. To do this, they need to keep track of sequence numbers.

Protocol Class 2

Protocol class 2 (two) assumes the same type-A flawless network as does class zero, but adds the ability to multiplex. This means that multiple conversations can be carried on at the same time over a single network connection. Multiplexing will be discussed in more detail later in this chapter.

Protocol Class 3

Protocol class 3 (three) takes the features of classes 1 and 2 and combines them. This enables multiplexing and recovery from N-RESETS. Basically, all a class 3 protocol really is is a class 2 multiplexing protocol with the ability to recover from N-RESETS. This means that with a class 3 protocol, you can multiplex on a type-B network. Class 3 protocols also use explicit flow control to keep the sending host from flooding the buffers of the receiving host.

Protocol Class 4

Protocol class 4 (four) pretty much does it all. It allows for recovery from N-RESETS, lost, garbled, or duplicate packets, and anything else you can think of. Class 4 *assumes* that there will be problems in the network and is thus designed to deal with them. Having to deal with all of these possible network problems in addition to allowing for multiplexing makes class 4 protocols significantly more complex. For most applications, class 4 protocols are over-engineered. Unless you absolutely have to guarantee that every single packet gets there, you probably do not need a class 4 protocol. Perhaps a live stock-ticker feed constantly pushing out transactions might use a class 4 protocol.

How Do I Know What Type and Class to Use?

What class of network and what type of protocol is used are more questions of what is acceptable for a particular network than of how reliable the network actually is. A network that occasionally drops a few packets may be considered a type A network and might require only a class 0 protocol if all we want to do is run e-mail across it. However, if the same network were used by NASA for telemetry data, it would be considered a type C network, and a class 4 protocol would be used. This is because, as you will recall, a type C network and a class 4 protocol both allow for unreliable service and potential network problems—allowances that are crucial for the type of work NASA performs. So, the question of what type of protocol is used comes down to the importance of the application that this protocol supports. You must ask yourself, "Can this application afford to miss a packet or two?"

Fortunately for the scope of this book, we really do not need to know what class of protocol is being used. It will be enough to be able to differentiate between connection-oriented and non-connection–oriented protocols.

Connection-Oriented versus Non-Connection-Oriented Protocols

There are two major types of protocols: connection-oriented and non-connection-oriented. Non-connection-oriented protocols are simpler to understand than are connection-oriented protocols.

> **Non-connection-oriented protocol**   Assumes that the correct receiving host will get data that has been passed out onto the network by the sending host. However, there is never any guarantee that the correct host ever receives the information. A non-connection-oriented protocol works much like e-mail. I can send you a message, but I never really know whether you will get it or read it.

Connection-oriented protocol   Requires that the receiving host send back some sort of acknowledgment to say that the data was received. This works much like a phone call or a face-to-face conversation: If I don't nod my head every so often or make some kind of noise to acknowledge that I am listening to you, you will assume that I am not paying any attention, and you will start to repeat yourself until you get completely fed up with me and give up. A connection-oriented session or communication must be established.

For example, TCP (Transmission Control Protocol) is a connection-oriented protocol that uses a three-way handshake to establish a connection before data is sent. This handshake is accomplished by using the SYN and ACK bits in the header of TCP segments, as shown in Figure 1.2.

Figure 1.2   TCP three-way handshake

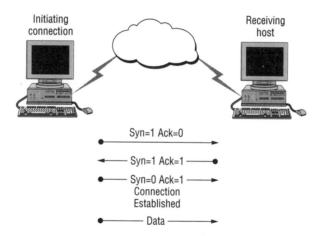

In order to establish a connection, the host that wishes to initiate the connection sends a TCP segment, with SYN set to 1 and ACK set to 0, to the host with which it wishes to communicate. The receiving host then sends back a TCP segment with SYN and ACK both set to 1 to tell the sending host it is ready to transfer data. The host that wished to send then replies to this segment with SYN set to 0 and ACK set to 1. The three-way handshake is now complete, and data transfer can begin.

Once data transfer has begun, congestion can arise. There are many causes for congestion. Someone might have a really fast computer that can generate traffic faster than the network can send it. Perhaps multiple computers are sending data through the same gateway simultaneously, or maybe the receiving host just cannot process data as fast as the sending host can get it through the network. For a short length of time, this excessive data is stored in memory buffers at the location of the congestion; but eventually these buffers fill and we need a way to slow down the data rate to prevent the loss of data. This is where flow control and *windowing* (discussed in the next section) come in.

When the receiving host realizes that it is receiving datagrams too quickly, a Transport layer function kicks in that allows the receiver to tell the sender to stop, as shown in Figure 1.3. This break in sending allows the receiver to process the datagrams that have been stored in its buffer. Once this processing is complete, the function tells the sender to go ahead and continue. This process continues until all the data has been sent.

Figure 1.3   Data flow control

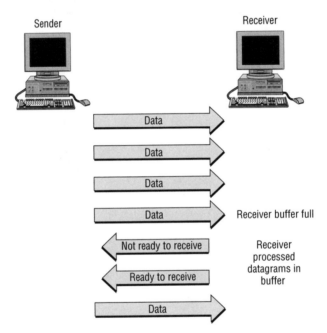

Windowing

Windowing is a method used to control the amount of data transferred between two hosts. The most basic connection-oriented protocols require that data segments be received in the same order in which they were sent. If every single one of these data segments must be acknowledged, efficiency will be very low. This is because the sender will have to wait until the receiving station has received the data and generated the acknowledgment, and the acknowledgment has traveled back through the network, before it can send its next segment. Although this kind of overhead is unavoidable in a connection-oriented communications protocol, where acknowledgments are necessary to ensure that data is received properly, windowing can reduce the amount of overhead substantially.

Within the transport header is a field called the Windowing field, which sets the window size. Right now we really don't need to concern ourselves with all the fields in the transport header; if you happen to be very interested in them, you should check out *Internetworking with TCP/IP Vol. I: Principles, Protocols, and Architecture* by Douglas Comer (Prentice-Hall, 3rd ed. 1995).

What the Windowing field does is set the window size for the sending host. An example is shown in Figure 1.4, where the window size is set to 1. This number basically represents the number of segments the sending host is allowed to send before it has to wait for an acknowledgment. When the window size is set to 0, the sending host must stop to allow the receiver to catch up.

Figure 1.4   When the window size is set to one, the sending host must wait for an acknowledgement after it sends each segment before it can send the next segment.

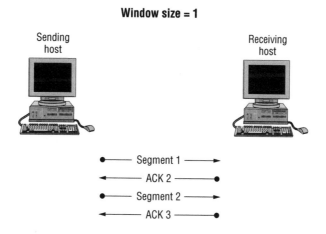

Window size = 1

When the window size is equal to 1, the sending host must wait for an acknowledgment for each segment it sends. Once the receiving host gets the segment, it responds with an ACK for the next segment. For example, if segment 5 had just been received, the response would be ACK 6. Translation: "I have received Segment 5, now send me segment 6." This means that for every segment there is a corresponding acknowledgment, so that 50 percent of the segments traveling between hosts are acknowledgments. Obviously this is not very efficient. In order to increase efficiency, we need to increase the window size. We've done so in Figure 1.5.

Figure 1.5   Communication with the window size set to 4

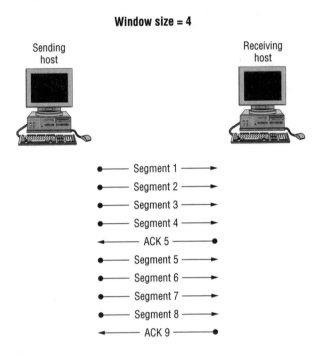

Window size = 4

With the window size set to 4, your sending host is allowed to send out four segments before it receives an acknowledgment. This means you only get one acknowledgment for every four segments. Obviously this involves considerably less overhead than the above example, where the window size was 1. As long as there are no errors, this works well.

Positive Acknowledgment with Retransmission   When the sending host sends out a segment, it sets a timer. If this timer expires before it receives the acknowledgment, it will resend the data under the assumption that it never made it there the first time. Depending on the protocol involved, the whole sequence may or may not have to be repeated. However, if only one segment out of a sequence is lost, it is possible to get just the lost segment resent. This system of resending just the lost segments is an extension of windowing known as *positive acknowledgment with retransmission.*

If the sender keeps track of all the segments it has sent until it receives an acknowledgment for them, then it is possible for the sender and receiver to coordinate which segments need to be resent and which do not.

Figure 1.6 demonstrates positive acknowledgment with retransmission at work. In the diagram, the first four segments are received correctly and acknowledged with ACK 5, which means the receiving host is asking for segment 5. Because the window size is 4, the sender now sends segments 5, 6, 7, and 8. The receiving host sends back ACK 6, which means it wants segment 6 resent. Since the sending host knows it sent 5,6,7, and 8, it sees the ACK 6 and realizes that something happened to segment 6 along the way. It resends segment 6. Once segment 6 is received, the receiving host sends ACK 9, which means that it has correctly received segments 5, 6, 7, and 8 and is now ready to receive 9, 10, 11, and 12.

Whether the entire window or simply an individual segment needs to be resent depends on the protocol. Different protocols—even those within the same class—have different criteria for resending data. Furthermore, many variables come into play when deciding on a window size, such as frequency of lost segments and how much data needs to be resent to recover from a lost segment, etc. Fortunately, when dealing with Cisco routers, we really don't need to know too much about how the window size is actually decided upon.

Figure 1.6 The receiving host misses segment 6 and needs to have it resent.

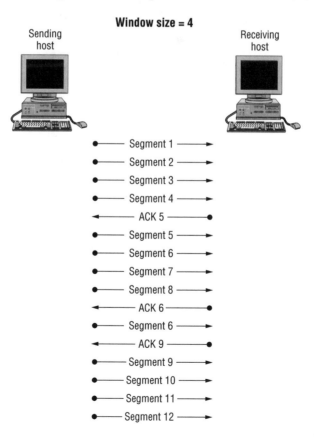

Multiplexing

Multiplexing is the capability for multiple applications to share the same transport connection. This is done at the segment level. Each application is allowed to send segments on a first-come–first-serve basis. The segments involved could be intended for the same or different hosts. This allows you to run multiple network applications on the same host at the same time. For example, I could Telnet to one device, FTP to another and mount an NFS drive to a third.

TCP uses port numbers to multiplex from the transport layer up to the application layer. These port numbers are listed in RFC 1700. There are two different port number ranges: Ports 1–1023 are in a category called the *well-known ports* and are generally assigned to specific services, such as Telnet or FTP. Ports 1024–65,535 are not assigned to any particular service. Typically, one side of the communication will be using one of the well-known ports (for example, the Telnet server), and the other side will be using a port above 1024. For example, a Telnet conversation might look like the one in the following graphic:

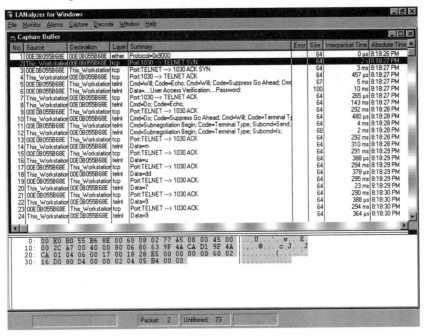

In this graphic, lines 2–4 show the TCP three-way handshake setting up the connection. We can see that this_workstation has chosen to use port 1030 to establish the connection, while the other device, 00E0B055B68E (which happens to be a router) is using the Telnet port, which is port 23. If we were to Telnet again, this_workstation would choose another port above 1024, while the router would still be using port 23, the well-registered Telnet port. It is also interesting to note that in the graphic, we can actually see the password that was used to log in to the router. The password is mudd799, which was passed as clear text across the LAN link.

It is important to understand that a client connects to a system using a well-known port number and the system will use a port above 1024 to respond. Figure 1.7 shows what a Telnet session might look like. The Telnet client sends a request to port 23 on the server with a source port of 1031. When the server replies, it will use port 23 as it source port and will reply back to port 1031, which is the port the client used to establish the connection in the first place.

Figure 1.7   A client system accessing Telnet services on port 23. The client is using port 1031 as its source port.

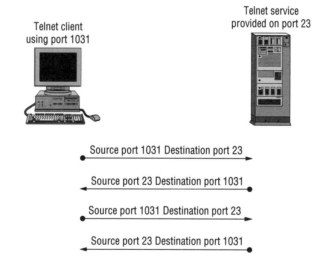

Telnet client
using port 1031

Telnet service
provided on port 23

Source port 1031 Destination port 23

Source port 23 Destination port 1031

Source port 1031 Destination port 23

Source port 23 Destination port 1031

It is almost impossible to predict from which port a client machine will try to connect to a well-known port. This concept will become important when we cover access lists later in the book.

A few of the well-known port numbers are shown in Table 1.3.

Table 1.3 Well-known Port Numbers

Port	Service
20	FTP data
21	FTP control
23	Telnet
25	SMTP
67	DHCP server
68	DHCP client
69	TFTP
80	HTTP
123	NTP
161	SNMP
162	SNMP trap

Layer 3: The Network Layer

The primary concern of the Network layer is getting data all the way from the source to the destination. The Network layer is the first layer we have looked at that actually has any real effect on the physical network. The Network layer is in a unique position because it provides the interface between user machines and the actual network. The layers above the Network layer (Transport, Session, Presentation, and Application) typically run on the user's machine. Meanwhile, the Network layer and the two layers below it (Data link and Physical), are actually responsible for controlling the network.

The functions implemented at the Network layer include routing, switching, flow control, data sequencing, and error recovery. Some of these functions may seem to duplicate those of the Transport layer, but, in fact, they do not. The Network layer's functions are concerned with end-to-end network connections, possibly spanning multiple network links. The Transport layer is not concerned with the intermediary links and devices like the Network layer is.

While we discussed flow control at the Transport layer, that type of flow control was concerned with the ability of the sending and receiving hosts to keep up with each other. Flow control at the Network layer is concerned not with the two end stations, but instead with the links and devices that the conversation is traversing. If too many packets are present at any one link at any given time, those packetss will interfere with each other, causing congestion errors and bottlenecks. Flow control at the Network layer is used to prevent those types of conditions from occurring, by trying to provide fair, orderly, and efficient access to network links.

The most important function of the Network layer is route determination, as illustrated in Figure 1.8. Without route determination, everything else the Network layer does would be useless.

Figure 1.8   The Network layer is responsible for selecting the best path through the network.

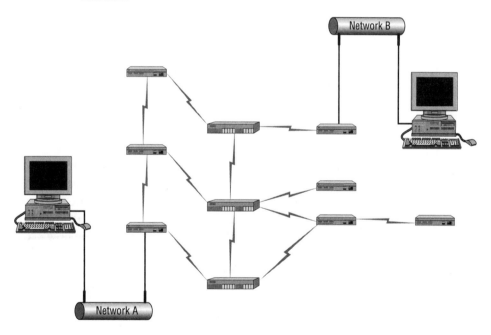

According to Figure 1.8, the Network layer determines the path that data will take to travel between a host on network A and a host on network B. What path is actually used depends on what routing protocols are used within the network. In an RIP network, the path may not be the same as one in an OSPF or EIGRP network. In fact, it is possible that each packet within the same conversation may take different paths to reach the same destination. All of this will be discussed in more depth as we move through the book and begin to look at how routers and routing protocols function.

Layer 2: The Data Link Layer

The Data Link layer is the layer that is responsible for moving data in and out across the physical network media. The layer is shown in Figure 1.9. There are two sub-layers located within the Data Link layer:

- The Logical Link Control (LLC) layer
- The Media Access Control (MAC) layer

Figure 1.9   The Data Link layer and its sub-layers

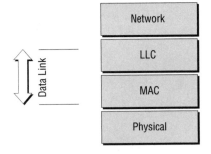

The Data Link layer is divided in this way so that the LLC does not have to be concerned with the specific LAN access method. The MAC deals with how to interface the physical media, while the LLC handles the interface to the Network layer. The LLC is responsible for assembly and disassembly of frames, addressing, address recognition, and CRC calculation and validation, while the MAC layer is responsible for defining how access is gained to the shared network media. This is dependent upon the type of network, while the LLC is protocol independent.

The Data Link layer as a whole is concerned with dividing output data into frames for transmission on the physical link, as shown in Figure 1.10. The Data Link layer provides framing, flow control, and error detection and correction. The Data Link layer concerns itself only with the current physical link.

Figure 1.10   The Data Link layer concerns itself with only one link at a time.

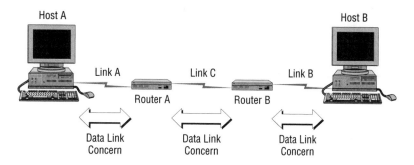

Figure 1.11 demonstrates that there are actually separate Data Link layer instances involved with the transfer of data from host A to B. There is data link functionality on links A, B and C. Each link has it own data link functionality to control data across the link.

While the Network layer would be concerned with flow for the whole path between host A and host B across links A, B, and C, the Data Link layer is only concerned with one link at a time. Host A will send out a frame, which is received by router A. Router A then strips off the Data Link layer header and reads the network address to figure out where to send the frame. In this way, the Data Link layer protocols of host A talk to the router until the data is transferred. Then router A talks to router B, and router B talks to host B.

According to the example in Figure 1.11, when host A is sending to host B, data flows down through the seven layers until it reaches the Data Link layer of host A. There it is chopped up into frames to be transmitted on the wire. Host A has realized that the network address of host B is different than its own, so it sends the data to router A. These frames are received by router A, which strips off the Data Link layer so it can read the Network-layer address. From the Network-layer address, router A determines where to send the packet. If router A realizes that the Network-layer address does not match that of any of its interfaces, it consults its routing table to determine where it has to send the packets. In our example, it has to send them to router B.

Figure 1.11 Where a device sits in the communication path will determine what layers of the OSI model are used.

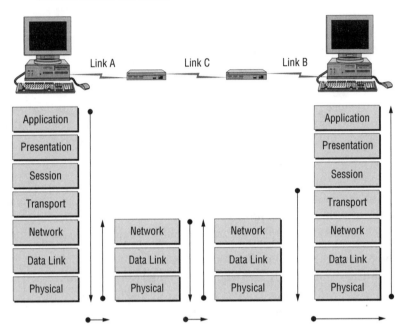

Once this is done, router A puts on a new Data Link header using its own Data Link address as the source address and puts the frame out on link C to router B. When router B receives these frames, the entire process is repeated. Router B strips off the Data Link layer and looks at the Network-layer address. It sees that the Network-layer address matches that of one of the interfaces on router B, so it determines that it needs to send the packet over link B to host B. Router B replaces the Data Link header, substituting its Data Link address for that of router A. Host B receives the data and passes it up the stack where the data is read and understood by whichever application requested it.

NOTE The way the hosts and the routers determine where to address the packets at the Data Link layer depends on the network protocol being run. With IP, Address Resolution Protocol (ARP) is used.

This stripping and replacing of the source and destination MAC address in the Data Link header occurs each time the packet transverses a routing device. This means that the original source MAC address is lost as soon as the packet crosses a router. It is important to note that data passing out of a router onto a local segment will have the router's MAC address as its Data Link source address.

> **NOTE** MAC addresses are unique addresses typically assigned by the hardware manufacturer. MAC addresses are made up of 48 bits, expressed as 12 hexadecimal digits. Each manufacturer has its own prefix, which comprises the first 6 digits of an assigned MAC address. For example, 00000C is one of the prefixes Cisco is licensed to use; so, if you see a MAC address starting with 00000C, you know that the device sending that data was made by Cisco. MAC addresses are administered by IEEE to ensure that no two vendors are using the same MAC address prefix. Many hardware manufacturers have more than one MAC address prefix assigned for their use.

Layer 1: The Physical Layer

The lowest layer of the OSI model is the Physical layer. By the time the data arrives at the Physical layer, it has been fully packaged, all the control and data fields have been set, and all the Physical layer needs to do is place the data on the wire. At the Physical layer, bits are transformed into signals on the transmission medium. It is the Physical layer that defines which signals on the wire constitute 1s or 0s, and which are just noise. Physical-layer specifications define things like allowable cable lengths, maximum transmit speeds, and the actual wiring of your network.

While it is important to understand the Physical layer, someone concerned with router management rarely delves too deeply into it. Some people consider modeling the inductance and RF gain on a particular length of wire to be interesting and necessary. The average person simply needs to know that the Physical layer sets certain limits on your networking environment. What the specifications are depends on the type of media—be it fiber optic cable, CAT5, shielded twisted pair, Thicknet, or what have you. Each different media type has different specifications.

> **TIP** When working with your Physical layer, be conservative with the specifications. For example, if a max cable length is specified at 100 meters, do not try to get away with 108 meters. It probably would work, but out-of-spec physical media cause some of the hardest problems to locate and correct.

Overall, it is important to note that as data travels downward through the stack, it is encapsulated within each layer's own header. This is illustrated in Figure 1.12.

Figure 1.12 As data passes through the layers of the OSI, each layer adds a header, which is removed as data passes up the stack on the receiving station.

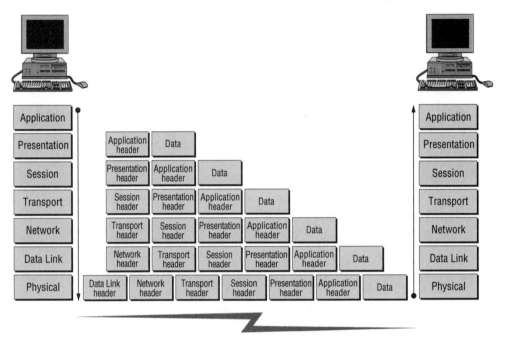

Data is encapsulated and passed in this way so that as it is passed up the stack by the receiving host, the layers of headers can be stripped off. This is so that each layer knows how to deliver the data to the next layer in the stack. When we are discussing the lower layers, it should be noted that data is referred to by different names at different points in the protocol stack:

OSI Layer	Layer Entity
Transport	Segments
Network	Packets
Data Link	Frames
Physical	Bits

What you call the data unit at each layer is less important than understanding what the functionality of the layer actually is. The data unit that the router is typically concerned with is the packet.

Switching versus Routing

The two major types of devices that make decisions about where data goes in the networking environment are switches and routers. Switches decide how frames should be directed based on the layer 2 address of the frame, which happens also to be the MAC address. Routers use layer 3 addresses, such as IP addresses, to determine where to send a given packet.

Many LAN administrators are converting their existing hubs to switches. This can offer significant performance improvements with very little effort on the administrator's part. A switch has the ability to learn about the environment in which it is placed so that it can make intelligent decisions about which of its interfaces it should forward frames to.

When a switch is first turned on, it knows nothing about the network it is on. The switch begins listening to traffic that is passing through it. By listening to the traffic, the switch begins to learn which MAC addresses are connected to which of its ports. This information is placed in a table so that the switch eventually learns of each device connected to it.

Figure 1.13 shows a simple switched environment.

Figure 1.13   An example of a simple switched environment

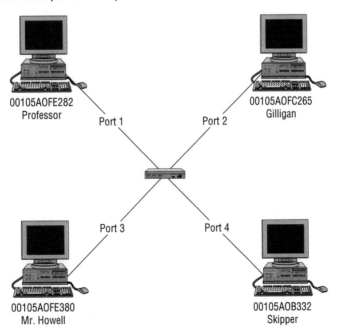

00105AOFE282
Professor

Port 1

Port 2

00105AOFC265
Gilligan

Port 3

Port 4

00105AOFE380
Mr. Howell

00105AOB332
Skipper

For example, suppose the Professor's machine in Figure 1.13 wants to talk to Gilligan's machine. The switch will see a frame with a source MAC address of 00105AFE282 coming into port 1. The switch will realize that this MAC address is connected to port 1 and add it to its switching table. Since the switch does not know about the destination MAC address in the frame, which is 00105A0FC265, it will flood the frame through all its ports except port 1, because it received the frame on that port. When Gilligan responds to the professor, the switch learns that Gilligan is connected to port 2. Now if Gilligan tries to talk to Mr. Howell, the switch will know where Gilligan is. Gilligan's first frame to Mr. Howell gets forwarded out all ports (1, 3, and 4) since the switch does not know where Mr. Howell (00105A0FE380) is connected. When Mr. Howell replies, however, the switch not only learns where he is, but it also knows that the reply is addressed 00105A0FC265 (Gilligan). This address is connected to port 2, so it only forwards the frame out port 2. This means that data never touched the links on ports 1 or 4, because it did not need to go there. This allows the switch to greatly increase efficiency in speed since it limits traffic to only those links where it needs to be.

This behavior, in combination with the fact that the backplane of the switch is significantly faster than the links to which it is connected, allows for increased data-transfer speeds under the right conditions.

Assume that links 1, 2, 3, and 4 are 10Mbps links, and that the Professor is transferring a file to Gilligan while Mr. Howell is transferring a file to the Skipper. Since the switch now knows where all the computers involved are, it can effectively create two 10-megabyte-per-second connections—one between the Skipper and Mr. Howell, and one between the Professor and Gilligan. Thus, you are actually getting 20Mbps of throughput on a 10Mbps LAN. This is the major advantage of a switch over a hub.

Switching is faster than routing, since a router has to strip off the Data Link header, read the network header, consult its routing table, replace the source address with its own, and finally re-create the header. A switch only has to read the header and look at its switching table, and, therefore, is much faster.

The main difference between a router and a switch lies in which layer of the OSI model they operate. Switches are primarily layer 2 devices, while routers are primarily considered layer 3 devices. The line between the two is beginning to blur as Application Specific Integrated Circuits (ASIC's) allow switches to perform more and more like routers.

Currently, a lot of the switching and routing technology is merging onto the same physical boxes. These devices, known as layer 3 switches, can perform as a normal switch, or can use the layer 3 header to actually perform routing functionality.

Layer 3 switching is one of the terms being thrown around a lot lately. Layer 3 switching is nothing more that routing. A layer 3 switch is just a switch that happens to contain a special processor to add routing functionality. The concepts behind layer 3 switching are the same as in routing. Most of the routing commands between a router and a layer 3 switch are similar, so that, although the focus of this book is not on switching, most of the principles involved in layer 3 switching will be covered as we progress through these chapters. For example, you could take all the concepts discussed in this book and apply them to configuring a Route Switch Module in a Catalyst 5500 switch.

2

LAN and WAN Technologies

Once your network is wired and operating, it is always tempting to sit back and say, "Cool, it's working, my job is done". Well, sorry folks—your job is never done. Just recognizing that it works is never enough. You have to ask yourself the following questions:

- Has everything been integrated properly?
- Are the LAN and WAN technologies wired and operating up to specifications?
- What's going to happen when more users are added to the network?
- What will happen when the amount of data exchanged in the network increases?
- What will happen when more of your users recognize the usefulness of the network and push its limits?
- As a network manager, what are you going to do to respond to these changes?

Routers are sophisticated devices. They perform integration tasks as well as segmentation activities. Aside from simply routing packets, in a large LAN environment they can be used to provide broadcast control, contention segmentation, and bridging functions. This chapter was designed to give you an understanding of some of the technologies that can be integrated into a routed or bridged environment as well as some of the issues you should be aware of when using these technologies.

Local Area Network (LAN) Technologies

In this section we will cover the following LAN technologies:

- Ethernet/IEEE 802.3
- Fast Ethernet
- Fast EtherChannel
- Token Ring
- Fiber Distributed Data Interface (FDDI)
- Gigabit Ethernet

Ethernet/IEEE 802.3

Among the most cost effective and simplest of LAN technologies, Ethernet is probably the one that is used the most. Ethernet is a LAN standard originally designed by Xerox Corporation back in the 1970s. It is a 10Mbps PC networking standard. Xerox, Intel, and Digital Corporations later made an improvement to the standard and called it Ethernet II. The original Ethernet standard would only carry packets that conform to the IPX/SPX protocol suite. It was initially only designed to carry Novell NetWare packets. Ethernet II is capable of carrying more than just one layer 3 protocol. The IEEE (Institute of Electrical and Electronic Engineers) also outlined a standard very similar to Ethernet called the IEEE 802.3 standard. It is in many ways compatible with the Ethernet II standard. Both standards use the same physical layer components. The differences are in the frame formats for each. We will discuss these later.

Ethernet/IEEE 802.3 Operation

Although there are various Ethernet frame types, all Ethernet networks operate in a similar fashion. It is a logical bus technology, and all devices communicate over a common communications channel. Only one device can communicate at any given time, and all devices receive the transmitted communications. The communications are in the form of a series of binary bits that make up a frame. Frame header information will include the Media Access Control (MAC) address of the destination device, as well as that of the source device. When the destination device reads the frame header and recognizes that the frame is addressed to it, that device will process the frame and send it up to its higher layers.

For instance, in Figure 2.1, let's say device A has information to send to device E. Device A will package (encapsulate) that information into a frame. The frame will be transmitted on a common bus for all devices to see. Devices B, C, and D will see the transmitted frame but will ignore it because the destination address in the frame header will not be theirs. Device E will also see the frame. Since it is Device E's MAC address that is in the destination-address field of the frame header, E's network interface circuitry will interrupt E's CPU, and the frame will be processed (decapsulated, etc.).

Figure 2.1   A simple bus network

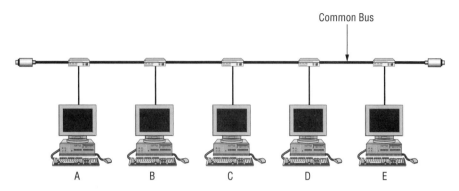

Carrier Sense Multiple Access with Collision Detection (CSMA/CD)

With Ethernet, multiple devices can share the same segment of media, but only one device can communicate on it at any given time. The way that Ethernet achieves this is by using a technology called CSMA/CD, or Carrier Sense Multiple Access with Collision Detection. When one station wants to transmit a frame, it will first listen to the bus. It will wait for an idle period. Only when no other devices are using the bus is frame transmission possible. Therefore, when that idle period happens, the device will start transmitting its frame. It is, however, possible that while one station is waiting for an idle period on the bus to send a frame, another station connected to the same bus is also waiting to send a frame. Both may try to transmit at the same time. If this happens, we will have a collision on the bus.

Collisions are bad things. When there is a collision, it generally means the competing frames did not complete their transmissions across the piece of media. While Ethernet devices transmit, they also simultaneously listen to the bus to detect collisions. If a collision occurs, both devices will send a *jam signal* across the bus to warn all other devices that there was a collision. The jam is a message to all stations indicating they should immediately cease all communications. Additionally, the devices that sent the colliding frames will set a random timer to establish a waiting period before transmission can resume.

The more devices that share the same piece of media, the higher the mathematical odds that there will be devices that want to communicate at the same time. Therefore, the more devices that are sharing the same bus, the more collisions the bus will have. Collisions cause more traffic to be generated. The more collisions the bus has, the more jam signals will have to be sent, and the more waiting periods will arise. While the collisions and jams are happening, more devices may be waiting to transmit. When the line is finally idle, they may, by chance, all attempt to transmit simultaneously and all collide. This process gets worse and worse as you add more devices and/or add heavier load to your network. For this reason, Ethernet doesn't perform well under heavy loads. It reaches critical mass somewhere between the 30 and 40 percent utilization point.

Ethernet/802.3 Frame Types

Ethernet/802.3 has the following frame types:

- Ethernet II frame
- IEEE 802.3 frame
- Logical Link Control header
- SNAP Solution

Ethernet II Frame   An Ethernet frame consists of the following parts, as shown in Figure 2.2:

Preamble   An alternating pattern of 1s and 0s that basically tells other devices on the network that a frame is on its way

Start of Frame (SOF)   A bit pattern ending in two successive 1s. It is used along with the preamble to signify that there is no more preamble on the way, and that everything that follows is frame header.

Destination MAC   The 48-bit hardware address of the destination device

Source MAC   The 48-bit hardware address of the sending device

Type   A 2-byte field that represents a layer 3 protocol. An example of what you may find in this field includes:

IP	0x0800
IPX	0x8137 – 0x8138
AppleTalk	0x809B
DECnet	0x6003
X.25	0x0805
ARP	0x0806

Data   Contains upper layer data usually consisting of a packet from a routed protocol

Frame Check Sequence   A field that contains a Cyclic Redundancy Check (CRC) that verifies the validity of the frame

Figure 2.2   An Ethernet frame

IEEE 802.3 frame   Both Ethernet II and IEEE 802.3 use the same preamble, SOF, and 48-bit addressing scheme. Both also have the same length restrictions. Frames are variable in size. They can be between 64 and 1518 bytes in length, not including the preamble and SOF. The 802.3 frame uses a length field in place of the Ethernet II type field. The length field represents the length of the LLC header and data. Possible values in this field will include 0x0040 through 0x05DC. An IEEE 802.3 frame is shown in Figure 2.3.

Figure 2.3   An IEEE 802.3 frame

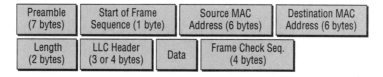

NOTE   A device distinguishes between Ethernet II and 802.3 by looking in the length field.

Logical Link Control (LLC) Header   In an 802.3 frame, protocol information is expressed in another set of fields called the Logical Link Control (LLC) header. The LLC header (shown in Figure 2.4) is outlined in the IEEE 802.2 standard. This very same information is found in the IEEE 802.5 Token Ring Standard and the 802.10 FDDI standard. The IEEE wanted a standard method of referring to upper-layer protocols, so they devised this 802.2 standard. They felt there were some limitations in the Ethernet II frame, in that a protocol could communicate only with the same protocol. Therefore, they devised the idea of a Service Access Point (SAP). SAP built on the same general idea as the Type in Ethernet II, but has added a Source SAP (SSAP) and a Destination SAP (DSAP) (Source Protocol and Destination Protocol fields). They also wanted the LLC header to optionally support flow control, as well as the ability to support sequenced and acknowledged communications. Ethernet doesn't need or use these capabilities, but the IEEE wanted the fields generic enough so they might be used with other technologies.

Figure 2.4   An LLC header

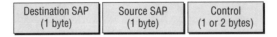

The IEEE liked their solution, but recognized that it does have some flaws. First, the DSAP/SSAP fields are only 1 byte each in length; therefore, even if every bit combination is used, there can be only 256 combinations of numbers to assign to protocols. So what should they do? As new protocols are developed, should they give out SAP numbers on a first-come–first-serve basis to every company that requests them, and leave those who requested them too late out in the cold? Maybe. In fact the IEEE did assign some protocols an SAP. Here are a few:

IP	0x06
XNS	0x80
IPX	0xE0
IBM Netbios	0xF0
IBM SNA	0x04 & 0x05

However, assigning SAPs isn't a good long-term solution. Since an SAP is an 8-bit field, there can be only 256 total combinations that can be addressed using an SAP field. With only 256 combinations allowed for protocols, it won't take long before all the available combinations run out. Once the combinations run out, we will have to reinvent the way we do things. Furthermore, another issue came up with the 1-byte SAP, in that some protocols needed the 2 bytes that were provided by the Ethernet II Type field. As an example, TCP/IP's ARP is represented by a type code of 0x0806. The IEEE obviously could not represent this particular numeral in a 1-byte field. They could potentially give ARP another number, and they did. Unfortunately, there were a number of legacy systems that could only use the type code for IP and ARP. They needed another, more practical, solution and so the SNAP frame solution was born.

SNAP Solution   The IEEE needed to define one SAP for those custom protocols not already defined by an SAP. As a catch-all solution, they decided to create a special kind of 802.3 frame, called a Sub-Network Access Protocol (SNAP) frame. If the DSAP and SSAP fields are set to 0xAA, and the Control field is set to 0x03, that frame is a SNAP frame. This is an indicator to devices that they should read 5 additional bytes into the data section, because that section includes additional information about upper-layer protocols. The additional information about these protocols consists of a 3-byte Organizational Unit Identifier (OUI), also known as a vendor code, and a 2-byte type identifier identical to the Type in the Ethernet II frame. The vendor code is the same 24-bit prefix that is used in a typical 48-bit MAC address.

The IEEE prefers that all manufacturers of Network Interface Cards (NICs) and protocols register with them (and pay a fee), and in return, those manufacturers receive a vendor code. Once the manufacturers have a vendor code, they can create thousands of custom protocols and assign to those protocols a 2-byte type at will. Figure 2.5 shows an LLC with a SNAP header.

Figure 2.5   LLC with SNAP header

Some examples of vendor codes follow:

Cisco	0x00000C
Novell	0x00000F
3Com	0x00608C
Intel	0x00AA00
Apple	0x000502
Network General	0x000065

Ethernet/IEEE 802.3 Physical-Layer Specifications

Ethernet networks can be wired using a number of different media types, each with its own benefits and drawbacks. Each is measured by the following factors:

- Total devices per segment
- Maximum segment length
- Media type used

Some popular specifications for Ethernet topologies are shown in Table 2.1.

Table 2.1   Specifications for Ethernet Topologies

Characteristic	Ethernet	IEEE 802.3 Values			
		10Base5	10Base2	10BaseT	10BaseFL
Total devices per physical segment	100	100	30	2*	2
Maximum segment length in meters	500	500	185	100	400 with MMF 2,000 with SMF
Media Type	50-ohm coax rg 9 or 11	50-ohm coax rg 9 or 11	50-ohm coax rg 58a	Unshielded twisted-pair Cat 3, 4, or 5	Fiber-optic

* Although only 2 devices can occupy one physical wire, 10BaseT can theoretically support up to 1024 maximum devices in one segment. This theoretical maximum in no way compares to the practical maximum.

Ethernet / IEEE 10Base5 (Thicknet)   An early flavor of Ethernet is 10Base5. Like all flavors of Ethernet, 10Base5 operates at 10Mbps. It uses a physical bus topology and can support up to 100 devices (workstations, repeaters, and bridges) per physical segment. The 10Base5 standard uses a very thick, very rigid type of coaxial cable (coax)—usually RG 9 or RG 11— to which we attach devices. For this reason, the cable is frequently known as *Thicknet*. Each node of Thicknet is connected to the coax using an external transceiver that is attached via a Vampire Tap. The minimum cable length between connections (or Vampire Taps) on the cable segment is 2.5 meters (about 8.3 feet). Thicknet coaxial cable can carry a signal for 500 meters (1640 feet). Every node is attached to the transceiver by an Attached Unit Interface (AUI) drop cable. The AUI cable has a maximum length limitation of 50 meters. The drop cable is connected to a device using a 15-pin AUI connector. Figure 2.6 is an example of a simple 10base5 network.

Figure 2.6   A simple 10base5 (Thicknet) network

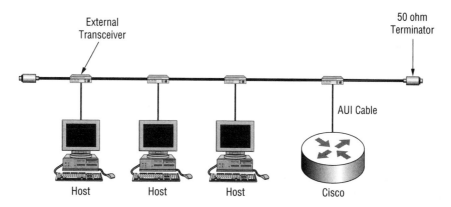

10Base2(Thinnet)   Thinnet is also a bus technology. It uses coaxial cabling (RG-58). The maximum cable length is 185 meters (about 607 feet) per segment. It allows up to 30 devices on each segment. Each device is connected via a BNC Connector on the 10Base2 Network Interface Cards (NIC). Thinnet is among the least expensive of all the networking media. It is also very limited in capacity compared to some of the other media.

Physical bus networks can be extended in length by the use of a device called a *repeater*. Actually, the repeater allows us to attach multiple segments so that they may act as one larger segment. We can, however, only grow physical bus networks to a certain total size. There is a rule in Ethernet that governs this called the *5-4-3 rule*. The 5-4-3 rule says that we may connect up to five (5) physical segments using four (4) repeaters, and only three (3) of the segments may be populated with devices. This basically means that we may extend 10Base5 segments to a length of 2500 meters and attach up to a total of 300 devices, including the repeaters. With 10Base2, we can have a total length of 925 meters and up to 90 devices on the entire network. Figure 2.7 is an example of a simple 10base2 network.

Figure 2.7   A simple 10base2 (Thinnet) network

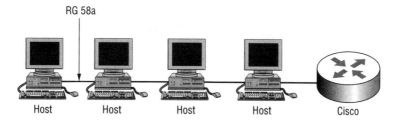

10BaseT   10BaseT is an Ethernet standard that uses unshielded twisted-pair (UTP) cable to provide LAN connectivity. As shown in Figure 2.8, the physical topology is wired as a star. Devices are connected via a hub. The cabling is attached at each end via an RJ-45 connector. Segments can be up to 100 meters (about 328 feet) in length. The minimum cable length between devices is 2.5 meters (about 8 feet). Only two devices can be connected at a time, although the entire network has a theoretical maximum of 1024 devices.

Ethernet and Cisco

Cisco routers can integrate Ethernet LANs with other Ethernet and non-Ethernet networks. To integrate them properly, it is important to understand some of the issues related to configuring, monitoring and testing Ethernet connections. One issue that can sometimes raise your blood pressure is the problem of routers that have dual media-types for the same interface. Cisco routers can come with one or more of any of the three media-type connectors that we talked about. It is common to find two different connectors that are used by the same router interface; however, only one connector can be used at any given time. Take the Cisco 4000 series for instance: On a Cisco 4000–4700 router you may have a Network Processor Module (NPM) that contains Ethernet ports. Each port may very well have 10Base5 AUI and 10BaseT RJ45 connectors. Well, it's common for most of us today to use the 10BaseT. Unfortunately, the default on that router is to attempt to use the 10Base5 connector. You could potentially want to rip your hair out troubleshooting a problem that doesn't even exist. To make matters worse, some of the newer routers that have dual media ports may indeed default to 10BaseT.

To remedy this, you may use the IOS media-type command at the interface you are configuring. In the following configuration we have issued the `media-type 10baset` command on Ethernet0 to change the connector type. Now on interface Ethernet0 the 10BaseT port is active and the AUI port is now inactive.

```
!
interface ethernet 0
  media-type 10baset
!
```

Extending Ethernet   All devices that share the same physical Ethernet segment compete for resources on that stretch of media. It is possible to extend the length of Ethernet segments using repeaters. You can extend any bus technology using up to four repeaters connected in series. For instance, using repeaters, we can extend a 10Base5 network to 2500 meters and attach up to 300 devices. This is a great feature, but all 300 devices still have to compete for the same logical bus. In addition, they must also contend for the same 10Mbps. Devices in these networks are said to be in the same *collision domain*, or even the same *contention domain*. When too many devices are placed in the same collision domain, it significantly slows network response for all devices and users on that segment. So, the question remains: What can one do if there are too many devices in the same collision domain? The textbook answer is segmentation. Divide your network into multiple contention domains or collision domains. In the Ethernet environment, the options for segmentation devices include bridges, switches, and routers.

The simplest segmentation device is the bridge, as shown in Figure 2.8. In the Ethernet environment, we use a transparent bridge for segmentation purposes. A transparent bridge gets its name from the fact that none of the devices connected to it actually needs to know it is there for the bridging functions to take place.

Bridges perform three basic functions:

- Address learning
- Forwarding/filtering
- Loop avoidance

A transparent bridge is a learning bridge. Over time, it will learn the MAC addresses of all the devices connected to each of its interfaces. Once the bridge learns which segment each device is on, it can forward or filter as necessary. This allows for simultaneous communications on each of the segments that it is connected to.

Figure 2.8   Transparent bridge

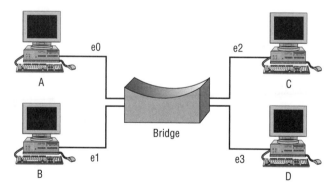

Initially, when the bridge is first turned on, it knows nothing of its environment. Let's suppose Figure 2.8's device A sends a frame destined for device D. The bridge has no idea where device D is so it has to forward that frame out of every interface with the exception of the one it came in on. Since the bridge had to forward the frame out of every interface, there was no segmentation benefit. However, the bridge learned something. It learned that device A is connected to interface E0. Let's suppose device C sends a frame to device

B. Again the bridge has to flood the frame out of all of its interfaces; but again the bridge learns. It has discovered that device C is associated with interface E2. The bridge maintains a MAC address table that stores MAC addresses with associated interfaces, as shown in Table 2.2. At this point, the MAC table would include two entries in our bridge.

Table 2.2   A MAC Table

MAC Address	Interface
MAC address for A	E0
MAC address for C	E2

Now let's suppose device D sends a frame to device A. The bridge looks in its MAC table and recognizes that device A is on interface E0. The frame is consequently sent out of E0 and filtered from the other interfaces, and therefore filtered from the other devices. The bridge has done its job. Over time, the bridge will learn the MAC addresses of all devices associated with all interfaces. As a result, the bridge can allow multiple, simultaneous conversation between devices on separate interfaces.

Bridging on a Cisco Router   A Cisco router can act as a transparent bridge. In fact, if all routing protocols are disabled, the router will automatically start bridging all frames. If there are routed protocols enabled, you can configure the router to perform concurrent routing and bridging. That functionality is not automatic. It must be configured to do so. Cisco routers support all of the features that a typical bridge would support, such as:

- Spanning Tree Protocol for loop avoidance; both the IEEE and the DEC versions are options in the IOS
- The ability to create multiple bridge groups for broadcast segmentation
- Translational Bridging to communicate with source-route bridged networks

Configuring for transparent bridging on a Cisco router is quite simple. The following is a working example:

```
!
bridge 10 protocol ieee
bridge 10 priority 1
!
```

```
interface ethernet 0
  bridge-group 10
!
interface ethernet 1
  bridge-group 10
!
```

In the above code listing, the first statement gives the bridge a bridge identifier of 10 and configures it to use the IEEE version of Spanning Tree. The second line is optional. We have decided to use it to set the priority of the bridge to 1. If all of the other bridges in the network have a higher priority, our bridge is sure to be elected as the Root Bridge by the Spanning Tree Protocol. The bridge-group commands add both Ethernet 0 and Ethernet 1 to the same bridge group.

> **NOTE** When you take a new router out of the box, it will not act like a bridge automatically. If you leave a blank configuration on the router, IP routing is still enabled. If you want the router to start bridging immediately, you must disable IP routing globally. All other protocols have to be explicitly turned on, but IP is on by default.

The following code is used to disable IP routing globally:

```
!
no ip routing
!
```

Fast Ethernet

As a popular higher-speed alternative to Ethernet, we have as an option Fast Ethernet. Fast Ethernet is technology that operates at 100Mbps. There are a number of different flavors of Fast Ethernet including 100BaseTX, 100BaseT4 and 100BaseFX.

In many ways, 100BaseTX is similar to 10BaseT. 100BaseTX technology uses the same basic framing format as 10BaseT. It also uses the same functionality of CSMA/CD. It operates in half-duplex operation in a collision environment, but can also be used in full-duplex in point-to-point links. They can both use some of the same physical media provided you are using a high enough quality of cable. Both use UTP, but only utilize two of the four pairs in the UTP cabling, specifically pairs 1-2 and 3-6. The other pairs, 4-5 and 7-8 of the four-pair wiring, sit idle.

The way 100BaseTX technology achieves the higher throughput is by shortening the time during which a bit exists on the media. This is done in a couple of ways. First, the equipment has to support the higher speeds. 10BaseT equipment cannot be used in a 100Base network unless bridging is done between them. Second, The media that carries the signals has to be of much higher quality. 10BaseT can utilize Category 3, 4, or 5 UTP where 100BaseT requires Category 5 UTP. Category 5 is much higher quality wiring than the lower categories. The total length of a 100Base network is much shorter than a 10Base. 100BaseT also uses a different signaling method than 10BaseT. Hubs that are able to mix 10BaseT and 100BaseTX, like the Cisco 112T or 124T hubs, actually perform store-and-forward bridging between 10 and 100 ports.

100BaseT4 achieves 100Mbps a little differently than its counterpart, 100BaseTX. Like 10BaseT and 100BaseTX, it uses UTP. It uses the same twisted pairs (1-2 and 3-6) of copper wire as the other technologies. The pairs are even used in half-duplex operation much like the other technologies. Where T4 differs is the fact that it also uses the other two twisted pairs (4-5 and 7-8) in the four-pair wire. In 100BaseTX, these pairs usually sit idle in full-duplex operation. Here's the kicker: It works with Category 3 wiring.

When *100Mbps to the desktop* was a huge buzzword in the industry a few years ago, many people ran right out to buy category 5 cable and accessories for their infrastructure to support 100BaseTX—when all along T4 was a thriving, viable standard. Now, what I didn't mention was that, in many cases, the price difference between rewiring and changing to TX equipment was still more attractive than paying for whatever T4 equipment was available at the time. This is because T4 uses a signaling technique that is different from TX, called the 4T+ signaling scheme. This scheme is incompatible with TX equipment. Intel Corp. does, however, sell TX/T4 equipment that can be set to use either signaling technique.

100BaseFX uses fiber optics to extend the total length of your 100Base network. With 100BaseT, the longest we can ask for is 100 meters. Using Multi-Mode Fiber (MMF) we can extend a segment to 400 meters. 100BaseFX is a point-to-point technology which makes it useful as an uplink between 100BaseT hubs and switches.

Table 2.3 summarizes the differences in the three flavors of Fast Ethernet.

Table 2.3   The Three Flavors of Fast Ethernet

Feature	100BaseTX	100BaseT4	100BaseFX
Segment Length	100 meters	100 meters	400 meters with MMF
Cable Type	Cat 5 UTP	Cat 3, 4, and 5 UTP	62.5/125 micron MMF

Table 2.3   The Three Flavors of Fast Ethernet *(continued)*

Feature	100BaseTX	100BaseT4	100BaseFX
Connector Type	RJ 45	RJ 45	ST or SC Fiber Attachment

Fast Ethernet and Cisco

Cisco supports both 10BaseT and 100BaseTX. Some of the routers support 10 and 100 in the same media connection. Additionally, if you like, you may configure a Fast Ethernet port for full- or half-duplex operation. You can even set a port to autonegotiate with the switch interface.

Half-Duplex Operation   To understand the concept of half-duplex operation, we use the analogy of the narrow one-way bridge. Anyone can cross in either direction, but only one person can cross at a time. It is the same with Ethernet (or Fast Ethernet). As you can see in Figure 2.9, all of the transmit circuits on all devices are logically connected to the receive circuits of all others. Only one device can transmit and all devices can hear it. When two devices try to communicate simultaneously, the collision-detection circuitry detects it and deals with it accordingly. An example of a configuration that sets an interface (fastethernet 0) into half-duplex mode is as follows:

```
!
interface fastethernet 0
   speed 100
   duplex half
!
```

Figure 2.9   Half-duplex Ethernet

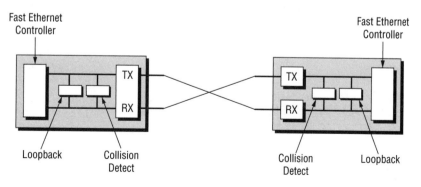

Full-Duplex Operation   If two devices are connected to each other in a point-to-point link and there is no chance for a collision to happen, then we can configure both devices in the point to point link to use full duplex. In full-duplex operation, all collision-detect and loopback circuitry in each device is disabled, because it is not needed. Each device can transmit and receive simultaneously. Figure 2.10 show us an example. By default, Fast Ethernet ports are configured to use 100Mbps and half-duplex operation. To change that, here is a sample configuration, which we'll call Example 1:

```
!
interface fastethernet 0
  speed 100
  duplex full
!
```

In Example 1, we have explicitly set the speed of the port to 100 Mbps and the duplex to full.

NOTE   Whatever the port in Example 1 is connected to must support, and be configured to use, those settings as well.

Here is another example, Example 2.

```
!
interface fastethernet 0
  speed auto
  duplex auto
!
```

In Example 2, the interface will negotiate speed and duplex with whatever device it is connected to. The default speed is 100. The default duplex setting is half-duplex.

Figure 2.10   Full-duplex Ethernet.

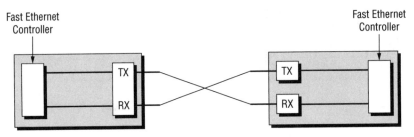

WARNING   Negotiating speed is an easy thing for 10/100 devices. Each uses a different signaling technique, and devices can easily tell them apart. Duplex, however, is a different story. Duplex mismatches are a common occurrence in 10/100 environments. It is difficult for a device to be accurate about the duplex setting of an adjacent device. To add insult to injury, ports with duplex mismatches may appear to work. It is likely that the actual throughput is very low due to errors, but when troubleshooting, it might still fool you into thinking the configuration is indeed correct.

A Trick: Discovering Problems Related to Duplex Mismatches:

You can look at certain counters available in Cisco routers and switches to get an indication of whether you are experiencing a duplex mismatch. A simple show interfaces command can be quite informative in this case.

When there *is* a duplex mismatch, one device will assume it can receive and transmit at the same time. The other will not.

Suppose router A is connected to switch B. Router A is configured for full-duplex. switch B is configured for half-duplex. In the midst of switch B sending a frame to router A, router A decides to send a frame to switch B. Immediately, switch B assumes there is a collision and ceases all conversations for a random amount of time. A duplex mismatch will cause certain types of errors to accumulate in our interface counters:

- On the full-duplex side, over time, we will accumulate frame check sequence (FCS) errors or cyclic redundancy checking (CRC) errors due to prematurely having communications cut off with the adjacent device while a frame is being received.

- On the half-duplex side, late collisions will accumulate. The half-duplex side will view any full-duplex activities as a collision.

Collisions usually happen within the first 64 bytes of an Ethernet transmission. Those collisions that happen after the first 64 bytes are called *late collisions*.

Fast EtherChannel

An ingenious technology that is receiving heavy support is *Fast EtherChannel*. Fast Ether-channel allows us to aggregate multiple Fast Ethernet ports to create one larger channel. Up to four Fast Ethernet ports may be combined for up to 400Mbps. The technology is a great solution for high bandwidth uplinks between switches. Additionally, with support from a number of NIC manufacturers, including Sun Microsystems, Intel, SGI, Compaq, and Adaptec, the technology has extended to the server arena as well.

Token Ring

IBM originally developed Token Ring in the 1970s. Later the IEEE released their own *token passing* standard closely based on the IBM standard. It was called the IEEE 802.5 standard. The two standards are compatible with each other.

Token Ring is a shared LAN technology that is very different than Ethernet. The technology is based on a logical ring rather that a logical bus.

How Token Ring Works

Token Ring operation revolves around the concept of *token passing*. All devices in a token ring network are logically assembled in a ring. A *token* is a special bit-pattern that is passed from one device to another around the ring. Each device can only send information to its downstream neighbor and receive information from its upstream neighbor. Information is passed around the ring in kind of a hot potato fashion, the token representing the potato. The token keeps these communications orderly by informing a device that it is next in line to transmit information. Each device is responsible for re-creating and transmitting the token to its downstream neighbor.

Only when a device receives a token does that device have the ability to transmit information around the ring. If a device has information to send, it must wait until a token is passed to it from its upstream neighbor. Once it receives a token, the device will change that token into an Information or Control Frame by setting a special bit called the *token bit* and adding additional data to it. Setting the bit basically creates a start-of-frame sequence in the token and makes it a real frame.

The frame is sent to its downstream neighbor, and the neighbor will re-create and pass it to its neighbor. The frame is retransmitted around the ring until it reaches the destination device. The destination device will read it and change a couple of bits in the frame and retransmit it to its neighbor. The frame will make its way around the ring until it gets back to the original sending device. Once the frame makes it back to the originating device, it is up to that device to remove the frame from the ring. It is also up to that device to now create a new token and pass it to its downstream neighbor.

Token Ring Frame Structure

As shown in Figure 2.11, a token only contains three fields: a 1-byte Starting Delimiter, a 1-byte Access Control field, and a 1-byte Ending Delimiter. The delimiters are special bit patterns that signify the beginning and ending of a frame. The Access Control field includes a token bit that tells an end station if the frame is a token or an information frame. It also has bits that allow us to set a priority on the token as well as to aid the Active Monitor in spotting a runaway frame.

Figure 2.11   A token

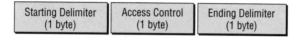

The priority and reservation bits are used to support a simple priority system that Token Ring can utilize. To distinguish a token from an information frame, end devices use the token bit. If the bit is set, the frame is recognized as an information frame. If the token bit is clear, the frame is considered a token. The monitor bit is used in the event that we have a runaway frame. When an end station seizes a free token and transmits an information frame, it is up to that end station to remove the frame once it returns from its transit around the ring. Well, what happens if a station sending a frame is removed from the ring before it has a chance to remove it? The frame has the potential to circle the ring forever. We elect one device on the ring to look for and fix this. We call this device the Active Monitor.

The Active Monitor is a device on the Token Ring that is elected to be the source of timing and to perform various control functions. One of the jobs of the Active Monitor is to watch all frames that are passed around the ring. Once a frame is sent to the Active Monitor, the monitor bit in the Access Control field (shown in Figure 2.12) should be clear. The Active Monitor will set the monitor bit and send the frame on its way. If a frame shows up and it has the monitor bit set, the Active Monitor knows it must be a runaway frame and removes it from the ring.

Figure 2.12   The Access Control field

In the Information/Control frame (or just Information frame) the Starting Delimiter, Ending Delimiter, and Access Control fields (as shown in Figure 2.13) have the same purpose as previously described in the "Token Ring" section. The Destination and Source Address fields hold the 48-bit MAC addresses of the sending and receiving devices. The addressing scheme is similar to that of Ethernet/IEEE 802.3, with two notable differences:

- Token Ring presents its bytes with the *most* significant bit first. Ethernet frames present their bytes with the *least* significant bit first. Ethernet's addressing is considered to be in canonical form.

- The very first (most significant) bit in a MAC address is the Unicast/Multicast bit. When this bit is set, it is presumed that the address is that of a group of devices. As a destination address this bit is only set for Broadcasts and Multicasts. The source address of the frame, however, will never be that of a group. Therefore, the first bit in the source address is not needed for addressing purposes. In fact, Token Ring uses it for a specific purpose. It is used to signify that this frame has information in its Routing Information Field (RIF). The RIF is used to provide enough information to route the frame through a source route bridged network and ultimately to the ring that contains its destination device.

Figure 2.13   The Information/Control frame

Starting Delimiter (1 byte)	Access Control (1 byte)	Frame Control (1 byte)	Destination Address (6 bytes)	Source Address and RII bit (6 bytes)
RIF (0 - 18 bytes)	Data	Frame Check Sequence (4 bytes)	Ending Delimiter (1 byte)	Frame Status (1 byte)

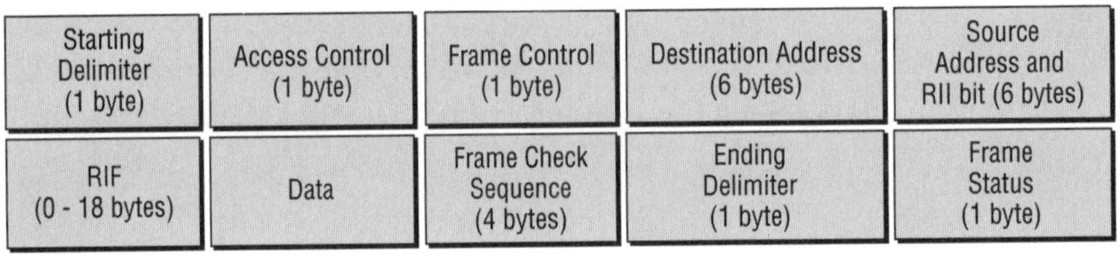

Ethernet works on the premise that we use dumb devices and smart bridges to perform bridging functions. Token Ring, on the other hand, uses dumb bridges and smart devices. They use Source Route Bridging (SRB). Each frame in an environment that uses SRB has to have explicit routing information to traverse the network. The information in the RIF field includes enough ring and bridge information for a frame to be forwarded to the proper destination ring to which a device is attached. There will be more on this topic later.

The Frame Status Field is there to communicate information to the sending device pertaining to how the frame was handled by the receiving device. The field has two significant bits that are used for this purpose; they are the Address Recognized bit and the Copied bit. The Address Recognized bit is used to signify that the destination device saw the frame. The Copied bit basically means the destination device has copied the frame into its buffers and hopefully used it.

Token Ring and Cisco

Cisco supports two Token Ring speeds: 4Mbps and 16Mbps. When enabling a Token Ring interface, the speed is a required parameter. The router will not allow you to enable the interface if a ring speed has not been specified. Here is an example:

```
!
interface tokenring 0
  ring-speed 16
!
```

Also, Cisco routers support early token release. Early token release strays from the concept of having one token or information frame on the ring at any given time. With early token release turned on, there can be multiple information frames on the ring at the same time. The way it works is as follows: If a station is configured for early token release, it does not have to wait until its information frame has made it completely around the ring before creating a token. It will transmit a free token as soon as it is through transmitting its information frame. The end result is that multiple information frames can reside on the ring, but only one free token can be passed around at any given time. We can experience an overall increase in throughput by using this technology.

Early token release is not enabled by default. It must be specified using the `early-token-release` command on the Token Ring interface.

```
!
interface tokenring 0
  ring-speed 16
  early-token-release
!
```

Source Route Bridging

As I mentioned earlier, in the Ethernet environment, we typically subscribe to the idealism that bridging should consist of dumb hosts and smart bridges—hence the idea of the transparent bridge. In the Token Ring environment, we basically subscribe to the opposite—that is, smart hosts and dumb bridges. We can use various types of bridging techniques in the Token Ring (TR) environment, including Transparent Bridging. Most commonly, however, in the TR we will use Source Route Bridging.

Source Route Bridging (SRB) allows multiple rings to be connected together for interoperability and segmentation purposes. By segmenting Token Ring devices using Source Route Bridges, we can cut down on the total number of end devices on each ring. As a result, response time increases for inter-ring communications. The way SRB works is based on the idea that the source host specifies the entire path through the bridged network in the frame header. This is very different from Transparent Bridging, where the source host has no idea the frame has been bridged. Using IBM Token Ring, we can attach seven bridges and eight rings. Using the IEEE 802.5 token-passing standard, we can attach 13 bridges and 14 rings.

In Figure 2.14, let's assume host A has a frame to send to host B. Initially, host A has no idea which ring host B resides on. First, host A will assume host B is on the same ring and send the frame around ring 5 only. When the frame makes it back around the ring, host A will recognize that it has not been read based on the settings in the Frame Status field. This will inform host A that the destination host B is not on its ring. As a result, host A will send out an All Rings/All Routes Explore frame. This explorer frame is used to map out a path (route) to the destination ring on which host B resides. The frame will be sent via every bridge to every ring. Once host B receives the explorer, it will set a special bit in the RIF field that will allow this frame to be sent back in the opposite direction from which it came. When the frame returns to its source, it will contain a complete route to the destination ring of host B.

Figure 2.14   Source route bridged network

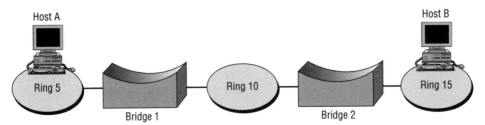

If there are multiple paths to host B, it is likely that host B will receive more than one Explorer frame from the same source. Host B will send every one it receives back to its source, and the source will use the path laid out by the first explorer frame that returns.

The Routing Information Field (RIF) is a field in the Token Ring frame that records the source route information. The RIF can be between 0 and 18 bytes in length, and is only read if a special bit called the Routing Information Indicator (RII) bit in the frame is set. The RIF is divided into two sections: the Route Control (RC) and the Route Descriptor (RD) portions.

The RC portion is 2 bytes in length and divided into the parts shown in Figure 2.15.

Figure 2.15   The RC portion of a Token Ring frame's RIF

Type of Packet (3 bits)	Length of the RIF (5 bits)	Direction Bit	Max Frame Size (3 bits)	Zero

The possible values in the Type of Packet field include:

0xx	The frame has a specific route to a destination
10x	The frame is an explorer
11x	The frame is a special explorer called a spanning explorer. Spanning explorers spread out across the network to minimize explorer traffic.

The Length field tells us the total length of the RIF in bytes. Possible values include:

00110	1 bridge
01000	2 bridges
01010	3 bridges
01100	4 bridges

The direction bit dictates in which direction the RIF should be read. A 0 value will tell devices to read the RIF from left to right. If the bit is set to 1, the RIF should be read from right to left.

The Max Frame Size field communicates the maximum frame size that may be transmitted across the network. Possible values include:

Size (bytes)	Value
516	000
1500	001
2052	010
4472	011
8144	100
11407	101
17800	110
64000	111

The final four bits of the RC field are always 0.

The Route Descriptor (RD) is the field that has the routing information needed by a source to deliver a frame to a destination. Source Route information is laid out in the following fashion:

RING | BRIDGE | RING | BRIDGE | RING | 0.

All Route Descriptors also end in 0. For instance, in Figure 2.14 the RD would be equivalent to:

Ring 5 | Bridge 1 | Ring 10 | Bridge 2 | Ring 15 | 0

The actual number is represented in hexadecimal. We reserve three digits for a ring number and one for a bridge ID. Here is what the RD field in our example would look like: 0051.00A2.00F0

Ring 0x005 | Bridge 0x1 | Ring 0x00A | Bridge 0x2 | 0x0

Fiber Distributed Data Interface (FDDI)

FDDI is a 100Mbps token-passing technology that works similarly to Token Ring. FDDI uses a dual-counter rotating ring for fault tolerance. In other words, it uses two rings, each with its own token. The token and other traffic on each ring is passed in opposite directions. The rings are considered primary and secondary rings. The primary ring is where data is usually transmitted. The secondary ring is idle until needed.

FDDI uses Multi-Mode Fiber (MMF) and Single Mode Fiber (SMF) for the propagation of bits. The rings may sustain up to 500 devices. Devices can be up to 60 kilometers apart using single mode fiber, and 2 kilometers apart using multi-mode. Devices on a FDDI ring can be considered either a dual-attached station (DAS) or single-attached station (SAS). Dual-attached devices have interfaces to both rings. If a device is dual-attached, it has the ability to participate in FDDI fault tolerance features. FDDI uses a concept called *wrapping* as a fault tolerance mechanism. Wrapping will be discussed in greater detail in the next section. Single-attached stations have to be connected to a FDDI Dual Attached Concentrator (DAC). An SAS cannot participate in wrapping operations.

FDDI Fault Tolerance

Two fault tolerance features of FDDI are wrapping and the *optical bypass switch*.

Wrapping   FDDI uses an ingenious fault tolerance mechanism called *wrapping*. The concept of wrapping uses a secondary ring to fall back on in the event of a break in the primary ring. Although FDDI needs only one ring for normal ring operation, a secondary ring is maintained in case there is a break in the primary ring. In the unlikely event of a break, each device that is affected by the break will create a logical path into the secondary ring. As a result, a new ring will be created for all FDDI devices using the connectivity provided by the secondary ring.

> **NOTE** Wrapping can only be performed by dual-attached stations and concentrators.

Optical Bybass Switch An additional fault tolerance feature of FDDI equipment is the ability to add an optical bypass switch (OBS). The OBS is a handy feature, because sometimes FDDI rings do not recover well when dual-attached devices go offline. An OBS is connected inline with the PHY A and PHY B connectors on the FDDI adapter or interface. When a DAS goes down, the OBS detects it and maintains continuity in the ring.

Most FDDI equipment comes with not only PHY A and B connectors, but also with a Mini-DIN connector to use for connectivity to an optical bypass. Although it is not required, the OBS is always recommended if you want to maintain a truly fault-tolerant FDDI environment. Figure 2.16 shows us an example of an OBS.

Figure 2.16 Optical Bypass Switch (OBS)

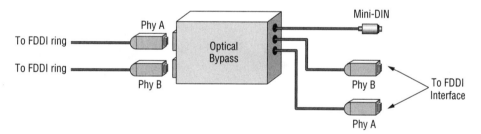

FDDI Connectors

As mentioned earlier, FDDI uses Fiber Optics for its transmission media. The connectors are different than those used by Ethernet or Token Ring. FDDI uses Fiber MIC connectors for a router's connectivity into a ring. ST connectors are used for Single-Mode fiber.

An FDDI interface has two physical ports: PHY A and PHY B. Connectivity between devices is achieved by connecting every PHY A to a PHY B—one connection for the primary ring, the other for the secondary. If you don't conform to this wiring requirement, FDDI will not initialize. You can verify that it works after performing physical connectivity by simply issuing a show interface command:

```
FDDI1# show interface fddi0/1
```

Look for the up/up status and for the PHY A and B to be active, as shown below:

```
FDDI1# show interface fddi0/1
Fddi0/1 is up, line protocol is up
```

```
Hardware is cxBus Fddi, address is 0000.0c01.2345 (bia 0000.0c01.2345)
Internet address is 10.4.0.1, subnet mask is 255.255.0.0
MTU 4470 bytes, BW 100000 Kbit, DLY 100 usec, rely 255/255, load 1/255
Encapsulation SNAP, loopback not set, keepalive not set
ARP type: SNAP, ARP Timeout 4:00:00
```

PHY A state is active, neighbor is B, cmt signal bits 008/20C, status ILS

PHY B state is active, neighbor is A, cmt signal bits 20C/008, status ILS

CFM is thru A, token rotation 5000 usec, ring operational 10:52:14

Upstream neighbor 0000.0c05.4321, downstream neighbor 0000.0c0A.BCDE

FDDI Frame Structure

The frame structure for FDDI is similar in many ways to Token Ring. Figure 2.17 shows an example of FDDI frame and an FDDI token. Each contains some of the following elements:

Start Delimiter and Preamble   A special bit pattern that indicates the beginning of a frame.

Frame Control field   Contains various informational and control data related to the frame, including size, and whether the data is asynchronous or synchronous.

Source and Destination MAC Address   A 48-bit MAC similar to Ethernet and Token Ring.

Frame Check field   Used to hold a Cyclic Redundancy Check (CRC) value that verifies the validity of the frame. The frame check informs end stations if the frame is damaged in transit and should be discarded.

End Delimiter   A bit-pattern that indicates the end of a frame.

Frame Status field   Used by an end station to indicate when a frame is recognized and read by the destination station.

Figure 2.17   FDDI Frame Structure

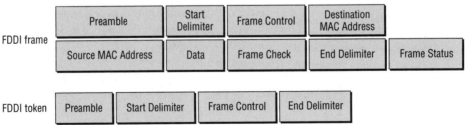

Gigabit Ethernet

An emerging technology is one called Gigabit Ethernet. It allows us to utilize 1000Mbps or 1 gigabit per second. Gigabit Ethernet is the product of incorporating two technologies: ANSI's FiberChannel and the IEEE 802.3 standards. The IEEE has standardized this technology and named it IEEE 802.3z. At layer 2 and above, Gigabit Ethernet operates like typical Ethernet. It uses the same frame formats as Ethernet. The speed advantage and differences come from the enhancements at layer 1.

Gigabit Ethernet uses Single Mode and Multi-Mode Fiber for connectivity. In both cases, an SC connector is used for physical attachment. Using SMF, we can span cable ranges of up to 10 kilometers in length. SMF uses a 1300-nanometer laser for bit propagation. Gigabit Ethernet using MMF spans shorter distances. It can use 50 or 62.5-micron fiber. Although work is currently underway on a copper wire version of Gigabit Ethernet, fiber is the only media available today.

Wide Area Network (WAN) Technologies

WAN technologies are available to span greater distances than we expect from our popular LAN technology. WAN protocols are typically point-to-point links and they use some telecommunications mechanisms for data transfer. There are three major WAN connectivity options:

- Leased lines
- Circuit-switched circuits
- Packet-switched circuits

Leased Lines

A leased line is a dedicated circuit that is up and available 24 hours a day and 7 days a week. It provides dedicated bandwidth and complete autonomy from any of your WAN provider's other customers. An example of a leased line is a T1 or E1 line. Once your WAN provider establishes the circuit, all dedicated bandwidth is available on a full time basis. This tends to be more secure than some packet-switched technologies. Additionally, there is no possibility of congestion in your WAN provider's network affecting your throughput.

Circuit-Switched Circuits

Circuit-switched technologies are those that are only established when needed and removed when not needed. An example of a circuit-switched technology is Integrated Services Digital Network (ISDN). ISDN uses a separate communications channel for out-of-band call setup and timing functions. (ISDN is discussed in greater detail later in this chapter.)

Circuit switched technologies typically need a mechanism for circuit setup, maintenance, and breakdown. We commonly use Dial on Demand Routing (DDR) with circuit-switched technologies. DDR allows us to create the link only when we need it and break it down when we don't. It is appropriate technology when your WAN traffic patterns are low in volume and periodic in nature.

Packet-Switched Circuits

Packet-switched circuits are based on the idealism that we can use a single-leased or circuit-switched connection to communicate with multiple locations using virtual circuits. Packet-switched technologies use permanent virtual circuits (PVCs) or switched virtual circuits (SVCs) to establish links from one point to another. They take advantage of the fact that your service provider has a network that spans a large geographical area. The network will consist of many connection points called central offices (COs). A virtual circuit can therefore be mapped either statically or dynamically to any location from any location in the provider's area of service. Overall, this technology tends to be less expensive than leased-line circuits over larger geographical distances. On the down side, however, sharing these COs with other clients tends to increase your security risks. Additionally, users of packet-switched technologies are at the mercy of occasional congestion on the provider's network. Some examples of packet-switched networks include X.25, Frame Relay, Switched Multimegabit Data Services (SMDS), and Asynchronous Transfer Mode (ATM).

High-Level Data Link Control (HDLC)

HDLC is a spin-off from IBM's Synchronous Data Link Control (SDLC) encapsulation. It uses a similar frame structure. HDLC is the default encapsulation for serial point-to-point links such as T1/E1 and ISDN on Cisco routers. Among the options for serial encapsulation on a Cisco router, HDLC is the most efficient WAN encapsulation overall. HDLC is an industry standard. The HDLC standard as used in the rest of the industry, however, only has the ability to carry a single layer 3 protocol. The Cisco implementation of HDLC is different. Cisco adds a proprietary field into their version of HDLC. This has the unfortunate side effect of making it completely incompatible with the routers of other manufacturers. (Not that any other manufacturers of routers exist. Right?) In these cases you may consider using PPP instead.

The HDLC frame format is shown in Figure 2.18. The Flag fields in the frame signify the start and end of the frame. They will always hold the binary value of 01111110. The Address field will contain either 0x01 for DCE or 0x03 for DTE, depending on functionality. The Control field can utilize bits for send and receive sequence numbers and a Poll

Final bit for indicating acknowledged communications. The Type field is a Cisco proprietary field. It is not present in normal HDLC. In the Cisco frame it holds upper-layer protocol information.

Figure 2.18   HDLC frame format

HDLC is easy to configure. It is on by default on most serial interfaces. To enable it in the event that you decide to change from a different encapsulation to HDLC, simply use the `encapsulation` command:

```
!

encapsulation hdlc

!
```

Point-to-Point Protocol (PPP)

For connectivity with other manufacturers of routers, one of the options available is PPP. PPP is an industry open standard available on many systems. It has many advantages over other WAN encapsulations. It is a very modular standard, meaning that it allows for many extra features that are not included with an encapsulation like HDLC. Some of the added features include:

- Authentication
- Error correction
- Compression
- Multilink

PPP Frame Structure is shown in Figure 2.19. The Flag fields contain the bit pattern 01111110. The Address field always contains 11111111. The Control field always contains 0x03. A 2-byte Protocol field comes after the Control. All of the really important information is stored in the LCP (described below). The Frame Check holds a CRC value to validate the frame.

Figure 2.19 PPP frame structure

The LCP Structure is shown in Figure 2.20. The first part of the LCP identifies one of the 12 packet types for PPP negotiation and configuration. The Identifier is a field used for synchronizing sequence numbers. The length specifies the length of the LCP fields. The Data field can be up to 1500 bytes in size. Actual size is negotiated during link establishment.

Figure 2.20 LCP structure

Enabling PPP is also quite simple. Issuing the `encapsulation ppp` command turns it on. Once it is enabled, additional features can also be enabled:

```
!
interface bri 0
   encapsulation ppp
!
```

One of the more popular options available with PPP includes authentication. Cisco's PPP supports two authentication methods, including Password Authentication Protocol (PAP) and Challenge Handshake Authentication Protocol (CHAP). PAP security is based on the exchange of a simple clear-text username/password pair. CHAP on the other hand exchanges an encrypted hash value that is based on the username and password.

Configuring CHAP authentication is a two-part process. First, we have to configure a USERNAME/PASSWORD entry referring to each router authenticated. These statements are placed in the running configuration of each router doing the authenticating. CHAP uses a two-way authentication process where all devices have to authenticate with each other.

The example below shows a working configuration for each router in Figure 2.21. Notice there is a USERNAME/ PASSWORD pair configured on each router that represents the opposite router. By default, all routers assume that their hostname is their USERNAME for authentication purposes. Also notice the password "secret" is the same on each. This is no coincidence. Cisco PPP CHAP authentication requires both ends to use a common password. In other words, both passwords *must* be the same.

Figure 2.21   Simple PPP configuration

```
!(configuration for router ROME)
hostname ROME
username LONDON password secret
interface bri 0
  encapsulation ppp
  ppp authentication chap
!


!(configuration for router LONDON)
hostname LONDON
username ROME password secret
interface bri 0
  encapsulation ppp
  ppp authentication chap
!
```

As mentioned, PPP also allows us to add capabilities to our link. If we want to, we can add additional error-checking, payload compression, and use multilink. The compress stac command tells the router to use the Stacker payload-compression algorithm. Another option would be to use compress predictor to specify the Predictor algorithm. Stacker tends to be more CPU-intensive where Predictor consumes more RAM. When using PPP, Van Jacobsen header compression is on by default. If both ends of the link support it, header compression will be used automatically. Quality and Magic Number are both error-detection technologies that can be turned on as an option. Multilink allows multiple channels of communications to be aggregated to act as one. This technology is very popular when using PPP with ISDN. In the example we have turned on stacker compression, Quality for error detection and Multilink for channel aggregation.

```
!
interface bri 0
  encapsulation ppp
  compress stac
  ppp quality
  ppp multilink
!
```

NOTE   PPP related RFCs include: 1220, 1378, 1494, 1549, 1552, 1570, 1661, and 1717.

Integrated Services Digital Network (ISDN)

ISDN is a WAN connectivity option that is gaining in popularity by leaps and bounds. When initially developed, ISDN was called the solution waiting for a problem. ISDN provides you with all-digital dial-up service. ISDN was designed to replace your existing telephone service. Basic rate ISDN service comes with two 64K bearer channels for data transfer and one 16K D channel for out-of-band call setup and timing. Two 64K channels give us a fair amount of bandwidth for data, voice, and video.

As stated earlier, ISDN is a circuit-switched technology that makes it perfect for Dial on Demand Routing situations. It is also a good dial back-up solution for leased lines and virtual circuits. ISDN call setup in most cases takes less than two seconds, as opposed to analog technologies that can take up to a minute or more to perform a call setup. Using Basic Rate ISDN, in tandem with PPP Multilink, both ISDN bearer channels can be aggregated for a total of 128K of bandwidth.

NOTE   ISDN is a broad topic and will be addressed in greater detail in Chapter 16.

Frame Relay

Another technology that has become a very popular choice for WAN services is Frame Relay. Frame Relay is a packet-switched technology that permits WAN implementations of up to T3 speeds. It uses virtual circuits (VC) that are nailed up either statically by your service provider, or dynamically when needed. Most implementations of Frame Relay use permanent virtual circuits (PVC). As far as an end user is concerned, a PVC, when established, operates just like a leased line. The circuit is mapped through the provider's network for you and theoretically does not change. A switched virtual circuit (SVC) has a call setup, a call maintenance, and a call breakdown process that needs to happen anytime it is used.

Virtual circuits use a layer-2 addressing scheme called a Data Link Connection Identifier (DLCI). A DLCI is a locally-significant address that allows us to refer to and utilize virtual circuits. For example, in Figure 2.22, when router ROME wants to send something to router LONDON, it simply sends it to DLCI 90, and it will come out of DLCI 80. DLCIs are only significant between the local CO and the router. They are basically there to distinguish between multiple VCs using one interface.

Figure 2.22 Frame Relay virtual circuits

In Frame Relay, a router keeps constant communications with the CO switch. The protocol that is used is called Local Management Interface (LMI). LMI frames are exchanged every 10 seconds by default. This means that every 10 seconds, the router sends a status enquiry to the switch, and the switch returns immediately with a status. There are two kinds of LMI frames: type 0 and type 1. Type 1 LMI frames are a keep-alive mechanism. Only sequence numbers and error counts are communicated. Every sixth LMI update will include a type 0 LMI. In type 0 LMI updates, the switch includes DLCI information so the router knows over what VCs it can communicate, as well as the status of the VC. In the example in Figure 2.23, the switch is sending an LMI that advertises local DLCI 90 as well as its status.

Figure 2.23   LMI operation

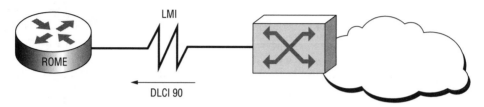

NOTE   Frame Relay is another *very* broad topic, and will be discussed in greater detail in later chapters.

3

Routed Protocols

This chapter will cover the protocols used in routing. For many readers this chapter will be review. Please feel free to skip ahead and refer to this chapter only when necessary. The protocols covered in this chapter include:

- TCP
- UDP
- IP
- IPX
- AppleTalk

The Internet Suite of Protocols

Connectivity to and interoperability with the Internet requires the use of the Transmission Control Protocol/Internet Protocol (TCP/IP) suite. TCP/IP was originally developed for the Advance Research Project Agency (ARPA) in the early 1970s. The project was funded by the Department of Defense (DOD) to provide a packet-switched network between various government and educational organizations. A protocol was needed to facilitate the communications. As a result, the TCP/IP suite was born. Over the years, ARPA's internetwork evolved to what we consider the Internet today.

The TCP/IP suite of protocols follows a conceptual model that is similar to the OSI model in functionality. It essentially includes four layers, as shown in Figure 3.1. The Application layer of the TCP/IP model concerns itself with things similar to those that concern the top three layers of the OSI suite. The Transport and Internet layer of the TCP/IP model have similar purposes as the OSI's Transport and Network layers, respectively. The lower layer of the TCP/IP model relates to the Data Link and Physical layers. This layer is sometimes known as the Network Access layer or may be referred to as the Data Link/Physical layer. TCP/IP doesn't concern itself with issues that relate to layers 1 and 2 of the OSI model as much as it does the upper layers.

Figure 3.1   The TCP/IP model

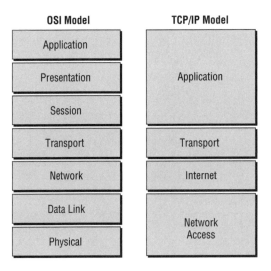

At the Transport layer, TCP/IP has two transport protocols: Transmission Control Protocol (TCP) and User Datagram Protocol (UDP). TCP is a connection-oriented transport where UDP provides connectionless services. At the Internet layer, TCP/IP uses the Internet Protocol (IP) for logical addressing and routing functions.

Transmission Control Protocol (TCP)

Transmission Control Protocol (TCP) is the connection-oriented Transport layer protocol for the TCP/IP suite. Many TCP/IP applications use TCP for transport, including Telnet, FTP, HTTP, and SMTP. TCP as a transport is commonly used by an application when reliability is necessary at the Transport layer. A comprehensive list of applications that use TCP can be obtained by downloading RFC 1700.

A TCP segment header provides us with a number of services including guaranteed delivery, sequencing, acknowledgments, windowing, and session control. Figure 3.2 breaks down a TCP segment.

Figure 3.2 A TCP segment

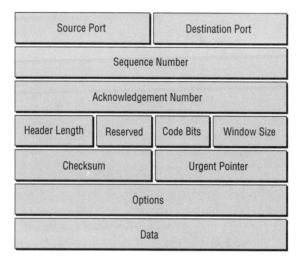

The fields of the TCP segment header are as follows:

The Source and Destination Port Number fields 16-bit fields that allow the TCP segment header to identify the source and destination applications that are communicating with each other.

The Sequence Number field A 32-bit field that identifies the sequence number of the first byte being sent in the data portion of the segment.

The Acknowledgement Number field A 32-bit field that identifies the next byte expected from a sender. TCP uses an expectational acknowledgement scheme where the receiver sends the sequence number of the next byte it is waiting for in the series of bytes being transferred.

The 4-Bit Header Length field Represents the length of the TCP segment minus any upper layer data. The value is represented as a number of 32-bit words in total. The TCP header will always be some multiple of 32.

The Code Bits field Allows the header to communicate any control-related functions that affect connection-oriented sessions such as setup and termination.

There are 6 bits in the field that may be set or clear at any given time, and therefore six control functions defined. They include:

SYN   The SYN bit is used to communicate that a transport session should be initiated. It signifies to a receiving host that the sender wishes the receiver to synchronize with the sender's sequence numbers.

ACK   The ACK bit communicates to a receiving host that, among other things, this segment is acknowledging receipt of a segment that has been sent.

RST   The RST bit signifies that a host is terminating a transport session.

URG   The URG bit makes the Urgent field in the segment significant. When the URG bit is set, the contents of the Urgent field become meaningful; otherwise, the field is ignored. It is typically set when the segment is part of urgent data.

FIN   The FIN bit is set by an application to signify that it has finished sending a data stream and the data can be sent to the destined application.

PSH   The PSH bit is set to signify a Push. It basically tells TCP to send any received data to the application even if it has not received the entire data stream.

The Window Size field   Communicates how much buffer space is available to receive additional segments from a sender. The number is specified as a byte value. The Window Size field is 16 bits long.

The Checksum field   Holds a value that represents the calculated checksum of the TCP segment. It is used to verify the validity of the segment. The Checksum field is 16 bits long.

The Urgent field   Used with urgent information. It holds the byte value of the end of urgent data. The Urgent field is also 16 bits long.

The Options field   A vendor-generic field that may or may not be used. It will commonly hold the maximum TCP segment size negotiated between the two hosts. If used, the Options field will be 32 bits long.

User Datagram Protocol

User Datagram Protocol (UDP) is the TCP/IP suite's connectionless transport. It is a very simple transport protocol with the least amount of overhead. There is no sequencing, acknowledging, control function, or windowing. The fact that it is connectionless implies that there are no reliability features in the protocol. Just send it and forget it. Applications that use UDP may implement reliability features at another layer, typically the Application layer itself.

As shown in Figure 3.3, the UDP header will always be 8 bytes in size, unlike the TCP header, which is 20 to 24 bytes in length. The following is a description of the fields:

The Source and Destination Port number fields   Allow the TCP segment header to identify the source and destination applications that are communicating. As in the TCP header, port number fields are 16 bits long.

The Length field   A 16-bit field that specifies the length of the segment.

The Checksum   A 16-bit field that validates the contents of the segment.

Figure 3.3   The UDP header

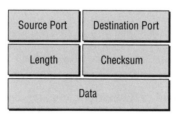

Internet Protocol

At the Internet layer, we concern ourselves with routing functions—getting packets from network A to network B. In an Internet Protocol (IP) packet header, we have fields that communicate things like logical addressing, path determination, and limited quality-of-service features. An IP packet can be 20 or 24 bytes in size. Figure 3.4 shows a breakdown of the fields in order.

Figure 3.4   The fields in an IP packet

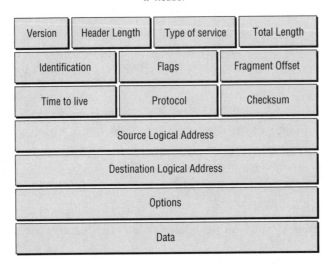

The fields in an IP packet are:

The Version field   4 bits; communicates what version of IP is being used. The current industry standard is version 4. Everything we will discuss in this chapter about IP is based on version 4.

The Header Length field   4 bits; communicates the length of the IP packet, minus upper layer data

The Priority And Type Of Service field   A field in which a series of 8 bits can be used to establish precedence for certain packets. It's a simplistic form of quality of service.

The Total Length field   16 bits; communicates the total length of the packet.

The Identification, Flags, and Fragment Offset fields   All used in the event the packet has to be fragmented by a router. The Identification field is a simple sequence number for fragments. The Flags field is 3 bits in size, but only two of these bits are used. They include the Last Fragment (LF) and Don't Fragment (DF) bits. The LF bit is set for the last fragment in a series. The DF bit can be set on packets that should not be fragmented. This can be a handy feature when testing for problems relating to Internetwork performance. Internetwork performance will be discussed in greater detail later in this book.

The Time-To-Live (TTL) field   8 bits; holds a value that represents hops/seconds. It is conceivable that due to network instabilities, a packet could get stuck in a routing loop. For this reason, we place a maximum life on a packet. A router always decrements a packet's TTL. If a router receives a packet with a TTL of 0, the router will discard the packet.

The Protocol field   Also an 8-bit field. It lists the protocol number for the Transport-layer protocol the packet is carrying. The protocol number for TCP is 6, and for UDP is 17.

The Header Checksum   A 16-bit field, it validates the packet.

Source and Destination logical fields   Hold a 32-bit source and destination IP address for the sending and receiving hosts, respectively.

The Options field   Can contain any of a number of IP options that are useful for various purposes including security and tracking functions. If used, the field will be 32 bits long.

The IP Address

IP involves the use of a special addressing scheme called an IP Address. An IP address is a 32-bit binary number that represents a network address, as well as a specific node on that network. Although there are a few exceptions, the IP address is typically represented in dotted decimal notation. An example of an IP address is 192.168.1.100.

The number is divided into four parts called octets or bytes. Each part is called an octet because it can be represented using eight binary digits. The binary equivalent to this number is as follows:

11000000 10101000 00000001 01100100

192 in decimal is 11000000 in binary

168 in decimal is 10101000 in binary

1 in decimal is 00000001 in binary

100 in decimal is 01100100 in binary

Even though we type the decimal version of the address when configuring IP hosts, the router actually interprets that as its binary equivalent. Converting binary to decimal and decimal to binary can be tedious work, but it is not hard as long as you understand some of the fundamentals.

We have all been taught to think using decimal numbers, or base 10. We get base 10 because the numbers used range from 0 to 9. In using the base 10 number system, all numbers increment in powers of 10. For example, they increment using:

... 100000, 10000, 1000, 100, 10, 1

Let's take for instance the number 2458. This number displays an 8 in the ones place, a 5 in the tens place, a 4 in the hundreds place, and a 2 in the thousands place. We can easily relate to that, right?

Digital devices like routers and computers, however, communicate using the binary number system. The binary number system is a base 2 system. The numbers used are 0 and 1 only. When counting in binary numbers, use increments as shown in Table 3.1.

Table 3.1   Binary Counting

Binary Number	Base-10 Equivalent	Binary Number	Base-10 Equivalent
0	0	1	1
10	2	11	3
100	4	101	5
110	6	111	7
1000	8	1001	9
1010	10	1011	11
1100	12	1101	13
1110	14	1111	15
10000	16	10001	17
10010	18	10011	19
10100	20	10101	21
10110	22	10111	23
11000	24	11001	25
11010	26	11011	27

Table 3.1   Binary Counting *(continued)*

Binary Number	Base-10 Equivalent	Binary Number	Base-10 Equivalent
11100	28	11101	29
11110	30	11111	31
100000	32	100001	33
100010	34	100011	35
100100	36	100101	37
100110	38	100111	39
101000	40	101001	41
101010	42	101011	43
101100	44	101101	45
101110	46	101111	47
110000	48	110001	49
110010	50	110011	51
110100	52	110101	53
110110	54	110111	55
111000	56	111001	57
111010	58	111011	59
111100	60	111101	61
111110	62	111111	63
...	...	11111111	256

Binary numbers increment in powers of 2 rather than 10. The number line is as follows:

... 128, 64, 32, 16, 8, 4, 2, 1

Knowing this, we can use this number line to perform conversions between decimal and binary. Let's take our original example of 192.168.1.100 and convert it to binary. Starting with 192: 192 is the result of adding 128 and 64. Therefore, we set 128 and 64 and clear 32, 16, 8, 4, 2, and 1, as shown. (If a place is set, it contains a 1. If it is clear, it contains a 0.)

128	64	32	16	8	4	2	1
1	1	0	0	0	0	0	0

For 168 we can add 128, 32, and 8 and therefore clear 64, 16, 4, 2, and 1, as follows.

128	64	32	16	8	4	2	1
1	0	1	0	1	0	0	0

To get 1, we set the 1 place and clear 128, 64, 32, 16, 8, 4, and 2, as follows.

128	64	32	16	8	4	2	1
0	0	0	0	0	0	0	1

To get 100 we add 64, 32, and 4 and therefore clear 128, 16, 8, 2, and 1.

128	64	32	16	8	4	2	1
0	1	1	0	0	1	0	0

Any decimal number between 0 and 255 can be represented using eight binary digits. Many calculators can perform these conversions for you, but there is a simple shortcut you can use to perform any conversions. Let's suppose we wanted to convert the decimal number 211 to its binary equivalent. We start by asking ourselves if we can subtract 128 from the 211. If so, we set the 128 position and do the subtraction. The result is 83. Next we ask ourselves if we can subtract 64 from 83. If so, we set the 64 position and do the subtraction. The result is 19. Can we subtract 32? The answer is no, so we clear the 32-bit position. Can we subtract 16? The answer is yes, so we set the 16-bit position and do the subtraction. Can we subtract 8? The answer is no, so we clear the 8-bit position. Can we subtract 4? The answer again is no, so we clear the 4-bit position. Can we subtract 2? The answer is yes, so we set the 2-bit position and perform the subtraction. Can we subtract 1? The answer is yes, so we set the 1-bit position and perform the subtraction. Once the result is a 0, we can stop.

$$
\begin{array}{r}
211 \\
- 128 \\
\hline
83 \\
- 64 \\
\hline
19 \\
- 16 \\
\hline
3 \\
- 2 \\
\hline
1 \\
- 1 \\
\hline
0
\end{array}
$$

The resulting binary number is 11010011.

Subnet Mask

As mentioned earlier, an IP address is a 32-bit address that represents a network address as well as a node on that network. Well, you may wonder, which part of the 32 bits is the network address and which is the node? We cannot tell by simply looking at our previous example of 192.168.1.100. We need more information. It is common practice to include more than just an IP address when configuring for IP. We also configure a subnet mask (also known as a *mask* or *netmask*). The job of the netmask is to identify the network portion of the address. Let's suppose we used the netmask of 255.255.255.0. If we apply this number, we can figure out which part of our address is network and which part is node.

By simply performing a logical AND function between the IP address and mask we can figure out the network address. The AND function is simple. When a 1 is ANDed with another 1, the result is a 1. Otherwise, the result will always be 0. The logic table is as follows:

Logical AND: 0 & 0 = 0

0 & 1 = 0

1 & 0 = 0

1 & 1 = 1

If we logically AND the IP address with its subnet mask, the result will be the network address. In Table 3.2, we have ANDed 192.168.1.100 with 255.255.255.0, and the resulting network address is 192.168.1.0. In this case, 192.168.1 is the network portion of the address and 100 is the node.

	Address	Network	Node
IP Address	192.168.1.100	11000000 10101000 00000001	01100100
Subnet Mask	255.255.255.0	11111111 11111111 11111111	00000000
Network Address	192.168.1.0	11000000 10101000 00000001	00000000

When the IP addressing standards were developed, the Internet community decided to separate ranges of addresses into five classes. Depending upon the first octet of the IP address, it will be part of one of these classes:

- If the first octet falls between 1 and 126, the address is class A.
- If the first octet falls between 128 and 191, the address is class B.
- If the first octet falls between 192 and 223, the address is class C.
- If the first octet falls between 224 and 239, the address is class D.
- If the first octet falls between 240 and 255, the address is class E.

The class A, B, and C addresses are the only addresses that may be used to address individual devices such as computers, printers, and router interfaces. Class D addresses are used for multicasting. These addresses are used in situations where one address is associated to more than one device. Some routing protocols like OSPF and EIGRP use a multicast address in the neighbor-discovery process. We will talk more about that in later topics. The class E has been reserved for scientific research.

Now, back to the class A, B, and C addresses. The Internet community wanted to come up with classes of addresses that were suited for large, medium, and small networks—class A addresses for the large networks, class B for the medium-size networks, and class C for the smaller ones. The differences are in the default subnet mask applied to any address in its class:

- Class A addresses have a default subnet mask of 255.0.0.0.
- Class B addresses have a default subnet mask of 255.255.0.0.
- Class C addresses have a default subnet mask of 255.255.255.0.

As mentioned previously, the subnet mask separates the network portion of an IP address from the node portion. That being the case, we have a total of 126 usable class A addresses, and each class A network can address 16,777,216 devices. Network 127 is reserved for local loopback addressing. We have 16,384 possible class B addresses, and each can potentially address 65,536 devices. We have 2,097,152 possible class C addresses, and each can address 254 devices.

If we went to our numbering authority and obtained a class C address, we would be able to address 254 hosts, assuming we used the default subnet mask in our organization. Let's suppose we were given the class C network address of 200.200.200.0. The available addresses would be as follows:

Available Address	Binary Version	What It Is
200.200.200.0	11001000 11001000 11001000 00000000	Network address
255.255.255.0	11111111 11111111 11111111 00000000	Subnet mask
200.200.200.1	11001000 11001000 11001000 00000001	First host address
200.200.200.2	11001000 11001000 11001000 00000010	Usable host address
.	.	.
.	.	.
.	.	.
200.200.200.253	11001000 11001000 11001000 11111101	Usable host address
200.200.200.254	11001000 11001000 11001000 11111110	Last host address
200.200.200.255	11001000 11001000 11001000 11111111	Directed broadcast

In the preceding list, the very first numeric combination of 200.200.200.0 is reserved to mean the actual network (wire) address. Any IP address with a node portion of all binary 0s is always a network address. The very last numeric combination of 200.200.200.255 is reserved as a directed broadcast address. A directed broadcast is an address that represents all devices on the 200.200.200.0 network. Any IP address with a node portion of all binary 1s is always a broadcast address. The other 254 numeric combinations in our example (the addresses 200.200.200.1 through 200.200.200.254) are valid addresses that can be used to address hosts, printers, and router interfaces.

IP Subnetting

In the previous example, we used a class C address and the default subnet mask. It allowed us to address 254 devices per network. What if we used a class B example such as 172.16.0.0? If we use the default subnet mask of 255.255.0.0, it will allow us to address 65,536 devices on one wire. How often can you get 65,536 devices to coexist on the same network? There are no technologies that I know of that will allow it. How about a class A network—16 million devices? No way! It is for this reason that we don't regularly use the default subnet mask for a network address. Sometimes the default subnet mask is feasible if you are using a class C address, but rarely is it so any other time.

Rather than using the default subnet mask and wasting a bunch of addresses, we can change the subnet mask and therefore allocate our numbers much more efficiently. We call this concept *IP subnetting*. In IP subnetting, we borrow some of the binary bits that were dedicated as node bits and turn them into additional network (subnet) bits. This allows us to make one network address usable by multiple networks.

Lets suppose we are given the class B address of 172.16.0.0. Using the default subnet mask of 255.255.0.0, we create the range of addresses 172.16.0.1 to 172.16.255.255. Based on this mask, we have one network address and 16 binary bits to use to address hosts.

Address	Network	Nodes	
172.16.0.0	10101100 00010000	00000000	00000000
255.255.0.0	11111111 11111111	00000000	00000000

Now if we change the subnet mask to something other than the default, we borrow some of the node bits to address additional networks. In the following example, we set 8 additional bits in the subnet mask and therefore borrowed 8 bits from the node side for more networks. Now we can address 254 networks, and each network can address 254 nodes.

Address	Network	Subnets	Nodes
172.16.0.0	10101100 00010000	00000000	00000000
255.255.255.0	11111111 11111111	11111111	00000000

This new subnet mask would result in these networks:

Address	Network	Subnets	Nodes
172.16.1.0	10101100 00010000	00000001	00000000
172.16.2.0	10101100 00010000	00000010	00000000
172.16.3.0	10101100 00010000	00000011	00000000
.		.	
.		.	
.		.	
172.16.253.0	10101100 00010000	11111101	00000000
172.16.254.0	10101100 00010000	11111110	00000000

> **NOTE** According to RFC, the first and last network in a series are invalid and therefore should not be used. In the Cisco environment, they are indeed valid and frequently used. The first network is valid provided you issue the global command `ip subnet-zero`, and the last subnet has always been valid without any action on your part.

> **NOTE** TCP/IP and IP subnetting are huge topics. If you need a detailed review of these topics, it may be a good idea for you to dig through some of the current RFC's, or pick up Sybex's *MCSE: TCP/IP for NT Server 4 Study Guide* by Todd Lammle.

Private Addresses

For a device to communicate using TCP/IP it needs a unique IP address. For a device to communicate over the Internet it needs a globally unique IP address. Where do we get these addresses? Well, most of us will lease or borrow one from our Internet Service Provider (ISP). Nowadays, IP addresses are much more difficult to obtain than they were 10 or 15 years ago. Today, they are in high demand and in limited supply. ISPs will closely control how many IP addresses are provided to you with your Internet service. They may even charge extra if you want more than a small number of them.

ISPs and firms that can prove they are worthy enough can go to the Internet numbering authorities and, for a fee, obtain new ranges of IP addresses. Those organizations that are deemed not worthy of new IP ranges are typically told to go to their ISP for addresses and/ or possibly use private (non-Internet-routable) addresses.

If your firm does not need Internet access, it is possible to pick any address range and use it without any problem. Doing this, however, could bring about problems later if your infrastructure changes and you do get Internet access. The Internet community prefers that you use one of a number of ranges set aside as "private" address ranges. These ranges will never be given out as Internet legal addresses by the numbering authorities. RFC 1918 outlines the following ranges:

- 10.0.0.0 to 10.255.255.255
- 172.16.0.0 to 172.31.255.255
- 192.168.0.0 to 192.168.255.255

These addresses can be used at will for private internal purposes. It is common in the industry to use protocols like Network Address Translation (NAT) to translate these private address ranges dynamically to globally unique (Internet-legal) addresses. We will discuss NAT in detail later in this chapter.

Configuring IP

Configuring a Cisco router for IP routing is easy. At a minimum, an IP address and subnet mask must be specified on each interface that will route IP. An example of a simple IP configuration is as follows:

```
!
interface ethernet 0
  ip address 10.2.3.1 255.255.255.0
!
```

Name Resolution

A large topic in the IP arena is that of name resolution. All TCP/IP applications are designed to use an IP address as a parameter. For instance: TELNET 102.45.23.76 or PING 9.23.7.45. People have a hard time remembering IP addresses, especially if they deal with a lot of them. For this reason, you also have the option to use a host name in place of an IP address for most TCP/IP applications. As an alternative, you can issue the command TELNET Chicago or PING Gateway1.mydomain.com. This is a good feature, but requires more work on your part. You have to configure some way to resolve these host names to IP addresses.

There are actually two ways that name resolution can be achieved. One method, of course, is to use Domain Name Services (DNS). By default, this feature is enabled on a Cisco router. However, also by default, the router has no idea what is the IP address of the DNS server. When a name resolution is needed and the router has not been configured with the IP address of a DNS server, the router will send a DNS query to the destination address 255.255.255.255 (a local broadcast). The server can receive the DNS request, provided the server and router are sharing the same network segment. It will not receive the request if the server is on a remote network.

To configure one or more IP addresses of DNS servers, use the global `ip name-server` command. A couple of examples are as follows:

```
ip name-server 1.2.3.4
ip name-server 10.2.3.4 172.16.3.2 192.168.1.2
```

As mentioned earlier, DNS resolution is on by default. This feature can sometimes be undesirable, however. When a command is issued to the command-line interface of a router, the command parser makes some assumptions. If a valid command is entered, it will execute it. If not, the parser assumes you want to initiate a Telnet session with a host named whatever you typed. This can be frustrating if you commonly misspell commands.

You can prevent these incorrect assumptions by disabling DNS resolution. To do this, issue the global `no ip domain-lookup` command. To re-enable DNS, use the command `ip domain-lookup`.

An alternative to DNS is to establish a local host table. A host table can be created by issuing one or more **ip hosts** commands. For instance:

```
!
ip host chicago 10.2.3.4
ip host sanjose 172.16.34.5 102.167.2.45
ip host newyork 192.168.1.2
!
```

Network Address Translation

A quickly growing problem in the IP community is that of IP address depletion. All devices that will communicate over the Internet need a unique IP address. IP addresses only afford us 32 bits of address space with which to work. Additionally, even with 32 bits available, a number of them are considered invalid address ranges. Considering the explosive growth of the Internet, if we hand out IP addresses to each and every device that will ever use Internet access, addresses will run out very soon. Consequently, a number of technologies have been developed that allow us to conserve addresses by decreasing the number of Internet-unique IP addresses required for all the users in a given firm to have Internet access. One of the more prominent of these technologies is Network Address Translation (NAT).

NAT allows us to translate non-Internet-routable addresses statically or dynamically to Internet-routable addresses. The benefit lies in that we do not need a one-to-one relationship for our addresses. We can translate a large number of illegal addresses into a small number of legal ones.

The concept revolves around a few basic features:

Inside Local addresses   Private addresses (Internet-illegal) that are translated to Internet-legal addresses

Inside Global addresses   Internet-legal addresses that are used by your organization for Internet access: NAT translates these addresses to and from Inside Local addresses.

Outside Global addresses   Internet-legal addresses used by hosts that are not part of your organization and are not being translated by your NAT service

Outside Local addresses   Internet-illegal addresses or private ranges used by other organizations.

For simple Internet access, a firm need only translate Inside Local addresses to Inside Global addresses. A router running the NAT service will change any source address in packets going out of your organization from an Inside Local to an Inside Global address. When a packet is coming from a host with an Outside Global address, the NAT router changes the destination address in the packet header from Inside Global to Inside Local. The router will store a dynamic table that associates these addresses to each other.

The example below displays a simple NAT configuration. Here we are translating the private pool of addresses between 10.1.0.0 and 10.1.255.255 to the globally unique addresses ranging between 200.200.200.16 and 200.200.200.31. The `ip nat pool` command is used to establish the pool of Inside Global addresses. We have given this pool of addresses the pool name `mypool`. The `ip nat inside source` command and `access-list 1` command work together to establish the range of addresses that are considered Inside Local and can be translated to the Inside Global addresses. Interface serial 0 is connected to the Internet; therefore, it is configured as the NAT outside interface. Interface Ethernet 0 is connected to the private side of the network and therefore is configured as the NAT Inside Interface.

```
!
ip nat pool mypool 200.200.200.17 200.200.200.30 255.255.255.240
ip nat inside source list 1 pool mypool
!
interface ethernet 0
  ip address 10.1.0.1 255.255.0.0
  ip nat inside
!
interface serial 0
  ip address 200.200.200.33 255.255.255.240
  ip nat outside
!
access-list 1 permit 10.1.0.0 0.0.255.255
!
```

The previous example is good as long as no more than 14 devices need Internet access concurrently. Cisco also supports address overloading on its Inside Local addresses.

What Cisco calls address overloading is sometimes known as Port Address Translation (PAT). The service is capable of storing not only source and destination IP addresses, but also source and destination port numbers. The net result is that, theoretically, we can have close to 65,000 private addresses utilizing one global address at the same time. The only thing required to enable address overloading is the addition of the keyword `overload` to the `ip nat inside source` command:

```
ip nat inside source list 1 pool mypool overload
```

The Advantages of NAT

In addition to allowing us to provide Internet access to a large number of devices when only a small number of legal addresses are available, NAT affords us other advantages as well:

- Since NAT provides translations from a single exit point in the network, it will hide your internal structure from the rest of the world. It is by no means a replacement for a good firewall solution, but can enhance your overall security solution.

- NAT makes a migration from one ISP to another very painless. Address ranges are typically owned by your ISP. If you decide at some point to change ISPs, you may not be able to take your IP addresses with you. If you have a large number of devices in your network that have been statically configured with the old ISP's IP addresses, you can use NAT to translate these addresses temporarily to your new range while migration is taking place.

- We can configure NAT to provide simple TCP load distribution. In other words, we can translate one IP address to many IP addresses to establish a server farm. For instance, suppose your organization has a Web site called www.myorg.com. DNS resolves this name to the IP address 200.200.200.1. Suppose that this site gets an extraordinary number of hits on a constant basis. One server alone cannot keep up with all the hits. What can you do? Well, you can use NAT to translate 200.200.200.1 to a number of addresses in round-robin fashion so that you can distribute the requests across multiple servers.

Below is a sample configuration of TCP load distribution. Here we have established the host address 200.200.200.1 as a virtual host using the `ip nat inside destination` command and `access-list 2`. We have created a pool of addresses called `webservers` that are the actual IP addresses of all of our 10 Web servers at 200.200.200.2 through 200.200.200.11. We have made this pool a `rotary` type pool to allow round-robin translations.

```
ip nat pool webservers 200.200.200.2 200.200.200.11 255.255.255.0
type rotary
```

```
ip nat inside destination list 2 pool webservers pool rotary
!
interface Serial0
 ip address 1.1.1.1 255.255.255.0
 ip nat outside
!
interface Ethernet0
 ip address 200.200.200.100 255.255.255.0
 ip nat inside
!
access-list 2 permit 200.200.200.1
```

Easy IP

An outstanding feature available in later versions of IOS is called Easy IP. Easy IP combines the features of NAT with the capability of assigning IP addresses dynamically using PPP. In other words, we can purchase a simple Internet dial-up account that provides only a dynamic IP address and configure the router to translate that one dynamic address to a number of Inside Local addresses. It will overload addresses in order to share that dial-up account with many users. Overall, this solution is great for smaller organizations that do not need Internet access too often. Simple dial-up accounts are among to least expensive of Internet access services.

NOTE Easy IP configuration will be discussed in detail in Chapter 10.

Internet Packet eXchange (IPX)

Internet Packet Exchange/Sequenced Packet Exchange (IPX/SPX) is a protocol suite that was developed in the early 1980s for Novell NetWare operability. Novell's NetWare product enjoys a huge market share in the Network Operating System arena. It is estimated that there are over half-a-million different implementations for NetWare worldwide. Cisco provides extensive support for IPX routing and NetWare interoperability. For these reasons, it is important to talk at least in some detail about IPX—even though the name of the protocol suite may imply it, IPX/SPX is not needed or used for access to the Internet.

IPX Packet Structure

IPX is the name of the Network-layer protocol in the suite. It provides the suite with logical addressing and routing capabilities. An IPX packet header is 30 bytes in length, and the fields are broken down as shown in Figure 3.5.

Figure 3.5   IPX packet structure

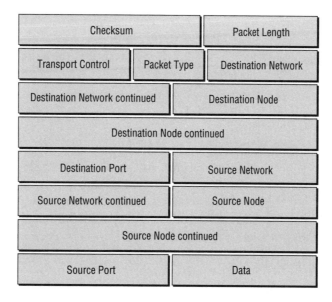

Here is a description of the fields in Figure 3.5:

The Checksum field   A 16-bit field that is normally set to 1s.

The Packet Length field   A 16-bit field that specifies the length of the entire IPX Packet. Length is always specified as a byte value.

The Transport Control field   An 8-bit field that indicates to a router how many other routers this packet has traversed. The value for the number of routers in this field rises incrementally when IPX packets are routed. IPX has a maximum hop count of 15. If this field exceeds 15 hops, the packet is discarded.

The Packet Type field   An 8-bit field that indicates which upper-layer protocol the packet is carrying. Two common upper-layer protocols carried are Sequenced Packet Exchange (SPX), with a protocol number of 5, and NetWare Core Protocol, with a protocol number of 17.

The Destination Network field   A 32-bit field that identifies the network address of the device for which the packet is destined.

The Destination Node field   A 48-bit field that identifies the MAC address or hardware address of the device for which the packet is destined.

The Destination Port field   A 16-bit field that identifies the service for which the packet is destined.

The Source Network field   A 32-bit field that identifies the network address of the device from which the packet came.

The Source Node field   A 48-bit field that identifies the MAC address or hardware address of the device from which the packet came.

The Source Port field   A16-bit field that identifies the service from which the packet came.

IPX Addressing Structure

IPX uses a very simple addressing scheme. As with IP, an IPX address is part network address and part node address. The network portion can be up to 32 bits in length, while the node portion is always 48 bits in length. The node portion of IPX is taken directly from the MAC address of the LAN interface. IPX addresses are displayed in hexadecimal. An example of an IPX address is as follows:

ABBADABA.0000.0C12.3456

> **NOTE**   Since a router's serial interfaces do not have MAC addresses burned in, the IPX node address needs to be configured. If it is not configured, the router will borrow the MAC address from the LAN interface with the lowest MAC address.

In the IPX environment, we assign a unique network address to every network. Devices on each network have to be configured to use the same encapsulation (frame type) to communicate. With some LAN media, we may have multiple encapsulations from which to choose. For instance, there are four Ethernet frame types that can carry IPX. If two devices in network ABBADABA want to communicate, they will have to be configured to use the same encapsulation. Based on Novell's given names, the four encapsulations are:

Ethernet 802.3   Novell's name for the original Ethernet standard. This standard has no basis in the IEEE. It is called 802.3 because it has the same length restrictions as the IEEE's frame.

Ethernet 802.2   Novell's name for the IEEE 802.3 standard. They call it 802.2 because all IEEE frames come with IEEE 802.2 LLC fields in the header.

Ethernet II   Novell's name for the Ethernet II standard developed by Xerox, Intel, and Digital.

Ethernet SNAP   Novell's name for an IEEE 802.3 frame with a SNAP header.

We do have the ability to communicate between devices that use different frame types. We let the router route between them. The trick behind this is that every encapsulation applied to the same wire must have a unique network (wire) address, as though it were a separate wire. Even though it is the same physical network, they are configured as separate logical networks.

Cisco also has its own unique way of referring to the four Ethernet frame types:

- What Novell calls Ethernet 802.3 Cisco calls *novell-ether*
- What Novell calls Ethernet 802.2 Cisco calls *sap*
- What Novell calls Ethernet II Cisco calls *arpa*
- What Novell calls Ethernet SNAP Cisco calls *snap*

This information will be valuable to you later when we discuss configuring the router for IPX operability.

Configuring IPX

Configuring a router to route IPX packets is a simple task. First and above all, *IPX must be enabled*. Unlike IP, IPX is not on by default and has to be enabled. Once the IPX service is enabled, it also enables IPX Routing Information Protocol (RIP). To allow an interface to route, it must be configured with an IPX network address. If it is expected that more than one encapsulation will be used for that interface, then each encapsulation will require a unique IPX network address.

The following is a simple IPX configuration.

```
!
ipx routing
!
interface ethernet 0
!
interface ethernet 0.1
   ipx network 99A encapsulation SAP
interface ethernet 0.2
   ipx network 88B encapsulation SNAP
```

```
!
interface ethernet 1
  ipx network 77F
!
interface serial 0
  ipx network AAA
!
```

- First we enable IPX using the `ipx routing` command. Once it is enabled, we can configure which interfaces will be routing IPX.

- On interface E1, we assign a network address of 77F. Since we don't tell the router which encapsulation to use, the router will default to using the novell-ether encapsulation.

- Serial 0 is configured similarly, but with a network number of AAA. Serial 0 will use HDLC encapsulation because HDLC is the default for serial interfaces.

- Ethernet 0 is configured to communicate with two logical IPX networks using subinterfaces. We do this so that Ethernet 0 can communicate using more than one frame type.

- Ethernet 0.1 has been assigned the IPX network number of 99A, with an encapsulation type of SAP.

- Ethernet 0.2 has been assigned the IPX network number of 88B, with an encapsulation type of SNAP.

Once these basic configurations are done, IPX packets will be routed. Since IPX RIP is automatically enabled along with IPX, routing will immediately commence. If you want to use a different routing protocol than RIP, that protocol will have to be enabled and RIP disabled. We will discuss another IPX routing protocol alternative called EIGRP in Chapter 8, "Hybrid Routing Protocols."

AppleTalk

Around the same time period that IPX was developed, Apple Corporation was working on a new protocol of its own. Apple engineers kept a couple of concerns in mind during development of this protocol. One concern was that their computer platform should have the capability to utilize computer networking. A second concern was that they create a protocol suite that would integrate networking into their familiar, easy-to-use interface. The result was called AppleTalk.

When AppleTalk was first developed, it was designed only for a smaller environment. In fact, the limitations are quite significant by today's standards. Each network received a unique wire address, much like the process in the IPX environment. Each network, however, only allowed for up to 256 total devices to be addressed. These addresses, though, were displayed in decimal rather than in hex, as is the case in IPX. Later, this standard was called officially *AppleTalk Phase 1*.

Today we have AppleTalk Phase 2. Phase 2 is much more scalable for larger internetworks. It allows us to associate a wire range to a network rather than a single wire number. Now, instead of giving a wire the wire address of 1000, we can give a wire the range of 1000 to1005. Each number in the range can be used for addressing purposes and can address 253 devices per number in the range. In the example of 1000 to1005 we have a range of six different wire numbers; therefore, the network can address up to 1,518 Apple/Macintosh hosts.

Apple has a 24-bit addressing scheme. 16 bits of it comprise an administratively assigned network address. The other 8 bits constitute the node address. Apple computers will choose a network address within the wire range provided, and then select a node address on that wire that has not already been used. The node selection process is completely dynamic.

AppleTalk arranges resources into logical groupings called *zones*. When Apple computers request resources, they do so using name-binding requests. Name-binding requests are only performed in a single zone. All resources such as printers, scanners, and file servers will belong to only one zone. When a request is made for one of these services, it must be directed to the zone in which that device resides.

Configuring AppleTalk

Configuring a router to route AppleTalk is quite simple. There are really only three required components to configure. First, AppleTalk needs to be turned on in order to operate. Unlike IP, AppleTalk is disabled by default on a Cisco router. The command to enable AppleTalk routing is simply `appletalk routing`. Once AppleTalk is enabled, Routing Table Maintenance Protocol (RTMP) is also turned on. RTMP is a simple distance vector routing protocol. It is commonly referred to as *Apple RIP*.

Once AppleTalk is turned on, the only items left to configure are the individual interfaces that will be routing AppleTalk. Each interface will need, at a minimum, a wire range and one or more zone names. An interface requires one wire range to be specified, but unlike Apple devices, each wire range can be part of more than one zone. An interface, therefore, can be configured with more than one zone name. It is up to the Apple administrator to choose to which zone an individual device will belong.

The following is an example of a simple Apple configuration. First we enable AppleTalk routing. Then at interface E0 we configure it with the wire range 500 to 505. Next, we associate wire address 500 to 505 to zone Ozone. Interface E1 is then assigned the wire range of 600 to 610. Devices on wire range 600 to 610 can be part of Ozone or Twilight Zone.

```
!
appletalk routing
!
interface ethernet 0
  appletalk cable-range 500-505
  appletalk zone Ozone
!
interface ethernet 1
appletalk cable-range 600-610
  appletalk zone Ozone
  appletalk zone Twilight Zone
!
```

Once these three basic steps are complete, AppleTalk packets will be routed. AppleTalk's RTMP is automatically turned on when AppleTalk is turned on; therefore, routing will immediately commence. If you want to use a different routing protocol than RTMP, that protocol will have to be enabled. We will discuss another AppleTalk alternative to RTMP called EIGRP in Chapter 8, "Hybrid Routing Protocols."

4

Network Design

When discussing network design there are no concrete right or wrong answers. The final network design becomes more a question of what the network goals are and what compromises you are willing to make. Show a network design to three different people and all of them will probably tell you how they would have done it differently. Some people may want to compromise efficiency for ease of understanding; others may sacrifice fault tolerance for cost.

Consider the example of a client who uses a full class C network on each of their point-to-point interfaces. Since they need only two addresses per link, they are essentially wasting 251 usable addresses. They could have taken one class C network and subnetted it out to address their point-to-point links, or even used IP Unnumbered on those particular links. This particular client, however, has a full class B address assigned to them, so address space is not a concern, and they find it easier to understand their network without having to worry about subnet masking.

The primary design considerations are:

- manageability
- scalability
- reliability

You want a network that is relatively easy to manage, is scalable so it can grow as your networking needs grow, and is reliable enough that you can go home and not have to worry about being beeped in the middle of the night because the network is down.

NOTE Unfortunately most of us get very little opportunity to actually design networks from the ground up. Typically there is some existing network we are either going to add onto or completely replace. When is the last time someone walked into your office and said, "I know we don't have a network today but we need to build one. Here is a bunch of money, and here are some specifications about what we need it to do. You have three months to design it"? Life would be so much easier if things worked this way. Designing around a pre-existing network uses the same concepts as starting from scratch but tends to impose more limitations on you. The same principles are used to modify a network—you just get to work a little harder to make all the pieces fit.

Scalability

Scalability is the flexibility to adapt and grow as necessary. A scalable network can be adjusted as required without requiring major modifications. With the network becoming more and more tightly imbedded into the business processes of today's companies, the increasing demand for network services requires that any network be easily adaptable to handle growth.

Scalable networks are typically built on the model of a hierarchy, as shown in Figure 4.1. At the top of this hierarchy are the backbone or core routers; in the middle are the distribution routers; and at the bottom are the access routers. Using a hierarchical model, each router fits into a specific class that performs specific functions. By defining each router's role in this way and adhering to those roles, you tend to avoid spreading different processing functions haphazardly throughout the environment. This makes it much easier to manage your environment, because you can tell what a router should be doing based on its role in the hierarchy.

Figure 4.1   A hierarchical design for a scalable network

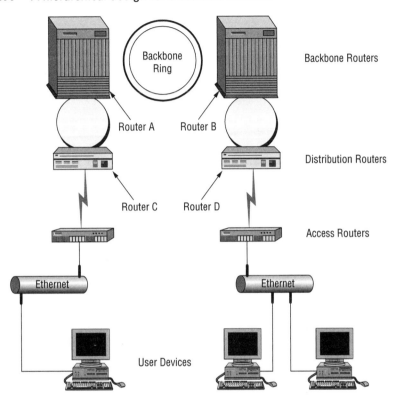

The Core Layer

The core layer is basically the heart of the network; it is responsible for optimizing network paths. Most of the data on your network will pass through the core routers, as will the routing protocol information. This means that your backbone environment must be able to withstand at least one of the core routers going down without impacting the network too much as a whole. In Figure 4.1, if one of the backbone routers does go down, half of the network will be lost. If, for example, we were to lose router B, then everything on the left-hand side of the diagram would be unable to talk to anything on the right-hand side of the diagram. This is obviously not a very fault tolerant design. If, however, we were to connect router A to router D and router B to router C, then we could deal with the loss of one of our backbone routers. Alternatively, we could connect routers C and D and get the same kind of functionality with only one link instead of two. See the example shown in Figure 4.2.

Figure 4.2 This design is more fault tolerant that the one shown in the previous figure.

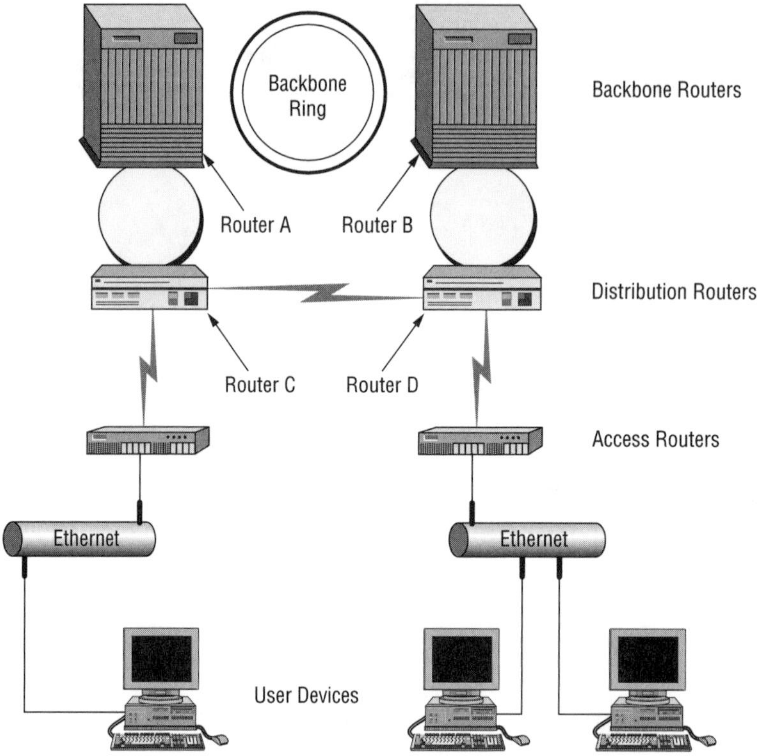

Now if either router A or router B goes down for some reason, we can still get into the core from both sides of the network by using the link between C and D. In this way, the network is capable of routing around the loss of either of the backbone routers, provided that the routing protocols involved are smart enough to realize that they need to use the link between C and D to do so. Most of today's modern routing protocols will recover from the loss of either of these two routers relatively quickly.

> **NOTE** If you are using static routes you will need to add the backup routes manually and apply an administrative distance high enough so these backups are not used when they don't need to be. The default administrative distance for a static route is either one or zero, depending on how you configure it. You can also use Hot Standby Routing Protocol (HSRP) to accomplish the same goal. HSRP will be discussed in more detail later in the book.

Core routers are typically Cisco 7000 and 12000 series routers. A lot of companies, however, are now going to layer 3 switched backbones with mission-critical devices hanging directly off switch ports, so that, basically, the core resides inside the switch.

Using a switch such as the Cisco Catalyst 6509 with a Multi Switch Feature Card (MSFC) provides the functionality of both a router and a switch in the same box, but with some added complexity. This type of core implementation is becoming more and more popular. With such a switch, you can not only break up your broadcast domains but also let the switching functions break up your collision domains to allow for excellent throughput. Cisco switching is outside the scope of this book, unfortunately. If you are looking to replace your core backbone, a layer 3 switch might be something worth looking into. Remember to plan for redundancy, though. You don't want your whole core to reside in one switch, because if that switch dies you are in big trouble. No matter what your core looks like, it needs to be fault tolerant, and a single switch does not offer that. This fault tolerance can be obtained using multiple switches in the proper configuration. Fault tolerance is discussed in more detail in the section "24seven Design," later in this chapter.

The Distribution Layer

Distribution routers typically provide access into the core and need to be able to select the best path to different locations in order to make the most efficient use of the available bandwidth. The Distribution router is responsible for quality of service to network applications trying to traverse the core. Often your Distribution routers will be using some sort of queuing mechanism or other means to provide as much consistency as possible in the quality of service.

Distribution routers are typically Cisco 3600 or 4000 series routers. The Cisco 4000 series routers have been phased out and are being replaced with the 3600 series.

The Access Layer

The Access layer is where your users typically gain access to the network. Access routers are used to limit broadcasts. Typically you will implement access lists on your access routers so that unwanted traffic is stopped before it can pass through the network. It makes no sense to allow a piece of data to be passed all the way to the core only to have it blocked and thrown away. If you are going to block traffic, you will want to block it as close to the source as possible.

Access routers are typically Cisco 1000, 2500, and 2600 series routers. Which router is used at which layer is less a matter of what model you are using than of the function that a particular router performs. You could use a Cisco 2500 router as a core router; however, this is only recommended for small networks. Small networks really do not need a full-blown hierarchy; you might need only core routers, or else a single router might serve multiple roles in the hierarchy. It all depends on your environment. It is important to remember that anything you design and deploy now will have to be modifiable to fit your needs a few years from now.

Manageability

Manageability should be a major concern when designing, implementing, or modifying you network structure. Typically a good design is relatively easy to manage, but there are things you can do to make it even more manageable. Most of the time your network is going to run on its own without too much outside help. When there is a problem, however, you are going to need to be able to solve that problem as quickly as possible, because most network problems impact many people and are very noticeable.

Out-of-Band Management

There is nothing worse than having a link down and not being able to get to the router to see what is going on. Unless you have someone on site who knows what is going on and can get into a router and look around, you might seriously want to consider setting up a dial-in modem on all your remote site routers. This is relatively simple to do and can save you a lot of headaches later on. Using a modem in this way is referred to as out-of-band management, because you are not using network bandwidth to connect to the router.

The one problem with leaving a modem connected to your router is that it can be viewed as a security risk. Using some form of more secure authentication, such as RADIUS server authentication, which Cisco supports, can minimize this risk.

In the case of a remote site, however, you may not be able to access the Remote Authentication Dial-In User Service (RADIUS) server for authentication. What you can do in this case is configure the modem and simply unplug the telephone line. When you have a problem and need to get into the router, have someone plug the line back in for you.

Sure, this is not the most beautiful solution, but it does beat having to get in a car or on a plane only to learn that the problem was something very simple. It is also much easier to walk someone through plugging in a phone line than to try to get them to help you troubleshoot the router over the phone.

Connectivity

You are going to want to be able to Telnet to every router within your environment to check things out and see what is going on. Most of the time your network will support IP. Because Telnet runs across TCP, if you are running IP then you will most likely be able to Telnet to your routers. If, however, your network does not support IP, you will probably want to enable it so that you can access your routers.

I have seen networks designed to support only IPX that had no IP addressing, so there was no way to change anything on the routers aside from using a console cable. This is fine if the routers sit under your desk, but it becomes a management headache if they are elsewhere in the building and a logistical nightmare if they are at remote sites. For this reason, you will most likely want to configure IP routing, even if it is only to manage your routers. A side benefit to running IP is that most of the modern management protocols, like SNMP, rely on IP services as their transport protocol.

Route Summarization

When designing the layout of your network, it is important to take *route summarization* into account. Route summarization allows you to keep your routing tables small, and to increase routing efficiency.

Suppose that your network looks like Figure 4.3 and you are going to use the 192.168.0.0–192.168.255.255 address range for it because it is not connected to the outside world. Obviously you can number the network pretty much any way you want to. If you want to optimize things, however, you can set it up so that the top router needs only two routes. To that end, if we keep 192.168.0.0–192.168.127.0 to the left and 192.168.128.0–192.168.255.0 to the right, we can summarize all the routes into just two: a route to 192.168.0.0–255.255.128.0 out S0 and a route to 192.168.0.0–255.255.0.0 out S1. The router will use the more specific route first, so this will work. Alternatively, you can specify two different major network routes: 192.168.0.0 and 192.168.128.0 with a 255.255.128.0 mask. We can continue this thought process as we move through the network so that we can summarize routes as we go. Looking at router B, we can apply address 192.168.0.0-192.168.63.0 out the S0 side and address 192.168.64.0–192.168.127.0 out the S1 side. This would also allow us to condense the routing table on this router.

NOTE There are many different ways this could have been done; this is just one example.

Figure 4.3 Route summarization

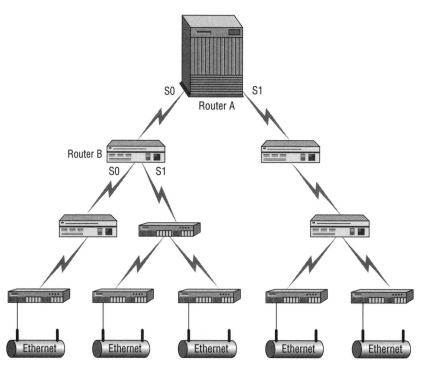

Figure 4.4 shows how you might address the network to allow for route summarization. Rather than defining what types of links exist between the routers, we have simply assigned a full class C network to each link. If these were point-to-point serial links, we could have used IP Unnumbered or subnetted out an address to use for them. The goal of Figure 4.4 is to make you think about route summarization and the constraints it places on your network addressing.

Figure 4.4   A network designed for router summarization might look like this.

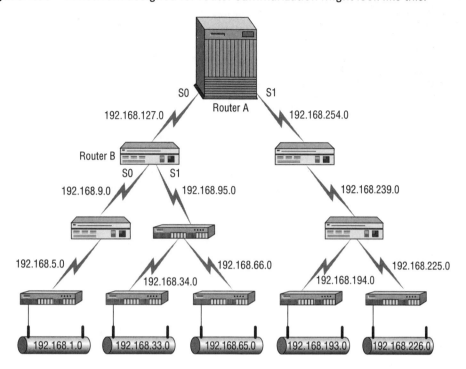

WARNING   Route summarization makes a lot of sense; however, you have to be careful that you have complete control over the network addressing if you are going to implement it. Because you are summarizing your routes, if you use the wrong addresses in the wrong places, those addresses you configured in the wrong places will most likely be unreachable. Therefore, it is very important to keep careful control over where you use your addresses. Placing an address in the wrong place may destroy all your route summarization efforts, or it simply may not be possible to route to those addresses that are incorrectly located. What actually happens depends on which routing protocols you are running.

Route summarization can be done with any class of address; I have simply used the above example to illustrate the general concept. It does not make any difference if you are working with multiple class C networks or if you are using a single class C and subnetting into multiple networks. Either way, you can still design a scheme which will allow for route summarization.

In my experience, route summarization is important to take into consideration, but do not get too carried away with designing the perfect network for summarization. It might be fun as an intellectual experience, but the time required to keep it up and the headaches involved are really not worth it. Pick a point and summarize as best you can to it but don't worry if it is not perfect.

Most protocols will AutoSummarize your routes for you. Because they do not carry subnet information, RIP and IGRP will summarize based on address class boundaries. EIGRP carries a subnet mask and will AutoSummarize routes for you as best it can. OSPF does not AutoSummarize routes, but you can configure the summarizations you want when you set it up.

Obviously you want as few routes as possible in your router, and summarization allows you to trim down the number of routes needed. However, it also takes away some of your freedom in assigning addresses to devices because you have to make sure that the summarized routes will work properly with the new addresses you are using. In fact, it is much easier to design for summarization when you first set up the network than to go in and try and summarize routes later. If your luck is anything like mine, your present network-addressing scheme will look like someone intentionally designed it to prevent any type of route summarization from working.

Route Redistribution

No matter how well you design your network for expandability, you may run across situations that are beyond your control, such as acquiring another company or being acquired yourself. Ideally, you want to have only one routing protocol in your environment per routed protocol.

Suppose, however, that you had to incorporate a RIP network into your existing OSPF network. Route redistribution allows you to take the routes discovered via one protocol and convert them into another protocol. For example, RIP routes can be converted into OSPF routes, and vice versa. Redistribution can be executed between almost any routing protocols. This is convenient when you are not allowed to change the routing protocol on the other system and seems like an ideal solution to the problem of different routing protocols having to work together. Unfortunately, we do not live in a perfect world. There are a couple of things you need to consider.

In Figure 4.5, we want router A to redistribute its RIP routes via OSPF, and we want router B to redistribute its OSPF routes to router A. This allows the routers within the OSPF environment to know about all the routes from within the RIP environment, and vice versa. Obviously, to redistribute routes, one of the routers needs to be running multiple routing protocols. In our case, router A is running both RIP and OSPF, so it knows about all the OSPF routes and all the RIP routes. Router A, therefore, handles the redistribution process. All it has to do is take the routes it has learned via the first routing protocol, and then advertise via the other routing protocol using the default metric you have defined statically. When you tell the router to redistribute its routes via another routing protocol, you have to assign the proper metric for the protocol to the redistributed routes. This means that every route that is redistributed to the other routing protocol will be given the same cost metric. For example, if we were redistributing OSPF into RIP and we assigned a cost metric of 3 hops for all OSPF routes (since RIP uses only hop count as a metric), then a router receiving the redistributed routes would see them as normal RIP routes 3 hops away. After adding these routes to its routing table, the router will add 1 hop to the cost and broadcast them out to all other RIP routers on segments it is connected to. This can cause poor route selection.

Figure 4.5   RIP-OSPF route redistribution

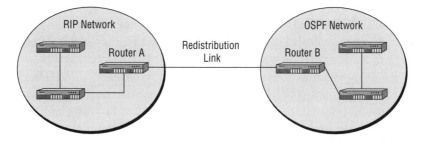

In Figure 4.6, suppose that routers C and D are redistributing their OSPF routes to RIP routes, and you have a hop count of 3 assigned for all OSPF routes redistributed into RIP. If router A wants to talk to router B in this scenario, which route will it take?

Figure 4.6   Route redistribution can lead to sub-optimal path selection.

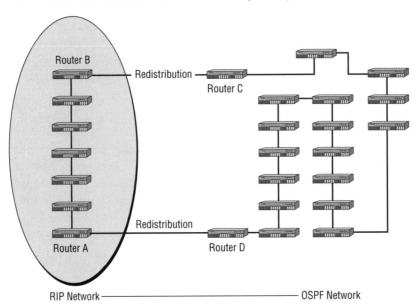

Router A will see a route to router B advertised through the RIP network with a distance of 6 hops. Router A will also see a route to router B advertised via RIP with a distance of 3 hops. Obviously there is no way to get from router B to router A in 3 hops. This 3-hop route is visible to A because router D knows how to get to router B, and D is redistributing all of its OSPF routes into the RIP environment with a metric of 3 hops. This means every route that router D knows about via OSPF, no matter how far away it is, is advertised in the RIP environment by router D as being 3 hops away.

Router A is going to choose the 3-hop route to B to add to its routing table because as far as it is concerned, 3 hops is better than 6 hops. It does not question the information it is receiving and assumes it will truly take only 3 hops to get to router B. Obviously we know that the 6-hop route is much shorter than taking a detour through router D to get to router B. As far as router A is concerned, however, the route through router D is the best one, even though it is more than twice as long as going directly to router B in 6 hops.

When configuring or deciding to use redistribution, you need to be careful in selecting your metrics. You also need to consider your topology. Once you set up redistribution, you should monitor your routing tables and the general responsiveness of the network for awhile to make sure the network is functioning as anticipated. You need to be very careful to make sure you select a proper metric, because that metric must be used when advertising all routes discovered via one protocol into the other protocol. Most of the time you can pick a spot in the middle of the network and determine the actual cost up to that point; then use that cost as your redistribution cost or metric.

WARNING   RIP has a max hop count of 15, so keep in mind that too high a redistribution cost could make some networks unreachable. For example, if we redistribute EIGRP into RIP with a default metric of 8 hops, then no router can be more than 7 hops away from the point of redistribution or the redistributed routes will become unreachable. If you were 8 hops away from the point of redistribution, you would have the 8-hop default metric plus the 8-hop distance from the point of redistribution, and this would give you 16 hops. A distance of 16 hops is defined as unreachable in RIP.

TIP   The metric you use to redistribute will depend on the actual metrics of the protocol into which you are redistributing. For example, the metric could be something relatively simple, such as cost in OSPF, or something more complex, such as bandwidth, delay, MTU, reliability, and loading. Remember that these values are set statically and globally for all redistributed routes on the router doing the redistribution.

Tunneling

Tunneling is a Cisco IOS feature that allows you to pass a specific protocol through an area that does not support that protocol, or to hide the given protocol within an another protocol as it traverses an area. Tunneling in its most basic form is the encapsulation of one protocol in another protocol. Through tunneling, the encapsulated protocol is hidden within the encapsulating protocol. This means that as far as any network devices are concerned, the whole encapsulated packet is merely data inside the encapsulating protocol's packet.

One way to think of this is to imagine that you have a sales guy at your office who travels between New York and Boston weekly. Let's call him Ted. In your office there is a backpack that Ted carries between New York and Boston for mail. If you are in Boston, and you address an envelope to someone in the New York office using their New York inter-office mail address and place it in Ted's backpack, it will get to the intended person in New York. Ted has no clue what is in the backpack. He knows only that it is mail, a.k.a. data, and that he has to carry it to New York with him. Now, as long as the mail is in the backpack (encapsulated) it is using Ted's source and destination address to determine where to go. So Ted gets on a plane and flies to New York, and when he gets to the New

York office he dumps the contents of the backpack into the interoffice mail. The actual interoffice addresses are visible again (no longer hidden in the backpack, or encapsulated) and the mail is delivered like normal interoffice mail. The entire time Ted had the mail in the backpack, however, its real addresses were not known; thus, we did not have to support mail between New York and Boston and only had to tell Ted to carry the backpack.

A common example of this is using IP to tunnel IPX across a network.

In Figure 4.7, there is a tunnel set up between router A and router B to allow IPX traffic to get across the network in the middle. Since the middle network does not support IPX, we have to hide the IPX traffic as it crosses through this network. The basic steps in setting up a tunnel for IPX are:

1. Create the tunnel interface.

2. Assign an IPX network number to the tunnel.

3. Define a tunnel source.

4. Define a tunnel destination.

5. Set the tunnel encapsulation type.

Figure 4.7   A tunnel is set up between router A and router B.

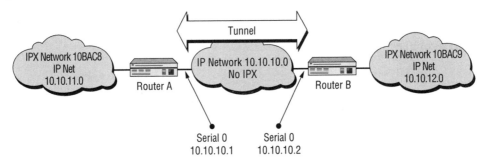

For example, on router A, the tunnel commands might look something like this:

```
interface Tunnel0
 no ip address
 ipx network 10BAD1
 tunnel source Serial0
 tunnel destination 10.10.10.2
```

The tunnel needs to be set up from both ends, so you would need to set up the tunnel in the opposite direction on router B. You do not see the tunnel encapsulation because we are using the default of GRE IP.

NOTE   A tunnel is not limited to spanning two directly connected hosts but can span multiple hops.

Tunneling allows you to get a protocol across an area where it is not supported without having to configure that protocol in the area in question. The tunnel does not care what is in the middle. So long as the carrier protocol is supported along the full length of the tunnel, what is in the middle does not matter. Tunneling obviously adds some overhead to your router and to the data but can be an ideal solution in certain situations.

Sizing

Two of the most often asked questions in network design are, "How much bandwidth do I need?" and "What types of routers should I use?"

Communication Lines

As far as the Local Area Network is concerned, you generally can use whatever speed transport medium you have available to you, whether that is 4, 10, 16, or 100Mbps, or more. The LAN speed is typically limited by your existing equipment and cabling. In general, when it comes to LAN bandwidth, it is easier and cheaper to over-engineer your LAN. You may only need to run 10Mbps Ethernet to support your user community, but it is not really that much more expensive to go to 100Mbps. LAN bandwidth is typically not like your WAN links where you are paying for the bandwidth every month. On the LAN, you are typically paying a one-time installation fee, so why not get as much bandwidth as you can afford?

It is a pain to realize that your category 3 wiring will not support 100Mbps when management finally decides the network needs to run at that speed. You will have to rewire your whole infrastructure, and there are many things in life more fun than ripping out wiring and running new cable. Try to make sure that whatever you put in will be able to grow with the environment. It may be fine to be running 10Mbps Ethernet or 4Mbps Token Ring, but make sure you can bump up that speed pretty easily if you have to.

WAN links are a lot different. With your WAN lines, you are paying your telecom company a fee each month based on the amount of bandwidth you have ordered, whether or not you use it. It makes little sense to pay for a full T-1 line if you are only going to sporadically push 56Kbps of data over it.

If you don't need a constant connection, you should look at something like ISDN with Dial-on-Demand routing (DDR). DDR only brings up the line when there is traffic that needs to be sent. This can provide a significant cost savings, provided you are not bringing the line up and down very frequently.

> **_WARNING_** Be very careful with ISDN. Although it can be a very cost-effective solution, it can get very expensive very fast. It is not a lot of fun to find out from a giant phone bill that your ISDN link was up continuously for a month. The ISDN carrier is not going to have any sympathy for you.

When you realize you need dedicated connectivity, you need to analyze the costs versus your actual needs. Most people who work with this stuff on a day-to-day basis want a T-3 link into their homes, but no one, as we all know, is willing to pay for this access speed; nor is it necessary for a home user. What you need to do is find a balance between what would be ideal and what is cost effective. There is a wide range of options available, and the technology you choose, along with the telecom carrier, will determine what is available. Not all services are available in all areas, and some options maybe prohibitively expensive based on geography.

A typical WAN leased line should be able to handle about two times the average bandwidth you are planning to run across it. This means that if you anticipate average bandwidth to be 56Kbps, you will want a line capable of at least 128Kbps. This is not a hard-and-fast rule, but rather a guideline. You want to make sure that you have enough bandwidth above your average traffic load to be able to support and recover from momentary peaks in traffic volume.

The best way to think of your WAN lines is as a highway. If you have a capacity of 6 cars per second on a given stretch of road and you are running at full capacity, with 6 cars entering this stretch per second, what will you do if 36 cars suddenly show up at once and try to get through? Assuming there is no accident, you now have traffic backed up and no way to recover because you are still getting 6 new cars per second. As long as you are still getting 6 new cars per second the road will never recover. However, if all of a sudden you start getting only 5 new cars per second, in 36 seconds, the road will have been able to transfer out those extra cars.

Actually figuring out your bandwidth requirements ahead of time is no simple task. The best way to determine this is to think about what kind of traffic is going to traverse the WAN links, and how much. Experience plays into this estimate a lot. This is one case where working with an existing LAN can be helpful: You can take your existing links and calculate the amount of traffic over them to try to extrapolate an average traffic value for your new links. Once you have this value, you can make a more informed decision about your bandwidth requirements.

Routers

There are many factors that need to be considered when choosing a router. You need to know the role of the router in your environment, whether it is a core, distribution, or access router. Cisco classifies their routers into these three groups, which does not mean a distribution class router cannot serve as a core router. In large environments, it is best to use the Cisco classes when choosing your routers. In smaller environments you don't need to use a 7000 series router as your core router; you can make do with a 3640.

The major factors when choosing a router are the number of ports and the port type. Your router needs to be able to handle all your connection needs and leave some room for expansion. For example, if you have four serial links and one Ethernet link, don't get a router with just four serial ports and one Ethernet port. If you do, you will have no room to grow and no extra ports available if one should happen to die. Most of the newer routers Cisco is making are modular, which means you buy the chassis and populate it with the interface cards you want. This allows for greater flexibility when configuring your router and also allows you to change things around down the line. For example, take out your FDDI ports and replace them with Fast Ethernet ports. This flexibility allows you to modify the physical configuration of the router to suit your present environment.

The determination of which router to use will usually boil down to how many ports you need. Obviously the 7000 series routers are more powerful than the 2600 series; but if you only need three or so ports, the 2600 should be able to support that without too much trouble. The cost differential is enough that you cannot justify buying the 7000 for only three ports.

Once you have the router, you are going to need to put flash memory and RAM into it. The amount of flash you need depends on the IOS you are going to run. Each IOS has specific flash requirements, which are typically located in the IOS documentation. You will need at least enough flash to hold the IOS image. Typically I like to have enough flash to hold two IOS images. This way I can bring in a new IOS during an upgrade without having to delete the old one.

When deciding how much memory to put into the router, you need to consider what you are actually going to run on the router. A router just routing IP traffic needs a lot less memory than a router configured for a VPN. These requirements are typically documented based on the IOS you are using. Some examples for IOS 12.0.7 on the 3640 router are shown in Table 4.1.

Table 4.1   RAM Requirements for IOS 12.0.7 on a 3640 Router

Platform	Release	Features	Flash	RAM
3640	12.0.7	IP/IPX/AT/DEC PLUS	8MB	32MB
3640	12.0.7	IP/IPX/AT/DEC	8mb	32MB
3640	12.0.7	Enterprise Plus	8MB	48MB
3640	12.0.7	IP	4MB	24MB

The more features you add, the larger the IOS image, and the more processing the router has to do. If you were to run the IP/IPX/AT/DEC PLUS and only run IP with it, you could probably get away with running less than 32MB of RAM. There are commands within the router that will show you how hard it is working and how much free memory it has. Ideally, you would rather have too much memory than too little. The Cisco guidelines for memory requirements are for the most part pretty good, provided you are working with a fairly normal router configuration. If you are using a lot of subinterfaces or anything intensive, you may need more memory; but for most cases the Cisco numbers are a good place to start.

> **TIP**   When sizing the memory on Cisco routers, make sure you also consider the number of routes. Estimate about 1.2KB for each route. This is not important for smaller networks (<500 routes). For those, the default memory is enough. With larger networks (>1024) that are running OSPF, and especially those running BGP, this calculation comes in handy.

Routing Protocols

Which routing protocol to run is largely a matter of personal choice, and you are going to have to be able to support the routed protocols required by your application servers. For example, if you are running AppleTalk, you are going to need to run a routing protocol that will support AppleTalk, such as Routing Table Maintenance Protocol (RTMP).

When selecting a routing protocol, you want to focus on efficiency and time of convergence. While RIP has been very popular in years past and is a well defined, well tested standard, it is generally not the best routing protocol to use based on efficiency or convergence time. Every 30 seconds, RIP broadcasts out the routers' entire routing table. If you have large routing tables, this can take up a significant amount of bandwidth. This broadcast is sent even if there is no change in the network, so information is being repeated over and over again. RIP also converges rather slowly because a new route always has to propagate through the network from router to router. Figure 4.8 is an example of a large RIP environment.

Figure 4.8   A large RIP environment can have very large convergence times.

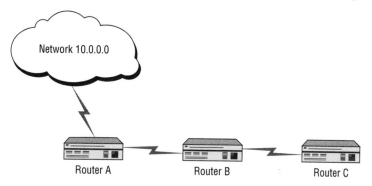

In Figure 4.8, if router A learns about a new route from network 10.0.0.0, it will add the new route to its routing table and then advertise the new route. Router A will add an additional hop to the cost of the route when it advertises it. When router B receives a copy of A's routing table, it will also receive the new route and will follow the same process of advertising the route and adding a hop when its RIP update interval expires. This means that router C may not see the new route for up to 60 seconds from the time A learns about it. (This is assuming that router A and B received the new route update just after they sent their RIP updates, and that the RIP update interval was set to 30 seconds.)

Sixty seconds is a long time in the networking world, and this example had only three routers. The convergence time only gets longer the more routers you add. Of course, because RIP assumes that a hop count of 16 signifies an unreachable network, there is a limit to how bad this time of convergence problem can get. The 15-hop limit can be a problem especially if you have a very large network. For these reasons, unless you have a small network and are not overly concerned about bandwidth utilization, you are probably better off not running RIP. RIP also only uses hop count as the sole metric for determining the best path.

In Figure 4.9, RIP will see the 56K link between A and C as the best route, because it can get from A to C in one hop. It is obvious to us, however, that in most cases it is preferential to get to C using the path through B. This is because even though you are adding an extra hop, you are at T1 speed (1.544Mbps) the entire way. Thus, unless you have a small network and are not overly concerned about bandwidth utilization or best path selection, you are probably better off not running RIP.

Figure 4.9 Because RIP only uses hops as a metric, it can choose sub-optimal paths very easily.

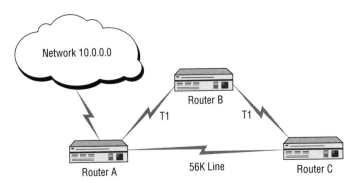

Most of the newer routing protocols address the shortcomings of RIP. The two protocols I see used most often for intranet routing are OSPF and EIGRP. OSPF offers the following benefits over RIP:

- Multicasting of routing updates
- Faster convergence
- No hop-count limit
- Better path selection

OSPF is able to converge faster than RIP, because when a router detects a routing change, it floods that change out on the network simultaneously with computing its new routing table. OSPF uses the Dijkstra algorithm to compute the best route between devices. Every interface is assigned a cost, and the path with the smallest cost is used. The default cost of an interface is $1*10e8$/interface speed. This means that a 10Mbps link will have a default OSPF cost of 10. This can cause problem since links with speeds of 100Mbps or more will all have a cost of 1. To deal with this you need to set the interface cost manually for those links that are faster than 100Mbps to something other than 1 if you want OSPF to be able to properly determine the most efficient path.

```
interface Serial0.18 point-to-point
 ip address 10.0.0.1 255.0.0.0
 ip ospf cost 4
```

Of course you may find it more of a headache to set all the high-speed interface costs than to allow the possibility that OSPF would choose suboptimum routes. When picking the interface cost to assign, you can use anything you want as long as you take into account what the default costs for your other links are. For example, you don't want to use 11 on a 100Mbps interface, but you could use 4 for 100Mbps interfaces, and maybe 2 for a 150Mbps interface.

OSPF uses the concept of areas to define where and how routing protocol information is propagated. When designing an OSPF network it is important to remember that there must always be an area 0. In a multi-area OSPF network, all inter-area traffic must cross area 0, which is known as the backbone area. This means that every area must have at least one router with an interface in area 0. When designing OSPF networks, it is important to keep this fact in mind. OSPF virtual links can allow you to span across an area to make OSPF think an area that is not connected to the backbone area 0 really is.

In Figure 4.10, a virtual link is used to connect area 2 to area 0. Traffic going from area 1 to area 2 still has to cross the virtual link into area 0 and come back out. The virtual link is useful when you are merging two companies who both run OSPF, and both have an area 0. You can use a virtual link to combine the two area 0s into one big area. You can also use a virtual link as shown in Figure 4.10 if you are faced with a situation where it is impossible to provide an area with an interface in area 0. Whenever possible, however, you want to avoid using virtual links.

Figure 4.10   A virtual link connects area 2 to area 0.

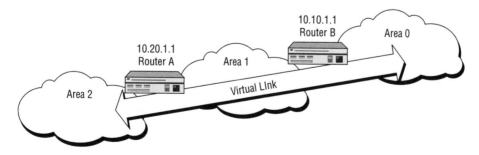

When setting up the virtual link you need to configure it from both sides so that both router A and router B will be configured for the virtual link. The virtual link from router A can be set up using the commands below. In this case, 44 is the OSPF process ID, which you choose, and 10.10.1.1 is the route ID of router B.

```
Router ospf 44
Area 1 virtual link 10.10.1.1
```

Router B would look something like:

```
Router ospf 83
Area 1 virtual link 10.20.1.1
```

In order to create a virtual link, the two routers involved must share a common area, and one of the two routers in question must be connected to the backbone area (area 0).

In order to limit the amount of overhead, OSPF uses the concept of a Designated Router (DR) to allow the multicasting of routing updates on multi-access links. This means that the routers on the segment send their routing information to the DR, and the DR sends this information out to the other routers on the segment. In this way, instead of each router having to establish an adjacency with all other routers, they need only establish adjacencies with the DR and BDR (Backup Designated Router). This significantly limits OSPF routing traffic. When multicasting, the OSPF routers all listen to address 224.0.0.5, and the DR and BDR also listen to 224.0.0.6. This means that only OSPF routers have to process this information. The merits of multicasting don't need to be discussed in any more detail than this for the purposes of this book.

> **NOTE** When running OSPF, the router ID is the highest IP address configured in the router, unless a loopback interface is specified. Always specify a loopback interface. If the interface that holds the address of the router ID goes down, then the router will stop routing data. Configuring a loopback interface eliminates this problem, because the loopback is not tied to any physical interface. As long as the router is up, the loopback interface is up. You don't want your router to stop working because one of your serial interfaces has gone down. You can either use a real IP address to which you have rights, or a bogus address. It really makes no difference as far as OSPF is concerned.

EIGRP offers many of the same advantages as OSPF. EIGRP is a Cisco proprietary routing algorithm that uses the Diffusing Update Algorithm (DUAL) for routing table calculation. The algorithm allows EIGRP to store backup routes when they are available so that if a route goes down, the router can quickly switch over to one of the alternates it has stored.

EIGRP does not use periodic updates as RIP does, but it does send partial updates when a path changes or when a route's metric changes. Updates are only sent about the link in question and are sent only to the routers that need the new information. EIGRP does not send out the whole routing table.

EIGRP supports AppleTalk, IP, and IPX. With IPX, EIGRP can send incremental SAP updates across point-to-point interfaces, as shown in Figure 4.11.

Figure 4.11   EIGRP can use be configured to use incremental SAP updates to conserve bandwidth.

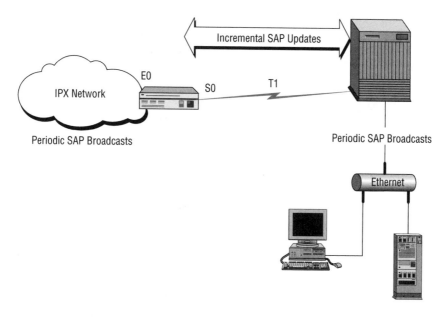

This allows you to limit the SAP traffic across your point-to-point links to those updates when things change. Your clients on the shared Ethernet, Token Ring, or FDDI network will still see the periodic SAP broadcasts, however. EIGRP by default uses periodic SAP broadcasts on these types of links so the clients and servers can properly maintain their SAP tables.

EIGRP supports automatic route summarization and variable length subnet masking. EIGRP also takes many factors into consideration when selecting the best route. By default, bandwidth and delay are used to calculate the best route; however, reliability, loading, and MTU (Maximum Transmit Unit) can also be used. This gives you added flexibility in defining how your routers are going to pick the best routes.

The biggest drawback to EIGRP is that it is Cisco proprietary, and so non-Cisco devices will not understand it. However, in an all-Cisco environment, it is an excellent protocol which looks a lot like RIP from a configuration point of view. If you have ever worked with RIP, figuring out how to set up EIGRP will not be too much of a leap.

> **NOTE**   If you enable EIGRP routing for IPX, remember to turn off IPX RIP. As soon as you enable IPX routing on a router, IPX RIP is enabled. If you don't turn it off you will still be wasting bandwidth on IPX RIP updates that are not needed. Since RIP has a higher administrative distance, you will not see these routes in the routing table, but the bandwidth will still be wasted on propagating them. It is also important to make sure that your IPX servers know how to get off the local segment if they need to. Novell servers listen to IPX RIP by default and cannot be configured to listen to EIGRP. This means you may have to run RIP on your local segments that have Netware servers on them. Fortunately EIGRP will automatically redistribute its IPX routes into IPX RIP. Of course if you don't want to run a routing protocol you can always set up static routes. While static routes do have their place, they are really not scalable to a large environment. Most environments end up using a routing protocol along with a few static routes.

There are obviously other routing protocols, but those I've mentioned are the most popular. When choosing a routing protocol, you want to make sure that it is efficient, scalable, will converge quickly, and will support the routed protocols in your environment. You can always change your routing protocol later. Keep in mind that it is much easier to change your routing protocol than, for instance, your IP addressing scheme. You are never really locked into a specific routing protocol once you deploy it. You can even run multiple protocols at the same time, a feature that makes it relatively easy to change routing protocols.

24seven Design

When designing a network or planning a design change, it is all too easy to overlook fault tolerance. Fault tolerance is perhaps one of the most important aspects of any design. Today's networks have become so imbedded in the business practices of the companies that rely on them that any down time is unacceptable. Unfortunately, the days when you could simply tell people that the network was down and they should pull out a pencil and paper and keep working are long gone. Today, all downtime has a cost associated with it.

As a network design architect you need to realize that faults will occur. The network needs to be able to recover quickly from all types of outages. Obviously you can not be expected to design a network that will recover from every outage imaginable. You probably do not have to worry too much about making sure the network can handle having

Godzilla and Mothra duke it out atop your corporate headquarters; however, the network will have to be able to handle mishaps like failed routers, power outages, dropped leased lines, cut cables, etc.

When you are working within the confines of your own building or buildings, adding in fault tolerance is pretty straightforward and not unreasonably expensive.

In Figure 4.12, the client PCs will still be able to access both the Mercier and Hammer servers on the FDDI ring so long as routers A and B or routers X and Y don't fail at the same time. If we completely lose router X, the clients can use the path through B and Y. So we have two completely separate communication paths between the Mercier server and, say, Bob's PC. The only common points are the two end points (the Mercier server and Bob's PC), the FDDI ring on which the Mercier server sits, and the Ethernet segment on which Bob's PC sits. FDDI already has some fault tolerance built into it, so we don't have to worry about it too much.

Figure 4.12   A fault tolerant design

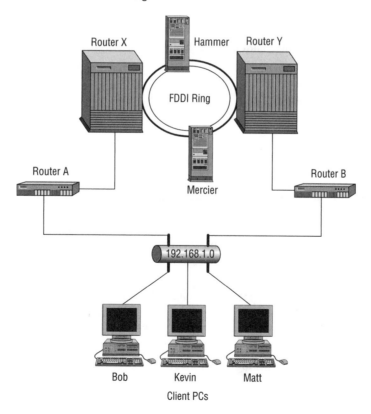

When designing a network to be fault tolerant you want to try to have multiple paths with no common elements whenever possible. We have all seen that a full mesh network is the most robust and fault-tolerant design possible, but it is also highly impractical. In most real-world situations you only need to provide two paths between any two given devices. When we deal with routing these devices we are providing multiple paths to what are really networks or segments. If done right, both paths will almost never go down at the same time.

> **NOTE** This book will not cover any of the fault-tolerant server technologies, such as clustering.

Suppose there is a 1 in 1000 chance that any of the components in the path from Bob's PC through router A through router X to the Mercier server will fail at any given time, and we have the same probability for the other path. The odds that a component will fail in both paths at the same time will therefore be 1 in 1,000,000. Can you live with a 1 in 1,000,000 chance that your network will fail? You probably can.

> **NOTE** Be sure to replace equipment that fails ASAP. Remember that devices have finite lives, and two devices put into service at the same time will probably fail at relatively close to the same time. Car headlights are a good example of this: If you don't change that burned-out headlight right away, you typically end up driving home in the dark a few weeks later when the other one fails.

When you get to do your own cabling on-site, the creation of these redundant paths is relatively easy and under your control. You probably will decide that some areas do not have to be fault tolerant or are not worth the effort. As long as you consciously make that decision before disaster strikes, you should be fine.

When creating redundant paths, try to think of all the things that could happen to take both paths down. For example, you don't want to run both links through the same conduit, because both cables could be cut at the same time. You don't want to power two routers with redundant links from the same UPS. There are many more examples possible. The most important thing to do is to make sure you think things through. Never assume a particular mishap won't occur. A network can fail for reasons as ridiculous as a toilet above the computer room overflowing and flooding the rack with both core routers in it. Yes, I have seen this, and it is really tough to have to explain. If possible, try to avoid having plumbing running above your computer room.

When you have to worry about leased lines and the telecom companies, things get a little more difficult because you no longer have full control. Your most frequent outages will probably occur on your WAN links. Digging can cut fibers, storms can knock down wires, cars can hit poles—there are tons of dangers out there waiting to take down your WAN service.

What you need to do to deal with this it to devise some kind of a backup link. This link can be as simple as an analog dial-backup link, an ISDN, or a separate leased line. Analog dial backup is for the most part pretty safe because it will typically run over different cabling than that used by leased lines. However, it most likely will not provide you with the bandwidth you need.

ISDN is a popular and cost-effective backup solution because you only pay a small monthly fee and a premium for the ISDN calls you make. Many people learned a hard lesson in 1999 when AT&T's high-speed data network went down. The ISDN data is carried across the same switches that comprise the AT&T Frame Relay service, so everyone expecting their ISDN links to take over for their lost Frame Relay service got a very unpleasant surprise when their links would not come up.

When ordering redundant links, you want to make sure that you have them diversified. This means that you don't want to have them go to the same central office (CO) or come in on the same path from the street. Often times it may even make sense to use a different carrier for the redundant links. You will still want to make sure that both carriers are not using the same CO, if possible.

Figure 4.13 represents a compromise between fault tolerance and cost. Take a look at the Attleboro and Boston routers. Both Attleboro and Boston are directly connected to the main office and to each other to form a triangle. Notice that three different carriers have been used to reduce the likelihood of losing two links at once. Also notice that the two sides of the triangle enter the main office on different routers. This allows us to lose any of the three links in the triangle and get by on the other two without experiencing a network outage. The smaller offices like Foxboro, which is connected to Attleboro, have only one link, but we have decided that adding a second link to Foxboro would be more expensive than the cost of a typical outage in Foxboro.

Figure 4.13 Finding the balance between fault tolerance and cost

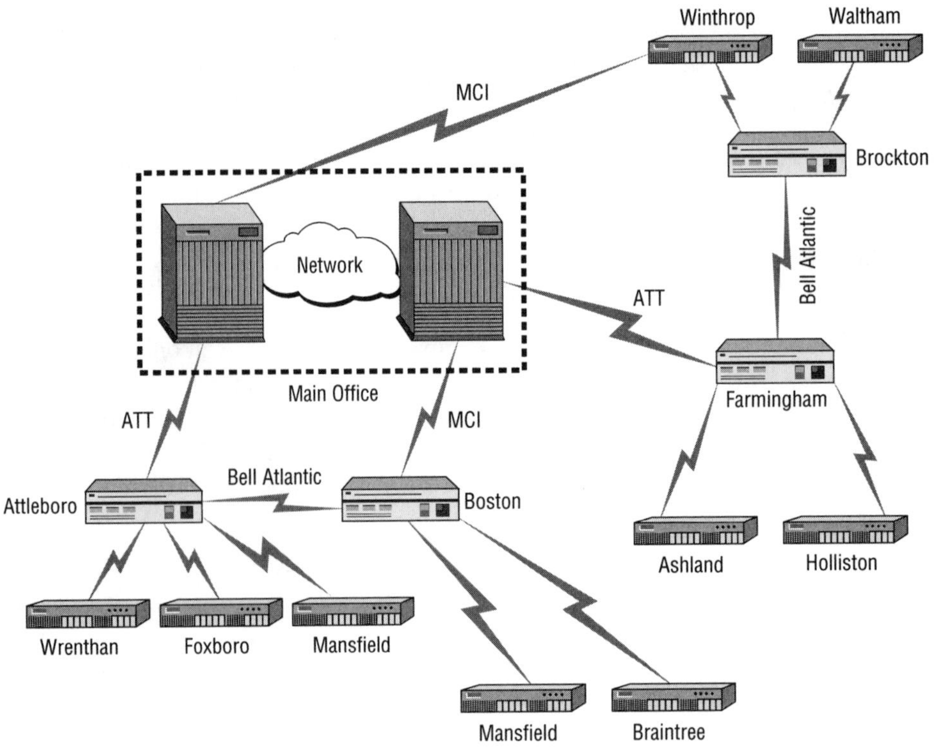

In the cases of Foxboro, Wrentham, Mansfield, and the other offices with only one connection, we are gambling that because these are smaller offices, any revenue lost due to a WAN outage on these links will be less than the cost of maintaining a redundant link to these sites. Obviously our routing protocols have to be set up to be able to route around problems when possible. Figure 4.13 gives us a good example of a compromise between cost and fault tolerance. You will never be able to justify a full, 100 percent fault tolerant system, but with a little planning you can come really close without a huge expenditure.

Designing a Simple Fault-Tolerant WAN

Suppose you have been contracted to design a WAN solution for Pinto Property. Pinto Property is a moderate-sized property management company with five remote offices throughout New England. The main office is based in Wrentham, Massachusetts, and there are approximately 75 users located in the main office. Each of the branch offices has between two and seven employees in the office at any given time. Currently, each office has only a LAN, and there is no connectivity between the offices. Pinto Property would like to streamline its business by adding a WAN to connect each of the remote offices to the main office.

First you need to take a look at where the remote offices are located. Office locations are:

- Bangor, Maine
- Lebanon, New Hampshire
- Wrentham, Massachusetts (corporate office)
- Wrentham, Massachusetts (small business office)
- Fairfield, Connecticut

Because the two Wrentham offices are very close together you are going to use a leased line to tie them together. You probably don't need that much bandwidth, so you will use fractional T1 service. Now the remote offices offer more of a challenge. You could just use leased lines, but it probably makes more sense from a cost standpoint to use Frame Relay. To further reduce costs, you will create a hub-and-spoke topology, with the corporate office as the hub. This will limit the number of PVCs or SVCs needed in the frame cloud. Also, most traffic will be between the corporate office and the remote office anyway.

Now that you know what type of network you are going to build, you need to think about redundancy on the links. Because Pinto Property did not previously have a network, they can probably get away with some down time, so you will not worry about redundant hardware. Because you are using Frame Relay for your primary connection, you might want to be wary about using ISDN as your backup solution; however, you are still going to use it. Assume that only one remote office will be down at a time. It is too hardware-intensive to be able to support all the offices on ISDN at the same time, and Mr. Pinto does not want to spring for that. So you will set up ISDN from the remote sites to be able to dial into the HQ router. For the HQ router you will use a Cisco 3640 with a NT1 BRI interface for ISDN. Each of the other offices will use a Cisco 2600 router.

Each of the remote offices will connect into the frame cloud, and you will have the frame provider map PVCs to entry points into the frame cloud from the Wrentham HQ office. You will also have them map PVCs to another frame switch, which will connect to the Wrentham business office. This way, if HQ loses contact with the frame cloud we can have data route through the cloud to the business office, and then go across the T1 to the HQ office. You are in no way prepared for a total frame failure, but as long as we explain that to Mr. Pinto we should be fine. Since this network is very simple we will use static routing; this gives us a little more security over dynamic routing protocols.

For the HQ and business office routers, you will create subinterfaces so that each office-to-office link will appear to be a complete end–to-end link. Taking this all into account, your design might look something like Figure 4.14.

Figure 4.14   Pinto Property proposed design

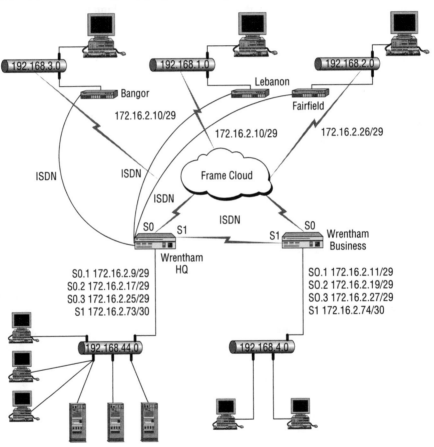

None of the IP addresses for the ISDN connections have been assigned. This is to keep the figure from getting cluttered. Any network could be used for those interfaces since they are not up most of the time. This design provides a decent amount of fault tolerance, while at the same time still being cost effective. Also it is very easy to grow this design: Adding another remote office is a fairly simple task.

The 3640 router used in the corporate office would work for awhile if you needed to create more of a backbone environment in that office. Pinto Property will most likely outgrow its office space before it outgrows the equipment. Based on the size of the company and the fact that it is only establishing a WAN environment, we want to keep things simple so that they can get a handle on managing their own network. Remember, sometimes it is fun to design a really complex solution, but there is always someone who has to support that design. As we've said before, you want to make sure that your designs are capable of being supported by someone other than yourself and can grow as the company grows.

5

The Cisco Router Product Line

This chapter is designed to help with an overview of the Cisco product line. Cisco offers a wide variety of products, from the simplest of networks connecting only a few computers together to complex, high-speed, multinational networks with built-in security and redundancy. Somewhere amongst this sea of products will be the solution that best fits your business' network. A solid understanding of the different products and the corresponding technologies will empower you to make the right decision about the right product that will provide the right service *and*, just as importantly, fit the budget.

The following topics will be discussed in this chapter:

- High-end routers
- Small/medium business solutions
- When to use which products

High-End Routers

Cisco products that are designed for the "core" of the network are obviously going to require the greatest amount of throughput and, undoubtedly, will carry the largest burden of network traffic. These routers are design to be a central connecting point in a large enterprise network or ISP. They may also be integrated as a major connecting point between large enterprises. The "high-end" classification of Cisco routers ranges from the 7000 series to the 12000 Gigabit Switch Router (GSR).

Cisco 12000 GSR Series

The Cisco 12000 (GSR) series routers comprise a scalable, carrier-class routing platform that allows ISPs and other providers of high-speed access to migrate their network infrastructure to 10Gbps (OC-192c/STM-64). The 12016 boasts an enhanced switch capacity of 80Gbps, with built-in scalability of up to 320Gbps and runs a service-provider–specific Internetwork Operating System (IOS) (version 12.0 as of this writing). The 16-slot chassis will host a plethora of different line cards that are backward-compatible to the earlier 12000 models.

A key feature of these workhorses is Cisco's new Dynamic Packet Transport (DPT) product that combines the bandwidth-efficient and services-rich capabilities of IP routing with the bandwidth-rich, fast restoration capabilities of fiber rings to deliver fundamental cost and functionality advantages over existing solutions. Cisco has also demonstrated the GSR 12000's ability to be directly connected to a wide range of third party optical transport products such as the TeraMux 128 channel DWDM system, Monterey Networks' 20000 Wavelength Optical Router (another recent Cisco acquisition) and the multi-terabit Corvis transparent optical switch.

Figure 5.1 shows a Cisco 12012 with redundant power supplies. The module on the far-left slot is the supervisor module, complete with a flash card slot, a console, and aux ports.

Cisco 12000 Terabit System

The new Cisco 12000 Terabit System will scale to an incredible 5 Terabits per second (Tbps). This new system is able to offer a non-disruptive system by using an advanced crossbar switch fabric architecture, and, because the system is managed as a single routing node, it simplifies POP (point-of-presence) architecture and reduces the cost of operation. This new high-speed technology utilizes the already proven components of the Cisco 12016 GSR series, such as the Cisco IOS, and provides many features at a carrier-class quality, such as VPN, Unicast, and Multicast services.

Cisco 7000 Series

Although Cisco announced the "end-of-sale" for the 70*x*0 series in July of 1997, there are still enough in deployment that it's worth mentioning here. Cisco has allowed for backward compatibility on many of the series' components and continues to offer line cards and replacement parts.

There are several other 7*xxx* routers that cover a wide range of high end and/or processor intensive duties.

Figure 5.1   Cisco 12012 GSR Switch Router

Cisco 12012

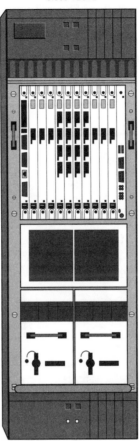

Cisco 7100 VPN Router

If you utilize this model of router, you will be able to create a Virtual Private Network (VPN). A properly designed VPN eliminates your need for a dedicated private network connection to all offices. This alleviates your access line costs and any subsequent toll charges, providing for a very cost efficient yet secure network design. For example, rather than providing a dedicated circuit from each remote office to the home office, you could provide each remote office with only a local Internet connection.

Figure 5.2 shows each of the remote locations with a dedicated link between. Most likely the links are more expensive the farther the distance between the locations. Figure 5.3

demonstrates connecting each site to a local ISP. Data can be transmitted securely over the public Internet with VPN security tunneling and encryption. Because the access charges are local, the costs are significantly less and, as with the dedicated link, there can be no charge for any additional distance. Communication from Chicago to Nashville, for instance, would cost the same as from Chicago to Athens.

Figure 5.2 Conventional hub-and-spoke network with leased lines for each location

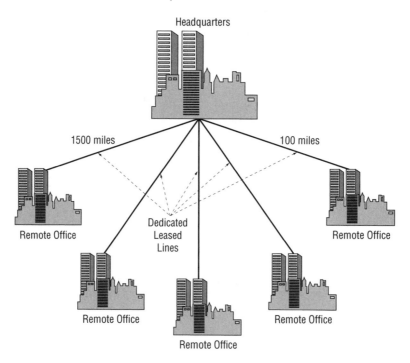

The Cisco 7100 Series router is designed specifically to provide a turnkey solution for VPNs with embedded Fast-Ethernet and WAN interfaces. It offers the full feature set of a regular 7x00 router but adds all of the benefits of a comprehensive suite of VPN services including tunneling, data encryption, security, firewall, and advanced bandwidth management.

Figure 5.3   A VPN network example, with each remote office maintaining only a local Internet connection. Data is kept secure with tunneling and encryption.

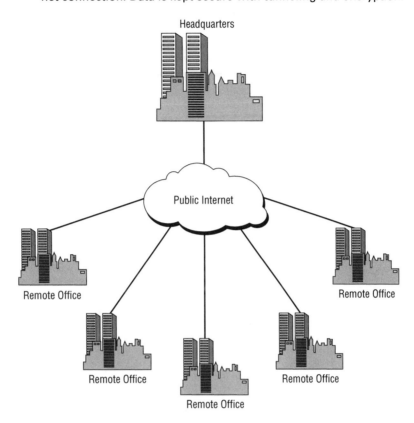

Cisco 7200 Multifunction Platform

The Cisco 7200 router is called a "Multifunction Platform" because it incorporates several different functions that heretofore occupied different devices throughout the network. Increased processor performance enables the 7200 to handle ISP distribution design layer functions and allow multiple processes such as security, traffic management, accounting, and support to compensate for the increased demands of high-density dedicated access and high-bandwidth interfaces. The 7200 packs all of the features of the 7000 Series of routers but there are a few that make it stand apart:

Gigabit Ethernet/Packet over SONET   For interconnection to high-performance switching fabrics such as the aforementioned Cisco 12000 GSR and the Catalyst family of switches. The addition of high-density multichannel interfaces means these capabilities will position the Cisco 7200 as a modular, cost-effective solution for enterprises and service provider (POPs).

Voice/data integration services   These enable end users to make voice calls to other locations without incurring toll charges. Many companies are allowing voice calls to ride on data lines that already exist and are seeing very quick return on investment dollars. The 7200 extends the multiservice capabilities to support Voice-over-IP (VoIP) services, in addition to ATM/Circuit Emulation Services (CES). These capabilities also support voice-processing extensions such as voice compression and private branch exchange (PBX) signaling. The Cisco 7200 supports multiservice aggregation of lower-end, or branch/CPE, applications.

Data center integration   This allows the support of IBM data centers and will support increased Token Ring enhancements and an IBM channel connection for direct connection to an IBM mainframe. Coupled with the wide range of mixed-LAN/WAN interfaces and IOS-based services, these developments underscore the multifunctional role of the Cisco 7200, becoming a cost-effective solution for IBM data centers.

The Cisco 7206VXR shown in Figure 5.4 is an enhanced version of the Cisco 7200 router. The Cisco 7206VXR routers up the ante by incorporating a multiservice Interchange (MIX) capability, allowing integrated multiservice extensions that will support future digital voice port adapters.

Figure 5.4   Cisco 7206 Multifunction Platform Router

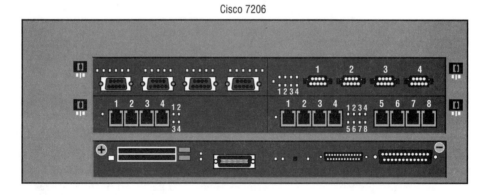

The VXR series is also available with the NPE-300 high-performance processor, which performs at approximately 300,000 packets per second (pps) in fast switching mode, a 50 percent increase over the NPE-200 processor's performance.

Cisco 7500

The Cisco 7500 series offers all of the reliability and serviceability features of the Cisco 7000 series and provides higher levels of performance, offering over 2Gbps of system bandwidth. Built on Cisco's new distributed switching architecture, the Cisco 7500 series integrates switching and routing functions in the Route Switch Processor (RSP) to deliver fast, multi-layer switching, increased peak performance, and scalability to very large networks. Cisco's new Versatile Interface Processor (VIP) provides increased port densities, better slot utilization, and increased functionality, as well as increased packet memory.

The Cisco 7500 series is available in three models: the Cisco 7505, the Cisco 7507, and the Cisco 7513. The entire line of the 7000 family can be built and configured to be fully redundant. It is even possible in this series to have a "router in a router." Everything from the power supplies to back planes to interface processors can be duplicated, increasing uptime to an all-time high.

Table 5.1 gives the specifications for the 7513, 7507, and 7505. Each of the family of 75*xx* comes with a 100-MHz R4600 processor, 16MB of memory expandable to 128MB, and 8MB Flash memory expandable to 40 MB. The system back plane of the 7505 is 1.066Gbps. The 7507 and 7513 both have a 2.132Gbps back plane. The last two digits of the model number indicate the chassis slot capacity (for example, the 7505 has five slots). One of these slots must be used for the RSP, leaving four slots to be populated by interface line cards. The 7507 and 7513 each will support redundant RSPs and will therefore hold 5 and 11 line cards, respectively.

Table 5.1 Specifications for the 7513, 7507, and 7505

Feature	Cisco 7513	Cisco 7507	Cisco 7505
Processor Type	100MHz R4600	100MHz R4600	100MHz R4600
System Processors	RSP2 and dual RSP2	RSP2 and dual RSP2	RSP1
Memory	RSP2; 16MB expandable to 128MB	RSP2; 16MB expandable to 128MB	RSP1; 16MB expandable to 128MB
Flash Memory	RSP2; 8MB expandable to 40MB	RSP2; 8MB expandable to 40MB	RSP1; 8MB expandable to 40MB

Table 5.1 Specifications for the 7513, 7507, and 7505 *(continued)*

Feature	Cisco 7513	Cisco 7507	Cisco 7505
System Bandwidth	2.132Gbps	2.132Gbps	1.066Gbps
Chassis Slots	13	7	5
Configurable Interface Slots	11	5	4

Figure 5.5 shows a Cisco 7513, both in front and rear view. The rear view exposes the interface slots.

Figure 5.5 Cisco 7513, front and rear views

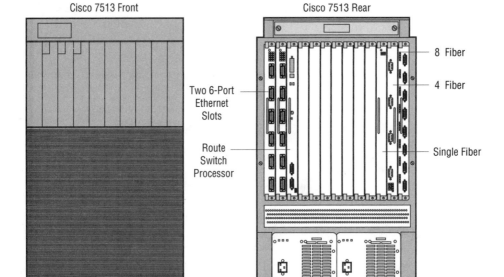

The example in Figure 5.5 is populated with a few different types of fiber modules, two 6-port Fast Ethernet modules, and an RSP card.

Small/Medium Business Solutions

Cisco Systems offers a wide variety of solutions for the small/medium-size business market, the selection and possible combinations of which are so immense that we cannot possibly discuss all of them here. (One recent version of the Cisco Product Catalog was over 900 pages!) In this section, we will define some of the most popular families of routers and their uses in an effort to help you familiarize yourself with the different classes, capabilities, and functionalities of the families.

Router families reviewed are:

- 800 ISDN Routers
- 1400 DSL Routers
- 1600 Modular Data Routers
- 1700 Modular Access Routers
- 2500 Fixed Configuration Data Routers
- 2600 Modular Voice/Data Routers
- 3600 Modular Voice/Data Routers
- 3810 Fixed-configuration voice/data access concentrators
- 4000 Modular Data Router

800/900 ISDN Routers

The 800 Series ISDN routers are intended for Small Office/Home Office (SOHO) use. They are ideal for telecommuters and offices that have a low bandwidth requirement. ISDN will support up to 128K (two 64K B Channels). There are multiple flavors of the ISDN routers, some of which support the full Cisco IOS, including security and VPN capabilities. The powerful software makes this router fully functional and can provide the same level of service as some of the higher-end routers at the lower bandwidth and cost. Additionally, some models offer an integrated hub to provide workstation attachment capabilities and Plain Old Telephone Service (POTS) ports to allow for voice access from one or both of the ISDN channels. Figure 5.6 shows such an example. The hub ports are labeled LX1–LX4, and the POTS ports are labeled PH1 and PH2.

Figure 5.6   Front view of a Cisco 800 ISDN router

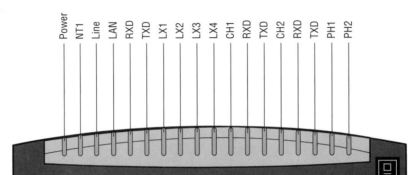

1400 DSL Routers

The *x*DSL market is growing ever popular, as users continually demand more and more bandwidth access from remote locations. The Cisco 1400 DSL routers, shown in Figure 5.7, are designed to meet these demands by offering always-on, high-speed Internet and corporate LAN access. The Cisco 1400 series also provides enhanced security with the Cisco IOS Firewall, ATM and IP quality-of-service (QoS), and extensive multimedia capabilities, as well as ease-of-use, management capabilities, and VPN. The speed of these boxes is remarkable as the Cisco 1417 router supports speeds of up to 8Mbps downstream to the user and 640Kbps upstream.

Figure 5.7   A rear view of a Cisco 1400 DSL router

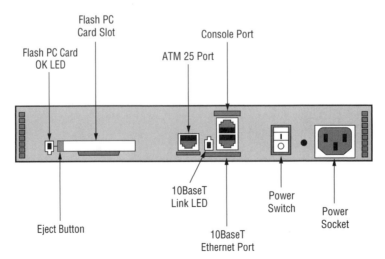

1600 Modular Data Routers

The Cisco 1600 series routers are intended for small offices that may have medium bandwidth requirements but still need a flexible solution that can provide some scalability and security. The 1600 series can connect an Ethernet LAN to several different WAN options, including ISDN, asynchronous and synchronous serial connections, Frame Relay, leased lines, Switched 56, Switched Multimegabit Data Service (SMDS), and X.25. Models are available with two Ethernet ports for LAN separation, as well as a possible WAN slot for upgrading or adding an additional circuit. Figure 5.8 shows both the front and rear view of a 1605 router.

Figure 5.8   Cisco 1605 Modular Data router

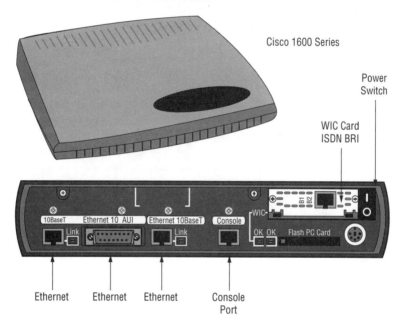

All models are available with the standard Cisco IOS for the extended Firewall feature set.

1700 Modular Access Routers

The Reduced Instruction Set Computer (RISC) chip-based processor of the 1700 family puts it at the top of the class of the 1*xxx* series Cisco routers. As with the 1600, several port configurations are available with the additional slot for the WAN Interface Card (WIC). This extra processing capacity of the 1720 makes it ideal for the horsepower-intensive VPN requirements. Such features include a VPN tunnel server and the optional integrated Firewall feature set. Integrated hardware options include DSU/CSU, as well as NT-1 for ISDN. Figure 5.9 shows the front and rear view of the Cisco 1700 Modular Access router.

Figure 5.9   The Cisco 1700 Modular Access router

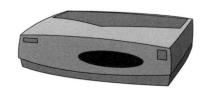

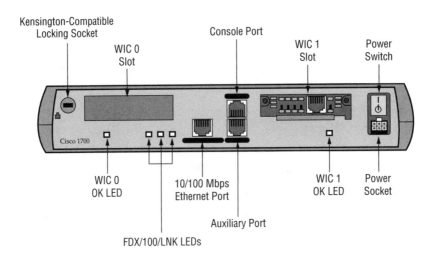

The 1750 flavor offers all of the robust qualities of the 1720 with the additional capabilities of voice/fax/data integration. All three Cisco 1750 models (1750, 1750 2V, and 1750 4V) offer three modular slots for voice and data interface cards, an autosensing 10/100BaseT Ethernet LAN port, a console port, and an auxiliary port. To help make upgrades less painful, it supports the same WAN interface cards as the Cisco 1600, 1720, 2600, and 3600 routers. These WICs support synchronous and asynchronous serial, ISDN BRI (Basic Rate Interface), and serial with DSU/CSU options. The 1700 also supports the same analog voice interface cards and voice-over-IP technology as the Cisco 2600 and 3600 routers. The voice interface cards include support for Ear & Mouth (E&M), Foreign Exchange Station (FXS), and Foreign Exchange Office (FXO).

2500 Fixed Configuration Data Routers

Likely the single most deployed of the Cisco routers, the 2500 Series is composed of fully integrated hub/routers that enable remote offices to provide both LAN and internetwork connectivity. As of January 2000, 1.5 million have been sold. These hub/routers combine the functions of a stand-alone hub and router in one chassis to provide simpler setup, improved serviceability and reliability, and integrated remote Simple Network Management Protocol (SNMP) network management, as well as dial backup capabilities to provide disaster recovery.

The 2500 family offers many LAN and WAN configuration options. Both Ethernet and Token Ring LAN options are available, including one of each, or single or dual of either. WAN options include high-speed synchronous or asynchronous serial interface, low-speed synchronous or asynchronous, and ISDN BRI. Integrated hub models are available in 8-, 14-, and 16-port flavors.

Access servers are also available in the 2509 or 2511 models. These routers make it easy to access several routers in a rack without requiring attachment and reattachment of the console cable. All connections are made through a central box.

> **NOTE** Those who intend to pursue a CCIE Certification should become intimately familiar with the access server and how to use it to access multiple routers.

The 2500 family supports the full range of IOS software. Versions range from the minimal IP only to the Enterprise (EN) software set that allows for IP, IPX, AppleTalk, and the rest of the full IOS protocol suite. Each features Autoinstall capabilities.

Figure 5.10 illustrates rear views of two different 2500 series routers. The top picture shows the 2509 Access Server with Dual serial ports, an AUI Ethernet, and, on the far left, an async port for the octopus cable that will connect to all of the other routers. Below it, we see a rear view of a 2513 router with a fixed configuration of one Token Ring, one Ethernet, two serial ports, and an ISDN BRI interface.

Figure 5.10 Cisco 2509 and 2513 rear views

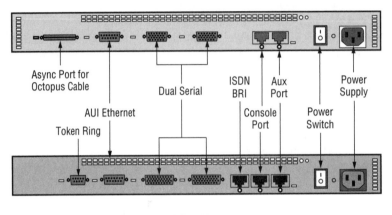

2600 Modular Voice/Data Routers

The 2600 family is basically an extension of the 2500 family with the integration of many multiservice platforms. Internet/intranet access with a firewall security feature allows for the use of a single box rather than necessitating a separate firewall. Multiservice voice/ data integration provides the aforementioned ability to let voice calls ride on existing data lines, perhaps saving long distance toll charges. The 2600 family also offers VPN access services for secure data transfers across the public Internet. If your local network has a switched environment, the Inter-VLAN routing feature will be useful to pass traffic between different VLANs. Figure 5.11 is a rear view of a router in the 2600 series.

Figure 5.11 Rear view of a Cisco 2600 router

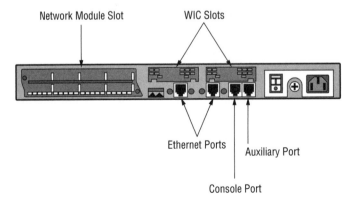

The Cisco 2600 series shares modular interfaces with the Cisco 1600, 1700, and 3600 series.

3600 Modular Voice/Data Routers

The 3600 series (as well as the 2600 series above) of multiservice platforms has been drastically improved by the addition of many voice capabilities such as: Voice over Frame Relay (VoFR) and Voice over ATM (VoATM-AAL 5) on the digital voice interfaces (T1 and E1). QSIG is also now supported on all digital interfaces, including T1/E1 and BRI, VoIP Frame Relay, and enhanced queuing functionality. There is also now an option to integrate these products to configure a gateway for the PBX and PSTN for IP telephony, and for enabling applications like call transfers, holds, and conferencing.

The Cisco 3600 series includes the 3660, the 3640, and the 3620 multiservice platforms. The Cisco 3600 series is fully supported by Cisco IOS software, which includes analog and digital voice capability, ATM access with T1/E1 IMA or OC-3 interfaces, dial-up connectivity, LAN-to-LAN routing, data and access security, WAN optimization, and multimedia features. The third number is the module slot capacity indicator (for example, the 3660 has six slots). Each chassis incorporates one or, optionally, two integrated 10/100 (Ethernet/Fast Ethernet) network module slots and will accept a variety of network module interface cards, including LAN and WAN mixed-media cards supporting additional Ethernet, Fast Ethernet, Token Ring, and a variety of WAN technologies. These cards provide the foundation of LAN and WAN connectivity on a single, modular, network module. An additional series of network module cards offering digital modems and asynchronous and synchronous serial, ISDN PRI, and ISDN BRI interfaces are also available. In addition to its six network module slots, the Cisco 3660 has two internal Advanced Integration Module (AIM) slots for support of such functionality as hardware-accelerated compression. The Cisco 3600 family can share WAN interface cards with the Cisco 1600, 1700, and 2600 series; with the latter series it can also share network modules and Voice Interface Cards.

Standard out-of-the-box hardware configuration includes 8MB of flash RAM, single inline-editing modules (SIMM) expandable to 32MB for the Cisco 3620/40 models. The 3660 flavor also comes with 8MB of flash in the enterprise models and 16MB in the telco models. Each is upgradable to 64MB. Personal Computer Memory Card International Association (PCMCIA) flash memory cards are also supported by all models, available in 4- to 16-MB sizes. The processors get stronger as the model numbers increase:

- Cisco 3620: 80-MHz IDT R4700 RISC
- Cisco 3640: 100-MHz IDT R4700 RISC
- Cisco 3660: 225-MHz RISC QED RM5271

Figure 5.12 shows both a front and rear view of a Cisco 3640 router.

Figure 5.12   Front and rear views of a Cisco 3640 router with voice module

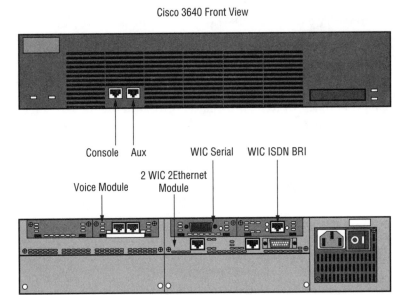

Cisco 3640 Front View

Cisco 3640 Rear View

Notice that from the rear view, you can see that the WIC slots in this example are populated with a serial, an ISDN, and dual Ethernet ports. Additionally, this 3640 has been populated with a singe voice module.

MC3800 Multiservice Router

The flagship product of the MC3800 family, the MC3810, is a compact, cost-efficient multiservice access device that integrates voice, data, and video traffic over a variety of services, such as Ethernet and analog or digital voice. The analog configuration allows 1 to 6 ports of analog voice. When configured for digital operation, the Cisco MC3810 will support up to 24 channels of compressed voice over ATM, Frame Relay, and Voice over IP. Additional fax and video services create a common communications network device that has the potential to reduce network costs by combining multiple network services into a single box.

With only a simple software change, the Cisco MC3810 series is designed to scale from low-speed leased-line environments starting at 56Kbps to high-speed 2.048Mbps Frame

Relay and T1/E1 ATM networks. To enhance the benefits of a single end-to-end networking solution, the Cisco MC3810 can also be integrated with the full line of Cisco routers and switches.

The standard hardware configuration consists of 32MB Dynamic Random Access Memory (DRAM). Flash memory is 8MB, expandable to 16MB with a 40-MHz MP860 Motorola PowerPC QUICC processor.

Figure 5.13 illustrates a very well populated Cisco 3810 router.

Figure 5.13   Cisco 3810 multiservice router with six phone ports

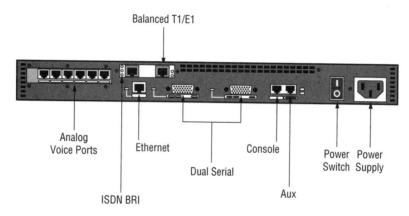

In addition to the usual Ethernet and two serial ports, the example in Figure 5.13 has been loaded up with an ISDN BRI port, a balanced T1 port, and six voice ports.

4000 Modular Data Router

This Cisco 4000 series is at the top of the food chain for the small/medium business routers. It is positioned as the core router for the medium-sized enterprise network. The latest flavors of the Cisco 4000 series consist of the 4500-M and 4700-M routers. Although still very popular and in large deployment, the Cisco 4000, 4000-M, 4500, and 4700 routers are no longer available; however, they are still supported.

The Cisco 4000 series routers support the full Cisco IOS software suite and can be loaded with the software image that best suits your business needs. For example, if you are only running TCP/IP, you would want the IP Only software option. However, if your environment also requires IPX or AppleTalk, you would want to purchase the enterprise versions of the software. A flash EEPROM (Electrically Erasable Programmable Read-Only Memory) is a standard feature on the 4000 series, allowing you to distribute new software releases from a central location. After the software is distributed, the routers can reboot from programs stored in local flash memory.

All models provide a configurable modular router platform by using Network Processor Modules (NPMs). NPMs are individual removable cards used for external network connections. Because the router's modules support many variations of protocols, line speeds, and transmission media, the Cisco 4000 series can accommodate many types of network computing environments. As Cisco introduces new modules, the Cisco 4000 series can be upgraded to keep pace with technological advances. Some of the standard features include three slots for NPMs, which can be Ethernet, Token Ring, FDDI, HSSI (High-Speed Serial Interface), ISDN BRI & PRI (Basic Rate Interface and Primary Rate Interface), ATM, or serial network interfaces. The 4700-M features a 133-MHz IDT Orion RISC processor, while the 4500 features a 100-MHz IDT Orion RISC processor. The NVRAM memory standard for each is 16MB and is expandable to 128KB. The flash memory standard is 4MB and is also expandable.

The 4500 Series router shown in Figure 5.14 is populated with three modules.

Figure 5.14   Cisco 4500 router front and rear view

Cisco 4500 Front

Cisco 4500 Rear

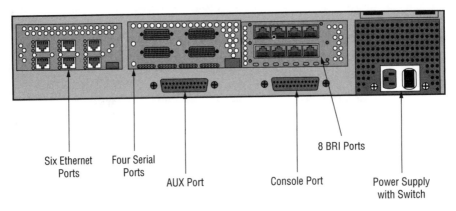

The module on the left contains six Ethernet ports. The middle provides four serial ports and the last module on the right is an 8-port ISDN BRI.

When to Use Which Model

With the vast selection of Cisco routers to choose from, making sure that you are choosing the right router can be tough. Even deciding among some of the most popular models listed in this chapter can be a challenge. As with any business decision, there are many approaches to the correct decision. In most companies, the bottom line budgetary allowance for any decision is exactly that—*the bottom line*. How this figure is viewed varies greatly from IS Manager to CIO to CEO. One may see only the cash layout for the initial purchase. Another may ask about the cost of future upgrades, and yet another may ask about the TCO (Total Cost of Ownership). If you are responsible for the network design, you had better have answers for all of these questions.

When you are designing a system and choosing which components to use, where, and when in the network, always consider the future. A great example, as out of context as it may seem, is the story of the local airport in Nashville, Tennessee. The local airport authority recognized a significant amount of growth with subsequent overcrowding and decided it should expand its facilities accordingly. They calculated the amount of growth over the previous three years and made a projection as to what the growth would be for the following three years. They made decisions about the amount of parking, ticket counters, thoroughfares, etc., that would be required and started the expansion project. Overall, *the project took four years*. By the end of the project, what they had built was already a year behind the capacity. Another project had to be started to compensate for the "new" capacity requirement, starting a vicious cycle. If a mistake like this is made in the communications industry, it is likely that what is purchased will no longer be useful by the end of its life and will require a *forklift upgrade*, which involves completely pulling out the old and installing something completely new in its place. You can imagine the expense of such a network project.

A better way to go about projects is to plan several years in advance. It is often difficult to take a company's past growth patterns and apply them to your design, because often the growth follows an upward curve instead of a linear pattern. Figure 5.15 shows a sample of such a growth pattern.

Figure 5.15 Typical network growth pattern

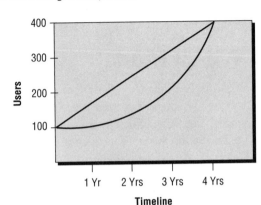

TIP Make a practice of working closely with business managers and other people within your organization who have an understanding of the potential company growth. This will help you design a network that will scale to your company's growth potential.

If after a company's third year of business the network was ready for an upgrade, and the designer looked at the history of growth, he might see that over the course of three years, the network had doubled in size from 100 to 200 users—certainly a substantial amount of growth for any network. But suppose that between the third and fourth years, the network size doubled again—this time inside of 12 months! The point is that the network designer must work very closely with the business and its management to help prepare for such anomalies and must always be forward thinking.

One common example of such forward thinking is a small company network with only two locations: one headquarters and one remote office. Suppose that after considering estimated traffic and bandwidth utilization, you determine a possible solution may be to put Cisco 1600 family routers at each end and install a serial link between the two locations as illustrated in Figure 5.16. This installation works successfully, and so this seems like a viable solution—*for now!*

Figure 5.16   A typical point-to-point network link

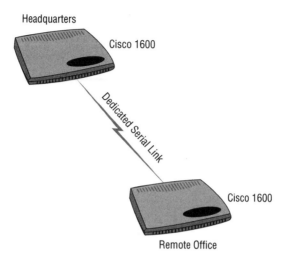

What if that company decides to add two more locations? The future design is a single headquarters with *three* remote offices. Hmmm, now what? Do you add more serial links to accommodate the other two sites? That would require two additional serial interfaces. Such a configuration is not available on the 1600 family routers that *you* picked. Have you just opened the door to a potentially costly forklift upgrade?

Let's go back and rethink our initial design, this time with a little forward thinking. Perhaps a Frame Relay link and use of subinterfaces on the headquarters router would be more appropriate to allow for future growth. But what about the equipment choice? You lucked out! You can still use both of the 1600 routers. The increased bandwidth may be a little much to keep one at the headquarters, though. Consider moving the current headquarters 1600 out to remote office 1 and acquiring a third 1600 for the remote office 2 location. To allow for even more growth, a 2500 family router for the headquarters would be ideal at this point. If the company network continues to grow, more 1600s can be added to the frame cloud from the future remote locations, as illustrated by Figure 5.17. As the 2500 begins to labor, consider moving it out to the largest of the remote sites and acquiring a 3600 or 4500 Series router to place at the headquarters.

Figure 5.17   The future network

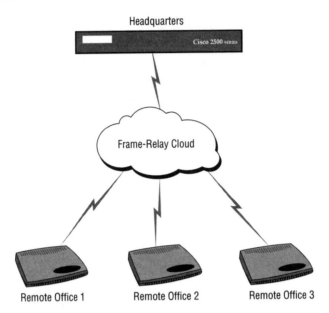

This type of forward thinking will keep your network users and managers happy. Rotating routers from the core out to the remote sites is very common and can be done with minimal down time. Another possible solution would have been to continue with additional serial links to each location. The line cost of doing so would likely be more expensive. Thus, the frame-relay solution was examined. Additionally, a minimum port configuration of three serials would have been required. Although a 4-port fixed configuration is available within the 2500 series family, for our example this would not scale as well as what was proposed.

Part 2

Routing Protocols

- Distance-vector protocols
- Link-state protocols
- Hybrid routing protocols

6

Distance-Vector Routing Protocols

Routers use routing protocols to exchange known network information with other routers. There are a number of classes of routing protocols, including distance vector, link state, and hybrid. Each exhibits different characteristics and is important for an internetwork engineer to understand. This chapter focuses on routing protocols that exhibit behavior consistent with distance vector protocols.

Distance-vector routing protocols are among the earliest routing protocols and have very simple characteristics. The most notable characteristic is the way they receive updates. Distance vector protocols get their updates on a frequent periodic basis in broadcast format. Additionally, the update is in the form of an entire routing table. In other words, a router running a distance-vector protocol will broadcast virtually all entries in its routing table every so many seconds whether a change has occurred or not.

Autonomous System

Before discussing routing protocols, it is first important to discuss the concept of an *autonomous system*. An autonomous system is a grouping of routers under common administration using a common routing strategy. Simply put, the sum of all the routers in an organization makes up its autonomous system. The Internet is nothing more than a bunch of autonomous systems intercommunicating.

Routing protocols are classified as either *interior* or *exterior gateway protocols*. Interior gateway protocols operate within an autonomous system. Their main job is to exchange information with other routers in your organization (within the same autonomous system). Some examples of interior gateway protocols include Routing Information Protocol (RIP), RIP version 2, Interior Gateway Routing Protocol (IGRP), Open Shortest Path First (OSPF), and Enhanced Interior Gateway Protocol (EIGRP). Exterior gateway protocols work between autonomous systems. Their main job is to advertise summaries of networks that represent other autonomous systems. Some examples of exterior gateway protocols include Exterior Gateway Protocol (EGP) and Border Gateway Protocol (BGP). The Internet is based on Border Gateway Protocol (BGP) version 4.

Some protocols require configuration with a unique autonomous system number. For instance, IGRP routers will only exchange updates with other IGRP routers that have been configured with the same autonomous system number. A valid autonomous system number is any number between 1 and 65,535. It serves to identify the system itself. To participate on the Internet, an autonomous system must have a globally unique autonomous system number in order to exchange exterior routing information. All first-tier ISPs have one or more autonomous system numbers registered through the IP numbering authorities.

If your organization will not be participating on the Internet using an exterior gateway protocol, it is safe to say that any autonomous system number can be used in your router configuration. However, this tends to be problematic down the road if Internet access does indeed come along. The Internet community has set aside a range of autonomous system numbers as private autonomous system numbers that will not be assigned to any organizations. RFC 1930 has reserved the range of 64,512 through 65,535 as available to all; these should be used in cases where a globally unique number is not needed.

Classfull versus Classless

Some IP routing protocols are considered *classfull* and others are *classless*. Classfull routing protocols do not include subnet mask information in their updates. All routers that receive updates using a classfull protocol have to assume they should apply the default subnet mask for the network class that was advertised. For instance, if the network address 10.1.0.0 is used with the subnet mask 255.255.0.0, any routers that receive updates for this network will not know what subnet mask to apply unless that router has an interface configured with a 10.0.0.0 address. If not, that router will have to assume it must use the default subnet mask for that class of address. The 10.1.0.0 network is a class A network and, therefore, has a default subnet mask of 255.0.0.0. This has the end result of classfull protocols automatically summarizing all subnetted networks by default. For instance, let's take a look at Figure 6.1.

In the following example we have an internetwork with four routers labeled A through D. Router A is attached to the 192.168.1.0, 172.16.1.0, and 172.16.2.0 networks. Router B is connected to the 172.16.1.0 and 172.16.3.0 networks. Router C is connected to 172.16.3.0, 172.16.4.0, and 10.1.0.0. And router D is connected to 172.16.2.0 and 172.16.4.0. All routers have attached interfaces in the 172.16.0.0 network. This being the case, all routers also know what subnet mask to apply to all advertised subnets in the 172.16.0.0 network. This is not the case for advertised subnets of the 10.0.0.0 network, though.

If we were using a classfull protocol, router C would advertise network 10.1.0.0 to routers B and D with no subnet mask. Routers B and D would have to assume the default mask should be applied. Because the default mask is applied, routers B and D place an entry in their routing table for the 10.0.0.0 network. Consequently, they will advertise 10.0.0.0 (not 10.1.0.0) to router A.

Figure 6.1   Simple internetwork with classfull routers

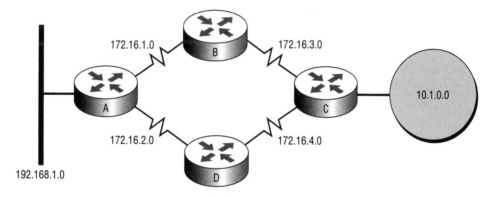

If we were using a classless protocol, router C would advertise 10.1.0.0 with a bit-count value that represents the subnet mask, for example, 10.1.0.0/16.

Some examples of classfull IP protocols include the following:

- RIP version 1
- IGRP

Some examples of classless IP protocols include the following:

- RIP version 2
- OSPF
- EIGRP

Administrative Distance

Cisco routers are capable of utilizing a number of different routing protocols at the same time. In other words, if desired, we could run RIP and OSPF and IGRP, as well as other protocols, all at the same time. Well, this is a great feature for flexibility's sake, but it brings up a question: What happens if more than one protocol learns about the same network? RIP might learn that a network is accessible by sending a packet in one direction, and IGRP might learn that the same network is accessible via a different direction. Which protocol do we believe? Cisco has resolved this issue by applying a value to each routing protocol to represent how believable or trustworthy that protocol is. That value is called *administrative distance*. Administrative distance is one among many of the things stored in a routing table. Some defaults for administrative distance are outlined in the following table. Note: A route with an administrative distance of 0 will take priority over a route with an administrative distance of 120. The lower the administrative distance, the more trustworthy the source.

Source	Administrative Distance
Directly connected route	0
Static Route	1
EIGRP	90
IGRP	100
OSPF	110
RIP	120

Routing Information Protocol (RIP)

RIP is probably the simplest, most widely available, and oldest of IP routing protocols. All systems that support routing functions probably support some variation of RIP. RIP is a distance-vector protocol; therefore, its updates include virtually all entries in the routing table with a certain exception. Cisco's RIP uses split horizon, so networks learned by an interface will not be advertised out of the same interface. (We will discuss split horizon in detail later in this chapter.)

RIP uses a simple hop count as a metric. A *hop* is a metric value measured by the number of other routers a packet must pass through to reach a destination network. RIP allows for a maximum hop count of 15 hops; a network that is 16 hops away is considered unreachable. IP RIP updates are advertised in broadcast format on a 30-second cycle. Each update is good for 180 seconds. If a route is not renewed after 180 seconds, that network is marked as possibly down. If that network is not advertised or has not come back up after 240 seconds, it is removed from the routing table. Advertisements from a neighboring router are based on that neighboring router's perspective. Each network is advertised with a metric that represents its distance plus one hop.

Configuring RIP

IP RIP is among the simpler of routing protocols to configure. Two steps are required. First, the routing protocol has to be enabled. This is done using the `router rip` command in global configuration mode. Once issued, the command-line interface will place you in an IP router configuration mode. The prompt will look like this:

```
Router(router-config)#
```

Once in this mode, it is necessary to tell the router which interfaces will be participating in the RIP process. This is done by listing all the classfull networks in which each interface will participate. The following is an example of a typical RIP configuration. In Figure 6.2, we have a router connected to two segments. One is configured as part of the 10.0.0.0 network; the other is part of the 172.16.0.0 network. Because this router has interfaces in each network, the router has to be configured to advertise both.

Routing Protocols

PART 2

Figure 6.2   Simple network with two network segments.

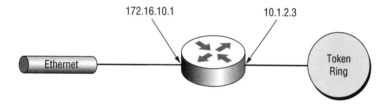

```
!
router rip
  network 10.0.0.0
  network 172.16.0.0
!
```

We have a useful show command that will allow us to verify our RIP configuration. The command is `show ip protocols`. The following is an example output of this command:

```
RouterA#show ip protocols
Routing Protocol is "rip"
    Sending updates every 30 seconds, next due in 3 seconds
    Invalid after 180 seconds, hold down 180, flushed after 240
    Outgoing update filter list for all interfaces is not set
```

```
Incoming update filter list for all interfaces is not set
Redistributing: rip
Default version control: send version 1, receive any version
   Interface          Send  Recv   Key-chain
   Loopback0            1     1 2
   Serial0              1     1 2
Routing for Networks:
   10.0.0.0
   172.16.0.0
Routing Information Sources:
   Gateway          Distance        Last Update
   172.16.1.2           120         00:00:14
Distance: (default is 120)
```

Notice that the output lists the update, invalid, and flush timers. It also lists whether an outgoing or incoming route filter has been applied. It will let you know whether the router has been configured to recognize and send RIP version 2 updates (more about that later). The default configuration has the router send version 1 updates but listen for version 1 and 2 updates. The output also has a section called "Routing for Networks." This section lists all the locally attached networks the router will advertise. These networks directly reflect the networks you configure the router to advertise. The section called "Routing Information Sources" lists all the IP addresses of other router interfaces from which this router has received RIP updates.

We can change the value of all the default timers RIP uses in normal operation. We do this by using the `timers basic` command. The following is an example of this command.

```
timers basic <update cycle> <invalid timer> <hold-down timer>
<flush timer>
```

Below we have changed the IP RIP interval to every 60 seconds and made each update good for up to 360 seconds. With the same command we have also changed the hold-down timer to 420 seconds and the flush timer to 600 seconds.

```
!
timers basic 60 360 420 600
!
```

NOTE The developers of routing protocols have carefully thought out the values for default timers. There are very few instances when it is appropriate to change these timers.

We also have the ability to monitor real-time RIP updates as they are happening. To do so, we enable the infinitely useful IOS debug feature. The command to monitor RIP is `debug ip rip`. The following is an example output of an IP RIP debug. Notice that each received update includes the source of the information and all known IP networks with a hop count. Sent updates go to the broadcast address 255.255.255.255. All updates are broadcast out of each RIP enabled interface. In this case that includes Serial0 and Serial1.

```
RouterB#debug ip rip
RIP protocol debugging is on
RouterB#terminal monitor
RouterB#
RIP: received v1 update from 172.16.1.1 on Serial1
        10.0.0.0 in 1 hops
RIP: received v1 update from 192.168.1.2 on Serial0
        10.0.0.0 in 1 hops
RIP: sending v1 update to 255.255.255.255 via Serial0 (192.168.1.1)
        network 172.16.0.0, metric 1
RIP: sending v1 update to 255.255.255.255 via Serial1 (172.16.1.2)
        network 192.168.1.0, metric 1
RIP: received v1 update from 172.16.1.1 on Serial1
        10.0.0.0 in 1 hops
RIP: received v1 update from 192.168.1.2 on Serial0
        10.0.0.0 in 1 hops
RIP: sending v1 update to 255.255.255.255 via Serial0 (192.168.1.1)
        network 172.16.0.0, metric 1
RIP: sending v1 update to 255.255.255.255 via Serial1 (172.16.1.2)
        network 192.168.1.0, metric 1
```

WARNING Be careful when using the IOS debug feature. Every time a debugged criterion is met, a message must be generated and sent to the console. If many of these messages are generated in a given time, the router must spend many CPU cycles processing the debugs and may not accomplish much routing. Additionally, when debug is used for most situations, all packets debugged must be route processed and are no longer eligible for fast switching. This too slows routing operations overall. The best policy to follow is to only use IOS debug for troubleshooting, not monitoring. Use it when you have a problem that you need to gather more information about. Once troubleshooting is over, turn off debugging.

WARNING Another important point about debug—you have a great deal of flexibility in what you may debug. Be very specific about what you choose to debug. The command debug all issued on a production router is rarely followed by good results. Be careful to only debug what you want to view.

TIP If you get in trouble with IOS debug, you can turn off all debugging by using the command u all. It is short for undebug all. If you come from the South, you can probably relate well to that command.

RIPv2

RIP version 2 was an attempt to overcome some of the shortcomings of RIP. It was actually created to support Classless Interdomain Routing (CIDR). Like RIP (which we will call RIP version 1 or RIPv1), it is a distance vector protocol. RIPv2 uses hop count as a metric like RIPv1. The update cycle is every 30 seconds like RIPv1. Where it differs is in the fact that it supports variable length subnet masks. RIPv2 updates include subnet mask information. This makes it a classless protocol. Some of the additional features include the following:

- Authentication using both clear text and MD5 password encryption
- Optional route summarization, unlike RIPv1, which always summarizes
- Variable-length subnet masks (VLSMs)

RIPv2 updates come by default in two parts. To be compatible with version 1 routers, RIPv2 will send typical RIP updates. It will, however, only listen to version 2 updates. As you may recall, version 1 updates are sent to a broadcast address (255.255.255.255). Version

2 updates, on the other hand, are sent to a multicast address. Updates are still sent every 30 seconds, but they are sent to the address 224.0.0.9. RIPv2 routers will by default ignore the broadcast updates and listen for the multicast ones only.

Configuring RIPv2 is similar to configuring version 1. There is one additional command required: the `version 2` command. The following is an example of a version 2 configuration:

```
!
router rip
  version 2
  network 10.0.0.0
  network 172.16.0.0
!
```

PART 2

The following is a debug output performed on a router running RIPv2. Notice each network update includes a bit count (/24) that represents the subnet mask applied to that network address. RIPv1 updates do not include this. Additionally, the updates are sent to a multicast address rather than a broadcast address.

```
RouterA#debug ip rip
RIP protocol debugging is on
RouterA#
RIP: received v2 update from 172.16.1.2 on Serial0
      192.168.1.0/24 -> 0.0.0.0 in 1 hops
RIP: sending v2 update to 224.0.0.9 via Loopback0 (10.4.1.1)
      192.168.1.0/24 -> 0.0.0.0, metric 2, tag 0
      172.16.0.0/16 -> 0.0.0.0, metric 1, tag 0
RIP: sending v2 update to 224.0.0.9 via Serial0 (172.16.1.1)
      10.0.0.0/8 -> 0.0.0.0, metric 1, tag 0
RIP: ignored v2 packet from 10.4.1.1 (sourced from one of our
      addresses)
RIP: received v2 update from 172.16.1.2 on Serial0
      192.168.1.0/24 -> 0.0.0.0 in 1 hops1
RIP: sending v2 update to 224.0.0.9 via Serial0 (192.168.1.1)
```

Routing Protocols

```
             172.16.0.0/16 -> 0.0.0.0, metric 1, tag 0
RIP: sending v2 update to 224.0.0.9 via Serial1 (172.16.1.2)
             192.168.1.0/24 -> 0.0.0.0, metric 1, tag 0
RIP: received v2 update from 172.16.1.1 on Serial1
             10.0.0.0/8 -> 0.0.0.0 in 1 hops
RIP: received v2 update from 172.16.1.1 on Serial1
             10.0.0.0/8 -> 0.0.0.0 in 1 hops
RIP: sending v2 update to 224.0.0.9 via Loopback0 (10.4.1.1)
             192.168.1.0/24 -> 0.0.0.0, metric 2, tag 0
             172.16.0.0/16 -> 0.0.0.0, metric 1, tag 0
RIP: sending v2 update to 224.0.0.9 via Serial0 (172.16.1.1)
             10.0.0.0/8 -> 0.0.0.0, metric 1, tag 0
RIP: ignored v2 packet from 10.4.1.1 (sourced from one of our
             addresses)
RIP: ignored v1 packet from 192.168.1.2 (illegal version)
RouterB#u all
All possible debugging has been turned off
```

Although not required, RIP version 2 comes with additional features. We can add authentication. We can also disable the automatic summarization of networks not directly attached. We can even have a version 2 router listen for version 1 updates as well as send them. The following is a configuration that disables the automatic summarization.

```
!
router rip
  version 2
  no auto-summary
!
```

In the following configuration example we have configured interface Ethernet 0 to listen for version 1 and 2 updates, and we have configured interface Serial 0 to listen for version 2 updates but only send version 1.

```
!
interface ethernet 0
  ip rip receive version 1 2
  ip rip send version 1 2
!
interface serial 0
  ip rip receive version 1 2
  ip rip send version 1
!
```

As an alternative to restricting which version of RIP is sent or received, we also have the ability to make an interface *passive*. A passive interface will listen for updates but will not send them at all. This is a popular option when redistributing between different protocols to avoid a looped environment. The following RIP configuration turns on RIPv2 and makes interface e0 passive.

```
!
router rip
  version 2
  passive-interface ethernet 0
!
```

NOTE   Redistribution will be covered in later sections of this book.

Interior Gateway Routing Protocol (IGRP)

Cisco's earliest answer to some of the limitations of RIPv1 was IGRP. IGRP is another distance vector routing protocol available via the Cisco IOS. It was developed by Cisco in the mid-1980s to allow for scalability in larger environments. As you may recall, RIP uses a simple hop count as a metric. Using a hop count can sometimes lead to the router using a suboptimal path. For instance, look at Figure 6.3. Using RIP, if router A wanted to send a packet to the 192.168.1.0 network, it would simply use the path with the fewest hops. In this case, the router would send the packet across the 56K path. However, we can see this is not the optimal path. A thinking person might say that the best path is across routers C, D, and E over the Fast Ethernet links because it has more bandwidth and less overall delay. In this case, however, IGRP is a more desirable option.

Routing Protocols

PART 2

Figure 6.3 Simple IGRP network

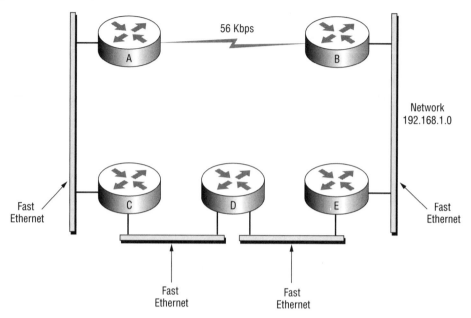

IGRP overcomes a number of the perceived limitations of RIP. Its benefits include the following:

- Sophisticated metric that includes bandwidth, delay, reliability, and load
- Less frequent update cycle
- Scalable to much larger networks
- Unequal cost load balancing

Configuring IGRP is almost as simple as configuring RIP. You must first enable IGRP on the router and then tell it which classfull networks it will advertise. To enable IGRP, you must issue the `router igrp <AS number>` command. The *<AS number>* will be replaced by an autonomous system number. IGRP will only exchange updates by default with other IGRP routers in the same autonomous system. Therefore, they all have to be configured with the same autonomous system number. Once the `router igrp <AS number>` command is issued, you will be placed in router configuration mode. The prompt will appear as follows:

```
Router(config-router)#
```

Once in router configuration mode, one or more classfull network statements are required to tell IGRP which interfaces will exchange IGRP updates. The following is a working example.

```
!
router igrp 65000
  network 172.16.0.0
  network 192.168.1.0
!
```

IGRP uses a composite metric to make its routing decisions. The metric comes from an equation that takes into account bandwidth and total delay of a route. With some tweaking it can even take factors including reliability and load into account as well. The composite metric is based on the equation below:

```
metric = [k1 * bandwidth + (k2 * bandwidth)/(256 - load) + k3 *
delay]


If k5 does not equal zero, then the metric = metric * [k5 /
(reliability + k4)]
```

This equation uses five variables: k1, k2, k3, k4, and k5. By default, k1 and k3 are given the value of one, and k2, k4, and k5 equal zero. The way it works out by default is that the IGRP router will take into account the cumulative delays on all the networks in a path and add it to the bandwidth of the slowest network. Bandwidth is measured as an inverse in bits per second. It represents the minimum bandwidth network of the path scaled by a factor of 10 times 10 to the tenth power. The range is from a 1200bps line to 10Gbps. Some examples of IGRP bandwidth values are as follows:

Link Type	Bandwidth
Ethernet	256,000
T1 (1.544Mbps)	1,657,856
64Kbps	40,000,000
56Kbps	45,714,176 bits

Delay is used in units of 10 microseconds. Different media will have different delay values assigned to them. The value is stored as a 32-bit field on the router. Each increment of that 32-bit field is given the value of 39.1 nanoseconds. A value of all ones (4,294,967,040 nanoseconds, or 168 seconds) is considered unreachable to IGRP. Some examples of typical delays are as follows:

Link Type	Delay
Ethernet	25,600 (or 1ms)
T1 (1.544Mbps)	512000 (or 20,000ms)
64Kbps	512000 (or 20,000ms)
56Kbps	512000 (or 20,000ms)

Reliability is continuously calculated and is given as a number between 1 and 255. A reliability factor of 255 implies that you have 100 percent reliability and, therefore, a perfectly stable link. Load is also calculated on a continuous basis and given as a number between 1 and 255. A load of 255 implies that you have a completely saturated link. Both reliability and load can be monitored by issuing the show interfaces command.

If you are really brave, you have it in your power to change how the composite metric does its thing by changing the values of the k variables. We do this by issuing the metric weights command. The following is the syntax:

```
metric weights <tos> <k1> <k2> <k3> <k4> <k5>
```

This command is issued in router configuration mode along with other IGRP-related commands. TOS stands for type of service. This variable is not currently used and must be set to zero. The k variables are the only part we are concerned with, as they change the behavior of the composite metric.

WARNING Changing the metric weights is tricky business. Be sure you really know how the change is going to affect your updates before you do it.

One of the ongoing complaints about RIP is its update frequency. RIP sends updates every 30 seconds whether there is a change or not. In the eyes of many engineers this tends to be excessive and wasteful of bandwidth. In contrast, IGRP sends its updates every 90 seconds. To make convergence happen as quickly as possible, IGRP also supports *flash updates*. A flash update is a regular update, but it happens when there is a change in the topology. Overall, in the eyes of many, this tends to be a more efficient strategy.

The following is an output from a debug ip igrp transaction command. Using this command we can get a picture of some typical IGRP updates. This command is also useful when troubleshooting IGRP update problems.

```
RouterA#debug ip igrp transactions
IGRP protocol debugging is on
```

```
RouterA#
IGRP: sending update to 255.255.255.255 via Loopback0 (10.4.1.1)
      network 192.168.1.0, metric=10476
      network 172.16.0.0, metric=8476
IGRP: sending update to 255.255.255.255 via Serial0 (172.16.1.1)
      network 10.0.0.0, metric=501
IGRP: broadcasting request on Loopback0
IGRP: broadcasting request on Serial0
IGRP: received update from 172.16.1.2 on Serial0
      subnet 172.16.1.0, metric 10476 (neighbor 8476)
      network 192.168.1.0, metric 10476 (neighbor 8476)
IGRP: edition is now 2
IGRP: sending update to 255.255.255.255 via Loopback0 (10.4.1.1)
      network 192.168.1.0, metric=10476
      network 172.16.0.0, metric=8476
IGRP: sending update to 255.255.255.255 via Serial0 (172.16.1.1)
      network 10.0.0.0, metric=501
IGRP: received update from 172.16.1.2 on Serial0
      network 192.168.1.0, metric 10476 (neighbor 8476)
RouterA#u all
All possible debugging has been turned off
```

IGRP is much more scalable for a larger internetwork. It does not have the same hop count limitation that RIP has. To RIP, 15 hops is maximum and 16 hops is considered unreachable. This means the maximum width of a RIP internetwork is limited to only 15 routers. IGRP has a configurable maximum hop count. The default is 100 hops and can be increased to 255. The command to do so is metric maximum-hops <*hops*>. This command is performed in router configuration mode with other IGRP commands.

RIP and IGRP both allow us to do load sharing over multiple equal-cost paths. In fact, we can load share over up to four paths by default and can even increase that to six in IP networks. This is a great feature. An added bonus with IGRP is its ability to do unequal-cost load sharing over multiple paths. For example, if you wanted to, you could have a primary T1 link and a backup link of 256K and use both links simultaneously. Rather than have one link idle waiting for the primary link to fail, we can use both—a more attractive option if you are paying for both. This concept requires us to configure a variable called *metric variance*.

Metric variance is a factor that represents how slow a secondary link can be and still allow a primary link to unequal-cost load share with it. For instance, the default metric variance on an IGRP router is one. With a metric variance of one, a primary line of 512K can only load share with another 512K line. If we change the variance to two, we can load share that primary 512K line with lines as low as 256K. Changing the variance to four will enable load sharing with as low as 128K lines, and so on. For example, if we did have a metric variance of four, the router would send four packets across the primary (512K) link and one packet across the secondary (128K) link in round-robin fashion.

The command for changing the metric variance is `variance <multiplier>`. This command is issued in router configuration mode with other IGRP commands. The following is a working example of the variance and metric maximum-hop commands. Here we have increased the maximum hop count to 200 and the metric variance to two.

```
!
router igrp 65000
  network 172.16.0.0
  network 192.168.1.0
  metric maximum-hops 200
  variance 2
!
```

The `show ip route` command shows us a routing table that is based on the IGRP routing protocol. Notice that the IGRP learned routes start with the letter I. Also notice the number used as a metric. The number 10,476 is the result of the composite metric. The 100 portion of the metric is the administrative distance for IGRP. One hundred is the default.

```
RouterC#show ip route
Codes: C - connected, S - static, I - IGRP, R - RIP, M - mobile, B -
BGP
       D - EIGRP, EX - EIGRP external, O - OSPF, IA - OSPF inter area
       N1 - OSPF NSSA external type 1, N2 - OSPF NSSA external type 2
       E1 - OSPF external type 1, E2 - OSPF external type 2, E - EGP
```

```
         i - IS-IS, L1 - IS-IS level-1, L2 - IS-IS level-2, * -
            candidate default
         U - per-user static route, o - ODR


Gateway of last resort is not set


      10.0.0.0/24 is subnetted, 1 subnets
C        10.3.1.0 is directly connected, Loopback0
C        192.168.1.0/24 is directly connected, Serial1
I        172.16.0.0/16 [100/10476] via 192.168.1.1, 00:00:25, Serial1
```

As with RIP, we can use the show ip protocols command to view how IGRP is configured on a router. In the following example we can see that this router is configured to be part of autonomous system 65000. Additionally, it is configured to send IGRP updates every 90 seconds. Each update is good for 270 seconds. The hold-down timer is 280 seconds and the flush timer is 630 seconds. Further down, we notice the values assigned to k1, k2, k3, k4, and k5. They are set to the default. It also lists the configured maximum hop count. The default is 100, but we previously changed it to 200. It displays the value of the metric variance. The default is 1(equal-cost load sharing only), but we increased it to 2 in the previous section. It is configured to advertise the 172.16.0.0 and 192.168.1.0 networks and has recently received updates from other IGRP routers with the interface addresses of 192.168.1.2 and 172.16.1.1. Last, it is configured with the default administrative distance of 100.

```
RouterB#show ip protocols
Routing Protocol is "igrp 65000"
   Sending updates every 90 seconds, next due in 68 seconds
   Invalid after 270 seconds, hold down 280, flushed after 630
   Outgoing update filter list for all interfaces is not set
   Incoming update filter list for all interfaces is not set
   Default networks flagged in outgoing updates
   Default networks accepted from incoming updates
   IGRP metric weight K1=1, K2=0, K3=1, K4=0, K5=0
   IGRP maximum hopcount 200
   IGRP maximum metric variance 2
```

```
Redistributing: igrp 65000
Routing for Networks:
    172.16.0.0
    192.168.1.0
Routing Information Sources:
    Gateway         Distance      Last Update
    192.168.1.2         100       00:00:13
    172.16.1.1          100       00:00:10
Distance: (default is 100)
```

Split Horizon

At the beginning of this chapter, we described a distance-vector update as including virtually every entry in the router's routing table. In actuality, Cisco protocols utilize a technique called *split horizon* to cut down on the possibility of inviting a routing loop if the internetwork becomes unstable. Split horizon keeps a specific interface from advertising a network that was learned from that interface. Let us suppose a router had three active interfaces. We will call them Serial 0, Serial 1, and Ethernet 0. The router learns about network 10.0.0.0 through Serial 1. Assuming split horizon is enabled, the 10.0.0.0 network will only be advertised out of interfaces Serial 0 and Ethernet 0.

It is recommended that split horizon be disabled for packet-switched networks like Frame Relay and X.25 when configured as a non-broadcast multi-access (NBMA) topology. An NBMA network is one where a number of routers are set up in a hub-and-spoke topology and are configured so that all interfaces connected to the packet-switched network are configured to be part of the same logical network. Figure 6.4 is an example of an NBMA network. Notice that all interfaces inside the network cloud are part of the 10.0.0.0 network. With these types of networks, all spoke routers (routers B, C, and D) rely completely on the hub router (router A) for communications between them. When there is a broadcast transmitted on any of the networks, it is up to router A to retransmit it on all other networks.

Let's assume router B sends a routing update to router A. It is up to router A to send that update to routers C and D. This means router A potentially learns about a network through the interface connected to the WAN and advertises that same network out the same interface for the other routers to learn it. Split horizon was developed to prohibit this exact scenario because it can potentially invite a routing loop into our environment. Unfortunately, the reality is that with an NBMA network we have no other choice than to disable split horizon. In fact, a router operating in a Frame Relay network configured as a multipoint network (NBMA) automatically turns off split horizon.

Figure 6.4   Hub-and-spoke network

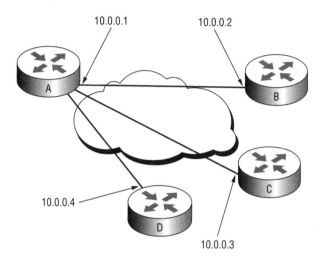

To verify that split horizon is enabled you can issue the command show ip interface. The following is an example output of this command.

```
RouterB# show ip interface serial0
Serial0 is up, line protocol is up
Internet address is 192.168.1.1/24
Broadcast address is 255.255.255.255
Address determined by setup command
MTU is 1500 bytes
Helper address is not set
Directed broadcast forwarding is enabled
Multicast reserved groups joined: 224.0.0.9
Outgoing access list is not set
Inbound access list is not set
Proxy ARP is enabled
Security level is default
```

Split horizon is enabled

ICMP redirects are always sent

ICMP unreachables are always sent

ICMP mask replies are never sent

IP fast switching is enabled

IP fast switching on the same interface is enabled

IP multicast fast switching is enabled

Router Discovery is disabled

IP output packet accounting is disabled

IP access violation accounting is disabled

TCP/IP header compression is disabled

Probe proxy name replies are disabled

Gateway Discovery is disabled

Policy routing is disabled

Network address translation is disabled

We have the ability to disable split horizon by issuing the `no ip split-horizon` command. Split horizon is enabled and disabled on an individual interface basis. Consequently, the command to disable it must be performed in interface configuration mode. The following is an example of disabling split horizon on an interface participating in an X.25 network.

```
!
interface serial 0
  encapsulation x25
  x25 address 310123456789
  no ip split-horizon
!
```

Both RIPv1 and IGRP use broadcasts to exchange network updates. By default, routers connected to non-broadcast networks do not propagate broadcast traffic onto them. In cases where broadcasted routing updates are required between routers over a nonbroadcast type of network, an additional configuration may be required. The IOS `neighbor` command was created for just such a reason. The following is an example of the use of the `neighbor` command (see Figure 6.5). Notice that router A is configured with the neighbor information of router B. Router B, in turn, is also configured with the IP address of router A, as its neighbor.

Figure 6.5   Neighboring routers

```
! Configuration for router A
interface serial 0
  ip address 10.0.0.1 255.0.0.0
  encapsulation frame-relay
  neighbor 10.0.0.2
!


! Configuration for router B
interface serial 0
  ip address 10.0.0.2 255.0.0.0
  encapsulation frame-relay
  neighbor 10.0.0.1
!
```

As previously mentioned, distance-vector protocols are among the earliest routing protocols. Although simple to configure, they tend to be a less desirable option than some of the more recently developed protocols. The frequent periodic nature of the updates tends to be somewhat wasteful of bandwidth. Additionally, these protocols can, in some cases, be unreliable. Distance-vector routing protocols have to rely on the information advertised by neighboring routers. If this information is correct, then distance-vector routers can make proper routing decisions. But if this information is incorrect for one reason or another, then distance-vector routers can make poor routing decisions, send packets down sub-optimal paths, or possibly even cause a routing loop. Last, most of the distance-vector protocols are classfull in nature and tend to be limited as to where they can be used.

Routing Protocols

PART 2

A response to some of the perceived limitations of distance-vector routing protocols has been the development of link-state routing protocols. Link-state routing protocols exhibit far different characteristics from distance-vector protocols. In the next chapter, we will discuss routing protocols such as OSPF, and NetWare Link Services Protocol (NLSP).

Classless Routing with RIPv2

John once had a client with a very interesting problem. They originally had a simple routed network with two physically sparse locations and had recently added a third remote office. They were using a mixture of protocols in their organization, mainly RIP and EIGRP in their 10.3.0.0 network, as well as on router A. The graphic below is a topological view of their network.

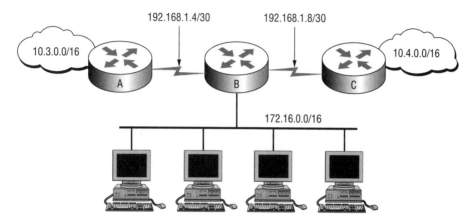

Routers A and B were both Cisco routers, and router C was that of another manufacturer. Routers B and C ran only RIP. Everything worked well until router C and the rest of the 10.4.0.0 network were added to the internetwork. Then performance slowed to an unacceptable level, and in some cases network access just didn't work. So John was assigned to figure out why. Shortly after arriving to the site that housed router B, John performed a number of show commands and Pings. The following output was the result of doing a Ping to any address in any 10.x.x.x network. After using the Ping utility to verify connectivity to addresses in both the 10.4.x.x and 10.3.x.x networks, he found that both resulted in half the packets being successful and the other half failing (U = unreachable, ! = success). Strange, he thought.

```
RouterB#ping 10.4.1.1

Type escape sequence to abort.
Sending 5, 100-byte ICMP Echos to 10.4.1.1, timeout is 2 seconds:
U!U!U
Success rate is 40 percent (2/5), round-trip min/avg/max = 32/32/32 ms

RouterB#ping 10.3.1.1

Type escape sequence to abort.
```

```
Sending 5, 100-byte ICMP Echos to 10.3.1.1, timeout is 2 seconds:
!U!U!
Success rate is 60 percent (3/5), round-trip min/avg/max = 32/32/32 ms
```

Upon performing a show IP protocols, John found that the following is what the routing table on router B looked like. From router B there were two next-hop addresses for the 10.0.0.0 network. The router makes no distinction between 10.3.x.x and 10.4.x.x even though they are in different physical locations.

```
RouterB#show ip route
Codes: C - connected, S - static, I - IGRP, R - RIP, M - mobile,
       B - BGP
       D - EIGRP, EX - EIGRP external, O - OSPF, IA - OSPF inter area
       N1 - OSPF NSSA external type 1, N2 - OSPF NSSA external type 2
       E1 - OSPF external type 1, E2 - OSPF external type 2, E - EGP
       i - IS-IS, L1 - IS-IS level-1, L2 - IS-IS level-2, * -
         candidate default
       U - per-user static route, o - ODR


Gateway of last resort is not set

R    10.0.0.0/8 [120/1] via 192.168.1.6, 00:00:01, Serial0
                 [120/1] via 192.168.1.10, 00:00:10, Serial1
C    172.16.0.0/16 is is directly connected, Ethernet0
     192.168.1.0/30 is subnetted, 2 subnets
C       192.168.1.4/30 is directly connected, Serial0
C       192.168.1.8/30 is directly connected, Serial1
```

It occurred to John that routers A, B, and C were running RIP version 1, a classfull routing protocol. He had found the problem. It seems RIP was summarizing the 10.0.0.0 network even in this case, when it was inappropriate.

Now all that was left was to come up with a solution. They could go with a classless protocol throughout the organization. The choices they had were OSPF, EIGRP, and RIPv2. Router B was a lower-end router that was really not suited for OSPF. EIGRP is a Cisco proprietary protocol and, therefore, could not be used on router C, which was not a Cisco router. Buying new routers really wasn't in the cards due to budget constraints. That left RIP version 2, which was supported by all the routers. It requires very little overhead and is classless.

After implementing RIP version 2 and configuring it to redistribute with the other protocols, everything worked great. The routing table listed individual entries for the 10.3.0.0 and 10.4.0.0 networks, and all Pings to the 10.0.0.0 networks were successful.

7

Link-State Routing Protocols

Link-state protocols exhibit characteristics that are significantly different from distance-vector protocols. You may recall from previous chapters that a link-state protocol typically uses change-based updates compared to the distance-vector's frequent periodic updates. In addition, link-state protocols usually maintain some kind of topology database. This makes updates more reliable and convergence much quicker. Distance-vector protocols rely on information communicated to them from their neighboring routers. This chapter discusses the following link-state protocols:

- Open Shortest Path First (OSPF)
- NetWare Link Services Protocol (NLSP)
- Intermediate System to Intermediate System (IS-IS)

With the recent growth of the Internet came a broad necessity for IP routing protocols in the industry. Administrators have found themselves looking more and more at IP routing protocols with the capability to grow with the times. Because of its capabilities, the use of OSPF in larger internetworks has grown by leaps and bounds. Because of the widespread interest in the topic, this chapter will focus mostly on the OSPF routing protocol.

Open Shortest Path First (OSPF)

OSPF is an interior gateway protocol used in IP networks. It was developed by the Internet Engineering Task Force (IETF) to support those internetworks that are larger than RIP can handle. OSPF's design incorporates a number of features that make it superior to RIP in many ways. These features include:

- Scalability to very large internetworks
- The ability to use a better metric than a simple hop count
- A fast convergence time
- The ability to support variable length subnet masks
- The ability to control how networks are summarized
- The ability to handle routes derived from external networks
- It is an open standard and therefore supported by most vendors of routing products

---

NOTE   OSPF version 2 is documented in RFC 1247.

OSPF Operation

Since it is a link-state protocol, OSPF's operation is significantly different from any of the distance-vector protocols. For example, OSPF does not send its updates on a frequent periodic basis like RIP or Interior Gateway Routing Protocol (IGRP). It first learns the topology of the internetwork, then uses change-based updates when there are networks and routers added or removed. Rather than relying on updates that are broadcasted out of every interface every so many seconds, OSPF establishes acknowledged adjacencies with other routers in the internetwork. Updates are sent only when required and only include information relating to changes in the topology.

The whole concept of OSPF revolves around the use of a topological database. All routers in the same OSPF area store a common topological database. The topological database is a dynamic information base of routers and links stored in the routers' RAM. An OSPF area is a logical grouping of OSPF routers. OSPF areas will be discussed in detail in the following section. Any time there is a change to the topological database, the change is communicated to other routers using Link State Advertisements (LSAs). When an OSPF router receives one of these LSAs, it will compare that information with what is in its topological database. If the advertisement changes the topological database, then the router will execute the SPF algorithm. The SPF algorithm, sometimes called the Dijkstra's algorithm (named after the man that designed it), calculates the new routing table.

NOTE You can view the topological database on an OSPF router by issuing the `show ip ospf database` command in Privileged Exec mode.

Maintaining Adjacencies

An *adjacency* is an acknowledged connection and is maintained on a continuous basis. All OSPF routers maintain adjacencies with other routers in their area for the sake of keeping up the topological database. To make this possible, OSPF relies on a special keep-alive mechanism called a Hello. Hello packets are multicasted on a periodic basis on all links between routers. This allows a router to keep track of the status (state) of a link. The Hellos also allow OSPF routers to learn about and establish adjacencies with other routers in their area.

Understanding Hello Packets

Understanding the contents of a Hello packet helps us to understand OSPF operation. A Hello packet includes the following information in its makeup:

- Router ID, which is the IP address used to identify the sending OSPF router. Router ID is used by the OSPF process for identification in the topology.

- Hello Intervals, which indicate how often Hello packets are sent.

- Dead Intervals, which indicate how long the router will wait without receiving a Hello from a neighbor before it declares that the neighbor is down. Hello and Dead Intervals must match on all routers attempting to establish an adjacency.

- Routers will add their neighbor's IDs in the Hello packet. An adjacency cannot take place until a router sees itself in the neighbor list of another router's Hello packet.

- Area ID indicates the area in which the sending router is configured to be. The area ID must match on all Hello packets from routers in the same area.

- Router Priority is used in the election of a designated router (DR) and a backup designated router (BDR). DRs and BDRs will be discussed in detail later in this chapter.

- Designated Router's ID, which is represented by a 32-bit IP address.

- Backup Designated Router's ID, which is represented by a 32-bit IP address.

- Authentication Info field, which is used to hold an authentication password. Authentication is optional. If used, the password must match with all neighbors establishing adjacencies in an area.

- Stub Area Flag, which is a field that is used to indicate that the area is a stub area. All routers in an area must agree on whether the area is a stub.

Network Types

OSPF recognizes three different network types: *broadcast multi-access*, *point-to-point*, and *non-broadcast multi-access* (NBMA). Each has different characteristics and each is handled a bit differently by OSPF. The most notable characteristic of a broadcast multi-access network is the fact that you can have many devices sharing the same media. All devices on the network hear any information sent. An example of a broadcast multi-access network is Ethernet. A point-to-point network type is any technology where only two routers can share a link. An example of a point-to-point is a serial connection. An NBMA network is a multi-access network where, by default, you can have multiple devices in the same broadcast domain but the technology is not truly a broadcast technology. Examples of NBMA networks are Frame Relay or X.25.

For each network type the hello and dead timers may vary. The following is summary of the default settings:

Network Type	Hello Timer	Dead Timer
broadcast multi-access	10 seconds	40 seconds
point-to-point	10 seconds	40 seconds
NBMA	30 seconds	120 seconds

OSPF routers communicate any changes in link states by sending the information to all routers with which they have an adjacency. This is good most of the time but can be inefficient in some circumstances. Take, for instance, an Ethernet network with six routers attached to it. When one router gets a Link State Update (LSU) as a result of a link state change, it will send that information to all five other routers with which it has an adjacency. They in turn will send that information to their adjacencies, and they in turn will send to theirs. The end result is that you have six routers receiving the same information up to six times. This wastes bandwidth and CPU cycles. OSPF addresses this by electing a Designated Router (DR) and a Backup Designated Router (BDR) on broadcast multi-access networks.

Rather than every router establishing an adjacency with every other router, on broadcast multi-access networks OSPF will elect a DR and a BDR with which all routers will establish adjacencies. Anytime a router receives an LSU, it will update its topological database and send an update to the DR and BDR. It is up to the DR to flood that information to all of its adjacencies. All in all this is a much more efficient way to deliver information. The BDR is there to take over the job of DR in the event that the existing DR goes down.

The DR and BDR are elected based on their priority. When necessary, all router priorities are compared, and the routers with higher priorities are elected. The DR is the router with the highest priority. The router with the next highest priority is elected as the BDR. The default priority for an interface is 1. In the event of a tie, the router's ID is used as a tie-breaker. Priorities can be set using IOS commands. The DR and BDR only change when the existing DR or BDR are removed from the network. If a router with a higher priority is placed on the network, it will not become a DR or BDR until one of the existing ones go down.

On point-to-point networks, there is no need for a designated router because there is only one adjacency per link. On NBMA networks you have to configure it to know where information will be flooded from.

OSPF Areas

With OSFP, design is 99 percent of the work. OSPF has its strength in the fact that it can scale to any size. There is a catch, however. OSPF is very dependent on a good hierarchical design. To allow an OSPF network to grow to really huge proportions, it must be designed to use as little of your router memory and bandwidth resources as possible. OSPF hinges on two design factors. They are:

- The definition of areas in your internetwork
- An IP addressing design that allows for good summarization

An *area* is a logical grouping of routers. Routers in a common area have to be connected in a contiguous manner. As was mentioned previously, all routers in the same OSPF area share a common topological database. As the topological database gets bigger, more memory will be required to store the database. Additionally, as the database gets larger, more bandwidth and CPU time will be required for synchronizing the contents of the database with other adjacent routers. Routers will only establish OSPF adjacencies with other OSPF routers in the same area.

A good hierarchical design starts with the backbone area. All inter-area traffic (traffic from one area to another) passes through this backbone area. In the design shown in Figure 7.1, area 0 is considered the backbone area. Every OSPF network design needs at least one area; one of those is area 0. All non-backbone areas in the same OSPF network have to be connected to the backbone area either directly or indirectly. Routers in area 0 store intra-area routes, external routes, inter-area routes, and default routes.

Area 0 is the only required area in an OSPF network. Other areas, though not required by OSPF, may be necessary for stability and scalability. The soft rule is that you should not have more than 50 routers in the same area. This will keep the topological database in one router from growing to an unmanageable size. Running the SPF algorithm is a very CPU-intensive process. The larger the database is, the more information the SPF algorithm has to deal with and, therefore, the greater the overhead on the router. When routers cannot keep up with the LSAs in an area, it causes a potentially unstable environment.

Any routers that are part of two areas at the same time are called Area Border Routers (ABRs). ABRs store multiple copies of multiple topological databases—one per area to which it is connected. In an ideal design, it is recommended that one router is part of no more than two areas. If necessary, a high-end router with lots of RAM can be part of three or four. ABRs also serve as the doorway into and out of an area. Area summarization, intra-area summarization, and advertisement are done by the ABR.

Configuring OSPF

This section will discuss configuration issues relating to OSPF. Figure 7.1 will be referred to as your configuration topology.

Figure 7.1 A Simple OSPF Topology

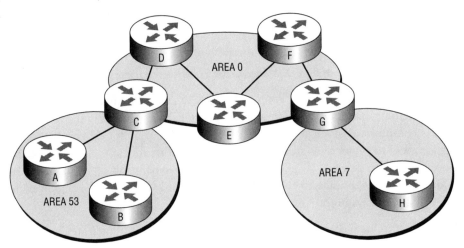

Configuring OSPF is significantly different from configuring RIP or IGRP. To start with, OSPF routers rely on a router identification number (RID) to identify it in the OSPF network. The RID of a router is, by default, the highest of all IP addresses assigned to all active interfaces. This scheme works fine as long as the interface stays up. If that interface experiences instabilities, so will OSPF.

An alternative to using the IP address of an existing interface is to create a *loopback interface*. A loopback interface is a virtual interface that stays up regardless of the state of any physical interface. Creating a loopback interface and giving that loopback an IP address forces the router to use that IP address as the RID. Overall, this adds stability to your OSPF network. The following is an example of the syntax for creating a loopback:

```
!
interface loopback 0
ip address 1.1.1.1 255.255.255.255
!
```

To enable OSPF, use the `router ospf <process id>` command at global configuration mode. The process ID is any number between 1 and 65535 that will uniquely identify each OSPF process that a router will execute per the autonomous system (AS) to which they belong. Unless your router will be part of more than one AS, you will more than likely have only one OSPF process on each router.

Once the `router ospf <process id>` command has been entered, the router will place you into router configuration mode for that OSPF process. Once in router configuration mode, you are required to specify which interfaces will participate in the OSPF process as well as which area each will be in. The network statements expect the following syntax:

```
Network <address> <wild card mask> area <area>
```

Address specifies the address of an interface or a summarized group of interfaces. The *wild card mask* is used when summarizing interface addresses. If an interface's exact IP address is used as the address parameter, the mask of 0.0.0.0 can be used. If desired, an IP address and wildcard mask that represent a grouping of addresses can also be used.

Let's take router D as an example. Router D is part of area 0 (the backbone area). Its configuration might look like one of the examples below. In Example 1, the specific IP address of each interface was entered with an area tag of area 0 and a wildcard mask of 0.0.0.0. This tells the OSPF service to enable OSPF only on interfaces with the IP address 10.2.2.1 and 10.2.3.1. In Example 2, the router was configured to enable OSPF for any interfaces that have IP addresses between 10.2.2.0 and 10.2.3.255. Both of these examples would work for the network in Figure 7.1.

Example 1

```
!
router ospf 1
network 10.2.2.1 0.0.0.0 area 0
network 10.2.3.1 0.0.0.0 area 0
!
```

Routing Protocols

PART 2

or

Example 2

```
!
router ospf 1
network 10.2.2.0 0.0.1.255 area 0
!
```

Router C is an area border router and therefore stores a topological database for both area 0 and area 53. As an area border, router C will have OSPF interfaces in different areas. Here is an example configuration for router C:

```
!Configuration for router C
router ospf 1
network 10.1.2.3 0.0.0.0 area 0
network 172.16.1.3 0.0.0.0 area 53
network 172.16.2.1 0.0.0.0 area 53
!
```

OSPF has no hop count limitation. It uses a cost value as a metric. Cost is an administratively assigned value based on whatever is important to you. By default, on a Cisco router the cost of a link is assigned based on its bandwidth. Cisco uses the equation 100,000,000/ bandwidth to figure out default cost. For example, a simple Ethernet link of 10,000,000 bits per second would be given the cost value of 10 (100,000,000 / 10,000,000 = 10). You can change this default using the `ip ospf cost <cost>` command. The `ip ospf cost <cost>` command is performed in interface configuration mode. The following is an example of an interface configuration that utilizes the `ip ospf cost <cost>` command:

```
!
interface serial 0
ip address 10.1.2.3 255.255.255.0
ip ospf cost 100
!
```

To view the OSPF link cost assigned to an interface, as well as other useful information including network type, priority, and the router ID of the DR and BDR on that interface, you can issue the `show ip ospf interface` command. The following is an example output of this command:

```
RouterA# show ip ospf interface ethernet 0
Ethernet 0 is up, line protocol is up
Internet Address 10.1.1.3, Mask 255.255.255.0, Area 0
AS 65000, Router ID 10.1.1.3, Network Type BROADCAST, Cost: 10
Transmit Delay is 1 sec, State OTHER, Priority 1
Designated Router id 10.1.1.1, Interface address 10.1.1.1
Backup Designated router id 10.1.1.2, Interface addr 10.1.1.2
Timer intervals configured, Hello 10, Dead 60, Wait 40, Retransmit 5
Hello due in 0:00:05
Neighbor Count is 8, Adjacent neighbor count is 2
Adjacent with neighbor 10.1.1.2    (Backup Designated Router)
Adjacent with neighbor 10.1.1.1    (Designated Router)
```

To cut down on total internetworking resources you can declare some areas to be *stub areas*. Routers in stub areas get updates that include inter-area routes, intra-area routes and default routes. To cut down on resources, routers in stub areas will not advertise and store external routes. External routes are those that are redistributed from other protocols or other OSPF services. A stub area can be any area as long as it meets the following criteria:

- That area cannot be the backbone area.
- That area cannot contain an Autonomous System Boundary Router (ASBR). An ASBR is a router that performs the redistribution from other routing protocols to OSPF.
- The area cannot be a transit area for a virtual link. Sometimes a virtual link is established through a non-backbone area to extend the size of the backbone area 0.

Making an area a stub is easy. Simply add the command `area <area id> stub` to all the routers in the stub area. Router C is a good candidate for making a stub. The following is an example of a configuration in which area 53 is a stub.

```
!Configuration for router C when made stubby
router ospf 1
network 10.1.2.3 0.0.0.0 area 0
```

```
network 172.16.1.3 0.0.0.0 area 53
network 172.16.2.1 0.0.0.0 area 53
area 53 stub
!
```

To go one step further, you can declare an area a *totally stubby area*. The concept of a totally stubby area is a Cisco proprietary concept; therefore, it is only available on Cisco routers running OSPF. Routers in a totally stubby area only advertise and store a default route and inter-area routes. A totally stubby area can be declared on any area with only one entry point and one exit point. In the following example, area 7 has been configured as a totally stubby area. All networks in area 7 will be advertised to both routers in area 7. All other networks will be accessible from router H using a default route to router G. Router G houses the topological database for both area 0 and area 7 and can reach all networks. As with a regular stub area, when configuring a totally stubby area all routers have to agree that the area is a stub. Only the ABR, however, needs to know it's a totally stubby area. The following is an example of a configuration for routers G and H. Notice on the configuration for router G that it has been declared a stub with the *no-summary* keyword. The no-summary keyword tells router G to advertise only a default route and any inter-area routes to router H. This in turn makes area 7 a totally stubby area.

```
!Configuration for router G
router ospf 1
network 10.4.4.2 0.0.0.0 area 0
network 192.168.1.5 0.0.0.0 area 7
area 7 stub no-summary
!

!Configuration for router H
router ospf 2
network 192.168.1.6 0.0.0.0 area 7
area 7 stub
!
```

Summarization is another extremely important issue when designing an OSPF network. A good OSPF design should have an IP addressing scheme that allows it to be summarized at area borders and autonomous system boundaries. For example, take a look at the internetwork in Figure 7.2. An addressing scheme has been chosen that allows you to summarize all of the subnets in area 53 as 172.16.0.0 /16. Notice also that area 7 has been summarized as 192.168.1.0/24. Even though there may be many subnets and a variety of subnet masks used in those networks, only 172.17.0.0/16 and 192.168.1.0/24 are advertised to routers in other areas. The idea is that if a subnet changes its link state (goes up or comes down), it does not affect the summary in another area; therefore, LSAs will not need to be generated. The fewer the LSAs that are generated, the fewer times the SPF algorithm has to be run. Overall, this will allow for a high amount of scalability.

Figure 7.2   Area Topology

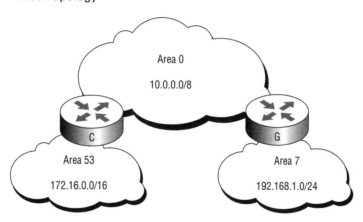

With OSPF, you have the ability to dedicate a router as the ASBR. An ASBR is a router that will redistribute other protocols from other autonomous systems to OSPF. It is also considered the router that can get us access to resources outside the AS. Commonly you will redistribute Border Gateway Protocol (BGP) routes (or exterior routes) with OSPF for Internet interoperability. The router on which you do this is the ASBR. The ASBR is then considered the AS's point of ingress and egress. This being the case, it is a perfect candidate for establishing a *default route*. Remember that a default route is your network of last resort. When you do not have specific knowledge in your routing table about a network, you send it in the direction of the default route. Today a default route is one that takes you a step closer to the external gateway of your network (maybe your gateway to the Internet).

A default network is a network that has been advertised to your autonomous system that will act as a network of last resort. It is usually a network advertised from an external source or from another autonomous system. It may even be in your autonomous system, but is redistributed from another protocol. Whatever the case may be, a default route has to be a valid and accessible route in your routing table. Any time you use the redistribute command on an OSPF router, it automatically becomes an ASBR. As far as OSPF is concerned, you need only tell the ASBR to advertise its redistributed information as default information using the `default-information originate always` command. An example is provided below:

```
!
router ospf 1
default-information originate always
network 10.1.1.1 0.0.0.0 area 0
redistribute static
!
```

Given the previous configuration and assuming it was applied to router A in Figure 7.3, you can assume that router A is the ASBR. Router A is configured to have Internet access via a static route to some network accessible in the Internet Service Providers facility. In the previous example code, you have redistributed the static route into the OSPF topology. Using the `default-information` command, you have flagged that network as a default network and will advertise it to other OSPF routers that way. Other routers will be informed of the network and will adjust all *gateways of last resort* to the next hop address that is in the direction of the advertised default route (the network that provides Internet access).

Figure 7.3 Area topology with a gateway to the Internet

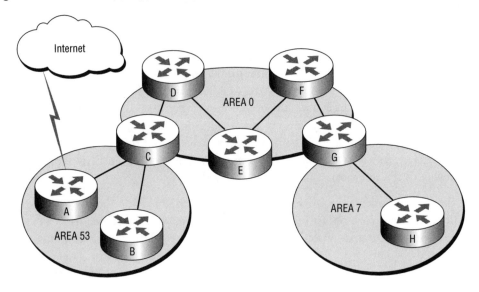

Verifying OSPF Operation

There are many commands available to help verify OSPF operation and configuration. Among the simplest is the `ping` command. The `IP ping` command will not be demonstrated here because it has already been discussed in detail. It is, and will remain, an engineer's favorite way to verify internetwork connectivity.

Another simple command is the `show ip route` command. Like the `ping` command, the `show ip route` command has already been discussed. However, since you are now using a different routing protocol, the output changes. Here is an example output of a `show ip route` command:

```
Router# show ip route


Codes: C  - connected, S - static, I - IGRP, R - RIP, M - mobile, B - BGP
       D  - EIGRP, EX - EIGRP external, O - OSPF, IA - OSPF inter area
       N1 - OSPF NSSA external type 1, N2 - OSPF NSSA external type 2
       E1 - OSPF external type 1, E2 - OSPF external type 2, E - EGP
       i  - IS-IS, L1 - IS-IS level-1, L2 - IS-IS level-2, * - candidate
            default
       U  - per-user static route, o - ODR


Gateway of last resort is not set


     10.0.0.0/8 is variably subnetted, 3 subnets, 1 masks
C    10.1.1.0/24 is directly connected, Serial0
O    10.2.2.0/24 [110/10] via 10.1.1.1, 00:32:16, Ethernet0
O    10.3.3.0/24 [110/10] via 10.2.2.1, 00:32:16, Ethernet1
O    10.4.4.0/24 [110/10] via 10.1.1.1, 00:32:16, Ethernet2
```

Another valuable command to issue on an OSPF router is the `show ip ospf`. The following is an example output:

```
Router# show ip ospf


Routing Process "ospf 1" with ID 1.1.1.1
```

Routing Protocols

PART 2

```
Supports only single TOS(TOS0) route

It is an area border and autonomous system boundary router

Redistributing External Routes from,

        igrp 65000 with metric mapped to 2, includes subnets in
redistribution

        rip with metric mapped to 2

Number of areas in this router is 2

Area 53

Number of interfaces in this area is 1

Area has simple password authentication

SPF algorithm executed 6 times
```

The output communicates the following information:

- OSPF process ID number and the router ID
- The router's role (whether it is a ABR or ASBR)
- The autonomous system number used
- The protocols redistributed into OSPF
- How many times the SPF algorithm has been executed

You also have the ability to view the contents of the topological database. To do so, issue the show ip ospf database command. The command lists all routers and links in all areas to which that router is configured. The following is a sample output:

```
Router# show ip ospf database


        OSPF Router with ID (1.1.1.1) (Process ID 1)


           Router Link States (Area 0)


Link ID        ADV Router    Age      Seq#         Checksum  Link count
1.1.1.1        1.1.1.1       302      0x80000002
10.1.1.2       10.1.1.2      224      0x8000002F   0x46D2       2
```

```
10.2.2.2     10.2.2.2     200     0x800000A4     0x1129     1
10.3.3.2     10.3.3.2     230     0x80000003     0xEFA2     4


              Net Link States(Area 0)


Link ID      ADV Router    Age      Seq#         Checksum
10.1.1.2     10.1.1.2      1152     0x80000067   0x0912
```

The show ip ospf neighbor command shows you information about neighboring routers. Here is an example:

```
Router# show ip ospf neighbor


Neighbor ID    Pri   State          Dead Time   Address    Interface
10.2.2.2       1     FULL/DR        00:00:31    10.1.1.2   Ethernet0
10.3.3.2       1     FULL/DROTHER   00:00:25    10.3.3.2   Ethernet1
10.4.4.3       1     FULL/DROTHER   00:00:54    10.4.4.3   Ethernet2
```

NOTE There are many show ip ospf commands. To see all the options, type **show ip ospf ?**.

NetWare Link Services Protocol (NLSP)

Another link state routing protocol is NetWare Link Services Protocol (NLSP). NLSP was designed for the IPX/SPX suite of protocols. It has its basis in the OSI suite's Intermediate System to Intermediate System (IS-IS) protocol. NLSP is an alternative to IPX RIP. It is superior to IPX RIP in many ways. NLSP is more reliable, less bandwidth-consuming, and more scalable than RIP.

Rather than sending updates every 60 seconds to neighboring routers like RIP, NLSP stores a complete map of the topology. Traditional RIP updates are followed by SAP updates as well. These updates happen whether there is a change or not. NLSP updates are communicated primarily when there is a change in the environment and in summary fashion every two hours. This goes not only for network information but also for SAP information. When NLSP learns of a service, it will store this service until there is a change in the internetwork.

Since NLSP is a NetWare routing protocol, configuring it requires a good knowledge of routing IPX. If you are not familiar with configuring a router for IPX routing activity, flip forward and read Chapter 10.

Configuring NLSP

For the purposes of this discussion, you can assume that IPX routing is already enabled and working. To properly configure NLSP, there are three main tasks that are required. Additionally, there are optional configuration activities that you may choose to perform if necessary. The required steps are:

1. The first step is to define an IPX internal network number. Defining an IPX internal network number is required by NLSP to identify that router on the NLSP network. The command to specify an IPX network number is `ipx internal-network <network number>`. This command is issued in global configuration mode.

2. The next step is to enable the NLSP routing process. This is done by issuing the command `ipx router nlsp`, which is issued in global configuration mode.

3. Next you must define an NLSP area number. To do so use the `area-address <network> <wildcard mask>` command. In NLSP, the area number specifies which networks will be included in the NLSP process. It is most common to use the command `area-address 0 0`. Using a network of 0 and a mask of 0 includes all networks.

4. Next configure all interfaces that will be participating. Once you are happy with the area number, the final required step is enabling NLSP at each interface that will use it. This requires you to issue the `ipx nlsp enable` command at each interface.

A sample configuration is as follows:

```
!
ipx routing
ipx internal-network 1A
ipx router nlsp
area-address 0 0
!
```

```
interface ethernet 0/0
ipx network 2B
ipx ipxwan
ipx nlsp enable
!
interface ethernet 0/1
ipx network 3C
ipx ipxwan
ipx nlsp enable
!
```

NLSP uses a metric based on a link cost. The link cost calculation is based on the throughput and delay of a link. Usually the cost is calculated using the results of the IPXWAN command. These variables can also be set by hand. The commands are as follows:

- To set the metric weight of a link, use the `ipx nlsp metric <metric-number>` command.

- To set the link delay on an interface, issue the `ipx link-delay <microseconds>` command.

- To set the throughput on an interface value, issue the `ipx throughput <bits-per-second>` command.

> **NOTE** Changing metric values in NLSP is not a recommended configuration task. Provided that you enabled IPXWAN, the protocol is smart enough to make proper decisions. For more information on IPXWAN, see Chapter 11.

Another optional command you can issue is the `ipx maximum-hops` command. By default, IPX has a maximum hop count of 15. Anything over 15 hops is considered unreachable. Using NLSP you can increase that to a maximum of 127 hops. Here is an example:

```
!
ipx maximum-hops 127
!
```

Verifying NLSP operation

You can use a number of valuable commands to verify NLSP operation. Here are two examples:

- **show ipx route**   Shows your IPX routing table. All NLSP learned routes will start with an "N." A sample output of the show ipx route command is as follows:

```
Router# show ipx route
Codes: C - connected primary network, c - connected secondary network
S - static, F - Floating Metric, L - Local (internal), W - IPXWAN
R - RIP, E - EIGRP, N - NLSP, X - External, s - seconds, u - uses


5 Total IPX routes. Up to 2 parallel paths and 16 hops allowed.


No default route known.


    L    1a is the internal network
    C    2b (NOVELL-ETHER),              Eth0/0
    C    3c (NOVELL-ETHER),              Eth0/1
    N    4d  [20]  [02/01] via           2b.0000.0c12.3456
    N    5e  [20]  [02/01] via           3c.0000.0c98.7654
```

- **ping ipx <*ipx address*>**   Using an IPX ping verifies IPX connectivity. This does not mean you can ping a Novell client or server, but you can ping the IPX address of another router configured with IPX.

```
Router# ping ipx 3c.0000.000c98.7654
Sending 5 100-byte Novell echoes to 3c.0000.000c98.7654, timeout is
2 seconds
!!!!!
success rate is 100%, round trip min/avg/max = 2/2/2 ms.
```

Integrated Intermediate System to Intermediate System (IS-IS)

Intermediate System to Intermediate System (IS-IS) is a link-state routing protocol developed by the International Organization for Standardization (ISO). It was developed for the OSI (Open Systems Interconnection) suite of protocols. Although IS-IS was developed to support the Connectionless Network Service (CLNS) protocol, Cisco's implementation of IS-IS makes it possible to use it as an IP routing protocol as well. Cisco calls it *integrated* IS-IS.

As with other link-state routing protocols, IS-IS floods the network with link state information in order to build a complete topology. To IS-IS there are two kinds of intermediate systems—*level 1* and *level 2* routers. Level 1 routers can only communicate with other level 1 routers in the same area. Level 2 routers have the ability to communicate with other areas and can therefore route between level 1 intermediate systems. Level 2 intermediate systems are used as backbone routers.

IS-IS uses a metric based on an arbitrary cost value. A link can have a cost between 1 and 64. Costs are recorded in a cumulative manner as the total cost of a path. In other words, all links are added along the way for a total cost. A path can have a total cost of up to 1024.

> **NOTE**   IS-IS is described in ISO 10589.

Configuring IS-IS

In this section we will outline the steps required for configuring integrated IS-IS.

- Enable IS-IS. Use the `router isis <tag>` command to enable the IS-IS service. The tag is a meaningful name for the routing process if you want to run more than one IS-IS process on the same router. The tag is optional, but, if used, it must be unique among all IP router processes for a given router.

    ```
    Router isis
    ```

- Configure a network entity type (NET) for the IS-IS process. A NET is an identifier that includes a 6-byte system ID and an area ID of up to 14 bytes in length. The command to configure a NET is `net <network entity title>`. An example of a NET is 4a.0001.0001.0001.0000.0c12.3456.00. The NET implies

Routing Protocols

PART 2

an area ID of 4a.0001.0001.0001and a system ID of 0000.0c12.3456. All NETs end with a zero byte. An example of the use of the net command is as follows:

```
Net 4a.0001.0001.0001.0000.0c12.3456.00
```

- Configure the IS-IS level at which the router will operate. There are two IS-IS levels, level 1 and level 2. A level 1 router is a station router. A level 2 router is an area router. A router can act as a level 1 only, a level 1-2, or a level 2 only. To set the IS-IS level, you must use the is-type <*level*> command.

    - Configured as level 1 only, the router can perform only intra-area routing.

    - Configured as level 2 only, the router acts as an area router only. It will not talk to L1-only routers in its own area.

    - Configured as level 1-2, the router acts as a station router and an area router. It will run an instance of the SPF algorithm for each level. The default level for a Cisco router is 1-2.

An example of the use of the IS-type command is as follows:

```
is-type level-2-only
```

The following example configures IS-IS for IP routing. First the router isis command enables the IS-IS protocol. Using the net command, assign a system ID of 0000.0000 .0003 and area ID of 01.0001. Lastly, use the interface command ip router isis to tell each interface that it is participating in the IP IS-IS routing process.

```
!
router isis
net 01.0001.0000.0000.0003.00
is-type level-1
!
interface ethernet 0
ip address 10.1.1.1 255.255.255.0
ip router isis
!
interface serial 0
ip address 10.0.0.5 255.255.255.252
ip router isis
```

The Hello-Interval Headache

John ran into an interesting problem one day. He was called to a client site to look at an OSPF problem. It seems that the client was using OSPF over a complex Frame Relay network. The network was a large hub and spoke network. All remote locations were configured as point-to-point configurations. In all, there were over 120 remote sites.

They had just added a new division that used to be a competitor but had been absorbed recently by this company as a result of a buyout. The new department had to be added to the OSPF network. The engineer that implemented it viewed its structure to be a good candidate for a multipoint configuration and consequently configured it that way.

The symptom of the problem was that the new portion of the network was not exchanging OSPF information with the existing OSPF backbone. As a result, the new department did not have connectivity to the corporate office. It seemed like a simple enough problem, so John went to look at it.

After performing a few show commands in an attempt to get a big-picture view, John discovered something interesting: Performing a show ip ospf interface command on the routers in the new department revealed that the Hello interval was different between point-to-point and non-broadcast (multipoint) networks. It seemed the Hello interval on the existing part of the internetwork was set for every 10 seconds. The default Hello interval for the non-broadcast network was every 30 seconds. This was keeping the new neighboring routers from establishing an adjacency and learning the new topology.

At the time, there was only one option for fixing this problem: adjusting the frequency of the Hello packets using the ip ospf hello-interval command and establishing a neighbor relationship using the neighbor command. So, John changed the Hello interval on the routers in the non-broadcast network to every 10 seconds and established the neighbor relationship between the routers by connecting the new network with the old one. Almost immediately the newly added routers converged with the rest of the internetwork, and routing started. An example of the configuration commands used is as follows:

```
!
router ospf 1
neighbor 192.168.1.6
!
interface serial 0
ip address 192.168.1.5
255.255.255.252
ip ospf hello-interval 10
!
```

Today Cisco has put in place another command to help with this problem, the ip ospf network point-to-multipoint command.

You can issue this command on any routers connecting point-to-point with non-broadcast multi-access networks. It will adjust timers and start exchanging Hellos as appropriate.

For further information about OSPF and other related topics see the following RFCs:

1584 – Multicast Extensions to OSPF

1587 – The Not-So-Stubby Areas (NSSA) Option

1793 – Extending OSPF to Support Demand Circuits

1850 - OSPF Version 2 Management Information Base

2328 – OSPF version 2

2329 - OSPF Standardization Report

2370 - The OSPF Opaque LSA Option

2740 - OSPF for IPv6

2676 - QoS Routing Mechanisms and OSPF Extensions

8

EIGRP: A Hybrid Routing Protocol

In this chapter we will discuss *hybrid routing protocols*. A hybrid routing protocol is one that exhibits characteristics of both a distance vector and a link state protocol. We will compare the characteristics of these protocols, focusing most of our attention on Enhanced Interior Gateway Routing Protocol (EIGRP).

Enhanced IGRP (EIGRP)

Enhanced IGRP (EIGRP) is another popular choice for routing protocols. EIGRP is a Cisco proprietary protocol. No other manufacturer of routing devices supports EIGRP as an option on their routers. What that means to us is if you want to use EIGRP in your organization, you can use only Cisco routers. That is not as bad as it sounds. EIGRP is in many ways superior to the routing protocols available in the industry. EIGRP offers the following features:

Fast convergence   EIGRP converges much faster than RIP or IGRP. EIGRP can accomplish in mere seconds what can take minutes using a distance vector protocol. Much like OSPF, EIGRP works by developing a topology view of the internetwork. It will keep track of alternative routes to a network. This way, if a primary route goes down, EIGRP will immediately implement the secondary path.

Incremental updates   EIGRP uses a system of incremental updates. When the status of a network changes, only the information that changed is advertised. Rather than triggering an update that will advertise a full routing table, EIGRP only sends partial information. This cuts down on total bandwidth use. Additionally, Enhanced IGRP will not send the update information to every router in the topology. Unlike a link state, Enhanced IGRP will only send the update to routers that need the information. This feature is viewed by some as an improvement even over link state protocols. Overall, this also requires less CPU usage than its counterpart IGRP. And, unlike with IGRP, full update packets will not have to be processed every 90 seconds.

Supports multiple routed protocols   EIGRP is protocol-independent. It supports IP, IPX, and AppleTalk. In this chapter, we will be discussing the configuration specifics for using EIGRP on all three routed protocols.

Variable-length subnet masks   EIGRP includes subnet mask information in its updates. IP networks are advertised with a bit count value. For example, 10.0.0.0/8 is a network that may be advertised. The "/8" represents an 8-bit subnet mask or 255.0.0.0. This feature makes EIGRP a classless routing protocol.

Forgiving of a bad network design   EIGRP can perform arbitrary route summarization wherever it thinks it can. It will try to make the best of any IP addressing scheme, even if the scheme is not the best design possible. This is one trait that makes EIGRP significantly superior to OSPF. OSPF relies on good design, whereas EIGRP can tolerate a bad one better than OSPF can.

Scalability   EIGRP scales to large networks. It can be used on networks with a diameter of up to 224 hops in width. This is a huge improvement over RIP with its 15-hop maximum.

Automatic redistribution   EIGRP will automatically exchange (redistribute) routing information with an IGRP process running on the same router. The only thing that is necessary is that they are configured to be part of the same autonomous system.

Composite Metric   Enhanced IGRP uses the same composite metric as IGRP. The metric is a value based on the bandwidth of the slowest link and the cumulative delay in a path. The composite metric is capable of also taking into account the reliability and load counters on an interface as well.

Multicast updates   Enhanced IGRP updates are sent out as multicasts, not broadcasts. Thus they do not cause interrupts on workstations.

EIGRP Operation: The DUAL Algorithm

EIGRP bases its entire operation around an algorithm referred to as the Diffusing Update Algorithm (DUAL), which you saw briefly in Chapter 4. This protocol technology was created by Cisco but was based on research conducted at SRI International. The DUAL algorithm was designed to provide a loop-free environment at every instance throughout the convergence process. Devices have the ability to compute and recompute network paths simultaneously. Not all routers in the topology have to learn about changes in the topology. Only routers that are affected by a topology change will perform recomputations using the DUAL. Overall, convergence time using EIGRP and its DUAL algorithm technology ranks with the fastest protocols available.

EIGRP routers perform a neighbor-discovery process that allows them to learn dynamically about all neighbors sharing directly attached networks. To do so, they periodically send out a small keep-alive packet called a Hello packet. You saw Hello packets briefly in Chapter 7. Although these are somewhat different, their purpose is almost the same. Using these Hello packets, routers know not only when new routers are added, but also when routers are removed. As long as all neighbors are sending and receiving Hellos, all routers can assume the network is stable. The lack of Hellos from a neighbor means the neighbor is down and convergence can commence.

A simple Hello is sent to a multicast address to cut down on total resource utilization on multi-access networks. EIGRP uses the address 224.0.0.9 as a destination for its Hellos. Using these Hellos, the router can create a table called the *neighbors table*. The Hellos are sent every 5 seconds on multi-access and point-to-point links and every 60 seconds on non-broadcast multi-access links. As a result, routers can learn about all other neighboring routers.

To learn how EIGRP learns routes, we can use the example in Figure 8.1. Notice that router A and router B are connected via a serial connection. Let's suppose router A has been up and operating for some time now, but router B has just been turned on. Both are configured with EIGRP. As soon as router B initializes, it will send a Hello packet out of all of its interfaces. Hearing this, router A will respond by sending router B all information it has about the topology. Router B will acknowledge the receipt of this information and populate its topology table with it. In turn, router B will send router A what *it* knows about the topology. Once this process has taken place, router B can use this information to create its routing table. Router A acknowledges, and convergence is achieved.

Figure 8.1   EIGRP Neighbors

EIGRP maintains three separate tables for each protocol configured. They are the neighbors table, mentioned earlier, a topology table, and, of course, the routing table. The neighbors table lists information about all neighboring routers. It is maintained using the Hello protocol. The topology table lists destination networks in the topology. These destinations may include primary routes (*successors*) and backup routes (*feasible successors*) if applicable. EIGRP maintains its routing table based on the information in the neighbors and topology table.

Whenever a router receives EIGRP updates or there is a topology change the DUAL is executed. The DUAL is run not only for the purpose of selecting the best route(s) to a destination, but also to identify backup routes. Primary and backup routes are stored in the topology table to facilitate much faster convergence in the event of a topology change. EIGRP recognizes next-hop routers as either successors or feasible successors.

Successors and Feasible Successors

A successor is a next hop router that has the best metric to a destination. We identify that router based on the lowest *advertised distance*. The advertised distance is the metric advertised between the next hop router and the destination. There can be multiple successors, provided each has the same advertised distance.

Feasible successors are next hop routers that have been identified as backups to the successors. We choose a feasible successor based on advertised distance and *feasible distance*. Feasible distance is the metric value that represents the path from your local router to the next-hop router. First we look at advertised distances to see if a router is a possible successor. If it is not, EIGRP looks at the feasible distance of existing successors. Feasible successors will be placed in the topology table, provided that their advertised distances are not greater than the feasible distance to the successor(s). There can be multiple feasible successors in the topology. Feasible successors do not have to have the same advertised distances.

If a successor is no longer available due to a topology change, a feasible successor can be promoted immediately. After a feasible successor is promoted, EIGRP must attempt to find new feasible successors. When a destination is no longer available and there is no feasible successor, EIGRP will flag that destination as "active" in the topology table and proceed with its attempt to find a successor.

In the active state, the router will send a query to all neighbors except the one from which it originally learned about the network (split horizon). The query is a request for information about an alternate route for the destination that went down. Each query requires a reply. The status of the query is tracked in the topology table. If one of the queried routers has a successor or feasible successor for the downed destination, that router will respond with this information. The querying router can then update its topology table with the new information. If not, the queried routers will query their neighbors, and a query ripple effect will happen in the internetwork. If no alternate path to the downed network is found, the router removes the entry from the topology table.

Configuring EIGRP for IP

Configuring EIGRP is only a little harder than configuring IGRP—specifically one character harder. The configuration requirements for EIGRP and IGRP are almost the same, except that EIGRP requires you to add an E in front of any references to *IGRP*. To configure EIGRP for IP, you must first enable EIGRP. Once it is enabled, you must tell the service which interfaces will be participating in the EIGRP service.

The EIGRP service is enabled using the `router eigrp <AS number>` command. The command requires an autonomous system (AS) number that represents your autonomous system. By default, EIGRP will only exchange updates with routers in the same autonomous system. An example is as follows:

```
Router(config)# router eigrp 65000
```

By issuing the `router eigrp` command, the command line interface (CLI) will place you into router configuration mode for that particular EIGRP process. In router configuration mode, you must specify which interfaces will be sending and receiving EIGRP updates. We identify these interfaces by issuing the `network <network number>` command along with the classfull networks we want to advertise. The following is an example:

```
Router(config-router)# network 10.0.0.0
Router(config-router)# network 192.168.1.0
```

If you think back to how we configure IGRP, you may notice that this is really similar. In fact, Cisco designed it that way. They wanted you as a network administrator to be able to migrate from IGRP to EIGRP with little effort. All that is required is for you to add an E in front of all references to *IGRP* in your configurations. It's that simple and it works fine.

There are a number of commands that, though not required for EIGRP to work, can be helpful from time to time:

eigrp log-neighbor-changes Enables logging of adjacency changes. You can use this command while in global configuration mode to enable EIGRP to log any changes to the neighbors table. This feature tends to help troubleshoot problems in the EIGRP topology.

ip bandwidth-percent eigrp *<AS number> <percent>* Gives you the power to change how much of your bandwidth is used up by EIGRP updates. By default, EIGRP can use up to 50 percent of your bandwidth for update traffic, but this command overrides this percentage. It is issued in interface configuration mode for the interface you want to control.

metric weights tos k1 k2 k3 k4 k5 Enables you to change the behavior of the composite equation by changing the metric weights. This command is issued in router configuration mode.

WARNING Only an experienced designer should tamper with changing the metric weights.

---

no auto-summary Disables route summarization. Although it is a classless protocol, EIGRP still automatically summarizes at classfull boundaries. To disable this feature, issue this command in router configuration mode.

ip summary-address eigrp *<AS number> <address> <mask>* Configures a summary aggregate address. If you want to summarize a number of networks into one network statement, you can do so by using this command in interface configuration mode for the interface that will be advertising the summary.

ip hello-interval eigrp *<AS number> <seconds>* and **ip hold-time eigrp** *<AS number> <seconds>* Change the values of the hello and hold timers, respectively. By default, the EIGRP hello timer for point-to-point and multi-access networks is 5 seconds, and the hold timer is 15 seconds. For NBMA networks, the hello timer is 60 seconds, and the hold timer is 180 seconds. The hello timer specifies how often, in seconds, the hellos are sent. The hold timer specifies how long to wait without hearing a hello before a neighbor is declared down. In a heavily congested network it may be necessary to increase the hello and the hold timer using these commands.

WARNING   Before using any of these optional commands, be sure you fully understand their impact. It is recommended that, before changing hello and hold timers, you contact Cisco TAC for assistance.

Verifying IP EIGRP

EIGRP provided us with a number of handy commands for verification and trouble-shooting. In this section, we will discuss these commands in detail. For the purposes of this discussion, we will be using a topology consisting of a series of routers connected via serial interfaces over point-to-point links. Figure 8.2 provides a visual.

Figure 8.2   Our sample topology

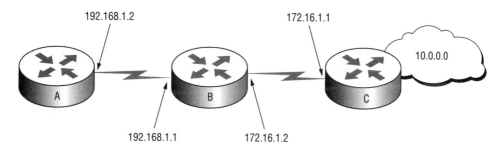

Refer to Figure 8.2 as you read the descriptions of each command's function.

Show IP Protocols

By issuing the privileged-mode command show ip protocols, we can view how EIGRP is configured. As we have already learned, show ip protocols will display parameters for every routing protocol configured. In our example we have both IGRP and EIGRP configured for the same autonomous system. The following is a partial display of the output on our router:

```
Router# show ip protocols
Routing Protocol is "eigrp 65000"
  Outgoing update filter list for all interfaces is not set
  Incoming update filter list for all interfaces is not set
  Default networks flagged in outgoing updates
  Default networks accepted from incoming updates
  EIGRP metric weight K1=1, K2=0, K3=1, K4=0, K5=0
```

Routing Protocols

PART 2

```
EIGRP maximum hopcount 100
EIGRP maximum metric variance 1
Redistributing: igrp 65000, eigrp 65000
Automatic network summarization is in effect
Automatic address summarization:
   192.168.1.0/24 for Serial0
   10.0.0.0/8 for Serial1
Routing for Networks:
   192.168.1.0
   10.0.0.0
Routing Information Sources:
   Gateway         Distance       Last Update
   192.168.1.1           90       00:00:09
Distance: internal 90 external 170
```

The output of the show ip protocols command tells us the following:

- We are routing in autonomous system 65000.

- We have no inbound or outbound route filters applied to this EIGRP process. If we had any, the number of the access list would be listed in the display.

- The EIGRP process will accept and pass along default network information.

- The K values are set to their defaults: K1 and K3 are set to 1, and K2, K4, and K5 are set to 0. As you may recall from the last chapter, the K values are variables used in the composite metric. In their defaults, the K values only take into account bandwidth and delay when computing the composite metric.

- EIGRP defaults to a maximum hop count of 100. It can, however, be configured to allow for up to 224 hops.

- Like IGRP, EIGRP allows the router to perform unequal-cost load sharing. This is dependent upon the value of the metric variance. With the variance set to 1, which is the default, the router will only implement equal-cost load sharing. The metric variance specifies how slow a secondary link can be and have EIGRP load share with it.

- EIGRP will redistribute automatically with IGRP, provided that both services are configured to be part of the same autonomous system. Since we have done that here, our router will convert IGRP-learned routes to EIGRP.

- Automatic summarization is in effect when possible.
- We have enabled EIGRP on all interfaces configured with IP addresses in the 192.168.1.0 and 10.0.0.0 networks.
- We received a packet from another EIGRP router with the address 192.168.1.1 nine seconds ago.
- EIGRP is assigning all interior EIGRP routes the administrative distance of 90. Any routes that are redistributed from other protocols to EIGRP are not considered trustworthy sources and are therefore assigned an administrative distance of 170.

WARNING All of these parameters can be changed using simple IOS commands if desired. Be careful to know what the effect will be before you make a change to EIGRP on a production router.

Show IP EIGRP

To view the Enhanced IGRP neighbors table, we can use the show ip eigrp neighbors command. This command is performed in privileged mode. The following is a sample output:

```
RouterB#show ip eigrp neighbors
IP-EIGRP neighbors for process 65000
H   Address            Interface   Hold Uptime   SRTT   RTO   Q   Seq
                                   (sec)         (ms)         Cnt Num
1   192.168.1.2        Se0         11 00:01:40      0   3000   0   3
0   172.16.1.1         Se1         14 00:02:11    844   5000   0   4
```

The table includes some important elements, including the neighbor's addresses, interface, hold time, uptime, smooth round-trip time, retransmission timeout, queue value, and a sequence number. Following are descriptions of each:

Address The IP address of the neighboring router

Interface The interface from which we received the remote router's hellos

Hold The length of time the router will wait without hearing hellos before it declares that the neighbor is down. The default is under 15 seconds on point-to-point links.

Uptime The length of time the remote router has been up and sending hellos

Smooth Round-Trip Time (SRTT) The time it takes, in milliseconds, to send a packet to the neighboring router and receive an acknowledgement

Q count The number of EIGRP update, query, and reply packets the router is waiting to send

Seq Number The sequence number of the last update, query, or reply packet received from that neighbor

To view the topology table, issue the `show ip eigrp topology` command in privileged mode. An example of the output of this command is as follows:

```
RouterB#show ip eigrp topology
IP-EIGRP Topology Table for process 65000


Codes: P - Passive, A - Active, U - Update, Q - Query, R - Reply,
       r - Reply status


P 10.0.0.0/8, 1 successors, FD is 2297856
        via 172.16.1.1 (2297856/128256), Serial1
P 192.168.1.0/24, 1 successors, FD is 2169856
        via Connected, Serial0
P 172.16.0.0/16, 1 successors, FD is 1
        via Summary (2169856/0), Null0
P 172.16.1.0/24, 1 successors, FD is 2169856
        via Connected, Serial1
```

The topology table gives us valuable information, including a code that represents the state of the table entry, the state of the destination network, and the number of successor routers available to access this network and their feasible distances. The following is a description of each:

Code Each entry starts with a code that represents the state of an entry. The possibilities include:

Code	State of the Entry	What it Means
P	Passive	No EIGRP computations are being performed for this destination at this time. This is a normal state for a destination to be in.

Code	State of the Entry	What it Means
A	Active	EIGRP computations are currently being performed for this destination.
U	Update	An update packet was recently sent to this destination.
Q	Query	A query packet was recently sent to this destination.
R	Reply	A reply packet was recently sent to this destination.
r	Reply status	An indicator that the router has sent a query and is waiting for a reply.

Destination network   A destination network in the topology

Successors   The number of successors that can provide access to that destination

Feasible Distance   The value is used in the feasibility condition check. If the neighbor's reported metric is less than the feasible distance, the feasibility condition is met and that path is a feasible successor.

Show IP Route

To display a routing table based on Enhanced IGRP, we simply use the show ip route command in privileged mode. You will notice that all EIGRP learned routes have a *D* as a source identifier. The *D* is the code for interior EIGRP routes. Also, the EIGRP-learned route has been assigned the administrative distance of 90 and a metric that is the result of the composite metric.

```
RouterB#show ip route

Codes: C - connected, S - static, I - IGRP, R - RIP, M - mobile, B - BGP
       D - EIGRP, EX - EIGRP external, O - OSPF, IA - OSPF inter area
       N1 - OSPF NSSA external type 1, N2 - OSPF NSSA external type 2
       E1 - OSPF external type 1, E2 - OSPF external type 2, E - EGP
       i - IS-IS, L1 - IS-IS level-1, L2 - IS-IS level-2, * -
          candidate default
       U - per-user static route, o - ODR


Gateway of last resort is not set


D    10.0.0.0/8 [90/2297856] via 172.16.1.1, 00:01:30, Serial1
```

Routing Protocols

PART 2

```
C     192.168.1.0/24 is directly connected, Serial0
      172.16.0.0/16 is variably subnetted, 2 subnets, 2 mask
D        172.16.0.0/16 is a summary, 00:01:07, Null0
C        172.16.1.0/24 is directly connected, Serial1
```

Refresher: The Composite Metric

Remember that the composite metric gets its output using the following equation:

If k5 equals 0, metric = [k1 * bandwidth + (k2 * bandwidth)/(256 - load) + k3 * delay]

If k5 does not equal zero, an additional operation is done: metric = metric * [k5 / (reliability + k4)]

More Show Commands

Some additional show commands that are valuable include show ip eigrp interfaces, show ip igrp traffic, and show ip igrp topology summary. Following are examples and descriptions of each.

Show IP EIGRP Interfaces   The show ip eigrp interfaces command displays information about all interfaces configured for Enhanced IGRP. A sample output is shown below:

```
RouterB#show ip eigrp interfaces
IP-EIGRP interfaces for process 65000
```

Interface	Peers	Xmit Queue Un/Reliable	Mean SRTT	Pacing Time Un/Reliable	Multicast Flow Timer	Pending Routes
Se0	1	0/0	0	0/15	50	0
Se1	1	0/0	844	0/15	4219	0

A description of each field is as follows:

Field	Description
Interface	Lists the interface designator for each interface configured for Enhanced IGRP
Peers	Lists the number of directly connected EIGRP neighbors

Field	Description
`Xmit Queue Un/ Reliable`	Lists the number of packets remaining in both of the two transmit queues. There is an Unreliable and Reliable transmit queue. Reliable is for activities that require acknowledgement, and Unreliable is for activities that do not.
`Mean SRTT`	Lists the mean smooth round-trip timer. This is the mean time in seconds it takes to send a packet and receive and acknowledgment.
`Pacing Time Un/ Reliable`	Lists the pacing time. This value is used to determine when EIGRP packets should be sent out the interface.
`Multicast Flow Timer`	Lists the maximum number of seconds in which the router can send multicast EIGRP packets
`Pending Routes`	Lists the number of routes in the packets sitting in the transmit queue waiting to be sent

Show IP EIGRP Traffic   The `show ip eigrp traffic` command displays the number and type of EIGRP packets sent and received. A sample output is shown below:

```
RouterB#show ip eigrp traffic
IP-EIGRP Traffic Statistics for process 65000
   Hellos sent/received: 68/62
   Updates sent/received: 8/9
   Queries sent/received: 1/0
   Replies sent/received: 0/1
   Acks sent/received: 6/3
   Input queue high water mark 1, 0 drops
```

Show IP EIGRP Topology Summary   The `show ip eigrp topology summary` command gives us summary information related to the topology and topology change activity. Here is a sample output:

```
RouterB#show ip eigrp topology summary
IP-EIGRP Topology Table for process 65000
Head serial 1, next serial 10
4 routes, 0 pending replies, 0 dummies
IP-EIGRP enabled on 2 interfaces, neighbors present on 2 interfaces
Quiescent interfaces:  Se0 Se1
```

Routing Protocols

PART 2

You can see what Enhanced IGRP show commands are available using the show ip eigrp ? command. For example:

```
RouterB# show ip eigrp ?
  Interfaces    IP-EIGRP interfaces
  Neighbors     IP-EIGRP neighbors
  Topology      IP-EIGRP Topology Table
  Traffic       IP-EIGRP Traffic Statistics
```

EIGRP for IPX

In addition to all its other capabilities, EIGRP can also be used as an IPX routing protocol. In fact, it is in many ways superior to the alternative IPX RIP. We can extend all of the same wonderful benefits that were available with IP to the IPX environment, including the fast convergence, the composite metric, the scalability to huge internetworks, etc.

Configuring EIGRP for IPX

Configuring IPX with EIGRP is simple but requires you to have some understanding of IPX. If you are new to IPX routing, read Chapter 11. Come back to this information after you have thoroughly acquainted yourself with IPX.

Once you have taken all required steps to configure a router for IPX routing, adding EIGRP support is simple. Take the following steps:

1. Enable the service using the ipx router eigrp <AS number> command. The <AS number> is not really an autonomous system number. It is actually a process ID. Like IP, all routers exchanging EIGRP updates have to use a common AS number in their configurations.

2. List the interfaces that will participate in the EIGRP service by identifying the network numbers using the network <network number> command.

Using the example in Figure 8.3, we can gain a better understanding of this process. In the Figure, router A is configured for access to networks 1A and 9F. Router B is configured to attach to 9F and 2B. Router A's configuration would look like the following:

```
! Router A's IPX configuration
ipx routing
!
```

```
interface ethernet0
  network 1a
!
interface serial0
  network 9f
!
ipx router eigrp 1
  network 1a
  network 9f
!
```

Because the routers are communicating with each other over a serial link, we may be inclined to configure just the serial link with EIGRP. We can do this by simply turning off IPX RIP on the serial interface. To turn off IPX RIP, issue the `no network 9F` command in the router configuration mode for the RIP service. Because all interfaces send and receive IPX RIP by default, it is up to us to tell RIP which interfaces to ignore. An example follows:

```
!
ipx router rip
 no network 9f
!
ipx router eigrp 1
 network 1a
 network 9f
! (network all work as well)
```

An alternative is to disable IPX RIP completely. We do this with the command `no ipx router rip`. This command is issued in global configuration mode. Example:

```
!
no ipx router rip
!
ipx router eigrp 1
```

```
network 1a
network 9f
!
```

Figure 8.3 EIGRP for IPX

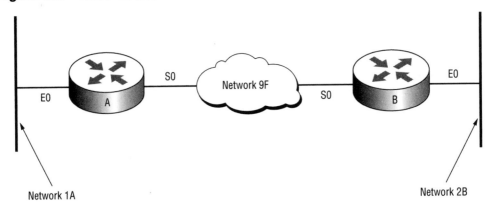

Incremental Service Advertisement Protocols (SAPs) In addition to all of the benefits already mentioned, we can also configure EIGRP to do incremental SAPs. If you are familiar with routing in an IPX environment, you probably know that IPX servers and routers periodically advertise networks and services by default every 60 seconds. Networks are advertised in the form of IPX RIP, and services are advertised in the form of Service Advertisement Protocol (SAP) packets. SAPs can consume a significant amount of bandwidth, especially if a number of services are advertised. On top of that, if we have to advertise these SAPs across serial links, they can become, potentially, a bandwidth issue.

When you configure a router to exchange EIGRP updates across a serial interface, it will automatically enable incremental SAPs. In other words, the interface only exchanges service information when services are added and removed. EIGRP even allows us to configure our LAN interfaces so that they support incremental SAPs. We do so using the `ipx sap-incremental eigrp <AS number>` command:

```
!
ipx sap-incremental eigrp 1
!
```

An option available to this command is to add the `rsup-only` statement at the end. By adding `rsup-only`, we are telling the router to use only RIP for network updates, but EIGRP for incremental SAPs. Example:

```
!
ipx sap-incremental eigrp 1 rsup-only
!
```

Some options that may be worth knowing about when configuring EIGRP for IPX:

Changing the maximum hop count for IPX   By default, any packets whose hop count exceeds the 15 hop maximum is discarded. We can change that using the `ipx maximum-hops <hop count>` command. A hop count can be increased to 254 hops. This command is issued in global configuration mode.

Changing how much of your bandwidth is used up by EIGRP updates   By default, EIGRP can use up to 50 percent of your bandwidth for update traffic. It is in our power to change this using the `ipx bandwidth-percent eigrp <as-number> <percent>` command. This command is issued in interface configuration mode for the interface you want to control.

Changing the redistribution behavior of RIP and EIGRP   By default, IPX RIP and EIGRP redistribute routes between them. You can disable this feature using the `no redistribute {rip | eigrp <AS number> | connected | static}` command. This command is issued in IPX router configuration mode for the protocol you want to affect.

Changing the hello and hold timers   By default, the EIGRP hello timer is 5 seconds and the hold timer is 15 seconds. The hello timer specifies how often in seconds the hellos are sent. The hold timer specifies how long to wait without hearing a hello before a neighbor is declared gone. In a heavily congested network, it may be necessary to increase the hold timer. We can change both these values using the `ipx hello-interval eigrp <AS number> <seconds>` and `ipx hold-time eigrp <AS number> <seconds>` commands.

WARNING   Before using any of these optional commands, be sure you fully understand their impact. It is recommended that before changing hello and hold timers you contact Cisco TAC for assistance.

Routing Protocols

PART 2

EIGRP for AppleTalk

Configuring AppleTalk with Enhance IGRP is simple but requires you to have some understanding of AppleTalk. If you are new to AppleTalk routing, jump ahead and read Chapter 12. Come back to this information after you have thoroughly acquainted yourself with AppleTalk.

Configuring Enhanced IGRP for operation with AppleTalk is done a bit differently from IP and IPX. Like IP and IPX, we have to enable the service and specify which interfaces will use EIGRP. How this is done is where the differences lie. The required steps for achieving the configuration are as follows:

1. Enable the EIGRP routing process. This is the first step to configuring EIGRP. The command to enable Enhanced IGRP for AppleTalk is `appletalk routing eigrp <router-number>`. The router number must be unique for all EIGRP routers in the network. This is quite different from what we have been doing in the past. With IP and IPX, all routers had to be in a common AS. This is not true for AppleTalk.

2. Enable EIGRP on each interface. This next step involves configuring each interface that will be participating in the Enhanced IGRP process. To do this, issue the `appletalk protocol eigrp` command in interface configuration mode for every interface that will be affected.

A sample configuration is as follows:

```
!
appletalk routing
!
interface serial0
  appletalk cable-range 100-120
  appletalk zone Ozone
  appletalk protocol eigrp
!
appletalk routing eigrp 1
!
```

To remove Enhanced IGRP for AppleTalk from an interface, use the no form of the command you used to enable it: `no appletalk protocol eigrp`. To disable Enhanced IGRP from the entire router, use the `no appletalk routing eigrp <number>` command.

WARNING Be careful when using the no `appletalk routing eigrp` command. If you disable EIGRP from a router and you have previously disabled RTMP on any of the interfaces, the AppleTalk configuration will be erased from those interfaces completely. The correct thing to do is first re-enable RTMP on all interfaces on which you have disabled it, and then remove EIGRP. The interface command to use is `appletalk protocol rtmp`.

Some options that may be worth knowing about when configuring EIGRP for AppleTalk are:

Changing the hello and hold timers   By default, the EIGRP hello timer is 5 seconds and the hold timer is 15 seconds. The hello timer specifies how often in seconds the hellos are sent. The hold timer specifies how long to wait without hearing a hello before a neighbor is declared gone. In a heavily congested network, it may be necessary to increase the hold timer. We can change both these values using the `appletalk eigrp-timers <hello-interval> <hold-time>` command.

Changing the active state time   By default, all AppleTalk routes have an active state time of 1 minute. Once that minute is reached, the router removes the route from the routing table. You can increase that time using the `appletalk eigrp active-time {minutes | disabled}` command.

Changing how much of your bandwidth is used up by EIGRP updates   By default, EIGRP can use up to 50 percent of your bandwidth for update traffic. We have it in our power to change this. We do so using the `appletalk bandwidth-percent eigrp <AS number> <percent>` command. This command is issued in interface configuration mode for the interface you want to control.

Changing the redistribution behavior of EIGRP and RTMP   By default, RTMP and Enhanced IGRP redistribute between each other. There are times when this can cause problems. We can disable this feature using the `no appletalk route-redistribution` command in global configuration mode.

Routing Protocols

PART 2

Load sharing with EIGRP

One of the organizations for which John did some work has a huge internetwork. We won't say who it is, but we will say that our tax dollars have funded their network. It consists of just about every routing protocol, as well as just about every routed protocol you can think of. John was asked to clean up some inconsistencies in a part of the topology where they were having problems with hop count maximums on RIP routers. They had poor area design, a bad IP addressing scheme, and an all-around no-good hierarchy in their OSPF backbone. They had a number of networks using a variety of protocols that were all attempting to redistribute into OSPF. It was a mess! You have to understand that the organization couldn't keep qualified engineers employed because government pay scales don't compare to the private sector. So, they had contract engineers trying to put band-aids on the network for a decade. (Seems like contractor pay is different money than payroll to the Feds.) Anyway, as far as the network was concerned, it finally came time to pay the piper.

After an in-depth analysis of the part of the topology over which John had control, it occurred to him that this network was a perfect candidate for Enhanced IGRP. The organization had an open-purchase contract with Cisco and a policy that precluded them from buying anything but Cisco routers. Cisco sales engineers recommended all of their hardware, so every router and switch in the place was far bigger and faster than it had to be. As Tim Taylor would say after a good

simian grunt, "More power!" Additionally, with IP addressing–related design problems, you tend to open a really big bag of worms that may be too much to handle if you decide to renumber everything. In retrospect, John probably should have done some renumbering throughout the organization, but at the time he couldn't justify the time spent with any real benefit. The obvious solution then was to implement EIGRP. EIGRP is very forgiving of a poor design. It will try to make the best of what you have.

Now folks, you are going to be disappointed because this story doesn't have a climax at the end. John ended up migrating 37 routers to EIGRP without a stitch of problem. This is the kind of protocol that EIGRP is. It makes our jobs eventless. It's kind of like being an honest accountant who doesn't make clerical errors: Your job isn't very emotional. The one bit of emotion came from the client, who thought John had been sent from the router gods to bless their network. To this day, the network runs fine and there is plenty of room for growth.

John did learn something interesting. The network had Frame Relay, ISDN, and an X.25 backbone as well. They had just funded two PVCs to one of their remote internal clients. They were currently using a Centrex ISDN connection at 64K. The PVCs were installed, but no one had configured them to work. One of the PVCs was T1 and the other was a 128K backup. John probably wouldn't have recommended a frame backup for a frame but he figured that because it was there he could play with it. Plus, because EIGRP supports it, he could setup unequal-cost load sharing.

The way John saw it, he could set it up to use all three paths. They weren't going to lose the Centrex connection for a while. There was one potential complication: John had only heard and read about unequal-cost load sharing and had never tried it. Because he wanted to load-share over three lines—one at 1.544MB, one at 128K, and a third at 64K—he needed to come up with a metric variance value that would work. It turned out to be simple. He divided the fastest line speed with the slowest and rounded up to the nearest integer. Based on these calculations, he configured all the affected routers with a metric variance of 24. After doing this, he was able to utilize all three links simultaneously. Cool!

The routing table listed all three routes as valid, each with a different metric. How neat! Additionally, he turned on debug ip packet, did a fairly lengthy ping, and watched the division of packets. Twenty-four packets would go down the T1 path. Then two would go down the 128K path. Then one went across the 64K path. The next series would again take the T1 path. The division was in round-robin fashion, just like all the books said!

Now the bad news with unequal-cost load sharing. Depending on the link technologies you use, enabling this feature has the potential to add a good deal of latency to your overall packet deliveries. We call the concept *pinhole congestion*. It is recommended that if you do indeed change metric variance, don't try to make it too high. Variance 24 is way too high. It was cute to play with, but in a production environment it might not help as much as you hoped it would.

Part 3

Router Configuration

- The Cisco IOS and command interface
- Configuring and troubleshooting TCP/IP
- Configuring and troubleshooting IPX
- Configuring and troubleshooting AppleTalk
- Configuring ISDN and DDR

9

Configuring a Router: An Introduction

The Cisco IOS software is the most important component of any router. The IOS is the program code that defines how the router functions. Without the IOS, the router cannot route data. Cisco's IOS software is one of their major strengths. All Cisco routers are configured essentially in the same way because, generally, they are running the same IOS or operating system. This is also true of the Cisco switches: They run the Cisco IOS and have configuration interfaces that look similar to the routers. The Cisco IOS is very feature-rich and provides a seamless interface across the range of Cisco routing products. If you have worked with a 2500 series router, there is no real difference between its interface and that of a 7500 series router. Because the IOS is the same no matter what the platform, once you get comfortable with the IOS on one router, you do not have to learn a new set of commands to work on a different router.

The Cisco IOS offers a streamlined command line interface for configuring routers that is fairly easy to navigate. The IOS is what really separates Cisco from its competition. The consistent interface in both basic and advanced routing features allows both the novice and the inexperienced user to accomplish their tasks with the same interface. Cisco's IOS is one of the major reasons that the company has managed to gain such incredible market share.

The Boot Sequence

There are several basic steps through which every router passes when it is turned on:

1. The first is Power-On Self Test (POST). During the POST, the router verifies that its internal components are functioning properly. These components include the CPU, the memory, and the interface circuitry.

2. Next, Bootstrap is executed from ROM on the CPU card.

3. The router looks at the boot field value of the router's config register to decide from where it should load the IOS.

4. The operating system determines the hardware and software components of the router and lists them on the console terminal.

5. The router loads the rxboot IOS in preparation for loading the full IOS that the router will run when it is operational. This can be thought of as a Bootstrap step. The rxboot IOS is loaded to help the router load the actual IOS it will run once it has finished the boot sequence.

6. The router finds and loads the IOS software. The IOS can either be booted from ROM or the router can be configured to look in NVRAM for user-defined commands specifying where to load the IOS from.

7. The configuration file you have specified loads. The configuration files defines how the router will function in your environment. If no configuration file exists, the router will enter Setup mode.

Figure 9.1 shows the router boot sequence.

Figure 9.1   Figure 9.1: The router boot sequence

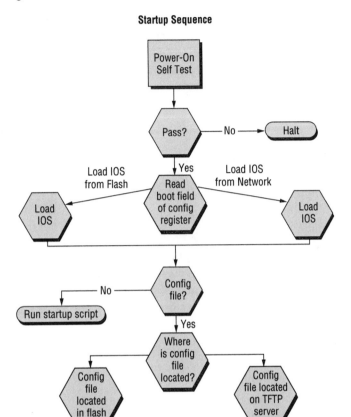

Startup Sequence

Your Router and Its Many Modes

In this section, we will discuss the various modes in which your router can run. These include:

- ROM Monitor mode
- Rxboot mode
- User Exec mode
- Privileged Exec mode
- Config mode

ROM Monitor Mode

If the boot sequence is not completely successful, the router may drop into one of two modes: the ROM Monitor (ROMMON) mode and the rxboot mode. The ROMMON mode is activated if the router cannot find an IOS to load or if the boot sequence is broken by user intervention. The ROMMON mode is signified by one of the following two prompts:

```
>
```

or

```
rommon >
```

A number of commands are available in ROMMON mode which will allow you to perform tasks such as loading a selected IOS image, showing the config register values and options, or running a test on the system memory.

You rarely have to enter ROMMON mode unless you need to set the config register so that the router will not read its config file when it boots. Forcing the router not to read the config allows you to bypass the router's passwords. This procedure is discussed in greater detail in Appendix C. ROMMON mode allows you to reset the router's password, among other things

Rxboot Mode

The rxboot mode is accessible by changing the config register settings and rebooting the router. Rxboot mode loads a subset of the IOS software to help you get the router running if it cannot find a valid version of the IOS. Rxboot allows you to configure the router enough so that you can load an IOS image onto it. The rxboot prompt looks like this:

```
Router<boot>
```

Rxboot mode is another mode in which you probably will not spend too much time. One of this mode's few uses is when swapping out flash memory in routers. Because the new flash does not have an IOS loaded, the router will boot up into rxboot mode. From rxboot, you can configure an interface so that you can then TFTP an IOS image onto the router.

User Exec Mode

User Exec mode is a read-only mode that allows users to enter the router and look around. No configuration changes can be made from within this mode. User Exec mode allows you to connect to other devices, perform some tests, and look at some statistics. It is the first mode you enter when you get to the router. To access the mode, you can either Telnet to the router or connect to the console port. User Exec mode is signified by the following prompt:

```
Router_name>
```

In order to be able to telnet to the router, you need to have set up a password on the vty lines or else you will not be able to get in. An exception to this is if you specify `no login` in the router's vty line configuration. This tells the router not to require a password when granting access via the vty line. The default configuration has the login command specified on the vty line, which forces the user to enter a password for vty access. Although you can set up the router so it will not require a password for vty access, we strongly discourage doing so.

Privileged Exec Mode

Privileged Exec mode allows you access to all of the commands in the router. Privileged Exec mode is signified by the following prompt:

```
Router_name#
```

You can access this mode only by first passing through User Exec mode. Issuing the command `enable` initiates the transition from User Exec mode to Privileged Exec mode.

From Privileged Exec mode, you can enter any of the configuration modes, perform any number of tasks, and enter any commands. Privileged Exec mode gives you access to everything in the router and unlimited access to the router's commands. It is also very easy to cause the router to function incorrectly from within this mode, so make sure you know what each command does before you execute it.

For example, issuing the command `debug all`, which turns on all possible debugging in the router, sounds like something you might want to do when trying to fix a problem. However, those two little words can take down a router completely. This is because the router gets so busy providing the console with debug output that it can do nothing else and will not allow you to get in and turn off debugging.

Also, by default, debug output goes to the console and will not be seen via a Telnet session. So, if you were to turn on debugging from a Telnet session, you would not see anything and you might forget you had turned it on. You can use the Privileged Exec command `Terminal monitor` to send the debug output to the terminal lines.

The most important `debug` command to remember is `No debug all`. Sometimes you cannot remember the necessary syntax to turn off the particular debug set you turned on. Other times it is difficult to see what you are typing due to debug output scrolling up the screen. The command `No debug all` will turn off any debugging that is turned on.

Router Configuration

PART 3

NOTE   We will devote more time to debug commands in Chapter 17, "Troubleshooting."

Config Mode

Config mode is where all the changes to the router's configuration take place. The Config mode contains several sub-modes, which suggests that Config mode is really a hierarchically structured set of different Config modes. The topmost Config mode is generally referred to as global config. From there, you can access sub-modes such as interface config, line config, and many others. These three are the most common.

NOTE   There are more than 17 different Config modes. Fortunately, if you know how one works, you know how they all work; the only difference is what you can configure in a particular mode.

When you are making changes in Config mode, you are simultaneously modifying the running configuration on the router. (The running configuration is defined in the next section.) These changes usually take effect immediately. There are, however, one or two exceptions to this rule. For example, when you change the config register, it does not register the change until after you boot the router.

Assuming you have not saved your changes, you can always reboot the router to restore it to where you were before you made the changes. A router that is up and running contains two versions of its configuration: the running configuration and the startup configuration. The startup config is stored in NVRAM and is loaded each time the router starts. When the router is powered on, it loads the startup config. Once the startup config is loaded, it becomes unnecessary, because the router is now using the copy it loaded into RAM as the running config. The startup config has therefore become the running config.

The concept behind the startup and running configs is important to remember. It is very useful to know that if you really screw something up, you can reboot the router and get back to where you started relatively quickly (assuming you have not saved the changes).

WARNING   Often after a power outage, the routers don't work properly when they come back up. This is because at some point someone made a change to the running config but never saved the new running config back to the startup config.

Use the following code to save the running config into the startup config. You should do this as soon as you are sure you want to keep the changes you made to the running config mode:

```
digger_router#copy running-config startup-config

Building configuration...

[OK]
```

Context-Sensitive Help in the Modes

Probably one of the most helpful features of the Cisco IOS is its ability to provide context-sensitive help. Typing a question mark from the command prompt will bring up all the commands that are available to that mode. This is very useful because it allows you to see what your options are. It gets even better, though: Suppose you want to look at the router's IPX routing table but you don't remember the exact command. You can enter the command show ipx ? in its place. The question mark indicates that you are in search of all the options available to complete the show ipx command, and a list of those options will appear. In this case, show ipx route is the one we want to use.

```
digger_router#show ipx ?
    accounting  The active IPX accounting database
    cache       IPX fast-switching cache
    eigrp       IPX EIGRP show commands
    interface   IPX interface status and configuration
    route       IPX routing table
    servers     SAP servers
    spx-spoof   SPX Spoofing table
    traffic     IPX protocol statistics
```

If you were to enter a partial command such as show c?, the router would respond by showing you all options that begin with the letter *c* and complete the command.

```
digger_router#show c?
clock  compress  configuration  controllers
```

This means that you will get different results depending on where you place the question mark. If you do not use a space, you will get back all possible ways the router knows about to complete the word you are typing. If you do add a space after the last word typed and then enter a question mark, when you hit Return you will get all the possible entries for the next part of the command you have entered. Often this is not a word, but it may tell you what type of input the command is expecting.

In the following example, you can see that you need to supply a subnet mask to the IP address:

```
digger_router(config-if)#ip address 172.29.1.0 ?
  A.B.C.D  IP subnet mask
```

You can also abbreviate commands as long as you enter enough of the command to make it unique. Here are some examples of common abbreviations:

Abbreviation	Command
Sh	Show
Int	Interface
Conf	Configure
Shut	Shutdown
Trace	Traceroute

Obviously, there are many more abbreviations that you could use. As long as you enter enough of the command that the router can tell what you mean, the router will execute that command. If you try to shorten your command too much, you will get the following output.

```
digger_router#t
% Ambiguous command:  "t"
```

This output indicates that the router needs more letters to figure out what to do.

> **TIP**   If you type enough of a command to make it unique and hit the Tab key, the router will fill in the rest of the word for you. This is an excellent feature because it allows you to see exactly what you are doing while still saving some time. This is especially beneficial for commands you use less frequently and with which you are therefore less familiar. More commonly used commands are easier to abbreviate.

Tools for Configuring Your Router

Of the several different ways to configure a router, each has its own advantages and disadvantages. The methods include the setup script, TFTP, Config Maker, the command line interface, and boot commands.

Configuring a Router Using the Setup Script

The most common way of configuring a router is to use the command line interface to enter the commands that create the configurations. If you start with a new router without a configuration, the router will ask you if you want to enter the system configuration dialog. The system configuration dialog is a setup script that asks you various questions in order to set up the router for you. The script will ask you what routed protocols (IPX, IP, AppleTalk, etc.) and routing protocol (RIP or EIGRP) you want to run and which interfaces you want to configure.

Once you have answered all the questions, the router will show you what it has in mind for a configuration and ask you if you want to use that configuration. If you say Yes, the router will load that configuration as the running configuration and will also save it as the startup configuration.

While useful, the setup script does not allow you to do too much more than set up some basic things, and for that reason it is almost never used. Some people may find it useful for a simple configuration or as a good starting point, but beyond that it really is not flexible enough for common use.

> **NOTE** When defining subnet masks in the setup script, you have to specify the number of bits past the classfull mask. For example, to put a 255.255.255.0 mask on 10.1.1.1, you need to specify 16 bits of subnet masking. While you have 24 total bits of masking, the first 8 are assumed, because 10.X.X.X addresses have, by default, a classfull, class-A mask of 8 bits. By adding 16 more bits, you get the 24-bit mask you wanted.

Configuring a Router Using TFTP

TFTP is a very effective way to configure a router. You can store a router configuration as a text file, edit it with any word processor, and then upload it to the router via TFTP. This means you can take a configuration from one router, modify it, and place it on another router. In an environment with more than one router this is useful because most of the configuration information is going to be the same anyway. Instead of creating a complete configuration for each router, you can make a working configuration by modifying an existing one from another router.

TFTP can also be used to modify a few lines in a configuration on a running router. These lines can be placed into a text file and TFTPed to the router with the following command:

```
digger_router#copy tftp running-config

Host or network configuration file [host]?

Address of remote host [255.255.255.255]? 10.1.1.2

Name of configuration file [digger_router-confg]? diconfig

Configure using digger-config from 10.1.1.2? [confirm]

Loading diconfig
```

The above commands take the contents of the diconfig file and load them into the running configuration.

NOTE   It is important to note that the running configuration is not overwritten, but instead the diconfig file and the running config are merged. This means anything that is not mentioned specifically in the diconfig file in the running configuration will be left unchanged. For example, this would be useful if you had to change the passwords in all your routers: You could create a partial configuration in a text file with just the new passwords specified and TFTP it to all your routers. Because the files are merged, you would only be changing the passwords.

Using TFTP for Backups

Tftp is also an excellent way to back up your configuration files. The following commands take the running configuration and copy it to the TFTP server running on host 10.1.1.1 into the file digger_router-confg:

```
digger_router#copy running-config tftp

Remote host []? 10.1.1.1

Name of configuration file to write [digger_router-confg]?

Write file digger_router-confg on host 10.1.1.1? [confirm]
```

If, for some reason, we had to replace the digger router, how long would it take to get a new one configured to replace it? If we had backed up the configuration previously to a TFTP server, all we would have to do would be to configure one interface on the new router with an IP address, and then we could TFTP the saved router configuration up to the new router.

Using TFTP for Backups *(continued)*

The dialog would look like this:

```
digger_router#copy tftp startup-config

Address of remote host [255.255.255.255]? 10.1.1.2

Name of configuration file [digger_router-confg]?

Configure using digger_router-confg from 10.1.1.2? [confirm]
```

Notice that we are copying the configuration to the startup-config. This is because TFTPing to the startup config means that the old startup config is replaced by what you are copying and is not merged as it is when you TFTP into the running config. Because we want to replace *everything* in the config on the router, we TFTP to the startup config and then reboot the router. This allows you to reconfigure and replace a router completely in under five minutes with very little effort.

Config Maker

Cisco has a piece of software called Config Maker that allows you to draw out a network with a Visio-like drawing tool. Based on how you draw the network, Config Maker asks you various questions. Using the topology and the answers you give to the questions, Config Maker builds the proper router configurations and allows you to push them out to your routers.

Command Line Interface

Even with all the tools available, most people perform the largest portion of the configuration work through the command line interface (CLI), which can be accessed either through a Telnet session or through a connection to the console port. If you can configure the router from the CLI, all the other methods only make things a little easier or faster. This book focuses on the CLI.

No matter what you are doing or where you are, you will always have access to the CLI; so it is important not to become dependent on any specific tool which may not be there when you need it. UNIX editors operate similarly: All UNIX systems typically have the VI editor, and if you have ever used VI, you might recall that working with it can be challenging. Editors such as Emacs and Pico are much more user-friendly. However, I often run across UNIX systems that have only VI installed. Therefore, knowing how to get around in VI makes your job a lot easier, since you can almost guarantee that any UNIX system you work on will have it installed.

Boot System Commands

The boot system commands specify from what location the router will load its IOS and the fallback sequence to use if it cannot load the IOS from the primary location. Boot system commands are executed in the order they are entered in config mode.

The following is an example of a boot system command sequence:

```
digger_router(config)##boot system flash cpa25-cg-1.110-6

digger_router(config)#boot system tftp image.exe 10.1.1.2

digger_router(config)#boot system rom

digger_router(config)#exit

digger_router#copy run start
```

This command sequence tells the router to first try to load the IOS file cpa25-cg-1.110-6 from the router's flash. If this fails, it will try to load the image.exe file off a TFTP server at address 10.1.1.2. Finally, if all else fails, it will load the IOS from ROM. If the IOS is loaded from ROM, it will most likely be a subset of the IOS and will be an older version. Because it is burned into ROM, it cannot be updated, and you are stuck with whatever Cisco was putting on the ROM chips at the time you bought the router.

In addition to specifying from what location the IOS is loaded, you can also tell a router from where it should pull its configuration. This is useful if for some reason you choose not to store your configuration file in NVRAM. The following command sequence will tell the router to load sparky-confg from a TFTP server at 192.168.1.100 as its running configuration:

```
service config
boot host tftp sparky-confg 192.168.1.101
```

Adding these two lines in global config mode will tell the router to pull the file sparky-config from the address 192.168.1.101 via TFTP to get its configuration. The service config command allows for the loading of configuration files from a network server. Without this command, the router cannot pull configuration files off the network. Most of the time, routers are set up to load their configurations out of NVRAM. Unless you have a good reason for pulling a configuration off the network, it is best not to—you don't want to have to worry about network integrity while a router is coming online. TFTP, RCP, and FTP can all be used to pull configuration files off the network. TFTP is the protocol most commonly used for this application.

The boot commands will also allow you to load a generic set of commands, and then a specific set for each individual router, as follows:

```
service config
boot network tftp generic-confg 192.168.1.101
boot host tftp sparky-confg 192.168.1.101
```

This will cause the router to load both the `generic-confg` and `sparky-confg` commands together. This approach gives you the flexibility to

- Use one base set of commands for the general configuration entities, which should be the same for all your routers in the boot network file.

- Specify those values that are specific to an individual router in the boot host file.

NOTE When `service config` is enabled and you have not specified both a boot network and boot host command, the router will go off looking for the default files' names. The defaults are `network-confg` and `cisconet.cfg` for the boot network files and *hostname*-cfg and *hostname*.cfg for the boot host files, where hostname is replaced with the host name of the router for which you have not fully specified the boot commands. For example, if you specify only a boot host location, the router will still try to load a network version of the config file using the default network config filenames. This will fail if the file does not exist. Because the router has loaded the host config, it will function properly if that file has the full config for the router. You do not need to specify a boot network file. However, keep in mind that the router will still look for the default network config files. Although this is not a problem, you should be aware of it because a message is written to the console when it goes out to look for the default files.

Passwords

The Cisco IOS allows you to set passwords on the console connection and the vty lines to control access to the router. The following commands set the vty password on vty line 0-4 to `ashland`. This is the password you would now use to telnet into the router.

```
digger_router#conf t
Enter configuration commands, one per line.  End with CNTL/Z.
digger_router(config)#line vty 0 4
digger_router(config-line)#password ashland
digger_router(config-line)#
```

Router Configuration

PART 3

By default, the router has five vty lines: 0, 1, 2, 3, and 4. This means it can support up to five vty sessions at once. You can easily increase the number of vty lines using the following command:

```
Digger_router(config)#line vty 0 8
```

By simply changing the 4 to an 8, you created nine vty lines: 0, 1, 2, 3, 4, 5, 6, 7, and 8. You can create separate passwords for each vty line or for sets of them; however, because it is impossible to tell on which line a Telnet session is going to come in, most people set all the lines to the same password.

TIP If you have multiple people administering your routers, it sometimes makes sense to configure the highest vty line with a separate password. Because vty lines are allocated sequentially, this ensures that if all the vty lines are filled, you can get still get into the router on the highest vty. The only way to tell you are on the highest line, however, is when the normal password fails, and the one you configured on that line works. This sets aside a vty line for use in case of emergency, which cannot be accessed unless the other password is known.

There is only one console line. This is the port on the router labeled *console*. The procedure for setting the console password is the same as that for setting the vty line's password.

```
digger_router(config)#line console 0
digger_router(config-line)#password ashland
digger_router(config-line)#exit
digger_router(config)#exit
digger_router#
```

The vty and console passwords control access to the User Exec mode and are, by default, stored in clear text.

```
Current configuration:
!
version 11.0
service udp-small-servers
service tcp-small-servers
!
hostname digger_router
```

```
!
!
!
interface Ethernet0
 ip address 10.1.1.1 255.255.255.0
!
interface Serial0
 no ip address
 shutdown
 no fair-queue
!
interface Serial1
 no ip address
 shutdown
!
!
line con 0
 password ashland
line aux 0
 transport input all
line vty 0 4
 password ashland
 login
!
end
```

Whether having the passwords stored in clear text in the config is a bad thing is debatable. Remember that they are not only stored in the config, but are also passed across the network in clear text. It is often a good idea to leave them this way because User Exec mode is fairly safe, and it is nice to be able to look at a hard copy of the configuration if you forget the passwords. You will need to be much more careful with the password into Privileged Exec mode. You should always use the enable secret password to control access to

Privileged Exec mode because it is encrypted. One way to encrypt your passwords is to use the following command:

```
digger_router(config)#service password-encryption
```

This will encrypt all the router passwords, (with the exception of the enable secret password, which is already encrypted) using a simple hash, so they are not in clear text. There are, however, numerous programs on the Internet that will crack these passwords. The encryption gives you a slightly increased level of security, but not much.

> **NOTE**   Once you have enabled service password encryption, the passwords will be stored in an encrypted form. Turning off service password encryption will not decrypt the passwords. In order to get the passwords back into clear text, you need to reset them.

It is also possible to set the access lines vty so that they will not require a password. This is done with the following command:

```
MMAGH(config)#line vty 0 4
MMAGH(config-line)#no login
```

This is definitely not recommended, however. You could also set up a stronger authentication method by configuring the vty line to use TACACS for authentication. This is covered in Chapter 15, "Securing Your Environment." The command for this is the following:

```
MMAGH(config)#line vty 0 4
MMAGH(config-line)#login tacacs
```

Getting into Privileged Exec mode, also referred to as Enable mode, requires a second password. There are two ways to set this password. The first is this command (still setting the password to ashland)

```
digger_router(config)#enable password ashland
```

This will set what is called the enable password. This password is stored in clear text in the configuration. Never set your enable password to the same word or set of characters as any of the other passwords in your router. The enable password generally should never be used—it still exists in the IOS for backward compatibility but has been replaced by the enable secret password.

The following command sets the enable secret password to `sparky`:

```
digger_router(config)#enable secret sparky
```

The enable secret password controls access to Privileged Exec mode in the same way as the enable password, but the enable secret password is encrypted using the MD5 encryption algorithm. It is *never* stored or exchanged in clear text. If the enable secret password exists, any enable password set up will be ignored. This makes the enable password useless for the most part.

TIP   It is useful to set the enable password to something that has nothing to do with your password scheme and that is not something you would normally see on the network. This way, if someone gets a look at one of your router configurations they will see the enable password and they might try to use it. Using an intrusion detection system and looking for the string that contains the useless enable password, you can detect people who have seen your configurations trying to get into the router. If you happen to have an intrusion detection system running, this is a simple way to catch a lot of internal people playing around.

Configuration and the IOS

As stated earlier, one of Cisco's major strengths is its IOS software, which makes it possible to configure all Cisco routers in basically the same way. The Cisco IOS software is the most important component in the router. The following sections highlight some of the basic concepts that are important in the Cisco IOS.

Backing Up the IOS

You always want to make sure that you have stored somewhere a back-up copy of the IOS that is running on your routers. This can be done easily by using Tftp to copy an image of the IOS down from the router to a server, as follows:

```
digger_router#copy flash tftp


System flash directory:
File  Length    Name/status
   1    3816576  cpa25-cg-1.110-6
[3816640 bytes used, 4571968 available, 8388608 total]
```

Router Configuration

PART 3

```
Address or name of remote host [255.255.255.255]? 10.1.1.2
Source file name? cpa25-cg-1.110-6
Destination file name [cpa25-cg-1.110-6]?
Verifying checksum for 'cpa25-cg-1.110-6' (file # 1)...  OK
Copy 'cpa25-cg-1.110-6' from Flash to server
   as 'cpa25-cg-1.110-6'? [yes/no]yes
```

You will follow these steps:

1. When the command `copy flash tftp` is entered, the router will display the contents of its flash.

2. The router will then prompt you for the address of the TFTP server. This can be another router or a remote computer running TFTP server software.

3. When you are prompted for the source file, enter the file that you want to download from flash.

4. For the destination file, you can enter anything you want; however, the name needs to be a valid file name on the system to which you are TFTPing. This means that if you are downloading the file to a DOS machine, you have to adhere to the 8.3 naming convention.

NOTE   Tftp has no authentication associated with it. However, on most systems, if you are trying to copy down a file called `test.exe` then the system to which you are copying the file must already have a file called `test.exe`. Typically, most TFTP implementations will not let you create a new file on the TFTP server, but will only let you overwrite an existing one. However, this is not true of Cisco's TFTP server for Windows machines. Cisco's implementation will allow you to create a new file via TFTP.

Updating the IOS

There are many reasons to upgrade your IOS. Typically, when you get a router, it is not loaded with the IOS you want on it, which means you have to upgrade. Or, there may be a bug in the current IOS version running on the router, and you will need to upgrade to fix it. Alternatively, you may realize that you need an IOS with more features than those contained in your present IOS.

As time moves forward, Cisco produces newer and newer IOS images. You should not upgrade just because a newer IOS exists—if everything is working, why mess with it?

However, certain versions eventually will be phased out and no longer supported; this will force you to upgrade. You don't want to be stuck with a piece of software that the manufacturer no longer supports.

You can check you current IOS version using the show version command, as follows:

```
digger_router#sh version

Cisco Internetwork Operating System Software

IOS (tm) 2500 Software (C2500-DS-L), Version 11.3(3)T, RELEASE
   SOFTWARE (fc1)

Copyright (c) 1986-1998 by cisco Systems, Inc.

Compiled Mon 20-Apr-98 18:04 by ccai

Image text-base: 0x0304310C, data-base: 0x00001000
```

....

The above router is currently running IOS 11.3 (3) T for the 2500 series routers. We can see when it was compiled and even that ccai compiled it.

The show version command also shows us the bootstrap version, the amount of time the router has been up, and the file that was used to boot the router (in this case 80272701.bin from flash memory).

```
ROM: System Bootstrap, Version 5.2(8a), RELEASE SOFTWARE

BOOTFLASH: 3000 Bootstrap Software (IGS-RXBOOT), Version 10.2(8a),
   RELEASE SOFTWARE (fc1)


digger_router uptime is 1 hour, 32 minutes

System restarted by reload

System image file is "flash:80272701.bin", booted via flash
```

Finally, we see that this is in fact a 2500 router. We can see how much memory is in it, and the specific interfaces 1 Ethernet and 2 serial. The current configuration register value is 0x2102. Remember that the config register controls how the system boots. 0x2102 is the default for the 2500 series routers. 0x2102 tells the router to read the boot system commands to determine from where to load the IOS and configuration file.

```
cisco 2500 (68030) processor (revision F) with 16384K/2048K bytes of
memory.
```

```
Processor board ID 05182340, with hardware revision 00000000

Bridging software.

X.25 software, Version 3.0.0.

1 Ethernet/IEEE 802.3 interface(s)

2 Serial network interface(s)

32K bytes of non-volatile configuration memory.

8192K bytes of processor board System flash (Read ONLY)


Configuration register is 0x2102
```

Cisco breaks up their IOS feature sets into several different types. Each feature set has a different set of capabilities. Which feature set to run is a function of what you are going to have the router do. For example, we use the IP/IPX/AT/DEC feature set fairly frequently; however, to implement Network Address Translation (NAT) you need to run the IP/IPX/AT/DEC PLUS feature set. When choosing a feature set, make sure that it has the capabilities you need. For example, don't go with an IP ONLY feature set if you need to run IPX and AppleTalk. The best way to determine which feature set up you need to run is to check out the documentation at www.cisco.com. There are far too many feature sets and feature combinations to enumerate here.

Updating the IOS Using CPSWInst

Cisco includes on each IOS CD-ROM they ship a tool for updating the IOS on their routers. This tool, known as CPSWInst, or the router software loader, facilitates the upgrade of the IOS on a router from any PC. The router must be connected to the PC via a crossover network cable, and the router and the PC must also be connected via the console port. The crossover connection does not have be completed with a crossover cable but could be accomplished through a hub or switch. However, because the router's address is going to be changing, a crossover cable ensures that no other hosts will be affected by the upload process.

The CPSWInst utility configures the router to the same IP network as that configured in your PC. For example, if the network card to which you have the crossover link connected is addressed as 172.16.1.25, the router software loader will configure the router to 172.16.1.1 on the Ethernet port you are using to connect the two devices. This is done via the console port. Once this is taken care of, the router's configuration can be TFTPed down if a backup is requested. Then a UDP session is established in the high port range to transfer the IOS image file to the router.

When launching the router software loader, the first thing you are asked is what type of network interface you will be using.

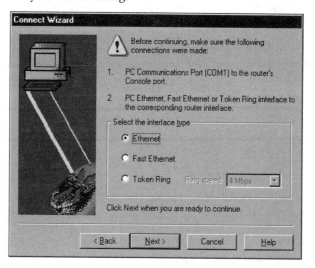

You are then asked if you are working with a new or a preconfigured router. A preconfigured router requires that the passwords be entered. Once this information is entered, the program will go out and learn what type of router you are working with.

The program then asks you for the IP address of the interface you wish to use. It will grab the first one it sees on your computer. You can change this, but typically your PC will have only one IP address.

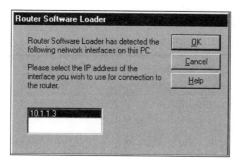

From there, you are presented with all the applicable IOS images you can load in the target directory. Select one and click Load Image.

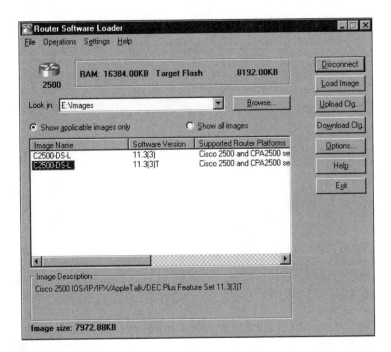

Next, the program asks if you want to back up the flash files, or if you want to erase the flash before you download the new flash to the router. If you have enough room in flash, it is a good idea not to erase the old flash image. The backup and erase options will typically be dictated by the amount of flash memory you have. With the lower-end routers, however, you will often have to erase the existing flash IOS image to make room for the new image. On higher-end routers, you can typically store multiple IOS images in flash.

When working with the requirement that a console cable be connected, you are by necessity close to the router, so if anything goes wrong, you are right there and can figure out a way to fix it. The biggest problems we have seen with the router software loaders is a tendency for the router to forget its temporary IP address just before the new IOS is downloaded. This can be corrected by removing the console connection for a second, placing it into a second PC, and resetting the router's IP address. This problem seems to occur more often with specific IP address ranges, such as 12.0.X.X. Trying a different IP network address for the router connection also generally fixes the problem.

Updating the IOS Using TFTP

You can also upgrade the IOS using the TFTP commands from the router. TFTP is by far the most common way to upgrade the IOS.

```
digger_router#copy tftp flash

                    ****  NOTICE  ****

Flash load helper v1.0

This process will accept the copy options and then terminate the
   current system image to use the ROM based image for the copy.

Routing functionality will not be available during that time.

If you are logged in via telnet, this connection will terminate.
```

```
Users with console access can see the results of the copy operation.
          ____ ******** ____
[There are active users logged into the system]
Proceed? [confirm]


System flash directory:
File  Length    Name/status
  1   8164224   80272701.bin
[8164288 bytes used, 224320 available, 8388608 total]
Address or name of remote host [10.1.1.3]? 10.1.1.2
Source file name? 80272701.bin
Destination file name [80272701.bin]?
Accessing file '80272701.bin' on 10.1.1.2...
Loading 80272701.bin from 10.1.1.2 (via Ethernet0): ! [OK]


Erase flash device before writing? [confirm]
```

The router will prompt for the host to pull the file from, the source file, and the destination file. Once this is done, it will validate that the source file exists and is retrievable. Next, depending on the model, the router may ask whether to erase flash before writing the new file. Most of the newer routers have the ability to store a second IOS image in flash, so there is no need to delete the existing one. Finally, the download begins.

Because the default on older routers, and low-end routers like the 2500 series, is to erase the old IOS before pulling down the new one, it is possible to run into problems. For the most part, however, TFTP is a very safe method for upgrading the IOS. Furthermore, the IOS will have to be upgraded from time to time, and TFTP is the most economical way to perform these upgrades.

WARNING   On a 2500 series router, once the router actually begins the TFTP file transfer procedure, it will use the ROM-based IOS image during the process. This means that the router will stop all routing during the file upload, and any Telnet sessions will be terminated.

A TFTP server can be any PC or even a router. A router can be told to allow TFTP access to its own flash. This allows for a complete IOS to be pulled out of the flash on one router and pulled into the flash on another router. This can be very useful if you have multiple routers across a slow link.

In Figure 9.2, if we have a new IOS on our PC and want to upgrade the IOS on router 2 and router 3, it does not make sense to send the upgrade twice across the slow 56K link if we don't have to.

Figure 9.2   Routers can be used as TFTP servers to reduce the bandwidth required for delivering IOS flash images.

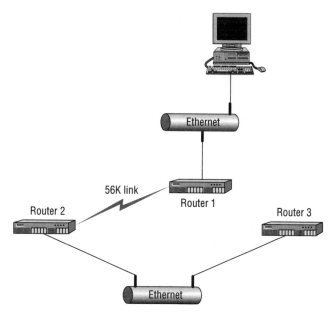

We could upgrade router 2 and then set it up as a TFTP server, allowing it to server out the new IOS file via TFTP:

```
digger_router(config)#tftp-server flash 80272701.bin
```

This command will allow any TFTP client to pull the file 80272701.bin from the flash on this router. It is possible to specify a file alias for this file or use a standard access list to limit who can access this file via TFTP:

```
digger_router(config)#tftp-server flash 80272701.bin 77
```

This command would only allow those hosts specified by IP access-list 77 to use the digger_router as a TFTP server.

Once router 2 is set up to allow TFTP access to the new IOS, we can pull the IOS onto router 3. This allows the use of the Ethernet segment for the file transfer. The 56Kbps line need only support the Telnet session between the host PC and router 3, which is used to start the TFTP session.

10

Configuring and Troubleshooting TCP/IP

A good understanding of TCP/IP and all of the protocols used by the IP stack is crucial to designing and, subsequently, configuring a successful 24seven networking infrastructure. In previous chapters, we covered the basics of IP, including addressing, masking, and basic configuration. In this chapter, we will assume that you have a thorough understanding of these basic concepts as we approach some of the more advanced subjects. We will be covering some techniques for using these tools to successfully configure and test your TCP/IP environment. We will also be covering some alternative methodologies for using some of the tools with which you may already be familiar to help diagnose and successfully troubleshoot problems.

Drawing Out the Logical Addressing of the Environment

In most areas of life, it is very important to know where you are going before you start off on any journey. As is it in life, so it is with your TCP/IP network. Starting with a solid diagram that plots out where you need to go will assist in the configuration of the network. Once the network is diagramed out and you can physically see all of the IP addresses, you may be able to code an entire router at one time, rather than going segment by segment and backtracking to the same router for each segment. Additionally, the troubleshooting process can be improved greatly with a visual layout of the network, as you can quickly find points of failure and trace them to the source.

If You Must Draw by Hand...

There are many tools available to help you with drawing out your network. None is more popular than the good old fashion pen and paper. Often while in a meeting, a situation will arise that will require a quick network drawing. The self-contained multicolor pens that were such a novelty in the fifth grade are particularly useful. These are the pens with the four different colors of ink in one casing, where you just push down on the color of choice and go to work. On a single piece of paper you can show IP addresses, OSPF areas, IPX networks, BGP domains, or whatever you choose, very quickly and in full color. Clearly, this does not scale well and is difficult to save electronically without the benefit of a color scanner, but it certainly has its place and can greatly help you communicate ideas quickly.

Software Network Drawing Solutions

For the larger networks, and for the more permanent type of network layout drawing, you will want something that is capable of producing professional-looking drawings. Of the many software packages on the market that can help you draw your network, none are as popular as Visio. Visio 2000 is the latest network version of the software and comes with most of the basic tools for drawing a network. More shapes are available from the Web site, and the shapes of most vendors are there, even some of the very obscure.

The Visio package mentioned above is great for "drawing" a network. However, you may require more horsepower than an artistic rendering of your network. Many network managers and consultants require a package that can go out and actively collect the data regarding the network and put it into a drawing for them. For such horsepower you will be required to dig a little deeper into the pockets. Visio has such an offering in their Enterprise edition. Figure 10.1 shows a sample screen from this software. There are a few others, such as NetSuite, that may offer an even more robust feature set with such tools as design validation, purchase order generation and order tracking. Information and demo versions of the NetSuite software are available at www.netsuite.com. Figure 10.2 shows some of what NetSuite has to offer.

Figure 10.1 A sample screen shot from Visio Enterprise edition

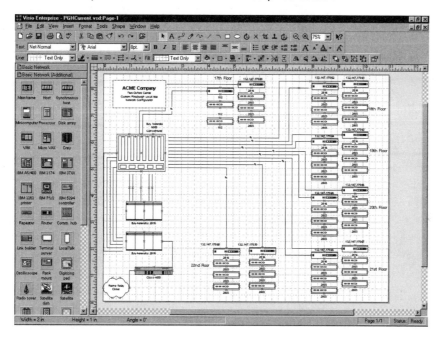

Figure 10.2 A sample screen shot from NetSuite

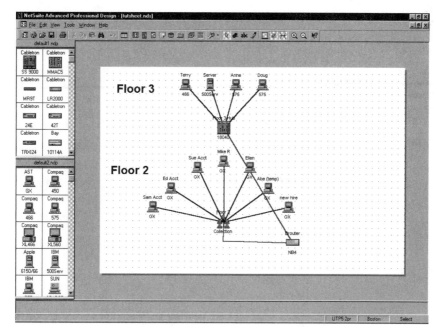

Cheater Chart

As mentioned in previous chapters, a binary chart is key to help successfully design and manage a TCP/IP addressing scheme. A full-blown binary chart may be cumbersome if you are trying to calculate masks and router summarization. However, you will find that as you are configuring your TCP/IP environment, an at-a-glance cheater chart helps greatly. For example, if during your configuration you come across a 29-bit mask, you know by looking at the chart that in decimal that mask is listed as 255.255.255.248. If you have the chart available, you will find that you have fewer errors, and that saves a great deal of time.

Table 10.1 is a sample chart that consists of bit positions and the powers of two as the headings and then the decimal equivalents and the placeholders as shown:

Table 10.1 An At-a-Glance Cheater Chart for TCP/IP Configuration

Bit Position per Octet	1	2	3	4	5	6	7	8
Power of 2	128	64	32	16	8	4	2	1
Mask	128	192	224	240	248	252	254	255
Decimal for Class C	25	26	27	28	29	30	31	32
Decimal for Class B	17	18	19	20	21	22	23	24
Decimal for Class A	9	10	11	12	13	14	15	16

A chart such as that in Table 10.1 can be cranked out in a matter of seconds and done right off of the top of your head. There is no mysterious information or rocket science going on here, but it is a very valuable tool to have posted beside your monitor as you are configuring so you can check yourself for accuracy as you go. It is also very likely that your chart may not need the level of detail shown here. If, for instance, you are working on a class C network, you will not need the bottom two rows.

Setting Up Your Routers

Once you have your network diagram completed with all of the information necessary for your network, you are actually ready to begin the physical implementation of your routers.

Verify That Everything Is Physically Connected First

As mentioned, we have already discussed how to add an IP address to your interfaces. We also discussed at great length several of the encapsulation options. When setting up any kind of routing, IP or otherwise, it is best to work your way up the OSI model starting with the Physical layer. Where possible, be sure that you have your physical connectivity established prior to any IP addressing scheme.

Frame Relay

You can test the Frame Relay environment for connectivity with the frame switch by using the `debug frame-relay lmi interface` command. The output from this command will give you positive verification that your router is in communication with the switch. Here is a typical Logical Management Interface (LMI) exchange:

Section 1:

```
Serial1(out): StEnq, myseq 8, yourseen 7, DTE up
datagramstart = 0x4031838, datagramsize = 14
FR encap = 0x00010308
00 75 95 01 01 00 03 02 08 07
```

Section 2:

```
Serial1(in): Status, myseq 8
RT IE 1, length 1, type 0
KA IE 3, length 2, yourseq 8 , myseq 8
PVC IE 0x7 , length 0x3 , dlci 20, status 0x2
```

Section 3:

```
Serial1(out): StEnq, myseq 9, yourseen 8, DTE up
datagramstart = 0x40315E0, datagramsize = 14
FR encap = 0x00010308
00 75 95 01 01 01 03 02 09 08
```

Router Configuration

PART 3

The first section describes the LMI request the router has sent to the switch. As indicated by the StEnq keyword, it is a status enquiry. Section 2 describes the LMI reply the router has received from the switch; it is a standard Status message. The third section shows the response to this request from the switch. The most important thing to notice here is that the sequence numbers are incrementing. The sequence numbers in section 1 are myseq 8 yourseen 7. In section 3 the router increments its sequence number with the STEnq message to 9 and the yourseen to 8. If there is a problem communicating with the switch, it is likely that the myseq will continue to increment while yourseen will not.

TIP Whenever possible, make sure that, prior to setting up your IP Addressing, you have physical connectivity to each of your end devices.

Cisco Discovery Protocol

A protocol-independent way of testing for direct connectivity is with the Cisco Discovery protocol. Cisco Discovery is a layer two proprietary protocol that gives information about your directly connected neighbors. The results will show you the device you are connected to. The output may reveal the router or the switch type. The following sample output shows that the Ethernet 0 interface is directly connected to module 0, port 5 of a Cisco Catalyst 2916M switch. If this were a router, the Capability Code would show an "R" rather than an "S."

```
Capability Codes: R - Router, T - Trans Bridge, B - Source Route Bridge
            S - Switch, H - Host, I - IGMP, r - Repeater


Device ID  Local Intrfce  Holdtme  Capability  Platform       Port ID
Switch     Eth 0          171      S           WS-C2916M-Fas  0/5
```

Interface Descriptions

Placing descriptions on interfaces is very helpful for simplifying complex networks. This practice is especially beneficial in large networks with many circuits. For example, if you have a Frame Relay network with multiple subinterfaces, it may be difficult to track which subinterface is for which circuit. More importantly, it is crucial to the efficiency of the network that other engineers coming in behind you who need to troubleshoot a failed circuit be able to identify each interface destination so they know where to start. After each address is configured, enter a description regarding that interface.

- Command line help display:

  ```
  #description ?
   LINE Up to 80 characters describing this interface
  ```

- Sample output of the show run command:

  ```
      interface Ethernet0
   description Interface to Inside Local Network
   ip address 149.166.6.101 255.255.255.0
   !
   interface Serial0
   encapsulation frame-relay
   !
   interface Serial0.1 point-to-point
   description Frame Cir to Dallas
   ip address 172.16.123.1 255.255.255.0
   !
   interface Serial0.2 point-to-point
   description Frame Cir to New York Park Ave. office
   ip address 172.16.14.1 255.255.255.0
   !
   interface Serial0.3 point-to-point
   description Frame Cir to New York Lexington office Contact
   Chandler Bing 202.781.3311
   ip address 172.16.15.1 255.255.255.0
   !
  ```

The above router configuration shows several different uses of the description command. The Ethernet description only indicates that it connected successfully to the local Ethernet network. The Serial 0.1 line is only a description of the city where the connection terminates. The final two lines are a bit more descriptive, both showing not only the city, but also a particular office location, with the final line giving the contact information of the person responsible for that circuit.

Point-to-Point Connectivity

Once you have diagrammed your network and tested for physical connectivity, it is time to start setting up the routers to communicate with IP. You will want to put the appropriate IP address on each end to see if they can communicate with each other.

Confirming Your Environment Is Working Properly

Configuring IP addresses on each side of the network does not necessarily mean that traffic is passing between the routers. You should test for connectivity with the router at the opposite end to verify that your line and protocols are both in an "up" state.

Useful Tools for Testing IP Connectivity

Cisco understands the importance of testing the availability and connectivity of TCP/IP connections. For this purpose, they have included several basic tools for testing, some of which are very common across other operating systems. The basic usage of these commands is also common. Cisco offers several advanced features for some of these commands, which will prove to be invaluable. Over the next few sections we will look into these command and their usage.

Ping and the ICMP Protocol

Ping is the basic tool for testing IP connectivity. It is a product of the Internetwork Control Message Protocol (ICMP) that was proposed in September of 1981 by RFC 792, which is a fairly readable document that goes into detail about packet formatting rules and so forth. ICMP messages are designed to help test and manage the network and can be classified into three categories: messages, queries, and responses. Table 10.2 shows the basic ICMP types as listed in RFC 792.

Table 10.2   ICMP Message Types

Type	Description
0	Echo Reply
3	Destination Unreachable
4	Source Quench
5	Redirect

Table 10.2   ICMP Message Types *(continued)*

Type	Description
8	Echo
11	Time Exceeded
12	Parameter Problem
13	Timestamp
14	Timestamp Reply
15	Information Request
16	Information Reply

Our concern will be focused on type 8, Echo, and type 0, Echo Reply. These types are synonymous with the ping test previously discussed. Upon successful completion of IP addressing on the routers on each end of the circuit, a final ping should look like this:

```
NashvilleHQ1#ping 124.5.191.142


Type escape sequence to abort.
Sending 5, 100-byte ICMP Echos to 24.5.191.142, timeout is 2 seconds:
!!!!!
Success rate is 100 percent (5/5), round-trip min/avg/max =
104/152/312 ms
```

This is a very common output, and much of the data in it is often overlooked. This output data tells us that 5 messages were sent that were 100 bytes in length. The destination was 24.5.191.142, and the timeout was 2 seconds.

The most important information to the connectivity of our environment is in the echo reply messages. Five out of five echo request messages that were sent were successful. This means that we have positively tested our environment for IP connectivity. In a production environment the last numbers are possibly the most overlooked. Travel time is very consequential to time-sensitive applications such as Telnet. The output shows us the time that the traffic took to get round trip. The first number is the minimum, or the fastest of the five. The middle is the average of all five packets sent, and the last is the time of the packet that took the longest. These numbers will always display left to right from lowest to highest. As we can see, the times in the example are acceptable for an Internet connection. If this were a private, point-to-point circuit or a LAN attachment, these times would not be acceptable, and we would need to research further the problems on the line.

NOTE   The examples show round-trip traffic times as 104/152/312 milliseconds, which is acceptable for an Internet connection. This is *not* acceptable for private or LAN connections. These times should be considerably less. A LAN connection should be less than 10 milliseconds.

There are several output characters for echo replies for a `ping` command. They are as follows:

!   Successful receipt of a reply

.   Network server time-out for each period displayed

?   Unknown packet type for each question mark received

&   Packet lifetime exceeded for each ampersand received

U   PDU error or Destination Network Unreachable

C   An ICMP congestion experienced packet was received

I   User Interrupted test

NOTE   The **ping** command can be followed by a name if there is a hostname configured or a DNS server set up.

TIP   You do not have to wait for the ping to time out completely before regaining control of the router. Ctrl+Shift+6 X will cancel the ping.

Advanced Pinging Techniques

In the previous example, we pointed out how the standard ping goes out, i.e., in five 100-byte packets. If we type `ping` without any designators after it, the router will prompt us for the input:

```
NashvilleHQ1#ping

Protocol [ip]:

Target IP address: 124.5.191.142

Repeat count [5]:
```

```
Datagram size [100]:

Timeout in seconds [2]:

Sweep range of sizes [n]:

Type escape sequence to abort.

Sending 5, 100-byte ICMP Echos to 124.5.191.142, timeout is 2
seconds:

!!!!!
```

Notice that the defaults we discussed previously are listed when each option is prompted. This is useful if we need information regarding throughput, for example. We may choose to manipulate the size of the pings by making them larger than the default 100 bytes. Any size can be used, up to 18024.

> **WARNING**   Be care not to make the size of the datagrams too large without increasing the timeout value accordingly, or the echo replies will not be allowed the time to make the trip.

One option that is listed with this use of the ping command is **sweep range of sizes.** This option will allow you to vary the sizes of the echo packets being sent. This capability is useful for determining the minimum sizes of the Maximum Transfer Units (MTUs) configured on the nodes along the path to the destination address. Packet fragmentation contributing to performance problems can then be reduced.

Extended Ping

In addition to the regular ping, Cisco also offers a more useful way to test connectivity: the extended ping. With the extended ping, Cisco enables you to change more than just the default information. With its extended options, you are able to test for more than just connectivity.

```
NashvilleHQ1#ping

Protocol [ip]:

Target IP address: 124.5.191.142

Repeat count [5]:

Datagram size [100]:

Timeout in seconds [2]:

Extended commands [n]: y

Source address or interface:
```

Router
Configuration

PART 3

```
Type of service [0]:

Set DF bit in IP header? [no]:

Validate reply data? [no]:

Data pattern [0xABCD]:

Loose, Strict, Record, Timestamp, Verbose[none]:

Sweep range of sizes [n]:

Type escape sequence to abort.

Sending 5, 100-byte ICMP Echos to 124.5.191.142, timeout is 2
seconds:

!!!!!
```

Traceroute

Traceroute uses the ICMP protocol the same way as ping to help you determine what path the packets are taking to get to their final destination.

The `trace` command takes advantage of the ICMP error messages generated by communication servers when a datagram exceeds its time-to-live (TTL) value. When you initiate a trace, it sends datagrams with a TTL value of 1. This will cause the first communication server to discard the probe datagram and send back an ICMP error message. The trace process will send out several probes at each TTL level and will subsequently display the round-trip time for each set of error messages. These probes are sent out one probe at a time, all of which will return one of two types of error messages:

Time exceeded	Indicates that an intermediate communication server has seen and discarded the probe.
Destination Unreachable	Indicates that the destination node has received the probe and discarded it, because it could not deliver the packet.

If the timer goes off before a response is returned, `trace` will report an asterisk (*). Do not be afraid to let several sets of these asterisks go by before you terminate the process. There are some issues with the `trace` command and how it works that are necessary in the functionality. As we mentioned earlier, `trace` operates based on the return of ICMP errors. Various implementations of the TCP/IP stacks on different products may cause the `trace` command to misbehave, in turn causing some hosts to respond with an ICMP *port unreachable* message. This is evidenced in a trace report that shows only a long sequence of asterisks resulting in an eventual process time-out, which is set to 30 hops by default.

Additionally, some TCP/IP hosts will reuse the TTL of the incoming packet, although they still generate an ICMP message. This reuse of the TTL (that is now set to 0) will prevent the packets from making it back to their source. When this occurs, it is possible for a block of TTL values to produce a set of asterisks. Eventually, the TTL value will get high enough that the ICMP messages can actually make it back to the source. For example, if you're trying to reach www.sampletrace.com from the NashvilleHG1 router, the result of your trace route looks like this:

```
NashvilleHQ1#trace www.sampletrace.com


Type escape sequence to abort.
Tracing the route to home.sampletrace.com (216.200.247.130)


1 149.166.6.100 4 msec 4 msec 4 msec

2 abcy-dmz.atm.testing.com (132.168.15.103) 4 msec 0 msec 0 msec

3 PVC1.INT.GW1.IND1.ALTER.NET (218.130.101.189) 8 msec 4 msec 24 msec

4 121.ATM2-0.XR2.CHIC4.ALTER.NET (146.182.208.166) 28 msec 16 msec 16 msec

5 194.at-1-1-0.TR2.CHIC2.ALTER.NET (155.63.65.74) 12 msec 28 msec 24 msec

6 126.at-5-1-0.TR2.SACS1.ALTER.NET (155.63.1.194) 72 msec 64 msec 76 msec

7 196.ATM6-0.XR2.PAWO1.ALTER.NET (155.63.50.105) 72 msec 92 msec 92 msec

8 188.ATM10-0-0.GW4.PAO1.ALTER.NET (148.188.148.93) 88 msec 64 msec 64 msec

9 abov-pao-gw.customer.ALTER.NET (137.130.195.214) 88 msec 80 msec 88 msec

10 sjc-pao-oc12.above.net (216.210.0.253) 108 msec 104 msec 108 msec

11 sjc2-main.co0.above.net (208.114.102.103) 108 msec 108 msec 104 msec

12 * * *

13 * * *

14 * * *

15 * * *

16 * * *

17 * * *

18 * * *

19 sampletrace-abovenet.1.above.net (216.200.254.106) !A * *
NashvilleHQ1#
```

In the preceding output, the destination host is 12 hops away, *not* 19 hops away. The timeouts are the result of the re-use of the TTL value. Eventually, the TTL value was increased enough by the probe packets that the host was able to respond.

A quick breakdown of line 11 would be as follows:

Output	Explanation
1	Sequence number
sjc2-main.co0.above.net	DNS resolved host name
(208.114.102.103)	IP address of the host
108 msec 108 msec 10 4 msec	Round trip time from source to this host

The termination of the trace command can occur on one of three instances: a response from the destination, when the maximum TTL value has been exceeded or when the command is cancelled by the user. To manually cancel a trace command, use the default Cisco break sequence, Ctrl+Shift+6 X.

Extended Trace

The extended trace utility offers the same power over the default values of the utilities as the extended ping utility. A sample of an extended trace would be as follows:

```
NashvilleHQ1#trace
Protocol [ip]:
Target IP address: www.cisco.com
Source address:
Numeric display [n]:
Timeout in seconds [3]:
Probe count [3]:
Minimum Time to Live [1]:
Maximum Time to Live [30]:
Port Number [33434]:
Loose, Strict, Record, Timestamp, Verbose[none]:
Type escape sequence to abort.
Tracing the route to www.cisco.com (198.133.219.25)

 1 149.146.16.100 0 msec 0 msec 4 msec
 2 id-dmz.atm.tst.edu (134.68.15.103) 4 msec 4 msec 4 msec
```

```
3 PVC.INT.GW1.NET (157.130.101.189) 4 msec 8 msec 4 msec

4 121.ATM.XR2.NET (146.188.208.166) 16 msec 8 msec 8 msec

5 194.at-2-1-0.TR2.CHI2.ALTER.NET (152.63.65.78) 12 msec 8 msec 12 msec

6 126.at-5-1-0.TR2.SAC1.ALTER.NET (152.63.1.194) 64 msec 60 msec 72 msec

7 196.ATM7-0.XR2.SJC1.ALTER.NET (152.63.51.49) 76 msec 76 msec 80 msec

8 192.ATM8-0-0.GW4.SJC2.ALTER.NET (152.63.51.125) 68 msec 68 msec 68 msec

9 cisco.customer.alter.net (157.130.200.30) 68 msec 80 msec 92 msec

10 192.150.47.2 88 msec 68 msec 68 msec

11 www.cisco.com (198.133.219.25) 92 msec 72 msec 68 msec
```

An interesting thing to note about the extended trace option is that it is initiated the same way as the extended ping. This means that if you enter only the command without the destination host name or IP address, you will be dropped into extended mode. An additional similarity between the trace and the ping is the ability in both to change the source, as you'll see in the case study at the end of this chapter. The ability to change the maximum time to live value enables you to extend the number hops before the eventual time out. The output of the extended trace does not vary from trace to extended trace.

Useful Debug Commands for IP

Debug commands can be invaluable tools to help you determine exactly what is going on in the router and what traffic is passing through the interfaces. It is very important to note that you should only use the debug commands to isolate problems or diagnose error messages for a short period of time. Debug should not be used to monitor normal network traffic. Extra special consideration should be taken when you are debugging in a production environment. Some of the debug commands demand an exceptional amount of processing power.

> **WARNING**   The improper use of debug commands on production routers can be critical, causing serious performance degradation and, possibly, connection loss.

The cycles required to debug can interfere with the user data traffic passing through the router. This can cause a serious degradation in performance, perhaps even to the point of a loss in connectivity. It is preferable to debug remotely from a Telnet session. By utilizing a Telnet session, you avoid the character-by-character processor interrupts that are generated by allowing the output to be sent to the console.

Router Configuration

PART 3

TIP Remember that of you issue a debug from a Telnet session the output will still be sent to the console by default. You must issue the exec command `terminal monitor` to change the debug output to the Telnet session.

Depending on the IOS version and feature set in your router you may find many different varieties of debug commands. Following is a listing of the possible debug commands from a 2501 router with IOS version 11.2, Release 14:

```
Router1#debug IP ?
  bgp      BGP information
  cache    IP cache operations
  cgmp     CGMP protocol activity
  dvmrp    DVMRP protocol activity
  egp      EGP information
  eigrp    IP-EIGRP information
  error    IP error debugging
  ftp      FTP dialogue
  http     HTTP connections
  icmp     ICMP transactions
  igmp     IGMP protocol activity
  igrp     IGRP information
  mcache   IP multicast cache operations
  mobile   Mobility protocols
  mpacket  IP multicast packet debugging
  mrouting IP multicast routing table activity
  nat      NAT events
  ospf     OSPF information
  packet   General IP debugging and IPSO security transactions
  peer     IP peer address activity
  pim      PIM protocol activity
  policy   Policy routing
  rip      RIP protocol transactions
  routing  Routing table events
```

```
rsvp      RSVP protocol activity
sd        Session Directory (SD)
security IP security options
tcp       TCP information
udp       UDP based transactions
```

As you can see, there are many categories available to you. As you are able to narrow down the problems further, you will be able to get more specific with the debug commands, making the output more valuable.

There are many options for the debug output. Debug output can be sent to the router buffers for later view. The buffer is circular, so new messages overwrite the old, but can consume valuable router memory and is not the method of choice. It is also possible to send the data to a log file by setting up a *syslog* server and pointing the debug data to it. The debug data can then be stored for review or archived for a point of reference.

> **NOTE**   For more detailed information on debug commands, consult the "Cisco Debug Command Reference" available on the Cisco Web site.

Debug IP Packet

The debug IP packet command is a very useful and, at the same time, *dangerous* command. It is quite possibly the most resource-intensive of the debug commands. It, however, can be extremely useful to find what is and is not working on the router. The debug IP packet command is the catch-all of the debug commands for IP. All IP traffic is recorded when this command is implemented.

> **WARNING**   It could almost be said that the debug IP packet command should never be used in a production environment.

In the following example, a simple ping has been executed to the www.cisco.com Web site. The pings have all come back successful, and with the debug IP packet on, we are able to see the echo request and reply packets.

```
NashvilleHQ1#debug ip packet
IP packet debugging is on IP packet debugging is on
NashvilleHQ1#
NashvilleHQ1#ping www.cisco.com
Type escape sequence to abort.
```

```
Sending 5, 100-byte ICMP Echos to 198.133.219.25, timeout is 2 seconds:
!!!!!
Success rate is 100 percent (5/5), round-trip min/avg/max = 72/73/80 ms
NashvilleHQ1#
IP: s=149.166.6.101 (local), d=198.133.219.25 (Ethernet0), len 100, sending
IP: s=198.133.219.25 (Ethernet0), d=149.166.6.101 (Ethernet0), len 100, rcvd 3
ICMP: echo reply rcvd, src 198.133.219.25, dst 149.166.6.101
IP: s=149.166.6.101 (local), d=198.133.219.25 (Ethernet0), len 100, sending
IP: s=198.133.219.25 (Ethernet0), d=149.166.6.101 (Ethernet0), len 100, rcvd 3
ICMP: echo reply rcvd, src 198.133.219.25, dst 149.166.6.101
IP: s=149.166.6.101 (local), d=198.133.219.25 (Ethernet0), len 100, sending
IP: s=198.133.219.25 (Ethernet0), d=149.166.6.101 (Ethernet0), len 100, rcvd 3
ICMP: echo reply rcvd, src 198.133.219.25, dst 149.166.6.101
IP: s=149.166.6.101 (local), d=198.133.219.25 (Ethernet0), len 100, sending
IP: s=198.133.219.25 (Ethernet0), d=149.166.6.101 (Ethernet0), len 100, rcvd 3
ICMP: echo reply rcvd, src 198.133.219.25, dst 149.166.6.101
IP: s=149.166.6.101 (local), d=198.133.219.25 (Ethernet0), len 100, sending
IP: s=198.133.219.25 (Ethernet0), d=149.166.6.101 (Ethernet0), len 100, rcvd 3
ICMP: echo reply rcvd, src 198.133.219.25, dst 149.166.6.101
IP: s=10.2.2.2 (local), d=10.2.2.5 (Ethernet0), len 41, sending
```

Much helpful information is presented in the output. The line heading starts with the protocol type. All outgoing packets will reflect only IP. Incoming packets, however, are a little more informative. In this example, the incoming packet type is ICMP echo reply, or ping response, which may show up as an echo reply.

The source address tells us the IP address that the data is using as the source. There is a source address issue in the extended ping case study at the end of this chapter. In the case study, you will see that a debug of the IP packets would have revealed the problem right away. We should also bring attention to the difference in the source address for the echo send and the echo reply.

The destination address tells us where the packets are going. Again notice the difference between the echo send and echo reply addresses. Additionally, you may see a debug output for a broadcast packet with a destination of 255.255.255.255 that looks like this:

```
IP: s=0.0.0.0 (Ethernet0), d=255.255.255.255, len 328, rcvd 2
```

Debug IP ICMP

Most of the time when you want to isolate errors and find problems you will want to be more specific. The debug ip icmp command is a prime example of that. In the previous example a ping command was issued so that we could see the packets go in and out of the router. This is a lab router, so we were able to allow only the ping traffic to get through. In a production environment, you may not be that fortunate. Let's say, for instance that you want to test the same ping but cannot afford the processing cycles of debugging all of the packets passing through the router. It would be beneficial to use the debug ip icmp command to see only the echo traffic. Notice that the following output lists only the traffic with the heading ICMP.

```
NashvilleHQ1#debug ip icmp
ICMP packet debugging is on
NashvilleHQ1#ping www.cisco.com

Type escape sequence to abort.
Sending 5, 100-byte ICMP Echos to 198.133.219.25, timeout is 2 seconds:
!!!!!
Success rate is 100 percent (5/5), round-trip min/avg/max = 68/72/84 ms
NashvilleHQ1#
ICMP: echo reply rcvd, src 198.133.219.25, dst 129.166.6.101
ICMP: echo reply rcvd, src 198.133.219.25, dst 129.166.6.101
ICMP: echo reply rcvd, src 198.133.219.25, dst 129.166.6.101
ICMP: echo reply rcvd, src 198.133.219.25, dst 129.166.6.101
ICMP: echo reply rcvd, src 198.133.219.25, dst 129.166.6.101
```

Debug IP UDP

As stated previously, the more specific you can be when using debug commands, the more valuable the data will be to you. Using the debug ip udp command can be useful for tracking data that is UDP based, such as DNS, TFTP, NTP, SNMP, and others. If UDP debugging is enabled and a DNS request is made, the output may look like this:

```
NashvilleHQ1#ping www.novell.com
Translating "www.novell.com"...domain server (134.68.7.4) [OK]
```

Router Configuration

PART 3

```
Type escape sequence to abort.
Sending 5, 100-byte ICMP Echos to 192.233.80.5, timeout is 2 seconds:
!!!!!
Success rate is 100 percent (5/5), round-trip min/avg/max = 40/43/48 ms
NashvilleHQ1#
```

UDP: sent src=149.166.6.101(4589), dst=134.68.7.4(53), length=60

UDP: rcvd src=134.68.7.4(53), dst=149.166.6.101(4589), length=227

To retain consistency with the other debug outputs, the protocol type is listed first. This output was received from a source address and port as well as a destination address and port. The predefined port for DNS is 53. Port 4589 is the response port that is set up dynamically and will vary for each connection. It may also be interesting to note the length of each of the packets. The DNS request packet is only 60 bytes in length. The reply packet is 227 bytes in length, as it must also carry the name.

Changing Your IP Addressing Scheme

In this day and age, companies seem to be merging, acquiring, and gobbling each other up at a phenomenal rate. All this activity can play havoc for network managers. Networks overall are personality-oriented, because if you give the exact same scenario to 30 people, you will very likely come up with 30 different solutions. One of the biggest variables in network designing is IP addressing. For a private network, you may see a knowledgeable designer use the proper private addressing scheme, or you may see someone not so knowledgeable at another company use a number based on their kid's birthday or who knows what. If these two companies merged, the first task at hand would be to make the networks talk to each other, which would be difficult given the inconsistent skill levels of their designers. One possible solution might be to use an NAT translation. In a permanent situation, however, you will want your network addressing to be consistent throughout. The remaining sections in this chapter will guide you through that process.

Deciding on IP Addresses

If you are connected to the Internet, not a lot of choice is involved in what IP addresses to use. The question becomes a matter of security: what do you want exposed, and what needs to remain private? This situation is a design and security issue and beyond the scope of what we are trying to accomplish here, which is a marriage of two different IP address schemes into a single, consistent design. TCP/IP addressing and network design has been covered in a previous chapter; thus, those topics will not be repeated here. We will focus instead on the implementation details.

Secondary IP Addresses

It is permissible to use two different IP addresses on a single interface while you are in the process of changing the IP addresses. Routers are often deployed in such a switched topology when traffic needs to jump from VLAN to VLAN. This is known as the "router on a stick." Traffic will pass in on one interface, go through the decision process, and pass back out on the same interface. This is the same principle we are trying to accomplish with the IP address changeover. In a well designed network, VLAN to VLAN routing is accomplished with subinterfaces. We should point out that secondary interfaces are a work-around, not a design guideline.

In Figure 10.3, there are two networks: 10.19.17.0 and 132.147.170.0. Each of these networks has several hosts that talk to each other on their respective networks but cannot talk to the other network. The solution is to place both IP addresses on the Ethernet 0 (e0) interface of the router. This will allow the router to "see" both networks.

Figure 10.3   An example of when a network might need a secondary IP address configured on the router.

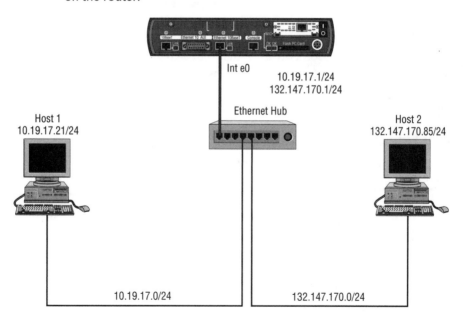

Int e0
10.19.17.1/24
132.147.170.1/24

Host 1
10.19.17.21/24

Ethernet Hub

Host 2
132.147.170.85/24

10.19.17.0/24   132.147.170.0/24

Distance-vector routing protocols such as RIP, IGRP, and EIGRP sometimes treat secondary addresses differently when sending routing updates. This is the issue of split horizon, which is enabled by default on all interfaces. An interface configured with secondary IP addresses might not be sourced by every secondary address. Only routing update

Router Configuration

PART 3

is sourced per network number. The solution for our example is to disable split horizon for the e0 interface. Depending on the routing protocol, the command syntaxes vary:

RIP   `no ip split-horizon`

IGRP   `no ip split-horizon`

EIGRP   `no IP split-horizon EIGRP` *`<autonomous-system number>`*

WARNING   Be careful when disabling split horizon on an interface. Be very deliberate in making sure that you are not opening up a can of worms, such as routing loops.

Setting Up a Simple Statically Routed Environment

Chances are that if you have a router and you are reading this book, you have the need to get traffic from one network to another network. If you have multiple networks and multiple routers, you are going to need some method of path determination. On most large networks, routing protocols are used, as covered in other chapters. This is by far the way of choice for large networks, but there is an occasional exception. Static routing is the least complicated way to determine a path and is also the most efficient, because static routing does not use any bandwidth.

Why Use Static Routing?

There are a few instances where static routing may be the method of choice. For example, suppose you have a hub-and-spoke environment with only the one hub router and, let's say, five spoke routers, and the bandwidth needs for your data are minimal, so you are dealing with 56K leased lines. A single static route out of each of the spoke routes to the hub, and vice versa, would preclude the need to pass any routing protocol traffic, thereby leaving the lines available for data.

The configuration in Figure 10.4 example would consist of five static routes at the hub location and a single static route at each of the spokes.

Figure 10.4   Hub-and-spoke topology

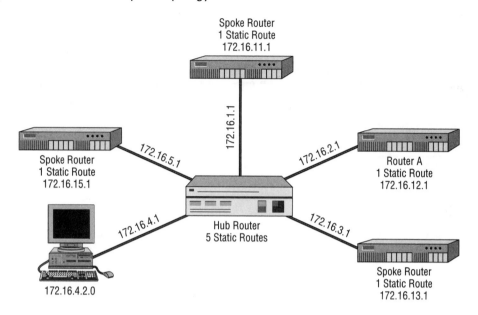

An example of a static route out of router A may look like this:

```
#ip route 172.16.4.0 255.255.255.0 172.16.2.1
```

The command breaks down as follows into four parts. The first part is the command itself: **ip route**. The second part is the destination IP address, or "where I want to go": 172.16.12.0. The third part is the subnet mask for the destination: 255.255.255.0. The fourth part is the next-hop address, 172.16.2.1, which could be called the "which direction address."

Most likely, the static routes configured on the spokes would be set up as default routes. A default route would be used as a path of last resort. If the router looks in its table and has no possible path to the intended destination, then it will attempt to send the traffic out the default route. Since our example only has a single entry and exit point, this would be an appropriate configuration. An example configuration of a default route should look like this:

```
#ip route 0.0.0.0 0.0.0.0 172.16.2.1
```

The breakdown of this address is no different than the previous. It is still 1) command 2) destination address 3) mask and 4) next-hop address. The difference, and what makes it a default route, is the use of "quad zeros" for both the address and the mask. This says to the router that any packet with a source address for which it does not have a path it should send to the next-hop address 172.16.2.1.

Advanced Static Routing for Route Backup

Often in a mission critical environment, you may have the need for a circuit to be up *all the time*. As we all know, circuits will fail, so it is good to have a backup plan. Static routes can be used to force traffic down a secondary path in the event of a failure. In Figure 10.5, you can see plainly that the best possible path for host A to communicate with host B is over the 172.16.14.0 network.

In a statically routed environment that may look like this:

```
#ip route 172.16.11.0 255.255.255.0 172.16.14.1
```

Figure 10.5 When static routing may be used

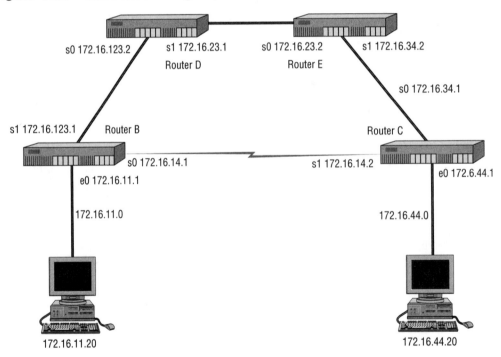

172.16.11.0 is the location the host network to which you want to get, and 172.16.14.1 is the next hop out of router C to router B. If the link between these two fails, all communication between these two hosts will be cut off. A solution for such a problem would be to install a second static route with an increased administrative distance for the less preferred route. The administrative distance for a route adds a weight value to allow more than one path to a destination to exist, but it allows only one used at a time. The lowest administrative distance wins the battle.

Our back-up solution, with an administrative distance set to 20, for the less preferred route through router E may look like this:

```
#ip route 172.16.11.0 255.255.255.0 172.16.14.1
#ip route 172.16.11.0 255.255.255.0 172.16.34.2 20
```

NOTE   The number 20 was randomly picked. Any number higher than zero would work in this situation.

WARNING   This backup scenario assumes that router E has knowledge of how to get to the 172.16.11.0 network.

A static route may also be listed with a next-hop interface rather than a next-hop address. Using an interface relieves the requirement that the next-hop address be reachable. In our example, the s1 interface is the closest and, consequently, the shortest path, so our command would look like this:

```
#ip route 172.16.11.0 255.255.255.0 s1
```

The difference in using the interface or the next-hop address is in how the administrative distance is handled.

- If only the interface is used, then the router does not consider itself in the distance calculation, so the administrative distance is defaulted to 0.
- If a next-hop address is used, then that hop is considered in the calculation, and the administrative distance defaults to 1

Knowing this, another possible alternative would be to use the interface number for the primary and a next-hop address for the secondary:

```
#ip route 172.16.11.0 255.255.255.0 s1
#ip route 172.16.11.0 255.255.255.0 172.16.34.2
```

DHCP in a Routed Environment

As popular and almost essential as Dynamic Host Configuration Protocol (DHCP) is in networking today, it is appropriate to discuss it here. By default, all Cisco routers will *not* pass broadcast traffic over its interfaces. Since DHCP is UDP-broadcast based, having a DHCP server on one side of the router and a series of hosts on the other side of the router that need to get their addresses from this server is going to require some attention.

First, we must enable the router to forward these UDP broadcasts. You can enable the forwarding feature by using the `ip forward-protocol` *<protocol type>* global configuration command, as follows:

```
#ip forward-protocol udp 67
```

The udp keyword of this command will enable several protocols by default, some of which are TFTP, DNS, Time service, NetBIOS Name Server, NetBIOS Datagram Server, and BootP (DHCP). If we wish to only forward the DHCP packets, we would additionally need to add the keyword to specify only the DHCP port number 67.

You must now tell the router which interfaces you wish to forward to and from. This is accomplished with the `ip helper-address` *<address>* interface configuration command:

```
#ip helper-address 172.16.41.1
```

TIP   If required by your environment, you can use more than one helper address per interface to point to multiple DHCP servers.

Extended Ping

An extended ping can be useful in the case of BGP routing. Let's say that your router (router A) is attached to the outside world and is running BGP with an inside Ethernet address of 172.16.20.1 and outside serial address of 172.16.10.1. You want to advertise *only* your inside network to the rest of the world and you do so by placing a network statement under the BGP configuration. (See BGP configuration for details).

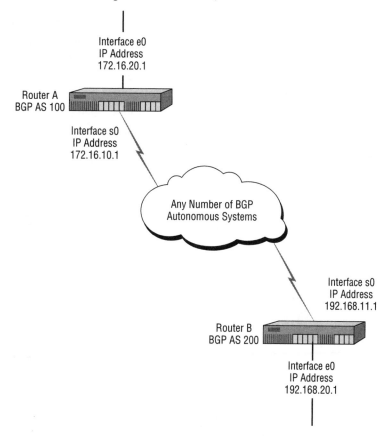

Now the neighboring BGP communities are able to see *only* your inside network. You can successfully see your BGP neighbors and they can see your network. Everything is working just fine. Just for kicks and giggles one day you decide to try a ping test from the router to one of your known BGP neighbors.

```
RouterA#ping 192.168.20.1
```

```
Type escape sequence to abort.
Sending 5, 100-byte ICMP Echos to 192.168.20.1, timeout is 2 seconds:
```

The ping fails. You panic! The network is down! You check the BGP neighbors and everything is still there. You check from your workstation and everything is still working. What is going on? The rule is that a ping will go out the closest interface. In our example, the ping would naturally go out of the Serial 0 interface of router A destined for router B. The source address of our sample ping packet will take on the address of Serial 0 172.16.10.1. The echo request packet makes it to router B just fine. *But when router B attempts the echo reply to the source 172.16.10.1, it has no route back.* You see, router B does not have an entry for the 172.16.10.0 network in its routing table. When the BGP was configured, you only allowed the inside network 172.16.20.0 to be advertised...*not the outside network.* Your ping test from the router was not testing from host network to host network. It was, in fact, testing from the outside address of router A to the inside of router B. Not the right kind of test for this situation.

The correct way to test the actual end to end connectivity is to do an extended ping as follows:

```
RouterA#ping
Protocol [ip]:
Target IP address: 192.168.20.1
Repeat count [5]:
Datagram size [100]:
Timeout in seconds [2]:
Extended commands [n]: y
Source address or interface:172.16.20.1
Type of service [0]:
Set DF bit in IP header? [no]:
Validate reply data? [no]:
Data pattern [0xABCD]:
Loose, Strict, Record, Timestamp, Verbose[none]:
Sweep range of sizes [n]:
Type escape sequence to abort.
Sending 5, 100-byte ICMP Echos to 124.5.191.142, timeout is 2
seconds:
!!!!!
```

By changing the source address to the inside interface of Router A, the ping is successful. Router B knows how to get to the 172.16.20.0 network because it is in its routing table, whereas it did not know how to get to the 172.16.10.0 network. So the network was never actually down.

Implementing New IP Addresses

Much care must be taken when changing IP addresses. The ultimate goal is to make the task as transparent to the users as possible. Let's take the ACME Vacuum Cleaner Company of Walla Walla, Washington. They have a 200-host network running DHCP for all of their users' PCs. They support 7 file servers, some of which have printing services. Third-party print devices provide additional printer services. They have also just been acquired by the ACME Networking Division and have lost a political battle, so they must now change their IP addressing from their current scheme of 132.147.**170**.0 to the newly allocated, legally private address of 10.19.**17**.0. Seems easy enough, and in concept it is quite simple. Executing is another story.

An overview list of the implementation strategy would be as follows:

1. Reduce current lease times on DHCP Servers to 3 hours.

2. Add secondary DHCP scope to reflect new scheme, and test.

3. Add secondary interface addresses on all affected router interfaces.

4. Make necessary changes to static devices, such as file and print servers, etc.

5. Apply secondary DHCP scope as primary.

6. Test user accounts for connectivity to all devices.

The first step would be to back the lease times down for your DHCP servers. When the hosts' leases expire, they will be handed a new lease with the reduced time. Of course, this makes for an inordinate amount of DHCP traffic, but it is temporary and will help things along. Some implementations of DHCP will check the DHCP server for active leases at boot, and if no active lease is found, then a new lease is generated with a new address. If this is the case, then backing down the lease times for the DHCP servers is not necessary. The ACME people are not sure and do not have the benefit of a lab in which to test this, so they are taking this extra precaution.

While we are working on the DHCP server we will need to create the new scope of addresses. Although we are not covering network design here, this is the schema adopted by ACME:

Subnet Number	10.19.17.0
Router Interfaces	10.19.17.1 to 10.19.17.10
File Servers	10.19.17.11 to 10.19.17.20
Printers	10.19.17.21 to 10.19.17.60
Workstations and other hosts	10.19.17.61 to 10.19.17.254

Router Interfaces   These addresses should be reserved only for router interfaces. It is recommended that you start with *n.n.n*.1, where *n* is the network number, and progress upward (i.e. *n.n.n*.2, etc.).

File servers   These addresses should be reserved only for file servers or other serving devices. They will be assigned statically and remain constant for the duration of their existence.

Printers   These addresses should be reserved only for print servers. They will be assigned statically and remain constant for the duration of their existence.

Next, we add secondary interface addresses on all affected router interfaces, allowing the router to see and pass traffic to and from both networks. On the interfaces, you need the ip address 10.19.17.1 255.255.255.0 secondary command. The show run output should look like this:

```
interface Ethernet0
  ip address 132.147.170.253 255.255.255.0
  ip address 10.19.17.1 255.255.255.0 secondary
```

If you are configuring your router from a Telnet session, make absolutely sure that you include the secondary keyword following the IP address. If you forget it, the address that you have configured will take the place of primary, and you will lose your connectivity.

Make sure also that if you are running any routing protocols, you include your newly added networks into their processes. For example, for RIP:

```
#router rip
  Network 10.19.17.0
#interface e0
  ip address 132.147.170.253 255.255.255.0
  ip address 10.19.17.1 255.255.255.0 secondary
  no ip split-horizon
```

Making necessary changes to static devices, such as your file and print servers, can be very cumbersome. Some devices, such as NT servers, will allow you to have multiple IP addresses on a single network interface card, which can certainly ease the transition by allowing a less panicky cutover process.

Once all of the static devices have their new addresses, you are ready to apply as the primary scope what was the new secondary DHCP scope. We would not recommend deleting the old existing scope just yet, to allow for some backout strategy. It is best just to inactivate it, and when all is working under the new addressing scheme, you can go back and delete. Because the ACME staff backed the lease times down a couple of days ago, as the users log in they will face immediate requests for a new addresses. The user will likely never know that there was a problem.

ACME has now reached the moment of truth: testing the user accounts for connectivity to all devices. Because they set forth a well-designed plan and executed it properly, all of the users connected without ever even knowing that their IP address changed, and all of the ACME IT people were able to keep their jobs.

Internet Packet Exchange (IPX)

This chapter discusses some of the advanced topics related to IPX routing and to verifying IPX activity. In this chapter we assume you have been introduced to IPX and are familiar with the basic process for configuring simple IPX routing. If you are new to IPX, we recommend you read the IPX section in Chapter 3 for a brief introduction before reading this chapter.

IPX RIP

When IPX routing is enabled, so is IPX RIP, a version of Routing Information Protocol (RIP) used in Novell NetWare/IPX-routed environments. IPX RIP has some similarities to and differences from IP RIP, which we will discuss in this section.

IPX RIP is a distance-vector protocol like IP RIP. As we learned in Chapter 6, IP RIP uses a simple hop count as a metric. By contrast, IPX RIP uses both a tick count and a hop count as its metrics. A tick is a time value of 55 milliseconds (or 1/18 of a second). A tick is used as the primary metric, and a hop count is used for tiebreakers. By default, a router assigns a tick count of 6 for all serial interfaces and a tick count of 1 for all LAN interfaces. It makes no difference what type of LAN you are using or at what speed the serial interface is operating. Without additional information, the interface will take on one of those defaults. We can change this default behavior using the IPXWAN IOS command. This command gives us the ability to have IPX interrogate a link and figure out a true tick value for an interface. We will learn how to use the IPXWAN command later in this chapter.

NetWare servers as well as Cisco routers propagate IPX RIP updates. NetWare describes these advertisements as *network updates*. These updates have a default update period of every 60 seconds. You may recall that this is also a bit different from IP, which has a 30-second update cycle. Like other distance-vector protocols on Cisco routers, an IPX RIP update is broadcast out of all interfaces with the exception of the interface it was learned on (split horizon).

IPX SAP

NetWare servers advertise their available services using a special protocol called *Service Advertisement Protocol* (SAP). SAP packets contain route information for individual services. A SAP contains enough information to allow a network device to learn the socket address and a metric of a specific service. Clients in a Novell network do not store this information. Clients do, however, frequently need to utilize the information in these SAP tables to access NetWare services. SAP entries are actually stored on NetWare servers and Cisco routers in what we call *SAP tables*.

Much like IPX RIP updates, NetWare servers broadcast these SAP updates every 60 seconds. Cisco routers listen for these SAP updates and store the information in their own SAP tables. As a result, the Cisco routers will be able to propagate these SAPs via a SAP advertisement. The entire SAP table is broadcast every 60 seconds for the benefit of other Cisco routers and NetWare servers.

There are four basic SAP types. They include:

- Type 0x1: General Service Query
- Type 0x2: General Service Response
- Type 0x3: Service Request
- Type 0x4: Service Response

Novell calls the information in a SAP packet an *object type*. These Novell object types are simply numbers that represent services. Although there are many types of services in a NetWare environment, some common numbers (object types) you will see in a SAP include:

- 0x4: File Server

- 0x7: Print Server
- 0x20: NetBIOS
- 0x26b: Time Synchronization Server (NetWare 4.x)
- 0x278: Directory Server (NetWare 4.x)

NOTE For a complete listing of Novell object types, you can access `ftp.isi.edu/in-notes/iana/assignments/novell-sap-numbers`.

Get Nearest Server (GNS)

Since IPX was designed to be a LAN protocol, many aspects of its operation reflect the fact that it was originally designed for use in a server-centric type of network. In earlier NetWare implementations, the availability of network resources completely relied upon the network server being operational. Early NetWare clients had no power on their own. Additionally, there was no concept of a directory tree that allowed multiple servers to work together to provide common network services. Without the NetWare server operational, we basically had no network. Although we don't think this way today, we still have to recognize that IPX is designed around this premise and still has many of the same characteristics it had when it was first developed.

When a NetWare client first initializes, it basically has no networking capabilities. Therefore, it needs a logical connection to a NetWare server. This logical connection is sometimes known as getting "attached." The connection allows the client to utilize all services offered by that server. It also allows the client to utilize the SAP table on the server to obtain services residing on other servers. This logical connection is created using a special SAP we call a *Get Nearest Server (GNS) request.*

It is up to a NetWare server to respond to a GNS request with a service response. In many cases, however, it is common to have clients in one broadcast domain and the server in another. In these cases, the router connecting the broadcast domains initially responds to the GNS for the server. The router will respond with a SAP that will include the exact socket information relating to the server that was requested by the client. The requested server will be whatever server name is specified on the client as a preferred server. It may also be a server that is part of the same tree in a specified preferred tree statement.

During initialization, earlier DOS clients broadcast a service request (SAP type 0x3) for an object type number of 0x4 (file server). If there is a preferred server statement in the clients' configuration, they will send a service request with an object type of 0x4 and include the server's name. If this request fails after a number of attempts, clients will do a general service query (SAP type 0x1) requesting all services available.

Clients using the DOS redirector and Client 32 software are capable of logging into a Net-Ware directory tree. Therefore, they do things just a little differently. They will first broadcast a service request for an object type of 0x278 (directory server). If this fails after a number of attempts, they will try a service request for an object type of 0x4 (file server). If the type 0x4 service request fails after a number of attempts, clients will do a general service query.

Cisco routers can respond to any and all of these queries. If a Cisco router receives a service request for an object type of 0x4 that includes a server name (assuming there is an entry for the server in the SAP table), the router will respond with a specific service response relating to that server. The client will be able to communicate directly with that file server because it now has a socket address. If the client does not identify a particular server, the router will respond with a service response that represents the file server that is closest to the top of the SAP table. The file server closest to the top is the one that was most recently learned. Once a client gets its response, it can start the process it has to go through to establish an attachment to a NetWare server.

Configuring IPX

For the rest of the chapter, all of the following configuration, show, and debug commands are going to be based on the simple IPX network topology displayed in Figure 11.1. The topology includes six networks labeled 1A, 2B, 3C, 4D, 5E and 6F. On network 4D, there are two Novell NetWare servers labeled Server1 and Server2. The networks are interconnected via three routers labeled A, B and C. All of the LAN segments are Ethernet. All point-to-point connections are T1 serial links.

Figure 11.1   A simple IPX network

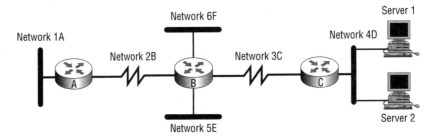

Some of the key issues to keep in mind when configuring IPX include:

- IPX addresses are 80 bits long and represented in hexadecimal.

- IPX network addresses can be up to 32 bits in length.

- The node portion of an IPX address is always 48 bits. On LAN interfaces, the node address is always the MAC address, which is hard-coded in the hardware. Since WAN interfaces do not have a MAC address but still need a 48-bit node address, one of two things may happen: The router will either assign the same MAC address as is assigned to the lowest LAN interface or will rely on an administratively assigned one. On routers with no LAN interfaces, an administrator is required to assign a node address to be used on all WAN type interfaces.

- There are four Ethernet encapsulations that can be used with IPX. They include:

Novell Name	Cisco Name
Ethernet_802.3	novell-ether
Ethernet_802.2	sap
Ethernet_II	arpa
Ethernet_SNAP	snap

- The default encapsulation type for an interface configured with IPX is novell-ether. The default encapsulation for a sub-interface is arpa. Novell servers running NetWare versions 3.11 and earlier default to supporting what Novell calls Ethernet_802.3 and what Cisco calls novell-ether. Novell servers running NetWare versions 3.12 and later default to what Novell calls Ethernet_802.2 and what Cisco calls the SAP encapsulation.

- Unlike IP routing, IPX has to be enabled when configuring IPX. Once enabled, it also enables IPX RIP. The command to enable IPX routing is simply `ipx routing`. This command is issued in global configuration mode.

- Each interface that will be participating in IPX routing will have to be configured with an IPX address and an associated encapsulation type. Since an Ethernet interface can have multiple encapsulation types assigned to it, we have to configure each encapsulation as its own logical network. This means that for every encapsulation we want to communicate with, we will need to assign it a unique IPX network address. We use the interface command `ipx network <network number>` encapsulation `<encapsulation type>`.

When enabling IPX services using the `ipx routing` command, we also have the option to specify what node address will be given to serial interfaces. The actual syntax for the enabling IPX is `ipx routing [optional node address]`. By using the node address option in the `ipx routing` command, we can assign a specific node address to all serial interfaces. The following is an example:

```
RouterA(config)# ipx routing BADD.BEEF.CAFE
```

When configuring a NetWare server, it is always necessary to supply it with an *internal network address*. The internal network address is used to identify a logical internal network. The server uses this logical network for internal routing purposes. The server treats this internal network as just another network. It is even advertised via RIP updates. All SAP advertisements come from the internal network with a node address of 0000.0000.0001.

A NetWare server is actually a software router. It perceives all the sending and receiving of information to and from the server as being routed to and from the server. Acting as a software router, the server can exchange network and service information with other routers on the network. Consequently, a Cisco router can exchange RIP and SAP updates with a NetWare server.

In some cases, as when configuring for NLSP, it is necessary to specify an internal network address on a Cisco router as well. We do so using the `ipx internal-network` command. The following is an example:

```
RouterA(config)#ipx internal-network A00001
```

Here are some additional commands that any administrator may want to be aware of:

`ipx ipxwan`   Rather than relying on the default tick count of a WAN interface, we can have IPX interrogate the link and figure out a more realistic tick value. We do so using the `ipx ipxwan` command. The `ipx ipxwan` command is performed in interface configuration mode. Here is a usage example:

```
Router (config-if)# ipx ipxwan
```

It is worthy to note, however, that the link interrogation only happens during a link change. Therefore, it is recommended that you issue the **shutdown** and **no shutdown** commands on the interface one immediately following the other.

NOTE   An alternative to shutdown and no shutdown is using `ipx down` and `no ipx down`. Convergence is quicker and it only affects IPX on the interface.

`ipx maximum-paths`   By default, IPX does no load sharing. If there are multiple equal-cost paths to a destination, we can instruct IPX to perform round-robin load sharing over the equal-cost paths. We do so by issuing the `ipx` `maximum-paths <1-64>` command. This command is issued in global configuration mode. An example of this command is as follows:

```
Router(config)# ipx maximum-paths 4.
```

This example will allow load sharing over four paths or fewer.

`ipx gns-round-robin`   Rather than have the router respond to service requests with the most recently learned server's information, we can have the router alternate between servers in a round-robin fashion. This is a nice feature because it allows us to spread the load of authenticating clients to more than one server. It does, however, have the unfortunate side effect of load sharing with servers that may not be an equal-cost distance away. We can enable this feature by issuing the global `ipx gns-round-robin` command; for example:

```
Router(config)#ipx  gns-round-robin
```

`ipx route`   As with IP, we can specify static routes for IPX, as well. To do so, we use the global `ipx route <network> <next hop address> <optional ticks> <optional hops>` command. An example is as follows:

```
Router(config)# ipx route 4d 2B.00e0.1454.f180
```

This example statically defines network 4D in the routing table and uses 2B.00e0.1454.f180 as the next hop address.

`ipx delay`   An alternative to using the `IPXWAN` command to change the default tick value on an interface is by statically setting it. We can do this using the `ipx delay <ticks>` command. Each tick is equal to 55 milliseconds. You may issue this command in interface configuration mode for the interface that you want to affect. An example is as follows:

```
Router(config-if)# ipx delay 12
```

The example assigns the interface a tick count of 12.

`ipx default-route`   To be able to forward all packets without an explicit route for them in the routing table, we use the `ipx default-route <network>` command. An example is as follows: `Router(config)#ipx default-route 2b`. In this example, we send all packets that we do not have a specific route for in the direction of network 2b. Of course, the router needs to know how to reach network 2b; there must be a valid entry in the IPX routing table for it.

Router
Configuration

PART 3

NOTE For additional information on IPX-related commands, access the Cisco documentation CD-ROM.

Filtering SAPs

By default, all SAPs are advertised to all routers. In a large internetwork, this can be a big waste of bandwidth. In many cases, there are services that will not be used by users in other parts of your network. For instance, there is no reason for users in Australia to be able to print to a printer located in the United States. There is no reason to advertise a print server to that part of the internetwork. For these cases, we employ SAP filters. A SAP filter is an access-list that can specifically control which SAPs will be filtered and which will be advertised to other routers.

Configuring a SAP filter is a two-part process. First, you must create a SAP filter. Then, you must apply the SAP filter to an interface. The following is description of each.

Creating a SAP Filter

You create a SAP filter like a typical access list. It is entered line by line and interpreted in a top-down process like any access list. The syntax for creating a SAP filter is:

```
access-list <list number> {deny or permit} <network[.node][service
type [server name]]>
```

The *list number* is any number between 1000 and 1999. The *network* portion is the IPX network and optional node address of the network and node we want to filter or permit. The optional *service type* and *server name* allow us to be even more specific in our control. The access-list command is performed in global configuration mode. An example of a SAP filter statement is as follows:

```
access-list 1000 permit 4D.0000.0000.1234 4 FSERVER1
```

In this example, we issued an access-list statement that will be part of access list 1000. We are permitting SAPs from network 4D, from node 0000.0000.1234—as long as it's a type 4 (file server) service, and from a server named FSERVER1. Pretty simple, huh?

The following is a working example of an entire list:

```
!
access-list 1001 permit 4d 4
```

```
access-list 1001 permit 4d 7
access-list 1001 permit -1 26b
access-list 1001 permit -1 278
!
```

Here, we have permitted file and print services (type 4 & 7) from network 4D, and time synchronization and directory services (26b & 278) from any network. The –1 is a unique way of representing all networks. All other SAPs will be denied. Without a SAP filter applied to an interface, all SAPs will be advertised by default. Once a SAP filter is applied, only SAPs that are explicitly permitted in the list will indeed be permitted. All other SAPs will be denied.

We chose this as an example because it is fairly realistic. You should be very careful when restricting object types 4, 26b, and 278, especially in a NetWare 4 or later environment. You could potentially keep servers from synchronizing and possibly keep clients from getting access to necessary services.

Applying a SAP Filter

We create a SAP filter in global configuration mode. But just creating it doesn't affect the flow of SAPs coming in and out of your routers. Once a SAP filter is created, it must be applied to an interface in order to take effect. There are two ways to apply a SAP filter: as an input-SAP-filter or an output-SAP-filter. If applied as an input-SAP-filter, a list will affect SAPs coming into the router. As such it also affects the contents of the SAP table on the router and consequently the SAPs advertised. If applied as an output-SAP-filter, a list will affect SAPs being advertised out of the router. Output-SAP-filters are more appropriate when you want to advertise some SAPs out of some interfaces and different SAPs out of others.

The commands used to apply SAP filters to an interface are `ipx input-sap-filter` `<list number>` and `ipx output-sap-filter <list number>`. The list number corresponds with the number used in the access-list you created. These commands are issued in interface configuration mode. Following is a working example where we apply the list we created earlier:

```
!
access-list 1001 permit 4d 4
access-list 1001 permit 4d 7
access-list 1001 permit -1 26b
access-list 1001 permit -1 278
```

Router Configuration

PART 3

```
!
interface serial 0
  ipx input-sap-filter 1001
!
```

In this example, we will only allow type 4 and 7 services from network 4D and any type 26b and 278 to enter our router via serial 0.

Verifying IPX Operation

We know that just configuring IPX is never enough. We have to be able to verify IPX configurations, as well. Cisco provides us with a number of good **show** and **debug** commands to help us verify all kinds of IPX activity. Some of the important ones include:

- show ipx route
- show ipx interface
- show ipx traffic
- show ipx servers
- show ipx access-list
- ping ipx
- trace
- debug ipx routing activity
- debug ipx sap activity
- debug ipx packet

The show ipx route Command

Cisco routers are capable of routing multiple routed protocols simultaneously. We call this concept "ships-in-the-night" routing. Each protocol is treated autonomously and does not interfere with the others. It's like two ships passing in the night. Each ship does not know about the other and does not care. Consequently, for each routed protocol, a Cisco router maintains a separate routing table. To view the routing table for the IPX service, we use the command **show ipx route**. The following is an example output:

```
RouterA#show ipx route
Codes: C - Connected primary network,    c - Connected secondary network
       S - Static, F - Floating static, L - Local (internal), W - IPXWAN
```

```
          R - RIP, E - EIGRP, N - NLSP, X - External, A - Aggregate
          s - seconds, u - uses


7 Total IPX routes. Up to 1 parallel paths and 16 hops allowed.


No default route known.


L       A00001 is the internal network
C          1A (NOVELL-ETHER),   Et0
C          2B (HDLC),           Se0
R          3C [07/01] via       2B.00e0.1454.f180,    32s, Se0
R          4D [13/02] via       2B.00e0.1454.f180,    33s, Se0
R          5E [07/01] via       2B.00e0.1454.f180,    33s, Se0
R          6F [07/01] via       2B.00e0.1454.f180,    33s, Se0
```

The IPX routing table is one of the first places we typically look when troubleshooting IPX-related routing problems. If a network is not in the routing table, then a router can't route IPX packets to it. Let's examine an entry in our output:

```
R          3C [07/01] via       2B.00e0.1454.f180,    32s, Se0
```

This entry is an example of a typical IPX RIP learned route. We know it is learned via RIP because it starts with an R (see the Codes chart at the top of the output). The entry is for IPX network 3C. The network is seven ticks and one hop away ([07/01]). The next hop IPX address is 2B.00e0.1454.f180. The invalid timer on that entry is 32 seconds, and the entry was learned from the interface Serial 0.

The show ipx interface Command

Another helpful command is show ipx interface. Using this command we can learn a great deal about how IPX is configured. The following is an example:

```
RouterA#show ipx interface Ethernet 0
Ethernet0 is up, line protocol is up
   IPX address is 1A.00e0.1454.cf60, NOVELL-ETHER [up]
   Delay of this IPX network, in ticks is 1 throughput 0 link delay 0
```

```
IPXWAN processing not enabled on this interface.
IPX SAP update interval is 1 minute(s)
IPX type 20 propagation packet forwarding is disabled
Incoming access list is not set
Outgoing access list is not set
IPX helper access list is not set
SAP GNS processing enabled, delay 0 ms, output filter list is not set
SAP Input filter list is not set
SAP Output filter list is not set
SAP Router filter list is not set
Input filter list is not set
Output filter list is not set
Router filter list is not set
Netbios Input host access list is not set
Netbios Input bytes access list is not set
Netbios Output host access list is not set
Netbios Output bytes access list is not set
Updates each 60 seconds, aging multiples RIP: 3 SAP: 3
SAP interpacket delay is 55 ms, maximum size is 480 bytes
RIP interpacket delay is 55 ms, maximum size is 432 bytes
IPX accounting is disabled
IPX fast switching is configured (enabled)
RIP packets received 0, RIP packets sent 15
SAP packets received 0, SAP packets sent 1
```

By issuing the show ipx interface Ethernet 0 command, we learned a lot about how Ethernet 0 is configured for IPX. For instance, in our display we learn that Ethernet 0 is assigned the IPX address of 1A.00e0.1454.cf60 and the encapsulation type of novell-ether. Since it is an Ethernet interface, it is assigned a tick count of 1. IPXWAN is not enabled. There are no packet filters, SAP filters, or network filters applied. SAP and RIP updates are exchanged in one-minute intervals. Rather than trying to analyze the running configuration, you can use the show ipx interface command and really know how it's configured.

The show ipx traffic Command

Another very helpful show command is show ipx traffic, which allows us to view how many IPX packets the router has handled. It divides the packet counts according to IPX packet type. The following is an example:

```
RouterA#show ipx traffic
System Traffic for 0.0000.0000.0001 System-Name: RouterA
Rcvd:   18 total, 2 format errors, 0 checksum errors, 0 bad hop count,
        2 packets pitched, 16 local destination, 0 multicast
Bcast:  15 received, 30 sent
Sent:   31 generated, 0 forwarded
        0 encapsulation failed, 0 no route
SAP:    2 SAP requests, 0 SAP replies, 0 servers
        0 SAP Nearest Name requests, 0 replies
        0 SAP General Name requests, 0 replies
        0 SAP advertisements received, 0 sent
        0 SAP flash updates sent, 0 SAP format errors
RIP:    1 RIP requests, 0 RIP replies, 6 routes
        13 RIP advertisements received, 19 sent
        6 RIP flash updates sent, 0 RIP format errors
Echo:   Rcvd 0 requests, 0 replies
        Sent 0 requests, 0 replies
        0 unknown: 0 no socket, 0 filtered, 0 no helper
        0 SAPs throttled, freed NDB len 0
Watchdog:
        0 packets received, 0 replies spoofed
Queue lengths:
        IPX input: 0, SAP 0, RIP 0, GNS 0
        SAP throttling length: 0/(no limit), 0 nets pending lost
route reply
        Delayed process creation: 0
```

Router
Configuration

PART 3

```
EIGRP:  Total received 0, sent 0

        Updates received 0, sent 0

        Queries received 0, sent 0

        Replies received 0, sent 0

        SAPs received 0, sent 0

NLSP:   Level-1 Hellos received 0, sent 0

        PTP Hello received 0, sent 0

        Level-1 LSPs received 0, sent 0

        LSP Retransmissions: 0

        LSP checksum errors received: 0

        LSP HT=0 checksum errors received: 0

        Level-1 CSNPs received 0, sent 0

        Level-1 PSNPs received 0, sent 0

        Level-1 DR Elections: 0

        Level-1 SPF Calculations: 0

        Level-1 Partial Route Calculations: 0
```

NOTE The show ipx traffic command can be helpful in many cases of troubleshooting performance-related problems. It is important to keep in mind that the counters increase on a continuous basis. To troubleshoot a problem using these counters, you may want to reset the values to zero and monitor them while the problem is occurring. The command to do so is clear counters.

The show ipx servers Command

To view the SAP table on the router, you can issue the show ipx servers command. In the example below, we have four entries in our SAP table. Two are type 4 (file servers), and the other two are type 7 (print servers). Notice that all of the services come from the servers on network 4D. It lists the server names where the services reside. It also lists the sockets used to access those services. All services from our perspective are 13 ticks and two hops away (Route =13/02). As far as the originating server is concerned, all SAPs are routed from the server's configured internal network. The Hops value represents how many hops, from the server's perspective, the SAP has traveled. The Hops value will normally be one hop higher than the hop count in the Route value. So, in this case, all SAPs have a Hops value of 3. And the SAPs were learned about via Serial 0 (Se0). The SAP table stores the interface that the SAP was learned on because split horizon is also applied when router sends SAP updates.

```
RouterA#show ipx servers
Codes: S - Static, P - Periodic, E - EIGRP, N - NLSP, H - Holddown,
       + = detail
4 Total IPX Servers


Table ordering is based on routing and server info
```

	Type	Name	Net	Address	Port	Route	Hops	Itf
P	4	FSERVER1	4D.0000.0000.1234:0471			13/02	3	Se0
P	4	FSERVER2	4D.0000.0000.4321:0471			13/02	3	Se0
P	7	FSERVER1	4D.0000.0000.1234:0471			13/02	3	Se0
P	7	FSERVER2	4D.0000.0000.4321:0471			13/02	3	Se0

The show ipx access-list Command

You can view all IPX access lists, including SAP filters created on a router. To do so we use the show ipx access-list command. The following is an example:

```
RouterA# show ipx access-list


IPX sap access list 1001
  permit 4D 4
  permit 4D 7
  permit FFFFFFFF
  permit FFFFFFFF
```

NOTE Both the show access-list and show ipx access-list 1001 commands would have shown us the same thing in the previous example. Show access-lists displays all access lists regardless of protocol. Show ipx access-list 1001 only displays that specific access list.

Other show ipx Command

You can get an idea of the other IPX show commands by issuing the show ipx ? command. The following is an example output:

```
RouterA#show ipx ?
   access-list  IPX access lists
   accounting   The active IPX accounting database
   cache        IPX fast-switching cache
   compression  IPX compression information
   eigrp        IPX EIGRP show commands
   interface    IPX interface status and configuration
   nasi         Netware Asynchronous Services Interface status
   nhrp         NHRP information
   nlsp         Show NLSP information
   route        IPX routing table
   servers      SAP servers
   spx-protocol Sequenced Packet Exchange protocol status
   spx-spoof    SPX Spoofing table
   traffic      IPX protocol statistics
```

The ping ipx Command

To test for IPX connectivity, we can use the ping ipx command. Very much like the IP ping command, this command sends five IPX echo packets to another IPX router and expects a response for each packet sent. An example output of this command is as follows:

```
RouterA# ping ipx 2B.00e0.1454.f180


Type escape sequence to abort.
Sending 5, 100-byte IPX cisco Echoes to 2B.00e0.1454.f180, timeout is
2 seconds:
!!!!!
Success rate is 100 percent (5/5), round-trip min/avg/max = 28/28/32 ms
```

Each favorable response will generate an exclamation point (!) as an output. Other outputs you may encounter are as follows:

.   A period indicates the ping timed out while waiting for a reply.

U   A destination unreachable error was received.

C   Congestion was experienced.

I   A user has interrupted the test.

?   The ping was of an unknown packet type.

&   The packet lifetime exceeded.

You will notice the `ping ipx` command is used with a full IPX address as a parameter. This tends to be a bit tedious when testing for IPX connectivity. We do have a shortcut, though. Rather than using the entire IPX network and node to test for connectivity, you can specify the network address along with a node address of ffff.ffff.ffff (all ones). An all-ones broadcast on the network you want to test will result in some reply. In most cases we really don't care which device answers, only that something from the destination network answers. Remember, routers route to wires, not hosts. If the packet makes it to the destination wire, the router has done its job. We really don't care which device on that wire responds. The following is an example of an IPX ping:

```
RouterA#ping ipx 4d.ffff.ffff.ffff


Type escape sequence to abort.
Sending 5, 100-byte IPX cisco Echoes to 3C.ffff.ffff.ffff, timeout is
2 seconds:
!!!!!
Success rate is 100 percent (5/5), round-trip min/avg/max = 56/56/60 ms
```

The trace ipx Command

A new feature available in IOS version 12.0 is the ability to do a trace using IPX. You may already know how useful the IP `trace` command is. We can now use it in an IPX environment, as well.

```
RouterA# trace ipx  2B.00e0.1454.f180
   Type escape sequence to abort.
```

```
Tracing the route to 2B.00e0.1454.f180

0 8 msec 8 msec 8 msec
```

The debug ipx Commands

We can view real-time IPX activities as they are happening, just as we can with many Cisco features. If you want you can use the debug ipx network activity and debug ipx sap activity commands to monitor RIP and SAP updates respectively. The following is an output of debug ipx routing activity:

```
RouterA#debug ipx routing activity

IPX routing debugging is on


RouterA# clear ipx route *

RouterA#

IPXRIP: Deleting network 3C FFFFFFFF in table-wide purge

IPXRIP: Marking network 3C FFFFFFFF for Flash Update

IPXRIP: Deleting network 4D FFFFFFFF in table-wide purge

IPXRIP: Marking network 4D FFFFFFFF for Flash Update

IPXRIP: Deleting network 5E FFFFFFFF in table-wide purge

IPXRIP: Marking network 5E FFFFFFFF for Flash Update

IPXRIP: Deleting network 6F FFFFFFFF in table-wide purge

IPXRIP: Marking network 6F FFFFFFFF for Flash Update

IPXRIP: General Query src=1A.00e0.1454.cf60, dst=1A.ffff.ffff.ffff,
        packet sent

IPXRIP: General Query src=2B.00e0.1454.cf60, dst=2B.ffff.ffff.ffff,
        packet sent

IPXRIP: positing flash update to 1A.ffff.ffff.ffff via Ethernet0
        (broadcast)

IPXRIP: positing flash update to 2B.ffff.ffff.ffff via Serial0
        (broadcast)

IPXRIP: update from 2B.00e0.1454.f180

IPXRIP: create route to 6F FFFFFFFF via 00e0.1454.f180, delay 7, hops 1

IPXRIP: Marking network 6F FFFFFFFF for Flash Update

    6F in 1 hops, delay 7
```

```
IPXRIP: create route to 5E FFFFFFFF via 00e0.1454.f180, delay 7, hops 1

IPXRIP: Marking network 5E FFFFFFFF for Flash Update

    5E in 1 hops, delay 7

IPXRIP: create route to 4D FFFFFFFF via 00e0.1454.f180, delay 13,
        hops 2

IPXRIP: Marking network 4D FFFFFFFF for Flash Update

    4D in 2 hops, delay 13

IPXRIP: create route to 3C FFFFFFFF via 00e0.1454.f180, delay 7, hops 1

IPXRIP: Marking network 3C FFFFFFFF for Flash Update

    3C in 1 hops, delay 7

IPXRIP: positing flash update to 1A.ffff.ffff.ffff via Ethernet0
        (broadcast)

IPXRIP: positing flash update to 2B.ffff.ffff.ffff via Serial0
        (broadcast)

IPXRIP: src=1A.00e0.1454.cf60, dst=1A.ffff.ffff.ffff, packet sent

    network 3C, hops 2,  delay 8

    network 4D, hops 3,  delay 14

    network 5E, hops 2,  delay 8

    network 6F, hops 2,  delay 8

IPXRIP: suppressing null update to 2B.ffff.ffff.ffff

IPXRIP: suppressing null update to 1A.ffff.ffff.ffff

IPXRIP: suppressing null update to 2B.ffff.ffff.ffff


RouterA#u all

All possible debugging has been turned off


depub ipx sap activity
```

RouterA#debug ipx sap activity
```
IPX service debugging is on


RouterA#clear ipx route *
```

```
RouterA#
IPXSAP: General Query src=1A.00e0.1454.cf60, dst=1A.ffff.ffff.ffff,
        packet sent
IPXSAP: General Query src=2B.00e0.1454.cf60, dst=2B.ffff.ffff.ffff,
        packet sent
IPXSAP: positing update to 1A.ffff.ffff.ffff via Ethernet0
        (broadcast) (flash)
IPXSAP: positing update to 2B.ffff.ffff.ffff via Serial0 (broadcast)
        (flash)
IPXSAP: Update type 0x2 len 288 src:1A.00e0.1454.cf60
        dest:1A.ffff.ffff.ffff(452)
 type 0x4, "FSERVER1", 4D.0000.0000.1234(471), 16 hops
 type 0x4, "FSERVER2", 4D.0000.0000.4321(471), 16 hops
 type 0x7, "FSERVER1", 4D.0000.0000.1212(471), 16 hops
 type 0x7, "FSERVER2", 4D.0000.0000.2121(471), 16 hops
IPXSAP: suppressing null update to 2B.ffff.ffff.ffff
IPXSAP: Response (in) type 0x2 len 288 src:2B.00e0.1454.f180
        dest:2B.00e0.1454.cf60(452)
 type 0x7, "FSERVER2", 4D.0000.0000.2121(471), 3 hops
 type 0x7, "FSERVER1", 4D.0000.0000.1212(471), 3 hops
 type 0x4, "FSERVER2", 4D.0000.0000.4321(471), 3 hops
 type 0x4, "FSERVER1", 4D.0000.0000.1234(471), 3 hops
IPXSAP: type 0x7 server "FSERVER2" distance lowered; new entry
        accepted [3/2/13]
IPXSAP: new SAP entry: type 7 server "FSERVER2" 3 hops [2/13]
IPXSAP: type 0x7 server "FSERVER1" distance lowered; new entry
        accepted [3/2/13]
IPXSAP: new SAP entry: type 7 server "FSERVER1" 3 hops [2/13]
IPXSAP: type 0x4 server "FSERVER2" distance lowered; new entry
        accepted [3/2/13]
IPXSAP: new SAP entry: type 4 server "FSERVER2" 3 hops [2/13]
IPXSAP: type 0x4 server "FSERVER1" distance lowered; new entry
        accepted [3/2/13]
IPXSAP: new SAP entry: type 4 server "FSERVER1" 3 hops [2/13]
```

```
IPXSAP: positing update to 1A.ffff.ffff.ffff via Ethernet0
        (broadcast) (flash)

IPXSAP: positing update to 2B.ffff.ffff.ffff via Serial0 (broadcast)
        (flash)

IPXSAP: Update type 0x2 len 288 src:1A.00e0.1454.cf60
        dest:1A.ffff.ffff.ffff(452)

 type 0x4, "FSERVER1", 4D.0000.0000.1234(471), 4 hops

 type 0x4, "FSERVER2", 4D.0000.0000.4321(471), 4 hops

 type 0x7, "FSERVER1", 4D.0000.0000.1212(471), 4 hops

 type 0x7, "FSERVER2", 4D.0000.0000.2121(471), 4 hops

IPXSAP: suppressing null update to 2B.ffff.ffff.ffff

RouterA#

RouterA#u all

All possible debugging has been turned off
```

NOTE We used the clear ipx route * command in both cases only to speed up the update process. It is not required in everyday use of the debug ipx commands.

Migrating to Ethernet 802.2

The ABC Corporation was a large user of Novell NetWare products. They had 14 NetWare servers for various purposes and supported over 800 users. The four main file servers had recently been upgraded from NetWare 3.11 to 4.1. Most of the clients were configured as DOS workstations using the Ethernet_802.3 encapsulation. Additionally, there were a number of Client 32 clients on Windows 95 and NT systems.

The IT development committee decided that the entire organization would go to Windows 98. In addition, all clients would be using Client 32 as their NetWare redirector software. To cut down on CPU utilization on the servers, all servers would standardize on only Ethernet_802.2 since it is the preferred encapsulation in NetWare 4 environments. All Client 32 stations would also have to be using only 802.2.

This job was no small task. All clients would have to be touched (configured and tested) to ensure they would adhere to the new corporate standard. Given limitations in manpower in the IT department, the migration could not be done over one weekend. It had to be done over several months' time. By far, the largest concern in the minds of the entire IT department was maintaining connectivity between clients and servers while the migration took place.

Thanks to the ingenuity of a young internetworking enthusiast, ABC was able to devise a wonderful solution to the potential connectivity problem. They configured their Cisco routers to basically convert packets carried by 802.2 frames into 802.3 frames and vice versa. This ensured that, no matter where they were in the migration process, all clients would have access to all servers.

They configured all router interfaces that connected to IPX segments with two IPX addresses —one based on the Ethernet_802.2 and one on the Ethernet_802.3. Any packets being carried by an 802.2 frame would be converted to an 802.3 and vice versa. A couple of examples of configurations they used are as follows:

```
!
ipx routing
!
interface ethernet0
  ipx network 1111 encapsulation novell-ether
  ipx network 2222 encapsulation sap secondary
!
interface ethernet1
  ipx network 3333 encapsulation novell-ether
  ipx network 4444 encapsulation sap secondary
!
```

This solution worked well and got the job done for the ABC Corporation. They finished their migration without a single occurrence of loss of connectivity.

The way ABC went about establishing multiple encapsulations was good, and it worked well. However, today Cisco recommends a more desirable alternative: to use subinterfaces rather than the secondary keyword on an interface. Cisco has promised to remove support for secondary keywords in the future. Therefore, it is best that we get used to it now. Using subinterfaces instead of the secondary keyword, our previous example would look like this:

```
!
ipx routing
!
interface ethernet 0.1
  ipx network 1111 encapsulation novell-ether
interface ethernet 0.2
  ipx network 2222 encapsulation sap
!
interface ethernet 1.1
  ipx network 3333 encapsulation novell-ether
interface ethernet 1.2
  ipx network 4444 encapsulation sap
!
```

AppleTalk

This chapter discusses some of the advanced topics related to AppleTalk routing and to verifying AppleTalk activity. In this chapter we assume you have been introduced to AppleTalk and are familiar with the basic process for configuring simple AppleTalk routing. If you are new to AppleTalk, before you read this chapter we recommend you read the AppleTalk section in Chapter 3 for a brief introduction.

Configuring AppleTalk

Throughout this chapter, all of the commands that relate to configuration and verification (show and debug) are based on the example of a simple AppleTalk network topology, illustrated in Figure 12.1. We have structured the chapter in this fashion because, in many cases, it is easier to implement a real-life configuration properly when there is an example to follow.

The topology includes six cable ranges, labeled as follows:

- 1000–1010
- 2000–2000
- 3000–3010
- 4000–4010
- 5000–5000
- 6000–6010

All cable ranges are part of an AppleTalk zone called Ozone. Cable range 1000–1010 is also part of a zone called zone1. Cable ranges 2000–2000, 3000–3010, 4000–4010, and 5000–5000 are also part of a zone named zone2. Cable range 6000-6010 is also part of a zone called zone3. On cable range 6000–6010 there are two Apple/Macintosh machines. Each is configured to be in zone3. The networks are interconnected via three routers labeled RouterA, RouterB, and RouterC. All of the LAN segments are Ethernet. All point-to-point connections are T1 serial links.

Figure 12.1   Simple AppleTalk Network

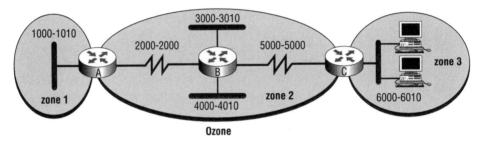

Required AppleTalk Configuration Activities

Some basic configuration tasks you *must* perform when configuring AppleTalk are:

- Enabling AppleTalk routing
- Assigning cable ranges
- Assigning zone names

Let's examine the configuration for one of our routers. Based on our topology, an example configuration for RouterA would look like the following:

```
!
appletalk routing
!
interface ethernet0
  appletalk cable-range 1000-1010
  appletalk zone Ozone
  appletalk zone zone1
!
interface serial0
```

```
appletalk cable-range 2000-2000
appletalk zone Ozone
appletalk zone zone2
!
```

Enabling AppleTalk Routing

The first thing we always do when configuring for AppleTalk routing is enable it. We do so using the global `appletalk routing` command. RouterA has two interfaces (Ethernet0 and Serial0) routing AppleTalk; therefore, we have to configure both. Every interface that will route AppleTalk will need to be configured with a cable range. All devices sharing the same broadcast domain must agree on a cable range. In our case, Ethernet0 is attached to cable range 1000–1010 and Serial0 is attached to 2000–2000. We assign a cable range using the `appletalk cable-range <range>` command in interface configuration mode for each affected interface.

Next we assign the zones that each interface will participate in. We do so using the `appletalk zone <zone>` command in interface configuration mode. In reality, we are actually associating cable ranges with zones. However, since each interface will only be part of one cable range, it is the same thing. A cable range can be in more than one zone and a zone can contain more than one cable range. (Figure that one out!)

In our example, all cable ranges belong to two zones. All are a part of the Ozone zone and one other. As a result, every interface must be configured according to which zone it is in. For instance, Interface Ethernet0 is connected to cable range 1000–1010. Cable range 1000–1010 is in the zones named Ozone and zone1, and therefore must be configured as such. Serial0 is attached to cable range 2000–2000 and is therefore in the zones named Ozone and zone2 and also must be configured as such.

The basic configuration displayed is enough in our case for AppleTalk packets to be routed. Once AppleTalk is enabled, so is Apple's Routing Table Maintenance Protocol (RTMP). RTMP is a simple distance-vector routing protocol commonly used in AppleTalk environments. Once RTMP is enabled, cable ranges and zones will be exchanged between AppleTalk routers, and, shortly thereafter, routing will commence.

Optional Configuration Activities

As with other protocols, AppleTalk also has its optional configuration capabilities. Every good administrator should know about these:

- Assigning a static node address

Router Configuration

PART 3

- Enabling discovery mode
- Selecting an alternate routing protocol
- Configuring AURP
- Tunneling AppleTalk
- Verifying AppleTalk Operation

Assigning a Static Address

We learned in Chapter 3 that, by default, AppleTalk uses a dynamic method of acquiring a node addresses for each Apple/Macintosh device on a network. This makes things easier for the administrator, who does not have to worry about keeping track of all Apple addresses and does not risk using the same AppleTalk address on two nodes. Overall, it's a great feature.

Dynamic node discovery does, however, have one down side. It makes the node address unpredictable. A node address could theoretically change from day to day. Most of the time this is not a problem, but in some cases, such as when you are using AppleTalk with X.25 or dial-on-demand routing (DDR), you have to map an AppleTalk address statically to a phone number or X.121 address. Common sense says that any time a manual mapping is required, so is a predictable AppleTalk address. You can provide a static Apple-Talk address to an interface by using the `appletalk cable-range` command. The syntax of this command is as follows:

```
appletalk cable-range  <range> <network>.<node>
```

Let's suppose we wanted to assign an address to interface Serial0 statically on RouterA. Because Serial0 is attached to cable range 2000–2000, we can just choose a node address in the available range. In the example code below, we have used the address 2000.128.

```
!
interface serial0
  appletalk cable-range 2000-2000 2000.128
!
```

> **WARNING**   Keep in mind that when you use static addresses on a network, you must be careful not to use the same address on two nodes. Doing so would keep them from communicating on the network.

Enabling Discovery Mode

A neat feature available to us on Cisco routers is called *discovery mode*. Rather than configuring all of our routers with cable range and zone information, we can have them discover this information for themselves. All that is needed is a seed router on the same network. A *seed router* is any device that has the capability of answering requests for cable ranges and zones. This is most commonly another router's interface that has not been configured for discovery mode. We can, however, even configure Microsoft and NetWare servers and Apple/Macintosh peers to perform this role.

To configure an interface to learn its cable range and zones, use the `appletalk cable-range 0-0` command. Issuing this command in interface configuration mode has an interesting result. The running configuration will include the commands for a static Apple address assignment and the zone or zones discovered. It also adds the command `appletalk discovery`.

An example is as follows:

```
!
interface ethernet0
  appletalk cable-range 6000-6010 6001.22
  appletalk zone Ozone
  appletalk zone zone3
  appletalk discovery
!
```

> **NOTE** Discovery mode only works on interfaces that are faster than T1. By design, it will not work on a typical serial interface.

Selecting Alternate Routing Protocols

Although RTMP is a good protocol when used in a simple environment, it is a distance-vector protocol and therefore suffers from the same limitations as do other distance-vector protocols. RTMP has an update cycle of every 10 seconds (yes, that's 10 seconds). It uses a hop count as a metric and has a maximum hop count of 15 hops. Therefore, its greatest weakness is that it is not very scalable.

You will be happy to know (if you don't already) that RTMP is not our only option. We can also use Enhanced IGRP or AppleTalk Update Routing Protocol (AURP) in conjunction with or in the place of RTMP. EIGRP is discussed in Chapter 8 of this book. If you

Router Configuration

PART 3

plan to use EIGRP in your AppleTalk network, please examine Chapter 8 carefully. We will take a closer look at AURP in the section to follow.

To add routing processes, we use the `appletalk protocol <protocol>` command. This command is issued in interface configuration mode. For example:

```
!
interface Serial0
  appletalk protocol aurp
!
```

To disable RTMP as a routing protocol, use the `no appletalk protocol rtmp` command.

WARNING   This command should not be used on LAN interfaces if the LAN segment contains Apple/Macintosh devices. Some devices rely on RTMP updates for gateway information.

AppleTalk Domains   To understand AppleTalk internetworking, it is important to understand the concept of an AppleTalk domain. A logical domain structure is used to support AppleTalk interenterprise routing. An AppleTalk domain is little more than an internetwork where all cable ranges are unique. There will be no physical or logical connection between domains unless connectivity is through a domain router. And yes, you guessed it—a Cisco router can act as a domain router.

We segment our internetwork into domains to overcome problems that relate to:

- Overlapping network ranges assigned to different parts of the internetwork. By implementing AppleTalk domains to remap remote network numbers that conflict with local network numbers, we can resolve address conflicts.

- Hop count limits. We can get around the 15-hop maximum imposed by RTMP and Datagram Delivery Protocol (DDP). As a packet is routed from domain to domain, its hop-count field is reduced to a value of 1.

Configuring AppleTalk Domains   There are three tasks usually associated with configuring a router to support AppleTalk domains. They are:

- Enabling the domain
- Remapping network numbers (when necessary)
- Reducing hop count (when desired)

We enable a domain by issuing two commands: one to declare it and another to associate the domain to an interface. To declare a domain, we use the `appletalk domain` *<number>* `name` *<name>* command. When we declare a domain, we assign it a unique name and number to which we may refer later. The domain is declared in global configuration mode. Once it is declared, the domain can be associated to one or more interfaces. The command to associate the domain is `appletalk domain-group` *<number>*. The number you use in the *<number>* field must correspond with the number of the declared domain. This command is issued in interface configuration mode for the interface you intend to affect.

When connecting two AppleTalk internetworks, it is possible to have conflicts between cable ranges. The two internetworks could easily have used the same or overlapping ranges. This, in turn, causes address conflicts between devices—and of course we know address conflicts are a very bad thing in networking. To remedy this, Cisco has provided us with the ability to remap addresses both coming into a domain and going out of a domain. We do so using the following IOS commands:

```
appletalk domain <number> remap-range in <cable range>
appletalk domain <number> remap-range out <cable range>
```

Both of these commands are issued in global configuration mode. The *<number>* field corresponds with the number of the declared domain. The *<cable range>* field corresponds to the range to which you want inbound and outbound packets to be changed.

When you join AppleTalk internetworks, the distances between individual segments can easily exceed the 15-hop maximum imposed by AppleTalk's Datagram Delivery Protocol (DDP). That said, you have the option to have your domain routers reduce the hop count for packets traversing it. To do this, issue the `appletalk domain` *<number>* `hop-reduction` command. This command can be issued in global configuration mode. Once enabled, it sets the hop-count field in all AppleTalk packets to a value of 1. An example configuration is as follows:

```
!
appletalk domain 1 name Jersey
appletalk domain 1 remap-range in 700-799
appletalk domain 1 remap-range out 800-899
appletalk domain 1 hop-reduction
appletalk domain 2 name York
appletalk domain 2 remap-range in 900-999
```

Router Configuration

PART 3

```
appletalk domain 2 remap-range out 100-199
appletalk domain 2 hop-reduction
!
interface Ethernet0
  appletalk domain-group 1
interface Serial 0
  appletalk domain-group 2
!
```

In this example, we have declared two domains, Jersey and York. Interface Ethernet0 is part of domain Jersey and interface Serial0 is part of York. All packets coming into domain Jersey (Ethernet0) will be remapped using the range 700–799. Any packets going out of the Jersey domain will be remapped to 800–899. All packets coming into domain York (Serial0) will be remapped using the range 900–999. Any packets going out of York will be remapped using the range 100–199. Additionally, on this router we have chosen to enable hop-count reduction for both domains.

> **NOTE** You cannot have more than one domain router attaching two domains. If you want to set up redundant links between domains, the only way it can be done is through multiple links on the same router.

AppleTalk Update Routing Protocol (AURP)

A routing protocol option we can use on AppleTalk phase 2 networks is AppleTalk Update Routing Protocol (AURP). AURP's primary purpose is to connect two non-continuous AppleTalk networks separated by a non-AppleTalk network (like IP). It is actually a tunneling protocol.

By definition, tunneling is taking one Network layer protocol's packet and carrying it as payload in the packet of another Network layer protocol. A source router configured to tunnel will encapsulate the AppleTalk packet in an IP packet and route it over an IP backbone to a destination IP router. The destination router will in turn decapsulate and route the native AppleTalk packet to its destination network. Later in this chapter we will look at an example of tunneling AppleTalk over IP.

AURP is configured on a tunnel interface. Once you have configured an AppleTalk domain, AURP allows you to extend that domain to other areas of your internetwork. AURP is typically used as a replacement to RTMP on the tunnel interface. It is a bit more efficient, with an update cycle of every 30 seconds, as opposed to RTMP's 10-second time interval.

Tunneling AppleTalk

Setting up a router for tunneling AppleTalk is simple, provided you are aware of all of the steps. The following is list of the procedures:

1. Declare a tunnel interface. To define a tunnel, use the `interface tunnel` *<number>* command. You issue this command in global configuration mode. It will, however, place you in interface configuration mode for the tunnel interface you created. Once in interface configuration mode, you can configure that tunnel as if it were a physical interface.

2. Create an AURP routing process. To turn on AURP while in interface configuration mode, issue the command `appletalk protocol aurp`.

3. Enable tunneling using the AURP protocol. To do this, while in interface configuration mode for the tunnel interface, type `tunnel mode aurp`.

4. Specify a tunnel source and destination. Do so by issuing the `tunnel source` `<source interface or ip address>` and `tunnel destination` `<destination ip address>` commands while in interface configuration mode for your tunnel interface.

5. Specify the number that represents the domain group in which this router's interface will participate. If there has been a domain group declared, you should specify the number used to identify it. Do so by issuing the `appletalk domain-group <group number>` command.

In the following example, we have declared AppleTalk domain Jersey and have created domain-group 1 to define all parameters related to domain Jersey. We chose to remap cable ranges for all inbound packets to 700–799 and for all outbound packets to 800–899.

To facilitate tunneling, we declared a tunnel interface called Tunnel 0. Under Tunnel 0 we have enabled AURP as the Tunnel protocol and have started an AURP routing process. We specified our tunnel source as interface Ethernet 1 and tunnel destination as IP address 123.213.210.100. Last, we have identified domain group 1 as the domain that Tunnel 0 will be participating in.

```
!
appletalk domain 1 name Jersey
appletalk domain 1 remap-range in 700-799
appletalk domain 1 remap-range out 800-899
!
```

```
interface Tunnel 0
  tunnel source ethernet 1
  tunnel destination 123.213.210.100
  tunnel mode aurp
  appletalk protocol aurp
  appletalk domain-group 1
!
```

Verifying AppleTalk Operation

The Cisco IOS provides us with many useful commands for verifying AppleTalk operation. A number of them are as follows:

- `show appletalk route`
- `show appletalk zone`
- `show appletalk interface`
- `show appletalk globals`
- `show appletalk traffic`
- `ping apple`
- `debug apple routing`
- `debug apple zip`

When verifying any Cisco router operation we typically start by issuing one or more **show** commands. The available AppleTalk **show** commands can be displayed by issuing the `show appletalk ?` command at the command-line interface. The following is a sample output:

```
RouterA# show appletalk ?
   access-lists    AppleTalk access lists
   adjacent-routes AppleTalk adjacent routes
   arp             AppleTalk arp table
   aurp            AURP information
   cache           AppleTalk fast-switching cache
   domain          AppleTalk Domain(s) information
   eigrp           AppleTalk/EIGRP show commands
   globals         AppleTalk global parameters
```

interface	AppleTalk interface status and configuration
macip-clients	Mac IP clients
macip-servers	Mac IP servers
macip-traffic	Mac IP traffic
name-cache	AppleTalk name cache
nbp	AppleTalk NBP name table
neighbors	AppleTalk Neighboring router status
remap	AppleTalk remap table
route	AppleTalk routing table
sockets	AppleTalk protocol processing information
static	AppleTalk static table
traffic	AppleTalk protocol statistics
zone	AppleTalk Zone table information

Whenever there is a problem that relates to routing AppleTalk the first place a systems administrator should always look is at the status of the AppleTalk routing table. To view the AppleTalk routing table, issue the show appletalk route command. The following is a sample output:

```
RouterA# show appletalk route
Codes: R - RTMP derived, E - EIGRP derived, C - connected,
A - AURP  S - static  P - proxy
6 routes in internet


The first zone listed for each entry is its default (primary) zone.


C Net 1000-1010 directly connected, Ethernet0, zone zone1
                Additional zones: 'Ozone'
C Net 2000-2000 directly connected, Serial0, zone zone2
                Additional zones: 'Ozone'
R Net 3000-3010 [1/G] via 2000.37, 9 sec, Serial0, zone Ozone
                  Additional zones: 'zone2'
R Net 4000-4010 [1/G] via 2000.37, 0 sec, Serial0, zone zone2
```

Router Configuration

PART 3

```
                      Additional zones: 'Ozone'
   R Net 5000-5000 [1/G] via 2000.37, 0 sec, Serial0, zone zone2
                      Additional zones: 'Ozone'
   R Net 6000-6010 [2/G] via 2000.37, 0 sec, Serial0, zone Ozone
                      Additional zones: 'zone3'
```

A routing table can be quite informative. Let's examine one entry in the table:

```
   R Net 3000-3010 [1/G] via 2000.37, 9 sec, Serial0, zone Ozone
                      Additional zones: 'zone2'
```

Based on this example, we can see the following:

- The R signifies that the route was learned via RTMP. This is evident from the codes in the display.
- The 3000–3010 is the cable range advertised.
- The [1/G] is a hop/state value. This route is one hop away and it is a Good route. The options for states include G: Good, S: Suspect, and B: Bad.
- 2000.37 is the next-hop AppleTalk address.
- The last update that included this cable range was 9 seconds ago.
- The route was learned via Serial0 and therefore will not be advertised out of Serial0, because of split horizon.
- The cable range is part of two zones, Ozone and zone2.

In addition to the routing table, the Zone Information Table (ZIT) is also available. The ZIT contains a listing of all the learned zones, as well as associated cable ranges in the internetwork. You can view it by issuing the **show appletalk zone** command. The following is an example output on RouterA. All zones and cable ranges in our internetwork are listed.

```
   RouterA# show appletalk zone
   Name                            Network(s)
   Ozone                           6000-6010 5000-5000
                                   3000-3010 4000-4010
                                   2000-2000 1000-1010
   zone1                           1000-1010
```

```
zone2                                    5000-5000 3000-3010
                                         4000-4010 2000-2000
zone3                                    6000-6010
Total of 4 zones
```

To display the status of an interface configured for AppleTalk, issue the `show appletalk interface` command. The following is a sample output:

```
RouterA#show appletalk interface ethernet 0
Ethernet0 is up, line protocol is up
  AppleTalk cable range is 1000-1010
  AppleTalk address is 1008.180, Valid
  AppleTalk primary zone is "zone1"
  AppleTalk additional zones: "Ozone"
  AppleTalk address gleaning is disabled
  AppleTalk route cache is enabled
```

From the output of the `show appletalk interface ethernet 0` command we learn the following:

- Ethernet0 is operational.
- The interface is attached to cable range 1000–1010.
- The AppleTalk address of the interface is 1008.180 and it does not conflict with any other AppleTalk node on the network. That it does not conflict is indicated by Valid keyword at the end of the AppleTalk address line. The keyword options are Valid, Probing, and Invalid.
- The primary zone is zone1.
- Another zone was configured called Ozone.
- AppleTalk *address gleaning* is disabled. AppleTalk uses a mechanism very similar to IP's ARP for resolving logical addresses to physical device addresses. Apple calls it AppleTalk Address Resolution Protocol (AARP). Gleaning, when enabled, tells the router to cache all AARP resolutions and store them in the AppleTalk ARP table. Gleaning is off by default.
- The AppleTalk route cache is enabled by default for increased performance.

We can view the AppleTalk ARP cache by issuing the show appletalk arp command. The following is a sample output:

```
RouterA# show appletalk arp

Address      Age (min)  Type      Hardware Addr      Encap     Interface

1008.180            -   Hardware  00e0.1454.cf60.0000  SNAP      Ethernet0
```

To display information related to AppleTalk settings we can issue the show appletalk globals command. The following is a sample output:

```
RouterA#show appletalk globals

AppleTalk global information:
    Internet is incompatible with older, AT Phase1, routers.
    There are 6 routes in the internet.
    There are 4 zones defined.
    Logging of significant AppleTalk events is disabled.
    ZIP resends queries every 10 seconds.
    RTMP updates are sent every 10 seconds.
    RTMP entries are considered BAD after 20 seconds.
    RTMP entries are discarded after 60 seconds.
    AARP probe retransmit count: 10, interval: 200 msec.
    AARP request retransmit count: 5, interval: 1000 msec.
    DDP datagrams will be checksummed.
    RTMP datagrams will be strictly checked.
    RTMP routes may not be propagated without zones.
    Routes will not be distributed between routing protocols.
    Routing between local devices on an interface will not be performed.
    IPTalk uses the udp base port of 768 (Default).
    AppleTalk EIGRP is not enabled.
    Alternate node address format will not be displayed.
    Access control of any networks of a zone hides the zone.
```

If you like, you can even display a count of all the AppleTalk packets the router has handled. To do so, we can issue the show appletalk traffic command. As you can see, all packet counts are displayed by type.

```
RouterA#show appletalk traffic
AppleTalk statistics:
  Rcvd:  154 total, 0 checksum errors, 0 bad hop count
      154 local destination, 0 access denied
      0 for MacIP, 0 bad MacIP, 0 no client
      6 port disabled, 0 no listener
      0 ignored, 0 martians
  Bcast: 0 received, 292 sent
  Sent:  307 generated, 0 forwarded, 0 fast forwarded, 0 loopback
      0 forwarded from MacIP, 0 MacIP failures
      0 encapsulation failed, 0 no route, 0 no source
  DDP:   154 long, 0 short, 0 macip, 0 bad size
  NBP:   33 received, 0 invalid, 0 proxies
      0 replies sent, 20 forwards, 33 lookups, 0 failures
  RTMP:  126 received, 10 requests, 0 invalid, 0 ignored
      281 sent, 0 replies
  ATP:   0 received
  ZIP:   5 received, 16 sent, 0 netinfo
  Echo:  0 received, 0 discarded, 0 illegal
      0 generated, 0 replies sent
  Responder:  0 received, 0 illegal, 0 unknown
      0 replies sent, 0 failures
  AARP:  0 requests, 0 replies, 0 probes
      0 martians, 0 bad encapsulation, 0 unknown
  AppleTalk statistics:
      20 sent, 0 failures, 0 delays, 0 drops
  Lost: 0 no buffers
  Unknown: 0 packets
  Discarded: 0 wrong encapsulation, 0 bad SNAP discriminator
  AURP: 0 Open Requests, 0 Router Downs
```

```
0 Routing Information sent, 0 Routing Information received

0 Zone Information sent, 0 Zone Information received

0 Get Zone Nets sent, 0 Get Zone Nets received

0 Get Domain Zone List sent, 0 Get Domain Zone List received

0 bad sequence
```

To test for AppleTalk connectivity between two AppleTalk routers, you can use the ping apple *<AppleTalk address>* command. The following is a sample output:

```
RouterA# ping apple 2000.37


Type escape sequence to abort.
Sending 5, 100-byte AppleTalk Echos to 2000.37, timeout is 2 seconds:
!!!!!
Success rate is 100 percent (5/5), round-trip min/avg/max = 28/29/32 ms
```

As an alternative to pinging a specific address, you can ping a directed broadcast address. AppleTalk reserves the node addresses 0, 254, and 255 as broadcast addresses. To test connectivity to cable range 5000–5000, use the following command:

```
RouterA#ping apple 5000.255


Type escape sequence to abort.
Sending 5, 100-byte AppleTalk Echos to 5000.255, timeout is 2
seconds:
!!!!!
Success rate is 100 percent (5/5), round-trip min/avg/max = 28/34/40 ms
```

Or

```
RouterA#ping apple 5000.0


Type escape sequence to abort.
Sending 5, 100-byte AppleTalk Echos to 5000.0, timeout is 2 seconds:
```

```
!!!!!
```

Success rate is 100 percent (5/5), round-trip min/avg/max = 28/29/32 ms

We can also view the current status and configuration parameters of our AppleTalk domains by using the **show appletalk domain** command. The following is a sample output for this command:

```
RouterA# show appletalk domain


          AppleTalk   Domain   Information:
     Domain 1          Name : Jersey

     ----------------------------------------

     State                           : Active
     Inbound remap range  : 700-799
     Outbound remap range : 800-899
     Hop reduction        : ON
     Interfaces in domain :
           Ethernet0      : Enabled
     Domain 2          Name : York

     ----------------------------------------

     State                           : Active
     Inbound remap range  : 900-999
     Outbound remap range : 100-199
     Hop reduction        : ON
     Interfaces in domain :
           Serial0        : Enabled
```

The output displayed is from a Cisco router that has been configured as a domain router. It is part of two domains, Jersey and York. In our configuration we have instructed the router to remap all routes outbound from Jersey to 800–899 and inbound to Jersey to 700–799; and outbound from York to 900–999 and inbound to York to 100–199. Although hop reduction is disabled by default, we have enabled it in this case for both domains.

Router Configuration

PART 3

Debugging AppleTalk

As with other protocols, AppleTalk allows you to view real-time events as they are happening. To get an idea of what AppleTalk options are available for debugging, you can issue the debug apple ? command. The following is a sample output.

```
RouterA#debug apple ?
  arp                    Appletalk address resolution protocol
  aurp-connection        AURP connection
  aurp-packet            AURP packets
  aurp-update            AURP routing updates
  domain                 AppleTalk Domain function
  eigrp-all              All AT/EIGRP functions
  eigrp-external         AT/EIGRP external functions
  eigrp-hello            AT/EIGRP hello functions
  eigrp-packet           AT/EIGRP packet debugging
  eigrp-query            AT/EIGRP query functions
  eigrp-redistribution   AT/EIGRP route redistribution
  eigrp-request          AT/EIGRP external functions
  eigrp-target           Appletalk/EIGRP for targeting address
  eigrp-update           AT/EIGRP update functions
  errors                 Information about errors
  events                 Appletalk special events
  fs                     Appletalk fast-switching
  iptalk                 IPTalk encapsulation and functionality
  load-balancing         AppleTalk load-balancing
  macip                  MacIP functions
  nbp                    Name Binding Protocol (NBP) functions
  packet                 Per-packet debugging
  redistribution         Route Redistribution
  remap                  AppleTalk Remap function
  responder              AppleTalk responder debugging
  routing                (RTMP&EIGRP) functions
```

rtmp	(RTMP) functions
zip	Zone Information Protocol functions

NOTE Remember that the debug command must be performed in Privileged Exec mode.

WARNING Be careful when using the IOS debug feature. Every time a debugged criterion is met, a message must be generated and sent to the console. If many of these messages are generated in a given time, the router must spend many CPU cycles processing the debugs and may not accomplish much routing. Additionally, when debug is used, in most situations all packets debugged must be route-processed and are no longer eligible for fast switching. This, too, slows routing operations overall. The best policy to follow is to use IOS debug only for troubleshooting, not monitoring. Use it when you have a problem about which you need to gather more information. Once troubleshooting is over, turn off debugging.

To view routing updates as they come in and go out you can issue the debug apple routing command. The following is an example of the output of this debug:

```
RouterA# debug apple routing
AppleTalk RTMP routing debugging is on
AppleTalk EIGRP routing debugging is on
RouterA#
AT: RTMP from 2000.37 (new 0,old 4,bad 0,ign 0, dwn 0)lear appl rou
AT: src=Ethernet0:1008.180, dst=1000-1010, size=40, 5 rtes, RTMP pkt sent
AT: src=Serial0:2000.64, dst=2000-2000, size=16, 1 rte, RTMP pkt sent
AT: Route ager starting on Main AT RoutingTable (6 active nodes)
AT: Route ager finished on Main AT RoutingTable (6 active nodes)te *
AT: src=Ethernet0:1008.180, dst=1000-1010, size=40, 5 rtes, RTMP pkt sent
AT: src=Serial0:2000.64, dst=2000-2000, size=16, 1 rte, RTMP pkt sent
AT: Route ager starting on Main AT RoutingTable (6 active nodes)
AT: Route ager finished on Main AT RoutingTable (6 active nodes)
RouterA#u all
All possible debugging has been turned off
```

> **WARNING** This particular debug will generate a significant number of messages and send them to the console. To turn it off you can issue the u all command. This command is the short form of undebug all.

Another useful debugging command is **debug apple zip**. This displays all zone traffic being sent and received in real time. The following is an example of the output of this command:

```
RouterA# debug apple zip

AppleTalk ZIP Packets debugging is on


RouterA#clear apple route 5000

RouterA#

AT: in CancelZoneRequest, cancelling req on 5000-5000...failed; not
on list

AT: NextNbrZipQuery: [5000-5000] zoneupdate 0 gw: 2000.37 n: 2000.37

AT: NextNbrZipQuery: r->rpath.gwptr: 60C7C4A4, n: 60C7C4A4

AT: maint_SendNeighborQueries, sending 1 queries to 2000.37

AT: 1 query packet sent to neighbor 2000.37

AT: Recvd ZIP cmd 2 from 2000.37-6

AT: 2 zones in ZIPreply pkt, src 2000.37

AT: net 5000, zonelen 5, name zone2

AT: net 5000, zonelen 5, name Ozone

AT: in CancelZoneRequest, cancelling req on 5000-5000...succeeded1

All possible debugging has been turned off

RouterA#
```

Tunneling AppleTalk

ABC Corporation (names have been changed to protect the innocent) has a huge internetwork consisting of locations in Baltimore, MD, Washington, DC, Philadelphia, PA, and Newark, NJ. Most of the internetwork is IP and IPX, with various parts using AppleTalk for peer-to-peer networking between local devices. The corporation uses an ATM backbone and has restricted its traffic to IP only.

One division in the company, publishing, is located in Baltimore and uses primarily off-the-shelf desktop publishing applications in their day-to-day activities. As desktop publishers, most of the employees in the department prefer to use Power Macs with Macintosh desktop publishing software.

ABC recently started an Internet Web-based publishing division in their Washington, DC office. The DC office's desktop publishing business was very slow and the management decided to refocus those resources on Internet Web Page design. The DC office had a large mix of Apple and Macintosh computers, spanning from earlier Apple IIs to top-of-the-line Power Macs. Well, to the delight of everyone, the Web-based publishing business took off. The amount of work they were receiving was more than double what the DC division could handle.

This was an easy problem for management to solve: Commit some of the resources in Baltimore to helping DC with Web-based publishing. This was a common sense solution that also made good business sense, because Baltimore was underutilized at

the time and had the resources to jump in and help.

However, it brought about other problems. ABC had to be able to exchange files between Baltimore and DC frequently and quickly. They had their ATM backbone in place and therefore had physical connectivity. The problem was in how they intended to transport these files. What protocol suite was best for the job?

After discussing all of the feasible options, they put a number of proposed solutions to a vote:

- Enable AppleTalk routing onto the backbone.

- Migrate all Apple/Macintoshes to MacIP and use TCP/IP as the only transport.

- Tunnel AppleTalk over the IP backbone between sites.

The first option was shot down almost as fast as it was suggested. The people managing the backbone were hardcore IP people who didn't want AppleTalk on their backbone. At first, it made little sense that they would reject this first solution, because it was a very logical idea. However, IP brings with it many benefits, especially manageability (via SNMP) that is not available with AppleTalk. The backbone people didn't want packets they couldn't monitor and control. Additionally, if they had to reconfigure all of their backbone routers, the job would become huge (they didn't want to work on Saturday).

24seven **CASE STUDY**

So the next option was considered. They could migrate completely to MacIP. The Baltimore office would have been no problem. They could enable MacIP on all the Power Macs because the Power Macs supported it just fine. The Washington office, however, would have required many of their machines to be replaced with current models. Most of them supported AppleTalk, but few of them supported MacIP. Management wasn't willing to replace that many machines this quarter, especially because (in their eyes) the machines worked just fine.

So that left one additional solution: tunneling AppleTalk over the IP network. The configuration required to the necessary routers was minor. Only the edge routers had to be configured. The backbone devices would route IP just as they normally do. They wouldn't have to buy new machines. The users could continue doing business just as before. It was a great solution. ABC set it up and it worked well for them.

ABC Corp. chose tunneling AppleTalk over IP because it was a solution that fit their specific circumstances. Today we are seeing a big trend in the industry where firms are migrating completely away from AppleTalk (and other protocols) and going to IP. A few of the many reasons include:

- A single protocol suite to learn and understand
- Less demand on the routers and hosts because they need only run one routed protocol service
- Better manageability via SNMP
- Total coverage of all of the broad services available via AppleTalk
- Universal e-mail using SNMP
- Access to the Internet

13

Configuring ISDN and Dial-on-Demand Routing (DDR)

In order to configure and administer ISDN, you need to understand some of the underlying technology. This chapter describes ISDN technology and provides detailed configuration information. We have included many examples to help you understand what is required for ISDN connectivity in both dial-on-demand and backup interface configurations.

ISDN Components

The physical components of an ISDN network include the following:

- Terminal equipment
- Terminal adapters
- Network-termination devices

ISDN terminals come in two flavors, classified either as terminal equipment type 1 (TE1) or terminal equipment type 2 (TE2). Data Terminal Equipment (DTE) devices that have native ISDN interface circuitry are considered TE1 devices. An example of a native ISDN interface is a Basic Rate Interface (BRI). If a router has one or more BRI interfaces, it is considered a TE1. If a DTE has no native ISDN connectivity but is used with ISDN, it is a TE2. A TE2 needs a terminal adapter (TA) for ISDN connectivity. An example of a DTE we would classify as a TE2 could be a router with no BRI interface. We would use a serial interface connected to a TA instead for connectivity.

Both TE1 and TE2 devices need a network termination device to help interface the TE to the local loop. The two kinds of network termination devices are the NT1 and the NT2. For connectivity to an ISDN WAN, an NT1 acts as the DCE and the TE acts as the DTE. The NT1 connects the four-wire subscriber wiring used by the DTE to the conventional two-wire standard used by the local loop. In North America, NT1 is considered customer premises equipment (CPE). In other parts of the world, the NT1 is included in your ISDN service. The NT2 is the point at which all ISDN lines at the customer's location are aggregated and switched. The functions of NT2 and NT1 are frequently provided in the same device.

ISDN Reference Points

ISDN identifies several reference points between each component. The reference points are the interfaces or connections between the TEs, TAs, NT2s, and NT1s. We identify them by using alphabetical characters:

R   The R interface is the reference point between non-ISDN equipment and a TA. This might include an EIA/TIA-232-C (formerly RS-232-C), V.24, or V.35 cable.

S   The S interface is the reference point between the TE and the NT2.

T   The T interface is the reference point between the NT1 and NT2 devices. Electrically, the S and T interfaces are the same and are commonly referred to as an S/T interface. The functionality for S and T is almost always provided in the same device.

U   The U interface is a reference point between NT1 devices and the local exchange of your ISDN service provider. The U reference point is only important in North America, because the NT1 functionality is considered part of the CPE and is therefore not included with your ISDN service.

NOTE   Many devices include the functionality of multiple ISDN components. Routers with a U interface have an NT1 built in and can be connected directly to the local exchange. Routers with an S/T interface need to be connected to an external NT1 device.

Basic Rate Interface (BRI)

ISDN comes in two variations: Basic Rate Interface (BRI) and Primary Rate Interface (PRI). ISDN BRI provides two 64Kbps bearer channels (B channels) and one 16Kbps D channel. The two B channels are designed to carry data, voice, and video. Any "user" data is transferred across the B channels. The D channel is used to communicate both control and signaling information. Data needed for call setup, maintenance, and breakdown is transmitted over the D channel. Because of its structure, we sometimes hear BRI referred to as 2B+1D.

ISDN uses a framing structure called Link Access Procedure on the D-Channel (LAPD) for communications across the D channel. Although the primary purpose of the D channel is call control, under certain circumstances it can carry user data as well. The encapsulation used across the B channels is up to you. Once the link has been set up via the D channel, the resulting link (or links) over the B channel(s) can use HDLC, PPP, or SLIP encapsulations.

> **NOTE** The BRI physical layer specification is outlined in ITU-T I.430. (ITU-T is short for International Telecommunication Union Telecommunication Standardization Sector. It was formerly the Consultative Committee for International Telegraph and Telephone or CCITT.) The standard can be obtained through the ITU-T.

Configuring BRI

BRI is a dial-up technology. Thus, configuring your routers for ISDN BRI support alone is not enough; you also need to configure a means to trigger the call. You will learn how to do that later in the chapter, when we talk about dial-on-demand routing. But for now it is important to identify the commands that are unique to using ISDN as your dial-up technology.

When configuring ISDN, you need to remember the three essential configuration tasks required for establishing a connection via ISDN:

- Identify an ISDN switch type.
- Configure all necessary SPIDs.
- Configure dialer statements to trigger and establish a call.

Identifying an ISDN Switch Type

There are many ISDN switch types throughout the world. Unfortunately, they all work a little differently. But thankfully, Cisco has done a good job of providing support for them. All that you need to do is identify which one you will be communicating with. To make that happen you use the `isdn switch-type <switch-type>` command. In older versions of the IOS, this command could be performed in global configuration only. Cisco soon learned, however, that there are situations when one router must communicate with multiple switch types, so IOS version 12 changed this command to work in global and interface configuration modes. North America uses the AT&T 5ESS, DMS-100, and National ISDN 1 (NI1) switches. To obtain a complete list of the switch types supported by Cisco, use the following command:

```
Router(config)# isdn switch-type ?
```

Configuring SPIDs

Depending on the switch type you use, you may be required to configure one or more Service Provider IDs (SPIDs). SPIDs are configured on the BRI interface itself. Without an SPID configured, some dialer interfaces will not accept incoming calls; some will not even come up initially when the BRI interface is first enabled. Assign SPIDs using the `isdn spid1 <SPID>` and `isdn spid2 <SPID>` commands. Since BRI comes with two B channels, it will also come with two phone numbers assigned, one per B channel. In addition to the phone numbers, the service provider will also assign two SPIDs, one per B channel. SPIDs are numbers based on the phone number—for example, 41055512121010.

Establishing a Call

Configuring for ISDN BRI alone is never enough. In addition to the BRI-specific information just described, you must also configure a means to identify when and where to call. Dial-on-demand routing (DDR) give us a mechanism to specify this information, as you'll see later in this chapter when we talk about the DDR configuration. Although DDR can be used with other dial-up technologies, all DDR examples in this chapter will use ISDN as the dial-up technology.

Primary Rate Interface (PRI)

ISDN Primary Rate Interface (PRI) is commonly used for higher-capacity applications. It is a popular solution for central offices that have many branch offices in remote locations. The central office can implement PRI, and the remotes can use the lower-capacity ISDN BRI. PRI provides a higher concentration of B channels for more simultaneous calls. In North America and Japan, PRI provides 23 B channels of 64Kbps each and one 64Kbps D channel for control and signaling. The aggregated bandwidth provides us with up to 1.544Mbps. In Europe, Australia, and other parts of the world, PRI provides 30 B channels and one 64Kbps D channel for an aggregate bandwidth of more than 2Mbps. The PRI physical-layer specification is outlined in ITU-T I.431.

Configuring PRI

Configuring PRI more closely resembles configuring a dedicated line like T1 than a dial-up technology like ISDN BRI. When a PRI interface is added to a router, it is added in the form of a PRI controller. All configuration commands relate to configuring the PRI controller. The following is an example configuration for PRI connectivity:

```
!
isdn switch-type primary-5ess
!
controller T1 1/0
 framing esf
 linecode b8zs
 pri-group timeslots 1-24
!
```

Most ISDN switch types support PRI as well as BRI. This example tells the router that it will be interfacing with an AT&T 5ESS switch and using the protocol for PRI. To configure a PRI controller, you must enter controller configuration mode for that controller. In our example, we use the PRI controller in slot 1 port 0 (controller T1 1/0). Once there, we can configure parameters such as framing, line-code, and the number of time slots set up for you by your provider. The PRI service provider should give you all of this information when the service is activated. If not, you will definitely want to ask.

Dial-on-Demand Routing (DDR)

Dial-on-demand routing (DDR) is commonly used with dial-up technologies, so it is frequently discussed in conjunction with ISDN. The basic concept of DDR is that you establish a WAN link when it is required, maintain it as necessary, and drop it when no longer needed. DDR is suitable for situations where WAN access is low-volume and needed only occasionally.

Configuring DDR

There are three steps required in configuring DDR:

1. Identify interesting traffic.
2. Establish static routes to remote networks.
3. Map next-hop layer three addresses to phone numbers.

Interesting Traffic

The first step is to identify *interesting* traffic—any traffic that, when detected at the router's interface, will trigger a call. When the router detects no interesting traffic for a specified time, the link can be dropped. While the link is up, all unfiltered traffic will be routed; traffic that is not interesting, however, will not maintain the open link. Interesting traffic can be identified by protocol, by address, or any combination of protocols and addresses. If you can create an access list, you can identify interesting traffic.

Establishing Static Routes

The second step in configuring DDR is to establish static routes to remote networks. Why do we need to do this? Since dial-on-demand networks are only up and routing part of the time, network updates cannot be received periodically as in a full-time link. It is also not feasible to have network updates trigger a link, because that could mean huge connection charges. For example, suppose you make RIP updates part of your criteria for interesting traffic. If your router is making calls every 30 seconds, at $.01 to $.10 a minute for ISDN connection charges, your monthly phone bill could be enormous (even worse if there are long distance charges involved). So, the answer is to use static routes in conjunction with DDR.

Mapping Layer Addresses

The third step is to map layer 3 addresses to phone numbers. A router configured for dial-on-demand has to know what phone number to call when a packet has to be sent to a specific next-hop address. This being the case, every IP, IPX, and AppleTalk next-hop address must be mapped to its respective phone number. A router can be configured with many mappings between next-hop addresses and phone numbers.

Figure 13.1 illustrates an example of a network topology that uses ISDN and DDR for connectivity. In addition, the working code demonstrates the configuration commands required to make DDR work on this network.

Figure 13.1   A Simple ISDN Network

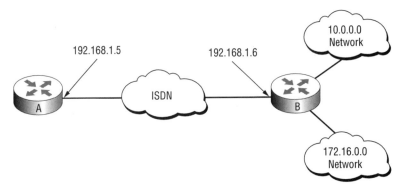

```
!
hostname A
!
isdn switch-type basic-5ess
!
interface BRI0
  ip address 192.168.1.5 255.255.255.252
  encapsulation ppp
  dialer map ip 192.168.1.6 5551111
  dialer-group 1
!
ip route 10.0.0.0 255.0.0.0 192.168.1.6
ip route 172.16.0.0 255.255.0.0 192.168.1.6
dialer-list 1 protocol ip permit
!
```

This code provides simple ISDN connectivity from router A to router B. We have identified the ISDN switch type to be an AT&T 5ESS. At the dialer interface (BRI0), we have assigned an IP address of 192.168.1.5 and PPP as the encapsulation type.

For DDR connectivity to take place, we had to identify interesting traffic; we did so using the global `dialer-list 1 protocol ip permit` command. Once the dialer list is created you must apply it to the dialer interface; the example uses the `dialer-group 1` command. The "1" parameter corresponds with the number in the dialer-list. These two statements result in defining all IP as interesting and applying that interesting traffic to BRI0.

Also notice that we created two static routes, one to the 10.0.0.0 network and one to the 172.16.0.0 network. The next-hop address in both of these is 192.168.1.6, which is the remote router's (router B) IP address. These static routes are not enough for router A to route packets to the remote networks. Router A also has to know what phone number to call to reach the next hop address of 192.168.1.6. To make this happen, we use the `dialer map ip 192.168.1.6 5551111` command.

Optional DDR Commands

Beyond the minimum configuration just described, with ISDN and DDR the Cisco IOS offers several optional but valuable commands:

- `dialer idle-timeout <time out in seconds>`

Router
Configuration

PART 3

- `dialer load-threshold <load>`
- `dialer wait-for-carrier-time <seconds>`
- `dialer map <protocol> <address>` name `<remote router> <speed 56> <broadcast> <phone number>`

The `dialer idle-timeout <seconds>` command tells the dialer interface how many seconds to wait after not detecting any interesting traffic before the call is dropped. Any time interesting traffic is detected, while the link is up, it resets the idle timer. When the idle timer reaches its predefined maximum, the call is dropped. The default without any configuration is 120 seconds.

The `dialer load-threshold <load> <direction>` command allows you to configure bandwidth on demand. If you have a multi-link bundle or a rotary group, you can aggregate links to add bandwidth to your existing connections based on your load. The load factor is specified as a number between 1 and 255. Load can be measured inbound, outbound, or in either direction.

For instance, you can issue the command `dialer load-threshold 191 either` on BRI0. Since BRI0 refers to ISDN with two B channels, we automatically have a bundle of two channels. This command tells BRI0 to activate the second channel when the load threshold reaches 75 percent in either direction.

NOTE By default, the two channels in ISDN BRI form a rotary group.

The `dialer wait-for-carrier-time <seconds>` command is necessary when you have to allow extra time for an interface to detect a carrier signal before, in the absence of a signal, it assumes something is wrong. The default is 30 seconds. You can increase this value to something that better serves your needs.

The `dialer map` command gives you some optional capabilities. The following is an example of the entire syntax:

```
dialer map <protocol> <address> [name <remote router>] [speed 56]
[broadcast] <phone number>
```

All of the parameters listed in brackets are optional. The name parameter allows you to specify a host name for the router you are connecting to. This parameter is only required if we plan to use CHAP authentication with our PPP encapsulation. The speed parameter allows us to use a speed of 56Kbps rather than the default of 64Kbps. Some service providers may require this. The broadcast keyword tells the router to allow broadcast traffic across this link when established. By default, the router does not broadcast out of that interface and across that link. You'll need to include the broadcast keyword if you plan to exchange routing updates across the link.

Following is an example of an ISDN and DDR configuration that includes some of these optional features:

```
!
hostname A
!
isdn switch-type basic-dms100
!
interface BRI0
  ip address 192.168.1.5 255.255.255.252
  encapsulation ppp
  isdn spid1 44455522221010
  isdn spid2 44455533331010
  dialer map ip 192.168.1.6 name B broadcast 5551111
  dialer-group 1
  dialer idle-timeout 60
  dialer load-threshold 191 either
  ppp authentication chap
!
ip route 10.0.0.0 255.0.0.0 192.168.1.6
ip route 172.16.0.0 255.255.0.0 192.168.1.6
dialer-list 1 protocol ip permit
!
```

In this example we are configured to connect to a DMS 100 switch, a type that requires SPIDs to be configured as well. We also added some options to the dialer map command. Because we are using PPP with CHAP authentication, it was necessary to add the *name* parameter. The name we use in this case is B, the host name of the next-hop router. We have also used the dialer idle-timeout and dialer load-threshold commands. The first of these tells the router to keep the dialer link up until interesting traffic has not been detected for 60 seconds, and the second tells the BRI interface to enable the second B channel when the load exceeds 75 percent (191) in either direction.

Router Configuration

PART 3

Access Lists

You can use an access list to replace the `dialer-list 1 protocol ip permit` command. For example:

```
!
dialer-list 1 list 99
access-list 99 permit any
!
```

Access lists provide us with a great deal of flexibility in identifying interesting traffic. Using them, you can specify traffic based on source and destination address, protocols, and even sockets. In the example code, we used the `dialer-list 1 list 99` statement to select access list number 99 as our interesting traffic criteria. Access list 99 is only one statement and permits all IP traffic but, if you want, you can create very specific criteria by creating a more sophisticated list.

Dialer Profiles

The commands and procedures discussed for configuring DDR actually relate to an earlier method. Consequently, Cisco likes to call it "Legacy DDR." Don't be fooled by the name; because of its simplicity, it is now and will probably remain the most popular way to configure DDR. Legacy DDR does, however, have a limitation: You must dedicate all dialer parameters to the physical interface itself. In other words, no matter what number you are dialing or location you are connecting with, your BRI's addresses, time-out values, encapsulation types, or interesting traffic cannot change. This is somewhat limiting if you have a highly diverse internetwork. To remedy this, Cisco provides a neat feature called *dialer profiles*.

Essentially, a dialer profile is a virtual dialer interface to use for connectivity to each of your remote sites. The physical interfaces, like the BRIs, are made part of dialer pools that the virtual dialer interface can use. The physical interface will never be permanently married to a specific subnet or circuit. It will be used as necessary by whatever virtual interface may need it.

You create the virtual dialer interface using the `interface dialer <number>` command. Once this command is issued, the dialer is declared and you are placed in configuration mode for that dialer interface. Once in interface configuration mode, you configure the dialer just as if it were any physical interface. Note, however, that for dialer profiles you must issue a few different commands compared to legacy DDR.

Once in interface configuration mode for the dialer interface, you can configure parameters such as:

- Dialer string
- Dialer pool
- Dialer group
- Dialer idle-timeout
- Any layer 3 addresses that will be associated with that dialer interface.

In legacy DDR, you associate a layer 3 address with a phone number using the `dialer map` statement. With dialer profiles, you don't use the `dialer map` statement at all. Just assign the IP, IPX, and Apple addresses along with one phone number on the interface. The idea is that a single dialer interface will never dial any other number. The command used to identify the dial string is `dialer string <phone number>`.

Since a dialer interface is a virtual interface, it has to be associated with a physical interface to do any useful work. When configuring dialer profiles, group your BRI interfaces into dialer pools and assign a dialer pool to whatever dialer interface may need it. To make this happen, use the `dialer pool-member <pool number>` command on the physical interface and the `dialer pool <pool number>` command on the dialer interface. For a dialer interface to use a physical BRI, the pool numbers in their configurations must match.

The dialer group, dialer idle-timeout, and addition of layer 3 addresses are done the same way as legacy DDR. The difference is that the parameters are assigned to a virtual interface and do not permanently affect the physical interface.

The following is an example of using dialer profiles for different physical connections:

```
!
isdn switch-type basic-5ess
!
interface BRI0
 encapsulation PPP
 dialer pool-member 1
!
interface BRI1
 encapsulation PPP
 dialer pool-member 1
 !
```

Router Configuration

PART 3

```
interface BRI2
 encapsulation PPP
 dialer pool-member 2
!
interface BRI3
 encapsulation PPP
 dialer pool-member 2
!
interface dialer0
ip address 10.1.2.1 255.255.255.0
ipx network 1a
 encapsulation ppp
 dialer idle-timeout 30
 dialer pool 1
 dialer string 5551111
 dialer-group 1
!
interface dialer1
ip address 10.1.3.1 255.255.255.0
ipx network 2b
 encapsulation ppp
 dialer idle-timeout 120
 dialer pool 2
 dialer string 5556666
 dialer-group 3
```

In this example we have four BRI interfaces and two locations the router will be calling. Since there are two locations to call, we create two dialer interfaces. Dialer0 will use dialer pool 1, and Dialer1 will use dialer pool 2. Each has its own IP and IPX addresses assigned, and each has its own interesting traffic assigned (as you can see by the `dialer-group` command). Since we have four BRIs, we can assign each dialer pool two interfaces. This way, if one is busy the router will automatically use the other. In addition, we'll be able to set up bandwidth on demand if we want to do that later.

Verifying DDR

When troubleshooting ISDN and DDR, Show and Debug commands are your friend. Some valuable ones include:

show dialer	Displays the status of a dialer interface, including how long it's been active.
show isdn status	Displays the status of an ISDN link.
show isdn active	Displays layer 1, 2, and 3 information about your ISDN configuration.
show interfaces	Displays interface-related counters and configuration parameters.
debug dialer	Shows real-time call setup and call tear-down activities.
debug isdn-q921	Shows ISDN layer 2 activity.
debug isdn-q931	Shows ISDN layer 3 activity.

The show dialer Command

This is among the more useful commands for verifying DDR operation. It gives you an idea whether the dialer has done its job. Specifically, it tells you whether the line is connected and if so why, to where, and for how many minutes. If show dialer indicates that you are connected, there is a good chance DDR and ISDN are both working properly. Here is an example output:

```
RouterA# show dialer interface bri 0
BRI0 - dialer type = ISDN
Dial String  Successes   Failures  Last called  Last status
5551111            1           0    00:01:39     successful
0 incoming call(s) have been screened.
BRI0: B-Channel 1
Idle timer (120 secs), Fast idle timer (20 secs)
Wait for carrier (30 secs), Re-enable (15 secs)
Dialer state is data link layer up
Dial reason: ip (s=172.17.0.1, d=10.0.1.1)
Interface bound to profile Dialer0
Time until disconnect 22 secs
Current call connected 00:01:39
Connected to 5551111 (B)
```

```
BRIO: B-Channel 2

Idle timer (120 secs), Fast idle timer (20 secs)

Wait for carrier (30 secs), Re-enable (15 secs)

Dialer state is idle
```

The show isdn active Command

Another useful command is `show isdn active`, which allows you to see information relating to all ISDN active calls on the router. It may be useful at times if your router or access server has many dialer interfaces. You can isolate and look at only the ISDN ones. The following is an example output:

Router# show isdn active

```
-----------------------------------------------------------------

                       ISDN ACTIVE CALLS

-----------------------------------------------------------------

History Table MaxLength = 100 entries

History Retain Timer = 15 Minutes

-----------------------------------------------------------------

Call Calling     Called       Duration  Remote   Time until

Type Number      Number       Seconds   Name     Disconnect

-----------------------------------------------------------------

Out              4445551111   Active(10)  B                  11

-----------------------------------------------------------------
```

The show isdn status Command

Another extremely useful command, especially when troubleshooting ISDN problems, is `show isdn status`. This allows you to view the status of ISDN as it relates to layers 1, 2, and 3 of the OSI model. If an ISDN problem occurs, you can use the output of this command to isolate it to one of these layers. The following output is an example of a working ISDN interface. If your output is similar to this, chances are ISDN has been configured correctly:

Router# show isdn status

```
Global ISDN Switchtype = basic-5ess
```

```
ISDN BRI0 interface
     dsl 0, interface ISDN Switchtype = basic-5ess
  Layer 1 Status:
    ACTIVE
  Layer 2 Status:
    TEI = 64, Ces = 1, SAPI = 0, State = MULTIPLE_FRAME_ESTABLISHED
  Layer 3 Status:
    0 Active Layer 3 Call(s)
  Activated dsl 0 CCBs = 0
```

NOTE The layer 1 status should be ACTIVE. The layer 2 status should include state = MULTIPLE_FRAME_ESTABLISHED. Layer 3 should not list any errors.

The show interfaces Command

As in all cases, the show interface command can be useful, showing you physical and data link layer information relating to the BRI interface. One thing to keep in mind, however: You need to look at BRI output carefully because it might lie to you. Each BRI interface is viewed by the router as being made up of three parts: two B channels and a D channel. In the example below, when we issue the show interface bri 0 command, the first line of the output tells us that the physical interface and the line protocol are both up; this is deceiving. The command only gives us a status of the D channel and is fooling the router into thinking a real data link is established. This is indicated by the word "spoofing" in the output. Any time the router is spoofing, it is fooling you into believing something that isn't true.

```
Router# show interfaces bri 0
 BRI0 is up, line protocol is up (spoofing)
  Hardware is BRI  Internet address is 192.168.1.5/30
  MTU 1500 bytes, BW 64 Kbit, DLY 20000 usec, rely 255/255, load 1/255
  Encapsulation PPP, loopback not set
  Last input 00:00:01, output 00:00:01, output hang never
  Last clearing of "show interface" counters never
  Input queue: 0/75/0 (size/max/drops); Total output drops: 0
```

Router Configuration

PART 3

```
Queueing strategy: weighted fair  Output queue: 0/64/0 (size/
  threshold/drops)
  Conversations  0/1 (active/max active)
  Reserved Conversations 0/0 (allocated/max allocated)
5 minute input rate 0 bits/sec, 0 packets/sec
5 minute output rate 0 bits/sec, 0 packets/sec
  609 packets input, 2526 bytes, 0 no buffer
  Received 0 broadcasts, 0 runts, 0 giants
  0 input errors, 0 CRC, 0 frame, 0 overrun, 0 ignored, 0 abort
  615 packets output, 2596 bytes, 0 underruns
  0 output errors, 0 collisions, 5 interface resets
  0 output buffer failures, 0 output buffers swapped out
  3 carrier transitions
```

We should have issued a show interface command that specifically addressed the B channels. The show interfaces bri 0 1 command below reveals that the first B channel is actually down (contrary to the show interfaces bri0 output). To view information relating to the individual B channels, you simply add the number of the B channel at the end of the normal show interface command:

```
Router# show interfaces bri 0 1
  BRI0:1 is down, line protocol is down
  Hardware is BRI
  MTU 1500 bytes, BW 64 Kbit, DLY 20000 usec, rely 255/255, load 1/255
  Encapsulation PPP, loopback not set, keepalive not set  LCP Closed
  Closed: IPCP  Last input never, output never, output hang never
  Last clearing of "show interface" counters never  Queueing
    strategy: fifo
  Output queue 0/40, 0 drops; input queue 0/75, 0 drops
  5 minute input rate 0 bits/sec, 0 packets/sec
  5 minute output rate 0 bits/sec, 0 packets/sec
    0 packets input, 0 bytes, 0 no buffer
    Received 0 broadcasts, 0 runts, 0 giants
    0 input errors, 0 CRC, 0 frame, 0 overrun, 0 ignored, 0 abort
```

```
0 packets output, 0 bytes, 0 underruns

0 output errors, 0 collisions, 7 interface resets

0 output buffer failures, 0 output buffers swapped out

0 carrier transitions
```

You will notice the first line of the `show interfaces bri 0 1` command tells us that the D channel number on the BRI0 is actually down. This is different from what we were told using the `show interfaces bri 0` command alone.

TIP   Look at the *Debug Command Reference* for examples of the debug `dialer`, debug `isdn-q921`, and debug `isdn-q931` command output. These are valuable commands and can really be helpful when troubleshooting ISDN problems. The reference is available on the Cisco Documentation CD as well as Cisco web site at www.cisco.com.

Snapshot Routing

As an alternative to using static routes in your DDR configurations, you can use *snapshot routing*. When snapshot routing is configured, routing updates are held during configured sleep times and exchanged during configured active times. You have complete control over when updates are exchanged. For instance, you can configure the router to sleep for an hour, connect for five minutes to exchange updates, and sleep for another hour. Also, if the router connects as a result of detecting interesting traffic, updates can be exchanged then as well. The result is that the routing table stays somewhat up-to-date but you don't have to pay connection charges for dialing up every 30, 60, or 90 seconds.

Configuring Snapshot Routing

Snapshot routing requires us to configure all routers that will participate. Each will be designated as either a snapshot server or snapshot client. For this chapter, we will configure our router A as a snapshot client and router B as the server.

Each router needs to be issued two commands. The client gets the following statements:

```
Snapshot client <active time> <quiet time> [suppress-statechange-
updates] [dialer]

  dialer map snapshot <sequence number> name <name> <phone number>
```

For the server, issue these statements:

```
snapshot server <active time> [dialer]
dialer map snapshot <sequence number> name <name> <phone number>
```

You will notice that with the `snapshot server` and `snapshot client` commands, we declare each device as either a server or client. On the client, we can specify active time and quiet time in minutes. The *active time* is the time in minutes the router will exchange routing updates, and the *quiet time* is the time in minutes the router waits before exchanging updates. We can even use the optional `suppress-statechange-updates` or `dialer` keywords. The `suppress-statechange-updates` keyword suppresses the exchange of routing updates even if there is a change in the link's state. The optional `dialer` command tells the router to dial up if (in the absence of normal interesting traffic) it hasn't been able to exchange updates. You may have noticed that a snapshot server is not configured with a quiet time. This is because there is no need for one.

The `dialer map snapshot` command includes a *sequence number*, remote router *name*, and a *phone number* as parameters. The client router uses the sequence number to prioritize the order in which the client calls all servers. The remote name is the host name of the called router, and the phone number is the number to dial to access the remote router.

Here is an example:

```
!Config for router A
interface BRIO
    snapshot client 5 120 dialer
    dialer map snapshot 1 name B 5551111
!


!Config for router B
interface BRIO
    snapshot server 5 dialer
    dialer map snapshot 1 name A 5552222
!
```

In our example we configured router A as a client and B as a server. On router A's BRI interface, we have specified an active time of five minutes and a quiet time of two hours (120 minutes). We have told it to dial in the absence of a normal connection. When appropriate, it will dial router B specifically at 5551111. Router B has been configured to accept calls from router A but only stay active for 5 minutes.

NOTE   When troubleshooting problems with snapshot routing, it is sometimes necessary to clear the quiet timer to facilitate an immediate active time. To do so you can use the `clear snapshot quiet-time` command.

Dial Backup

In networking, redundancy is sometimes a requirement. You can provide redundancy to WAN links using an IOS feature called *dial backup*. The dial backup feature allows you to dedicate one interface on a router as a backup to another interface.

ISDN is a great candidate for a dial backup solution. For instance, you can have a T1 line as a primary WAN link and dedicate an ISDN BRI interface as its backup. While the T1 is operational, the BRI interface stays idle and is not used. When the T1 link goes down, the router uses typical DDR commands to establish an alternate connection. The bandwidth provided by an ISDN connection may not be substantial enough to replace the T1 line but can keep essential systems connected and operational while the T1 is being fixed.

Configuring Dial Backup

Configuring dial backup requires you to understand three basic commands:

- `backup interface <interface>`
- `backup load <enable threshold> <disable threshold>`
- `backup delay <enable delay> <disable delay>`

Only the `backup interface <interface>` command is truly required for dial backup to work. You use this command to specify which physical interface will serve as a backup to a selected primary interface.

The `backup load` command allows you to specify a load threshold that the router will wait for before activating a backup link. The `backup delay` command identifies a delay time before a backup link is activated and before a backup link is dropped when no longer needed. You impose some delay before a backup interface becomes active because you don't want a simple network burp or a flapping interface to activate the backup link. Because you still have to pay connection charges on your calls, you want to be sure they are warranted.

Let's look at an example:

```
!
interface BRI0
 encapsulation PPP
```

```
   dialer pool-member 1
!
interface dialer0
ip address 10.1.2.1 255.255.255.0
 encapsulation ppp
 dialer pool 1
 dialer string 5551111
 dialer-group 1
!
interface serial 0
 ip address 10.1.1.1 255.255.255.0
 backup interface dialer 0
 backup delay 10 30
 backup load 50 10
!
```

In this example we have created a backup to interface serial 0. We have done this by using a virtual interface called dialer0. Dialer0 is configured to use dialer pool 1. We've configured BRI0 to be a member of this group with the `dialer pool-member 1` command. Now, rather than configuring BRI0 directly, we can configure dialer0 instead. This allows us to add more physical interfaces to the dialer pool at any time if we later need to.

The `dialer string` command here configures dialer0 to dial 5551111 when the backup interface becomes active and interesting traffic is detected. Interesting traffic in this case is defined in dialer-list 1 (not listed), as indicated by the `dialer-group 1` command on the interface.

Interface serial 0 has been configured to use dialer0 as the backup interface in the event that its link should fail. For this we used the `backup interface dialer 0` command. We also established a delay for both the times before it becomes active and before it is dropped after dialing, using the `backup delay 10 30` command. This tells the router to wait 10 seconds before activating dialer0 after serial0 goes down. If it has been active but is now no longer needed, the router will wait 30 seconds before the ISDN link is dropped. Finally, we have configured the interface with the `backup load 50 10` command. This command tells serial 0 to activate BRI0 when the load threshold reaches 50 percent and drop the secondary link when the load drops below 10 percent.

Dial Backup for Frame Relay

ABC Corporation wanted a way to back up their Frame Relay PVCs in the event that one or more should go down. Initially, they set up a dial backup configuration using ISDN as the backup interface. When they first implemented the backup solution, they tested it by unplugging the CSU/DSU from the smart jack in their wiring closet. That seemed as good a way to test a downed line as any other. The backup interface went active and established an alternate link. It seemed to test OK, so everyone was happy.

Later that month, a router located in one of ABC's remote sites went down, and so access to the site via Frame Relay was cut off. At the central location, the backup interface never became active. The result was that network access to the remote site was down for almost four hours before a contractor came on site to fix the problem. The outage alone cost them thousands of dollars in sales.

ABC brought in a savvy contractor first to figure out why the dial backup didn't work and then to do whatever was needed to prevent the problem from happening again. Once he got on site, it didn't take him long to figure out the problem. He found the following:

Configuring conventional dial backup for a Frame Relay link tends to work only under certain circumstances. If the physical WAN link to the central office goes down, dial backup will work. If the CSU/DSU is faulty or disconnected, dial backup will work. If LMI updates are no longer received from the CO, dial backup will work. However, if a router goes down on an opposite part of a hub-and-spoke network, it will not trigger a dial backup. The only time the dial backup will happen is if the connection to your CO goes down or stops sending LMI messages.

Losing access to the router at the remote site didn't affect LMI updates to the router in ABC's central location. As a result, the router at the central site thought everything was fine and didn't trigger the ISDN interface to place a call. As it turned out, it wasn't the router that went down at all. The fault was in the local loop between the remote location and the central office. But since the administrators at the remote site had not set up a dial backup solution on their end, there was still no redundancy under this circumstance.

Now ABC knew why it didn't work. Next they needed a solution to this problem. They couldn't tolerate any more four-hour network outages. This meant an alternative to traditional dial backup was required.

The solution was to back up Frame Relay with a *floating static route*. They set up a typical DDR link to all the remote sites with one small variation. They set an administrative distance of 200 for all static routes to the remote locations. This made the static routes less desirable than the routes learned via their routing protocols. The nice thing about this solution is that the static route is only used when the dynamic route goes away—for example, when another router goes down.

Today, ABC functions well with their backup solution. They learned a valuable

CASE STUDY

24seven

lesson, however: They should have tested their backup solution a little more thoroughly. That should be a lesson to all of us. When implementing a backup solution, test, test, test! Finding out it doesn't work when it is too late can cost you time, money, your reputation, and business.

Part 4

Optimization and Maintenance

- Traffic prioritization and queuing
- Making your router a bastion host
- Access lists as a security tool
- Router management using Syslog and command-line tools
- Using SNMP and other management protocols
- Using basic and advanced troubleshooting tools
- Disaster planning and preparedness
- Using the Cisco Technical Assistance Center effectively
- Hot Standby Router Protocol (HSRP)
- The Firewall feature set

14

Traffic Prioritization and Queuing

There are many types of network applications, and they all have different needs and sensitivities. Some applications may not be able to tolerate delay well, while others are not at all disturbed by it. For example, with a large FTP data transfer we are not too concerned about the nature of the delay imposed by the networks so long as the delay is not large enough to cause the session to time out. A video stream, however, is very delay-sensitive, because video needs a constant delay or else it will appear choppy. The same is true for voice and many other network applications.

As computer networks have grown and begun to span larger distances, companies have started to see their existing networks as money-saving tools. Instead of having people go to meetings in remote cities, companies are now using their networks to videoconference. Sure, this saves money, but it also significantly increases the demands on the network. Voice data is now being carried across traditional network links to minimize long distance charges. These are great advances, but these types of applications require a large amount of bandwidth and are very sensitive to the variable delays imposed by most networks. When voice data travels across a network, for instance, it needs to sound as clear as if it were traversing normal dedicated voice circuits.

Besides voice and video, many other applications have requirements that can strain the typical network. The big question is how to deal with these requirements. More bandwidth is an option; so is using a dedicated network for your voice and video needs. However, in many cases, traffic prioritization offers a cost-effective solution.

Traffic Prioritization

Traffic arriving at a router is handled by protocol-dependent switching mechanisms. These switching processes include the delivery of traffic to an outgoing interface buffer. The typical method for processing traffic from these outgoing interface buffers is a first-in first-out (FIFO) algorithm. This means very simply that packets will be sent out in the order in which they were received. FIFO was the default on all router interfaces until Cisco's IOS version 11.1. In that version, Cisco switched from using FIFO on all interfaces and changed the default queuing type for all interfaces with speeds less than 2Mbps to weighted fair queuing. The major problem with FIFO queuing is that once the interface buffer fills up, the router will discard anything that does not fit into the buffer. There is no intelligence to decide which traffic should be discarded and which should not be. Instead, whatever traffic gets there when there is no more room is discarded.

NOTE   FIFO queues use a discard mechanism much like musical chairs: If Michelle is left standing when the music stops, then Michelle is out. It makes no difference how important Michelle is to the game: Once the music stops and she is left standing, the rules say that she must stop playing because there are no more chairs for her. Michelle could, however, be saved by the concept of prioritizing. By changing the queuing type, we could give Michelle a higher priority than all other people in the game. Thus, she would be allowed to sit down first, with everyone else forced to wait until she is seated before they can scramble for their chairs. This would ensure that Michelle was not discarded. (Of course this might make Michelle happy, but it defeats the whole purpose of the game of Musical Chairs.)

In a real-world environment you might find it both useful and necessary to bump up the priority of a specific type of traffic to help ensure it is not discarded. In Figure 14.1, for example, the AppleTalk traffic has been given a higher priority than IP or IPX traffic, so it is processed from the queue first. Normally, the IPX packet would be processed first since it arrived first and is on the bottom of the queue. The increased priority of the Apple-Talk protocol, however, overrides the typical FIFO behavior and allows the AppleTalk packet to get out onto the network first.

Figure 14.1   Setting priorities by protocol

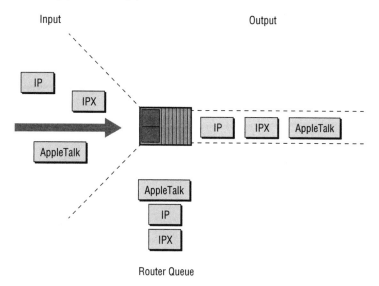

Router Queue

Typically, traffic is prioritized to first allocate bandwidth to ensure that those applications needing to get through the network quickly are not compromised by other network applications that can handle more delay. The classic example of this is a Telnet or terminal emulation session versus a large data transfer.

When people type into their Telnet or terminal emulation session, they do so erratically. They may type a couple of lines rapidly, then stop and think, and then quickly type a few more lines. These types of applications therefore tend to accumulate characters for a short period of time and then send them. Once the receiving application gets these characters, it acknowledges them in some form. This acknowledgement may be an answer to a query or, in some cases, a repeat of the data the receiving application received. Typically, new transmissions are held until the sending application has received an acknowledgement from its peer application. This type of application is therefore very delay-sensitive.

What would happen, for example, if a large FTP session was in progress while someone else was running a Telnet session? The FTP session represents a constant data stream, while the Telnet session represents small bursts of data. Without any type of traffic prioritization, the FTP session could clog the outgoing interface queue and thus severely impact the Telnet session. Inevitably, the FTP session is going to keep the interface queue very full. Some Telnet traffic will be able to sneak through, but the FTP traffic will monopolize the queue. Prioritizing the traffic will allow both these applications to play well together.

Prioritization is most effective on links that have bursts of traffic combined with relatively low average data rates. If the link is constantly congested, traffic prioritization probably will not solve the problem.

WARNING   On uncontested links, prioritization actually degrades performance. There is no need to prioritize traffic on links that do not experience congestion. Enabling prioritization simply wastes CPU cycles on the router.

Types of Queuing

Cisco's IOS supports several different types of queuing algorithms. The three most common are:

- Weighted fair queuing
- Priority queuing
- Custom queuing

Which queuing option you use depends largely on the traffic needs of your network. Each queuing option has drawbacks and benefits. In order to determine the best queuing option, you should ask a few questions about the network.

- Is the network congested? If the network is not congested, there is no need for any type of queuing. Congestion occurs in a router when the amount of traffic coming into the router exceeds the router's ability to send traffic out. The border router in Figure 14.2 has no reason to be queuing, because there is only one input interface and one output interface. The speeds of these two interfaces are the same; thus there is no threat of congestion.

- Is strict control needed over how the data is queued? If strict control is not needed over how the data is queued and processed, then the default of weighted fair queuing is probably the best answer. Weighted fair queuing is discussed in the next section. If strict control is needed, either priority queuing or custom queuing must be implemented.

Figure 14.2   In this situation there is no need for queuing, because there is no threat of congestion.

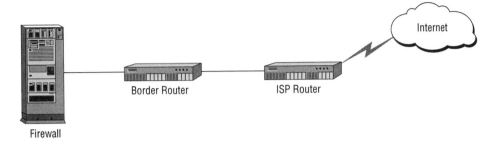

> **NOTE**   In order to exercise strict control, you must define a queuing policy. A queuing policy is developed by analyzing the existing data on a network and knowing what each network application needs in terms of bandwidth. Each network scenario is different and calls for a different queuing policy.

The three queuing methods can be ranked from most favorable to least favorable. For almost all network implementations, the default queuing option of weighted fair is probably the correct one to use. Someone obviously thought that weighted fair queuing was useful enough to have it turned on by default on all interface with speeds less than 2Mbps.

The next in order of desirability is custom queuing, used when some delay can be tolerated by the network application. As you'll see, with custom queuing there is generally some type of delay associated with most traffic on a congested link.

If you cannot tolerate delay, you are forced to use priority queuing. Priority queuing, however, is usually the least favorable queuing method of the three to use. Priority queuing will service all high-priority traffic first, which may sound great; but it also means that if there is always high-priority traffic present, no lower-priority traffic will get through. The first few RIP packets don't really need to get through, but if none get through because they are not defined as high priority, then routes will start to age out of the routing tables.

The following sections discuss these queuing options in greater detail.

Weighted Fair Queuing

Weighted fair queuing is the simplest queuing type to configure because it does not require the creation of any queue lists. Instead, traffic is sorted into messages that are part of conversations, and the queue is serviced based on conversation. Weighted fair queuing makes sure that high-bandwidth conversations do not monopolize the link by giving low-volume traffic priority over high-volume traffic. This is done by breaking up packet trains, which are groups of packets that travel together and are generated by high-volume network applications. Weighted fair queuing divides up traffic into conversations. Conversations are categorized by things like source and destination MAC address, source and destination network address, source and destination port numbers, frame relay DLCIs, etc.

Traffic from various conversations is placed into the queue. The order of removal from the queue is based on the virtual time of delivery of the last bit of the packet. This means that smaller packets, which take less time to arrive on the interface, get priority. While a large packet may arrive at the router before a smaller packet, what really matters is which packet finishes arriving first. The packet that gets completely into the router first will have priority in being removed from the queue and forwarded.

Low-volume conversation packets get priority over high-volume conversation packets, and the first of these packets to arrive gets priority. This means that bandwidth is shared among the various conversations. Large file transfers with large packet sizes end up being interleaved among each other while small packets in low-volume conversations are given priority and sent through.

Because of this bias toward small, low-volume conversations, weighted fair queuing is not suitable for high-speed interfaces. It is, however, perfectly suited for interfaces with speeds lower than 2Mbps. Weighted fair queuing is enabled by default on these interfaces, and nothing needs to be done to configure it. Because weighted fair queuing is a default, it does not show up when you list the running configuration, as shown below.

```
interface Serial0
 ip address 172.16.1.1 255.255.255.0
 no ip route-cache
 no ip mroute-cache
```

The command dialog below shows that Serial 0 is in fact using weighted fair queuing.

```
digger_router#show queue s0
  Input queue: 0/75/0 (size/max/drops); Total output drops: 0
  Queueing strategy: weighted fair
  Output queue: 0/1000/64/0 (size/max total/threshold/drops)
    Conversations  0/0/256 (active/max active/max total)
    Reserved Conversations 0/0 (allocated/max allocated)
```

The `show queue interface` command shows you the queuing that occurs on a given interface. The router in this example is running weighted fair queuing, with the current size of both the input and output buffers displayed along with the maximum size of these buffers. The default size of the output buffer is 64 messages. This output buffer size can be changed as necessary, as shown in the following example code:

```
interface Serial0
  ip address 172.16.1.1 255.255.255.0
  no ip route-cache
  no ip mroute-cache
  fair-queue 512 256 0
```

In this example, `Fair-queue 512` sets the congestion discard threshold to 512 messages. Congestion discard applies only to high-volume conversations to try and prevent high-volume conversation from monopolizing the link. Once an individual conversation queue has reached the congestion threshold, it will not be allowed to place any more messages in the queue until the queue is emptied to one fourth of the discard threshold. In the case of a discard threshold of 512, the conversation can begin to fill the queue again once it gets down to 128 messages.

The discard threshold can be any number between 1 and 4096. The `fair queue` command has several other options that can be configured, such as the option to set a number of dynamic conversation queues and the number of reserved conversations. The following example shows a `fair queue` command with these numbers set:

```
fair-queue 512 256 10
```

This command would set the discard threshold to 512, the number of dynamic conversation queues to 256, and the number of reservable conversation queue to 10. In most cases, the default of 64 256 0 will work fine. Be very careful when changing the queuing options. Making the queue sizes too big or too small can severely impact network performance. Do not change the queuing values unless there is a good reason to do so.

To turn off weighted fair queuing on an interface that has been configured by default to use it, issue the following command:

```
no fair-queue
```

Priority Queuing

Priority queuing works by breaking traffic into four separate queues: high, medium, normal, and low. The queues are serviced in the order implied by their names. The high queue is serviced first. When the high queue is empty, the medium queue is serviced. Once the medium queue is empty, the normal queue is serviced. And finally, when the normal queue is empty, the low queue is serviced. This means that if the high queue always has data in it, then no other queue will be serviced. Data could end up sitting in the lower-priority queues until it is no longer useful to the application that requested it. In this case, the application may request the same data again or, if congestion is bad enough, may just give up.

Priority queuing is used to ensure that critical data is given the best chance of getting through the network in a timely fashion. Obviously, if all data is defined as critical and placed in the high queue, then nothing happens. You end up with the same situation you had before you decided to enable priority queuing. It is therefore important to properly define the queues that are being used. All of the queues do not need to be used; you could have only a high and a normal queue. A good queuing strategy is one that gets your critical data through while not starving your less critical data.

Data is placed in queues by defining a priority list in the router. We do this in Global Configuration mode, as shown in the following example:

```
priority-list 1 protocol ip high tcp telnet

priority-list 1 protocol ip low udp tftp

priority-list 1 protocol ipx medium

priority-list 1 interface Serial1 medium

priority-list 1 protocol stun low

priority-list 1 protocol ip medium tcp 1352

priority-list 1 default normal
```

The priority list number can be anything between 1 and 16, and you can have multiple priority lists. However, only one priority list can be applied to a given interface at any one time. The above priority list specifies that all Telnet traffic will be placed in the high queue. The medium queue will get all IPX traffic, all traffic coming into the router from interface serial1, and all traffic for TCP port 1352. The normal queue will handle all traffic not specified in the priority list. The low queue will handle TFTP data and Serial Tunnel (STUN) traffic. Obviously, Telnet is the most important application on this network, and STUN is the least important.

NOTE When setting up a priority list make sure to specify a default queue.

Once you have created the priority list, you need to apply it to an interface. This is done with the `priority group` command shown here:

```
digger_router(config)#int s0
digger_router(config-if)#priority-group 1
```

In this example, we are using priority list 1 on interface serial 0.

Each queue has a default queue size:

- High: 20 datagrams
- Medium: 40 datagrams
- Normal: 60 datagrams
- Low: 80 datagrams

While these queue limits can be changed, it is generally not a good idea to do so. Changing them can have adverse results, such as starving the lower-priority protocols.

If you decide to change the default queue sizes, you do so from the Global Configuration mode. The following is an example of doubling the queue sizes:

```
priority-list 1 queue-limit 40 80 120 160
```

The `queue-limit` command is used to specify the size of the high, medium, normal, and low queues for a given priority list. The queue-list command applies only to the specified priority list.

Priority queuing can make troubleshooting difficult. Given the above priority list, what would you do if STUN and TFTP did not work? You would probably assume they were being starved since they are both in the low queue. However, Telnet, Ping, and other applications could still work. If the company's router people don't work closely with the application support people, it could take a long time to find the root cause of why STUN and TFTP are not working.

Priority queuing works fine if you keep an eye on it. But as traffic patterns change over time, it is easy to forget that priority queuing is running. When problems start, they are very difficult to track down because they become intermittent based on traffic loads at a given time. For this reason, we generally use weighted fair or custom queuing instead.

Optimization and Maintenance

PART 4

You can monitor how the queues are being processed with the following command:

```
Debug priority
```

```
PQ: Serial0 output (Pk size/Q 45/0)
PQ: Serial0: ipx -> medium
PQ: Serial0 output (Pk size/Q 104/1)
PQ: Serial0 output (Pk size/Q 56/0)
PQ: Serial0: ip (tcp 23) -> high
PQ: Serial0 output (Pk size/Q 45/0)
PQ: Serial0: ipx -> medium
PQ: Serial0 output (Pk size/Q 104/1)
PQ: Serial0: ip (tcp 23) -> high
PQ: Serial0 output (Pk size/Q 45/0)
PQ: Serial0: ipx -> medium
PQ: Serial0 output (Pk size/Q 104/1)
PQ: Serial0: ip (tcp 23) -> high
PQ: Serial0 output (Pk size/Q 45/0)
PQ: Serial0: ip (tcp 23) -> high
PQ: Serial0: cdp (defaulting) -> medium
PQ: Serial0 output (Pk size/Q 308/1)
PQ: Serial0 output (Pk size/Q 56/0)
```

In the second line of the output from the debug priority command, we can see that the router begins servicing IPX traffic from the medium queue. Then, at line 5, a Telnet packet goes into the high queue, so the router has to switch from servicing the medium queue to servicing the high queue. Once the high queue has been serviced, the router goes back to servicing the medium queue. The debug output allows us to see what queues are being serviced and what is being serviced from that queue. In the example above, we see that CDP is being serviced from the medium queue because medium is the default and CDP was not defined in the priority list.

Notice that the low and normal queues were not serviced when we captured this output. That is because none of the lower-priority traffic happened to hit the router while we were looking at it. The important thing to look for in this debug output is that the queues you expect to be serviced are actually being serviced. A good way to test this is to set to the low-priority queue a protocol for which you can easily generate packets, and then make sure it can get through the router. This way you can easily look at the debug output and see if the low queue is being serviced. If you create low-priority traffic and never see that the low queue is being processed, then constant congestion exists and more bandwidth or a different strategy may be needed. Though the lower queues can go unserviced for short periods of time, they should eventually be taken care of. If there is traffic that is of such low priority that no one will notice if it ever got through, try to alleviate congestion by eliminating that traffic rather than queuing it.

Custom Queuing

The final queuing option offered by Cisco is custom queuing. Configuration of custom queuing is much the same as the configuration of priority queuing. Lists are defined to classify data and place that data into specific queues based on the list definitions.

Custom queuing services each of the defined queues on a round-robin basis. This means that a certain amount of data is guaranteed to be processed from each queue in every time interval. By default, each queue is allowed to place 1,500 bytes onto the network each time it is processed. Assume four queues have been defined in Figure 14.3.

Figure 14.3 Custom queue operation

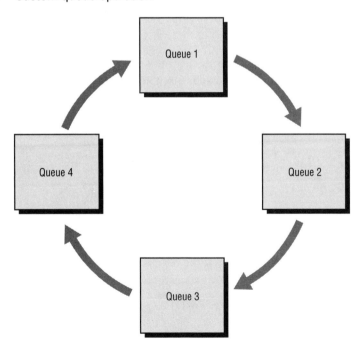

First, the router will look at queue 1, and if there is data, it will send data from the queue onto the network until its byte-count limit has been reached. By default the byte-count limit is 1,500 bytes. This means that once 1,500 bytes have been sent, the router will finish sending the packet it is working on and move on to process data from queue 2. Unless queue 2 is empty, its data will be processed until the byte-count limit is reached. Then the router will move on to queue 3, then queue 4, and finally back to queue 1.

By limiting what traffic is placed into which queue, we can give certain traffic preferential treatment. There is a maximum of 16 custom queues available. Actually, there are 17; queues 1–16 are user-defined queues, and queue 0 is a special system queue that is used for time-critical traffic. The following traffic types use queue 0:

- Spanning tree keep-alives
- ISO IGRP Hellos
- ESIS Hellos
- ISIS Hellos
- DECnet Hellos
- EIGRP Hellos
- SLARP Hellos
- OSPF Hellos
- Router Syslog messages

Queue 0 is emptied before any other queues are processed. This means if there is any data in queue 0, the queue will be immediately emptied. The other 16 possible queues all have a lower priority than queue 0. The way the router deals with queue 0 is much like priority queuing. Queue 0 would correlate to the high queue, and all the other queues would be a large medium queue that is broken up into smaller queues that are serviced when queue 0 is empty. Since queue 0 exists by default and does not need to be configured, there is really no cause to be concerned with it. The types of traffic placed into queue 0 should constitute a minimal percentage of network data.

Traffic can be given preferential access to the network in one of two ways. If, for example, two queues are configured, and IP traffic on port 1352 goes into queue 1 while all other traffic is placed in queue 2, then queue 1's traffic will effectively get half the bandwidth. Port 1352 traffic is guaranteed half of the bandwidth because each queue is serviced the same number of times and allowed to transmit 1,500 bytes. Another way to increase a protocol's access to the network is to modify the queue sizes. Four queues could be set up with different byte counts since each queue is serviced the same number of times per time interval. The size of the queue determines how much of the bandwidth that queue's data is allowed to use.

Take the simple example of three queues, 1, 2, and 3, with byte limits of 1,500, 3,000, and 4,500 bytes respectively. This means that 9,000 bytes are processed each time the router goes around and services the queues. Queue 3 would be able to use 1/2 of the bandwidth, queue 2 would be able to use 1/3, and queue 1 would have access to 1/6 of the bandwidth. These amounts are not exact since the packet being transferred when the byte count is reached is finished before processing of the next queue begins. Also, if a queue is empty, the router moves on to the next queue.

Since the router completes the packet it is working on when the byte count is reached, an understanding of packet sizes is necessary when changing the byte-count variable. Assume your router is sending large FTP packets from an Ethernet interface where the MTU is 1,500 bytes. With a byte count of 1,500, the router will send one packet each time the queue is processed. Now, increase the byte count to 1,510. What happens? That seemingly insignificant increase now allows the router to send two 1,500-byte packets. Since the first packet is processed before the byte count is reached, and the second packet is being processed when the byte count is hit, the router has to finish the packet it is working on before it can move to the next queue. So, even though the byte count is 1,510, it is effectively 3,000, assuming you are dealing with 1,500-byte packets.

To set up custom queuing, create a queue list in Global Configuration mode as follows:

```
queue-list 4 protocol ipx 4

queue-list 4 protocol ip 1 tcp telnet

queue-list 4 protocol ip 1 udp tftp

queue-list 4 protocol ip 2

queue-list 4 interface Serial0 3

queue-list 4 default 5
```

The above queue list places all IPX traffic into queue 4. Telnet and TFTP traffic is placed into queue 1. All other IP traffic is placed into queue 2. Any traffic arriving on interface serial 0 is placed into queue 3, and anything not defined by the queue list is placed in the default queue 5.

WARNING Always remember to specify a default queue.

Right now, we have five queues, all with the default byte count of 1,500. Suppose we want to allow queue 1 to be able to send twice as much traffic. Use the following command:

```
queue-list 4 queue 1 byte-count 3000
```

This command will increase the byte count of queue 1 in queue-list 4 to 3,000 bytes. Now queue 1 will be able to send twice as much data as any of the other queues specified. Obviously, the byte counts of any of the queues can be changed.

It is also possible to change the size in bytes of a particular queue. To change the size of queue 3 so it could hold 4,876 bytes, use the following command:

```
queue-list 4 queue 3 limit 4876
```

This command specifies the amount of data that can be placed in the queue before the router has to discard the data. If the queue is full, the router will discard all data attempting to go into that queue until there is space in the queue.

A queue list is applied to an interface using the following command:

```
digger_router(config)#int s1
digger_router(config-if)#custom-queue-list 4
```

This applies the queue-list 4 created above to interface serial 1.

The show queuing custom command will show you what is configured for custom queuing:

```
digger_router#show queueing custom
Current custom queue configuration:


List    Queue   Args
4       5       default
4       4       protocol ipx
4       1       protocol ip         tcp port telnet
4       1       protocol ip         udp port tftp
4       2       protocol ip
4       3       interface Serial0
4       1       byte-count 3000
4       3       limit 4876
```

Notice that all of the queuing information from the queue command shows up. The same information can be obtained by looking at the running configuration.

Executing the Exec mode command show interface will show the queuing strategy for a particular interface:

```
Serial1 is up, line protocol is up
  Hardware is HD64570
  MTU 1500 bytes, BW 1544 Kbit, DLY 20000 usec, rely 255/255,
    load 1/255
  Encapsulation HDLC, loopback not set, keepalive set (10 sec)
  Last input never, output never, output hang never
  Last clearing of "show interface" counters never
  Input queue: 0/75/0 (size/max/drops); Total output drops: 0
  Queueing strategy: custom-list 4
  Output queues: (queue #: size/max/drops)
      0: 0/20/0 1: 0/4876/0 2: 0/20/0 3: 0/20/0 4: 0/20/0
      5: 0/20/0 6: 0/20/0 7: 0/20/0 8: 0/20/0 9: 0/20/0
      10: 0/20/0 11: 0/20/0 12: 0/20/0 13: 0/20/0 14: 0/20/0
      15: 0/20/0 16: 0/20/0
  5 minute input rate 0 bits/sec, 0 packets/sec
  5 minute output rate 0 bits/sec, 0 packets/sec
      0 packets input, 0 bytes, 0 no buffer
      Received 0 broadcasts, 0 runts, 0 giants, 0 throttles
      0 input errors, 0 CRC, 0 frame, 0 overrun, 0 ignored, 0 abort
      0 packets output, 0 bytes, 0 underruns
      0 output errors, 0 collisions, 3 interface resets
      0 output buffer failures, 0 output buffers swapped out
      0 carrier transitions
      DCD=down  DSR=down  DTR=down  RTS=down  CTS=down
```

Not only is the queuing strategy shown, but all 17 queues are shown along with the amount of data in them and their maximum size, even though we have only configured queues 0–5 for use.

Optimization and
Maintenance

PART 4

An interface running priority queuing gives much the same output, in terms of queuing information, from the `show interface` command:

```
Input queue: 0/75/0 (size/max/drops); Total output drops: 0

  Queueing strategy: priority-list 1

  Output queue: high 0/40/0, medium 0/80/0, normal 0/120/0,
    low 0/160/0
```

Another Traffic Control Mechanism: Weighted Random Early Detection (WRED)

Weighted random early detection is a flow control mechanism that takes advantage of the traffic control mechanisms in TCP. WRED interacts with TCP flow control and windowing to randomly drop packets prior to a period of high congestion. By dropping these packets, WRED tells the sending host to slow down. Since TCP is connection oriented, the sender can monitor whether its packets are getting through or not. If the sender notices it is not getting some packets through, it will slow down. Basically, the router is manipulating the size of the TCP sliding window to control the amount of traffic the sending host places on the wire and thus into the router queues.

A host using a TCP sliding window is constantly adjusting the window's size to try to maximize its use of the bandwidth. If all of the sender's packets get through, the window is expanded; if packets are dropped, the window is contracted. The window size is adjusted in this way throughout the course of the transmission. At the beginning of the transmission, the adjustments are much larger than when the TCP session has been up and running for a while. Think of this algorithm as the divide-and-conquer algorithm used to guess a number when given the responses of "higher" or "lower" after each guess. For a number between 1 and 100, you would guess 50 and get a response of "higher," guess 75 and get a response of "lower," then guess 63, etc. This would continue until you got the correct number. Though a sliding window works a little differently, the important thing to realize is that the deltas of the window sizes for each change get smaller as the sender and receiver zoom in on the correct window size. They never really find the correct size since a network is a dynamic entity, but they continue to dynamically adjust throughout the length of the transmission.

WRED drops packets based on IP precedence. Packets with lower IP precedence are more likely to be dropped than those with high IP precedence. Hence the term "weighted" in Weighted Random Early Detection. It is possible to configure the router to ignore IP precedence value and thus have only RED (Random Early Detection). Typically, WRED is used on the core routers in your environment, since the edge routers are the ones that actually set the IP precedence.

WRED is only really useful with IP traffic because the TCP protocol assumes a dropped packet means congestion or some other network problem, which then causes the sending host to slow down its transmission rate. Other protocols may ignore dropped packets or continue to resend those packets at the same rate. Obviously, if the sending host simply resends the lost data and does not adjust the rate at which it is sending data, the problem becomes worse, since bandwidth is being wasted in an already congested network. Non-IP traffic is assigned precedence 0 and is thus most likely to be dropped. Obviously, an assumption has been made that IP traffic is more important than any other traffic on the network. On a network where most of the traffic is non-IP, WRED can cause performance problems since the non-IP traffic will be dropped first.

The benefit of WRED is that it manipulates how traffic is dropped. Without WRED, all new traffic is dropped as soon as the transmit buffers on the router are full. This means that all TCP hosts on the network immediately decrease their window sizes and continue to do so until the congestion clears and packets start getting through again. At this point, all the window sizes begin to increase again. This produces an effect like waves breaking on the beach. Short periods of congestion are followed by periods when the link is not fully utilized, which are followed by short periods of congestion, which are followed by periods when the link is not fully utilized. This pattern is very inefficient because the link has bandwidth to spare, but the hosts who need this bandwidth cannot use it. Then, during the wave of congestion, packets are dropped and will have to be resent later.

To prevent this inefficient pattern, WRED begins to selectively drop packets when the output interface starts to show indications of congestion. This prevents the buffer from becoming full and indiscriminately dropping all packets. In turn, this minimizes the chance that the sending hosts will become synchronized in the adjustments of their window sizes. Hosts sending a larger number of packets have a higher probability of having packets dropped simply because they have more packets that could be dropped. This means the hosts that send more traffic and use more bandwidth are the hosts that are most likely to be slowed down by WRED.

Average queue size is used to determine when WRED will drop packets. Average queue size is calculated with the following equation:

Average=((old_average * (1–1/2^n))+(current_queue_size*1/2^n))

N=exponential weight factor configured by the user

From this equation we can see that as N goes to infinity, we get the following equation:

Average=(old_average * (1–0) + current_queue_size * 0)

Thus, the larger the value of N, the slower the average size changes. The N variable basically controls how fast WRED adjusts the calculated Average. A value of N that is too high will not allow the calculated average to adjust fast enough to be useful.

Optimization and Maintenance

PART 4

When a packet arrives, the average queue size is calculated via the above equation. If the calculated value is less than the minimum queue threshold, then the packet is queued. If the calculated average is above the maximum queue size, then the packet is dropped. This indicates the router is already congested. When congestion occurs, all new packets are dropped; WRED functionality is not used again until the congestion abates. If the calculated average value is between the minimum and maximum queue threshold, then the packet is either queued or dropped. The decision to drop or not drop the packet is based on the packet drop probability.

Packet drop probability is a linear function related to where the calculated average sits in relation to the minimum and maximum queue sizes.

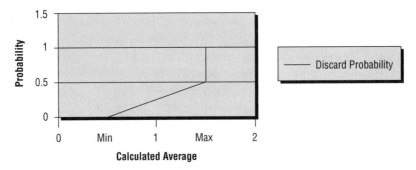

As the calculated average increases, the odds of any one packet being dropped increase. At the point where the calculated average is equal to the maximum queue threshold, all new packets are dropped. Since the minimum and maximum values define the drop probability, care needs to be exercised when selecting these values. The maximum value should be set high enough to maximize utilization of the link—if this value is set too low, packets will be dropped unnecessarily. The difference between the maximum and minimum values should be large enough to prevent the sending hosts from making synchronized window size adjustments.

There are many options available in the configuration of WRED. To simply enable WRED on an interface, use the following command:

```
digger_router#conf t
Enter configuration commands, one per line.  End with CNTL/Z.
digger_router(config)#int s1
digger_router(config-if)#random-detect
```

There are several other options you can specify with WRED, including the following:

```
(config-if)#random-detect precedence 1 2000 4096 40
```

This sets the minimum queue size to 2,000, the maximum queue size to 4,096, and the mark probability to 40. The mark probability sets the value of the denominator for the drop probability when the queue depth is at the maximum value. Here, the 40 means that 1 out of every 40 packets will be dropped. Essentially, this value defines the slope of the linear function that connects the minimum and maximum queue values. Mark probability is the point that defines the triangle between minimum, maximum, and drop probability. It is the maximum probability of any one packet being dropped before the router gives up on WRED and starts dropping all packets. Remember that if the calculated average is above the max queue threshold, the router drops all packets until the congestion begins to abate, and during this period of time the router is not using WRED.

Being able to modify these values within the WRED configuration gives the flexibility to modify the values that goes into calculating the average value. All the values in the commands used above are measured in packets.

```
(config-if)#random-detect exponential-weighting-constant 2
```

The above command sets the value of *N* in the average queue size equation. Typically, the IP precedence is set by your edge router using the IOS Committed Access Rate features (CAR). CAR also allows you to limit the amount of traffic going into or coming out of a given interface, as the following example illustrates:

```
digger_router(config-if)#rate-limit input access-group 144 500000
45000 45000 conform-action set-prec-transmit 5 exceed-action set-prec-
transmit 0

digger_router(config-if)# rate-limit input access-group 145

300000 20000 20000 conform-action set-prec-transmit 5 exceed-action
drop

digger_router(config-if)# rate-limit input 300000 2000 2000
conform-action

    set-prec-transmit 5 exceed-action drop
```

The above sets of commands define the IP precedence and rate limits for traffic into this interface. We also could have defined the IP precedence on an output basis by replacing the word *input* with *output*:

```
Rate-limit (input|output) <bps> <burst> <max> conform-action action
exceede-action action
```

The two important actions here for WRED are conform and exceed. If the traffic adheres to the specified rate limit standards, it is processed through the conform action, and if it does not, it is processed through the exceed action.

The possible actions are:

- Continue: Go to next rate limit command.
- Drop: Drop the packet.
- Transmit: Transmit the packet.
- Set-prec-continue: Set the IP precedence to X, then run the continue action on the packet.
- Set-prec-transmit: Set the IP precedence to X, then run the transmit action on the packet.

The above example sets the IP precedence to 5 for traffic, which matches access-list 144 and 145, so long as it adheres to the rate limit guideline. If not, then the precedence is set to 0 for access-list 144, and the packet is more likely to be dropped. For access-list 145 and all other traffic going into this interface, the `exceed` limit tells the router to drop the packet if it exceeds the `rate` limit. This allows us to specify how much bandwidth any one IP-based application type or set of IP-based application types can take up.

WRED has a few more features that can be configured, but they become platform specific and begin to tie into Cisco's switching software. This section gives you a general overview of WRED functionality and some configuration information, and covers most of the situations that you would run into in the real world.

Traffic Prioritization for Specific Protocols

Both Frame Relay and IPX present some further considerations for traffic prioritization. The following sections explore these issues.

Frame Relay Traffic Shaping

Frame Relay traffic shaping (FRTS) is a quality-of-service mechanism designed especially for use with frame relay. Frame Relay has its own congestion notification mechanisms, the FECN and BECN (forward and backward congestion notification). FECNs are generated when traffic is sent out of a congested interface. BECNs are generated if the queue in the opposite direction is large enough to create an FECN. Hence, if the inbound queue on an interface is full enough to create an FECN, then a BECN will be created on traffic outbound through that same interface. The BECN and FECN are actually created by setting bits in a frame relay frame. The job of the BECN is to tell the sending host to slow down. However, if the traffic is flowing one way, then the sending host will never see a BECN because there is no frame being sent back to the sending host where the BECN bit can be set.

Frame Relay lines have two important numbers that control how they function. These are the committed information rate (CIR) and the port speed. The port speed is the maximum amount of data that can be placed on the link. The CIR is the amount of data guaranteed to get through. Each Frame Relay frame contains a bit called the discard eligible bit. If this bit is set, then the frame relay network has the right to throw that particular packet away if it becomes congested at any point. Generally, CIR is not really enforced in North America, and very little traffic with the discard eligible bit set is thrown away. However, this could change at any time. When you begin to work with Frame Relay on an international scale, you see a lot more enforcement of CIR. This is especially true for links that span oceans. The CIR value can be anything from 0 up to the port speed of the link. Typically, the CIR value is much less than the port speed because most of the time the frame carrier will allow bursts of data up to the port speed of the link. It is cheaper not to pay for the extra CIR, because that data above the CIR will probably not be discarded anyway. In essence you are gambling here, but in most cases it is a safe gamble, the exception being international Frame Relay links. A common port speed/CIR configuration is a 56K port speed with a 16K CIR.

Frame Relay traffic shaping helps to control how the router sends traffic onto the Frame Relay link to make sure that the data transfer is as efficient as possible. To configure Frame Relay traffic shaping on an interface, use the following command:

```
digger_router(config-if)#frame-relay traffic-shaping
```

The Map Class

When configuring Frame Relay traffic shaping, you can define a map class to specify how the router will handle frame relay traffic. The command below will create a map class:

```
digger_router(config)#map-class frame-relay example_class
digger_router(config-map-cla)#
```

Once this command is entered, the router goes into Map Class Configuration mode. From here, there are various things that can be configured, but the map class must first be specified.

```
digger_router(config-map-cla)#frame-relay custom-queue-list 1
```

This command assigns custom-queue-list 1 to the map class, which allows custom queuing to also be used in the Frame Relay map class.

```
digger_router(config-map-cla)#frame-relay priority-group 1
```

Optimization and
Maintenance

PART 4

This command assigns a priority group to the map class, thus enabling priority queuing on the map class.

```
digger_router(config-map-cla)#frame-relay cir in 56000
digger_router(config-map-cla)#frame-relay cir out 56000
digger_router(config-map-cla)#frame-relay cir  56000
```

The first command above defines the inbound CIR and 56,000 bits/sec. The second command defines the outbound CIR to 56,000 bits/sec, and if no direction is specified, defines the given value for both incoming and outgoing CIRs.

```
digger_router(config-map-cla)#frame-relay mincir 45000
digger_router(config-map-cla)#frame-relay mincir  out 45000
```

These commands allow the minimal CIR to be set again if no direction is specified. The command sets both the incoming and outgoing CIR values.

The outgoing or incoming committed burst size and excess burst sizes can also be set with the following commands. The committed burst value is the maximum data transfer rate the line can jump up to in order to deal with a burst of data. The interface will send no more data than the defined committed burst size when using average shaping. The excess burst size is used with peak shaping. It allows more data than the committed burst size to be sent during a time interval under certain conditions. In these cases the total amount of data the interface can put on the line is the committed burst size plus the excess burst size. Excess burst is generally used with peak traffic shaping, not adaptive or average shaping, although it is probably still a good idea to define a value for the excess burst. The default is 7,000 bits for both commands. If no direction is specified, the command is applied to both incoming and outgoing traffic.

```
digger_router(config-map-cla)#frame-relay bc 8000
digger_router(config-map-cla)#frame-relay bc in 98000
```

The map class command `frame-relay adaptive-shaping becn` or `frame-relay adaptive-shaping foresight` defines whether the router will use BECNs or foresight messages as the backward congestion notification mechanism to adapt how it sends data.

NOTE Prior versions of the IOS used `frame-relay becn-response-enable` to tell the router to use BECNs to adapt how it sends traffic. This command has been removed in IOS 12, and `frame-relay adaptive-shaping becn` should now be used.

The difference between a BECN and a foresight congestion notification is that a BECN needs data to carry it, because it is only the setting of a bit in the Frame Relay frame containing user data. Foresight messages do not require user data to carry them. It does not matter which type of message the router receives; it still reacts the same. Foresight is a network traffic control feature of Cisco Frame Relay switches and is not enabled by default. When FRTS is set up on the router, foresight is enabled automatically but still has to be enabled on the switch. In an environment that is not entirely comprised of Cisco equipment, it is best to use BECNs since they are part of the Frame Relay standard.

When configuring FRTS, it is often helpful to set up the enhanced local management feature (ELMI). This feature allows the Frame Relay switch and router to exchange QOS values such as CIR burst size and excessive burst size. Once the router receives this information from the Frame Relay switch, it can use them to control its traffic shaping. This only works between Cisco devices. The following command enables ELMI on a given interface:

```
(config-if)#frame-relay qos-autosense
```

Configuring ELMI prevents the possibility of choosing incorrect traffic shaping values.

An example of a map class is as follows:

```
map-class frame-relay cir_class
  frame-relay traffic-rate 9000 18000
  frame-relay adaptive-shaping becn
```

The `traffic-rate` command defines the CIR as 9,000 and the burst size as 18,000. We can see that BECNs are being used to control which congestion notifications the router reacts to. Instead of specifying adaptive shaping we could have used peak or average shaping. Adaptive shaping is the most common and useful because you are allowing the network to attempt to optimize itself.

Here is another example of a map class with the CIR burst size and excessive burst size set:

```
map-class frame-relay example_class
  frame-relay adaptive-shaping becn
  frame-relay cir 16000
  frame-relay bc 45000
  frame-relay be 58000
```

Optimization and Maintenance

PART 4

Once a map class has been created, it needs to be applied to an interface. To apply our example_class to interface serial 1, the following commands would be used:

```
digger_router#conf t
digger_router(config)#int serial 1
digger_router(config-if)#frame-relay class example_class
```

Now that the class is applied to the interface, the router will begin to use the defined class to shape Frame Relay traffic on that interface.

Configuring Discard Eligibility

The router has the ability to set the discard eligible bit for user-specified traffic. This allows you to define which traffic will be dropped first if there is congestion in the Frame Relay switch. Discard eligible traffic can be defined by the UDP or TCP port number, the interface the traffic arrived on, packet size, an access list, or if the packet is a fragment.

```
frame-relay de-list 1 interface Serial0
frame-relay de-list 1 protocol ip tcp www
frame-relay de-list 1 protocol ip tcp talk
frame-relay de-list 1 protocol ipx list 800
frame-relay de-list 1 protocol ip gt 50000
```

> **NOTE**   There is a bit in the TCP packet that tells you if the packet is a fragmented part of a larger packet or not.

The above discard eligible list shows that the discard eligible bit will be set for all traffic arriving from interface serial 0 and any TCP traffic destined for the talk (517) or www (80) ports. All traffic matching the conditions in IPX access list 800 will be discard eligible, as well as all IP traffic with packet sizes greater than 50,000. The total packet size referred to here includes the MAC header, which the router will rewrite.

Discard lists are applied to specific DLCIs from the Interface Configuration mode. To apply our discard eligible list to serial interface 1 and DLCI 978, the following commands would be used:

```
digger_router#conf t
digger_router(config)#int serial1
digger_router(config-if)#frame-relay de-group 1 978
```

IPX Traffic Considerations

Though IP is the most common network protocol used today, IPX is a popular alternative. One of the major concerns with IPX is that it is not very efficient in its use of bandwidth. IPX servers periodically send SAP broadcasts to advertise the services they can provide to the other systems on the network. While the congestion control mechanisms discussed above are very useful, the best way to avoid congestion with the IPX protocol is to keep as much unnecessary data as possible from being sent across the network.

Problems with SAP

Although it might be nice for someone working in accounting to be able to print to a printer in engineering on the other side of the country, it is doubtful that anyone can really justify the need. The problem with SAP broadcasts is that, if left unchecked, they can consume a large portion of network bandwidth. Each service that is available on a network sends out SAPs to inform other network devices of what network services are available. SAP broadcasts are typically propagated as broadcast packets. This is fine on the local segment, but routers do not forward broadcasts. To get around this, Cisco routers build their own internal SAP tables that can be viewed with the following command:

```
show ipx servers
```

Rather than forwarding each SAP broadcast as it arrives, the Cisco router will collect all the SAPs it receives and then broadcast out its whole SAP table in one big SAP broadcast through all the router interfaces configured for IPX. Split horizon is adhered to in this forwarding, so SAPs are not broadcast back out the interface they were received on, but instead go out every other IPX interface. This behavior is both good and bad. There is obviously less overhead required to send out the full SAP table all at once in a few big packets than to use lots of small packets. Consider the environments shown in Figure 14.4.

What is going to happen to the 56K link every time the router goes to broadcast its SAP table to the satellite router? Assuming there are a lot of Novell servers running in the Corporate Headquarters, each server will have multiple SAPs to place on the wire. This means that the HQ router's SAP table can get very large. When the HQ router broadcasts this SAP table across the 56Kbps link, it is possible that the link will become saturated.

Optimization and Maintenance

PART 4

Figure 14.4 SAP propagation can consume a large chunk of bandwidth

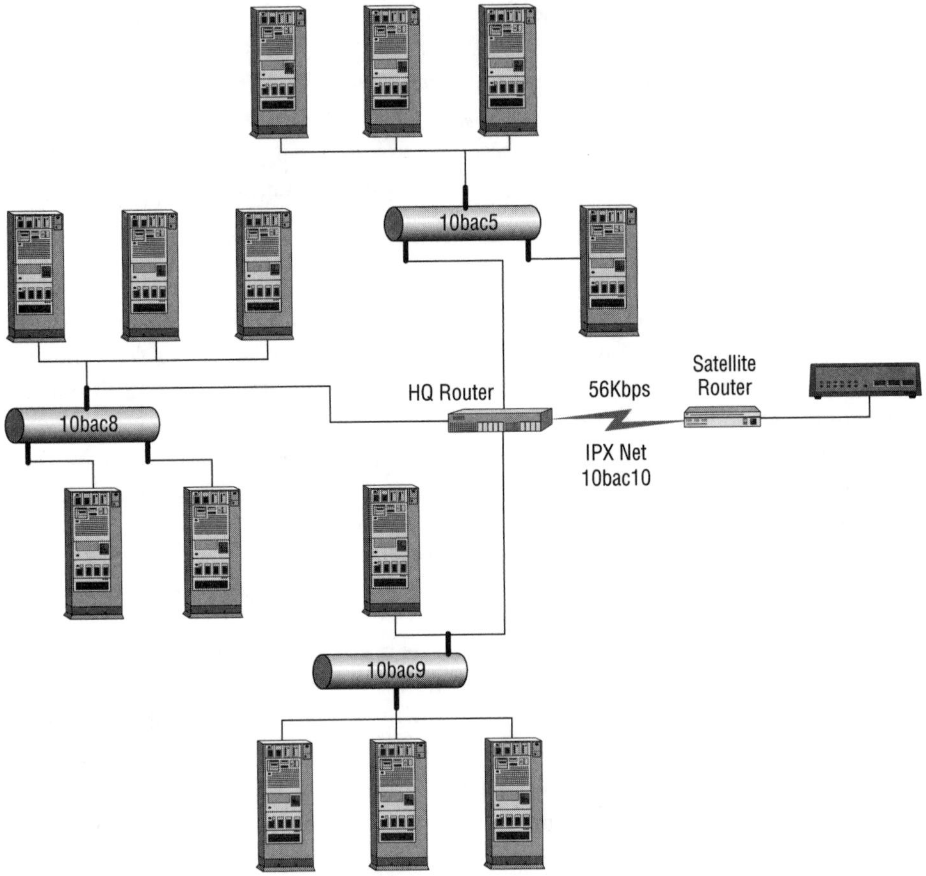

Link Saturation

This actually happened to one of this book's authors once. His company was connecting into a new client who had a couple hundred Novell servers. The client had not thought to set up any mechanisms to control the amount of SAP traffic sent across the 56K line. Every so often the link would appear to go down and the author's company would not be able to get any data through for 10–15 seconds. Then things would be fine for a while, and the pattern would repeat.

Link Saturation *(continued)*

They finally figured out what was going on by timing the interval between the periods when the link first appeared to drop. It turns out that this interval was almost exactly 60 seconds, which is the default SAP update interval. With this knowledge, it was a simple matter of limiting the number of SAPs that were broadcast across the link.

Of course, there were are a lot of other ways to solve this type of problem, but it was kind of cool to be able to figure out what the problem was without really even looking at the router!

The important thing to realize here is that Cisco routers do forward SAPs, but they build a table and forward that table every 60 seconds by default. Understanding this concept is important because it makes troubleshooting IPX problems much easier. It is can be very helpful to look at the router's own SAP table to determine if your SAPs are even getting across the intermediary links.

Configuring the SAP Update Interval

The interval at which the router sends out SAPs can be modified. Typically, the SAP update interval is increased from the default of 60 seconds. The interval can be decreased also, but there is really no reason to set the update interval to below 60 seconds. The main reason for increasing the SAP update interval is to conserve bandwidth by sending SAPs less frequently. Over low-speed links, it often makes sense to increase the SAP update interval. In a local area environment, increasing the update interval will probably not make a big difference. The following command sets the SAP update interval to 5 minutes.

```
digger_router(config-if)ipx update interval sap 300
```

The router will now send out its SAP table every 5 minutes instead of every 60 seconds. Make sure that the SAP update interval is not set so large that SAP entries are timing out of the tables of remote hosts. The update interval is set on a per-interface basis. This allows you to set your WAN links to a long update interval while leaving the local network interface at a quicker update speed.

As long as the router that is sending its table does not time any of its entries out of the SAP table, the proper table will be forwarded every time the SAP update interval occurs. When adjusting the update interval, make sure that the new update interval is not causing SAP entries to time out of any tables. SAPs typically time out of the router after three times the SAP update interval. This is the default but it can be changed, as shown by the following:

```
digger_router(config-if)#ipx sap-multiplier 6
```

This commands tells the router to age SAPs out of its table after six times the SAP update interval instead of three times. Increasing the SAP update interval and the SAP multiplier can be useful to cut down on the amount of overhead traffic.

In Figure 14.5, the WAN link has been configured with a larger SAP update interval and increased SAP multiplier. Their values have to be configured on the WAN link interfaces on both routers. This decreases the amount of SAP traffic crossing the WAN link. Though SAP updates are not needed very often for a stable network, it is important to make sure that devices on the local segments are getting SAPs frequently enough to handle their responsibilities properly. For this reason, the WAN link is the only point where the SAP timers have been increased. The only drawback to this approach is that if a server across the WAN link goes down, the local router will continue to advertise it locally every 60 seconds until the SAP eventually times out of the local router. In Figure 14.5, this would be the SAP multiplier of 6 times the SAP update interval of 600. The local router could still be advertising a remote IPX server for up to an hour after that service disappeared.

Figure 14.5 The SAP update interval can be modified

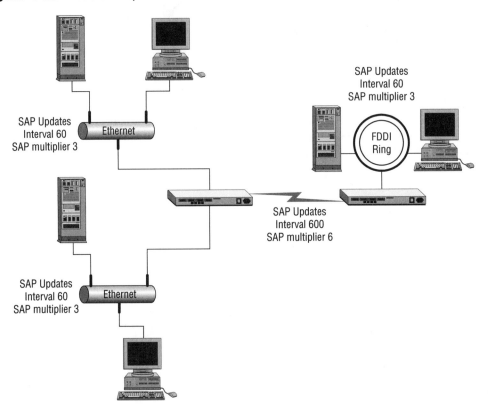

Modifying the RIP Interval

It is also possible to modify the IPX RIP interval to decrease the frequency with which RIP packets are sent as well as the aging time for the RIP routes in the router. The following commands illustrate how to adjust these values. The RIP multiplier is set to 6 while the RIP update interval is set to 300 seconds. This means that RIP broadcast will be sent every 300 seconds and RIP routes will be valid in this router for 30 minutes.

```
digger_router(config-if)#ipx rip-multiplier 6
digger_router(config-if)#ipx update interval rip 300
```

The defaults for these values are the same as those for SAP. IPX RIP packets are sent out every 60 seconds by default.

It is possible to have the router send out its SAP table right after it sends out its RIP routing table. This is beneficial because if the router receives a SAP for a service but has no route to get to that service, the SAP will be rejected and not placed in the router's SAP table. By sending SAPs directly after a RIP broadcast, it is less likely the router will receive a SAP for which it does not have a route. This becomes very important on links where the SAP update interval has been greatly increased. If a link has just come up and the far-end router happens to forward its SAP table before it sends an IPX RIP broadcast, the SAP table that was just received will most likely be ignored because the router does not have any route to the networks for which it is seeing SAPs advertised. It may be several minutes before the next SAP update comes along. If the first one is discarded, those services in the far end router's SAP table will not be accessible until the second SAP gets to the router. This assumes you are using RIP as your IPX routing protocol. The following command configures the router interface to send SAP broadcasts after it sends IPX RIP broadcasts.

```
digger_router(config-if)#ipx update sap-after-rip
```

> **NOTE**   As soon as IPX is configured on a router, IPX RIP is enabled.

Significant time will often be spent setting up a routing environment to limit SAP and RIP traffic generated by IPX. Often, we will see environments where NLSP or EIGRP are configured to try to conserve bandwidth by not using IPX RIP. However, people will often forget that IPX RIP was enabled on their router as soon as they configured IPX. So, not only are they using bandwidth to support NLSP or EIGRP updates and keep-alives, they are also wasting bandwidth on RIP updates that are not even being used. Instead of making things better, they have made them worse.

The following global configuration command will shut off IPX RIP for the whole router:

```
no ipx router rip
```

Alternately you could stop specific networks from being advertised via RIP:

```
digger_router(config)#ipx router rip

digger_router(config-ipx-rou)#no network 55

digger_router(config-ipx-rou)#no network 66
```

These commands will stop RIP from advertising networks 55 and 66. If you intend to use a protocol other than RIP when working with IPX, be very careful to make sure that the router is not sending out RIP updates. You can check this by using the following command:

```
digger_router#debug ipx routing activity
```

RIP is probably not the best protocol to run for your IPX routing needs; however, it does work and is rather simple. Other IPX routing options are EIGRP and NLSP. Both of these protocols are more scalable than RIP and require much less overhead. NLSP is discussed in more detail in Chapter 7.

NOTE It is very difficult to get away from IPX RIP completely. RIP or NLSP is needed on local segments with Novell servers because Novell servers think they are routing devices and they really do not understand any IPX routing protocols other than RIP and NLSP, and static IPX routing is really not an option. Basically, NetWare listens to the RIP updates to figure out how to get to other IPX networks. Because of this you will probably be stuck running IPX RIP on some segments. In general if you are concerned with bandwidth and overhead you should run IPX RIP only where absolutely necessary.

Running EIGRP

EIGRP allows for incremental SAP updates. The router can send only incremental changes across slower links and can provide normal periodic SAP updates on the faster local links. This is done by configuring the router to send only incremental SAPs on the WAN interface (as shown in Figure 14.6) and then setting EIGRP not to send incremental SAPs on the LAN interfaces.

Figure 14.6 EIGRP can be configured to send incremental SAP updates

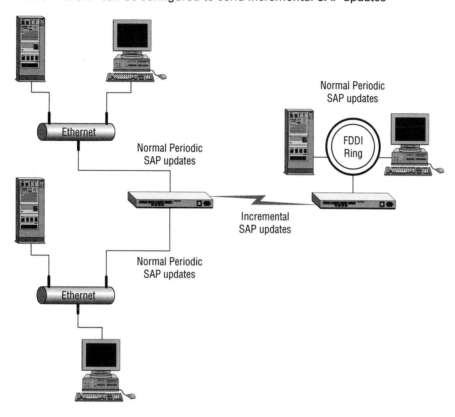

We configure the sending of incremental SAP updates interface by interface. Here the router is set to send incremental SAP updates on interface serial 0 with 55 as the autonomous system where serial 0 is located:

```
sparky(config)#int s0
sparky(config-if)#ipx sap-incremental eigrp 55
```

This configuration saves a significant amount of bandwidth because SAPs are only sent when they need to be. There is no reason the same information needs to be repeated every 60 seconds across the WAN link. On a LAN interface, it is typically easiest to allow the router to process SAP via the default method of broadcasting every 60 seconds. This way, you don't have to worry about whether other network devices that need to see the SAPs can deal with a decreased SAP update interval or incremental SAPs. When only routers are involved, things are very straightforward. But once you get to the local environment, the router administrator tends to lose control of network activities. For this reason, and because LAN links are generally at least 10 times faster than WAN links, we usually don't modify the SAP behavior on interfaces connecting to LAN segments.

Normal IPX RIP SAP updates still need to be run on segments populated by Novell servers. Across WAN links, however, we can run only EIGRP, which will significantly reduce the amount of overhead on the link. The router sends out normal RIP SAP updates on the LAN port, but only sends changes and periodic keep-alive packets for SAP traffic across the more expensive bandwidth on the WAN links.

Using EIGRP means that you really end up having to run both EIGRP and IPX RIP for segments with Novell servers on them. Compared to RIP, the amount of overhead caused by EIGRP is insignificant. If you can take IPX RIP off of even one segment, you come out ahead. Although this is slightly more difficult to configure, it saves a lot of bandwidth that would otherwise be wasted by IPX RIP traffic.

SAP Filtering

Not all SAPs need to propagate throughout the whole network. Many are only relevant in specific areas or may only need to be present on the local segment. Cisco routers have the ability to block SAPs based on source network, or source node and SAP type. This can greatly reduce the amount of traffic on your network since you may only need one or two SAPs outside the local segment. SAP filtering access lists are created in Global Configuration mode and use the 1000–1099 list number range. The following code creates an SAP access list:

```
access-list 1002 permit 10BAC8 4
access-list 1002 deny FFFFFFFF 47
access-list 1002 deny FFFFFFFF 7
access-list 1002 permit FFFFFFFF 107
```

This access list permits type 4 (file server) SAPs from network 10BAC8. Type 47 (advertising print server) and type 7 (print server) SAPs are denied from all networks, and the type 107 (rconsole) SAPs are permitted from all networks. All other SAP types are denied due to the explicit deny located at the end of all access lists. Knowing this, we could shorten access-list 1002 to just the following two lines:

```
access-list 1002 permit 10BAC8 4
access-list 1002 permit FFFFFFFF 107
```

NOTE To specify all networks in an IPX access-list command, use –1.

SAP filters are applied to a specific interface in Interface Configuration mode, as follows:

```
digger_router(config-if)#ipx output-sap-filter 1002
digger_router(config-if)#ipx input-sap-filter 1003
```

These two commands apply SAP filter 1002 to outbound traffic on the interface and 1003 to inbound traffic on the interface.

Sending GNS Requests

NetWare clients use Get Nearest Service (GNS) requests to locate a Novell server. When the client gets a response to its GNS request, the first reply it gets becomes the client's nearest server. This nearest server is responsible for telling the client about all the network services it knows about on the network. In this way the GNS server is kind of like a big brother telling the client where to find services on the network.

By controlling what responds to these requests and how, it is possible to control which servers become nearest servers for Novell client machines. This is important because becoming a nearest server for a client places additional demands on the Novell server which you may or may not want it to handle. In the Novell world someone has to be a nearest server for the client machines, but you may want to control which servers are allowed to undertake that extra work.

When responding to a GNS request, the router will choose the server with the best metric. If there are multiple servers with the same metric, then the router chooses the server from which it most recently received the SAP. This gives preference to the newest information, which is most likely to be correct. The following command can be used to see how the router is going to respond to GNS requests:

```
digger_router>show ipx servers unsorted
```

The `show ipx servers unsorted` command will show the SAP table top to bottom with the most recent information at the top and the oldest information at the bottom.

If there is a server on the local segment, the router will not respond to GNS requests. If there is no server on the local segment, the default response time to a GNS request for the router is 0 milliseconds. This means that the router responds as soon as it receives the GNS request. This delay can be changed to allow servers not located on the local segment to respond. To do so, use the following command:

```
digger_router(config)#ipx gns-response-delay 60
```

Optimization and Maintenance

PART 4

This command sets the GNS response delay to 60 milliseconds, which means the router will wait 60 milliseconds before it responds. The NetWare client is going to use the first response it gets because it assumes that whichever device responds to it first is the closest and thus most efficient to use. So, by increasing the GNS response delay, the router is less likely to be involved in selecting the nearest server for the client. The IPX GNS response delay can also be configured on an interface-by-interface basis as well as globally for the router.

NOTE The GNS response from the router only gives the client the name and address of a Novell server it can use as its nearest server. The router does not handle the responsibility of being a nearest server but rather volunteers a Novell server it knows about to be the GNS server for the client that sent the GNS request's nearest server.

To disable the router from responding to any GNS requests on a given interface, use the `config` command, as follows.

```
digger_router(config-if)#ipx gns-reply-disable
```

This command will prevent the router from replying to GNS requests on an interface-by-interface basis.

In versions of the IOS prior to 11.2, a command called `ipx gns-round-robin` was on by default.

```
digger_router(config)#ipx gns-round-robin
```

This global `config` command configures the router to respond to GNS requests in a round robin fashion.

The router's SAP table for the router in Figure 14.7 might look something the following (it is obviously simplified since the SAP types have been left out):

Server A

Server X

Server B

Server Y

Figure 14.7   GNS round-robin

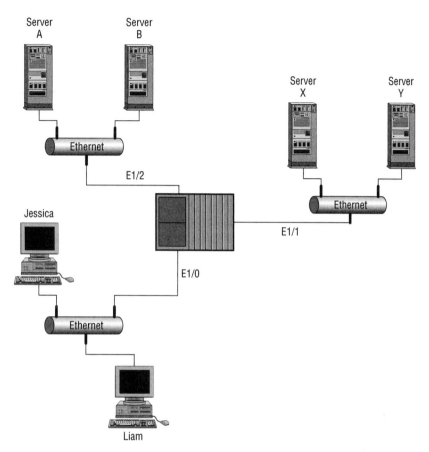

With IPX gns-round-robin configured on the router, requests will be handled as follows: for the first GNS request that the router receives, it will reply with Server A. The second request will get a response of Server X, and so on. The idea behind this it to distribute the load across the servers in the Novell environments. If this is such a great idea, why is GNS round robin no longer on by default? The problem is that round robin does not take location into account and will allocate remote servers when there are closer ones that can handle the task. So, while this does distribute the work among servers, it does not make sense to send network traffic over longer distances to save a few CPU cycles on a server. In Figure 14.7, this problem would not occur because all the servers are the same distance away from Liam and Jessica's client PCs. Of course, if we put a Novell server on Liam and Jessica's local segment, it would handle all the GNS requests no matter how the router was set up.

Further control over the GNS process can be gained through the use of GNS filters. These are standard IPX SAP filters (access-lists 1000–1099) that are applied with the following interface config command:

```
ipx output-gns-filter 1001
```

Only the information that is allowed by the GNS filter can be sent out by the router in response to a GNS request.

Suppose one of the servers in Figure 14.7 was a mail server and we were worried about its utilization. Obviously, we would not want it to be the response to a GNS query from any of the client PCs. Figure 14.8 shows what this would look like.

Figure 14.8 GNS filters can be used to control which servers perform GNS functions for client machines.

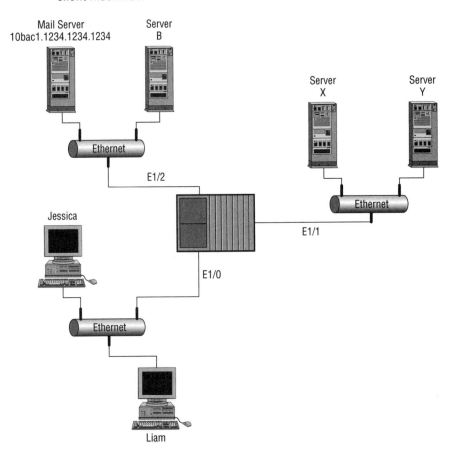

We could use the following access list as a GNS filter to prevent the router from replying with the mail server in response to a GNS request.

```
access-list 1004 deny 10BAC1.1234.1234.1234 0
access-list 1004 permit -1
```

Access list 1004 would deny all SAP service types from our mail server (specified by the 0). Now we would apply this access list as an output GNS filter on interface E0/1, since this is the segment that has the clients on it. Now the mail server will never have to worry about GNS requests from client PCs on Liam and Jessica's segment. If a client PC had been placed on the same segments with the mail server, the mail server could still respond to a GNS request. If the traffic is local and does not have to pass through the router, there is no way that it can be controlled with the router.

The example in Figure 14.8 is pretty simple. More complex SAP access lists can be applied as a GNS output filters. Since you are using an IPX SAP filter, the same flexibility that exists with SAP filters exists with GNS output filters. Therefore, you could filter out individual nodes, whole networks, or even specific service types.

Optimization and Maintenance

PART 4

Queuing

Esposito Enterprises is a currently having intermittent problem with response times to their Lotus Notes server from office across their WAN links. This is a major problem because Esposito Enterprises is using Lotus Notes as their core business application. For periods during the day the Note servers appear unreachable or response time is unacceptable. Figure 14.9 show what the Esposito network looks like.

Figure 14.9   The Esposito network layout

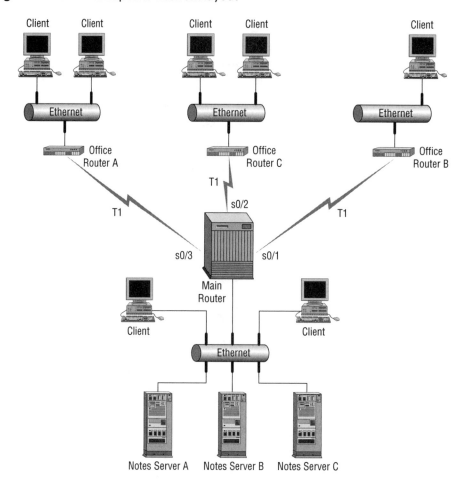

Recently the company has begun to do some large FTP file transfers between the offices and some users are watching video broadcasts from the Web. Since Notes is the primary business application, we need to make sure that this other traffic does not impact the Notes communication. The web video broadcasts are a problem we can address in either of two ways. We can simply block that traffic from the network or we can drop its priority down.

The solution we are proposing is to use custom queuing to guarantee that the Notes traffic has enough bandwidth. In order to do this we will configure the main office router to support custom queuing on all of its serial interfaces.

We would create a queue-list as follows:

```
queue-list 4 protocol ip 1 tcp 1352
queue-list 4 protocol ip 3 tcp ftp
queue-list 4 protocol ip 3 tcp ftp-data
queue-list 4 protocol ip 2
queue-list 4 default 4
```

This create four queues with Lotus Notes traffic (tcp port 1352) being placed in queue 1. Remember that by default 1,500 bytes are processed each time a queue is serviced. We are going to bump this up for the Notes traffic in queue 1.

queue-list 4 queue 1 byte-count 4500

By doing this, we guarantee half of the available bandwidth to Notes traffic if there is any present. Now we just need to apply the queue-list to the serial interfaces on the main router:

```
main_rtr(config)#int serial 0/1
main_rtr(config-if)#custom-queue-list 4
main_rtr(config-if)#exit
main_rtr(config)#int serial 0/2
main_rtr(config-if)#custom-queue-list 4
main_rtr(config-if)#exit
main_rtr(config)#int serial 0/2
main_rtr(config-if)#custom-queue-list 4
```

Now that we have assigned the queue-list to the serial interface, this should help to guarantee that Notes traffic gets through across the WAN links in a timely fashion. We have not really done anything to decrease the amount of traffic on the network but have instead specified which traffic will be given how much bandwidth when there is congestion. We could have made a decision to remove all the extraneous traffic from the network. There is no real need for users to be able to watch streaming video on their computers. However, as long as the Notes and FTP traffic gets through and the users do their job, it does not really matter. The crusade to get rid of the streaming video traffic can be taken up at a later time. Besides, video performance is going to be significantly degraded during periods of congestion anyway since it ends up in queue 2, which is handling all other IP traffic besides Notes and FTP.

SAP Filtering

Take a look at the network in Figure 14.10. Suppose that people in the Boston office print out orders in the Anchorage office, but no one from Anchorage ever prints in the Boston office. The printer SAPs from the Boston network do not have to get to Anchorage, so we can block them to preserve bandwidth. We use the following commands:

```
access-list 1005 deny 10BAC6 47
access-list 1005 deny 10BAC6 7
access-list 1005 permit FFFFFFFF
```

This access list could be applied to boston_rtr on either the E0 interface inbound or S0 outbound, it does not make much difference. The question is whether you want to have the SAPs in the router table. For troubleshooting purposes, we would block outbound traffic on the serial link. It helps to be able to see what IPX SAPs the router knows about. The following commands apply the access list we created above as an output SAP filter on Serial 0:

```
boston_rtr(config)#int s0
boston_rtr(config-if)#ipx output-sap-filter 1005
```

Figure 14.10 Often it makes sense to block certain SAPs

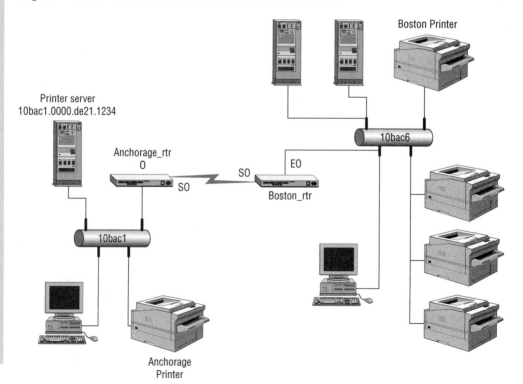

Another way we could accomplish the same task would be to set up a static SAP for the Anchorage printer in `boston_rtr` and not allow the printer SAP from the Anchorage printer across the WAN link. The following global configuration command sets up a static type 4 SAP for a server called `anchorage_pserver` with an IPX address of 10bac1.0000.de21.1234. The service is located on socket 454 and is one hop away from the router:

```
ipx sap 4 anchorage_pserver 10bac1.0000.de21.1234 454 1
```

By creating a static SAP, you can block all SAP traffic and still be able to use service advertised by SAPs since the router is generating the SAPs for the local segment. The problem with this is if that service ever goes away, the router will continue to advertise it unaware. Also, what happens if someone swaps out the network card in the `anchorage_pserver`? The printer server will get a new IPX node address and the static SAP will no longer work. Static SAPs should be used with caution because they can become an administrative nightmare. Remember, static SAPs always override those learned dynamically even if the dynamic SAP has a lower hop count. The router will also not advertise a static SAP unless it knows of a route back to that network.

15

Securing the Environment

In a perfect world, we would never have to worry about security, because people would respect our boundaries. However, the world we live in is far from perfect and things are only getting worse for network security. The incredible growth of the Internet, the rapid pace at which new software is pushed into the market, and the development of a class of computer users who have no idea about security are all conspiring to make securing your network a much more difficult task than it used to be. Ten years ago, you never heard much about computer viruses, hackers, or operating system insecurities. You also had far fewer people using computers and even fewer accessing the Internet.

This rapid explosion has virtually redefined the way we work and live. We now have people in positions that require the use of a computer who have no idea how a computer functions, why they can get e-mail, or even how to format a floppy disk. These people simply know how to use the one or two applications that their job requires. Some of these people see no problem with leaving PCAnywhere running on their office PC so they can access it at home across the Internet. These types of users are very difficult to protect—how often have you heard of someone launching an e-mail attachment and finding out that it was some sort of a Trojan horse?

It is important to define a network security policy. This policy will define how much risk you want to expose your network to. The only way to create zero risk is to shut everything off and go home; the minute the network begins passing data between hosts it is vulnerable to all sorts of attacks. These attacks range from the 10-year-old kid who downloads a hacker script off the Internet to the systems programmer with 30 years of experience writing special programs that help him or her get into your network. It is also important to remember that a large portion of network attacks come from inside the company or organization.

This chapter will not focus on general network security, but instead on how security applies to the routing environment. We will also cover how to augment your existing security policy using the features within your routers. A router can never replace a good firewall maintained by a competent security administrator. An argument can be made that a router running IOS 12.0 with the Firewall and IDS feature sets can provide the same level of security as a Cisco PIX firewall. For the purpose of this chapter, however, we will put the Firewall feature set aside. The Firewall feature set is a great tool, which we will cover in Chapter 19.

The router is simply not designed for that type of functionality. However, there are things that can be done to help secure the networking environment. Remember, the best security approach is a layered one, involving multiple devices providing security. This way, if one layer is breached, there are still other layers protecting the environment.

Making Your Router a Bastion Host

Routers provide a huge amount of network functionality. A compromised router can be used to take down a whole network, reroute data, or open new security holes. For these reasons and many more, it is important that every possible step be taken to make sure that your routers are secure.

Console Port

The router console, by default, does not have a password configured. You should set one using the following commands:

```
sparky(config)#line console 0
sparky(config-line)#password agh11
```

Although setting a console password will slow down anyone attempting to gain access on the console port, it will not stop them. The console port has the capability to send the break sequence to the router during boot up, which means that with console port access, the password recovery sequence can be started and the router can easily be compromised.

Therefore, care must be taken in allowing console port access. Ideally, the router should be in a locked room with nothing connected to the console port. Network devices, such as modems and terminal servers, are sometimes attached to the router's console port. Care must be taken to prevent an unauthorized user from accessing these devices with console port access. If an attacker can gain access to one of these devices and then crash the router causing it to reboot, they can take over the router.

There are valid reasons for attaching devices to the router console port—for example, if you're using terminal servers to access a console session on the router or connecting a modem for a dial backup link.

Care should be taken to restrict access to these devices. Unless there is a really good reason to do so, it is a good idea not to connect anything to the router's console port.

Telnet Access

Telnet is the most frequently used method of gaining interactive access to a router. However, it is not the only method; rlogin and SSH may also be supported, depending on the IOS version and the router configuration. Non-IP-based protocols may also provide interactive access the router. Protocols such as LAT, X.29, MOP, and a few others can give interactive access to the router. Care should be taken not to open security holes with these other protocols.

Interactive access is generally gained across the router's VTY lines. These lines should be password protected. The default on the router is to specify no password on these lines. This will prevent anyone from logging in using the virtual lines:

```
digger_router#telnet 10.1.1.3
Trying 10.1.1.3 ... Open



Password required, but none set


[Connection to 10.1.1.3 closed by foreign host]
```

This output is from an attempt to Telnet to a router without a password set on its VTY lines. Obviously, most of us want to be able to Telnet to our routers, so it makes sense to set up a password on our VTY lines. When configuring the VTY lines to allow access, care should be taken. The exec-timeout should be set on all VTY lines so that connected sessions will time out in a reasonable amount of time.

Optimization and Maintenance

PART 4

```
digger_router(config)#line vty 0 4
digger_router(config-line)#exec-timeout 2
```

Here we have set the VTY lines to time out all inactive connections after two minutes. This really does not do much from a security standpoint. It does help protect open Telnet sessions being left around, and it's useful in tearing down orphaned sessions, but does little to increase the security of your router.

Standard IP access list can be used to control which IP addresses are allowed to access the VTY lines. For example, it would make sense to allow Telnet VTY access only from your network:

```
sparky(config)#access-list 30 permit 10.1.1.0 0.0.0.255
sparky(config)#access-list 31 permit 10.1.1.44 0.0.0.0
```

These commands create two access lists: 30 and 31. Access list 30 permits IP traffic from any host on the 10.1.1.0 network. Access list 31 permits IP traffic only from the host 10.1.1.44, which happens to be the administrator's workstation. Now we need to apply these access lists to the VTY lines.

```
sparky(config)#line vty 0 3
sparky(config-line)#access-class 30 in
sparky(config)#line vty 4
sparky(config-line)#access-class 31 in
```

With these access lists applied, using the `access-class` command only hosts on the 10.1.1.0 network can get to the router's VTY lines with IP. This gives you the ability to control which hosts are allowed to Telnet into your routers. Also notice that we configured VTY line 4 with access class 31, which only allows 10.1.1.44 in. This is done so that while 10.1.1.44—the administrator's workstation—can access any of the VTY lines because it is part the 10.1.1.0 network, only it can access VTY line 4. In this way, if there is a problem, the administrator is guaranteed to have a VTY line free on the router to get in and look at the problem, because we have limited access to that VTY line to his or her workstation only.

Creating a Warning Banner

When allowing Telnet to a router, you should set up a banner stating that only authorized users are allowed to access the system and that all users' actions will be monitored. This is more a legal issue than anything else, and you should consult with your legal department to determine the proper wording of your banner. Never have a banner that says, "Welcome."

Creating a Warning Banner *(continued)*

Setting the banner is a simple matter of using the global configuration mode command banner and a delimiting character. Below < is used as the delimiting character to mark the beginning and end of the banner:

```
banner <Legal Mumbo Jumbo so we can monitor and prosecute<
```

This will set the banner for all connections to the router. Alternately, a banner can be set on individual access points or transitions to alternate access levels. Generally, one banner is enough and should be global to the router. This way, anyone accessing your router will be presented with the message.

TACACS

Cisco's IOS allows for the setting up of local usernames and passwords on routers. We do that using this command:

```
7000_HSSI(config)#username ahami password 0 sparky
```

This would set up the username ahami on the router with a password of sparky. If service password encryption is enabled, this will be stored in the router as:

```
username ahami password 7 0518160E33475749
```

The 7 specifies that an already encrypted password follows, so if you were to cut and paste the configuration into the router you would not have to worry about an already encrypted password being encrypted again.

By specifying this type of authentication, you require anyone attempting to Telnet to the router to provide both a valid username and password. To force this, you need to change the default authentication scheme. This can be done with the following global configuration command:

```
aaa new-model
```

This will force the Telnet session to ask for a username and not just a password. This increases the security level, because now both a username and password combination is needed. There are various other password options. In most cases, however, the combination of access classes and password should deter any attacker. Certainly one would not want to allow Telnet access to a router from the Internet or any other untrusted network. Because in even the largest environment there are usually only a few people responsible for managing routers, an elaborate scheme of usernames and passwords is probably not

Optimization and Maintenance

PART 4

necessary. If you are looking for this type of functionality, then TACACS is probably the way to go.

TACACS (Terminal Access Controller Access Control System) is an authentication method that can be used by routers to provide a centrally located database for user authentication.

Cisco currently supports three versions of TACACS:

TACACS (RFC1492) Provides password checking and authentication, along with notification of user actions for security and accounting purposes. TACACS is incompatible with TACACS+.

TACACS + Provides detailed accounting information and more flexible control over the authentication process. TACACS is used through the AAA (Authentication, Authorization, and Accounting) commands.

Extended TACACS An extension of TACACS that provides some additional information about router and protocol translator use. Extended TACACS is incompatible with TACACS+.

In order to use TACACS for router authentication, a TACACS server must be set up and administered. What this does is allow for a centrally managed host to provide the authentication for the routers in the environment. This way, passwords do not have to be updated on all routers but need only be modified on the TACACS server.

Setting up standard and extended TACACS on the VTY line is pretty simple:

```
sparky(config)#tacacs-server host 10.1.1.2

sparky(config)#tacacs-server last-resort password
```

This tells the router that the TACACS server is located at 10.1.1.2. The second line is very important: if the router cannot talk to the TACACS server, the default is not to allow the user in. To avoid this, `last-resort password` allows the router to use the enable secret password to authenticate you if it cannot talk to the TACACS server. Another option is `last-resort succeed`. Never use this: it authenticates the user automatically if the TACACS server is unreachable. All an attacker has to do is crash the TACACS server and the router will automatically authenticate her. "Cool! I don't even have to crash the TACACS server. I just have to prevent it from talking to the router long enough to get authenticated." This could be done with a denial of service attack, an ICMP redirect attack, or various other ways.

The lines that are going to use TACACS need to have the command `login tacacs` applied to them:

```
sparky(config)#line vty 0 4
```

```
sparky(config-line)#login tacacs
sparky(config-line)#exit
sparky(config)#line con 0
sparky(config-line)#login tacacs
```

Once TACACS is configured, moving to extended TACACS is trivial. Just add the global configuration command `tacacs-server extended`:

```
sparky(config)#tacacs-server extended
```

TACACS+ is mainly used if you want to track what users are doing on your routers. TACACS+, along with AAA features, gives you the ability to audit what users are doing on the routers with far more granularity than extended TACACS. To configure TACACS+, enter these global configuration commands:

```
sparky(config)#aaa new-model
sparky(config)#tacacs-server host 10.1.1.2
sparky(config)#tacacs-server key encryption_string
```

The command `aaa new-model` sets up the AAA features on the router.

The command `tacacs-server key encryption_string` sets up the encryption string for the router. This `encryption_string` value must match the one configured on the TACACS server or else the router and TACACS server will not be able to talk.

With this configuration, it is possible to force authentication for every command entered in the router by adding the following line to force authentication for all commands privilege level 1–15:

```
sparky(config)#aaa authorization commands 15 default tacacs+ none
```

With `aaa enabled`, a lot more auditing and authentication functionality is added. Authentication can be required to run a command at a specific level, enter enable mode, start an outbound Telnet or rlogin session, or any type of network-related service request. The following command will set up logging to the TACACS server to any commands entered:

```
aaa accounting commands 15 default start-stop tacacs+
```

There are many authorization and accounting commands that can be used. Once you get AAA and TACACS set up, they are self-explanatory. To work with accounting configuration, start with `aaa accounting`, and for authorization, start the command with

Optimization and Maintenance

PART 4

`aaa authorization`. From there, use the context-sensitive help to show all of the options.

Being able to track what people are doing on your routers is a good idea, and AAA provides some great functionality. It is always nice to be able to tell who did what and when, especially when you are trying to troubleshoot a problem.

Other Router Access Methods

It is all well and good to lock down the normal interactive methods of configuring a router, but there are a few other methods that need to be discussed because they are often overlooked. By default, version 12 of the IOS has the global command:

```
ip http server
```

This command allows the router to act as an HTTP server for configuration. Fortunately, the router password is needed to gain access to the router. Unless you are going to actively configure your router through the Web interface, this command should be disabled.

```
sparky(config)#no ip http server
```

The Web interface currently does not give any real added functionality over the command line interface. Besides, the command line will always be there, while you may not have access to a Web browser when you really need it.

If you decide you really need to use the Web interface, there are steps that can be taken to make it more secure. First move the HTTP service off the default port of 80 so unwanted guest will not find it as easily.

```
sparky(config)#ip http port 1056
```

This command sets the HTTP server for the router to port 1056. Be careful not to use a port required by the router. However, any port not used by the router could be used. This will not stop a competent attacker but might slow him down for a minute or two.

To increase security further, we can apply an access class to the HTTP server:

```
sparky(config)#ip http access-class 30
```

This command uses the same standard IP access list we used earlier to limit access to our VTY lines.

Access to the HTTP server can also be controlled using a TACACS server, using this command:

```
sparky(config)#ip http authentication tacacs
```

Using TACACS authentication for the router HTTP server will significantly increase the security of this access method.

WARNING Once a Web browser has authenticated to the router HTTP server, it will remain authenticated until the Web browser is shut down. Care should be taken not to leave a Web browser authenticated to the router sitting around.

SNMP

SNMP (Simple Network Management Protocol) has become all the rage of late. As networks have become more critical to businesses and the economy, it has become more important to be able to model their behavior. SNMP allows the querying of statistical information that can be used to gauge network health; it can also be used to configure devices or read information from those devices that support SNMP.

Entire management systems have been based around SNMP. These systems include HP Openview's Network Node Manager, Provision, and even CiscoWorks. Although SNMP can be a useful tool, it can also be the biggest security hole in a network. Fortunately, Cisco does not enable SNMP by default, unlike some other hardware vendors. However, configuring SNMP is one of the options in the install script for all Cisco routers.

By all means don't think SNMP is a bad thing; in fact, it is a very useful tool, which will be discussed in more detail in Chapter 16. However, you need to realize that a would-be attacker can gain a wealth of information from SNMP. Finding a host with SNMP enabled under the right conditions can be a field day for an attacker.

SNMP version 1, which is the default when you configure SNMP, uses only community strings for authentication. There are two types of community strings: read-only and read/write. Read-only will allow access to look at any statistics or MIB (Management Information Base) variables contained in the router. Although this may not seem like a big deal—it probably does not matter that someone can see that the router has output 7553 packets—the whole routing table and all the interface addresses can be learned by anyone who knows only the SNMP read-only community string. It is a fairly trivial task to map out a whole network using only SNMP read access queries.

The read/write community string gives a lot more access to the router. Someone can reload the router, force the router to TFTP its configuration to a host, or modify virtually anything in the router configuration if they know the SNMP read/write community string. So why would you ever enable the read/write community string? To gain full functionality from CiscoWorks and CiscoView, you need to have it enabled.

```
digger_router(config)#snmp-server community warren ro

digger_router(config)#snmp-server community fairfield rw
```

These global configuration commands set the read-only community string to `warren` and the read/write community string to `fairfield`. When setting a read/write community string, take care to keep the string secret; this is difficult because it is passed in clear text across the network. Also, SNMP traffic should never be allowed into your network from an untrusted network.

The biggest problem with SNMP is that typically people use the default community names. The default community string for read-only access is public, and unfortunately it is used everywhere. Eighty percent of the clients we have worked for who use SNMP will be using `public` as the read-only community string. It may be that read-only access is not a big deal, and in most cases SNMP requests are not allowed to come in from untrusted networks. The big problem here is the read/write community string, which has a default of `private` in many devices. Fortunately, Cisco does not have a default value for the read/write community string. However, many other devices do use `private` as their default. We know of at least two hosts directly connected to the Internet that are running SNMP with `private` as the read/write community string. Obviously, this is not very secure; anyone could easily go in and take over these devices using SNMP. The fact that `private` and `public` have been used so often as community strings makes them the first guess for any would-be hacker trying to use SNMP. Besides, what is a network administrator going to do if he or she sees SNMP traffic probing his network? Sure, the administrator could try to track the source down, but who's to say it is not an improperly configured SNMP management station doing a discovery on the Internet? Even worse: SNMP is based on UDP, which means it is not connection-oriented. This means no ACK has to be sent back, so a hacker who just wanted to change a variable and knew the read/write community string could easily spoof their IP address and be virtually anonymous.

WARNING   Be careful with read/write community strings. They can very easily be used for evil.

Typically with SNMP, there will be only a few management stations on the network that will be making legitimate queries to routers in the network. Knowing this, if you are going to use SNMP version 1, you should at least restrict those stations that are allowed to talk SNMP to the routers. There are two ways to do this; the first is to create an extended access list and limit the hosts who can send data to the router on the SNMP ports 161 (SNMP)—the SNMP trap port of 162 does not need to be blocked:

```
access-list 101 permit udp host 192.168.1.5 any eq snmp
access-list 101 permit udp host 192.168.1.6 any eq snmp
```

This access list will permit 192.168.1.5 and .6—our two management stations—to talk SNMP to the router. This would be applied inbound on all interfaces. Remember, there is an implicit deny any any at the end of this list, so you would have to permit the other traffic you want to allow through the router. This approach has an added benefit: because a destination of "any" is specified, all the devices behind the router are also protected. This is because the router, in an effort to protect itself, is dropping all SNMP traffic that tries to enter the network.

Another way of defining the hosts that can use SNMP on a router is to assign an access list to a given community string, defining which addresses are allowed to use that community string. In Figure 15.1, suppose that for some reason it was important to allow all hosts on the 10.1.1.0 network to read SNMP information from the router, but only the management station would be allowed read/write access. This could be done by limiting access to the community strings.

Figure 15.1   You can limit access to community strings based on IP address.

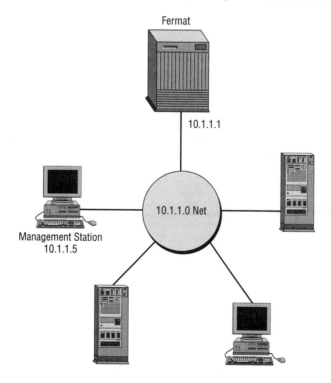

The following two access lists would be created:

```
access-list 5 permit 10.1.1.0 0.0.0.255
access-list 6 permit 10.1.1.5
```

Access list 5 would permit all hosts on the 10.1.1.0 network, while access-list 6 would only permit the 10.1.1.5. Now these access lists would be applied to the community strings using the following global configuration commands:

```
snmp-server community pub_community RO 5
snmp-server community priv_community RW 6
```

Only those hosts that are permitted by the access lists can use that community string. So all hosts on 10.1.1.0 can use pub_community to gain read-only SNMP access, but only 10.1.1.5 has access to the read/write community string. Multiple community strings can also be set up, so there could be more than one read/write community string with a different access list applied to each community string. The same goes for read-only community strings: there probably is no need to have multiple community strings in your router, but it is nice to know the functionality exists even if you never find a need for it.

This solution does not get around the issue of spoofed IP addresses, but we will look at ways to stop spoofing later.

SNMP and network management are still emerging technologies. SNMP version 1 is completely insecure and should be treated as such. SNMP version 2 addresses some of the security flaws in version 1, but the large majority of implementations of SNMP management are still using SNMP version 1. Care should be taken when using any management protocol. In order to manage something effectively, you need to have control over it; so care must be taken to make sure that only those who should be managing the environment are actually managing it.

Possibly Insecure Services

The default configuration for a Cisco router supports NTP (Network Time Protocol), Finger, and CDP. NTP and Finger are really not very dangerous services, but if they are not serving any function, why leave them enabled? It is possible that an attacker may be able to find a use for them. Use the following commands to disable NTP and Finger:

```
digger_router(config)#no ntp
digger_router(config)#no service finger
```

CDP (Cisco Discovery Protocol) is a much more dangerous service to have running on a router. The following is an example of type of output CDP can give you:

```
Device ID: sparky
```

```
Entry address(es):
 IP address: 10.1.1.3

Platform: cisco 2500, Capabilities: Router

Interface: Serial0, Port ID (outgoing port): Serial0

Holdtime : 150 sec


Version :

Cisco Internetwork Operating System Software

IOS (tm) 2500 Software (C2500-D-L), Version 12.0(8), RELEASE SOFTWARE
(fc1)

Copyright (c) 1986-1999 by cisco Systems, Inc.

Compiled Mon 29-Nov-99 14:24 by kpma
```

Notice that the router host name, the IP address, and the type of port on the neighboring router are displayed, along with the IOS version and the router model. This type of information can be used to design attacks against a network. CDP is normally used to provide some network management functions and can provide useful information, so you may not want to completely disable it. CDP information is only broadcast onto the local segment. This means that CDP information cannot get off the local segment and is only shared by devices with interfaces on the same segment. If CDP is not being used on the network, it should be disabled. CDP can be disabled either globally for the whole router or on an interface-by-interface basis.

To disable CDP globally:

```
digger_router(config)#no cdp run
```

To disable CDP for a given interface:

```
digger_router(config-if)#no cdp enable
```

Chargen, Echo, and Discard

In IOS versions 11.3 and lower, these services were all enabled by default. In IOS versions 12.*x*, these services are disabled. Chargen, echo, and discard are services left over from the old days of networking. Today, they have very few legitimate uses, which is why new versions of the IOS have them disabled. In version 11.3 and lower, you can disable these services with the following commands:

```
digger_router(config)#no service tcp-small-servers
digger_router(config)#no service udp-small-servers
```

Optimization and Maintenance

PART 4

It is important to disable both the UDP and TCP versions of these services; this is the reason for the two commands above.

Discard is really not something we have to concern ourselves with. It is exactly what it sounds like: you send packets to discard and they disappear. Think of it as routing traffic to the null interface.

Most of us know what the echo port on a device does: it sends back whatever it receives to the source. Chargen (character generator) works in somewhat the same way: for every packet sent to the chargen port, the complete ASCII alphabet is sent back to the sending host. This may be useful for testing; however, it also leads to one heck of a denial of service attack. For example, look at the simple network shown here and assume that both routers support echo (port 7) and chargen (port 19):

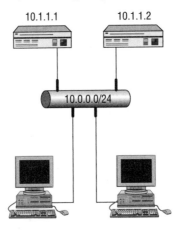

Now suppose a packet was created with source address of 10.1.1.2 and a source port of 7, and this packet was sent to host 10.1.1.1 destination port 19.

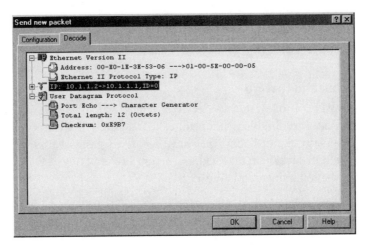

When the chargen port on 10.1.1.1 receives the packet, chargen will echo back the entire ASCII character set. This is sent back to the echo port, which just sends what it receives back to the source. The source happens to be the chargen port on 10.1.1.1. Now we have a cycle that will not end: each packet received is generating traffic that continues the cycle. Injecting only a few of the above packets into the network can quickly flood the entire bandwidth and deny service to all hosts on the network. The packet shown in the graphic was generated without using either of the two routers and could have been sent from a remote network segment or even from the Internet. This kind of attack could be done using two echo ports or two chargen ports. The main thing an attacker is looking for with this type of attack is to create traffic that can generate new traffic, thus creating a self-sustaining traffic flow.

A quick and easy way to illustrate this is to try Telnetting to a router that supports chargen on port 19:

```
telnet 10.1.1.1 19
```

Once you do this, sit back and relax—you need not even type anything, in fact you probably will not be able to type anything. Remember that Telnet uses TCP, and TCP is connection-oriented so that data received is ACKed. Each ACK hits the chargen port and generates more traffic. The only way to stop this is to kill the Telnet session or shut down the router.

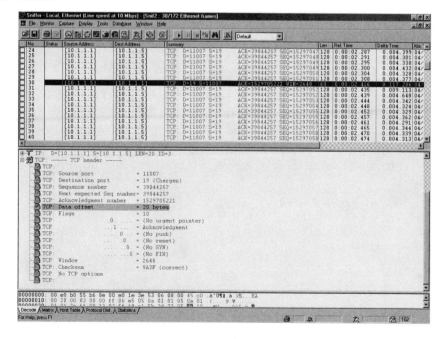

Optimization and Maintenance

PART 4

This graphic displays the results of Telnetting to the chargen port on a router. Notice that the ACK generates more traffic out of the chargen port and that the chargen output generates an ACK from the host to create a newer ending cycle. The best way to prevent this type of attack is to disable the echo and chargen services as discussed above.

Directed Broadcasts

Versions of the Cisco IOS prior to 12.0 supported IP directed broadcasts by default. This means that if you had a network of 172.16.8.0/24, it was possible to send a packet to 172.16.8.255 and the router would forward this on as an IP broadcast onto the 172.16.8.0 segment. Remember that one of the main functions of routers is to break up broadcast domains. Directed broadcasts sound like a good idea, right? What if you wanted to send a message to every system on a remote segment? You could use a directed broadcast. A router that will pass a directed broadcast offers an attacker a great chance for a denial of service attack.

Take a look at the scenario in Figure 15.2. Wilson Consulting is a huge firm with a full class B network connected to the Internet via a T1 line. Wilson Consulting probably has a lot of network devices, considering that they are using a class B address. Suppose that for some reason an attacker wanted to hurt Matt's Ice Cream. Maybe the attacker owned an ice cream truck and wanted to hurt Matt's business, in order to cut down on his competition. What would happen if the attacker created an ICMP echo request addressed to 172.16.255.255 and gave it the source address of 192.168.1.25? Every single host, at Wilson Consulting is going to try and reply; this is a maximum of 65536 hosts, each sending back an echo-reply packet. An echo reply is 78 bits, so one packet input can generate a maximum of 5,111,808 bits of reply data. Now this reply data is not going to go back to the attacker but is heading off for the Web server at Matt's Ice Cream.

Matt's Ice Cream only has a 56K Internet link so it is going to take something like 91 seconds to get all those echo replies across that 56K link. Because Ping is often used for performance testing, most hardware vendors have optimized their systems to give echo and echo-reply high priorities to get them through quickly. This means Matt is probably not going to get any data until all those echo replies are sent across his 56K line.

Figure 15.2   Matt's Ice Cream is vulnerable to a Smurf attack.

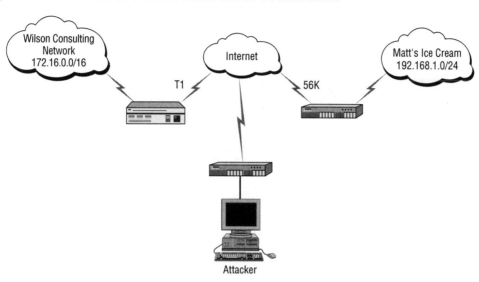

With only one packet, the attacker has now shut down all of Matt's Internet access for 90 seconds. Sending more packets would only keep Matt down longer. Now, when Matt sees all these echo replies he is going to try and track down where they are coming from. It looks like Wilson Consulting is attacking Matt; however, the attacker is only using Wilson Consulting to generate the echo-reply traffic. What can Matt do to prevent this? The answer is nothing. Matt has no control over the traffic until it reaches his router at the end of the 56K line, and by then it is too late—the line has already been flooded with the data. The fact that the destination for the echo replies is Matt's Web server at 192.168.1.25 is incidental. The destination address need only route into Matt's network; it does not need to be a valid host. This type of attack is know as a Smurf attack and is very difficult to stop because the victim does not have the ability to prevent the attack and has no idea who is actually attacking. Cooperation with the relay site is necessary to stop the attack and to attempt to find the perpetrator.

The only way to prevent this is for Wilson Consulting to stop allowing directed broadcasts. This can be done on an interface-by-interface basis with the command:

```
digger_router(config-if)#no ip directed-broadcast
```

To help Matt's Ice Cream, Wilson Consulting should set this up on the interface that connects them to the Internet to prevent their network from being used as a Smurf relay. Most network devices will not reply to a directed broadcast echo request, but there are

Optimization and Maintenance

PART 4

still enough out there that this type of attack is still a problem. Ping does not have to be the service used it this attack—it could be done with many other services. Ping just happens to work well because network devices tend to treat it with a high priority.

Source Routing

IP supports the option to allow the datagram sender to define the route the given datagram will take to its destination, and generally this route is simply reversed for the return trip. This is dangerous because if an attacker can define the routes his or her packets take, it is possible to sidestep the security systems in place. Source route packets can also be used to crash some systems that do not deal with them properly. There are rarely legitimate uses for source routed IP packets, so unless you know you are using source routed packets in your environment, disable IP source routing (which is on by default):

```
digger_router(config)#no ip source-route
```

Remember, part of a router's job is to select the best path through the network; source routing moves that functionality to the host device.

> **NOTE** IP source routing should not be confused with SRB (source route bridging). They are separate, although many of the theories are the same. IP source routing applies to a routed environment and not a bridged environment.

Access Lists

Now that we have discussed how to make the router itself more secure, we need to discuss how to also protect the devices behind the router. As a piece of networking equipment, the router has a special role in network security, because all data traveling between different layer 3 network addresses must pass through a routing device.

In Figure 15.3, we can see that a router must be used to connect differently addressed network areas. These areas do not have to be just IPX or IP, but could be DECnet, Apple-Talk, etc.

Figure 15.3   All network data traversing segments must pass though a routing device.

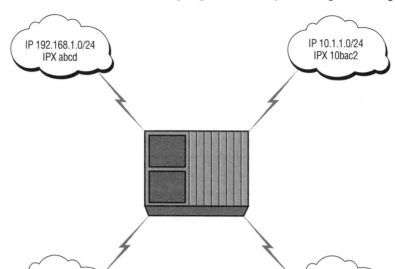

Because all traffic traversing segments must pass through a router, the router offers a unique opportunity for examining and classifying data. The router gives us the ability to discard data that does not match acceptability criteria before it crosses into a new segment. This is kind of like Liam at the county fair who checks to make sure everyone getting on the roller coaster is over a certain height. For Liam, this is a safety issue because someone who is too short might not fit properly in the seat and might fall out. The router has a similar type of function: it can check for a multitude of criteria to try and prevent unwanted data from getting through. This functionality is created through the use of access lists. We have already seen some access lists in previous chapters; however, the next few pages will cover them in much more detail. You probably have some experience with both standard and extended access lists, so we will not spend too much time on things you already know.

There are two main categories of access lists:

> **Standard access lists** allow filtering by source address only.

> **Extended access lists** allow filtering by source and destination address and service.

In older versions of the IOS, an access list's type is defined by its number:

Number	Protocol	Type
1–99	IP	Standard
100–199	IP	Extended
200–299	Ethernet Type Codes	N/A
300–399	DECnet	Either
600–699	AppleTalk	Either
700–799	Ethernet Addresses	N/A
800–899	IPX	standard
900–999	IPX	Extended
1000–1099	IPX	SAP Filters

> **NOTE** Vines also uses the access list ranges 1–100 and 101–200. However, we use a different command to create a Vines access list, so it does not overlap with IP access lists. The command is `vines access-list 104`.

Newer IOS versions allow for named access lists, which allow you to specify the type when you create an access list. The concepts covered in this chapter are exactly the same whether you are using numbered or named access lists.

Standard Access Lists

Standard access lists are simpler than extended access lists, and they allow you to filter only by the source address. Standard access lists should be placed as close to the destination you are trying to protect as possible.

For example, refer to Figure 15.4. If we wanted to prevent anyone on Dave's segment 192.168.50.44 from accessing server D using a standard access list, we would have to apply the access list to router D.

Figure 15.4   Standard access lists need to be applied as close as possible to the destination you are protecting.

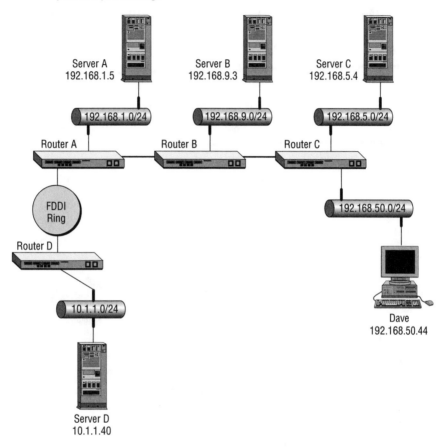

Because you can only specify source address with standard access lists, any data coming from that source will be blocked:

```
router(config)#access-list 44 deny 192.168.50.0 0.0.0.255
router(config)#access-list 44 permit any
```

> **NOTE** Remember that access list masks are exactly backward from subnet masks. Therefore, a 0 means, "match this bit," while a 1 means "don't worry about this bit of the address." So, to match 10.0.0.0–10.255.255.255, you would use a mask of 0.255.255.255.

If we were to apply this access list to the router connecting to server B's segment (router B) inbound on interface serial 0 so that anyone on the 192.168.50.0 segment could not get any IP data past router B, this would prevent Dave from talking to servers A and B. In order to prevent the 192.168.50.0 segment only from talking to server D while allowing those hosts to talk to any other segments, we would need to place the access list outbound on the Ethernet 0 interface of the router connecting to server D's segment (router D).

The standard access lists only being able to block based on source addresses is sort of like a locked door. Until you reach that locked door, you are not stopped; care must be taken with where the locked door is placed so as not to stop legitimate access. In most cases, this is very wasteful. Imagine if the link between router B and C were a satellite link, as in Figure 15.5.

Figure 15.5   Standard access lists are wasteful of bandwidth.

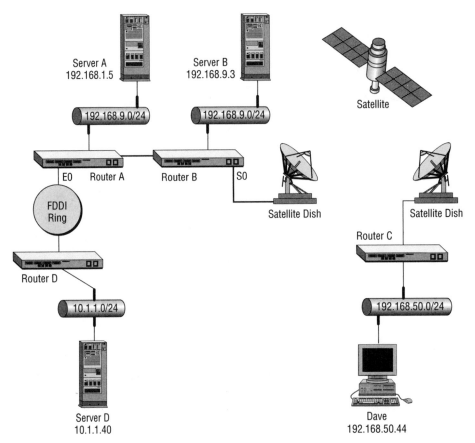

With a standard access list, the traffic that will be blocked is permitted to travel up to the satellite and back down all the way to router D before it is discarded. Why would you want to pay to have data travel that kind of distance only to be blocked at router D? It does not make any sense—it would be much more efficient to stop the data at router C. However, standard access lists do not provide this functionality. But, under the right conditions you don't even need an access list to provide destination-based filtering.

Null Interface

If you wanted to deny all traffic from the 192.168.50.0/24 network from getting to the 10.1.1.0/24 network, you could create a static route to 10.1.1.0/24 and point it at the null interface:

```
sparky(config)#ip route 10.1.1.0 255.255.255.0 null0
```

This will send all data destined for the 10.1.1.0/24 network to the null interface, which means, "discard the traffic." Remember, the administrative distance on a static route is 1 or 0. In this case, because the route is pointed at an interface with an administrative distance of 0, this route will always be the preferred route, no matter what routing protocol is being run.

A router is optimized to route data and not process access lists, although it does a good job with access lists. It is much faster to throw data into the null interface because all the router has to do is read the destination address, which it does anyway as it tries to figure out how to send the data.

The null interface cannot always be used. Because a route is global to the router, we cannot determine which end hosts use a given route, but we can determine how specific the route is. For example, we could create a route for a single host address and point it to null0. What we cannot do is specify that a single end host or even a single segment, if multiple segments are attached, should use the null interface route while other hosts use the real route. Routes apply to all data going through the router; you cannot pick and choose which data uses which route.

Extended Access Lists

Extended access lists provide the ability to filter traffic based on source destination and service type. Access-list filtering uses the data contained in the protocol header to decide whether to pass the traffic. There are two types of filtering that can be done by access lists: *static* and *dynamic packet filtering*.

Static Packet Filters

Static packet filtering is the most commonly used because it was all that was supported initially; only recently has Cisco begun to support dynamic packet filtering. A static packet filter makes the decision whether to drop a packet based solely on the packet it is looking at. An extended access list can look at many things in the packet to determine what to do. We will concentrate on IP, TCP, and UDP because these are the most common and you are probably already familiar with them. Most of us have probably never written a DECnet access list.

As we have discussed in previous chapters, the TCP segment contains a set of flags in the TCP packet header. These flags can be used as criteria for an access list. As illustrated in Figure 15.6, the following TCP bits are supported for access list matching in IOS 12:

ACK   Data is in response to a data request and there is useful information in the acknowledgment field.

FIN   Transmitting system wishes to close the communication session. Both sides should issue a FIN.

PSH   Used to prevent transmitting systems from queuing data before transmitting; also tells the receiving station not to queue the data, but to immediately push it up to the higher layers.

RST   Resets the state of the session: TCP three-way handshake must be done again.

SYN   Only used during the three-way handshake, to set up a connection; it should never be seen during an existing session.

URG   Data received is urgent and should be processed before any other data in the queue.

Now that we can filter based on all this flag information, how useful is it really? Although Cisco has allowed you to use all the flags as criteria in access lists, most likely you will only be interested in a few of them. Remember, from a programming point of view it is just as easy to check the SYN bit as it is to check the PSH bit. However, looking at the SYN bit is a lot more useful than looking at the PSH bit.

In Chapter 1 we discussed the TCP three-way handshake, shown again in Figure 15.7 to refresh your memory.

Figure 15.6 TCP used as access list criteria

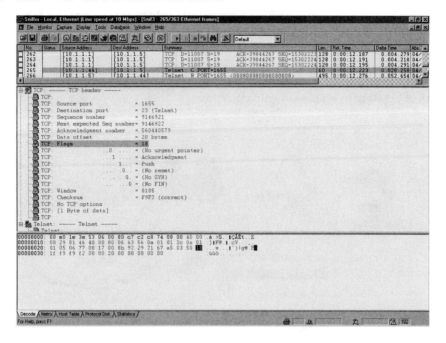

Figure 15.7 The TCP three-way handshake

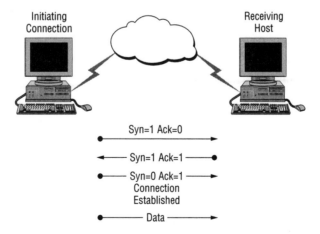

Notice that the host initiating the connection starts with syn=1 ack=0. This is the only time this ever happens. So anytime we see syn=1 ack=0, we know it is a host trying to start a session. Suppose we have a network that looked like Figure 15.8 and we want to allow the host behind our router to initiate a TCP session to the Internet but not allow the external hosts to access TCP services on our network.

Figure 15.8 Establishing a one-way connection

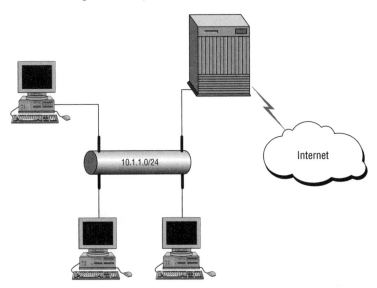

We would create an access list that denies any packets with syn=1 ack=0 from coming in through the router. Blocking this initial connection request would prevent an outside host from ever establishing a TCP connection:

```
access-list 101 permit tcp any any established
access-list 101 deny tcp any any
```

Thus we have allowed only one-way establishment of a connection. That is, only devices on the trusted side of the router are allowed to establish connections. This access list would be applied on the interface connecting to the Internet inbound. Generally, we would also specify a port number range of 1023 and greater because most communications should be coming back to random ports above 1023. This is because our hosts are accessing known services and picking high ports for their side of the connection. Back in Figure 15.6, you can see that 10.1.1.44 connected to port 23 on 10.1.1.1 using port 1655.

```
access-list 101 permit tcp any any gt 1023 established
```

When specifying a port number you can indicate a range of port numbers:

```
access-list 101 permit tcp any any range 23 52
```

This permits any ports between 23 and 52. Or you can use the operators gt (greater than), lt (less than), eq (equal to), or neq (not equal to) with a port number.

WARNING Remember that communication is a two-way process so you cannot block everything inbound from the Internet. Although this would be a really good security stance, it would probably upset a lot of people.

Static packet filtering is not the best way to lock down security. It is far too easy for an attacker to modify the TCP flags to trick a static filter into allowing malicious traffic through. For example, rather than using SYN=1 ACK =0 to scan for services, many attackers are now using a FIN scan, which uses FIN=1,ACK=1 in the TCP header. They cannot see if the host will return a SYN=1 ACK=1 (because the SYN=1 ACK=1 is blocked the FIN=1, ACK=1 is used). ACK=1 RST=1 will be returned if there is no service on the port; however, if ACK=1 FIN=1 is returned (the other host being scanned is agreeing to close the session), then the attacker knows a service exists at that port. We could block TCP packets with FIN=1 ACK=1, but then we start to mess up the mechanism of how TCP tears down connections. This is not really something you want to do.

The problem with static packet filtering is that it is static, which means the filter only knows about the current packet it is working on. A static packet filter will let a FIN=1 ACK=1 packet in because it has no idea that there is no active session on that port that needs to be closed.

This problem only gets worse when we start working with UDP; because UDP is not connection oriented, the flags for session control that exist in TCP are not present.

This means that UDP can only be controlled by destination port numbers, because source and destination port numbers are really the only information contained in the UDP header. Sometimes this can be done—for example, it works fine for TFTP. You can stop TFTP sessions from being initiated by blocking port 69 from getting through your router to hosts providing TFTP services. However, some services use the same source and destination port. DNS uses port 53 on both ends of the communication, so it is impossible to allow DNS traffic to be originated in one direction. Figure 15.10 illustrates the DNS communication process.

Figure 15.9 UDP packet decode

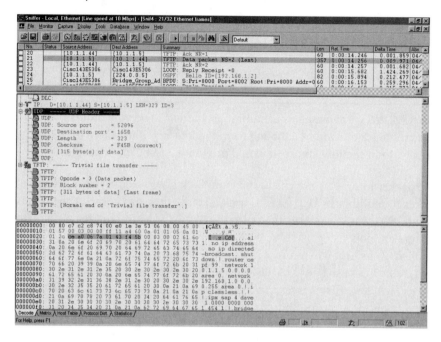

Figure 15.10 Both sides of the DNS communication process use port 53.

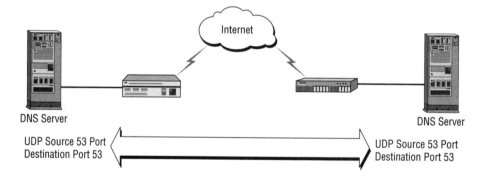

Because the replying host is not using a port number above 1023 but is actually using port 53, we cannot use static packet filtering to allow one-way DNS communication. There are several other services that also use the same port numbers for both side of the communication process. We use DNS here as an example because too often people break DNS while trying to configure static packet filtering.

ICMP Filtering   ICMP (Internet Control Message Protocol) provides background support for the IP protocol. You are probably familiar with using Ping to test end-to-end connectivity between systems. However, there is a lot more to ICMP than just Ping.

ICMP does not use service ports the way UDP or TCP do. Instead, it uses type and code fields. Some packet filters allow you to filter only on the type field. Cisco allows you to filter on both the type and the code. This gives you a great deal of granularity. There are far too many ICMP types and code field to cover in this chapter. Appendix B lists the possible ICMP type and code combinations.

One you should be aware of is the ICMP redirect. This tells a router or host that there is a better way to get somewhere. ICMP redirects should not be able to traverse more than one network hop and should never be sent by an end station. Thus, a valid redirect will only be sent to a local segment by a router. However, an attacker can violate these rules and there are several attacks based on using ICMP redirects.

In Figure 15.11, suppose host A wants to talk to server B. What will happen? Host A sends a packet to its default gateway, which is router C. Router C receives the packet and now looks at its route table and sees that the next hop is router D at 10.1.1.2. Well, router C has to send the packet out the same interface it just received the packet from. Router C assumes that a routing table is screwed up somewhere, forwards the packet to Router D, and sends an ICMP redirect to host A to tell it that it does not want the traffic to 172.16.0.0/18. Instead, host A should send all traffic for 172.16.0.0/18 to router D. Host A receives the redirect and modifies its routing table. Now all traffic for server B is sent directly to router D and not the default gateway router C.

> **NOTE**   Different operating systems handle ICMP redirects differently. Unix will change its route when it receives a redirect. Win95 and NT will change their routing tables for awhile, but the route created by the redirect will timeout after a few minutes and the default gateway will be used again to start the process over and reestablish the correct route again via an ICMP redirect.

Optimization and Maintenance

PART 4

Figure 15.11 ICMP redirects can modify the routing tables of hosts.

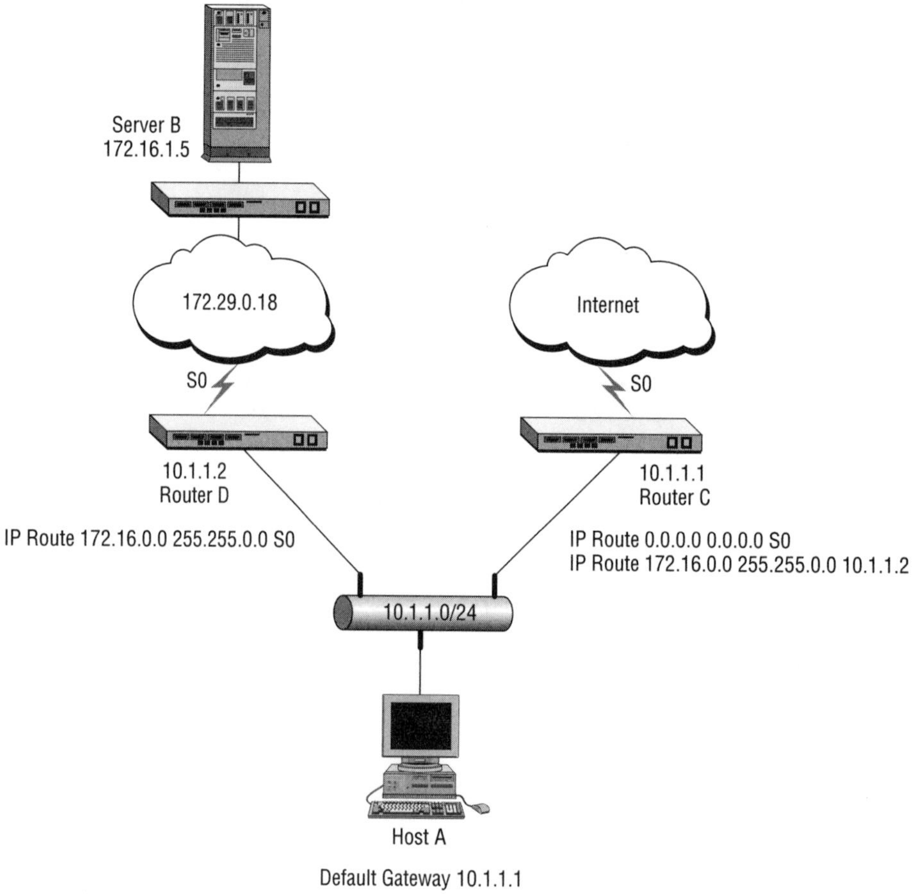

Because redirects can reconfigure a host's routing table, they should be blocked from coming inbound off an untrusted network:

```
access-list 101 deny icmp any any redirect
```

Obviously, you will want to allow redirects on your local segments. Remember, in a properly configured network, routers should not be listening to redirects, and redirects should not leave the local segment. Knowing this, you can block redirects inbound on every router interface and not impact network performance.

Dynamic Packet Filters

Dynamic packet filtering offers a major improvement over static packet filtering. A dynamic packet filter creates a state table, which contains information about all established connections. A `FIN=1 ACK=1` scan packet will not get through, because the filter will receive the packet and not see an entry for that communication session. Because there is no communication session, there is no reason an outside host should be tearing down the session, so the filter will drop the packet.

Dynamic packet filters include the same functionality as static packet filters but also allow the router to create a state table. This state table allows the router to make decisions based not solely on the present packet it is processing but also by comparing it to other traffic it has seen to make sure it makes sense. Basically, a dynamic packet filter is context sensitive. Obviously, a dynamic packet filter is more resource intensive on the router, because it has to create and maintain a state table in memory.

IOS 12.0 gives us the major improvement of allowing dynamic packet filtering for all types of IP traffic, not just TCP as with version 11.3.

Dynamic filters are created a little differently than static filters, because you also need to create a state table:

```
ip access-list extended inbound_filter
 permit tcp any host 10.1.1.34 eq 25 reflect smtp
 permit tcp any host 10.1.1.44 eq 80 reflect http
```

This is an example of dynamic packet filtering. We are creating two state tables an SMTP for mail to 10.1.1.34 and an HTTP for HTTP traffic to our Web server. All hosts are allowed to connect to these two devices via the specific service they are providing. Now that we have applied the rules for inbound traffic, we need to create rules for outbound traffic:

```
ip access-list extended outbound_filter
 evaluate smtp
 evaluate http
```

This access list will allow response traffic back for those connections created in the state tables. This can obviously be extended for any service you wish to evaluate, and you could add in nonreflexive access list entries for that data that you want to use a static filter for.

When working with reflexive access lists, you can use the `show ip access-lists` command to see what the router is actually doing in the background with the dynamic access-lists.

A partial output from this command appears below:

```
Reflexive IP access list ipfilter

permit tcp host 172.16.225.6 eq http host 10.89.193.221 eq 1045
(12 matches) (time left 887)

permit tcp host 172.16.225.72 eq http host 10.89.193.221 eq 1154
(11 matches) (time left 781)

permit udp host 172.17.128.127 eq domain host 10.89.193.209 eq domain
(6 matches) (time left 756)

permit udp host 172.18.31.4 eq domain host 10.89.193.209 eq domain
(2 matches) (time left 753)
```

From this output you can see that the router is creating access list entries for specific hosts and ports. In the first line you can see that someone at 10.89.193.221 has gone out to a Web site at 172.16.225.6. The router allowed this traffic through. Then the dynamic part of the filter took over and created the rule we see in the second line above. The router noticed that 10.89.193.221 was using port 1045 to get to the Web site on 172.16.225.6. So it created a rule that says "since I know port 1045 on 10.89.193.221 is talking to the Web site at 172.16.225.6, I need to allow traffic from 172.16.225.6 to get back to port 1045 on 10.89.193.221." The router has learned what port 10.89.193.221 is using to go to that Web site and has created a rule to allow only traffic via the HTTP port (80) on 172.16.225.6 to come back to the port on the host that requested the data. This allows the router to make intelligent decisions about what data it should and should not allow through. Without dynamic filters, we would have to allow TCP traffic coming in on ports above 1023 with the established bit set to come back through the filter. Obviously, the dynamic packet filter is much more secure because it is making access-list rules based on the outgoing traffic to allow the responses through the filter.

Creating Security: A Stance with Access Lists

Remember, your router is not a firewall. Although it does offer some nice security functionality, it should not be used as your only method of securing your network from the Internet unless there is absolutely no other choice. The best security stance is a layered one, in which you are using the router to help augment the functionality of a firewall.

IP Access Lists

When creating an access list, you should strive never to use a `permit any any` rule to override the explicit deny. It is much easier to define the scope of traffic you wish to allow than to try to define everything you wish to block. You will certainly miss something, and it is much safer to get caught not allowing enough services through the router than to allow too many services through.

Augmenting Your Firewall with Router Access Lists

Assume we have a firewall protecting our network. What should we block? Some people think the firewall should be the only source of protection, because that is what it is designed for. This view does have merits: a firewall provides a central point for administration and logging. However, to connect to the Internet you need a router, so why not use some of its capabilities? Of course, you still want the firewall to be secure and it should be configured as if nothing was being filtered by the router. Suppose we had an Internet connection like the one shown in Figure 15.12.

Figure 15.12 A router can augment the security mechanisms of a firewall.

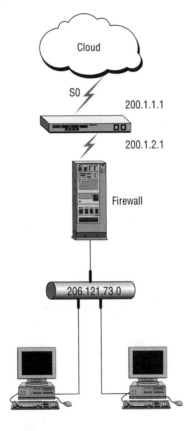

We would want to create an access list something like the following:

```
access-list 101 deny ip 206.121.73.0 0.0.0.255 any
access-list 101 deny ip 172.16.0.0 0.15.255.255 any
```

Optimization and
Maintenance

PART 4

```
access-list 101 deny ip 192.168.0.0 0.0.255.255 any
access-list 101 deny ip 10.0.0.0 0.255.255.255 any
access-list 101 deny ip 127.0.0.0 0.255.255.255 any
access-list 101 deny ip 224.0.0.0 7.255.255.255 any
access-list 101 deny ip host 0.0.0.0 any
access-list 101 deny icmp any any echo
access-list 101 deny icmp any any redirect
access-list 101 deny udp any any eq snmp
access-list 101 deny tcp any host 200.1.1.1 eq 23
access-list 101 deny tcp any host 200.1.2.1 eq 23
access-list 101 permit ip any any
```

WARNING   Only add an implicit permit in a layered security environment.

This access list would be applied to interface S0 inbound. The first line will prevent any traffic using our internal addresses as the source address from coming inbound from the Internet. This is done to prevent spoofing, which is also the purpose of the next four lines (2–5). These are not valid addresses and there is no reason they should be showing up at our Internet router. Line 6 is used to block multicast traffic; if you are actually using multicast, you will have to remove this line. Line 7 blocks any traffic that does not have a source IP address. Line 8 prevents Ping from getting in so that no one can map our network. This may not be very cooperative, because systems administrators tend to use Ping to test all kinds of connectivity issues. If you want, you could enable Ping to the router only. Then you are only giving away the address of the router. It is impossible to hide all your addresses anyway, because you are going to have Address and MX records in DNS anyway. But Ping should not be allowed to come through the router to just any device.

In line 9, we are preventing ICMP redirects because we don't want any ICMP redirects coming in off the Internet. The next line prevents SNMP so that an attacker cannot probe our network via SNMP. Remember, we probably don't want to enable SNMP on our Internet router. If you decide to do so, never put a read/write community string on that router. Lines 11 and 12 protect the router so that no one can Telnet to it from the outside. Notice that we need to protect both the inside and outside interface.

Line 13 lets all other traffic through, because we are assuming the firewall will deal with it. If we did not have a firewall, we would never consider doing this—it is far too dangerous. However, we have already hardened the router at the beginning of the chapter, so we should be pretty safe. If there were any other services we wanted to protect we could add them into the access list. Perhaps if the firewall did not deal with a particular service very well we could use the router to block that service before it gets to the firewall.

> **NOTE** Create your access list in an editor and paste it into the route. This will make things much easier. Also, never save the running configuration until you have tested the access list. Forgetting about the implicit deny has locked many people out of their routers. If all you have to do is reboot to recover, it is not too bad a mistake. However, if you save the config before you realize you have locked yourself out, then your will really get to test you ingenuity.

Blocking Traceroute Probes   Another method attackers use to gather data is traceroute. Implementations of traceroute are different for Unix and Windows. Unix uses high port numbers while Windows uses ICMP, so how the heck do we block it if Unix is going to use random high port numbers? Well, the truth is you let it through but block the responses going back out. Remember, traceroute works by reading ICMP time expired messages. Because it is incrementing the TTL value so that each successive packet will die one hop further away, each device that tosses the packet due to the TTL expiring must tell the sending host it killed the packet. All you have to do is kill these responses:

```
access-list 104 deny icmp any any time-exceeded
access-list 104 permit ip any any
```

This would be applied outbound to interface S0 to prevent traceroute from working for either Unix or Windows systems.

Access List Counters   To see how many packets are hitting each line of a given access list, the following command can be used:

```
sparky#sh ip access-lists 103
Extended IP access list 103
  deny tcp any any eq telnet log-input (2 matches)
  deny tcp any any eq smtp log-input
  permit ip any any (162 matches)
```

```
deny tcp any any eq 135

deny tcp any any eq 137

deny tcp any any eq 138

deny tcp any any eq 139

deny udp any any eq 135

deny udp any any eq netbios-ns

deny udp any any eq netbios-dgm

deny udp any any eq netbios-ss
```

Notice that you see not only each line of the access list but the number of packets that have matched each line as well. Look at the `permit any any` line. Notice that no line below it has any matches; this is exactly what we would expect from this access list. No data should ever get past this line to match any of the other access list conditions.

Access List Logging   All of this data blocking is great, but we have just lost the capability to track down an attacker because we are not logging anything other than the number of packets that match each line in the access list. Fortunately, logging access-list behavior is simple—just add the word `log` or `log-input` to the end of the access list lines you want to log:

```
access-list 101 deny ip 206.121.73.0 0.0.0.255 any log

access-list 101 deny ip 172.16.0.0 0.15.255.255 any log

access-list 101 deny ip 192.168.0.0 0.0.255.255 any log

access-list 101 deny ip 10.0.0.0 0.255.255.255 any log

access-list 101 deny ip 127.0.0.0 0.255.255.255 any log

access-list 101 deny ip 224.0.0.0 7.255.255.255 any log

access-list 101 deny ip host 0.0.0.0 any log

access-list 101 deny icmp any any echo log

access-list 101 deny icmp any any time-exceeded log-input

access-list 101 deny icmp any any redirect log-input

access-list 101 deny udp any any eq snmp log-input

access-list 101 deny tcp any host 200.1.1.1 eq 23 log

access-list 101 deny tcp any host 200.1.2.1 eq 23 log

access-list 101 permit ip any any
```

The difference between `log` and `log input` is that `log input` will record the interface the packet came through, in addition to the normal logging information. If you plan to do access list logging, you will want to have your router log to a syslog server. There are many shareware syslog servers, and most Unix implementations come with one (as does CiscoWorks). Setting up logging to a syslog server is simple. Use this global configuration command:

```
sparky(config)#logging 10.1.1.4
```

where 10.1.1.4 is replaced with the IP address of your syslog server.

An access list can be removed by entering the command

```
No access-list access-list#
```

This will delete the complete access list. Modifying an existing access list in the router can be tricky. Imagine you have this simple access list:

```
access-list 103 deny tcp any any eq telnet log-input
access-list 103 deny tcp any any eq smtp log-input
access-list 103 permit ip any any
```

Now you decide to add a few more lines without deleting the list and starting over. You decide you need to block file and print sharing in a Windows environment. But you forget to delete the access list and just go in and add the lines. You end up with the following access list:

```
access-list 103 deny tcp any any eq telnet log-input
access-list 103 deny tcp any any eq smtp log-input
access-list 103 permit ip any any
access-list 103 deny tcp any any eq 135
access-list 103 deny tcp any any eq 137
access-list 103 deny tcp any any eq 138
access-list 103 deny tcp any any eq 139
access-list 103 deny udp any any eq 135
access-list 103 deny udp any any eq netbios-ns
access-list 103 deny udp any any eq netbios-dgm
access-list 103 deny udp any any eq netbios-ss
```

What have you accomplished? Nothing. Look at line 3. Because access lists are processed top to bottom and processing stops on the first match, no IP packet will ever get past line 3. Because all IP packets will be permitted by line 3, all the lines we just added are useless and in fact they are dangerous, because looking quickly, someone might not see the permit ip any any, invalidates the rest of the access list. Order is very important, with access lists. You want to deny as much as possible first; then, when you permit, you need to start with the specific and move toward the general, as shown in Figure 15.13.

Figure 15.13 Access lists should be created so that traffic matches as soon as possible.

Access list permit statement should start with the specific and move toward the general.

Access list deny statement should start with the general and move toward the specific.

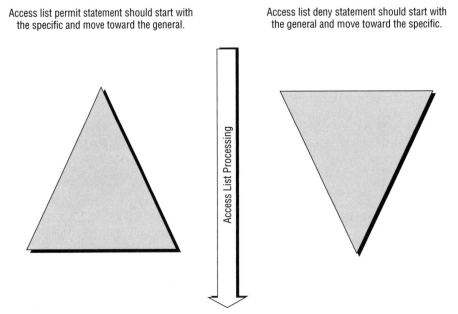

Access List Processing

This is done to make the list more efficient: the fewer lines the router has to compare the packet to, the more quickly it can move on to the next packet. Permit statements need to be ordered with the most specific appearing first, so that traffic that should be denied is not inadvertently permitted. In many cases, you will only use permit statements and let the implicit deny handle the rest of the traffic.

NOTE Applying an empty access list to an interface should not block any traffic, but certain versions of the IOS will block all traffic due to the implicit deny. Be careful: the correct behavior according to Cisco is to let all traffic through, but experience shows that this behavior is not consistent across all IOS versions.

Applying this access list:

```
access-list 103 deny tcp any any eq telnet log-input
access-list 103 deny tcp any any eq smtp log-input
access-list 103 permit ip any any
```

to a router and trying to access the Telnet and SNMP ports creates the following entries in the log:

```
08:23:28: %SEC-6-IPACCESSLOGP: list 103 denied tcp 10.1.1.1(59394)
(Ethernet0 00

e0.b055.b68e) -> 10.1.1.3(23), 1 packet

08:24:01: %SEC-6-IPACCESSLOGP: list 103 denied tcp 10.1.1.1(59906)
(Ethernet0 00

e0.b055.b68e) -> 10.1.1.3(23), 1 packet
```

Notice that we can see the time, the list that denied the packet, the source and destination addresses of the packet, and also a MAC address. Remember, the MAC address will be the MAC address of the most recent router and probably not the MAC address of the host that tried to violate the access list. We also see the interface that the packet came in on. This is useful if we are using the same access list on multiple interfaces. If your IOS version supports log input as an option and you are going to apply the same access list to multiple interfaces, it would make sense to use this option. If not, the simple log option works just as well.

TIP Sometimes it is a good idea to add a deny any any line to the access list. This is because the implicit deny does not log any information. You might not care about logging every single packet, but you might want to know how many packets are being dropped by the last line of the access list. Unless you add the deny ip any any, the show ip access list command will not give you any information about the implicit deny.

Protecting Your Network Without a Firewall

If we have a firewall, we don't have to worry too much about security. Anything missed in the router will be caught by the firewall. What do you do if you don't have a firewall? Well, if you do not have a firewall, we will assume you are not running a great many services accessible from the outside world, and you are definitely not running any e-commerce applications.

Let's assume we have the simple environment shown in Figure 15.14.

Optimization and Maintenance

PART 4

Figure 15.14 Perimeter protection without a firewall

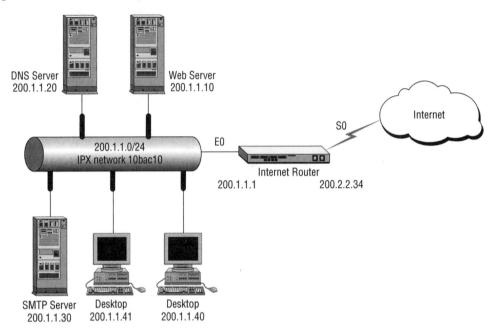

The first thing we need to do is define the types of traffic we need to support and in which direction should we support them. This would include the following:

- Inbound Web server requests and outbound replies from the Web server.
- Inbound connection requests from external mail systems to our SMTP server for mail delivery and the responses from our SMTP server.
- Outbound mail connections from our SMTP server for mail delivery.
- Outbound DNS queries from our DNS server.
- Inbound DNS replies to our DNS server.
- Outbound TCP connections for all internal hosts.
- Inbound TCP responses to connections established by our internal hosts.

Because this is going to be our only line of defense, we will want to use dynamic packet filtering. This will require the use of named access lists. We will also need an inbound and outbound access list:

```
ip access-list extended inbound_filter
permit tcp any host 200.1.1.10 eq www reflect webfilter
```

First we create the above access list line to allow HTTP traffic to the Web server and put those connections into our state table. Now we need to set up the outbound filter to allow the replies back out. We do this by evaluating the state table created by the inbound HTTP connections above:

```
ip access-list extended outbound_filter
evaluate webfilter
```

Now that we have handled HTTP, the rest follows the same pattern. To fulfill the requirements set out here, we would use an access list like this:

```
ip access-list extended inbound_filter
 permit tcp any host 200.1.1.10 eq www reflect web filter
 permit tcp any host 200.1.1.30 eq telnet reflect smtpfilter
 evaluate dnsfilter
 evaluate tcpfilter
ip access-list extended outbound_filter
 permit udp host 200.1.1.30 any eq domain reflect dnsfilter
 permit tcp 200.1.1.0 0.0.0.255 any reflect tcpfilter
 evaluate webfilter
 evaluate smtpfilter
```

However, there are some things we should add from some of the security measures we discussed above. Because we have only used permit statements, there is really no reason to add these extra security measures—the traffic will still be dropped. However, we don't have a firewall and it would be nice to be able to log what is going on, so you might use something like this (the added lines are highlighted in boldface):

```
ip access-list extended inbound_filter
 permit tcp any host 200.1.1.10 eq www log reflect webfilter
 permit tcp any host 200.1.1.30 eq telnet log reflect smtpfilter
 deny ip 200.1.1.0 0.0.0.255 any log-input
 deny ip 172.16.0.0 0.15.255.255 any log-input
 deny ip 192.168.0.0 0.0.255.255 any log-input
 deny ip 10.0.0.0 0.255.255.255 any log-input
 deny ip 127.0.0.0 0.255.255.255 any log-input
```

```
deny ip 224.0.0.0 7.255.255.255 any log-input
deny ip host 0.0.0.0 any log-input
deny icmp any any echo log-input
deny icmp any any redirect log-input
deny udp any any eq snmp log-input
deny tcp any host 200.1.1.1 eq telnet log
deny tcp any host 200.1.2.1 eq telnet log
deny ip any any log
evaluate dnsfilter
evaluate tcpfilter


ip access-list extended outbound_filter
permit udp host 200.1.1.30 any eq domain reflect dnsfilter
permit tcp 200.1.1.0 0.0.0.255 any log reflect tcpfilter
deny icmp any any time-exceeded log
evaluate webfilter
evaluate smtpfilter
```

Now all you need to do is apply the access list to the proper interfaces. In Figure 15.14 we would apply this to the S0 interface:

```
sparky(config-if)#ip access-group inbound_filter in
sparky(config-if)#ip access-group outbound_filter out
```

NOTE Only one access list per protocol per direction can be applied to any one interface at a time.

In the previous access list example, we set up logging on almost everything. The amount of logging you decide to do depends on how much you want to know about what is going on with your access lists.

It is always better to have too much information than not enough. What you want to log is entirely up to you. However, if you do not have a firewall, we recommend you log extensively.

You are really going to want to know what is going on at your borders, and logging is the only option. Also, because there are only two interfaces being used on the Internet router, we really did not have to specify log input. Because we know which interface the access list is applied on, we can be pretty sure which interface the data hitting the access list came in on.

IPX Access Lists

This chapter has focused on IP and IP security simply because the Internet is the one of the largest security holes networks today face, and the Internet is simply a big IP network. IPX and most other protocols have access list functionality, but generally IPX is only run on trusted networks within the corporate environment. Generally, when setting up security for IPX, you either allow the traffic into a location or deny that traffic.

The use of extended access lists in IPX does give you the ability to block specific sockets from specific hosts. All IPX packet filtering is static packet filtering; there is no dynamic packet filtering option. For the most part, IPX access lists work exactly like static IP packet filtering: you can do basically all the same things; the only difference is that the addressing scheme used in IPX is different from that used by IP.

If for example we wanted to prevent network 1234 from sending any SPX traffic we could use the following named access list:

```
ipx access-list extended list1
 deny spx 1234 all any
 permit any 1234 all any
```

The all is used to specify all sockets; however, we could specify individual IPX sockets. The following list shows some of the registered socket numbers:

451	NCP Process
452	SAP Process
453	RIP Process
455	Novell NetBIOS packet
456	Novell diagnostic packet
456	Novell serialization packet
4000–7FFF	Dynamically assigned sockets used by end station for interaction with network servers
85BE	IPX EIGRP
9001	NLSP

Optimization and Maintenance

PART 4

9004	IPXWAN
9086	IPX Ping

For the most part, when creating an IPX access list, you are not going to worry too much about masking the host portion of the address because IPX host addressing uses MAC addresses. This does give you the ability to block, say, all Compaq network cards, but the ranges tend to be too random to be of much use unless you are using them for specific network card manufacturers. Masking uses *F*s and *0*s; for example, to deny network 33333300–333333FF the following statement would be used:

```
deny 33333300 ffffff00
```

The following access list would permit any IPX/SPX traffic from network 4444, and permits only traffic with a protocol number of RIP or SAP from network 3333:

```
access-list 902 permit any 4444 all any all

access-list 902 permit rip 3333 all any all

access-list 902 permit sap 3333 all any all
```

Your access lists for IPX will almost always be blocking traffic from either an entire network or a specific server. Just as with IP access lists, you have the option to log extended IPX access lists.

> **NOTE** Logging cannot be used with standard IPX access lists. Attempting to do so creates unexpected results and the access list probably will not work.

Virtual Private Networks

With the growth of the Internet and the need to connect remote offices, VPNs (Virtual Private Networks) have become all the rage. Think about how cool it would be if you could have the Internet provide you with all you office-to-office connectivity needs, and only have to pay for the connection to the Internet.

Figure 15.15 shows a simple VPN connection.

Figure 15.15 A simple VPN topology

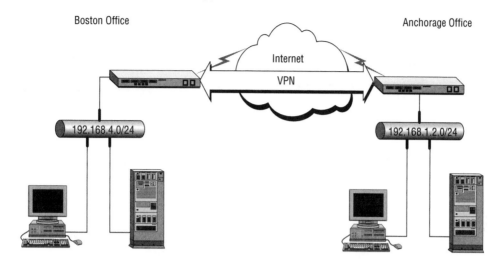

The Internet is used to connect the Boston and Anchorage offices. This connection looks the same as if you had a leased line connecting Boston and Anchorage but is significantly cheaper. A VPN is basically an encrypted tunnel. A packet gets to the VPN interface, is encrypted, and is placed inside an IP packet that is sent across the Internet to the other end where the IP header is stripped and the packet is unencrypted. Now you have the original packet on the other side of the VPN with all the proper header information to find its way to the intended destination. If you remember our discussion of tunneling, just take the packets you are going to tunnel and encrypt them and you have a VPN. There is no real magic to a VPN.

What the VPN does is expand on the Frame Relay cloud model where you lease a line to get your data into the cloud. Once it is in the cloud, you have no control over what happens to that data until it comes out the other end. Frame Relay does use PVCs (Permanent Virtual Circuits) and SVCs (Switched Virtual Circuits) so there is some control over how the data traverses the frame cloud. If you are having a frame problem, you can call your frame provider, who should be able to fix it. Frame Relay also guarantees you a CIR so you know you will be able to maintain a certain data rate through the cloud.

When you talk about running a VPN across the Internet, there is no such thing as a CIR. Your traffic is no more important than anyone else's. If someone at Columbia decides that they need to target Brown for a Smurf attack and your data happens to go across a link being flooded by that attack, too bad for you. If things stop working, who do you call? Sure, you can call your ISP, and they can confirm whether the link to the Internet is

Optimization and
Maintenance

PART 4

working, but if there is a backbone outage in Colorado that prevents you from getting to the Anchorage office, then who do you call? You cannot call anyone. Who owns the Internet? Once you dump packets into the Internet you have no control whatsoever. To get from Boston to Anchorage, your packets may go through a router in Korea (they probably won't, but they could) and you have no control. Anyone sitting in the right place on the Internet has an opportunity to snag your packets. True, they are encrypted, and it is unlikely anyone will be able to decrypt them, but you never know.

Another common use of a VPN is for remote access. Figure 15.16 displays this configuration.

Figure 15.16 Remote access VPN topology

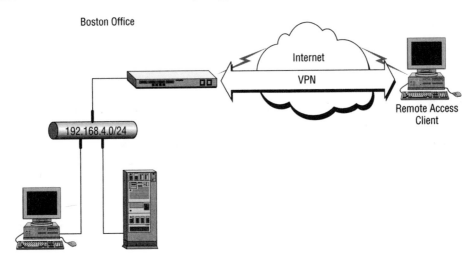

This type of VPN allows a remote user to access the corporate network via an ISP and appear as if they are directly connected to the network. It does not eliminate any of the issues discussed above for using a VPN to connect remote offices, but because you are scaling back to a single user, the impact of downtime is significantly reduced. True, if Liam—the project manager—cannot get on the network to update a spreadsheet, it may impact some people. However, this is typically not on the same scale as losing the link between two offices. From a security standpoint, it is important to note that Liam is now on the Internet, where we cannot protect him. His PC may have any number of programs on it that would allow hackers to monitor his activities. Thus, by allowing Liam to run VPN client software and connect to our network, we now have to worry about Liam's PC being an uncontrolled network access point that an attacker could potentially use to get into our network.

In Figure 15.17, once Liam connects his PC, he is on the Internet with a VPN link to our corporate network. All an attacker has to do is compromise Liam's PC, and the whole network is compromised. The attacker simply gets into Liam's PC and uses it as a relay point into our network. This is not to say that a client VPN solution is necessarily a bad thing.

Figure 15.17 VPN clients can offer backdoor access to attackers.

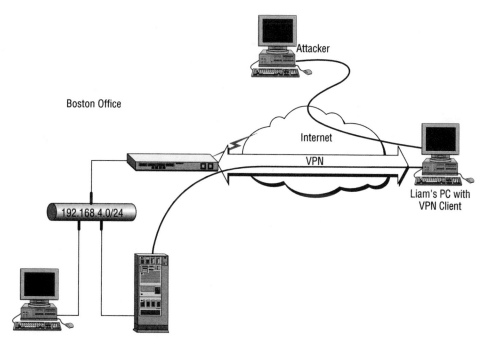

It is important to understand what you are getting into with a VPN, whether its purpose is to link remote offices or to allow users remote access to the network. VPNs can offer an interesting and cost-effective solution to high leased-line costs. However, they are far from a perfect solution. As with anything in life, there are trade-offs. Nothing is ever free.

VPN Configuration

Let's walk through the configuration of a remote office VPN link. Figure 15.18 shows the configuration we will be working with.

Optimization and Maintenance

PART 4

Figure 15.18 VPN topology to be configured

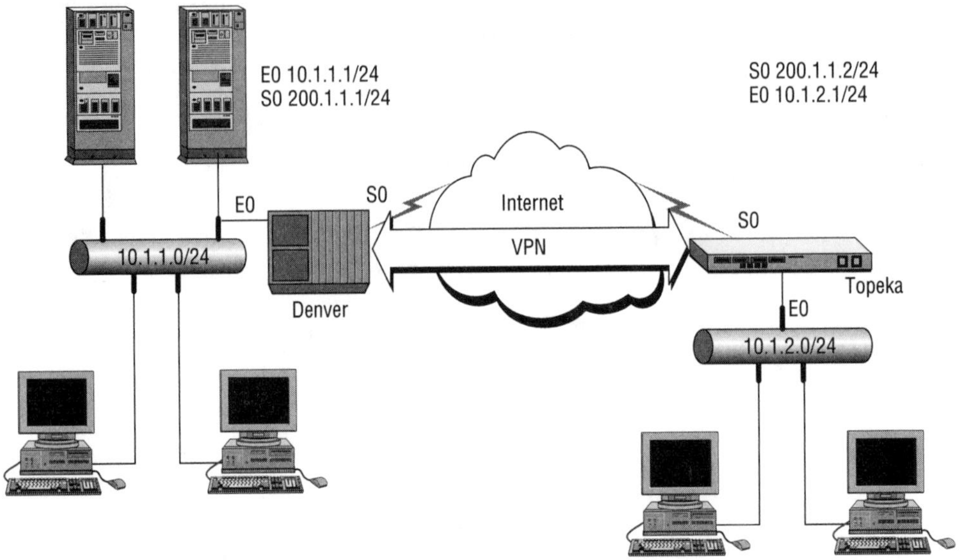

First we need to configure encryption:

```
DENVER(config)#crypto isakmp policy 1

DENVER(config-isakmp)#encryption des

DENVER(config-isakmp)#hash sha

DENVER(config-isakmp)#authentication pre-share

DENVER(config-isakmp)#group 1

DENVER(config-isakmp)#lifetime 14400
```

Here we are creating iskamp policy number 1. In the second line we have chosen to use DES encryption; we could have used the keyword 3des to specify using triple DES encryption. Line 3 specified the hash algorithm to be used, in our case, sha although we could have used md5. Line 5 specifies the Diffie-Hellman group. The identifier 1 specifies we are using 768-bit Diffie-Hellman; with a 2 we would get 1024-bit Diffie-Hellman. Finally, the lifetime entry specifies how long this the security association will be good for. In our case we are specifying 14400 seconds or four hours.

Now we need to configure a keying method. For this example, we are going to use a pre-shared key of 654321, although we could have used RSA signatures that would have involved configuring our router to get keys from a CA (Certification of Authority), and that would only confuse matters here. To specify our pre-shared key, we need to use the following commands:

```
DENVER(config)#crypto isakmp identity address
DENVER(config)#crypto isakmp key 654321 address 200.1.1.6
```

Line 1 specifies the ISAKMP identity the router will use when communicating with the remote router. In this case, the Denver router will use its IP address. Instead of the address, we could have specified hostname topeka to use the hostname of the topeka router. Line 3 specifies that the key 6534321 will be used with the remote peer 200.1.1.6. The same thing needs to be done on the topeka router. We can use the same key with multiple hosts, but generally it is a good idea to create unique keys for each pair of hosts.

> **NOTE** When you specify hostnames as ISAKMP identifiers, the routers must be able to resolve each other's hostname via either DNS or static host entries.

Currently, we are using the default security association lifetimes. We could change these to expire based on either traffic volume or time. Our present configuration looks like the following:

```
topeka#show crypto ipsec security-association-lifetime
Security association lifetime: 4608000 kilobytes/3600 seconds
```

To modify these values use the following global configuration commands:

```
crypto ipsec security-association lifetime seconds <value>
crypto ipsec security-association lifetime kilobytes <value>
```

Now that we have set up an encryption policy and created the pre-shared key on each host, we need to define what traffic is encrypted. We do this using an access list. Because we know we want to encrypt all IP traffic between DENVER and topeka, we would create an access list like the following:

```
DENVER(config)#access-list 111 permit ip host 200.1.1.5 host
200.1.1.6
DENVER(config)access-list 111 permit 10.1.1.0 0.0.0.255 200.1.1.0
0.0.0.255
DENVER(config)access-list 111 permit 10.1.1.0 0.0.0.255 10.1.2.0
0.0.0.255
```

This access list will catch all traffic between the DENVER and topeka routers. For the topeka router, you would just reverse the source and destination address; or, for simplicity, because we are using permit statements we could put the topeka statements in the same access list without hurting anything:

```
access-list 111 permit ip host 200.1.1.5 host 200.1.1.6

access-list 111 permit ip host 200.1.1.6 host 200.1.1.5

access-list 111 permit ip 10.1.1.0 0.0.0.255 200.1.1.0 0.0.0.255

access-list 111 permit ip 10.1.2.0 0.0.0.255 200.1.1.0 0.0.0.255

access-list 111 permit ip 10.1.1.0 0.0.0.255 10.1.2.0 0.0.0.255

access-list 111 permit ip 10.1.2.0 0.0.0.255 10.1.1.0 0.0.0.255
```

We want to encrypt all data between the two routers. By using this access list, we ensure that data going elsewhere on the Internet will not be encrypted. That is what we want, because Internet hosts do not know what key we are using.

We now need to define a *transform set*. When two hosts begin the ipsec negotiation, they need to agree on a particular transform set to use to protect their data flow. A transform set is just a combination of security protocols and algorithms. Multiple transform sets can be specified and you can use multiple transform sets in a crypto-map. When the peers negotiate an SA (security association), they look for a transform set that they have in common to use to protect the data. If a transform set is changed, it is only applied to those crypto-maps which reference that transform set, and any existing SAs are left unaffected. SAs will only use the new transform set when they are reestablished or are establishing new SAs. If a router has established an SA, changing the transform set will not affect that transform set until the SA is torn down and the router goes to reestablish it.

We will create the following transform set:

```
DENVER(config)#crypto ipsec transform-set tset1 esp-des ah-sha-hmac
esp-md5-hmac

DENVER(cfg-crypto-trans)#mode tunnel
```

The first line specifies the actual transform. The following options exist for transforms:

```
DENVER(config)#crypto ipsec transform-set tset1 ?
  ah-md5-hmac AH-HMAC-MD5 transform

  ah-rfc1828 AH-MD5 transform (RFC1828)

  ah-sha-hmac AH-HMAC-SHA transform

  esp-des ESP transform using DES cipher (56 bits)
```

```
esp-md5-hmac ESP transform using HMAC-MD5 auth

esp-null ESP transform w/o cipher

esp-rfc1829 ESP-DES-CBC transform (RFC1829)

esp-sha-hmac ESP transform using HMAC-SHA auth
```

When we set the mode in line 2 above, we have the option of specifying tunnel or transport. The difference is that the transport mode only encrypts the data and leaves the addresses alone; tunnel mode encrypts the original IP address. This protects you from having an attacker learn about your internal addressing scheme by looking at the packets running across the VPN. Transport mode has less overhead because it only has to add a couple of bits to the header. Also, because the original IP address is still present, a QOS mechanism can be used within the VPN. We are going to use tunnel mode here; it is the default. Alternately, you could create a tunnel between the two routers and just apply the crypto-map to that interface, effectively encrypting all traffic within the tunnel. Creating a tunnel and then encrypting the traffic is a very common way of doing the same thing we are doing here. Figure 15.19 illustrates the difference between tunnel and transport mode.

Figure 15.19 Tunnel mode vs. Transport mode

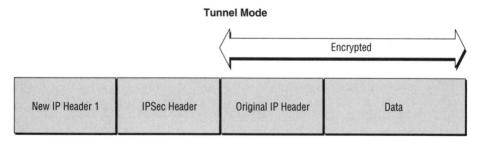

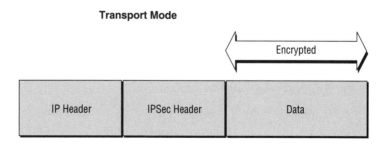

To see the transform sets you have configured, use this **show** command:

```
topeka#show crypto ipsec transform-set
Transform set tset1: { ah-sha-hmac }
 will negotiate = { Tunnel, },
 { esp-des esp-md5-hmac }
 will negotiate = { Tunnel, },
```

Now we need to create a crypto-map:

```
topeka(config)#crypto map cmap1 local-address serial 0
topeka(config)#crypto map cmap1 1 ipsec-isakmp
topeka(config-crypto-map)#match address 111
topeka(config-crypto-map)#set peer 200.1.1.5
topeka(config-crypto-map)#set transform-set tset1
```

The first of these commands creates crypto-map **cmap1** and specifies serial 0 as the local address. Then in line 2, we set the crypto-map to use IKE to establish SAs and **cmap1** with a sequence number of 1. Line 3 specifies the use of access list 111 to define the data to be encrypted, and line 5 specifies that the transform set we created (**tset1**) will be used to negotiate the SA. You need to create a crytpo-map for all routers involved in the VPN. To check the crypto-map, use the **show crypto map** command:

```
DENVER#show crypto map
Crypto Map: "cmap1" idb: Serial0 local address: 200.1.1.5

Crypto Map "cmap1" 1 ipsec-isakmp
 Peer = 200.1.1.6
 Extended IP access list 111
 access-list 111 permit gre host 200.1.1.5 host 200.1.1.6
 Current peer: 200.1.1.6
 Security association lifetime: 4608000 kilobytes/3600 seconds
 PFS (Y/N): N
 Transform sets={ tset1, }
```

Now all we need to do is to apply the crypto-map to an interface. We need to apply the crypto-map to the interfaces at each end of the tunnel. Because only data passing the access list is encrypted, nothing except the traffic on the link between the two routers will be encrypted. Ipsec is handling the creation of the tunnel for us, so we can consider all the data passing between DENVER and topeka to be tunneled. Also, we could create our own tunnel between the two routers and simply apply a crypto-map to the tunnel interfaces. When doing this, make sure you properly set up the tunnel interfaces as peers:

```
DENVER(config)#int s0
DENVER(config-if)#crypto map cmap1
```

The exact same steps are used to apply the crypto-map to the topeka router. To validate that the SA has been established, use the following command:

```
topeka#sh crypto isakmp SA
 dst src state conn-id slot
200.1.1.6 200.1.1.5 QM_IDLE 2 0
```

As you can see, we have a valid SA with the destination of 200.1.1.6 and a source of 200.1.1.5. We are in the QM_IDLE state and have a connection ID of 2.

The configurations for the router would appear as shown next. We have taken out everything except the information needed to create the VPN but have included a set of tunnel interfaces in the configuration to demonstrate how a tunnel configuration would be created. None of the routes to use the tunnel have been added.

NOTE When using a tunnel interface, be sure to add the proper routes to get data to go down the tunnel.

The Denver router's configuration would look like this:

```
!
service timestamps debug uptime
service timestamps log uptime
no service password-encryption
!
hostname denver
!
```

```
enable secret 5 $1$6Nat$3TUzHaxYq5TgRkrD32e9l/
!
!
!
crypto isakmp policy 1
 hash md5
 authentication pre-share
crypto isakmp key 654321 address 200.1.1.6
crypto isakmp key 654321 address 192.168.1.2
!
!
crypto ipsec transform-set tset1 ah-md5-hmac esp-des esp-md5-hmac
!
 !
 crypto map cmap 1 ipsec-isakmp
 set peer 200.1.1.6
 set peer 192.168.1.2
 set transform-set tset1
 match address 111
!
!
process-max-time 200
!
interface Tunnel0
 ip address 192.168.1.1 255.255.255.0
 tunnel source 200.1.1.5
 tunnel destination 200.1.1.6
 crypto map cmap
!
```

```
interface Ethernet0
 ip address 10.1.1.1 255.255.255.0
!
interface Serial0
 ip address 200.1.1.5 255.255.255.0
 no ip mroute-cache
 no fair-queue
 crypto map cmap
!
interface Serial1
 no ip address
 shutdown
!
ip classless
!
access-list 111 permit ip host 200.1.1.5 host 200.1.1.6
access-list 111 permit ip host 200.1.1.6 host 200.1.1.5
access-list 111 permit ip 10.1.1.0 0.0.0.255 200.1.1.0 0.0.0.255
access-list 111 permit ip 10.1.2.0 0.0.0.255 200.1.1.0 0.0.0.255
access-list 111 permit ip 10.1.1.0 0.0.0.255 10.1.2.0 0.0.0.255
access-list 111 permit ip 10.1.2.0 0.0.0.255 10.1.1.0 0.0.0.255
!
line con 0
line aux 0
line vty 0 4
 password s
 login
!
end
```

The Topeka router's configuration would look like this:

```
!
service timestamps debug uptime
service timestamps log uptime
no service password-encryption
!
hostname topeka
!
enable secret 5 $1$11RC$V7hkC8EtYJLvucIxJGDAH1
!
!
!
crypto isakmp policy 1
 hash md5
 authentication pre-share
crypto isakmp key 654321 address 200.1.1.6
crypto isakmp key 654321 address 200.1.1.5
crypto isakmp key 654321 address 192.168.1.1
!
!
crypto ipsec transform-set tset1 ah-md5-hmac esp-des esp-md5-hmac
!
 !
 crypto map cmap 1 ipsec-isakmp
 set peer 200.1.1.6
 set peer 200.1.1.5
 set peer 192.168.1.1
 set transform-set tset1
 match address 111
 !
```

```
!
process-max-time 200
!
interface Tunnel0
 ip address 192.168.1.2 255.255.255.0
 tunnel source 200.1.1.6
 tunnel destination 200.1.1.5
 crypto map cmap
!
interface Ethernet0
 ip address 10.1.2.1 255.255.255.0
!
interface Serial0
 ip address 200.1.1.6 255.255.255.0
 no ip mroute-cache
 no fair-queue
 clockrate 800000
 crypto map cmap
!
interface Serial1
 no ip address
 shutdown
!
ip classless
!
access-list 111 permit ip host 200.1.1.6 host 200.1.1.5
access-list 111 permit ip host 200.1.1.5 host 200.1.1.6
access-list 111 permit ip 10.1.1.0 0.0.0.255 200.1.1.0 0.0.0.255
access-list 111 permit ip 10.1.2.0 0.0.0.255 200.1.1.0 0.0.0.255
access-list 111 permit ip 10.1.1.0 0.0.0.255 10.1.2.0 0.0.0.255
```

```
access-list 111 permit ip 10.1.2.0 0.0.0.255 10.1.1.0 0.0.0.255
!
line con 0
line aux 0
line vty 0 4
 password s
 login
!
end
```

Address Translation

There are many reasons you would want to use some form of address translation. The most common is connecting to the Internet. With the way we are running out of legal IP addresses, it is almost impossible for a company to assign a legal address to each PC that needs Internet access. Typically, the address translation is done by a firewall; however, you can also translate addresses with a router.

Often it is much more secure to hide the actual addresses of internal hosts as they go out to communicate with untrusted networks. This means that from the outside it is much more difficult to map what the internal network looks like because all traffic going to the outside world appears to be coming from one or two addresses. There are several NAT (Network Address Translation) features supported by Cisco IOS 11.2 and above:

Static address translation   A one-to-one mapping of an internal address to an external legal address. This would be used for any systems that needed to be accessed from the outside would. For example, a Web server could have a real address of 172.16.1.1 but to make it accessible to the world we would have to use a legal Internet address and statically map that address.

Dynamic address translation   Translates local address to external address from a pool. In this mode, the number of addresses that need to be translated must be the same as the size of the pool of outside addresses allocated for translation. The router will create the translations as needed.

Address overloading   Allows you to conserve addresses by allowing multiple addresses to be translated to the same address. Using overloading you could make it look like all Internet traffic has the same source address. Address overloading uses TCP and UDP port numbers to keep track of which traffic is for which internal host.

Let's walk through setting up a NAT scheme for the network displayed in Figure 15.20.

Figure 15.20 Address translation

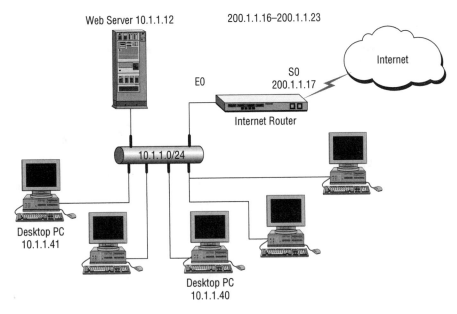

The first thing we need to do is establish which interfaces are inside and which are outside. For convention, *inside* will refer to our internal network and *outside* will refer to the Internet side of our router. It really does not matter which is which as long as you have an inside and outside interface so the router knows how to handle the translation.

The following commands set the serial 0 interface to be our outside NAT interface and the Ethernet 0 interface to be the inside:

```
inet_rtr(config)#int s0
inet_rtr(config-if)#ip nat outside
inet_rtr(config-if)#int e0
inet_rtr(config-if)#ip nat inside
```

Let's assume we have been given the network 200.1.1.16/29 for legal Internet access. Now, although Figure 15.20 shows only four host PCs, let's assume we have at least 20. That means we do not have enough addresses to set up static translations for all of them; nor can we not translate their addresses, because they are using private address space.

Optimization and
Maintenance

PART 4

We need to set up the Web server with a static translation; because this address is going to be published in our DNS record, we cannot have it dynamically changing or else no one will be able to get to our Web site. We can choose to translate the Web server to any of our registered addresses. Remember, though, that we need a registered address for the serial port on the router. Let's use 200.1.1.17 for that. Now we have left 18,19, 20, 21, and 22 as possible addresses. We'll use 18 for the Web server. To set up the translation, we specify an internal source address and the external address and specify that the translation is static. It is really pretty simple:

```
inet_rtr(config)#ip nat inside source static 10.1.1.12 200.1.1.18
```

If we wanted to add more statically translated devices—perhaps a DNS or FTP server— we would do exactly the same thing.

Now we need to set up the translations for the host devices. First we need to define what addresses will be translated. We do this by using a standard IP access list to define the hosts we wish to translate. Let's assume that all our hosts that require translation for Internet access are 10.1.1.32 and above. To specify these hosts, we would create the following access list:

```
access-list 1 permit 10.1.1.32 0.0.0.31
```

Once we have created the access list to define those addresses that need to be translated, we need to set up the translation parameters in global configuration mode:

```
ip nat translation timeout 3600
ip nat translation tcp-timeout 3600
ip nat translation udp-timeout 240
ip nat translation finrst-timeout 50
ip nat translation dns-timeout 50
```

Line 1 sets the translation timeout to 1 hour; the default is 24 hours. The second line sets the TCP timeout to 1 hour; this value specifies when a TCP port translation will time out. The default is 24 hours. Udp-timeout is the same as tcp-timeout, except that for the UDP protocol the default is 5 minutes; we have set it to 4 minutes. The finrst-timeout specifies the timeout value that applies to the FIN and RST TCP packets, which are used to terminate a connection. The default is 60 seconds; here we have set it to 50 seconds. Finally, the dns-timeout value specifies how long it will take for connections to a DNS server to time out. The default value for dns-timeout is 60 seconds; we have lowered it to 50 seconds.

To use the default values, you don't need to issue any of the commands above. They are only necessary when you wish to change the default values. There are many good reasons to change the default values; Cisco's default values for address translation tend to be very conservative. However, they do work. Most likely you will be using static or overload translation, which are unaffected by the timeouts anyway. However, if you use a dynamic translation with the defaults, then when a host gets a translated address, that translation will exist for 24 hours. If you have enough addresses, this is no problem; if you don't, then 24 hours could be an awfully long time. In this situation, you will want to use overloading. However, there will be situations when you are using dynamic translation and will need to decrease these intervals.

Because we are going to be doing an overload translation, we don't need to specify any of the timeout values; they are not applied to overload translations.

NOTE   In an address overload translation, timeout values are not used.

Now let's create our NAT pool and translate the addresses for our hosts PCs. We will use the 200.1.1.20–200.1.1.22 for our pool. This will leave us the 200.1.1.19 address in case we need to add another statically translated host. You don't really need to leave an address open—it is easy enough to pull an address out of an existing pool to use later on if needed.

To create the pool, use this global configuration command:

```
ip nat pool inet_pool 200.1.1.20 200.1.1.22 netmask 255.255.255.248
```

We have now created an address translation pool called `inet_pool`. Now all we have to do is apply the access list we created above to the pool and we are off and running. We do that using this global configuration command:

```
ip nat inside source list 1 pool inet_pool overload
```

We specify `inside source` because the source for the translation will be the inside address. Then, `list 1` specifies that we are using access list 1 to define the addresses to be translated, `pool inet_pool` tells the translation to use addresses from the pool `inet_pool` we've just created, and `overload` specifies that we are going to use address overloading.

A complete listing of the commands used to set up this translation would be as follows:

```
!Set the inside and outside interfaces
inet_rtr(config)#int s0
```

```
inet_rtr(config-if)#ip nat outside
inet_rtr(config-if)#int e0
inet_rtr(config-if)#ip nat inside
!Define the addresses to translate
inet_rtr(config)#access-list 1 permit 10.1.1.32 0.0.0.31
!set the time out values not necessary with address overloading
inet_rtr(config)#ip nat translation timeout 3600
inet_rtr(config)#ip nat translation tcp-timeout 3600
inet_rtr(config)#ip nat translation udp-timeout 240
inet_rtr(config)#ip nat translation finrst-timeout 50
inet_rtr(config)#ip nat translation dns-timeout 50


!Define the translation pool
ip nat pool inet_pool 200.1.1.20 200.1.1.22 netmask 255.255.255.248


!Apply the pool to traffic defined in the access list
ip nat inside source list 1 pool inet_pool overload
```

In most cases, you will either be using overloading or static translations, so you really don't have to worry about the timeout values. They have been included in this example solely for completeness. You should know they are out there and they can be helpful with dynamic translations.

Sointu Salvage

Let's suppose we have been contacted by Sointu Salvage to lock down security on the router connecting them to the Internet. Sointu Salvage has already invested a significant amount of money in a firewall to protect themselves from outside attacks but would like to use their Internet router to further enhance the security stance of the company.

Figure 15.21 shows the configuration we will be working with.

Figure 15.21 The Sointu Salvage Internet connection

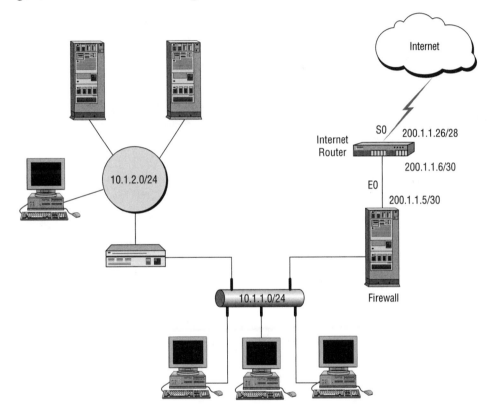

The first thing we want to do is turn off all the unnecessary services in the router:

```
Inet_rtr(config)#no ip http server
Inet_rtr(config)#no ntp
Inet_rtr(config)#no service finger
Inet_rtr(config)#no cdp run
```

24seven **CASE STUDY**

```
Inet_rtr(config)#no service tcp-small-servers
Inet_rtr(config)#no service udp-small-servers
```

We want to prevent Sointu Salavage from being used as a Smurf relay, so we add this command:

```
Inet_rtr(config)#int s0
Inet_rtr(config-if)#no ip directed-broadcast
```

to the serial 0 interface to prevent directed broadcasts from coming in off the Internet. Next we want to disable IP source routing for the entire router:

```
Inet_rtr(config)#no ip source-route
```

Now that we have protected the router, we probably want to filter some traffic coming inbound through the Serial 0 interface. There are no hosts on the Sointu Salvage network that should allow Telnet to them, so we can block all traffic with Telnet as the destination port from coming in through S0 this will protect the router and anything behind. If we had to support Telnet into the network, we could use an access class to limit Telnet access to the router to specific hosts. We also want to deny ICMP redirects from the Internet. Because there is a firewall behind the router, we will not worry about dynamic packet filtering but will use static packet filtering.

We create the following access list. Because Sointu Salvage is using private address space, we don't have to add its addresses to the anti-spoofing filter; but if it was not, we could add those addresses to the filter:

```
!Anti Spoofing
access-list 101 deny ip 10.0.0.0 0.255.255.255 any
access-list 101 deny ip 172.16.0.0 0.15.255.255 any
access-list 101 deny ip 192.168.0.0 0.0.255.255 any
access-list 101 deny ip 127.0.0.0 0.255.255.255 any
access-list 101 deny ip 224.0.0.0 7.255.255.255 any
access-list 101 deny ip host 0.0.0.0 any

!Deny services we want to allow
access-list 101 deny icmp any any redirect
access-list 101 deny udp any any eq snmp
access-list 101 deny udp any any eq snmptrap
access-list 101 deny tcp any any eq telnet

!permit the rest of the traffic to get to the firewall
!where it will be processed
access-list 101 permit ip any any
```

Access list 101 would be applied to serial 0 inbound. Now we want to protect Sointu Salvage from anyone running a traceroute to try and map their network. To do this, we create access list 102 and apply it outbound on serial 0:

```
!break traceroute functionality
access-list 102 deny icmp any any time-exceeded
access-list 102 permit ip any any
```

Finally, we want to prevent anyone from being able to ping the network. We will let the outside world ping the router, but nothing more. To do this, we are going to stop icmp echo requests from going through the Ethernet0 interface inbound:

```
!stop ping
access-list 103 deny icmp any any echo
access-list 103 permit ip any any
```

Finally, because this is a router connected to the Internet, we will use only static routes so that the router cannot be tricked into listening to improper routing protocol packets. This way, we don't have to worry about a RIP, OSPF, EIGRP, or any other routing protocol packet coming in and modifying the routing table. Static routes are by far the most secure routing protocol, but they are a pain to manage. However, on an Internet router the number of routes is generally very small. For Sointu Salvage we need only the following route statements:

```
Inet_rtr(config)#ip route 0.0.0.0 0.0.0.0 s0
Inet_rtr(config)#ip route 10.1.0.0 255.255.0.0 200.1.1.5
```

We could have made the 10.1.0.0 route more specific but because 10.x.x.x will not route outside of the Sointu Salvage network, it does not matter; because all of the 10 net is behind the firewall, we could have even used a class A mask if we wanted to.

Below is the complete configuration for Sointu Salvage. Notice that some of the commands such as no service tcp-small-servers don't show up because they are defaults. If this were IOS 11.X, the router configuration would look slightly different since the defaults are different.

You should always be careful to note what the default state of a command is, because it can change between IOS releases. It is fine not to worry about TCP-small-servers in IOS 12.0(8), but who is to say the default value will not change in the next IOS release? You want to make sure that the router is functioning as you expect it to no matter what the default configuration. In some cases, such as security, it makes sense to enter the command even if it is a default, just to make sure.

24seven **CASE STUDY**

The Sointu Salvage Internet router configuration is as follows:

```
Current configuration:
!
version 12.0
service timestamps debug uptime
service timestamps log uptime
service password-encryption
!
hostname Inet_rtr
!
enable secret 5 $1$8hLg$QY5TZ7GTD/wArbYOIs4Oj/
!
ip subnet-zero
no ip source-route
no ip finger
!
!
!
interface Ethernet0
 ip address 200.1.1.6 255.255.255.252
 ip access-group 103 in
 no ip directed-broadcast
!
interface Serial0
 ip address 200.1.1.26 255.255.255.240
 ip access-group 101 in
 ip access-group 102 out
 no ip directed-broadcast
 no ip mroute-cache
!
interface Serial1
 no ip address
 no ip directed-broadcast
 shutdown
!
ip classless
ip route 0.0.0.0 0.0.0.0 Serial0
ip route 10.1.0.0 255.255.0.0 200.1.1.5
!
```

```
access-list 101 deny ip 10.0.0.0 0.255.255.255 any
access-list 101 deny ip 172.16.0.0 0.15.255.255 any
access-list 101 deny ip 192.168.0.0 0.0.255.255 any
access-list 101 deny ip 127.0.0.0 0.255.255.255 any
access-list 101 deny ip 224.0.0.0 7.255.255.255 any
access-list 101 deny ip host 0.0.0.0 any
access-list 101 deny icmp any any redirect
access-list 101 deny udp any any eq snmp
access-list 101 deny udp any any eq snmptrap
access-list 101 deny tcp any any eq telnet
access-list 101 permit ip any any
access-list 102 deny icmp any any time-exceeded
access-list 102 permit ip any any
access-list 103 deny icmp any any echo
access-list 103 permit ip any any
no cdp run
banner motd ^C

This device is the property of Sointu Salvage. Access by any
individuals
other than those specifically authorized by Sointu Salvage is
unlawful.
All sessions on this device can and may be monitored. If you are not
authorized to have access to this device, leave now.
^C
!
line con 0
 transport input none
line aux 0
line vty 0 4
 password 7 0215
 login
!
end
```

24seven **CASE STUDY**

16

Router Management

Once you've set up the network environment, you need to develop a way to monitor and manage it. How you go about this task depends largely on your environment. If you only have one or two routers, you can easily keep track of what is going on. In an environment of this size, it is fairly easy to tell when a link has gone down or when other types of network problems arise.

In a larger environment, it is much more difficult to keep track of how the network is functioning. Imagine that instead of two routers you have 50. Now how do you detect if a link goes down or if you are having many collisions on a given segment? Due to the size of the environment, you are going to need some kind of help to keep a handle on things. Don't worry, though, it is a fairly trivial task for one individual to be able to keep track of a huge routed environment, provided they know what they are doing.

Network management has become a hot topic lately. All of a sudden, IT staffs are being asked to monitor and provide data on everything from the amount of disk space consumed daily on a Microsoft Exchange mail server to the number of broadcast packets on a given network segment. This results in much more work than the days when management was only concerned with whether the network was functioning or not. In days past, an outage per day was considered acceptable. Today, an outage of even a few minutes is completely unacceptable for many networks.

Now that business functions are so closely tied to the network, it has become important to not only limit the amount of downtime exposure, but to also justify IT budgets. IT individuals are no longer seen as those weird people who like to play with computers and are nice to have around. We are now an important part of the business organization. Being so ingrained in the business practices of a company has advantages and drawbacks. Salaries for people with computer skills are at an all-time high. IT professionals are demanding higher salaries and companies that recognize how important these people are to running a successful business in the twenty-first century are awarding them.

The drawback is that IT professionals are now being asked to provide all kinds of data to justify network related expenditures and are being held accountable for network downtime.

Proper router management not only allows us to detect issues and deal with them quickly; it can also help us to develop the data necessary to justify design changes to the network.

Syslog

Cisco routers support the use of system logging (syslog) for storing information from the router. Normally, a router will post certain event messages to the console screen; if you are not attached to the console when the message goes by, you will miss that message. These messages can be very valuable for troubleshooting purposes and should be saved.

Buffered Logging

Sometimes it is enough to take a piece of the router's memory and buffer these messages. To set up a buffer for log messages, use the following command:

```
inet_rtr(config)#logging buffered 4096 debugging
```

This will create a 4KB log buffer into which all system messages at the debug level or lower are written. Thus, by selecting debugging, which is level 7, we are actually enabling all possible logging since all the other logging levels are lower. Since debugging level logging with a 4KB buffer is the default in IOS versions 11.3 and higher, entering this command will not change the behavior of the router at all. Previous versions of the IOS did not let you select the logging level. Table 16.1 shows the logging levels.

Table 16.1 System logging levels

Level #	Keyword	Syslog Definition	Description
0	Emergencies	SYS_EMERG	System is unstable
1	Alerts	SYS_ALERT	Immediate action required
2	Critical	SYS_CRIT	Critical conditions

Table 16.1   System logging levels *(continued)*

Level #	Keyword	Syslog Definition	Description
3	Errors	SYS_ERROR	Error conditions
4	Warnings	SYS_WARNING	Warning conditions
5	Notifications	SYS_NOTICE	Normal condition but significant
6	Informational	SYS_INFO	Informational only
7	Debugging	SYS_DEBUG	Debugging messages

When a logging level is selected, all messages at that level or lower will be recorded. Thus, selecting debugging logging will cause all possible messages to be recorded. If we were to select errors, then only Errors, Critical, Alerts, and Emergencies would be written to the log.

Newly recorded messages are appended to the end of the log. Once the log becomes full, the oldest messages at the head of the log are removed as new messages are placed at the end. This means that your log time span will depend on how fast you are having messages written to your log. A log with a 4KB size can store messages anywhere from 1 minute to 6 months depending on the number of messages the router is writing in the log.

By default, when a message is written to the log, as shown below, it is not time stamped.

```
ANWCS-2#show logging
Syslog logging: enabled (0 messages dropped, 0 flushes, 0 overruns)
     Console logging: level debugging, 21 messages logged
     Monitor logging: level debugging, 0 messages logged
     Trap logging: level informational, 25 message lines logged


%SYS-5-CONFIG_I: Configured from console by vty0 (10.1.1.1)
%LINEPROTO-5-UPDOWN: Line protocol on Interface Ethernet0, changed
state to down
%LINEPROTO-5-UPDOWN: Line protocol on Interface Ethernet0, changed
state to up
```

In this log output we can see that the line protocol on interface Ethernet0 went down and came back up. But since there are no time stamps, we don't know how long this outage lasted. There are two ways of time stamping the log messages. We can time stamp based on router up time. This is basically a counter that keeps track of the amount of time the router has been up. To set log time stamping based on router uptime, use the following command:

```
ANWCS-2(config)#service timestamps log uptime
```

This tells the router to record the system uptime whenever it writes a message to the log. Here is some sample log data using uptime time stamping.

```
6d05h: %LINEPROTO-5-UPDOWN: Line protocol on Interface Ethernet0,
changed state

to down

6d05h: %LINEPROTO-5-UPDOWN: Line protocol on Interface Ethernet0,
changed state

to up
```

The above excerpt from the log shows that the Ethernet0 interface went down 6 days and 5 hours after the router was last booted, and came back up 6 days and 5 hours after the router was last booted. So, we can tell the outage was less than an hour. While this is an improvement over no timestamps, it would be pretty cool if we could know the date and time of day this outage occurred. We can do this using the following command:

```
inet_rtr(config)#service timestamps log datetime
```

We can specify a couple of options after datetime, as shown in the following excerpt:

```
inet_rtr(config)#service timestamps log datetime ?
  localtime      Use local time zone for timestamps
  msec           Include milliseconds in timestamp
  show-timezone  Add time zone information to timestamp
  <cr>
```

None of these options are going to add much value. We really do not need to know the time down to the millisecond, and we have never found time zone information to be that useful. What you really want to know is what time the event occurred in relationship to the clock in the router. The following example shows this:

```
*Mar  7 05:34:36: %LINEPROTO-5-UPDOWN: Line protocol on Interface
Ethernet0, changed state to down

*Mar  7 05:34:53: %LINEPROTO-5-UPDOWN: Line protocol on Interface
Ethernet0, changed state to up
```

With datetime specified, we can see that the Ethernet0 interface went down on March 7, at 5:34:36 AM, and came back at 5:34:53 that same day. This means the outage lasted only 17 seconds. Based on this early morning time frame and the duration of the outage, it is doubtful that anyone would notice this outage.

We do have to ask ourselves what caused this outage, and knowing what time it occurred can be very helpful for figuring that out. We had a client who used to lose the link to their Chicago field office every day around 10 PM Boston time. Since no one was in the office at 10 PM, we were only able to discover this was happening by looking through the log on the Boston router. When we looked at the Chicago router, it seemed to be rebooting in correlation with the Boston router losing its link to Chicago. Watching the logs on the Boston side, we learned that this happened around the same time every night but not on the weekends. It turns out that the person who cleaned the office in Chicago at night was unplugging the router to vacuum the room and plugging it back in when they were done.

Syslog Servers

The problem with buffered logging is that if the router is rebooted, you lose all your log information. This is less than an ideal situation because you also have to get to the router console and enter the show logging command to be able to see the log messages.

Syslog servers address both these issues. Setting up a syslog server is a fairly straightforward task. Most Unix systems will come with syslogd, the Unix syslog daemon that allows the Unix system to function as a syslog server. If you are running NT you can download a shareware syslog server. If you happen to own Cisco Resource Manager, it comes with a syslog server and some pretty neat tools for analyzing syslog data. Once you have set up the syslog server, you will need to configure the router to send its log messages to that server. This is a very simple process. Assuming our syslog server is at 10.1.1.2, the following commands would be used:

```
logging trap debugging
logging facility local6
logging 10.1.1.2
```

In the first line, we set the logging level to debugging. This means all messages will be written out to the syslog server. Obviously, if we wanted fewer messages in the log, we could use a lower level of logging. Most often, though, it is not going to hurt you to run the logging level at debugging. In fact, it takes the router less CPU time to write to a syslog server than it does to write to the console. If your router is writing a huge number of messages to the syslog server, then you have a problem with the router or network that needs addressing anyway. A possible exception is access list logging, which will most likely generate a large number of log entries.

`Logging facility local6` tells the router how to interact with the syslog server. `Local6` is the default, but you could use uucp, mail, news, the line printer system, or various other logging facilities to interact with the syslog server. Using `local6` is the most common way to work with all types of syslog servers. Finally, `logging 10.1.1.2` specifies the IP address of our syslog server. All log entries will be written to this address, and it is possible to set up multiple logging destinations by simply using the logging command with another IP address. For example, if you added another syslog server at 192.168.4.44, you could set the routers up to log to both 10.1.1.2 and 192.168.4.44 by specifying two logging destinations, as follows:

```
logging 10.1.1.2
logging 192.168.4.44
```

Typically, we like to also set up buffered logging in addition to using a syslog server. If the router cannot get to the syslog server, you are going to lose that message. But the combination of using buffered logging and syslog provides a good means of making sure you have the information you need to troubleshoot a problem.

The major benefit of syslog servers is that now all your log entries are in a text file, and there can be entries from more than one router in that file. Typically, you would set all your routers up to log to the same syslog destination and thus create one big log file with all the log entries from all the devices on your network. The following example illustrates this point:

```
1/23/00,9:53:56 PM,10.1.1.1,???,LOCAL6,NOTICE,30: 1d00h: %SYS-5-
CONFIG_I: Configured from console by vty0 (10.1.1.2)

1/23/00,9:53:59 PM,10.1.1.3,???,LOCAL6,NOTICE,46: 1w0d: %LINEPROTO-5-
UPDOWN: Line protocol on Interface Tunnel0, changed state to up

1/23/00,9:54:02 PM,10.1.1.1,???,LOCAL6,NOTICE,31: 1d00h: %LINEPROTO-
5-UPDOWN: Line protocol on Interface Tunnel0, changed state to up

1/23/00,9:54:28 PM,10.1.1.3,???,LOCAL6,WARNING,47: 1w0d: %CRYPTO-4-
IKMP_NO_SA: IKE message from 200.1.1.5 has no SA and is not an
initialization offer

1/23/00,9:54:59 PM,10.1.1.3,???,LOCAL6,NOTICE,48: 1w0d: %LINEPROTO-5-
UPDOWN: Line protocol on Interface Serial0, changed state to down

1/23/00,9:55:00 PM,10.1.1.3,???,LOCAL6,NOTICE,49: 1w0d: %LINEPROTO-5-
UPDOWN: Line protocol on Interface Serial0, changed state to up
```

```
1/23/00,9:56:19 PM,10.1.1.1,???,LOCAL6,ERROR,32: 1d00h: %LINK-3-
UPDOWN: Interface Serial1, changed state to up

1/23/00,9:56:20 PM,10.1.1.4,???,LOCAL6,ERROR,37: 2:05:54: %LINK-3-
UPDOWN: Interface Serial0, changed state to up

1/23/00,9:56:20 PM,10.1.1.1,???,LOCAL6,NOTICE,33: 1d00h: %LINEPROTO-
5-UPDOWN: Line protocol on Interface Serial1, changed
```

Notice that there are three routers logging information in the output. Most of it contains lines going up and down, but you can also see a warning message about ISAKMP traffic and where we configured the router 10.1.1.1 from 10.1.1.2. This is pretty cool, because now we can get all our log messages in one place, which makes many other tools available.

Text files are pretty easy to manipulate. It would be pretty simple to run AWK, SED, or PERL on this log file to get a good idea of what is going on in the network. Generally, we run syslog servers on Unix, schedule a CRON job to go out, and parse the log file at 7 AM to look for troubling conditions such as excessive collisions. We then output this information to a text file and mail it to the router administrators.

By having all the log output in one easily accessible place, you can do lots of really cool things in terms of processing the data, or just archive the log until you need it. We had a problem with a local telecom company, which will remain nameless, where they were blowing fuses on one of our fractional T1 lines about every week. After about a month of this, we were able to go to them and give them exact times and durations of the outages using our syslog data. Until we were able to produce this data, everyone at the telecom company was content to fix the problem and forget about it, until it happened again. It took about four weeks worth of data to prove the frequency of the outages we were seeing to actually get this fixed. (During week five, we suffered a momentary planned outage while our circuit was moved to another line.)

Getting Router Health Information via the Command Line

Cisco offers you many different options for checking the health of your router from the command line. Typically, information obtained directly from the router is more believable than information gathered through other means.

Optimization and Maintenance

PART 4

You will be interested in looking at things like the router CPU utilization, which can be viewed with the **show processes** command:

```
Core_rtr1#Show processes
CPU utilization for five seconds: 9%/5%; one minute: 7%; five minutes: 6%
 PID QTy       PC Runtime (ms)    Invoked    uSecs    Stacks TTY Process
   1 M*          0        532        304       1750 9408/12000   2 Virtual Exec
   2 Lst 601347A4    9238796     374184      24690 5764/6000     0 Check heaps
   3 Cwe 6011E860       9732       1220       7977 5652/6000     0 Pool Manager
   4 Mst 60160DA8         0          2          0 5612/6000      0 Timers
   5 Mwe 601E7E44      1560          3     520000 1596/3000      0 OIR Handler
   6 ME  602401D8         0          1          0 5840/6000      0 IPC Zone Manager
   7 ME  6024014C         0          1          0 5856/6000      0 IPC Realm Manage
   8 ME  6023FF94       992    1109099          0 5840/6000      0 IPC Seat Manager
   9 Lwe 60245F64   71987740  184772036        389 5072/6000     0 ARP Input
  10 Mwe 6005E174         0          1          0 5652/6000      0 SERIAL A'detect
  11 Mwe 601DEE34       168          3      56000 5276/6000      0 Microcode Loader
  12 HE  602E007C         0          1          0 5844/6000      0 ATM ILMI Input
  13 ME  602D90F0         0          2          0 5856/6000      0 ILMI Process
  14 Mwe 60231940         0          1          0 5636/6000      0 IP Crashinfo Inp
  15 Lwe 6023E520         0          1          0 5660/6000      0 DSX3MIB 11 handl
  16 Lsi 6022931C     18296    5172868          3 2712/3000      0 Chassis Daemon
  17 ME  600D32B8         0          1          0 5860/6000      0 IPC CBus process
  18 Mwe 6021B5F0         0          1          0 5648/6000      0 MIP Mailbox
  19 Mwe 60224B2C         0          1          0 5648/6000      0 CT3 Mailbox
  20 Hst 600554D8      7856   22150279          0 5756/6000      0 FBM Timer
  21 Hst 60055150         0          1          0 5776/6000      0 FDDI FDX Timer
```

Notice that the first line shows you the current CPU utilization, the one-minute average CPU utilization, which is 7 percent, and the five-minute average CPU utilization, which is 6 percent. The current CPU utilization is really not a very important statistic because, as you would expect, the value moves all over the place since the router will have to work hard to process a bunch of traffic and then slow down for a while. This output happens to be from a Cisco 7000 core router on a day when most of the office was sent home due to a snowstorm. So, an average of 6 percent utilization is low because the network was fairly quiet. However, during prime shift this router typically runs at an average CPU load of between 10 and 15 percent.

In the above output you can also see the various processes running in the router as well as some information about them. The **show processes** command can be used to show how various processes are using memory or about what percent of the processor each individual process is using. For example, here's what the output of **show processes memory** looks like:

```
denver#show processes memory
Total: 7289932, Used: 1437328, Free: 5852604

PID  TTY  Allocated     Freed   Holding   Getbufs   Retbufs Process
  0    0      35120      1256   1044788         0         0 *Init*
  0    0        264     16960       264         0         0 *Sched*
  0    0    2256456   1035096     55212    324864         0 *Dead*
  1    0        268       268      1740         0         0 Load Meter
  2    2      73488     72824      5404         0         0 Virtual Exec
  3    0          0         0      2740         0         0 Check heaps
  4    0         96         0      2836         0         0 Pool Manager
  5    0        268       268      2740         0         0 Timers
  6    0        268       268      2740         0         0 Serial Background
  7    0        264        84      3004         0         0 ARP Input
  8    0        268       268      2740         0         0 DDR Timers
  9    0         96         0      2836         0         0 SERIAL A'detect
 10    0       3368         0      6044         0         0 IP Input
 11    0     404076    402604      4212         0         0 CDP Protocol
 12    0          0         0      2740         0         0 PERUSER aux
```

Notice that now you can see the memory usage for each process, including the amount of space that process has allocated, the amount it has freed, and the amount it is holding.

To see process information broken down by CPU utilization, use the **show processes cpu** option:

```
denver#Show processes cpu
CPU utilization for five seconds: 13%/7%; one minute: 8%; five minutes: 8%

PID  Runtime(ms)  Invoked  uSecs    5Sec    1Min    5Min TTY Process
  1        61784    33544   1841   0.00%   0.00%   0.00%   0 Load Meter
  2         2680      273   9816   4.09%   0.59%   0.23%   2 Virtual Exec
  3       296208     3003  98637   0.00%   0.24%   0.17%   0 Check heaps
  4            0        1      0   0.00%   0.00%   0.00%   0 Pool Manager
  5            0        2      0   0.00%   0.00%   0.00%   0 Timers
```

6	0	2	0	0.00%	0.00%	0.00%	0	Serial Background
7	68	2846	23	0.00%	0.00%	0.00%	0	ARP Input
8	4	3	1333	0.00%	0.00%	0.00%	0	DDR Timers
9	0	1	0	0.00%	0.00%	0.00%	0	SERIAL A'detect
10	4948	5505	898	0.16%	0.02%	0.00%	0	IP Input
11	12656	22423	564	0.08%	0.01%	0.00%	0	CDP Protocol
12	0	1	0	0.00%	0.00%	0.00%	0	PERUSER aux
13	0	1	0	0.00%	0.00%	0.00%	0	PPP IP Add Route
14	0	1	0	0.00%	0.00%	0.00%	0	X.25 Encaps Manage
15	8	23	347	0.00%	0.00%	0.00%	0	TCP Timer
16	16	4	4000	0.00%	0.00%	0.00%	0	TCP Protocols
17	0	1	0	0.00%	0.00%	0.00%	0	Probe Input
18	4	1	4000	0.00%	0.00%	0.00%	0	RARP Input
19	0	1	0	0.00%	0.00%	0.00%	0	BOOTP Server
20	47376	170529	277	0.00%	0.06%	0.07%	0	IP Background
21	4	2797	1	0.00%	0.00%	0.00%	0	IP Cache Ager

Show processes CPU will allow you to see how much of the CPU each individual process is using. This can be very useful in figuring out what is going on with the router. No one process should be monopolizing the CPU. Any one process consuming a large portion of the CPU generally indicates a problem of some sort. You want your router average CPU utilization to be somewhere around 50 percent maximum. Once you start getting up around 60 and 70 percent, it is time to think about getting a more powerful router or redistributing the load.

The show interface command can give you some information on how much data is passing through a given interface, as shown in the following output:

```
Core_rtr1#show interface hssi0/0
Hssi0/0 is up, line protocol is up
  Hardware is cxBus HSSI
  Internet address is 192.168.139.254/24
  MTU 4470 bytes, BW 45045 Kbit, DLY 200 usec, rely 255/255, load 6/255
  Encapsulation HDLC, loopback not set, keepalive set (10 sec)
  Last input 00:00:00, output 00:00:00, output hang never
  Last clearing of "show interface" counters 4d02h
```

```
Queueing strategy: fifo
Output queue 0/40, 0 drops; input queue 0/75, 0 drops
5 minute input rate 324000 bits/sec, 421 packets/sec
5 minute output rate 1083000 bits/sec, 500 packets/sec
    66157200 packets input, 2038153098 bytes, 0 no buffer
    Received 101770 broadcasts, 0 runts, 0 giants
            0 parity
    0 input errors, 0 CRC, 0 frame, 0 overrun, 0 abort
    71718965 packets output, 1442031389 bytes, 0 underruns
    0 output errors, 0 applique, 0 interface resets
    0 output buffer failures, 0 output buffers swapped out
    0 carrier transitions
```

In this output, we can see things like the number of broadcasts (101770), the total numbers of packets input and output, and the five-minute average input and output packet rates. The input and output rates are important because by adding the two together we can get a good idea of how loaded the link is. This interface is averaging 324000 bps inbound and 1083000 bps outbound, which is 1407000 bps average throughput. Convert that number to bytes and you get 175875 Bps or about 171Kbps. Obviously, we are not coming close to maxing out this HSSI (High Speed Serial Interface) interface. Of course, this information was gathered after most people had gone home for the day, so it's not representative of peak use, or even the average use for this link.

The show interface command will also provide information on errors that the interface is seeing—things like carrier transitions, collisions (if applicable to the interface type), runts, giants, CRC errors, etc. When you are looking at this type of information, you are looking for something specific. Most of this information is only really useful in real time. Do you care about the total number of broadcasts or the total number of packets through the interface? Not likely, although the ratio of packets to broadcast packets is an interesting metric for measuring network efficiency. The total number of broadcast should be a very small fraction of the number of packets—typically less than 1 percent.

What these router statistics are good for is looking for problems or looking at a quick snapshot of how the router is functioning. It is very difficult to take this information and extrapolate it out over a long period of time, because it really only gives you a momentary glimpse of what is going on with the router. Normally when working with these commands, you will execute the clear counters command either globally for the router or for a specific interface and then watch what is happening for a given period of time. For example, the number of collisions occurring over a 5-minute period might be useful, but it doesn't matter how many collisions occurred since the router's counters were last reset. There could have been one bad period skewing the results, and you have no way of knowing that with any of the router's show commands. The following command output illustrates how to clear the counters for all interfaces and how to clear the counters for just the serial 0 interface.

```
denver#clear counters

Clear "show interface" counters on all interfaces [confirm]

denver#clear counters s0

Clear "show interface" counters on this interface [confirm]
```

While show processes and show interfaces are the most useful commands you can use to get statistical information out of the router, there are a few others. You could use show environment to check the router's environmental probe, if it has one. This can alert you to problems with things like heat and humidity. In a well-designed computer room it is doubtful you would need to at look environmental information with any great frequency. Here's a typical show environment dialog:

```
Core_rtr1#show environment

All measured values are normal
```

You can view traffic statistics on a protocol basis with the command

```
show protocol traffic
```

where *protocol* is replaced with the protocol you want to see information on. Here's an example:

```
ANWCS-2# show ipx traffic

System Traffic for 10BACEE.0000.0000.0001 System-Name: ANWCS-2

Rcvd:   0 total, 0 format errors, 0 checksum errors, 0 bad hop count,

        0 packets pitched, 0 local destination, 0 multicast

Bcast:  0 received, 8771 sent

Sent:   8771 generated, 0 forwarded

        0 encapsulation failed, 0 no route

SAP:    0 SAP requests, 0 SAP replies, 0 servers

        0 SAP advertisements received, 0 sent
```

```
              0 SAP flash updates sent, 0 SAP poison sent
              0 SAP format errors
   RIP:       0 RIP requests, 0 RIP replies, 3 routes
              0 RIP advertisements received, 8729 sent
              12 RIP flash updates sent, 0 RIP poison sent
              0 RIP format errors
   RIP:       0 RIP format errors
   Echo:      Rcvd 0 requests, 0 replies
              Sent 0 requests, 0 replies
              0 unknown: 0 no socket, 0 filtered, 0 no helper
              0 SAPs throttled, freed NDB len 0
Watchdog:
              0 packets received, 0 replies spoofed
Queue lengths:
              IPX input: 0, SAP 0, RIP 0, GNS 0
```

The show commands in the router offer a wealth of information, but it is a pain to get this information unless you know what you are looking for and why you are looking for it. You probably don't have the time to keep track of the number of broadcasts on each segment in your network, by using the show interface command. These commands come in very handy when you are troubleshooting a problem, but they are not designed to collect management information over any length of time for trend analysis.

SNMP and Other Network Management Protocols

Until 1987, there were really no mature network management protocols. Internet Control Messaging Protocol (ICMP) was typically used to test if a device was reachable and look at delay. ICMP is not really designed as a management protocol, but through the use of the Ping utility, ICMP can be utilized to determine if a device is reachable and what the round trip delay is to that device.

In November 1987, the Internet was just beginning to grow, and the predecessor of today's management protocols, Simple Gateway Monitoring Protocol (SGMP), was introduced. SGMP did not have a lot of functionality built into it, and people soon started to develop more advanced management protocols.

As the demand for better management protocols grew, several proposals were put to the Internet Architecture Board. These proposals included:

- High Level Entity Management System (HEMS): A generalization of the Host Monitoring Protocol (HMP)
- Simple Network Management Protocol (SNMP): An enhanced version of SGMP
- CMIP over TCP/IP (CMOT): Common Management Information Protocol over TCP/IP

Though HEMS was more capable than SNMP, it was abandoned because CMOT was seen as the long-term solution. SNMP was viewed as a temporary solution because implementing it was relatively simple. It was deemed a waste of effort to adapt HEMS if it was going to be phased out by CMOT anyway. Now, 13 years later, SNMP is the most widely used network management protocol. Most people don't even know that CMOT exists.

Looking at SNMP

SNMP is an Application layer protocol designed to allow management information to be passed between networked devices. There are several RFC documents referring to SNMP. The actual SNMP protocol is defined by RFC 1157, while SNMP objects contained in MIB II are defined by RFC 1213. MIB II defines a lot of information that is relevant to a wide range of networking devices—interface counters, system counters and information, TCP and UDP statistics, and many other things. There are many other RFCs that deal with SNMP, but these two are the most common.

Systems in SNMP are broken down into two distinct classes:

Management Stations   Devices that actively poll for SNMP information or receive traps

Management Agents   Devices that are queried by management stations or send traps to management stations

SNMP has three major methods for passing data:

Gets   Queries made by a management station to obtain information about variables on another system with a management agent.

Sets   Allow the management stations to change MIB object values on agent systems. Require read/write access.

Traps   Messages sent by an agent system to a predefined management station or stations, also known as trap targets when a certain threshold or condition is met.

Traps are used by the sending system to try and alert someone that it is in trouble. In a trapping mode, the managed system monitors itself and sends a trap when an error or pre-defined threshold occurs. This works like our 911 system. You have to make a call before anyone knows anything is wrong.

Gets are the opposite of traps. One system queries another system about some information it has. This information includes CPU utilization, packet rates, etc. Often this information is gathered and compared to a given threshold. If that threshold is exceeded, then an alarm is raised. Obviously, this is not the most effective way to manage anything, but many network management systems are based on this idea. Imagine that 911 worked this way; you would have to hire a bunch of people to continually call everyone in town to ask if they were OK.

SNMP Sets are used infrequently, primarily in configuration rather than management. They are not useful enough to describe in detail here.

SNMP Traps

Many people have tried writing agents to monitor statistics on operating systems, but most routers do not allow you to define a threshold and trap on it. Cisco does not provide this kind of functionality in its IOS, though it does allow you to query the router, which should be fine for most purposes. Cisco also allows you to send traps on various events occurring in the router.

Suppose, for example, you wanted to send a trap to a given host every time someone made a configuration change on a router. You would use the following global commands:

```
snmp-server enable traps config
snmp-server host 10.1.1.2 traps public
```

The first line enables traps for configuration changes, while the second line specifies which host to send the traps to and the community string to use when sending them. You can send traps on many things besides just configuration changes, as the following example shows:

```
denver(config)#snmp-server enable traps ?
  bgp          Enable BGP state change traps
  config       Enable SNMP config traps
  dlsw         Enable SNMP dlsw traps
  entity       Enable SNMP entity traps
  frame-relay  Enable SNMP frame-relay traps
```

Optimization and Maintenance

PART 4

```
isdn          Enable SNMP isdn traps

rtr           Enable SNMP Response Time Reporter traps

snmp          Enable SNMP traps
```

Some of the above options have additional parameters that can be selected during the configuration process. For example, you could enter the following:

```
denver(config)#snmp-server enable traps snmp ?

authentication   Enable authentication trap

<cr>
```

You can see that you have the option of enabling SNMP authentication traps or just sending SNMP traps.

Traps are very useful, but unfortunately Cisco has not done a very good job in giving you flexibility with their traps. SNMP is usually an afterthought when writing software, and we may have to live with poor trapping functionality. But Cisco's IOS tends to be very robust, so we really don't need all that much trapping anyway.

SNMP Gets

While SNMP is probably not the most efficient way to monitor information on a network, you can use it to poll thousands of statistics. These statistics are stored in the MIBs (Management Information Base). MIBs are organized into a basic structure often referred to as the MIB tree, which is partially displayed in Figure 16.1.

You can query for information using the tree. You can either query a specific instance using an SNMP Get or Get Next command or you can pick a point and walk down the tree from there. Figure 16.1 only shows the basic tree form. Most of the information we are interested in is going to be in the MIB II or the Cisco proprietary section of the tree. There is far too much information under `.iso.ord.dod.internet.private` `.enterprises.cisco` or MIB II to even attempt to display all the leaves of the tree.

Most SNMP-capable systems will allow you to do an SNMP Get, Get Next, or Walk. For example, to do an SNMP Walk of the system section under MIB II, we would enter the following:

```
Snmputil walk 10.1.1.1 public.iso.org.dod.internet.mgmt.mib-2.system
```

Figure 16.1 SNMP MIB Tree

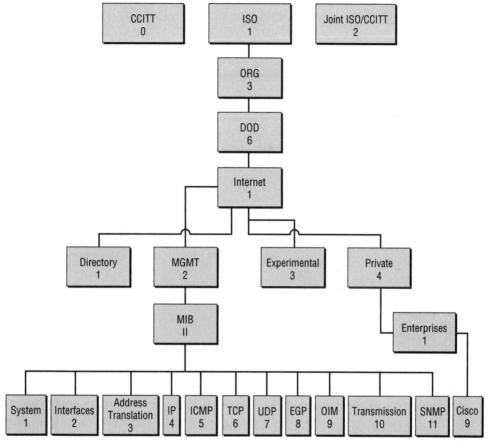

This is done using an NT system with the following files off the NT resource kit: mgmtapi.dll, mib.bin, snmpapi.dll, and snmputil.exe. For Unix systems, everything you need should be in your /usr/sbin directory. The syntax will be slightly different on (for example) an HP 10.20 system:

```
snmpwalk -c public .iso.org.dod.internet.mgmt.mib-2.system
```

Or

```
snmpwalk -c public system
```

However, it is the same concept. You need to specify what information you want, and SNMP will go get it for you, provided you have a community string specified on the router. The following command will set the SNMP community string to `public`:

```
denver(config)#snmp-server community public ro
```

> **NOTE** `Public` is used only as an example of a community string here. Many networking devices come with SNMP enabled by default with a read-only community string of `public`. Although Cisco does not enable SNMP by default, it is a good idea not to use `public`. Hackers often search for devices that will respond to these default SNMP community strings.

The output from our Get of the system leaf of the SNMP MIB tree would look something like this:

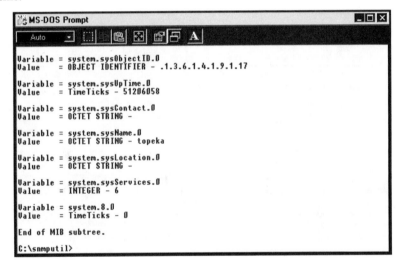

This output is really not that interesting. However, based on the object identifier of .1.3.6.9.1.4.9.1.17, we can see what kind of device we queried. If you traverse the MIB tree, 1.3.6.1.4.9.1.17 is .iso.org.dod.internet.private.enterprises.cisco.17. The last item defines the type of device that we have queried; in this case it's 17, a Cisco 2501 router. Some other things we can see in this output are the system uptime, the system name, the system contact, and the system location. Most of this information has not been filled in. The most useful metric here is system uptime (`sysuptime`). System uptime is useful for detecting if a device has crashed and been reset. Most management systems use reachability to determine if a device is up or not. However, if a router interface goes down, the router may still be up but will be unreachable from the management station. By looking at sysuptime, you can determine if the router crashed and took down all the lines attached to it or if the loss of a single line prevented the management station from getting to the router. If the management station cannot reach the router, you cannot get sysuptime until connectivity is restored. However, if you lose contact for 5 minutes and the sysuptime value is very large, then the router has not crashed or been rebooted.

NOTE Sysuptime is measured in time ticks and not seconds. A time tick is 1/100th of a second. For example, a minute is 6000 time ticks.

While making individual SNMP queries can be lots of fun, most of the information you receive is not very useful by itself. Sure, you can do cool things with SNMP, like query for a routing table or an ARP cache, but generally it is easier to just log into the router to get the information. What makes SNMP attractive is that with minimal effort you can set it to go out and periodically get information about the health of your network. This does require you to write some code and think about what information you want to query for.

You could periodically go out and do an SNMP Walk on the whole MIB tree, but this would generate a huge amount of traffic. It is best to poll only the variable you are interested in. Obviously there is no need to query the system location with any great frequency because it is unlikely to move and, even if it did, whoever moved it would probably forget to modify the system location variable.

Management Systems

Today, many software companies are writing network management systems, such as HP OpenView, Cabletron Spectrum, and Concord Network Health. All of these products use SNMP for gathering data about the health of your network. Figure 16.2 shows the typical network management topology. One management system will typically be responsible for the whole network or a large portion of it.

Optimization and Maintenance

PART 4

Figure 16.2   Management topology

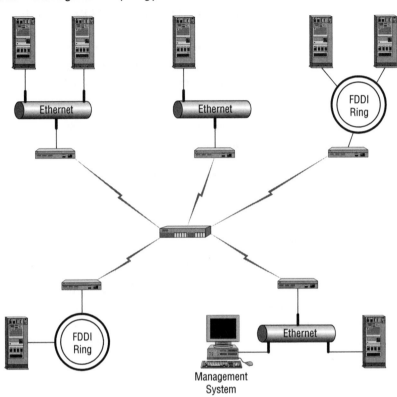

To get any significant value from these products, you'll need to invest a large amount of time to adapt the system to work with your environment.

One of the big moves in network management today is the total outsourcing of the management function. Companies are paying other companies to come in and manage their network environment for them. In many cases this makes sense. By not having to deal with maintaining or setting up a management system, the client corporation is able to tap the expertise of people whose main job is network management. In the typical network environment, network management is something you do only after everything else is taken care of. Outsourcing this function allows the corporate staff to concentrate on running the network, while someone else is collecting and analyzing the management data.

Many companies that have gone out and purchased very expensive management systems have never gotten around to implementing them. Because network management is important, it is easy to justify the expense. However, once you decide how you want to handle your network's management, it often becomes difficult to follow through. When designing a management solution that can be realistically implemented and maintained, it is important to remember that your network management solution should tie together the many different entities that compose a network, such as routers, switches, servers, applications, and hubs.

When investigating network management products, you should always evaluate the products before you purchase them. Four years ago, when we first started getting into network management, many of the products out there looked good in demos and marketing materials but would not hold up in a real environment. One product had a fundamental design flaw that allowed the misconfiguration of a remote agent piece to take the whole management system down. We have since written our own network management system, to help overcome some of shortcomings of the traditional management products.

Things have come a long way in the last four years, but you still want to be careful to make sure that the management system you envision using can be adapted to work effectively in your environment.

HP OpenView Network Node Manager

HP OpenView Network Node Manager (NNM) is an SNMP-based network management system that allows you to collect and graph SNMP data. For example, you could look at something like the number of bits per second through a router. To do that, issue a Get on an MIB variable with a defined frequency that can be adjusted:

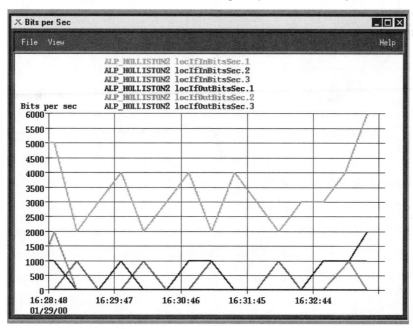

Here we see the bits per second travelling through the router ALP_Hollison2. The actual MIB variable being queried is locIfInBitsSec and locIfOutbitsSec. Notice that there are three interfaces being queried here. By looking at the traffic rates over time, we can get a good idea of what is going on with the network. Though this graph is polling every 15 seconds, we could also set one to poll every 30 minutes, and instead of displaying that information, we could have it write the information off to a database for further reference.

NNM also allows for the creation of thresholds for any MIB variable it can query. So, we could have the management system generate an event any time the number of bits per second went above 8000. We could do the same thing with things like CPU utilization of broadcast packets or any variable that can be queried. This is a great way to detect exceptions within the network environment.

NNM also has a discovery function that will go out and map your environment using SNMP and ICMP. In addition to developing a topology map, NNM will also keep track of the status of objects it has discovered by polling via ICMP echoes. In a large environment, it is very difficult to detect if a link goes down without some kind of help. Depending on what you have defined as an action for an event, NNM will create and send a page or e-mail or generate an audible alert, when an object becomes unreachable or a threshold has been met.

In Figure 16.3, we see an OpenView NNM topology map. Suppose we were having problems with getting to devices on the 192.168.240 segment. NNM uses color to display the status of a network device with green meaning OK and red meaning down. Suppose that ALP_BEDFORD1 was red. We can see from the topology that this is the device that connects to the segment in question. Since we can see that ALP_BEDFORD1 is down and it handles the connection to the 192.168.240.0 subnet, looking at this router is probably a good place to start the troubleshooting process.

Topology mapping with some kind of state status indicator can significantly speed up troubleshooting and fault detection. This is very useful in large environments because it enables you to get a high-level picture of the overall health of the environment from a single view.

Figure 16.3   An NNM topology map

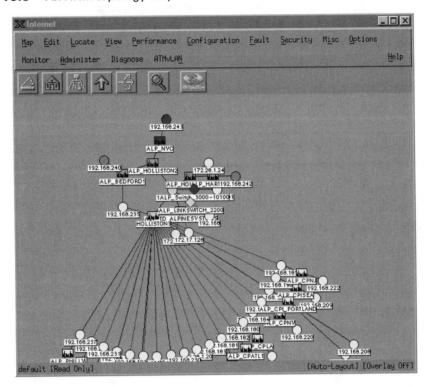

CiscoWorks

CiscoWorks is Cisco's entry into the world of network management software. Cisco-Works can be a great tool for router management. However, it does not allow you to do anything that you cannot do from the router command line. What it does is combine tasks to make things easier for you.

The early versions of CiscoWorks required that it be integrated with a management platform like HP OpenView or Sun Netmanager. CiscoWorks made use of the topology mapping and state monitoring of the underlying management system while providing Cisco-specific tools on top. These tools include inventory management, a configuration manager for collecting storing and comparing configurations, a traceroute utility for displaying loads across the various links, IOS software distribution, and various other useful functions.

Also bundled with CiscoWorks is CiscoView. CiscoView is an SNMP tool that will give you a view of the backplane of any router in its database.

In the above graphic, we can see the backplane of a Cisco 4500 series router. By querying the router, CiscoView will give you a view of exactly what is in the router. We can see that this router has two BRI ports, six 10Mbps Ethernet ports, and four serial ports. The color of the port defines its state. Green signifies Line up Protocol up, red signifies the port is down, and orange signifies the port is administratively down.

If we were to give CiscoView a read/write community string for the router, we could do some configuration through the CiscoView GUI:

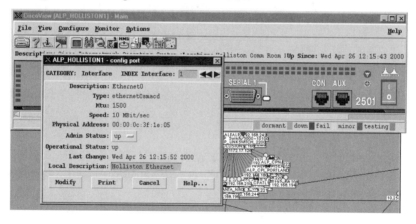

In the above graphic, we can see all kinds of information about the Ethernet 0 interface. From here we could set the interface to an administratively down state, or change the local description. This is a very limited configuration functionality. CiscoWorks allows you to modify whole router configurations. This is done using a text editor, and then CiscoWorks uses TFTP to load the new configuration up to the router.

CiscoView also has a router health monitor built into it. By selecting a device and running the CiscoView health monitor, you can see a graphical representation of ten health metrics.

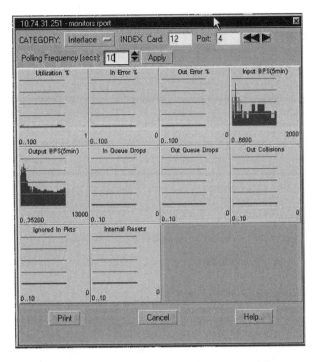

The above graphic shows the output of the CiscoView health monitor. As you can see, things like utilization, percent of errors, queue drops, and bits per second are displayed. This is useful for real-time troubleshooting but is not a particularly good long term planning tool.

To allow your routers to work with CiscoWorks and CiscoView, you only need to set up SNMP community strings in them. To take advantage of the full functionality of these products, read/write community strings are required.

CiscoWorks 2000 CWSI Campus

CiscoWorks 2000 is the newest version of CiscoWorks and functions slightly differently from previous versions. CW2000 can now be used as a stand-alone management system; it does not need to sit on top of another management platform, although it can be used that way. To use CW2000 as stand-alone, you simply specify one or more seed devices. A seed device is one that you tell CiscoWorks to go out and discover. Once CiscoWorks has discovered this seed device, it queries it to learn about other network devices. As each new device is discovered, CiscoWorks queries it to find out if it knows of any devices on the network CiscoWorks has not discovered. This process allows CiscoWorks to discover the whole network with minimal intervention. The discovery process discussed above is used by most management systems to learn about the environment they are connected to.

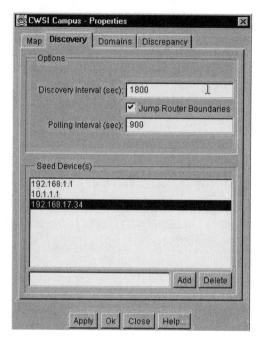

In the above image, 192.168.1.1, 10.1.1.1, and 192.168.17.34 have been specified as seed devices. Once the seed devices have been specified, CW2000 uses CDP to discover additional devices on the network. For this to work, CDP must be enabled on your routers, which it is by default. If it is not, you can always enable it with the following command:

```
topeka(config)#cdp run
```

In order to determine if CDP is enabled or not, use the following command:

```
topeka#sh cdp
```

You should get back an output that looks something like the following:

```
Global CDP information:
        Sending CDP packets every 60 seconds
        Sending a holdtime value of 180 seconds
```

Once CW2000 has discovered the environment, it will show you a map like the one shown here:

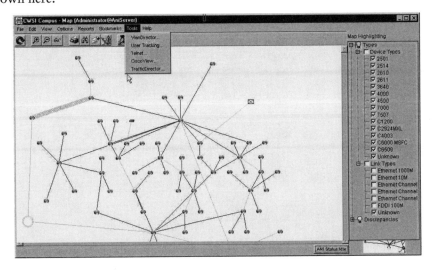

This is the same concept as the OpenView topology map. Not only is the topology laid out, but the state of each device is shown. A red X is placed through unreachable devices. By using CDP, CW2000 does a better job at discovery since it is not locked into using logical TCP/IP addressing to define its topology. This allows CW2000 to make much better decisions when dealing with things like overlapping address spaces and VLSM.

By selecting a device and then running the device ports report, we can see what the selected device has for ports and what the states of those ports are at the present moment.

Port	Name	Type	AdminStatus	OperStatus	Linking?	Trunking?	Speed	Protocols Enabled	Protocols Seen
	Hs0/0	propPointToPointSerial	up	up	true	false	45M	ALL	N/A
	Se1/0	propPointToPointSerial	up	up	true	false	1M	ALL	N/A
	Se1/1	propPointToPointSerial	up	up	true	false	1M	ALL	N/A
	Se1/2	propPointToPointSerial	down	down	false	false	1M	ALL	N/A
	Se1/3	propPointToPointSerial	down	down	false	false	1M	ALL	N/A
	Se1/4	propPointToPointSerial	down	down	false	false	1M	ALL	N/A
	Se1/5	propPointToPointSerial	down	down	false	false	56K	ALL	N/A
	Se1/6	propPointToPointSerial	down	down	false	false	1M	ALL	N/A
	Se1/7	propPointToPointSerial	down	down	false	false	1M	ALL	N/A
	Fd2/0	fddi	up	up	false	false	100M	ALL	N/A
	Fd3/0	fddi	up	up	true	false	100M	ALL	N/A
	Se4/0	propPointToPointSerial	up	up	true	false	1M	ALL	N/A
	Se4/1	propPointToPointSerial	up	up	true	false	1M	ALL	N/A
	Se4/2	propPointToPointSerial	up	up	true	false	56K	ALL	N/A
	Se4/3	propPointToPointSerial	up	up	true	false	1M	ALL	N/A
	Se4/4	propPointToPointSerial	up	up	true	false	1M	ALL	N/A
	Se4/5	ppp	up	up	true	false	1M	ALL	N/A
	Se4/6	propPointToPointSerial	up	up	true	false	1M	ALL	N/A
	Se4/7	propPointToPointSerial	up	up	true	false	1M	ALL	N/A

19 row(s)

Optimization and Maintenance

PART 4

We can see that the router selected in this graphic has eight ports in it. Six of them are fast Ethernet, with three of those being down. There is also a 45Mbps HSSI port that is down and an FDDI port, which is the port we connected to in order to get this information (as signified by the lightning bolt). There are many other reports we can run. For example, we can run a report on device attributes for multiple devices by simply selecting the devices and selecting the device attributes report from the menu.

IPAddress	Type	Module	NumPorts	Version(s)
192.168.111.253	2610	default	4	N/A
192.168.120.253	2610	default	4	N/A
192.168.105.253	2610	default	4	N/A
192.168.56.253	2610	default	4	N/A
192.168.165.253	2501	default	3	N/A
192.168.202.254	7000	default	16	N/A
192.168.24.253	2611	default	5	N/A
192.168.105.254	4000	default	6	N/A
192.168.58.253	2610	default	4	N/A
192.168.149.254	4000	default	6	N/A
192.168.16.250	4000	default	6	N/A
192.168.151.253	2610	default	4	N/A
192.168.35.253	2610	default	4	N/A

From this report we can see the IP address, router model, and number of ports we have for each router discovered in the topology map. We can do the same type of thing with links.

This is a great tool for keeping track of and documenting what is in the environment. CiscoWorks 2000 also comes with another set of tools known as Resource Manager Essentials, which contains a Web-based interface that allows you to perform various functions, including the following:

Availability Lets you monitor the reachablility and response time of devices on your network.

Change Audit Lets you track and report on network changes.

Configuration Management Allows you to access configuration files in flash file systems.

Contract Connection Helps you keep track of which devices are covered by your Cisco maintenance contract and which ones are not.

Inventory   Helps you keep track of the devices you have in your network. Also provides a neat but now thoroughly useless Y2K compliance report.

Job Approval   Controls when other application jobs within Resource Manager are allowed to run.

Software Management   Automates the process of downloading software images.

Syslog Analysis   Allows you to run various reports against the syslog server contained within Resource Manager.

Setting Up Your Routers to Use CiscoWorks and Resource Manager

In order to maximize the functionality of these applications, you will need to make a few changes on your routers. You will need to set up a read and read/write community string. Be sure to specify an access list to limit access to the read/write string. 10.1.1.2 is the address of the CW2000 station. The following commands set up a read/write community string and specify that only those devices permitted by access list 5 are allowed to use that community string. In this case only 10.1.1.2 is allowed to use the read/write community string Secret_squirrel.

```
topeka(config)#access-list 5 permit 10.1.1.2

topeka(config)#snmp-server community Secret_squirrel rw 5
```

Next you want to make sure CDP is enabled:

```
topeka(config)#cdp run
```

You also may need to modify the routers to enable RCP so that configurations can be archived. This is done with the following global configuration commands:

```
ip rcmd rcp-enable

ip rcmd remote-host remote_username 10.1.1.2 local_username enable
```

The values of remote_username and local_username should be those that will be used by the RCP process. The default for CW2000 is *cwuser*.

WARNING   Notice that we have just set up RCP with a default username. If an attacker knew you were running CW2000, which he could probably determine by doing a simple packet capture and looking at the traffic patterns, he could then spoof the management station address and get RCP to work with the default username he pulled out of the Cisco documentation. Where access is concerned, it is never a good idea to use the defaults.

You do not need to enable RCP to get CiscoWorks 2000 to work. You can get some pretty decent functionality with just CDP and read SNMP access. Unless you are actually going to use the CiscoWorks 2000 options that use RCP, we would recommend that you not enable it on your routers. Most of the time you probably will not use the CiscoWorks 2000 functionality provided by RCP anyway.

RMON

Remote Network Monitoring (RMON) is defined by four documents: RFC 1513, RFC 1757, RFC 2021, and RFC 2074. With SNMP we could only look at statistics related to the device we were monitoring. RMON allows us to collect statistics on a device for every packet it sees or on those packets that cross through the device, depending on how we configure it.

The RMON MIB is divided into 10 different groups:

Statistics   Collects low-level statistics about each subnet monitored by the agent.

History   Records periodic samples from the statistics group for long-term trending.

Alarm   Allows the management console user to set sampling intervals and alarm thresholds for various statistics.

Host   Contains counters for various traffic types between hosts on the managed subnet.

HostTopN   A sorted version of the host group.

Matrix   Displays error and utilization in the form of a host-to-host matrix so the information or traffic between two individual hosts can easily be obtained.

Capture   Allows for the capturing of data packets.

Filter   Allows for the defining of filters for traffic. These filters can either define traffic to be captured or traffic to record statistic on.

Events   Creates a table of events generated by the RMON probe.

TokenRing   Collects statistics and configuration information about token ring networks.

The information collected via RMON can be gathered in the same way we collected SNMP data since it is stored in a MIB. RMON information is very useful because it can give us data about what is going on with the local segment, not just what it passing through the router. We can also define thresholds with RMON and make the router send traps or create RMON events when these thresholds are met.

RMON is enabled on an interface basis. This is done using the following interface command:

```
MMAGH(config)#int e0
MMAGH(config-if)#rmon promiscuous
```

There are two RMON modes supported by Cisco: promiscuous and native. Promiscuous will collect statistics on all data the interface sees, while native will only collect information on packets passing through the interface. If you choose to use native RMON, the interface command would be this:

```
MMAGH(config-if)#rmon native
```

There is a queue that holds packets for analysis by the RMON agent. By default, it holds 64 packets, but if you want to increase the queue size, use the following command:

```
MMAGH(config)#rmon queuesize 444
```

You would use this command if you wanted the queue to hold 444 packets. Obviously, monitoring all this traffic will put a load on the router, so be careful. Also note that the RMON queue is taking away memory space from other routing functions, so you do not want to make it too large.

As we discussed above, Cisco's IOS does not allow much in the way of SNMP threshold configuration or monitoring. Luckily, RMON addresses this issue. RMON gives us the ability to monitor any MIB object. In order to set a threshold on an RMON statistic, we would use the following syntax:

```
MMAGH(config)#rmon alarm 1 mib_object 30 absolute rising-threshold
500 1 falling-threshold 300 2
```

The number 1 specifies the alarm number we are creating. You would replace `mib_object` with the actual name of the MIB object you are interested in. The number 30 specifies how often we are going to look at the MIB object, which ends up being the sampling rate. `Absolute` specifies what type of value we are looking for. We can specify either `absolute`, which creates an alarm if the sampled value surpasses the threshold value, or we could replace `absolute` with `delta`, which would compare the current reading to the last sample and create an alarm if the difference was greater than the value specified. Our threshold value is 500, which is a number with no units. The units are those of the actual MIB instance. So if we were looking at sysuptime, the units would end up being ticks, but if we were looking at input interface throughput, the units would be bits per second. The 1 after the 500 specifies that the RMON alarm number 1 should fire if this threshold is

Optimization and Maintenance

exceeded. The falling threshold specifies the threshold has a low border on for the metric. Finally, the 2 specifies that the alarm number 2 should fire on the falling-threshold.

Having both a falling and rising threshold gives us a great deal of flexibility with our alarms. The alarms will fire only when the threshold is crossed in the proper direction. For example, a rising-threshold alarm will only fire if the previous value is below it and the current value is above it so that the threshold is crossed in a rising direction. The opposite is true for the falling threshold. The following command could be used to configure an RMON alarm with both rising and falling thresholds:

```
rmon alarm 1 ifOutOctets 60 delta rising-threshold 10000
falling-threshold 50
```

This command would configure an alarm if the router saw more than 10000 ifOutOctets in the last minute or less than 50 ifOutOctets in the last minute.

Now that we have created the alarm, we need to create an RMON event. To create the event for our alarm 1, we would use the following command:

```
MMAGH(config)#rmon event 1 description ifoctets_alarm trap public
```

This would create an event for alarm 1 with a description of ifoctets_alarm and send a trap on that alarm with a community string of public. We could also generate an RMON alarm entry by using the following command:

```
MMAGH(config)#rmon event 1 description ifoctets_alarm log
```

Or, if we want to create both a log entry and a trap, we could use the following command:

```
MMAGH(config)#rmon event 1 description ifoctets_alarm log  trap
public
```

RMON requires a lot of processing power, and alarms and events require even more. Unless you are looking for a specific condition, you probably don't want to set up RMON alarms. They are great troubleshooting tools, but most likely you will want to set them up for a short period of time and then remove them. For example, if you know a line is becoming saturated, you can set an RMON threshold and trap when the line becomes saturated and then try and figure out what is saturating the line at that given time. The RMON HostTopN group can be very helpful for showing who is using the most bandwidth at a given time.

SNMP as a Diagnostic Tool

We have a client who is constantly having problems with their routers crashing every few weeks. Using SNMP we were able to determine the cause of this behavior. What we ended up doing was polling various router health statistics every 15 minutes for a few weeks. Then we analyzed this data. What we discovered by looking at the amount of free memory in the router was rather interesting, as you can see in the graphic below. This device happens not to be a Cisco router.

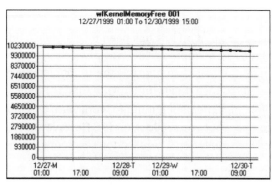

We can see that the statistic wfKernelMemoryFree is slowly trending down over the three days for which the graph is displaying data. Free memory should bounce up and down as the router's processing load changes. A continually decreasing trend in free memory over time, as indicated in this graph, suggests a memory leak. Once we discovered this we began to focus on the memory in the routers. What we saw was that there was a continual trend in the free memory statistic. Occasionally there would be a large drop in the amount of free memory, as displayed in graphic below.

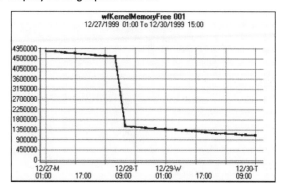

Here, some process on the router took hold of a big chunk of memory and then did not properly release it back to the free memory pool. But even before and after that dramatic drop, the downward trend still exists. Looking at this data over time on all of the customer's

24seven **CASE STUDY**

routers we were able to identify what we believe to be a memory leak in a certain version of routing software. We initially recommended they upgrade the software on all of the routers. However, the customer is not prepared to do this right now. So by carefully calculating the rate of decay of wfKernelFreeMemory on the routers, we extrapolated that in the worst case the router will run out of memory about every four weeks.

When the router runs out of memory, it crashes and ends up rebooting itself, so the process starts all over again. This means that some time about every four weeks the routers will crash and reboot. If this happened at 3 AM it might not be such a bad thing. But as we all know, crashes never happen at a good time.

Our recommendation to the client on this has been to schedule a time every three weeks to plan an outage and reboot the routers. This way, they can control when the inevitable outage occurs. The long-term plan is to upgrade the routing software and possibly even replace the current routers in their environment with Cisco routers.

SNMP is not always the most interesting thing to work with, and often you have to pore through lots of data to find what you are looking for. However, by collecting data over a long period of time and then analyzing it, you'll often see trends that you would miss in real time become obvious.

17

Troubleshooting Tools

Troubleshooting is the area of network administration where you probably spend most of your time. The router is an integral part of today's networks; unfortunately, it is often one of the least understood parts. As a result, many problems that are not router-related end up being blamed on the routers. In some companies, this has become almost a knee-jerk reaction—if a support person sees a problem they don't immediately understand, they will try to blame it on the network routers. This means that before you can even start solving the problem, you may need to demonstrate that it is not router-related. This can be very frustrating at times. Of course there will be times when there actually is a problem with the router: things break, configuration mistakes are made, and so on. At some point, you will have a router problem.

Good troubleshooting skills are essential for quickly locating and fixing the inevitable problems as they occur. What constitutes good troubleshooting skills? That is a hard question to answer, because it depends on a lot of factors. The way you troubleshoot a particular problem depends a lot on the information you have about the problem and your past experience.

Troubleshooting is a very hard skill to teach. You need to think logically and be able to break a problem down into its component parts. Obviously, we cannot tell you how to troubleshoot every network problem. The most important thing in troubleshooting is to understand how the network is supposed to function and the roles your routers play. With the previous chapters under your belt, you should have a good understanding of how your network works.

Spend some time observing the network when things are working properly. The more familiar you are with the way a given environment functions, the better you will be able to troubleshoot that environment. Experience also plays a huge role in the troubleshooting process. The best way to learn how to troubleshoot effectively is to do it. There is no substitute for experience.

Troubleshooting Philosophies

Most people will tell you to take a slow, methodical approach to troubleshooting and slowly break down the problem. That is a valid approach and definitely has its place. In a moment, we'll look at a couple of different systematic methods. First, however, there is an important "yes, but": many problems are simple things that you see over and over again, and you can often forgo the methodical approach for a few minutes to try a few things that might be causing the problem. Of course, if you are wrong, you have thrown away some valuable time. But as long as you keep track of what you are doing, these educated guesses don't hurt anything; and as your experience grows, you will be able to hit the correct solution more and more often.

Does it make sense to run through a methodical troubleshooting process that may take an hour when you can take 10 minutes to go with your instincts and experience and try a few things? If you are wrong, you have just wasted 10 minutes and now have that whole troubleshooting process still in front of you. If you are right, however, you have saved yourself maybe 50 minutes. So if you are right only once out of every six times, you still come out even. Most likely you will be able to achieve a better success rate than 1/6.

When you are using this "seat of the pants" approach to try solving a problem quickly, be careful to keep track of what you are doing and to make sure that you don't make the problem worse. Also be careful to set a time limit on what you are doing. This approach is valid only if you can solve the problem quickly. If your instincts send you off on a tangent, sticking to a time limit can help you pull yourself back. It is very important to make sure you don't end up rushing down the wrong road at full speed for too long.

Suppose you have exhausted your quick-resolution interval or run up against a problem that you just don't know where to start diagnosing. That's when you need a systematic troubleshooting approach. There are two ways of doing this: You can start at the very basics ("Is the power working?") and move forward, or you can start higher ("Are my OSPF routers establishing adjacencies?") and move back toward the more basic things ("Is there power? Is the line up?") The route you choose depends on how well you understand the environment. If you are very familiar with the environment, you will probably want to start at the top and work down. If not, you will probably want to start at the bottom and work up.

Working from the bottom up will fill in most of the information about how the environment works as you work towards the problem. This may take slightly longer than starting at the top and working backward, but they are both valid approaches. It's also very helpful to keep a notebook with you while troubleshooting a problem. During the troubleshooting process, write down what you are doing and why, and what you expect to see. Also keep careful track of any changes you make during the troubleshooting process. This makes it much easier to put things back together after you have located and fixed the problem. Reading over your notes from old troubleshooting encounters also helps you to improve your troubleshooting skills.

One of the most important questions you can ask in troubleshooting a problem is "What has changed?" If everything was working yesterday, but today something is not functioning properly, most likely something happened in the last 24 hours to create the problem you are working to fix. Finding out what changed will often lead you to the solution rather quickly. There is nothing more frustrating than spending a few hours troubleshooting a network problem to find out that someone was in one of the communication closets redoing some cabling and knocked the FDDI cable connection out of the back of the router.

> **NOTE** Network problems are inevitable, and often these problems can be compounded by mistakes made by end users or even IT staff. When this occurs, it is important not to get angry with anyone; just fix the problem and move on. Don't make anyone afraid to admit an error. You want people to let you know when they have made a change or done something that could cause a problem with the network. This is the type of information that can save you hours.

In troubleshooting, there is no substitute for familiarity with the environment. If you know how the environment should function normally, you can easily pick out problems. (Chapter 16 discussed the most important monitoring tools available for Cisco routers.) You should also have a detailed diagram of the network. This type of information is invaluable in a troubleshooting situation and you will want to make sure you have it in advance. Obviously, keeping up-to-date documentation and diagrams on your network can be time-consuming; and the last thing most of us want to do is documentation. However, all the work you put into documenting will pay off when you get into a difficult troubleshooting situation, and it makes your job much easier in the long run.

Basic Troubleshooting Tools

There are many tools we can use to troubleshoot network problems. Those covered in this section are the more common ones that you can use to troubleshoot most of the network problems that you will run into. Things like CDP, ping, and traceroute are very useful for tracking down network problems. In order to get the most out of the troubleshooting tools you have been given, you need to understand how they work and what they are trying to tell you. As we progress through this section, we will discuss several of the more common troubleshooting tools.

Ping

The most common troubleshooting tool is the ping command. As we all know, ping works by sending out an ICMP echo-request and listening for an ICMP echo-reply. If you can ping a device, you know that there is an IP route to that device and that the cabling between your device and the other device is working. We often use ping both to verify that a path exists between two devices and to check the response time of the network.

Here's an example:

```
MMAGH#ping 10.1.1.3


Type escape sequence to abort.
Sending 5, 100-byte ICMP Echos to 10.1.1.3, timeout is 2 seconds:
!!!!!
Success rate is 100 percent (5/5), round-trip min/avg/max = 4/4/4 ms
```

In the above ping output you can see that we sent the default five ICMP echorequests to 10.1.1.3 and received back five ICMP echo replies—a success rate of 100 percent. We can also see the round trip times for the average, max, and min response values. They happen to all be 4ms. The round trip time for a ping depends on many factors, including the number and type of intermediary devices and the types of media involved. The 4ms response time we are seeing tells us that we are probably either on the same segment as 10.1.1.3 or one hop away. Delays can crop up in all different places. For example, if you have to cross between FDDI and Ethernet there is a delay, since FDDI addresses are canonical and Ethernet addresses are noncanonical. Routers add delay because they have to readdress the layer 2 header, and the sending device must also wait until the network is clear before it is allowed to send. When a router is allowed to place data on the wire depends on the layer 2 protocol running on that interface. All of these factors can contribute to the round trip delay. Typically, though, the round trip delay should be relatively small. For example, we are currently monitoring a device in Irvine, California from Holliston, Massachusetts. The round trip delay to ping this device is between 75 and 100ms depending on what else is going on in the network when the ping is issued.

Using Ping on Cisco Routers

The ping implementation on a Cisco router gives you a lot of flexibility. There are actually two versions of ping on Cisco routers. The first is a version in user mode that allows only basic functionality, like you would get on a workstation. The second type of ping, available only in privileged exec mode, has a lot more functionality built into it. For example, you can choose the protocol you wish to use. AppleTalk, Apollo, DECnet, IPX, IP, VINES, Connection Less Network Service (CLNS), and XNS are all supported. Here's an example of the extended ping command:

```
MMAGH#ping
Protocol [ip]:
Target IP address: sointu.com
Repeat count [5]: 10
Datagram size [100]: 300
Timeout in seconds [2]:
Extended commands [n]: y
Source address or interface: 10.1.1.3
Type of service [0]:
Set DF bit in IP header? [no]:
Validate reply data? [no]:
Data pattern [0xABCD]:
Loose, Strict, Record, Timestamp, Verbose[none]:
Sweep range of sizes [n]:
Type escape sequence to abort.
Sending 10, 300-byte ICMP Echos to 172.16.1.5, timeout is 2 seconds:
!!!!!!!!!!
Success rate is 100 percent (10/10), round-trip min/avg/max = 4/5/8 ms
```

As you can see from the ping dialog above, the extended ping command lets you specify the protocol to use, the target address (sointu.com in this case), the number of packets to send (10), the datagram size, the type of service, and whether to set the DF (do not fragment) bit in the IP header. We can also set the 16-bit hexadecimal data being sent. The default is ABCD, but it is often useful to change this to all 1s or all 0s in order to detect CSU/DSU or cabling issues. Cable runs that experience a lot of crosstalk will often corrupt the data in these packets, and with the data pattern set to all 1s or all 0s it is much easier to pick up these Physical-layer problems.

The Loose, Strict, Record, Timestamp, and Verbose options allow you to set various IP header options, which are described in RFC 791. The default is None. The Record option is interesting because it forces the router to keep track of the address of each hop the packet has gone through. When using the Record option, you will be asked the number of hops to record; the default is 9. A `Ping` with the Record option between IP addresses 10.1.1.3 and 192.168.1.1 could produce an output like the following:

```
Sending 1, 100-byte ICMP Echos to 192.168.1.2, timeout is 2 seconds:
Packet has IP options:  Total option bytes= 39, padded length=40
 Record route: <*> 0.0.0.0 0.0.0.0 0.0.0.0 0.0.0.0
         0.0.0.0 0.0.0.0 0.0.0.0 0.0.0.0 0.0.0.0


Reply to request 0 (8 ms).  Received packet has options
 Total option bytes= 40, padded length=40
 Record route: 192.168.1.1 192.168.1.2 10.1.1.5 10.1.1.3
         <*> 0.0.0.0 0.0.0.0 0.0.0.0 0.0.0.0 0.0.0.0
End of list
```

You can see that in the outgoing packet there are nine sets of 0.0.0.0 addresses; these are where the address of each device in the route will be recorded. In the response packet you can see that the packet went first to a device with IP address 192.168.1.1 and was then sent to 192.168.1.2, which was the destination. Then it went to 10.1.1.5 and finally returned to 10.1.1.3, the source address. This looks odd. Why didn't the packet come back over the same route it went out? Remember that the router is allowed to pick the best route to a given host for each packet. The fact that a packet takes one route does not always mean the next packet will go the same way. In many cases all of the packets will take the same path between two given points, but it certainly does not have to be this way. In fact, the end destination IP addresses could be multiple devices sharing the network load.

Cisco routers use a number of special symbols in `ping` responses. There is a set of these symbols, for each protocol supported by the extended `ping` command. For the most part the symbols are pretty much the same between protocols. The most common ones are IP, whose symbols are show in Table 17.1, and IPX, whose symbols are shown in Table 17.2.

Table 17.1   IP Ping Response Symbols

Symbol	Description
!	Echo-reply was successfully received from host.
.	Router timed out while waiting for echo-reply.
U	ICMP Destination Unreachable message was received by the router.
N	ICMP Network Unreachable message was received by the router.
P	ICMP Protocol Unreachable message was received by the router.
Q	ICMP Source Quench message was received by the router.
M	ICMP Could Not Fragment message was received by the router.
?	ICMP Unknown Packet Type message was received by the router.

Table 17.2   IPX Ping Response Symbols

Symbol	Description
!	Reply was received.
.	Router timed out waiting for reply.
U	Destination Unreachable PDU was received by the router.
I	User interrupted the test.
C	Congestion Experienced packet received by router.
?	Unknown packet type.
&	Packet life exceeded message received by router.

Optimization and Maintenance

PART 4

The `ping` responses for the other protocols are for the most part the same as for IP. Obviously, you will need to specify the proper protocol address to be able to `ping` a device. What you are doing with a `Ping` is validating that a route exists between the two end stations and that the link is between the two stations is valid.

NOTE The IPX `Ping` from a Cisco router sends Cisco Proprietary IPX `ping` messages by default. Novell IPX devices will not respond to these `ping` messages. To `ping` a Novell device via IPX, you need to answer Yes when asked whether to send Novell standard echoes. Another option is to change the default IPX `ping` protocol by using the global `config` command, as shown here:

`Router(config)#ipx ping-default Novell`

When Ping Is Unsuccessful or Intermittent

Sometimes it happens that some `ping` messages are successful while others are not. For some applications this is not a problem, but for others it can be. For example, Novell's DS Repair is very sensitive to lost packets and will simply not work over lines where packets are being dropped. Telnet, by contrast, will work as long as some data is getting through. It is important to understand this. If you send out 10 `ping` messages and nine are successful, you probably have an intermittent problem with something in the network and should investigate further.

NOTE Often the first `ping` sent out will be unsuccessful, producing output like this:

`.!!!!`

The first `ping` timed out because of the delay involved in the ARP process. This is normal; don't worry about it. You should, however, be worried if you get output that looks like this:

`!!..!!.!`

This output would signify that the network is dropping packets and we should investigate to discover the cause of these dropped packets.

Traceroute

The `traceroute` command is an ICMP-based tool that attempts to map out the path between source and destination. Along the way, `traceroute` will give you information about the latency on each leg of the route. `Traceroute` takes advantage of the fact that when a device kills a packet because the TTL (Time to Live) value has expired, that device is supposed to send an ICMP TTL-expired message to the host that originated the packet. TTL is used to prevent packets from being stuck in an endless loop in the network forever.

Each time a packet goes through a routing device, the packet's TTL value is decremented by 1. When the TTL value of a packet has decremented to 1, the next router to receive it throws the packet away and sends a TTL Expired message to the source network address. Figure 17.1 illustrates how `traceroute` uses TTL to map a network path.

Figure 17.1   IP traceroute uses ICMP TTL Expired messages to map out network paths.

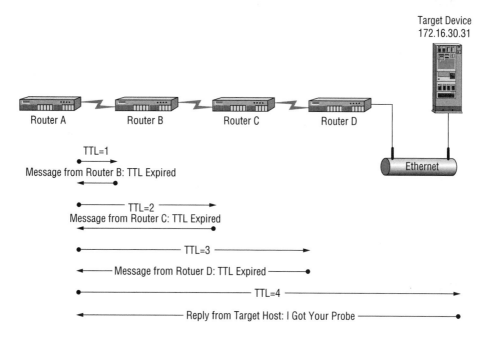

In Figure 17.1, we have issued the `traceroute` command from router A, specifying 172.16.30.31 as the destination device. The router first sends a packet destined for 172.16.30.31 with a TTL of 1. Router B receives this packet and decrements the TTL. It then realizes the new TTL is 0, kills the packet, and sends back a TTL Expired message to router A. By looking at the source address of the TTL Expired message, router A learns that router B is the first hop. Now router A sends out a packet destined for 172.16.30.31 with a TTL of 2. Router B receives the packet, decrements the TTL from 2 to 1, and sends it to router C. When router C receives the packet it decrements the TLL from 1 to 0, throws the packet away, and sends a TTL Expired message to router A. Router A now knows the first two hops. This continues until a packet reaches the target host. Once the target host gets the probe packet, it responds to router A, saying it received the packet. This tells router A it has mapped the full route.

It is important to remember that not all packets have to take the same route to a destination. Suppose we had a network like Figure 17.2. In this case the first packet with TTL=1 again goes to router B. Router B would kill the packet and send out a TTL expired message. Router A now knows that the first hop is router B. Now it sets the TTL to 2, but the packet goes to router E. Because the TTL is 2, router E passes it to D, and D kills the packet and sends a TTL Expired message to router A. So router D is recorded as our second hop. Router A sends a packet with the TTL set to 3. This time it goes through router B and router C. When router D gets it, the TTL is 1, so D kills the packet and sends a TTL expired message to router A. Router A now records router D as the third hop. Now looking for the fourth hop, router A sets the TTL to 4. This time, the packet goes to router E, then to router D, and from D to the target host. The TTL is 2 when it gets to the target host, but the host does not care—it just responds to the probe that router A has sent. Router A gets the response and assumes it is done. The path that ends up being reported is router A to router B to router D to router D to the host.

Figure 17.2 Not all packets take the same route to the destination.

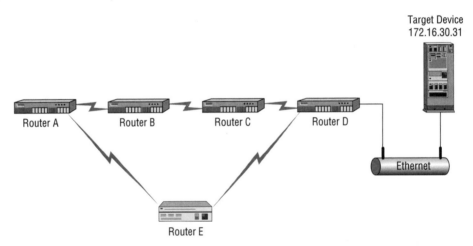

This is obviously not correct: router E never shows up, and neither does C. Looking at the reported path you would think that router B is connected directly to router D, but in fact router C is in the middle. Most of the time this will not happen, but you need to be aware that `traceroute` can report erroneous results. All it is looking for is ICMP TTL Expired messages. As long as it gets them, or a reply to its probe packet, it is happy.

Using traceroute on Cisco Routers

Cisco routers offer an extended version of the `traceroute` command, which allows you some additional options. A sample dialog looks like this:

```
AGH1#traceroute
Protocol [ip]: ip
Target IP address: 192.168.1.2
Source address: 10.1.1.5
Numeric display [n]:
Timeout in seconds [3]:
Probe count [3]:
Minimum Time to Live [1]:
Maximum Time to Live [30]:
Port Number [33434]:
Loose, Strict, Record, Timestamp, Verbose[none]:
1 10.1.1.7 4 msec 8 msec 8 msec
2 172.16.1.5 5 msec 7 msec 9 msec
3 192.168.30.1 15 msec 21 msec 25 msec
4 192.168.33.3 20 msec 27 msec 35 msec
5 192.168.1.2 4 msec 8 msec 8 msec
```

The supported protocols for `traceroute` are AppleTalk, CLNS, IP, Vines, and—in the newer Cisco IOS implementations only—IPX. The Numeric Display option lets you instruct the router not to resolve hostnames via DNS. If you answer Y to this option, you will only see the IP address for each hop; otherwise, you get both an IP address and a host name. You should be aware that trying to resolve DNS names will slow the `traceroute` process down. Other options you can specify include the number of probes for each TTL value, the timeout, and the max and min TTL values.

Choosing the Strict routing option lets you specify a list of nodes; only these nodes may be traversed in going to the destination. This option is not useful if you are using `traceroute` to trace a route, but it may come in handy when you are trying to locate the break in a known path. The Loose routing option allows you to specify certain nodes that must be passed through on the way to the destination. This is useful to guarantee that you are getting a proper `traceroute`. If, when we traced the network in Figure 17.2, we had specified that router C needed to be passed through, we would have gotten a much more accurate trace result.

There are two implementations of `traceroute`. UNIX hosts and Cisco routers use a UDP Probe packet with a source port above 30,000. (On a Cisco router, the default port is 33434.) Windows systems use ICMP echo requests as the probe packet. This distinction is not important for troubleshooting, but it does come into play when you are trying to prevent intruders from using `traceroute` to map out your environment. This is discussed in more detail in Chapter 15.

The Address Resolution Protocol (ARP)

As discussed in Chapter 1, the Address Resolution Protocol maps IP addresses to MAC addresses. Here's how it works: When a network device sends a packet, it needs to know what Data Link layer address to send the packet to. Remember from Chapter 1 that the network address is hidden by the data link header. Suppose host A wants talk to 10.1.1.2. We need to know the layer 2 address of 10.1.1.2. To find this, host A would send out a frame to the Data Link layer broadcast address and the network address of 10.1.1.2. All hosts on the same segment are going to receive this packet and pass it up their protocol stacks because they are all listening to the layer 2 broadcast address. Once the frame gets to the Network layer, all the devices on the segment host A is on will throw away this packet except the device that has 10.1.1.2 as its IP address. 10.1.1.2 is going to reply to host A. Since 10.1.1.2 got the ARP with host A's data link address, it will send a layer 2 Unicast frame back to that address, as a reply to the ARP. When host A receives this response from 10.1.1.2 it learns the data link address of 10.1.1.2 from the data link header of the response frame.

If the destination address were not on the same network as host A, the routers on host A's segment would consult their ARP tables. If the router had an entry for 10.1.1.2, it would reply with the data link address of its interface on host A's segment. If the router did not have an entry for 10.1.1.2 it would consult its routing table and if it had a route for the 10.1.1.x network, the router would send out its own ARP for 10.1.1.2 through the proper interface as defined by the router's routing table. This process will continue until either a router can get 10.1.1.2 to respond or a timeout occurs. Since a router and not 10.1.1.2 responded to host A's ARP, host A would then think that the remote device's data link address was that of the router that replied to the ARP. This is cool because host A is now sending Unicast layer 2 frames to the router, which is passing them up its protocol stack reading the Network layer addresses and using its routing table to properly forward the frames.

The `show ARP` command can often be useful in troubleshooting; it displays the contents of a router's ARP table or cache.

```
MMAGH#sh arp
Protocol  Address          Age (min)  Hardware Addr   Type   Interface
Internet  10.1.1.2                 2  0060.8cf3.b5ed  ARPA   Ethernet0
Internet  10.1.1.3                 -  00e0.b055.b68e  ARPA   Ethernet0
Internet  10.1.1.4                 5  0000.0c4a.53c8  ARPA   Ethernet0
Internet  10.1.1.5                31  00e0.1e3e.5306  ARPA   Ethernet0
Internet  192.168.31.1             5  00e0.b055.b68e  ARPA   Ethernet0
```

Every address in a router's ARP cache is a device that has, at some point, communicated with the router. The ARP table can be used for tasks like tracking down duplicate IP addresses. Each entry in an ARP table consists of an IP address, the corresponding hardware address, and the interface that hardware address is located on. However, this information is relevant only to the local segment. Because a router replaces each packet's original hardware address with its own MAC address, the ARP data is partly misleading once the packet crosses a router. At best, you can see that the router knows about the IP address, and you can determine which interface the router believes that IP address is connected to. ARP can be a good place to start when troubleshooting IP problems. Sometimes you may even want to flush the ARP table to clear out old entries and force the table to rebuild. Clearing the ARP table can be useful in troubleshooting because ARP entries are only created for devices that talk to the router. To do this, enter

```
ANWCS-2#clear arp
```

Cisco Discovery Protocol (CDP)

CDP is a Cisco proprietary protocol that was developed by Cisco and runs only on Cisco devices. It allows Cisco devices to exchange certain information among themselves—platform type, network capabilities, IOS version, and the like. CDP communicates via a layer 2 multicast with an address of 01-00-0C-CC-CC. Because it is a layer 2 multicast, CDP information will only be exchanged on the local network segment and will not be routed. This allows Cisco devices to learn about all their neighboring Cisco devices.

CDP is independent of both media and protocols. It does not care if it is running across FDDI, ATM, Token Ring, Ethernet, or other media. Because it is also protocol independent, two hosts running different protocols can talk CDP; they need not support a common protocol. Thus a router supporting IP can talk CDP to another router that is only running IPX or even to a Catalyst switch that is only performing layer 2 switching. This can be very useful in verifying connectivity. If a router can see its CDP neighbor across a link, then obviously there is a connection between the two devices, allowing CDP information to pass.

Optimization and Maintenance

PART 4

To see the Cisco devices a router knows about via CDP, use this command:

```
MO_rtr#sh cdp neighbors
```

The system will reply with the following display:

```
Capability Codes: R - Router, T - Trans Bridge, B - Source Route Bridge
                  S - Switch, H - Host, I - IGMP, r - Repeater


Device ID        Local Intrfce    Holdtme   Capability  Platform  Port ID
MMAGH               Eth 0           140          R        2500      Eth 0
BOS_r               Ser 0           120          R        3600      Ser 0
```

You can see that this router has two neighbors. One is a Cisco 2500 series router with a hostname of MMAGH connected off the Ethernet 0 port. The other is the BOS_r router connected off the serial 0 port. Under the Capability heading we can see what capabilities the device actually has. Since both of the CDP neighbors are routers, we see an R. The possible Capability codes are displayed before the actual CDP output.

You can get even more information by using the detail option with the show cdp neighbors command:

```
KAH_RTR#show cdp neighbors detail

------------------------

Device ID: MMAGH

Entry address(es):
   IP address: 10.1.1.3

Platform: cisco 2500,  Capabilities: Router

Interface: Ethernet0,  Port ID (outgoing port): Ethernet0

Holdtime : 130 sec


Version :

Cisco Internetwork Operating System Software

IOS (tm) 2500 Software (C2500-IO-L), Version 12.0(8), RELEASE
SOFTWARE (fc1)

Copyright (c) 1986-1999 by cisco Systems, Inc.

Compiled Mon 29-Nov-99 16:22 by kpma
```

We can see that the neighbor device is MMAGH and it is a Cisco 2500 router with an IP addresses of 10.1.1.3. The router learned about it via Ethernet 0. We can also see what version of the IOS the neighbor is running; in this case it happens to be C2500-IO-L version 12.0(8).

This information can be useful in the initial gathering of information as you begin the troubleshooting process.

Advanced Tools

The following section will cover those tools that are typically used to troubleshoot problems after the tools discussed above have failed to provide the solutions. There is really no distinction between a basic and an advanced troubleshooting tool. Depending on how well you know a tool, it could end up being used as either an advanced or a basic tool. The following tools require a greater understanding of how things should function in a networking environment to be useful.

Debug Commands

Cisco routers offer a large number of **debug** commands, which can be very helpful in troubleshooting. Administrators are often reluctant to use the **debug** commands, because they can cause significant overhead on the router. You need to weigh that overhead against the help they can provide in tracking down problems. You certainly do not want to run **debug all**, because doing so will almost guarantee that the router becomes unusable. However, you can use **debug** commands specifically tailored to the problem at hand. For example, if you were troubleshooting a problem with OSPF, you might want to enable one of the OSPF debugging commands:

```
KAH_RTR#debug ip ospf events

OSPF events debugging is on

KAH_RTR#

1d22h: OSPF: Rcv hello from 192.168.1.1 area 0 from Serial0 192.168.1.1

1d22h: OSPF: End of hello processing

1d22h: OSPF: Rcv hello from 192.168.31.1 area 0 from Ethernet0 10.1.1.3

1d22h: OSPF: End of hello processing
```

From this output we can validate that the router is receiving OSPF Hellos from other routers in the OSPF environment. This is a simple example; there are many **debug** commands available to you in the router. The following command output shows many of the options for the debug command:

```
KAH_RTR#debug ?
  aaa                 AAA Authentication, Authorization and
                      Accounting
  access-expression   Boolean access expression
  all                 Enable all debugging
  apple               Appletalk information
  arap                Appletalk Remote Access
  arp                 IP ARP and HP Probe transactions
  async               Async interface information
  backup              Backup events
  callback            Callback activity
  cdp                 CDP information
  chat                Chat scripts activity
  compress            COMPRESS traffic
  condition           Condition
  confmodem           Modem configuration database
  cpp                 Cpp information
  custom-queue        Custom output queueing
  decnet              DECnet information
  dhcp                DHCP client activity
  dialer              Dial on Demand
  dnsix               Dnsix information
  domain              Domain Name System
  dxi                 atm-dxi information
  eigrp               EIGRP Protocol information
  entry               Incoming queue entries
  ethernet-interface  Ethernet network interface events
  frame-relay         Frame Relay
  interface           interface
```

ip	IP information
ipx	Novell/IPX information
lapb	LAPB protocol transactions
lex	LAN Extender protocol
list	Set interface or/and access list for the next debug command
llc2	LLC2 type II Information
modem	Modem control/process activation
mop	DECnet MOP server events
nhrp	NHRP protocol
ntp	NTP information
nvram	Debug NVRAM behavior
packet	Log unknown packets
pad	X25 PAD protocol
pcbus	PCbus interface information
ppp	PPP (Point to Point Protocol) information
printer	LPD printer protocol
priority	Priority output queueing
probe	HP Probe Proxy Requests
radius	RADIUS protocol
rif	RIF cache transactions
rtr	RTR Monitor Information
serial	Serial interface information
smf	Software MAC filter
smrp	SMRP information
snapshot	Snapshot activity
snmp	SNMP information
spantree	Spanning tree information
standby	Hot standby protocol
tacacs	TACACS authentication and authorization

tbridge	Transparent Bridging
telnet	Incoming telnet connections
tftp	TFTP debugging
token	Token Ring information
tunnel	Generic Tunnel Interface
v120	V120 information
vg-anylan	VG-AnyLAN interface information
vprofile	Virtual Profile information
vtemplate	Virtual Template information
x25	X.25, CMNS and XOT information
x28	X28 mode

Obviously, the type of debugging you will enable will depend on the problem you are trying to resolve. You are not going to turn debugging on for IPX SAP activity if you are dealing with an IP EIGRP problem.

> **NOTE** In order to see debug output from a Telnet session, you need to enter the command terminal monitor from user exec mode. This will copy all console messages to the Telnet session and can be a very useful command. To disable terminal monitoring, simply enter no terminal monitor.

With the default logging setting in a router, the output from your debug commands is copied not only to the console but also to the log. This is useful if you want to catch some debugging information that is going across the screen rather quickly. You can enable the type of debugging you want and let it write to the log for a minute of two. Then enter the no debug all command to stop all debugging. It is generally easier to stop all debugging than to try and get the right command through a screen full of debug information. Once the debug info you want is in the log, you can look through it at your leisure by using the show log command.

Protocol Analyzers

Protocol analyzers are another important part of troubleshooting a network. As you probably know, protocol analyzers look at the traffic passing by them on a network and record certain information about it. They can also perform packet captures and decodes. Many of the better ones will also allow you to resend captured traffic out onto the network or generate your own traffic. Some of the more common protocol analyzers are

Network General's Sniffer, Novell's lanalyzer, and Etherpeek. The are lots of different protocol analyzers out there. To define which one is the best would be an impossible task since they all have strengths and weaknesses. We generally use Network General's Sniffer Basic. This tool was also used to create the protocol analyzer screen captures in this chapter.

> **NOTE**   Software-based protocol analyzers generally need special NICs capable of operating in promiscuous mode. In this mode, errored packets that would normally be thrown away by the network adapter can be recorded and seen by the protocol analyzer. Because invalid packets on a network are generally thrown away before they are processed up the protocol stack, a software-based protocol analyzer will not see any error packets unless it is running with a NIC in promiscuous mode.

Protocol analyzers can give you an idea of the traffic breakdown for your network. Most of them categorize the traffic by protocol, as illustrated here:

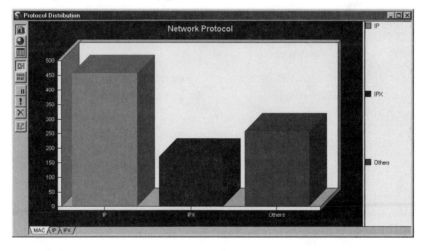

This type of information can be useful in determining what types of traffic are running on your network and in what quantities. Obviously the network illustrated is running mostly IP with some IPX. The "Other" classification is for things that don't fit into the protocols the analyzer knows about, such as BPDUs for bridging.

You can also get a view of how many packets are being sent through the network and the size of those packets.

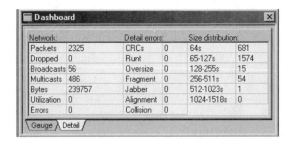

You can see that most of the traffic in this network is in small packets. Although small packets are inefficient, the utilization here is very low. What you are actually seeing is OSPF Hello and BPDU packets on a network that is really not doing anything at the moment.

Perhaps the most important function of a protocol analyzer is the packet decode, shown next. This is important because sometimes you will need to get down to the packet level to see exactly what is going on.

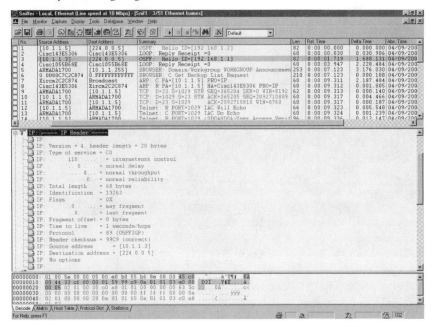

This graphic shows part of the protocol decode for an OSPF Hello packet. You can also see the start of a Telnet session including the ARP process to locate the Layer 2 address to use for the communication. Of course, for any of the information a protocol analyzer can provide to be useful, you need to understand how a network should function and what to look for. Fortunately, most protocol analyzers will let you filter traffic based on various criteria like source or destination address or network protocol.

NOTE In order to capture and report on all the traffic passing by, protocol analyzers need to be able to see that traffic. Plugging into a switch segments the collision domain and only allows traffic to and from the analyzer to be seen. To correct this, you need to set up a SPAN (switch port analyzer) or port monitor port on a port on the switch. Most switches, including all the newer Cisco switches, support this feature.

Troubleshooting Specific Elements of the Network

The following section will cover the methods used to troubleshoot the actual interfaces on the router. Determining why an interface is not functioning properly is a very important task. If the interface does not come up properly, there is no need to worry about any of the other functionality the router provides. Without properly functioning interfaces to send and receive data, a router is pretty useless.

Troubleshooting the Physical Layer

The physical layer is the easiest layer to troubleshoot, since you are only looking to see if the cabling is working properly. From a standpoint of what you are looking for it is pretty straightforward; you are not worried about anything really dynamic. Cable troubleshooting for routers is the same as for any other device. Most of us who have worked our way up into the router end of networking are intimately familiar with cable testers and have traced our fair share of cables. The more organized you keep your physical cable plant, the better off you will be in the long run. In a reasonable amount of time you should be able to figure out where each cable goes or be able to swap out that cable. You don't want your cable plant to look like the one shown on the next page.

To learn about how the interfaces are actually functioning, you can use the show interface (usually shortened to sh int) command. This can give you a lot of information about not only how the interface is performing but also how the network attached to the interface is performing.

```
KAH_RTR#sh int s0
Serial0 is up, line protocol is up
  Hardware is HD64570
  Internet address is 192.168.1.2/24
  MTU 1500 bytes, BW 1544 Kbit, DLY 20000 usec, rely 255/255, load 1/255
  Encapsulation HDLC, loopback not set, keepalive set (10 sec)
  Last input 00:00:02, output 00:00:00, output hang never
  Last clearing of "show interface" counters never
  Input queue: 0/75/0 (size/max/drops); Total output drops: 0
  Queueing strategy: weighted fair
  Output queue: 0/1000/64/0 (size/max total/threshold/drops)
    Conversations  0/1/256 (active/max active/max total)
    Reserved Conversations 0/0 (allocated/max allocated)
```

```
5 minute input rate 0 bits/sec, 0 packets/sec
5 minute output rate 0 bits/sec, 0 packets/sec
    6822 packets input, 408799 bytes, 0 no buffer
    Received 6822 broadcasts, 0 runts, 0 giants, 0 throttles
    0 input errors, 3 CRC, 0 frame, 0 overrun, 0 ignored, 0 abort
    6821 packets output, 411535 bytes, 0 underruns
    0 output errors, 0 collisions, 1 interface resets
    0 output buffer failures, 0 output buffers swapped out
    2 carrier transitions
    DCD=up  DSR=up  DTR=up  RTS=up  CTS=up
```

Particular attention should be paid to the error counters (highlighted above), as these will generally signal a Physical layer issue. Problems like CRC errors, framing errors, or overruns can usually be attributed to bad physical cabling. The sh int command can be used to display any type of interface on the router, and the type of output you get will depend on the specific interface type you are looking at.

Client Issues When Connecting to Switches

One problem we are seeing a lot lately occurs when hubs are replaced with switches. Although it is not strictly related to routing, it occurs often enough that it should be mentioned. Switch ports process through the blocking, listening, and learning states before they start forwarding traffic. This is done to allow Spanning Tree to learn about what is connected to the port to prevent network loops. However, this process takes about a minute to transition from blocking to forwarding. This can cause problems with NT and NetWare clients, which both send out important traffic in the first 60 seconds. The NetWare client, for example, sends out GNS request in this time frame. If it does not get a response, it gives up, and the login splash screen will not come up. The user can still log in but needs to do so manually. (Believe me, you don't want to try retraining all your end users to specify their full context.) The way to fix this is to modify how Spanning Tree operates on ports directly connected to end nodes. On these ports you will want to enable portfast, which lets the port go from blocking directly to forwarding. You can do that because you are assuring the switch that this port only connects to end stations. Since the port gets to the forwarding state much faster, that initial traffic gets through.

Optimization and Maintenance

PART 4

Client Issues When Connecting to Switches *(continued)*

The moral? If you replace a hub with a switch, don't assume it functions the same. Even though it looks similar and works with the same servers and the same general functions, it does things a little differently. Too many people assume that you can just take out a hub and put in a switch. That is when the problems start.

For example, an Ethernet interface will give you a different set of error counters than a serial interface:

```
KAH_RTR#sh int e0
Ethernet0 is up, line protocol is up
  Hardware is Lance, address is 00e0.1e3e.5306 (bia 00e0.1e3e.5306)
  Internet address is 10.1.1.5/24
  MTU 1500 bytes, BW 10000 Kbit, DLY 1000 usec, rely 255/255, load 1/255
  Encapsulation ARPA, loopback not set, keepalive set (10 sec)
  ARP type: ARPA, ARP Timeout 04:00:00
  Last input 00:00:00, output 00:00:00, output hang never
  Last clearing of "show interface" counters never
  Queueing strategy: fifo
  Output queue 0/40, 0 drops; input queue 1/75, 0 drops
  5 minute input rate 0 bits/sec, 0 packets/sec
  5 minute output rate 0 bits/sec, 0 packets/sec
     5255 packets input, 668184 bytes, 0 no buffer
     Received 4251 broadcasts, 0 runts, 0 giants, 0 throttles
     0 input errors, 0 CRC, 0 frame, 0 overrun, 0 ignored, 0 abort
     0 input packets with dribble condition detected
     7886 packets output, 738760 bytes, 0 underruns
     0 output errors, 41 collisions, 11 interface resets
     0 babbles, 0 late collision, 0 deferred
     0 lost carrier, 0 no carrier
     0 output buffer failures, 0 output buffers swapped out
```

Most of you are probably very familiar with the Ethernet error conditions, which are usually caused by cabling issues. One that is particularly hard to track down is the late collision. When a sending station has finished sending a packet but before that packet has fully traversed the wire, it collides with another station that is sending data. Because the sending station has stopped transmitting before the collision occurs, it has also stopped listening for a collision and assumes its packet got through. Although attenuation and other factors come into play, the risk of late collisions is what really defines maximum Ethernet cable lengths. To see how this works, take the two most distant points in a network and call them points A and B. If point A sends a minimum-size packet across the network, point B on the other side of the network must see the beginning of that packet before A stops sending. If not, then after A has finished sending a packet, B might start sending because it has not seen A's packet. When B starts sending, a collision occurs. So B sends a jam signal and backs off. However, A thinks its packet got through. This obviously causes problems. If `sh int` reports many late collisions, it generally means your cabling is out of spec.

Another useful command is `show controllers`. It can give you further insight into what is going on with the physical cabling, and it displays information about what is going on with the controller driving the interface, including information about memory management and errors seen by the interface controller:

```
KAH_RTR#sh controllers serial 0

HD unit 0, idb = 0xCC5C8, driver structure at 0xD1A50

buffer size 1524  HD unit 0, V.35 DTE cable

cpb = 0x61, eda = 0x4864, cda = 0x4878

RX ring with 16 entries at 0x614800

00 bd_ptr=0x4800 pak=0x0D3ED0 ds=0x61C460 status=80 pak_size=286

01 bd_ptr=0x4814 pak=0x0D32B8 ds=0x619BF8 status=80 pak_size=286

02 bd_ptr=0x4828 pak=0x0D36C0 ds=0x61A970 status=80 pak_size=286

03 bd_ptr=0x483C pak=0x0D34BC ds=0x61A2B4 status=80 pak_size=22

04 bd_ptr=0x4850 pak=0x0D2AA8 ds=0x618108 status=80 pak_size=22

05 bd_ptr=0x4864 pak=0x0D50F4 ds=0x6200FC status=80 pak_size=22

06 bd_ptr=0x4878 pak=0x0D3CCC ds=0x61BDA4 status=80 pak_size=0

07 bd_ptr=0x488C pak=0x0D30B4 ds=0x61953C status=80 pak_size=0

08 bd_ptr=0x48A0 pak=0x0D5700 ds=0x621530 status=80 pak_size=0

09 bd_ptr=0x48B4 pak=0x0D42D8 ds=0x61D1D8 status=80 pak_size=0

10 bd_ptr=0x48C8 pak=0x0D54FC ds=0x620E74 status=80 pak_size=0

11 bd_ptr=0x48DC pak=0x0D4EF0 ds=0x61FA40 status=80 pak_size=0
```

```
12 bd_ptr=0x48F0 pak=0x0D3AC8 ds=0x61B6E8 status=80 pak_size=0

13 bd_ptr=0x4904 pak=0x0D4CEC ds=0x61F384 status=80 pak_size=0

14 bd_ptr=0x4918 pak=0x0D52F8 ds=0x6207B8 status=80 pak_size=0

15 bd_ptr=0x492C pak=0x0D40D4 ds=0x61CB1C status=80 pak_size=0

16 bd_ptr=0x4940 pak=0x0D2CAC ds=0x6187C4 status=80 pak_size=0

cpb = 0x61, eda = 0x5014, cda = 0x5014

TX ring with 1 entries at 0x615000

00 bd_ptr=0x5000 pak=0x000000 ds=0x630F68 status=80 pak_size=22

01 bd_ptr=0x5014 pak=0x000000 ds=0x630F68 status=80 pak_size=22

0 missed datagrams, 0 overruns

0 bad datagram encapsulations, 0 memory errors

0 transmitter underruns

15 residual bit errors
```

Troubleshooting the Telecommunication Line

In a WAN environment, there are times when your telecommunication lines will go down
for unknown reasons. Most often these outages have nothing to do with the router but
are caused by something that has happened on the telecommunication carrier's side. You
can usually resolve a problem of this type by simply calling your carrier and asking them
to look at the line.

How do you determine that you have a problem with the telecommunication line? When
you run the show interface command on a serial interface, it can display several possible states for the interface.

Serial0 is up, line protocol is up   This indicates that the interface is functioning
properly. There is no overt problem with this line. There may still be errors on it,
but some data can get through.

Serial0 is up, line protocol is down   This indicates that the interface hardware is
up and is seeing a carrier detect signal (CD) from the CSU/DSU. However, the
software process that handles the line protocol considers the line unusable for
some reason. The first thing you should do upon seeing this state is put the CSU/
DSU in local loopback mode. If doing this causes the line protocol to come up
then the problem is with either the phone company or the remote router. If you
can put the remote CSU/DSU in remote loopback mode and the line comes up, it
is not a telecommunications problem. If it does not come up, then most likely you
have a problem on the line.

Serial0 is down, line protocol is down   Assuming a DTE interface, this generally indicates that the router is not seeing a carrier detect signal from the CSU/DSU. You should check the LEDs on the CSU/DSU and see if they are active. If the CSU/DSU also indicates a problem, such as loss of frame, contact the provider and have them look at the line.

NOTE   When the phone company is testing a line, they typically will ask you to authorize "intrusive testing." This allows them to take the line all the way down. Although it's a drastic step with an obvious potential business impact, if you have a problem this is often necessary to help them locate the problem. And of course, if the line is already down, it does not matter what they do to the line in the process of fixing it.

Serial0 is up, line protocol is up (looped)   This indicates that there is a loopback somewhere on the line. Check to make sure your CSU/DSU and interfaces are not looped; then call the provider and ask them to remove the loopback. Often you will see this on new circuits. The telecommunications provider will put the circuit into loopback to test it and either forget to take the loop out or deliberately leave it in so they don't get alarms because you have not yet connected anything to the circuit to bring it up.

Serial0 is up, line protocol is down (disabled)   This indicates that the router has disabled the port because it has received more than 5000 errors in a keep-alive interval. This will only occur on 7000 and AGS+ series routers.

Serial0 is administratively down, line protocol is down   This indicates that the interface is in the shutdown state. Configure the interface with the no shut command so the router will try to bring the interface up.

CSU/DSUs and Serial Lines

Channel service units/digital service units provide a wealth of information about your serial lines. These devices sit in front of the router and convert the data on the line into something the router can understand. Most CSU/DSUs have their own error counters to keep track of what is going on with the line. These are often more valuable than the router's counters because the CSU/DSU's sole job is to control the serial line. Also, since it is directly connected to the line, it has a firsthand view of what is going on with the line.

We often overlook the CSU/DSU when troubleshooting serial line problems and concentrate on the router. Generally this is a mistake; the CSU/DSU is a fairly simple device that can quickly give you an idea whether you need to call your telecommunications provider. The CSU/DSU's configuration typically does not change, so you don't have to worry

Optimization and
Maintenance

PART 4

about what has changed to cause the problem you are seeing. Also, the CSU/DSU does not do much dynamically—unlike the router, which is constantly building routing tables, buffering packets, and so on.

The CSU/DSU may tell you where to start looking for the problem. For example, the Paradyne Acculink 3160 can give a loss-of-signal (LOS) indicator and can specify where the LOS occurred, either at the DTE side or the network side. Remember that when you're dealing with a CSU/DSU, the network side is the telecommunications link and the router is the DTE device.

You can also get information about how the circuit is behaving. Most CSU/DSUs will report on the errors seen on the line. These are the most common error counters; depending on the type of CSU/DSU you are using, you may see others:

Errored Seconds (ES)   These are seconds that each contain one or more errors.

Unavailable Seconds (UAS)   These are seconds during which service was unavailable.

Severely Errored Seconds (SES)   These are seconds that each had 320 or more CRC errors or any second with an out-of-frame event (OOF).

Bursty Errored Seconds   These are seconds that each had more than one CRC error but less than 320. In terms of severity, this is the midpoint between an ES and a SES.

These types of error typically indicate something that is wrong with the line. A CSU/DSU will only report errors it is receiving and not detect errors it may be sending. Thus, if you see a lot of errored seconds on a CSU/DSU, the cause of those errors is most likely upstream from the CSU/DSU you are looking at. First you should look at the CSU/DSU on the other end of the line. If both CSU/DSUs are seeing errors, most likely they are being caused somewhere between the two devices.

CSU/DSUs also offer two loopback modes— local and remote—for testing certain portions of the circuit. Figure 17.3 illustrates both concepts.

Figure 17.3   CSU/DSUs allow both local and remote loopbacks.

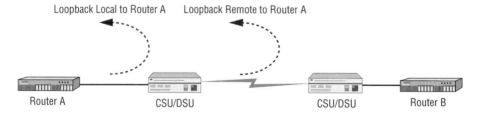

Local loopback will test the cabling from the router to the CSU/DSU. If the interface protocol does not come up when you create a local loop, there is a problem between the router and the CSU/DSU. Remote loopback will test everything up to the remote CSU/DSU. With this type of loopback, you are trying to determine where the problem is along the communication path. You may also need to run the same loopback tests from router B to see different test points.

Frame Relay

Frame Relay is a little more complex to troubleshoot than serial lines. Since leased lines are used to connect to the Frame Relay cloud, you can use the same type of loopback tests just described for normal serial lines. However, a Frame Relay network often has multiple links or PVCs terminating on one DLCI. This means that one physical serial interface may be subinterfaced to support multiple frame links. It becomes a little harder to troubleshoot the links because a single link may support more than one remote link. Figure 17.4 shows a common Frame Relay topology.

Figure 17.4   Typical Frame Relay topology

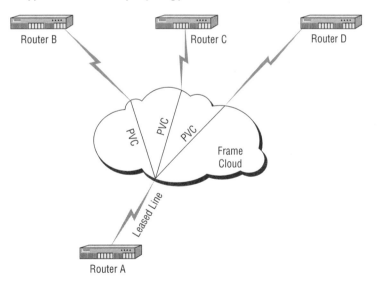

In this network, if you lose the leased line between router A and the frame cloud, you will lose all of the other routers. You would deal with this type of outage in the same way as with any other leased line outage, by contacting the provider. However, with Frame Relay there is one more element—the Frame Relay switch. The conventional "frame cloud" in networking diagrams represents a collection of frame relay switches. When you connect into a Frame Relay cloud, you also need to make sure you are interfacing with these switches properly.

A signaling protocol called Local Management Interface (LMI) is used to maintain this connection between the router and the Frame Relay switch. LMI is responsible for providing a keep-alive mechanism for the frame network, by providing a multicast service that in turn provides the DLCI information for the frame cloud, and by providing a mechanism to keep track of the status of the various DLCIs in the frame cloud.

When a router comes up on a Frame Relay network, it sends an LMI status inquiry message to its local Frame Relay switch, asking for the status of any remote routes. The switch responds with the status of all the remote routers it knows about and their DLCI information. Once the new router has this DLCI information, it sends out a RARP (Reverse ARP) packet to all of these remote routers. This RARP packet gives the remote routers the new router's addressing, which is contained in the packet header. The remote routers will then reply to the RARP packet. In doing so, they will give the new router their network layer addresses.

For each router that replies to the RARP packet, the router will create a map entry in its Frame Relay map table. This entry includes the remote router's network address and the DLCI locally configured on the router creating the table. It looks a lot like an ARP table entry; essentially, it maps a DLCI to a network address. This RARP process is carried out every 60 seconds to keep track of the state of each remote router. Every 10 seconds the Frame Relay switch and the router exchange LMI keep-alive messages to make sure the connection is still active.

There are different types of LMI:

- Cisco
- ANSI
- Q933a

The Frame Relay switch and the router must be configured to use the same type of LMI, or the connection will not work. Your Frame Relay provider should be able to tell you the type of LMI used by the frame switch. However, in Cisco IOS versions 11.2 and higher, the router will autosense the LMI type, so you don't really have to worry about it.

There are a few commands that help with Frame Relay troubleshooting. For example, here's the output from `show frame-relay lmi`:

```
FRAME_RTR#show frame-relay lmi
```

```
LMI Statistics for interface Serial1/0 (Frame Relay DTE) LMI TYPE =
ANSI
    Invalid Unnumbered info 0        Invalid Prot Disc 0

    Invalid dummy Call Ref 0         Invalid Msg Type 0

    Invalid Status Message 0         Invalid Lock Shift 0

    Invalid Information ID 0          Invalid Report IE Len 0

    Invalid Report Request 0         Invalid Keep IE Len 0

    Num Status Enq. Sent 17365       Num Status msgs Rcvd 17365

    Num Update Status Rcvd 0         Num Status Timeouts 0


LMI Statistics for interface Serial1/1 (Frame Relay DTE) LMI TYPE =
CISCO
    Invalid Unnumbered info 0        Invalid Prot Disc 0

    Invalid dummy Call Ref 0         Invalid Msg Type 0

    Invalid Status Message 0         Invalid Lock Shift 0

    Invalid Information ID 0          Invalid Report IE Len 0

    Invalid Report Request 0         Invalid Keep IE Len 0

    Num Status Enq. Sent 17362       Num Status msgs Rcvd 17363

    Num Update Status Rcvd 4         Num Status Timeouts 0
ARMSMAIN_RTR#
```

This will show you what is going on with the LMI between the frame switch and the router. Along with other information, you can see the number of Status timeouts, which will tell you how often the router failed to receive a keepalive message from the switch within the given keepalive interval. To see the information contained in the LMI packet, you need to use a protocol analyzer. Generally, though, the information displayed by this command is enough to determine whether the router is receiving LMI for the frame switch.

The show frame-relay map command is used to troubleshoot the mapping of DLCI to Layer 3 addressing in the same way we use the show ARP command.

```
FRAME_RTR#sh frame-relay map

Serial1/0.1 (up): point-to-point dlci, dlci 100(0x64,0x1840),
broadcast, IETF

        status defined, active
```

Optimization and Maintenance

PART 4

```
Serial1/1.51 (down): point-to-point dlci, dlci 991(0x3DF,0xF4F0),
broadcast, IETF
        status deleted
Serial1/1.1 (up): point-to-point dlci, dlci 955(0x3BB,0xECB0),
broadcast, BW = 1
6000
        status defined, active
Serial1/1.4 (up): point-to-point dlci, dlci 985(0x3D9,0xF490),
broadcast, BW = 3
2000
        status defined, active
Serial1/1.6 (up): point-to-point dlci, dlci 997(0x3E5,0xF850),
broadcast, BW = 1
6000
        status defined, active
Serial1/1.12 (up): point-to-point dlci, dlci 980(0x3D4,0xF440),
broadcast, BW =
16000
        status defined, active
Serial1/1.10 (up): point-to-point dlci, dlci 975(0x3CF,0xF0F0),
broadcast, BW =
16000
        status defined, active
Serial1/1.3 (up): point-to-point dlci, dlci 995(0x3E3,0xF830),
broadcast, BW = 1
6000
        status defined, active
```

The show frame-relay pvc command provides status information for all the DLCIs the router has learned about from the frame switch. This command shows the current state of a DLCI (active, inactive or deleted), when the PVC was created, and when its status last changed. Information about the traffic through the PVC is also displayed.

```
FRAME_RTR#sh frame-relay pvc
```

PVC Statistics for interface Serial1/0 (Frame Relay DTE)

DLCI = 100, DLCI USAGE = LOCAL, PVC STATUS = ACTIVE, INTERFACE =
Serial1/0.1

    input pkts 467960   output pkts 526863   in bytes 43948026

    out bytes 41161429   dropped pkts 0   in FECN pkts 0

    in BECN pkts 0   out FECN pkts 0   out BECN pkts 0

    in DE pkts 55606   out DE pkts 0

    out bcast pkts 2900   out bcast bytes 1127392

    pvc create time 2d00h, last time pvc status changed 2d00h

PVC Statistics for interface Serial1/1 (Frame Relay DTE)

DLCI = 910, DLCI USAGE = LOCAL, PVC STATUS = INACTIVE, INTERFACE =
Serial1/1.50

    input pkts 0   output pkts 32   in bytes 0

    out bytes 9427   dropped pkts 0   in FECN pkts 0

    in BECN pkts 0   out FECN pkts 0   out BECN pkts 0

    in DE pkts 0   out DE pkts 0

    out bcast pkts 30   out bcast bytes 9345

    pvc create time 2d00h, last time pvc status changed 2d00h

DLCI = 920, DLCI USAGE = LOCAL, PVC STATUS = ACTIVE, INTERFACE =
Serial1/1.2

    input pkts 827760   output pkts 962529   in bytes 68660790

    out bytes 75729664   dropped pkts 0   in FECN pkts 0

    in BECN pkts 0   out FECN pkts 0   out BECN pkts 0

    in DE pkts 0   out DE pkts 0

Optimization and Maintenance

PART 4

```
       out bcast pkts 5830        out bcast bytes 1345368
       pvc create time 2d00h, last time pvc status changed 2d00h


DLCI = 921, DLCI USAGE = UNUSED, PVC STATUS = ACTIVE, INTERFACE =
Serial1/1

       input pkts 0            output pkts 0          in bytes 0
       out bytes 0            dropped pkts 0          in FECN pkts 0
       in BECN pkts 0          out FECN pkts 0         out BECN pkts 0
       in DE pkts 0            out DE pkts 0
       out bcast pkts 0        out bcast bytes 0
       Num Pkts Switched 0


       pvc create time 2d00h, last time pvc status changed 2d00h


DLCI = 940, DLCI USAGE = LOCAL, PVC STATUS = ACTIVE, INTERFACE =
Serial1/1.11

       input pkts 2097990     output pkts 2116206     in bytes
       182923353
       out bytes 165579602    dropped pkts 0          in FECN pkts 0
       in BECN pkts 0          out FECN pkts 0          out BECN pkts 0
       in DE pkts 0           out DE pkts 0
       out bcast pkts 17579    out bcast bytes 6027040
       pvc create time 2d00h, last time pvc status changed 2d00h
```

Troubleshooting an IPX Problem

In the network illustrated below, everything runs fine for the first month or so. Then a problem starts cropping up: Client X starts taking an excessively long time to log into the Novell NDS tree. For some reason you cannot Rconsole into server X from client B, but if you initiate a remote control session to client X, you can Rconsole to server X. The act of creating the remote control session to client X confirms that the communication path is good. We know that IP connectivity is functioning properly, since we are using an IP remote control product.

From router X you can IP ping server X and you can IPX ping both its internal and network addresses. From router A you can IP ping server X and you can IPX ping its internal network number but not its real IPX network address. (Remember, you have to specify to use Novell IPX echoes, and we've done that.)

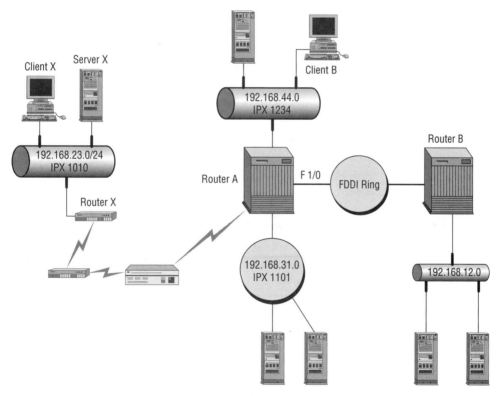

Now we have determined that because router A cannot IPX ping server X, we probably have an IPX issue. From server X we try to IPX ping one of the Novell servers in the core environment, which are providing a catalog service for login. This fails, so now we know why server X cannot talk to other Novell servers via IPX, and this is causing the login problem client X is experiencing. This, however, is only a symptom of the problem. Next we check the IPX SAP table in the router to see if the router knows about the other NetWare servers in the environment. We do this using the show IPX servers command, which reports that they are all there.

Since this seems to be an IPX problem, we should start looking at the IPX routing tables. The table on router X seems OK, but when we look at router A's IPX routing table, IPX network 1010 claims to be located off a FDDI port and is two hops away. This does not make sense. What we need now is to run a traceroute and check the path to IPX network 1010. Unfortunately, router A's IOS version does not support IPX traceroute. So instead we look at the IPX routing table for router A and realize that IPX network 1010 is located off port FDDI 1/0. Since FDDI 1/0 connects to router B, we Telnet to router B and check out the IPX routing table. The IPX routing table on router B, it reports that network 1010 is directly connected to Ethernet 1/4. Checking the router configuration, we see that Ethernet 1/4 is configured with IPX network 1010.

Now we know what has happened. Someone added a new network segment and mistakenly gave it an IPX network number that was already in use. Since IPX RIP was the routing protocol, all of the core routers used this new segment as the route to 1010 because it is closer. However, router X still had IPX network 1010. But all traffic from the Client X segment was getting into the core but its reply traffic was going back to the new IPX network 1010 because all the core routes identify this as a preferential route.

Once this was figured out, simply changing the IPX network on the new segment of router B fixed the problem. Remember, it is important to keep track of the addresses you are using. Unfortunately the individual who made the change had made it just before leaving the night before, and then took the next day off. So when the problem began to manifest itself the next day, we did not know there had been a change to the network. Had we known, that change would have been the first place we started to look, and the problem most likely would have been resolved sooner.

Broadcast Storm Troubleshooting

In the network shown below, we need to support LAT traffic to the mainframe, so all the router interfaces are in bridge group 1. Bridge group 1 is running the DEC Spanning Tree protocol to prevent bridging loops. This creates one big bridged domain. Every protocol that is not routed or has no network layer addressing will be bridged. Not the best of circumstances, but it does addresses the issue of LAT connectivity to the mainframe.

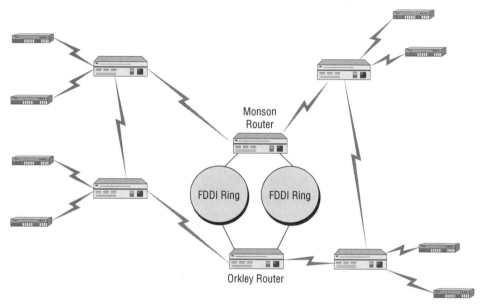

A problem started to occur on a Friday morning. The serial interfaces on the Orkley and Monson routers started to bounce up and down. The first step was to check the CSU/DSUs to see if they were losing the links. They were not; the CSU/DSUs were reporting no errors. Looking at the router, we saw that the CPU utilization was way above normal. Using the show process cpu command, we were able to see that the bridge processes were consuming a large portion of the CPU time. We took note of that, but set it aside for a while. We then began to look more closely at one of the serial links that was bouncing. We picked the one that connected to the office with the least number of users so the impact of our troubleshooting would be minimal. We pulled one of the links off the main router and connected it to a spare router to see if the link would still go up and down. It did not, so we knew that the equipment from the CSU/DSU out was good.

At this point we started to look for similarities between the lines that were having problems. There were not really any. Some were microwave links and some were T1 links from two different carriers.

Since the links were going up and down, and this creates a lot of routing protocol recalculation, we decided to break the redundant links to try to reduce the router CPU utilization. This helped a little; however, we left the redundant FDDI link in the core up. At this point we started looking at the bridge Spanning Tree to see if there was a loop. In a bridged network with redundant links, Spanning Tree should allow only one link to be in the forwarding state; all the other redundant paths should be in the blocking state. The network should look something like this if Spanning Tree is working properly:

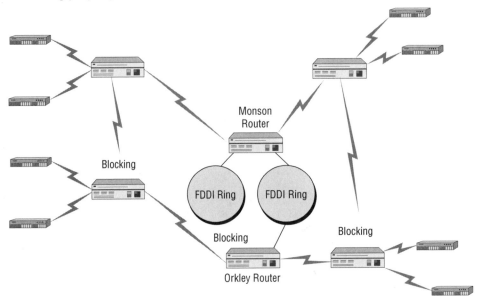

We carefully went through the network, looking at each router with the show spanning-tree command. We looked at the port states and whom the router thought was the designated root bridge. This showed that one of the loops was not being properly broken by Spanning Tree. This was causing a broadcast storm, which was building on itself and starting to destroy the network.

To get this under control quickly, we removed bridging from all the routers. This broke LAT connectivity but allowed other protocols to use the network again. Then we slowly started to reenable bridging in selected areas, making sure we did not create any redundant paths. After the network was fully up and running with no redundant paths, we left it alone since it was up and running. On Saturday we came in and worked to determine the cause of the problem. We reenabled the redundant bridge links one at a time and looked to make sure the Spanning Tree was recalculated properly. In the course of doing this, we were able to determine that if bridging was enabled on a certain link, a broadcast storm would result. Further effort was concentrated on that local segment, and we found that one of the switches on that segment was sending out bad BPDU information and was causing the problems we were seeing. This device was replaced and the network was back to normal.

18

Disaster Recovery

In today's world of computer dependence, everybody needs a network infrastructure that is highly available, scalable, and most important, *dependable*. As data networks become more and more prevalent in our lives, naturally our expectations of them rise as well. The telephone, for example, is probably the most common "luxury" in use today. Everybody has one. It is considered unusual if you do not.

When we pick up the phone, we not only expect it to work, we expect to have every possible function available. If something does not work, we immediately get upset and start looking for someone to be at fault, be it the phone manufacturer and/or the service provider. People are beginning to have the same expectations of their data networks.

Users expect the network to always be available. For example, they want to get their e-mail all of the time. Nobody in tech support gets a call to say, "Hey, guess what, I received all of my e-mail today. Thank you." It just does not happen. But if somebody can't get connected, you can bet they will get on the phone and it will not be to say "Thanks." This chapter will help you think through the issues that may keep your network up, or at least keep the downtime to a minimum.

Planning for the Worst

If anything can go wrong, it will. Sound familiar? Sure it does, and data networks are no exception to Murphy's Law. This is why we must prepare for the absolute worst-case scenario. You may also have heard that "an ounce of prevention is worth a pound of cure."

This means that the planning stage is the most important stage of disaster prevention. A well-designed network should have disaster prevention in mind as well as disaster recovery so that an outage may only be a mere inconvenience rather than a complete disaster.

Disaster recovery plans range from the very minimal plan to the very elaborate plan for catastrophic events.

A minimal plan may be appropriate for a small network that has only a single WAN link. Perhaps an ISDN DDR line would help keep the network operational during a main link failure. A more elaborate plan may entail outsourcing a network operation center in different parts of the country in case the building is somehow damaged or destroyed by weather or some other disaster.

The biggest issue with the entire disaster prevention/recovery plan is money. We all want the network to be up all of the time. Many IT managers will require a 99.97 percent availability but will not be willing to budget for it. Where is the dollar value and return on investment dollars for having a second circuit installed that you may never need? Where is the cost justification for putting in the minimal redundant power supply to the ultimate second router? These are valid questions that are very difficult to answer. In April 1998, *CIO Magazine* ran a story about the cost analysis of system downtime in several different industries. The average financial impact per hour of interrupted computer operations findings looked like this:

Retail brokerage firms	$6.45 million
Credit card sales authorization	$2.6 million
Catalog sales centers	$90,000
Airline reservations	$85,500

These numbers may be a little higher than what you would expect and may not reflect your business; but you must ask yourself the following questions: Would I be able to do business without the network? If so, for how long? If not, how much revenue am I giving up while the network is down? Per day? Per hour? Per minute? Once you have estimates of these numbers, you should be on your way to figuring out what kind of budget for redundancy and disaster recovery you need. Obviously, if your network will cost you $2.6 million if it is down for an hour, spending $1 million doesn't seem like a very high price to pay for redundancy and guaranteed uptime.

Redundancy in Hardware

Hardware redundancy is the backbone of disaster planning. Hardware has a finite life span and will eventually fail—especially any piece of hardware with moving parts, such as power supplies. Here are some options offered by a few of the Cisco product lines to consider when designing your network. Although only a few are mentioned here, there are hundreds of redundancy and backup options. Many of these options for Cisco products can be found on the Web site, www.cisco.com. There have also been many articles on hardware, circuit, and other types of redundancy in the common trade publications.

Power Supplies

Most of the medium- to high-end Cisco routers will offer some level of redundancy in power. For example, the 4000 series offers an RPS (Redundant Power Supply) option. Some of the higher-end models will support Hot Swappable Redundant Power Supplies. This is a great feature because any of the power supplies can be pulled out and be replaced without interruption to the router.

7000 Series Redundancy

The Cisco 7000 supports redundancy in power supplies, power access, and OIR (Online Insertion and Removal) of system components. The 7507 and 7513 models also provide a dual RSP (Route Switch Processor) architecture, which is supported by HSA (High System Availability) software.

In the first phase of HSA, the primary RSP is able to utilize the packet memory of the secondary RSP during normal operation, and the secondary RSP will monitor the performance of the primary RSP. Upon detection of a failure condition, the secondary RSP will automatically take over control and initiate a soft boot of the system without user intervention, thus minimizing network interruption.

A Cisco 7500 series with dual RSP cards can give the user the ability to double the packet memory size and increase the overall aggregate switching decision performance. By default, each RSP will ship with 2MB of packet memory. Users will be able to take advantage of the additional 2MB of memory on the slave RSP for a system total of 4MB of packet memory. You can also use the switching engine of the second or slave RSP to increase performance by allowing load sharing.

12000 Series Redundant Gigabit Route Processor

On the very high end, you can imagine that the system availability requirement is extremely important and thus, so are the redundancy features. For example, in the 12000 series router, the GRP (Gigabit Route Processor) redundant processor feature allows you to install two gigabit route processors. One GRP functions as the *primary processor* and will support all normal GRP operations.

The other GRP will function as the *secondary processor*. The secondary GRP will be in a passive state and will only monitor the primary GRP. In the event the primary fails, the secondary GRP will take over normal GRP operations.

The GRP redundant processor feature is not a hot standby system. Thus, the secondary GRP does not duplicate the state of the primary GRP. This non-mirroring feature is designed to prevent a software failure from affecting both processors. The tradeoff is that network services will be temporarily disrupted while the secondary GRP takes over. This recovery time for the secondary GRP is much faster than the cold boot time for the entire router.

Backing Up the Router Image and Configuration

It is very important with any system, be it a file server or a router, to keep things backed up as part of your disaster preparedness. With Cisco routers, there are a few different ways to go about getting a good backup. You must remember not only to back up the configuration file but also to get a good backup of the often-overlooked IOS image. Restoring the router will be covered in the next section.

Backing Up the Router Image

When you buy a Cisco router, you will most likely purchase a software image as well. This software image contains the router's Internetwork Operating System (IOS). It should be loaded on the router at the factory, and all you should need to do when you receive the new router is plug it in. However, in the event of a router failure, it is important to have made backup files for each image that is implemented on the network. When you replace a router, you will want to make sure that the same image is put back into production on the replacement router that was on the old router. This being said, keeping a log containing the names and version numbers of all of the software images on each router should be standard practice.

WARNING   Recovery from a system failure is not the time to be performing system upgrades. Get things back up and working with what is proven first.

The most popular way to back up an image file from a router is to use a TFTP server. Before performing the backup, you must gather the information necessary to perform the copy. First, you will need the host name or the IP address of the TFTP server. If you do not have a TFTP server, the basic server software is easily acquired from the Internet as shareware. Second, a show version command on the router you wish to back up will return the filename of the image you want to copy.

```
800Router#sho ver

Cisco Internetwork Operating System Software

IOS (tm) C800 Software (C800-G3-MW), Version 12.0(1)XB1, RELEASE
SOFTWARE (fc1)


TAC:Home:SW:IOS:Specials for info

Copyright (c) 1986-1998 by cisco Systems, Inc.

Compiled Wed 30-Dec-98 13:34 by ayeh

Image text-base: 0x000E9000, data-base: 0x004F5000


ROM: TinyROM version 1.0(2)

800Router uptime is 13 hours, 12 minutes

System restarted by power-on

System image file is "flash:c800-g3-mw.120-1.XB1"


Cisco C804 (MPC850) processor (revision 0) with 47356K bytes of
virtual memory.

Processor board ID JAD03142341

CPU part number 33

Bridging software.

Basic Rate ISDN software, Version 1.1.

1 Ethernet/IEEE 802.3 interface(s)

1 ISDN Basic Rate interface(s)

8M bytes of physical memory (DRAM)

8K bytes of non-volatile configuration memory

8M bytes of flash on board (4M from flash card)


Configuration register is 0x2102
```

Optimization and
Maintenance

PART 4

Once you have this information, you are ready to copy the flash memory to the TFTP server and follow the prompts:

```
800Router#copy flash tftp

Source filename []? c800-g3-mw.120-1.XB1

Address or name of remote host []? 10.0.0.7

Destination filename [c800-g3-mw.120-1.XB1]?

!!!!!!!!!!!!!!!!!!!!!!!!!!!!!!!!!!!!!!!!!!!!!!!!!!!!!!!!!!!!!!!!!!!!!!
!!!!!!!!!!!!!!!!!!!!!!!!!!!!!!!!!!!!!!!!!!!!!!!!!!!!!!!!!!!!!!!!!!!!!!
!!!!!!!!!!!!!!!!!!!!!!!!!!!!!!!!!!!!!!!!!!!!!!!!!!!!!!!!!!!!!!!!!!!!!!
!!!!!!!!!!!!!!!!!!!!!!!!!!!!!!!!!!!!!!!!!!!!!!!!!!!!!!!!!!!!!!!!!!!!!!
!!!!!!!!!!!!!!!!!!!!!!!!!!!!!!!!!!!!!!!!!!!!!!!!!!!!!!!!!!!!!!!!!!!!!!
!!!!!!!!!!!!!!!!!!!!!!!!!!!!!!!!!!!!!!!!!!!!!!!!!!!!!!!!!!!!!!!!!!!!!!
!!!!!!!!!!!!!!!!!!!!!!!!!!!!!!!!!!!!!!!!!!!

2314996 bytes copied in 24.616 secs (96458 bytes/sec)
```

Notice that we entered the copy flash tftp command, after which a series of prompts lead us through the process. First, we were prompted for the filename c800-g3-mw.120-1.XB1, which we retrieved from the show version command.

TIP   Cutting and pasting the image filename will prevent costly typing mistakes.

Next, we needed to enter the IP address or the hostname of the TFTP server. In this case, we just entered the IP address. The destination filename prompt will default to the same filename that we entered for the source. In this example, we used this filename as the default. In your environment, you may wish to be more specific and also indicate a router location or other information with the filename. Once you hit the Enter key, away the copy goes. Just as with ping results, an exclamation point indicates a successful transfer of data. When the copy process is complete, the vital statistics are shown, including total bytes copied and the amount of elapsed time as well as an average bytes per second.

Backing Up the Router Configuration

It is very important to keep good backups of your router configurations in the event that someone accidentally saves changes that were not intended to be saved, or if you lose your router memory or lose the entire router.

Cut and Paste

One way to back up your router is with the simple cut and paste method. From either a Telnet session or a direct console session, you can issue the show run or show startup command to display the entire configuration for your router. You will probably need to use the spacebar to scroll to the end of the configuration. You will know you are at the end of the configuration because you will be returned to the command prompt. Take your mouse and left-click the bottom of the configuration and drag it up to just below the show run command you just issued.

Next, you need to copy this data to the Clipboard. From Microsoft HyperTerminal there are a few different ways to copy the text you have marked to the Clipboard:

- Right-click and select Copy.
- Select Edit from the toolbar and then Copy from the menu.
- Press Ctrl+C.

Your only option from a Microsoft Telnet session is to choose Edit and then Copy. Once you have copied the information onto the Clipboard, you may paste it into your word processor of choice. Many prefer Notepad because it is simple and defaults to plain text, although it has a limited capacity. Some of the larger configurations will require Wordpad at a minimum because of their sheer size. Whichever word processor you choose, select the Paste option and save the file as text. This will successfully make an adequate backup of your router configuration files.

Figure 18.1 shows an example of a HyperTerminal session with router text ready to be selected and copied.

Figure 18.1   A Microsoft HyperTerminal session

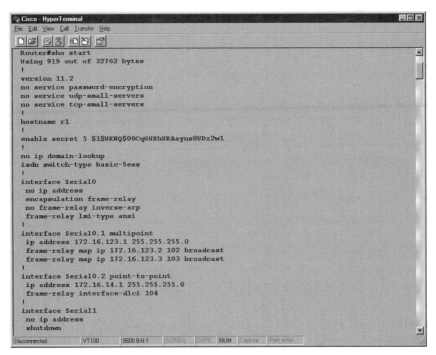

Using a TFTP Server for Configuration Backup

It may be more beneficial to utilize a TFTP server for backing up your configurations. If you have Telnet access to all of your routers, you could effectively sit in one chair and backup all of them. The process is very similar to copying the image file. You will need the hostname or the IP address of your TFTP server before you begin.

```
800Router#copy run tftp

Address or name of remote host []? 10.0.0.7

Destination filename [running-config]?

!!

1423 bytes copied in 2.348 secs (711 bytes/sec)
```

A simple `copy run tftp` command will start the process. You are then prompted for the TFTP server IP address. The default destination filename is `running-config`. This is undoubtedly a little vague if you have more than one router, and you will probably want to change it to a schema that fits your environment. It is always a good idea to be as descriptive as possible. You can rely on the date stamp of the software to give you the "when" portion. You may want to include the router name and location. For example:

```
Cisco804MainStOfficeCfg.txt
```

The configuration file size is much shorter than the image file size, so the whole process only took 2.348 seconds.

Swapping Out a Router

Physically swapping out a router should be just a matter of "out with the old and in with the new." Most smaller installations will have the extra rack space to accommodate both at the same time. If not, a little extra time should be allowed for the full replacement process of taking the old router out and mounting the new one. You may want to consider mounting all of the physical aspects in place before you begin, such as router rack ears and perhaps getting cables where they go.

It is very important to note the model number and serial number from the new router for your records in case you need to contact the TAC (Technical Assistance Center), which is covered later in this chapter.

Replacing the Router Image

The first thing to do is to replace the image on the "new" router with image that you have backed up from the "old" router. As mentioned, a system outage is no time to be upgrading software. A new IOS version may introduce unknown bugs into a system that you may not be familiar with, causing you a longer outage than necessary. The assumption is that you are replacing like hardware with like hardware.

The most popular way to replace the image is with the TFTP server. Image replacement can also be done over the console cable, but the images are typically large and the console connection is very slow and not really designed to pass large amounts of data. The first step is to power up the new router and give it an IP address. Next, you will want to investigate the size of the memory in the router to see if it will hold the new image without erasing the old one first, which is the method of choice. If not, you will should consider backing up this image, just in case. A ping test from the new router to the TFTP server is a good test of connectivity before you proceed with the file copy.

```
800Router#copy tftp flash

Address or name of remote host []? 10.0.0.7

Source filename []? c800-g3-mw.120-1.XB1

Destination filename [c800-g3-mw.120-1.XB1]?

Accessing tftp://10.0.0.7/c800-g3-mw.120-1.XB1...

Loading c800-g3-mw.120-1.XB1 from 10.0.0.7 (via Ethernet0):
!!!!!!!!!!!!!!!!!!!!!!!!!!!!!!!!!!!!!!!!!!!!!!!!!!!!!!!!!!!!!!!!!!!!!!!
!!!!!!!!!!!!!!!!!!!!!!!!!!!!!!!!!!!!!!!!!!!!!!!!!!!!!!!!!!!!!!!!!!!!!!!
!!!!!!!!!!!!!!!!!!!!!!!!!!!!!!!!!!!!!!!!!!!!!!!!!!!!!!!!!!!!!!!!!!!!!!!
!!!!!!!!!!!!!!!!!!!!!!!!!!!!!!!!!!!!!!!!!!!!!!!!!!!!!!!!!!!!!!!!!!!!!!!
!!!!!!!!!!!!!!!!!!!!!!!!!!!!!!!!!!!!!!!!!!!!!!!!!!!!!!!!!!!!!!!!!!!!!!!
!!!!!!!!!!!!!!!!!!!!!!!!!!!!!!!!!!!!!!!!!!!!!!!!!!!!!!!!!!!!!!!!!!!!!!!
!!!!!!!!!!!!!!!!!!!!!!!!!!!!!!!!!!!!!!!!!!!!!!!!!!!

2314996 bytes copied in 24.459 secs (96423 bytes/sec)
```

In much the same way as the image file went out to the TFTP server, so it comes back into the router. We enter the commands and follow the prompts for the TFTP server name and source filename. The default destination filename will be the same as the source just as before. The exclamation points indicate the successful transfer of data, and upon completion we are given the vital statistics: bytes copied, number of seconds, and the average bytes per second.

Catastrophic Software Failure

You may have only a software failure, without damage to your hardware. If both the boot and system images have been erased and/or damaged and only the ROM monitor is available, you can use the ROM monitor command xmodem to copy a Cisco IOS image to flash memory from the console. The console connection can be made through the console port, or can be made remotely through an external modem connected to the auxiliary port.

Optimization and Maintenance

PART 4

> **NOTE** Copying a Cisco IOS image from the console is a very slow process. This procedure should be used only in an emergency and is not recommended for normal Cisco IOS image upgrades.

Console Requirements

The console must have at minimum a terminal emulation program supporting one of the following file transfer protocols: Xmodem, Xmodem-CRC, Xmodem-1K, Ymodem, and a Cisco IOS image file.

Copying the Image from the Console

First, you want to make sure your console connection is in place in either the aux or the console port of the router. Next, you want to power-on the router. If your console connection is successful, you should begin to see the display results of the power-on self-test diagnostics. This initial test is run and the boot ROM searches for a valid boot image and Cisco IOS image in flash memory. If the boot image and Cisco IOS image are not found, the boot ROM monitor prompt is displayed:

```
rommon 1>
```

Next, you will enter the xmodem command and the name of the source file containing the Cisco IOS image:

```
rommon 1> xmodem filename
```

Additional xmodem Command Options

In addition to the *filename* optional keyword, specifying the source file containing the Cisco IOS image, you can use any of the following command options:

-c   Use cyclic redundancy check (CRC-16).

-y   Use Ymodem transfer protocol.

-r   Copy image to DRAM for launch.

-x   Do not launch image on completion of download.

When you enter the command, the system will search for the source file. Once it finds that file, the following message should appear:

```
Do not start upload program yet...
File size Checksum File name
2537948 bytes (0x26b9dc) 3620-boot-1


WARN: This operation will ERASE bootflash. If the xmodem
download to bootflash fails, you will lose any good image
you may already have in bootflash.
Invoke this application only for disaster recovery.


Do you wish to continue? [yes/no]:
```

A response of *Yes* will initiate the copy of the Cisco IOS image into flash memory. Messages similar to the following should appear:

```
Ready to receive file prog
Erasing flash at 0x3000000
program flash location 0x3000000
Transfer complete!
```

Replacing Router Configuration

There are a few different options for recovering a router configuration. Which one you use will depend on the severity of the failure.

Copy and Paste

As mentioned earlier, the router configuration files are simple plain text files and are very easy to manipulate. Open your router configuration file with your text editor of choice. Select the entire configuration and cut it to the Clipboard. Once in the Clipboard, you are ready to switch to either your console session or your Telnet session and paste the configuration. This seems simple enough, but there are a few "gotchas" you will want to be familiar with.

Configuration Mode   You need to sign on to your router, enter enable mode, and get to the configuration terminal prompt before you paste your configuration.

```
User Access Verification

Password:
800Router>en
Password:
800Router#conf t
Enter configuration commands, one per line. End with CNTL/Z.
800Router(config)#
```

Adjust Your HyperTerminal   The default setting for HyperTerminal will cause the text file to be pasted so fast that some of the longer lines may not be fully executed in the router and it is impossible to monitor the commands as they are printed across the screen. To adjust this, select File and then Properties from the main screen. This will display a dialog box with Phone Number and Settings tabs across the top. Select the Settings tab, as illustrated in Figure 18.2.

Figure 18.2   Hyperterminal Properties

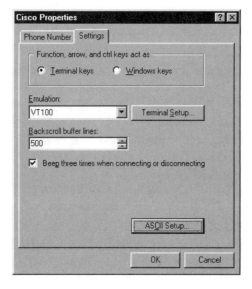

Under the ASCII Setup button you will find the options for Line Delay and Character Delay. A good rule of thumb is 500 and 10, respectively, as illustrated in Figure 18.3.

Keep in mind that these settings will hold true for all of your sessions. Some prefer to come back and return these to the default when the pasting process is complete.

Figure 18.3   Hyperterminal ASCII Setup

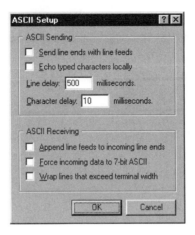

Potential Interface Problems   By default, all of the interfaces on the router are in an administratively shut down state. The most obvious problem with the cut-and-paste method is that when the configurations are complete, your interfaces will still be down and you will have to go in after the fact and perform a no shut to enable them.

The less obvious problem is that with several of the IOS versions, some of the routing protocols, such as OSPF, require at least one interface to be enabled for their configurations to be allowed. For example, if you just pasted the configuration into the router without enabling an interface, all of your configuration would be pasted but the OSPF would not "stick" to the router configuration and would require manual re-entry.

A show run command would confirm that none of the OSPF configuration data is there except the process ID number. The solution for this problem is to enable each of the interfaces that will be used *before* you paste the configuration.

WARNING   Perform a no shut on all of the used interfaces *before* you paste a configuration.

Once these setting are complete, you are ready to begin the paste process. You should be able to watch each of the lines as they go in and see that each command is taken by the router and that no error messages are returned.

Optimization and
Maintenance

PART 4

Using TFTP

If you have a TFTP server up with your configurations on it, it may be easier to pull larger configurations from this central location. Of course, you will need to put a very basic configuration on the router first. At minimum, you will need an IP address and mask for the segment that your TFTP server is on, as well as a no shut on that interface.

We see many similarities between pulling the configuration down to the router and putting the configuration up to the TFTP server. In this example, we use the copy tftp run command and follow the prompts for the remote host which will be the IP address or host name of the TFTP server and the source filename. Notice that because we specified in the initial command the destination of Run, the default destination filename is running-config.

```
800Router#copy tftp run

Address or name of remote host []? 10.0.0.7

Source filename []? Cisco804MainStOfficeCfg.txt

Destination filename [running-config]?

Accessing tftp://10.0.0.7/Cisco804MainStOfficeCfg.txt...

Loading Cisco804MainStOfficeCfg.txt from 10.0.0.7 (via Ethernet0): !!
[OK - 1423/2048 bytes]


1423 bytes copied in 2.848 secs (711 bytes/sec)
```

The output of the process will again show us exclamation marks for the successful pass of data as well as the data transfer amount and the time and bytes-per-sec statistics.

In large environments, routers are often configured in one location and shipped to another. In this case, you may want to copy the configuration to the startup-config rather than the running configuration. Doing so will allow you to keep your running configuration intact, and you will not lose your connection to your local network until that startup-config is placed into running-config or until the router is rebooted.

```
800Router#copy tftp start

Address or name of remote host [10.0.0.7]?

Source filename [Cisco804MainStOfficeCfg.txt]?

Destination filename [startup-config]?

Warning: copying this config directly into nvram from a network server
may cause damage to the startup config. It is advisable to copy the
```

```
file into the running-config first, and then save it using copy run
start.
Do you still wish to proceed? [no]: yes
Accessing tftp://10.0.0.7/Cisco804MainStOfficeCfg.txt...
Loading Cisco804MainStOfficeCfg.txt from 10.0.0.7 (via Ethernet0): !
[OK - 1423/2048 bytes]


1423 bytes copied in 2.848 secs (711 bytes/sec)
```

Notice the process is the same as copying to the running-config with the exception of the start keyword in the initial command. That is, until the router realizes that you are attempting to write directly to the NVRAM and a "sanity check" is returned for you to confirm that this is truly your intention. The file copy was a success, and no loss of connection to the local network occurred. A show start command will verify the configuration was transferred correctly. The router is now ready to be shipped to its final destination.

Contacting Cisco Technical Assistance Center

There are problems that even the best of the best are not able to solve, at which point it comes time to contact the "creator." Cisco has three different ways to be contacted about problems. One is via the Cisco Web site, which is excellent for getting questions answered. You can also send TAC (Technical Assistance Center) an e-mail message and wait for a response, or if you have a more urgent issue you can contact Cisco via its 24-hour support line.

Before you open a case number with Cisco, it requests that you have as much of the following information gathered as possible:

- Chassis type and serial number.
- Maintenance agreement and/or warranty information.
- Type of software and version number.
- Date you received the chassis.
- Brief description of the problem.
- Brief explanation of the steps you have taken to isolate the problem.

Cisco Web Support

Everybody is familiar with the Cisco Connection Online at www.cisco.com (affectionately known as "CCO"), and it is no mystery that a wealth of information can be found

Optimization and Maintenance

PART 4

there. Also available to you from the Cisco Web site is a channel to the TAC. Go to www.cisco.com/support and as a registered user you will be given the option to login and go directly to TAC and open a case.

Once you've logged in to TAC, you can specify what your inquiry is about, provide some detail, and give the family of products and technologies for which you are having a problem. Generally, the results will first try to guide you through some possible documentation solutions.

Another option is to try to place the problem out on the open forum. This is a location where Cisco employees as well as many Cisco users answer questions. The last option is the "one-to-one" support, which will actually lead you through the process of opening up a case number.

E-Mail Cisco TAC

The e-mail address for Cisco TAC in the United States is TAC@Cisco.com. The more information you include in your e-mail, the timelier your response will be. You will also want to include any contract numbers you have and any additional "reply to" information you may require. It is also a good idea to include a phone number where you can be reached in the event they need to call you for assistance. Cisco's global presence requires several different languages, a few of which are listed here:

Language	E-Mail Address
English/Spanish	tac@cisco.com
Hanzi (Chinese)	chinese-tac@cisco.com
Kanji (Japanese)	japan-tac@cisco.com
Hangul (Korean)	korea-tac@cisco.com
Thai	thai-tac@cisco.com

WARNING Do not rely on e-mail to submit network down emergency problems to Cisco. The fastest response time will be by telephone.

Telephone Support

The phone number for United States Cisco Technical Assistance Center is 1-800-553-2447. Again, when you call you will want to have all of the available information that was mentioned at the beginning of this section, as well as a support contract number if you have one. Cisco truly is an international company and has support numbers for just about everywhere in the world. If you are in the US and you call the US number late at night, be prepared to speak to someone in Australia or another part of the world because Cisco routes its call centers accordingly.

Table 18.1 shows an alphabetical listing of TAC phone numbers by geographic location.

Table 18.1 TAC Phone Numbers by Geographic Region

Region	Telephone
Asia-Pacific	+61 2 8448 7107
Argentina	0-800-555-4288, then dial 888-443-2447
Australia	1 800 805 227
Brazil	000814-550-3333
Chile	1230-020-0240
China	10810, then 800 501 2306 – Mandarin 10811, then 800 501 2306 – English 800 810 8886 - In country TAC support
Columbia	9809-154424
Costa Rica	0800-012-0043
Europe	+32 2 704 5555
France	0800 907 594
Hong Kong	800 96 5910
India	000 117, then 888 861 6453
Indonesia	001 800 61 838
Japan	0066 33 800 926
Korea	00798 611 0712 – Seoul 00 911, then 888 861 5164
Malaysia	1 800 805880

Optimization and Maintenance

PART 4

Table 18.1   TAC Phone Numbers by Geographic Region *(continued)*

Region	Telephone
Mexico	001-8884026569
New Zealand	0800 44 6237
North America	800 553 2447 408 526 7209
Philippines	1800 611 0056
Singapore	800 6161 356
Taiwan	0080 61 1206
Thailand	001 800 611 0754
UK	0800 960 547
Venezuela	8001-4724

How TAC Works

The Cisco TAC is designed to provide worldwide support for all of Cisco's product lines. Once a call or an e-mail is received, it is logged, given a call number, and assigned to a Customer Support Engineer, who will work with the customer to attempt to answer the question, give advice on system use, help with system configuration, or correct a system malfunction.

If you have a current Smartnet Support contract and it is determined that there is a hardware issue and the problem requires field assistance then the Customer Support Engineer will contact the Cisco local third-party service provider and the local service provider will *acknowledge* the dispatched schedule of a Field Engineer to the site within four hours. Any replacement parts that are needed will also be dispatched, most likely by overnight delivery.

Opening a Case with Cisco TAC

Again, you will want to have all of the information mentioned at the beginning of this section as well as your maintenance contract number. A brief description of your problem will also assist the dispatcher (also known as the CRC-Customer Response Center) to get your call to the appropriate CSE Customer Support Engineer, formerly known as CERT (Customer Engineering Response Team). It is also a good idea to tell the dispatcher what the priority level of the problem is; we will explain priority levels shortly. Depending on how backed up they are, you will either be connected directly to an available customer engineer, or one will call you back.

Cisco Customer Support Engineering Product Groups

When you call Cisco to open a case number, they will take your information to the appropriate group. It is useful to know what groups they have and what each group's responsibilities are:

Desktop: Novell, Banyan Vines, AppleTalk, FDDI

Rp (Routing Protocol): DECNet, OSI, OSPF, BGP, CLNS

WAN: WANs, X.25, CPT, ISDN, FRAME RELAY, SMDS

IBM: IBM Support, SRB, Translational Bridge, RSRB

NMS (Network Management): Ciscoworks, Config Builder, Netview

LAN Switching (Workgroup Business Unit): Concentrator, HUB, CDDI, Catalyst, Adapter

Access-Dial and ISDN

WAN Switching: IGX, BPX, AXIS (8000 series WAN switches)

Software Applications: GeoTel, WebLine

Priority Levels

In order to make sure that all of the calls coming in get serviced in the correct order, it is necessary for Cisco to prioritize the calls. For example, someone who has a general BGP design question should not get a call back before an engineer whose thousand-user network is down.

Priority 1: A priority 1 condition is to be used only when your production network is down. This is for production and potential loss of business.

TIP   Priority 1 calls will get the highest level of attention regardless of time of day. All other calls are handled during Cisco regular business hours, 6 AM to 6 PM Pacific time Monday through Friday excluding holidays. However, Cisco's customer support "follows the sun." Depending on your location, calls outside those hours may handled from another Cisco site, such as Brussels, that is open at that time.

Priority 2: A priority 2 circumstance could be when the production network performance is severely degraded.

Priority 3: A priority 3 situation is when network performance may be degraded, but most business operations continue.

Optimization and Maintenance

PART 4

Priority 4: Priority 4 calls are for general questions regarding design, installation, and configuration of Cisco products or other information.

TIP If you are not satisfied with the response you are getting, you can contact the *TAC Duty Manager* and have your call escalated or put back into the queue.

Configuring a Spare Router

Take the case of WeeBee Boats, a medium-size network with a central site and several remote sites. It is not beyond the realm of possibility that one of the remote sites could fail. In a well-designed and implemented network, such as WeeBee Boats, all of the remote sites have the same type of routers, or at least have a commonality for each type of site. For example, each site with fewer than 50 users may only require an 800, medium-size sites with 51 to 250 users may have a 2600, sites with 251 to 500 users may have a 4000, and so forth. Another major factor in the design, and an often-overlooked consideration, is that WeeBee needs to allocate the budget to keep a spare router of each type at the core site. In the event of a failure, it would be possible for the technical staff at the core to configure the spare and overnight deliver it to the failed location. At that point, a "power user" from the failed remote site could be walked through the physical hardware replacement, and that would be that. Let's look at some of the steps that we would need to take to make such a scenario happen.

First, we need to be sure that all of our router configuration and image files are backed up. Without this first step, none of the rest of our plan works, so it is clearly very important to keep things backed up. Unlike data, router configurations do not change very often once the router is up and running, so additional backups are necessary only when there is a configuration change. Directories have already been created on our server for all different locations to make our files easy to find.

NOTE   Once you learn of a failure, it is important to go through all of the troubleshooting techniques described throughout this book to determine whether you have a software configuration or perhaps a line failure. After the problem is determined to be a hardware failure, you can begin down the road of router replacement.

Before we initiate additional backup steps, we need to set up a TFTP server. The steps for this are simply to place the configuration file and necessary image files into the outbound directory, with the file names *exactly* as they appear, and to record the IP address for the server.

Next, the backup spare router should be set up for local network access to be able to pull the configurations down. From the console port of the router, go into enable mode. Once there, set up an IP address for the local side and test ping your TFTP server to validate your connectivity. Now you are ready to start pulling files.

It is important to know the statistics from the router you are starting out with. A show version command would be a good place to start:

```
800Router#sho ver

Cisco Internetwork Operating System Software
```

```
IOS (tm) C800 Software (C800-G3-MW), Version 12.0(1)XB1,  RELEASE
SOFTWARE (fc1)
```

```
TAC:Home:SW:IOS:Specials for info

Copyright (c) 1986-1998 by cisco Systems, Inc.

Compiled Wed 30-Dec-98 13:34 by ayeh

Image text-base: 0x000E9000, data-base: 0x004F5000
```

```
ROM: TinyROM version 1.0(2)

800Router uptime is 8 weeks, 1 day, 11 hours, 39 minutes

System restarted by power-on

System image file is "flash:c800-g3-mw.120-1.XB1"
```

```
Cisco C804 (MPC850) processor (revision 0) with 47356K bytes of
virtual memory.

Processor board ID JAD03142341

CPU part number 33

Bridging software.

Basic Rate ISDN software, Version 1.1.

1 Ethernet/IEEE 802.3 interface(s)

1 ISDN Basic Rate interface(s)

8M bytes of physical memory (DRAM)

8K bytes of non-volatile configuration memory

8M bytes of flash on board (4M from flash card)
```

Configuration register is 0x2102 We will need to examine the amount of flash memory in the router to know if you have enough room to hold the old image and the new image at the same time or if we need to delete the existing image first. From the console prompt, we can check the available flash memory in the router with a show flash command.

```
800Router#sho flash:
Directory of flash:/
```

```
0  ----     49096    Nov 03 1998 01:14:21  TinyROM-.0(2)
1  -r-x     2314996  Dec 30 1998 21:37:19  c800-g3-mw.120-1.XB1


8388608 bytes total (5963776 bytes free)
```

You can see by the output here that we have a total of 8388608 bytes of total flash memory, and the image only takes up 2314996, so both images will fit in flash.

> **NOTE**   It would be better to leave the existing image in place until we verify the new image transferred completely and error free. However for our case study and for further demonstration purposes we be deleting the old image and copying in the new one.

Had we not had enough room on the flash, we would need to delete the old image to make the necessary room. This would be done with the delete flash command.

```
delete flash:c800-g3-mw.120-1.XB1
```

Now that the old image is gone, we can copy the new one over:

```
800Router#copy tftp flash

Address or name of remote host []? 10.0.0.7

Source filename []? c800-g3-mw.120-1.XB1

Destination filename [c800-g3-mw.120-1.XB1]?

Accessing tftp://10.0.0.7/c800-g3-mw.120-1.XB1...

Loading c800-g3-mw.120-1.XB1 from 10.0.0.7 (via Ethernet0):
!!!!!!!!!!!!!!!!!!!!!!!!!!!!!!!!!!!!!!!!!!!!!!!!!!!!!!!!!!!!!!!!!!!!
!!!!!!!!!!!!!!!!!!!!!!!!!!!!!!!!!!!!!!!!!!!!!!!!!!!!!!!!!!!!!!!!!!!!
!!!!!!!!!!!!!!!!!!!!!!!!!!!!!!!!!!!!!!!!!!!!!!!!!!!!!!!!!!!!!!!!!!!!
!!!!!!!!!!!!!!!!!!!!!!!!!!!!!!!!!!!!!!!!!!!!!!!!!!!!!!!!!!!!!!!!!!!!
!!!!!!!!!!!!!!!!!!!!!!!!!!!!!!!!!!!!!!!!!!!!!!!!!!!!!!!!!!!!!!!!!!!!
!!!!!!!!!!!!!!!!!!!!!!!!!!!!!!!!!!!!!!!!!!!!!!!!!!!!!!!!!!!!!!!!!!!!
!!!!!!!!!!!!!!!!!!!!!!!!!!!!!!!!!!!!!!!!!!!!!!!!!!!!!!!!!!!!!!!!!!

2314996 bytes copied in 23.959 secs (96423 bytes/sec)
```

It is now time to copy the configuration file over. Remember that there are a few different ways to go about bringing in the configuration file. Since you already have the TFTP setup and you may have your console session connection to the router on the same box as your TFTP server a copy and paste option here is not very likely so it is best to stick with the TFTP method. Further notice that we are copying the configuration file directly to startup-config, *not* to running-config. If we were to copy the configuration over the running-configuration, we would lose the local connectivity to the router, because the IP address that we configured will be replaced with the address for the final destination of the router. That being said, this is what it would look like:

```
800Router#copy tftp start

Address or name of remote host [10.0.0.7]?

Source filename [Cisco804AntiochCfg.txt]?

Destination filename [startup-config]?

Warning: copying this config directly into nvram from a network
server may cause damage to the startup config. It is advisable to
copy the file into the running-config first, and then save it
using copy run start.

Do you still wish to proceed? [no]: yes

Accessing tftp://10.0.0.7/Cisco804AntiochCfg.txt...

Loading Cisco804AntiochCfg.txt from 10.0.0.7 (via Ethernet0): !
[OK - 1423/2048 bytes]


1423 bytes copied in 2.848 secs (711 bytes/sec)
```

You are now complete with transferring the necessary files into the router. You can reboot the router to verify that the image is booting correctly.

NOTE Remember that at this point when the router is rebooted you will lose your local connectivity because of the IP address differences between your location and the remote site, so you will have to verify your work from the console connection.

Once the router has completely rebooted, a show version command again will show the boot image. The last step would be a show running-config command to verify the configuration. We are now ready to ship the router out and have a local person plug the cables in. We have saved the day!

19

Advanced Topics

This chapter brings together a number of advanced topics that do not necessarily fit nicely into categories—the Hot Standby Router Protocol (HSRP), some advanced Border Gateway Protocol (BGP) issues, and the Firewall feature set. As such, it is something of a miscellany. Most of the topics we will discuss are subject areas that may be required for CCIE candidates.

Hot Standby Router Protocol (HSRP)

What is HSRP (Hot Standby Router Protocol) and why do I need it on my network? These very legitimate questions are the very topics of this chapter. After these questions are answered, we will go into detail about how the HSRP protocol works and touch on a few system integration issues that are fairly common.

What Is HSRP?

HSRP was introduced by Cisco in its IOS (Internetwork Operating System) version 10.0. This protocol is intended to provide a mechanism to accommodate a circuit failure, yet keep it transparent to the user community. HSRP will allow you to take two or more routers and make them appear to the network as a single point or a "virtual router" to use as the default gateway.

Why Do I Need HSRP?

HSRP is a valuable tool in environments where there are critical applications running and there is a need for a fault-tolerant network. Prior to Cisco's HSRP, there were four possible ways for hosts to "find their way out" of the network or a default gateway.

IRDP (ICMP Router Discovery Protocol) is a method by which the host itself is configured to run the IRDP protocol to find and maintain outside connectivity. IRDP will be covered later in this chapter. With ProxyARP (Address Resolution Protocol), a network host has the ability to find a router by using an ARP request to search for MAC addresses that are not on its directly connected segment. To use this method, you would configure the default gateway router to respond to the hosts' ProxyARP requests. The hosts would then use that router as the exit point for the network. This is a functionally sound method; however, if there are multiple exit points, ProxyARP falls short. In order to keep down the ARP traffic on the network and increase the speed, most hosts will cache their ARP tables for a specified time, some even indefinitely. Whichever exit point responds to the ProxyARP request first will be the default gateway, and upon a failure the host is left to either time out the ARP cache or restart to continue communications. The most popular method for exit path determination is probably the manual configuration of the default gateway option, either on the host as a static entry or by way of DHCP. This is probably the easiest method, but it is not at all fault tolerant. If the manually configured default gateway failed, each host would lose connectivity and a manual reconfiguration either of the hosts or the DHCP server would be required to inform them of the alternate path.

The last and probably least popular method of router discovery mechanisms is through the use of RIP (Router Information Protocol). This requires RIP-speaking hosts on the network, brings a lot of overhead, and can take over 60 seconds to failover.

Clearly, each of these methods of router discovery falls short of complete redundancy, which is where HSRP comes into play. HSRP works in concert with the manual configuration or DHCP mode to allow the easy integration and maintenance of the default gateway.

How Does HSRP Work?

The core functionality of HSRP is the sharing of an IP address and a MAC address by two or more routers. These routers appear to the rest of the network as one virtual router. Any of the routers configured in the group are then able to seamlessly take over the default gateway responsibilities within a few seconds in the event of a circuit failure or administrative outage. The hosts on the network that are configured with the virtual gateway address will continue to forward traffic to a consistent IP and MAC address regardless of the HSRP group situation.

HSRP relies on the exchange of multicast packets that deliver priority values and other information among all of the routers in the HSRP group. There are three types of multicast messages used by HSRP:

Hello   The hello messages are used to remain in constant communication with the other HSRP speaking routers. Hello messages can include priority information and router status.

Resign   If you are fortunate enough to have a router gracefully come down, it will attempt to send a multicast resign packet. A resign packet can also be initiated by learning of a router with a higher priority.

Coup   When the standby router realizes an active-forwarder failure, it will take on the roll of the active-forwarder. Upon doing so, it will let all of the other router know that it has assumed this role by sending out a coup multicast.

Through the use of these multicast packets, one of the routers within the group will be selected as the *active-forwarder*. The active-forwarder is the router that has assumed the forwarding responsibilities for the entire HSRP group and will additionally be responsible for handing out the hello timer and dead timer values. The hello timer value is the time interval between the HSRP hello packets to the other routers. The default hello timer value is 3 seconds. The dead timer is the value that tells the router how long to wait before declaring the active forwarder to be dead and carries a default value of 10 seconds. These values can be manipulated to increase the convergence time upon the unavailability of the active-forwarder but at the expense of increased network traffic. If the defaults are changed, the same values must be configured on all routers in that HSRP group.

A different router in the group will be selected as the *standby-router*. This router sits ready to take over the forwarding duties of the current active-forwarder in the event it is no longer available. The standby-router will listen for the standby IP address that will be shared for all of the routers in the HSRP group. Statically configured hello timer, dead intervals, and standby IP addresses will take precedence over those learned by the HSRP protocol.

The roles of the active-forwarder and the standby-router can be configured manually by the administrator setting priority values. The higher value will become the active-forwarder. In the event there is a tie, the highest IP address will win. The default priority is 100. If you wish for a particular router to be the default, then you set only that router to a higher priority, leaving all of the other routers set to the default value of 100. As stated earlier, we can have more than two routers in an HSRP standby group.

In addition to the active-forwarder and standby-router states already discussed, there are two more states that you need to be aware of: the *speaking-and-listening* state and the *listening* state. The speaking-and-listening state indicates that the HSRP speaker is both

Optimization and Maintenance

PART 4

sending and receiving hello messages, and the listening state denotes that the router is only receiving hello messages.

The standard configuration for HSRP leaves one router active, one router in standby, and all of the other routers in the HSRP group in a passive mode. There can be as many as 255 Hot-Standby groups on an Ethernet or FDDI network, but only three groups on a Token Ring network; therefore, the number of HSRP-speaking routers can grow quite large. This is hardly an efficient use of the hardware. In IOS 10.3 and later versions, the HSRP protocol will allow multiple groups to be configured per interface. This new flavor, called M-HSRP (Multiple-HSRP), allows you to configure multiple redundant gateways while still fully utilizing each of the routers. Each router could serve as a backup for the other in one group, all the while performing load sharing for the other.

In the following example, the HSRP protocol can be used to create redundancy for each of the two different networks while at the same time performing load sharing.

In Figure 19.1, you can see that there are two separate networks using two separate address spaces.

Figure 19.1   An example of HSRP configuration

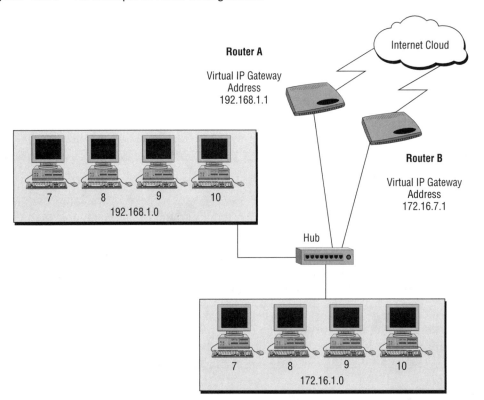

These networks are each attached to a hub that is additionally attached to both router A and router B. The configuration for router A might look like this:

```
interface Ethernet0
 ip address 192.168.2.2 255.255.255.0
 ip address 172.16.7.2 255.255.255.0 secondary
 standby 10 ip 192.168.2.1
 standby 20 ip 172.16.7.1
 standby prempt
 standby 10 priority 192
 standby 20 priority 172
 standby 10 authentication cisco
 standby 20 authentication san-fran
 standby 10 timers 2 6
```

Let's look at the configuration line by line:

1. The IP address 192.168.2.2 is the actual IP address of the interface.

2. The IP address 172.16.7.2 is the secondary IP address that will be used by HSRP to communicate with the router B and the 172.16.7.0 network hosts.

3. The `standby` command is followed by the HSRP group number 10 and the IP address that will be used for the virtual gateway for the router A 192.168.2.0 network. All of the other routers in HSRP group 10 should have the same standby IP address.

4. The `standby` command for the secondary network will be group number 20, with the virtual gateway address of 172.16.7.2.

5. The `standby preempt` command allows the router to become the active-forwarder if its priority level is higher than all of the other HSRP routers in its group. The absence of this command will make the router ineligible to become the active-forwarder.

6. Standby priorities are set with this command. Remember, the higher priority will be the default active-forwarder. For router A, we want our local group to be active, so we set HSRP group 10 to the higher priority.

Optimization and Maintenance

PART 4

NOTE We have used the first octet of the IP address for the priority numbers for clarity. This is a good idea only if your IP addresses match, as ours do. If you have the luxury of designing the IP addressing scheme, you may want to consider this. Remember that the tiebreaker is the higher IP address.

---

7. The gateway for which router A will be the backup will take the lower standby priority number of 172.

8. The optional `standby authentication` interface configuration command is enabled to secure the HSRP protocol. HSRP authentication inserts into each multicast packet an unencrypted eight-character field whose value is specified by the trailing keyword. Each router in the HSRP group must have the identical password. Thus, all routers in group 10 will require the password `cisco`.

9. Notice the use of a different HSRP password, `san-fran`, for the other network.

10. The `standby timers` command is used to alter the default interval in seconds for hello timer and hold down timer. If the default values are changed, then every router within the group must be changed to match. In our example, we have decreased the default times for a faster failover convergence.

Router B's configuration might look like this:

```
interface Ethernet0
  ip address 172.16.7.2 255.255.255.0
  ip address 192.168.2.3 255.255.255.0 secondary
  standby 20 ip 172.16.7.1
  standby 10 ip 192.168.2.1
  standby prempt
  standby 10 priority 172
  standby 20 priority 192
  standby 10 authentication cisco
  standby 20 authentication san-fran
  standby 10 timers 2 6
```

Again, we can walk through this configuration line by line. Each item corresponds to the equivalent line in the router A configuration, so we don't need to go into as much detail:

1. The primary IP address for the Ethernet interface is 172.16.7.2.

2. The secondary IP address for the interface is 192.168.2.3.

3. The HSRP group 20 virtual IP address is set to 172.16.7.1.

4. The HSRP group 10 virtual IP address is set to 192.168.1.1.

5. The `standby prempt` command allows this router to become primary.

6. This line sets the standby priority to 172. This is the backup for group 10, so it has been set to the lower priority.

7. This sets the standby priority to 192. This is the primary for group 20, so it has been set to the higher priority.

8. The standby password for group 10 must match the router A password of `cisco`.

9. The standby password for group 20 must match the router A password of `san-fran`.

10. Standby timers must match for all routers within the group. Group 10 on router A was set to 2 for hello and 6 for hold, so that's what we use here.

Notice that group 20's timers were not changed, so the defaults should be intact.

HSRP Issues

There are several issues anyone planning to implement HSRP should be aware of, including problems with MAC addresses, the use of HSRP in combination with other protocols, the disabling of ICMP, and problems with using HSRP and HP's OpenView software.

MAC Addresses and HSRP

When you configure HSRP on a group of routers, the routers will recognize at least two MAC (Media Access Control) addresses: their own native address and the HSRP group MAC address.

Some Ethernet controllers on lower-end Cisco routers are only able to recognize a single MAC address, and subsequently will use the HSRP learned MAC address while they are the active-forwarder only. If this same router is in the standby or listening state, the router will use its BIA (Burned In Address). You can force the router to use its BIA all of the time by issuing this interface command:

```
standby use-bia
```

This command will allow only one HSRP standby group because only one MAC address is available. This command will also prevent the MAC address from changing, whether it is in an *active* or *listening state*, potentially causing an issue with existing ARP cache entries. The entries that may already exist in the ARP (Address Resolution Protocol) table may need to be changed and such a change would take time and may cause a period of disconnectivity. To alleviate this issue, when the standby router becomes active it sends out a gratuitous ARP to force the hosts to update their ARP cache entries allowing the nondisruptive fail-over.

HSRP will use the MAC address 0000.0c07.ac*XX*, where the last two digits (*XX*) are reserved for the group number for all interfaces except Token Ring. In our example earlier, the MAC address for group 10 would be 0000.0c07.ac10. Up to 255 groups are available, because the last two digits can only be as high as FF in hex, which is 255 in decimal.

Token Ring handles multicast traffic a little differently than Ethernet. Token Ring networks rely on *functional addresses* for forwarding of multicast traffic. Many of these functional addresses are reserved for other uses, and because of the limited number available, Token Ring networks will allow only three HSRP groups, using the following MAC addresses:

c000.0001.0000 (group 0)

c000.0002.0000 (group 1)

c000.0004.0000 (group 2)

HSRP and Other Protocols

HSRP was designed for IP networks and functions very well in that arena but can cause some issues when implemented in a multiprotocol environment.

DECnet and XNS   HSRP relies heavily on the MAC addresses, as do DECnet and XNS. With these protocols all interfaces must "share" a specified MAC address for the entire router. The standby `use-bia` command is required to force HSRP to use the BIA. Doing so in this situation will prohibit the use of M-HSRP and may have an impact on these protocols on the LAN. The exceptions here are the Cisco 7000 and 7500 routers, as they have special hardware required to support multiple MAC addresses.

Banyan Vines   The lower-level functionality of a Banyan Vines network does not conform to topology changes very well. In the case of a failed router, the Banyan traffic will pause for no more than 90 seconds. Some of the sessions will need to be reestablished, and *all* serverless clients that have obtained their layer 3 addresses from the defunct router will require a new layer 3 address; this calls for a reboot of that host. Again, the exception is if the new active-forwarder is a 7000 series router. As mentioned earlier, the 7000 series has special hardware that will permit it to have more than one MAC address at the same time.

IPX In the case of IPX, a Novell 4.*x* host can discover a new active-forwarder in less than 10 seconds. Novell 2.*x* or Novell 3.*x* hosts might require more time to adapt. Another potential issue with IPX is the addressing. The IPX addressing format is

```
IPXNetwork# .MACaddress
```

Some companies choose to adapt an IPX addressing scheme by changing the MAC address to reflect perhaps the IP network and node numbers to make network sniffing and reporting simple. If these MAC addresses have been manipulated, then you will be looking at similar problems as the other protocols using HSRP.

ICMP When you set up HSRP on an interface, ICMP is automatically disabled for that interface. Hosts on the directly connected network may cache entries resulting from ICMP redirect packets, and may hamper the changeover of an HSRP router from standby to active.

HSRP and HP OpenView

One of the most common network management platforms is HP OpenView. This tool, along with the NNM (Network Node Manager), is often used in larger networks where HSRP also lives, so it seems appropriate to mention a very important issue here.

It is very common to receive *Duplicate IP Address messages* in the event browser when HSRP enabled routers are on the same network. It is most common in a network where two RSM (Route Switch Modules) are enabled with HSRP. There are two possible solutions for this problem.

The fastest way to terminate this problem is of course unsupported by HP but nonetheless is still functional. Gather all of the HSRP Standby address on the network and create a file called `netmon.noDiscover` in the `/etc/opt/OV/share/conf` directory. This will cause OpenView's discovery mechanism to disregard your standby address before it initiates the polling process. This can limit some of the functionality of OpenView.

The second way is to tell OpenView to poll the routers with an incorrect community string. The problem with this method is that these routers could respond to the incorrect polling with *Authorization Failure Traps* and could flood the management station. Great care should be taken to restart the process and clear all caches after this has been set up. For more detailed instructions on this process and for more information on HSRP and OpenView, go to:

```
http://www.openview.hp.com
```

Optimization and Maintenance

PART 4

ICMP Router Discovery Protocol (IRDP)

As we just learned with our HSRP studies, hosts must learn a "way out" of their network if they wish to communicate beyond their boundaries. IRDP (ICMP Router Discovery Protocol) has been established in RFC 1256 to provide a dynamic way for our hosts to discover such an exit point, alleviating the need for manual default-gateway configurations. IRDP uses ICMP [10] messages on all multicast links. It is independent of all routing protocols and is fully dynamic, so no manual configuration of workstation parameters is required.

IRDP Functionality

The ICMP protocol uses two methods to communicate router information: *router advertisements* and *router solicitations*. An IRDP-enabled router will announce the IP address or addresses of its interfaces by sending router advertisements every 7 to 10 minutes out of each of its multicast enabled interfaces using the multicast address 224.0.0.1. These routers will also send out these updates during startup as well to make themselves available without waiting for the periodic update or waiting to be "asked."

An IRDP-enabled host needs merely to listen for these router advertisements to receive information on its neighboring routers. Additionally, when a host boots up, it may send a *router solicitation* using the multicast address 224.0.0.2 in effort to learn of its routing neighbors. If the host receives no response to the request, it may ask again but then cease. Once a host learns of a router, the entry will have a default lifetime of 30 minutes.

Although it does have some of the same characteristics, IRDP is not a routing protocol. IRDP discovery messages are often compared to routing protocol updates, but there are components missing that keep IRDP very lean. IRDP contains no *preference level* for routing advertisements; thus there is no option for an ICMP redirect. Additionally, IRDP contains no *lifetime field* specifying the age of a route advertisement.

The use of IRDP allows each router to specify *both* a priority and the time after which a device should be assumed to be down if no further packets are received.

When a host discovers a router via IGRP, it is assigned an arbitrary priority value of 60. The list of entries is scanned and a change in the gateway will be made on three conditions: First, if the host discovers a router with a higher priority value; second, if the current default gateway neighbor goes down; third and last, if excessive retransmissions are about to cause a TCP connection to time out. As this value gets higher, the host will flush the ARP cache and the ICMP redirect cache in an attempt to find a better way out. It is also possible for the router to "proxy-advertise" other IRDP speakers, although this is problematic because these proxy advertisements update timers are set so high that the advertised host could be down, making the proxy advertisement bogus.

IRDP Application

Although still not overwhelmingly popular, IRDP is mostly seen in the Unix world. Some Unix vendors include an IRDP daemon with their operating systems. Cisco's flavor of IRDP fully conforms to the industry standard and will only receive router solicitation packets when acting as a host but will transmit router advertisements when set as an IRDP server.

IRDP Basic Commands

IRDP is not enabled on Cisco routers by default. The `ip irdp` interface command is used to enable IRDP on the interface. To disable IRDP, use the negation form of this command: `no ip irdp`.

```
interface Ethernet0
 ip irdp
```

> **WARNING**   If the `ip irdp` command is not issued on the interface first, none of the other commands will hold in the router configuration, although no error message will be generated when they are entered.

The `ip irdp` command alone without any parameters will accept all of the defaults. At a minimum, you will probably want to specify a priority level. The following sample IRDP configuration illustrates the parameters that you will most likely want to change from their defaults. As usual, we'll follow the command listing with a brief line-by-line explanation:

```
ip irdp
ip irdp preference 200
ip irdp maxadvertinterval 500
ip irdp minadvertinterval 200
ip irdp holdtime 3600
ip irdp address 172.16.1.1
ip irdp address 172.16.2.2 50
```

1. The first line enables IRDP on the interface.
2. This increases the router preference to 200. If all of the other routers are left at the default values, this router will be the preferred gateway. The allowed range is 0 to 255.

Optimization and Maintenance

PART 4

3. Sets the maximum time between advertisements to 300 seconds (5 minutes); the default value is 600 seconds. By default, if the maxadvertinterval value is modified, the minadvertinterval and holdtime values will also be modified. The minadvertinterval value will be reset to two-thirds of the max value, unless otherwise specified, and the hold time value will default to three times the maxadvertinterval value.

4. Sets the minimum time between advertisements to 300 seconds. The default value is 400. This sets the interval between advertisements.

5. Advertisements received are believed to be good for 3600 seconds. This value should be three times the maxadvertinterval value but cannot be greater than 9000 seconds.

6. Proxy-advertises 172.16.1.1 with the default router preference.

7. Proxy-advertises 172.16.2.2 with a preference of 50.

Checking for IRDP Configuration Settings

Use show ip irdp to display IRDP configuration settings. Here's what the output would look like for our example configuration:

```
Router A> show ip irdp


Ethernet0 has router discovery enabled


Advertisements will occur between every 200 and 500 seconds.

Advertisements are sent with broadcasts.

Advertisements are valid for 3600 seconds.

Default preference will be 200.

Proxy for 172.16.1.1 with preference 0.

Proxy for 172.16.2.2 with preference 50.


Serial 0 has router discovery disabled


Ethernet 1 has router discovery disabled
```

Advanced BGP Topics

BGP (Border Gateway Protocol) is a widely used path-vector routing protocol. It has many features and functions, and consequently can become very complex. This section is designed to offer some insight into some of the more advanced features of BGP and how they may be implemented. In order to address these advanced topics, we assume that you already have a very solid understanding of BGP, including configuration, route-maps, and BGP attributes.

BGP Communities

The BGP routing protocol controls the distribution of routing information based on the IP address prefixes or sometimes uses part of the AS_PATH attribute. A BGP *community* is designed to group destinations so that the forwarding decisions can be based on the group itself and not on each of the community's members. Clearly, the ability to group numbers of members together into a single update would greatly simply the configuration and give more control of BGP traffic.

BGP community attributes are global as well as optional, meaning that they are not required for normal BGP operation. They are also transitive. If we set the T bit to 1, the community attribute will be passed on.

An example of a strategic use of BGP communities is if a service provider had multiple BGP autonomous systems and wishes to make them available to each other without permitting the information beyond its boundaries.

Typically, we see an aggregate prefix as well as any more specific network addresses when routes are advertised. Once learned, these routes are populated to the other BGP speakers. If the network numbers are contiguous, then a simple aggregate address might be useful to control these updates. If not, things can be a little trickier. The use of BGP communities provides a simple BGP attribute that could be used to filter these values.

A BGP community is defined as any group of BGP-speaking routers that share a common attribute. The autonomous system administrator can assign each BGP speaker to belong to a single community or to multiple communities simultaneously if that is a necessary part of design. The community information is carried in the community attribute and by default is set to the general Internet community and use type code 8. This attribute contains a set of four octet values that each specify a community.

The well-known communities are as follows:

INTERNET   All routes received will contain this community attribute and it shall be forwarded to other BGP peers.

NO_EXPORT (0xFFFFFF01)   All routes received carrying a community attribute containing this value must *not* be advertised outside a BGP confederation boundary. (A stand-alone autonomous system that is not part of a confederation should be considered a confederation itself.)

NO_ADVERTISE (0xFFFFFF02)   All routes received carrying a community attribute containing this value must not be advertised to other BGP peers.

NO_EXPORT_SUBCONFED (0xFFFFFF03)   All routes received carrying a community attribute containing this value must not be advertised to *external* BGP peers (this includes peers in other members' autonomous systems inside a BGP confederation).

The community attribute can be used for several purposes in routing information. For example, you can specify which BGP routing updates will be allowed or disallowed. Or, you can set which update you wish to distribute or set a preference for. BGP speakers are allowed to modify the community attribute based on policy. It can initially set the attribute, modify, or append the attribute with new information. All of these things can be done as the router handles the BGP updates, i.e. the advertising, learning, or redistribution. If permitted by the policy, the attribute will produce an aggregate containing all of the information.

As we stated earlier, one of the purposes for creating communities in the first place was to keep things simple. To create a community list, use this configuration command:

```
ip community-list [community-list-number] [permit | deny]
[community-number]
```

We can use route maps to set the community attributes. In the following pair of examples, we see that we can set the community attribute either by matching an IP address defined in an access list or by matching an as-path list. Without the `additive` keyword, a value of 400 will replace any existing value. With this value set, 400 will be added to the community.

```
route-map com_attrib_access-list

match ip address 1

set community no-advertise
```

Or

```
route-map com_attrib_as-path

match as-path 1

set community 200 additive
```

The first configuration works as follows:

1. Defines a route map named `com_attrib_access-list`.
2. Defines where to find the IP address to match.
3. Sets the community attribute to `no-advertise` (see above definition).

The second configuration does this:

1. Defines a route map named `com_attrib_as-path`.
2. Defines which as-path list to match.
3. Sets the community to 400 with the `additive` keyword.

These processes have defined the attribute only. If we wish to send this community information to our BGP neighbors, we need to additionally use the `send-community` keyword of the `neighbor` command and use the `route-map` keyword to specify what to send. It will not be sent by default.

```
router bgp 62359
neighbor 172.16.3.1 remote-as 62323
neighbor 172.16.3.1 send-community
neighbor 172.16.3.1 route-map com_attrib_as-path out
```

BGP Community Filtering

One of the reasons BGP community attributes were created was to provide a method for allowing or disallowing routes. This can be done using route maps to filter wanted or unwanted routes. We will not attempt to teach route maps here, but we can show how to use route maps in conjunction with BGP filtering. At least one `match` or `set` command is required in the route map configuration.

```
route-map communityfilter permit 10
    match community-list 250 exact
```

This example `route-map` command demonstrates a basic configuration. This command could be broken down by its elements. A route map with the name COMMUNITY-FILTER will match the community-list attribute 250 exactly.

Sample Configurations

In Figure 19.1 we wanted router B to set the community attribute to the BGP routes it is advertising such that router A will not propagate these routes to its external peers (router C). Following are examples of the three ways we can do this.

Example 1: Example 1 shows how the `set community no-export` community attribute is used.

```
RouterB#
router bgp 11
network 192.168.20.0
neighbor 192.168.250.5 remote-as 10
neighbor 192.168.250.5 send-community
neighbor 192.168.250.5 route-map set_comm_att out
route-map set_comm_att
match ip address 1
set community no-export
access-list 1 permit 0.0.0.0 255.255.255.255
```

Note that we have used the `route-map set_comm_att` command to reference an access-list that includes all IP addresses and set the community to **no-export**. As mentioned earlier, after we set the attributes we wish, we must also configure the attributes to be populated, using the `neighbor send-community` command in order to send this attribute to router A. When router A gets the updates with the attribute **no-export**, it will not propagate them to its external peer, router C.

Example 2: In Example 2, router B sets the community attribute to `12 11 additive`. The value 12 11 will be added to any existing community value before being sent to router A.

```
RouterB#
router bgp 11
network 192.168.20.0
neighbor 192.168.250.5 remote-as 10
neighbor 192.168.250.5 send-community
neighbor 192.168.250.5 route-map set_comm_att out
route-map set_comm_att
match ip address 2
set community 12 11 additive
access-list 2 permit 0.0.0.0 255.255.255.255
```

Router C will see its own AS number in the AS_PATH and think that this is a routing loop and not allow the route to be added to its table.

By definition, a community is a list of routers that have a common attribute. We need to be able to define those communities and we do so with a community list. This list will allow us to filter or set attributes based on different lists of community numbers.

```
ip community-list [community-list-number] [permit|deny]
[community-number]
```

For example, we can define the following route map, named `matchcommunity`:

```
route-map matchcommunity

match community 10

set weight 20

ip community-list 10 permit 11 10
```

Here's a line-by-line explanation:

1. Defines a route-map called `matchcommunity`.
2. The community-list number is 10.
3. Sets the weight attribute to 20.
4. The community number is 11 10.

We can use the above example to filter or set certain parameters such as weight and metric based on the community value in certain updates.

Example 3:   In example 2, router B was sending updates to router A with a community of 12 11. If, in addition, router A wants to set the weight based on those values, we could do the following:

```
RouterA#

router bgp 10

neighbor 192.168.250.6 remote-as 11

neighbor 192.168.250.6 route-map check-community in


route-map check-community permit 10

match community 1

set weight 20

route-map check-community permit 20
```

Optimization and Maintenance

PART 4

```
match community 2 exact
set weight 10
route-map check-community permit 30
match community 3

ip community-list 1 permit 12
ip community-list 2 permit 11
ip community-list 3 permit internet
```

In Example 3, all routes that have 12 in their community attribute will match list 1 and will be assigned a weight of 20. Any route that has only 11 as community will match list 2 and will have weight 20. The keyword exact states that community should consist of 11 only and nothing else. You must remember the implicit deny rule of access lists and include the last community to ensure that other updates are not dropped. Remember that anything that does not match will be dropped by default. The keyword internet means all routes, because all routes are members of the internet community.

The Firewall Feature Set

Cisco has integrated several firewall features into their version 11.2(11)P and later versions. This feature set gives you the opportunity to maximize your IT dollars by requiring only a single box at the edge of your network that can provide multiprotocol routing as any Cisco router would, yet also furnish perimeter security, intrusion detection, VPN functionality, and per-user authentication and authorization.

Versions and Compatibility

The Enhanced (Phase I +) version of the feature set is available in IOS version 12.0(5)T and is compatible with the Cisco 800, uBR900, 1600, and 2500 routers. Features for this Phase I + include:

- Context-based Access Control (CBAC)
- Java blocking
- Denial of Service detection and prevention
- Real-time alerts and audit trail

Phase II of the Firewall feature set is available in IOS versions 12.0(5)XE and 12.0(6)T and is compatible with Cisco 1720, 2600, 3600, 7100, and 7200 routers. Additionally,

Phase II is available for version 12.0(5)T and is compatible with Cisco 2600, 3600, and 7200 routers. Phase II is packed with all of the possible features:

- Context-based Access Control (CBAC)
- Java blocking
- Denial of Service detection and prevention
- Real-time alerts and audit trail +
- Dynamic port mapping
- Configurable alerts and audit trail
- SMTP attack detection and prevention
- MS Netshow support +
- Intrusion detection (59 signatures)
- Dynamic per use authentication and authorization (authentication proxy)

Adding the Firewall feature set to the multiservice flavors of the Cisco family has added a new dimension to security integration. Cisco 1720, 2600, 3600, 7100, and 7200 routers are now capable of offering advanced security for dialup connections, integrated routing and security for data, voice, and dial access.

Firewall Features

If you are planning to implement the firewall features, it is very important to understand what each of the features does. The following section will give a description of each of the major features along with some hints and configuration tips.

Context-Based Access Control (CBAC)

One of the most important features of the Cisco firewall is CBAC (Context-based Access Control). With CBAC, sessions must be initiated from the protected side of the firewall for the traffic to even be allowed. CBAC can intelligently look as far enough into frames to see the application layer information to learn about the TCP and UDP information. This provides support for applications that use multiple channels, like FTP, RPC, and SQL*Net. Additionally, CBAC will discover and manage state information for these TCP and UDP sessions. In doing so, it can create temporary holes in the firewall to allow returning traffic and session establishment as long as these sessions are originated from the inside or protected side of the firewall.

In Figure 19.2 we see that the firewall is configured to deny Telnet traffic from the outside network. Any Telnet traffic that is attempted from the unprotected side of the firewall will be blocked. However, if a user opens a Telnet session from inside the protected network the Telnet traffic is allowed out. In order for the Telnet traffic to be allowed back through, CBAC will create a temporary hole in the firewall to allow only the return traffic for that session back through. Access lists are dynamically created and deleted for the firewall interfaces, according to the information maintained in the state tables. These entries create temporary openings in the firewall to permit only traffic that is part of a permissible session. As a packet is inspected, a state table will be created and updated to include the information about the state of the packet's connection. Return traffic will only be permitted back through the firewall if the state table contains information indicating that the packet belongs to a permissible session. The dynamic access-lists are temporary entries only and are never saved to NVRAM, keeping them secure.

Figure 19.2 CBAC overview

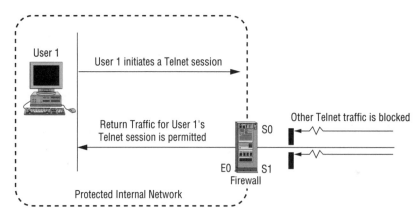

> **NOTE** This is functionally the same as using the established keyword for extended access lists but uses an inspection of the packets rather than port numbers.

It is important to note that CBAC uses less than approximately 600 bytes of memory per connection. Because of the stringent memory requirements, CBAC should only be used where necessary and you should calculate your memory requirements prior to deployment. It also takes more processing power to constantly maintain these security features, which should also be a design consideration.

The configuration of CBAC requires that you specify which protocols need to be inspected, an originating interface, and an interface direction (in or out). Each of the protocols specified will be inspected in both directions through the firewall. If an access list exists that denies the protocols that you specified for CBAC from entering the router, those packets will be dropped and not inspected. The payload of the protocols specified will *not* be inspected. CBAC will only inspect the TCP or UDP control channels. UDP is handled differently than TCP, because it is connectionless. CBAC will improvise a session by examining the UDP packets for similarities such as source or destination address port numbers and time-out values.

The configuration steps for CBAC are as follows:

1. Select an interface to inspect packets.
2. Configure IP access-lists for the protocols to be inspected.
3. Set necessary timeouts and thresholds.
4. Define an inspection rule.
5. Apply the inspection rule to an interface.

Select an Interface to Inspect Packets   You must decide which interface to inspect and whether to configure CBAC on an internal or external interface of your firewall. An *internal interface* refers to the originating side of the traffic and is often referred to as the *protected side*. An *external interface* is considered the unprotected side of the firewall and will not allow sessions to originate.

Often, network managers will be required to offer public services such as Web servers, FTP sites, or DNS; and they must allow public access to these services without compromising the security of the internal network. In these cases a DMZ (demilitarized zone) is set up. Figure 19.3 shows what a common simple Firewall design may look like.

Figure 19.3   A simple firewall

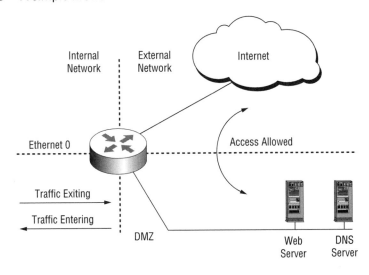

Configure IP Access Lists at the Interface   CBAC requires the use of *extended access lists* to enable inspection and to permit the creation of the temporary dynamic access list. When configuring the access list, remember that if an access list denies a protocol, that protocol will not be inspected but dropped. All access lists that evaluate traffic leaving the protected side of the network should be configured to permit that traffic to be inspected.

In the following example, access-list 101 is applied to interface Ethernet 0 and would be on the internal or protected side of the network. This access-list permits all traffic that should be CBAC inspected and also provides anti-spoofing. The access list is deliberately set up to deny unknown IP protocols.

```
access-list 101 permit tcp 192.168.10.0 0.0.0.7 any

access-list 101 permit udp 192.168.10.0 0.0.0.7 any

access-list 101 permit icmp 192.168.10.0 0.0.0.7 any

access-list 101 deny ip any any


interface Ethernet0

description Protected interface

ip address 192.168.10.1 255.255.255.248

ip inspect trafficlist in

ip access-group 101 in
```

Set Necessary Timeouts and Thresholds   CBAC uses globally configured timeouts and thresholds to determine when to drop sessions that do not become fully established and how long to manage state information for a session. The values are global; therefore they will be applied to all sessions. For most installations these TCP and UDP default values are acceptable. If they need to be changed, they can be overridden for specified application layer protocols' sessions by using the following syntax:

```
ip inspect [name] [value]
```

You can set any of these options back to their default values by using the no form of the command. The following is a sample of some of the commands; placeholders for the keywords are in italic and their default values are in brackets:

```
ip inspect tcp synwait-time seconds [30]

ip inspect tcp finwait-time seconds [5]

ip inspect tcp idle-time seconds [3600]

ip inspect udp idle-time seconds [30]
```

```
ip inspect dns-timeout seconds [5]

ip inspect max-incomplete high number [500]

ip inspect max-incomplete low number [400]

ip inspect one-minute high number [500]

ip inspect one-minute low number [400]

ip inspect tcp max-incomplete host number [50]

block-time seconds [0]
```

Define Inspection Rules   Inspection rules specify which application-layer protocols will be inspected by CBAC at the interface. The rule can contain several statements, each listing a protocol and specifying the same inspection rule name. You will need to use the rule to specify any TCP or UDP traffic. Unless you are using the firewall between an extranet and protect from both directions, you will likely need only one inspection rule. Except for Java (covered in the next section), use the following syntax for defining rules:

```
ip inspect name [inspection-name] protocol [timeout seconds]
```

This command should be repeated for each of the protocols desired. Examples of the supported protocols are below. As we indicated earlier, some of the timeout and threshold values can be modified on a per protocol basis.

```
ip inspect name trafficlist cuseeme timeout 3600

ip inspect name trafficlist ftp timeout 3600

ip inspect name trafficlist http java-list 51 timeout 3600

ip inspect name trafficlist rcmd timeout 3600

ip inspect name trafficlist realaudio timeout 3600

ip inspect name trafficlist smtp timeout 3600

ip inspect name trafficlist tftp timeout 30

ip inspect name trafficlist udp timeout 15

ip inspect name trafficlist tcp timeout 3600
```

Apply the Inspection Rule to an Interface   Once you have all of the values set and the rules in place, the last step is to assign these rules to an interface. This is functionally much the same as applying an access list to an interface. CBAC rules for an external (unprotected) interface should be placed on an outbound traffic. CBAC rules for an internal (protected) interface should be applied to the inbound interface. The only exception here is if you are using the firewall to protect in each direction in the case of an extranet, for example. The syntax is as follows:

```
ip inspect [inspection-name] [in|out]
```

In the following example, we are applying the CBAC rules and lists that we have created at this point to the Ethernet interface:

```
interface Ethernet0
description Protected interface
ip address 192.168.10.1 255.255.255.248
ip inspect trafficlist in
ip access-group 101 in
```

Use the no form of the command to remove the rule from the interface:

```
no ip inspect trafficlist in
```

Java Blocking

Java blocking requires the use of CBAC to inspect and filter Java applets at the point of entry into the network. Users will be prevented from running Java applets that originate from the protected (inside) side of the firewall.

You can define a specific list of friendly (trusted) external sites and deny all others, or you can take the converse approach and allow all sites and deny only those that you feel are hostile (untrusted). The former of these two choices is the more secure, but it is also the most restrictive to your users. It is important to reiterate that Java blocking uses CBAC, which does not inspect payload. Thus, any applets encapsulated in .zip or .jar files, or that enter via FTP or HTTP, will be allowed by the firewall as content data and will not be detected as a Java applet. Java blocking uses an access list along with the global CBAC commands with syntax as follows:

```
access-list access-list-number [deny|permit] source
[source-wildcard]
ip inspect name inspection-name http [java-list access-list]
[timeout seconds]
```

You will want to use the same *inspection-name* as you used in the other rules that you specified for the other protocols so only one application will be required on the interface.

The example below will specifically deny unfriendly 172.25.1.125 and 172.25.2.198, specifically permit 192.168.10.0 and deny all others.

```
access-list 10 deny 172.25.1.125

access-list 10 deny 172.25.2.198

access-list 10 permit 192.168.10.0 0.0.0.255

access-list 10 deny any


ip inspect name trafficlist http java-list 10 timeout 3600
```

Denial of Service (DoS) Detection and Prevention

A Denial of Service (DoS) attack can bring a site to its knees. It is like making a bunch of phone calls to one number to keep it "busy" so that no one else can get through. These continual attempts are not necessarily connections into the site. They are likely half-open sessions. These means that the TCP three-way handshake was not completed or in the case of UDP there was simply no return traffic. A high number of these half-open sessions, either by absolute count or by incoming rate, could indicate a DoS attack. Once per minute, CBAC will measure the total number of current half-open sessions and the rate of attempts.

When CBAC detects that the number of half-open session is above the `max-incomplete high` threshold it will begin to delete these sessions until the session count is below the `max-incomplete low` parameter. Additionally, when CBAC detects that the *new connection attempt* rate is rising above the *one-minute high* threshold, it will also begin to delete half-open session until the number is below the *one-minute low* parameter. Examples of the global configuration commands are as follows:

```
ip inspect max-incomplete high number [500]

ip inspect max-incomplete low number [400]

ip inspect one-minute high number [500]

ip inspect one-minute low number [400]
```

Real-Time Alerts

CBAC will provide you with real-time alerts that can be sent to a syslog server. Some of the warnings include Denial of Service attack attempt, Java blocking notifications, and SMTP attacks notification.

Optimization and Maintenance

PART 4

Here's the sample output for a DoS attack:

```
Mar 1 14:32:07 sifi-5 108: %FW-4-ALERT_ON: getting aggressive,
count(25/25) current 1-min rate: 110

Mar 1 14:32:37 sifi-5 109: %FW-4-ALERT_OFF: calming down, count (9/
10)current 1-min rate: 112

Mar 1 14:33:35 sifi-5 111: %FW-4-ALERT_ON: getting aggressive,
count(25/25) current 1-min rate: 102

Mar 1 14:34:10 sifi-5 112: %FW-4-ALERT_OFF: calming down, count (9/
10)current 1-min rate: 102

Mar 1 14:35:48 sifi-5 113: %FW-4-ALERT_ON: getting aggressive, count
(25/25) current 1-min rate: 89

Mar 1 14:36:24 sifi-5 114: %FW-4-ALERT_OFF: calming down, count (9/
10)current 1-min rate: 120

Mar 1 14:41:52 sifi-5 116: %FW-4-ALERT_ON: getting aggressive, count
```

Each aggressive listing is the attack and each calming is the firewall deleting the half-open session to bring the router back to a safe level.

Dynamic Port Mapping

The dynamic port mapping feature allows all CBAC-supported applications to run on nonstandard ports, keeping them safe. This is all done behind the scenes.

SMTP Attack Detection and Prevention

The use of CBAC with SMTP can help protect mail servers from attacks by using intrusion detection designed especially for SMTP. Enabling SMTP inspection causes CBAC to inspect SMTP packets for illegal commands. All packets containing legal commands will be allowed and all others dropped, causing the SMTP session to hang and eventually timeout. The following is an alphabetical list of legal SMTP commands:

DATA

EHLO

EXPN

HELO

HELP

MAIL

NOOP

QUIT

RCPT

RSET

SAML

SEND

SOML

TURN

VRFY

In the event that an SMTP attack is detected, the real-time alerts would look something like this:

```
Mar 1 15:10:07 sifi-5 22: %FW-4-SMTP_INVALID_COMMAND: Invalid SMTP
command from initiator (192.168.10.3:52419)
Mar 1 15:11:58 sifi-5 23: %FW-4-SMTP_INVALID_COMMAND: Invalid SMTP
command from initiator (192.168.10.3:52420)
```

Microsoft NetShow Support

The latest release of the Firewall feature set will now provide support for Microsoft Net-Show applications. To utilize this feature, use the global configuration command `ip inspect` with the `netshow` keyword:

```
ip inspect name trafficlist netshow timeout 3600
```

If you are using Microsoft NetMeeting, you will be required to configure inspection for TCP as well as the H.323 protocol, because NetMeeting uses additional TCP ports that are outside the H.323 specification.

Authentication Proxy

The authentication proxy feature allows you to use a CiscoSecure ACS, other RADIUS, or TACACS+ authentication server to apply specific security policies on a per-user basis. With this feature, users can be identified and authorized based on customized per-user policy rather than the previous group oriented policy method. Furthermore, these profiles will only be active when these authenticated users are passing traffic. Authentication proxy is compatible with CBAC, NAT (Network Address Translation), IP Sec (IP Security), and VPN client software.

Intrusion Detection System (IDS)

An IDS (Intrusion Detection System) is available on the higher-end Cisco platforms such as the Cisco 2600, 3600, 7100, and 7200. It is kept independent of the CBAC, but these tools work better together. The IDS is capable of identifying 59 signatures of the most common and severe attacks in effort to identify patterns of network traffic misuse. Functioning as an *in-line* intrusion detection sensor, the router will scrutinize dataflows in search of any match to an IDS signature. If a match is found, the IDS system can send an alarm to the syslog server or to a Cisco NetRanger Director, drop the packet or reset the TCP connection. Drops and resets are best when used together.

Once IDS is enabled on a router, it is considered a security device and no traffic will be allowed to pass through it without inspection. This can drastically affect router performance, so special consideration should be given to the amount of traffic passing through the router as well as other processor-intensive features such as encryption.

You will need to create *audit rules* to tell the router which informational or attack signatures to apply to the packets. You can specify the rules to apply all known signatures, no signatures, or to only apply or deny specific signatures. This flexibility is convenient in the event IDS is reporting false positives due to a specific application behavior. As these packets are passed through the interface, they are matched against the audit rules. If they match, they are then passed through a series of "modules," beginning with IP and then, depending on the packet content, they may be handed to TCP, UDP, ICMP etc. and then on to the Application level.

IDS Configuration

To configure the IDS on a router, use the following steps:

1. Initialize the Cisco IOS IDS.
2. Initialize the post office.
3. Configure audit rules.
4. Apply audit rules.

Initialize the Cisco IOS IDS   The first step to configuring IDS is the initialization of the IDS feature set. From the global configuration mode we use the ip audit smtp command. You will want to be sure to set the threshold to a number greater than the number in which spamming in e-mail messages is suspected. The syntax is as follows:

```
ip audit smtp spam [recipients]
```

The recipients keyword is the maximum number of recipients in an e-mail message. Without a keyword specified, the default of 250 is used.

Or, if you are using the Cisco NetRanger product in your network, the `ip audit po max-events` command will set the threshold beyond which queued events are dropped:

```
ip audit po max-events number_events
```

The `number_events` keyword is used to define the total number of events stored in the event queue. Be careful here. Each event stored in the queue will take 32Kb of memory and can quickly add up.

Initialize the Post Office   After you have enabled the IDS system, you must initialize the IDS post office system using the `ip audit notify` command. Doing so will enable you to send event notifications or alarms to your syslog server.

```
ip audit notify log
```

If you wish to send alarms to a NetRanger Director, use the `nr-director` keyword:

```
ip audit notify nr-director
```

If you are using NetRanger, the router will require a few additional steps. On the router you will need to define post office parameters:

```
ip audit po local hostid [host-id] orgid [org-id]
```

The `hostid` keyword should identify the router with a unique number between 1 and 65,535. The `orgid` keyword will also be a unique number within the same range and will define the organization that each the router and the NetRanger belong to, meaning that it should be the same on both.

The NetRanger itself will require some additional work as well:

```
ip audit po remote hostid [host-id] orgid [org-id] rmtaddress [ip-
address] localaddress [ip-address] port [port-number] preference
[preference-number] timeout [seconds] application [application-type]
```

NOTE   The above example is all one command and would be entered on a single line.

The `host-id` and `org-id` are the same keywords as used on the router. The `rmtaddress` would be the IP address of the NetRanger, and `localaddress` would be the *ip-address* *of* the router's interface. The optional `port` keyword identifies the UDP port on which the NetRanger will be listening for alarms. Absence of this keyword will cause the router to

Optimization and Maintenance

PART 4

use the default port of 45000. The `preference` keyword is also optional and is the relative priority of the route to the NetRanger. The default is 1. If there is more than one route to reach the same Director, you must define a primary route (preference 1) and a secondary route (preference 2). The `timeout` keyword will define the number of seconds the Post Office will wait before it determines that a connection has timed out. This keyword is optional and carries a default value of 5 if not used. The last of the optional keywords is `application` and it will require a value of `director` or `logger`, depending on whether you are using NetRanger Sensors in your network.

WARNING   Post Office configuration changes require reloading the router.

For monitoring purposes, it may be necessary to view any alarms on the console as well as sending them to the syslog server. Remember that this takes valuable router cycles and should only be used temporarily. Use the global configuration command:

```
logging console info
```

You will want to disable console logging as soon as you are finished. Use the no form of this command:

```
no logging console info
```

TIP   In addition to the commands we have covered here, several NetRanger software configurations are also required; you implement these using the nrConfigure tool.

Configure Audit Rules   As we mentioned earlier, we need audit rules to define signatures to apply to the data. To do this we will use the `ip audit info` and `ip audit attack` commands. These commands specify the default actions for information and attack signatures. Either type of signature can use the `alarm`, `drop`, or `reset` functions:

```
ip audit attack action alarm
ip audit info action alarm drop reset
```

TIP   Remember, the keywords `drop` and `reset` are most effective when used together.

To create the rules, you will use the `ip audit name` command to create audit rules. The *auditrule-name* will be the name of the rule that you assign. You will want to use the same name for attack and information signatures.

```
ip audit name auditrule-name info
ip audit name auditrule-name attack
```

You can use access lists with the `ip audit name` command to define hosts or networks that you wish to bypass the audit process using the following syntax:

```
ip audit name auditrule-name [info|attack] list [access-list#]
```

In the example below, the access list 1 is not denying traffic from the 192.168.10.0 network. Rather, it is only defining that hosts from this network will not be audited. This may be helpful to define trusted networks that pass heavy traffic through the router. Keeping them from unnecessarily being audited will preserve valuable router processing cycles. The `permit any access-list` entry will "permit" all other traffic to be audited.

```
ip audit name auditrule1 info list 1


access-list 1 deny 192.168.10.0 0.0.0.255
access-list 1 permit any
```

If it is necessary to disable signatures from the audit process, you can do so with the `ip audit signature` command:

```
ip audit signature [signature-number] disable
```

The *signature-number* value is the number of the signature. You need to be aware that this is a global command and the signature that you remove will no longer be included in any audit rules. If you later wish to reinstate a disabled signature, use the no form of the command.

```
No ip audit signature [signature-number]
```

Very much the same way we used access lists with the audit rule names, we can apply access lists to signatures using the ip `ip audit signature` command with the `list` keyword:

```
ip audit signature [signature-number] list [access-list#]
```

In the following example, we see the similarities in the application of the access-list. The 198.168.10.0 network is not being denied, but rather is being used to define the network hosts that are trusted and will not be filtered through the signature. This may also be helpful for applications that routinely cause false positives under normal operation. Rather than disable the signature globally for all hosts, it would be more secure to remove only those particular hosts or networks that are causing the problems. Note again the use of the `permit any access-list` entry, causing all other traffic to be audited by the signature.

```
access-list 2 deny 192.168.10.0 0.0.0.255
access-list 2 permit any
```

Apply Audit Rules   Now that we have all of the rules and signatures setup, it is time to apply the audit rules to an interface with the following syntax:

```
interface Ethernet0
ip audit [auditrule-name] [direction]
```

You will need to use the `auditrule-name` keyword to indicate the name of the rules that you have just setup and indicate the direction of the traffic that wish to audit by the `direction` keyword is either *in* or *out*. For example:

```
interface Ethernet0
ip audit auditrule1 in
```

The last step in applying the audit rules is to issue the `ip audit po protected` command to define which network should be protected by the router. The *ip-address* value is the address you wish to protect.

```
ip audit po protected [ip_address] [to ip_address]
```

In the following example, the 192.168.10.0–192.168.12.0 network will be protected.

```
ip audit po protected 192.168.10.0 192.168.12.0
```

Appendices

Password Recovery/ Resetting

Eventually, you will lose a router password and have to reset the password. The term "password recovery" is a misnomer, because you cannot really get the password back. All you can do is overwrite it with a new one.

There are two main password recovery techniques for Cisco routers. Which technique you use will depend on the router you are working with.

2000, 2500, 3000, 4000, 7000 and AGS Series Routers

For 2000, 2500, 3000, 4000, 7000 and AGS series routers running IOS 10.0 or greater, follow these directions:

1. Connect a console cable to the router. Hopefully, you know the config register's setting; most likely, it is 0x2102. If you have no password on the console line or if you know the console line password, you can use the show version command to see the config register value.

2. Power the router off and turn it back on.

3. When the router starts to boot, hit the Break key to stop the boot sequence. This must be done in the first 60 seconds after you turn the router on.

4. This will bring the router up to the > prompt. From here, you will want to select whether you want to boot from flash (specified by 0x42) or from the boot ROM (specified by 0x41). Most likely, you will want to boot from flash, so set the config register to 0x42 by using this command:

   ```
   o/r 0x42
   ```

5. Then enter **I** to initialize the router with the new config register setting. This process will look something like the following:

   ```
   2d19h: %SYS-5-RELOAD: Reload requested
   System Bootstrap, Version 11.0(10c), SOFTWARE
   Copyright (c) 1986-1996 by cisco Systems
   2500 processor with 6144 Kbytes of main memory


   Abort at 0x10A85F0 (PC)
   >o/r 0x42
   >i


   System Bootstrap, Version 11.0(10c), SOFTWARE
   Copyright (c) 1986-1996 by cisco Systems
   2500 processor with 6144 Kbytes of main memory
   ```

   The router will now boot without reading the config.

6. Once the router finishes booting, you will be asked if you want to run Setup; tell it No.

7. Go into enable mode. There will be no password since the router has not read the configuration.

8. Load the startup config into memory by typing **copy start run**. This will merge the empty config with the startup config. Since the empty config has all the router interfaces in the administratively down state, you will have to use the **no shutdown** command for all your interfaces to re-enable them.

9. Reset the passwords and enable your interfaces.

10. Reset the config register from global config mode.

    ```
    MMAGH(config)#config-register 0x2102
    ```

    It is very important to make sure you remember to reset the config register. If you do not, the next time the router boots, it will not load a configuration.

11. Copy the running config to the startup config.

12. Reload the router, making sure you remember what you set as the passwords.

1003, 4500, 3600, and 2600 Series Routers

For 1003, 4500, 3600, and 2600 series routers, do the following:

1. Connect a console cable to the router. Hopefully, you know the config register's setting; most likely, it is 0x2102. If you have no password on the console line or if you know the console line password, you can use the show version command to see the config register value.

2. Power the router off and turn it back on.

3. When the router starts to boot, hit the Break key to stop the boot sequence. This must be done in the first 60 seconds after you turn the router on.

4. You will be presented with the rommon> prompt. Enter **confreg**.

5. This will bring up a config script. Enter y for Do you wish to change the configuration[y/n]?

6. Answer No for all other questions until you get to Ignore system config info[y/n] Answer Yes for this.

7. Answer the rest of the questions with No until you get to change boot characteristics[y/n]? Answer Yes to this question.

8. At the enter to boot: prompt, type **2** and then hit the Enter key.

9. A config summary will be printed and you will see the do you wish to change configuration? prompt again. Say No.

10. This will take you back to the rommon> prompt. Type **reset**. The router will now boot without reading the config.

11. Once the router finishes booting, you will be asked if you want to run Setup. Tell it No.

12. Go into enable mode; there will be no password since the router has not read the configuration.

Appendices

13. Load the startup config into memory by typing **copy start run**. This will merge the empty config with the startup config. Since the empty config has all the router interfaces in the administratively down state, you will have to enter no shutdown for all your interfaces to re-enable them.

14. Reset the passwords and enable your interfaces.

15. Reset the config register from global config mode:

```
MMAGH(config)#config-register 0x2102
```

It is very important to make sure you remember to reset the config register. If you do not, the next time the router boots, it will not load a configuration.

16. Copy the running config to the startup config.

17. Reload the router, making sure you remember what you set as the passwords.

B

ICMP Types and Codes

ICMP provides a great deal of information about what is going on with the network. In order to properly interpret this information you need to know what the ICMP type and code combination you are seeing means. The following is a list of the possible ICMP type and code combinations you might run into.

Table B.1   ICMP Types and Codes

Type	Code	Name
0		Echo reply
1		Unassigned
2		Unassigned
3		Destination unreachable
3	0	Net unreachable
3	1	Host unreachable
3	2	Protocol unreachable

Table B.1 ICMP Types and Codes *(continued)*

Type	Code	Name
3	3	Port unreachable
3	4	Fragmentation needed and none set
3	5	Source route failed
3	6	Destination network unknown
3	7	Destination host unknown
3	8	Source host isolated
3	9	Communication with destination network administratively prohibited
3	10	Communication with destination network administratively prohibited
3	11	Destination network unreachable for type of service
3	12	Destination host unreachable for type of service
3	13	Communication administratively prohibited
3	14	Host precedence violation
3	15	Precedence cutoff in effect
4		Source quench
5		Redirect
5	0	Redirect datagram for the network
5	1	Redirect datagram for the host
5	2	Redirect datagram for the type of service and network
5	3	Redirect datagram for the type of service and host
6		Alternate host address

Table B.1   ICMP Types and Codes *(continued)*

Type	Code	Name
7		Unassigned
8		Echo
9		Router advertisement
10		Router selection
11		Time exceeded
11	0	Time to live exceeded in transit
11	1	Fragment reassembly (time exceeded)
12		Parameter problem
12	0	Pointer indicates the error
12	1	Missing a required option
12	2	Bad length
13		Timestamp
14		Timestamp Reply
15		Information request
16		Information reply
17		Address mask request
18		Address mark reply
19		Reserved (security)
20–29		Reserved
30		Traceroute
31		Datagram conversion error

Appendices

Table B.1 ICMP Types and Codes *(continued)*

Type	Code	Name
32		Mobile host redirect
33		ipv6 where-are-you
34		ipv6 i-am-here
35		Mobile register request
36		Mobile request reply
37		Domain name request
38		Domain name reply
39		Skip
40		Photuris
40	0	Reserved
40	1	Unknown security parameter index
40	2	Valid security parameters, but authentication failed
40	3	Valid security parameters, but decryption failed
41–255		Reserved

Common Cable Pinouts

You will occasionally run into situations where you need a specific type of cable and there does not happen to be one handy. This appendix shows the pinouts for cables commonly needed with routers. These pinouts should enable you to craft your own cable should the need arise. These tables list only the pins that need to be modified; if a pin is not mentioned, there is no change for that pin.

Tables C.1-C.7 show some common cable pinouts.

Table C.1   Ethernet Crossover Cable

Near End Pin	Connect to Far End Pin
1	3
2	6
3	1
6	2

If the gold contacts are up and facing away from you, then pin 1 is on the LEFT.

Table C.2 Cisco Rollover Console Cable

Near End Pin	Connect to Far End Pin
1	8
2	7
3	6
4	5
5	4
6	3
7	2
8	1

Table C.3 Cisco Null Modem Cable 9 Pin to 9 Pin

Near End 9 Pin Male	Connect to Far End Pin
3	2
2	3
1,6,8	4
4	1,6,8

Table C.4 Cisco Null Modem Cable 9 Pin to 25 Pin

Near End Pin 9 Pin Male	Connect to Far End 25 Pin
3	3
2	2
5	7
1,6,8	20
4	5,6,8

Table C.5 1-1 Modem Cable 9 Pin to 25 Pin

Near End 9 Pin Male	Connect to Far End 25 Pin
1	8
2	3
3	2
4	20
5	7
6	6
7	4
8	5
9	22

Table C.6 CSU/DSU to CSU/DSU Crossover Cable

Near End Pin	Connect to Far End Pin
1	4
2	5
4	1
5	2

If the gold contacts are up and facing away from you, then pin 1 is on the LEFT.

Table C.7 CSU/DSU to Telecom Demarcation Point

Near End Pin	Connect to Far End Pin
1	1
2	2
4	4
5	5

Notice this is just a standard straight-through cable. Any normal UTP cable can be used for the CSU to demarcation point connection.

Index

Note to the Reader: Page numbers in **bold** indicate the principal discussion of a topic or the definition of a term. Page numbers in *italic* indicate illustrations.

Numbers and Symbols

1-1 modem cable 9-pin to 25-pin connections, *591*
5-4-3 rule, 37
9-pin to 9-pin null modem cable connections, *590*
9-pin to 25-pin 1-1 modem cable connections, *591*
9-pin to 25-pin null modem cable connections, *591*
10Base2 (Thinnet) Ethernet standard, 36, 37, *37*
10Base5 (Thicknet) standard, 36, *37*
100BaseFX Ethernet standard, 42–43
100BaseT4 Ethernet standard, 42–43
100BaseTX Ethernet standard, 41–43
800/900 ISDN routers, 129, *130*
802.3 Ethernet standard, **30–41**. *See also* Ethernet networks
    5-4-3 rule, 37
    10Base2 (Thinnet) standard, 36, 37, *37*
    10Base5 (Thicknet) standard, 36, *37*
    10BaseT standard, 36, 38
    Attached Unit Interface (AUI) cable drops, 36
    bridges and, 39–41, *39*
    Carrier Sense Multiple Access with Collision Detection (CSMA/CD), 31–32
    Cisco routers support for, 38
    Cisco routers as transparent bridges, 40–41
    collision domains and, 38–39
    collisions and, 31–32
    contention domains and, 39
    defined, **30**
    Destination SAPs (DSAPs) and, 33–34, *34*
    Ethernet 802.3 frames, 33–34, *33, 34,* 85
    Ethernet II frames, 32, *33,* 85
    extending Ethernet segments, 38–40, *39*
    how 802.3 Ethernet works, 30–31, *31*
    jam signals, 31
    Logical Link Control headers in Ethernet 802.3 frames, 33–34, *34*
    Organizational Unit Identifiers (OUIs) and, 34–35
    Physical layer specifications, 35–36
    repeaters and, 37, 38–39
    SAPs (Service Access Points) and, 33–34
    segmentation devices, 39
    SNAP (Sub-Network Access Protocol) frames, 34–35, *35,* 85
    Source SAPs (SSAPs) and, 33–34, *34*
    transparent bridges and, 39–41, *39*
    Vampire Taps, 36

1000 series routers, 94, 583–584
1400 DSL routers, 130, *130*
1600 modular data routers, 131, *131,* 140–141, *141*
1700 modular access routers, 131–132, *132*
2000 series routers, 581–583
2500 fixed configuration data routers, 94, 133, *134,* 141–142, 581–583
2600 modular voice/data routers, 94, 105, 134–135, *134,* 583–584
3000 series routers, 581–583
3600 modular voice/data routers, 93, 106, 135–136, *136,* 141, 583–584
MC3800 multiservice routers, 136–137, *137*
4000 modular data routers, 93, 137–139, *138,* 141, 581–584
7000 series routers, **93, 105, 122–128,** 581–583
    7100 VPN router, 123–124, *124, 125*
    7200 Multifunction Platform router, 125–126, *126*
    7206VXR router, 126, *126*
    7500 series routers, 127–128, *128*
    hardware redundancy in, *525*
    network design and, 93, 105
    overview of, 122
    recovering and resetting passwords, 581–583
12000 series routers
    12000 GSR series, 122
    12000 Terabit System, 122
    12012 GSR switch router, 122, *123*
    hardware redundancy in, 525–526
    network design and, 93
? (question mark) command, 221–222, 304–305, 312–313

A

AAA features of TACACS (Terminal Access Controller Access Control System), 389–390
abbreviating commands, 222
ABRs (Area Border Routers), **174**
Access Control field of tokens, 47–48, *47*
access lists, **386, 400–426.** *See also* security
    access list masks, 403
    access list types and numbers, 402
    access-list command, 80, 278–279, 326, 372
    and configuring Dial-on-Demand Routing (DDR), 326
    and configuring Virtual Private Networks, 431–432

defined, **400–402**, *401*
extended access lists, **401–402**, **405–414**
IP access lists, **414–425**, 568
IPX access lists, **425–426**
named access lists, 402
Network Address Translation and, 442
versus routing data to null interfaces, 405
show ipx access-list commands, 285
for SNMP (Simple Network Management Protocol),
    392–394, *393*
standard access lists, **401–405**
Telnet security and, 386
access routers, **93–94**
acknowledgments
    ACK flag in TCP headers, 406–408, *407*
    positive acknowledgment with retransmission, 14–
    15, *15*
Active Monitor in Token Ring networks, 47
active-forwarder routers, **549**
adding
    interface descriptions, 246–247
    to firewall security with IP access lists, 415–417, *415*
addresses. *See also* IP addresses
    address overloading, 80–81, 440, 443, 444
    ARP (Address Resolution Protocol)
    BIAs (Burned In Addresses), 553
    internal network addresses for NetWare servers, 276
    IPX addresses
        defined, **84–85**
    MAC addresses
        defined, **22–23**
    mapping Layer 3 addresses to phone numbers in
        Dial-on-Demand Routing, 322–323, *322*
    Network Address Translation (NAT), **77**, **79–82**,
        440–444
    RARP (Reverse Address Resolution Protocol), 514
    static addresses in AppleTalk networks, 298
adjacencies in OSPF protocol, **171–173**
administrative distance, **148**
administrative services, **7**
advanced ping techniques, 250–251
advertised distances, **194**
AGS series routers, 581–583
alerts in CBAC, 571–572
Alerts level in system logging, 452
AppleTalk protocols, **7**, **86–88**, **208–209**, **295–316**. *See
    also* protocols
    appletalk bandwidth-percent eigrp command, 209
    AppleTalk domains, **300–302**
    appletalk eigrp active-time command, 209
    appletalk eigrp command, 208
    appletalk eigrp-timers command, 209
    appletalk protocol eigrp command, 208

AppleTalk Session Protocol (ASP), 7
AURP (AppleTalk Update Routing Protocol), **299–
    300**, **302–304**
    configuring, **87–88**, **295–304**
    configuring EIGRP routing for AppleTalk networks,
        208–209
    debugging, **312–314**
    defined, **86–87**
    no appletalk protocol eigrp command, 208–209
    no appletalk route-redistribution command, 209
    Phase 1 versus Phase 2 protocols, 87
    RTMP (Routing Table Maintenance Protocol) or
        Apple RIP
    tunneling AppleTalk
        explained, 302–304
        tunneling AppleTalk over IP case study, 315–316
    verifying AppleTalk operation, **304–311**
    zones
Application layer of OSI model, **4–5**
application processes, **4**
applying
    CBAC inspection rules to interfaces, 569–570
    IDS audit rules, 574, 578
    SAP filters to interfaces, 279–280
    standard access lists to routers, 404
Area Border Routers (ABRs), **174**
area-address command, 184
areas in OSPF protocol, **173–174**, **177–178**
ARP (Address Resolution Protocol)
    defined, **496–497**
    ProxyARP (Address Resolution Protocol), 548
ASBRs (Autonomous System Boundary Routers), **177**,
    179–180
ASCII character set, 5
ASP (AppleTalk Session Protocol), 7
ASs. *See* autonomous systems
assigning in AppleTalk networks
    static addresses, 298
    zones and cable ranges, 297
at-a-glance cheater charts of TCP/IP networks, 244
Attached Unit Interface (AUI) cable drops, 36
attributes of BGP communities, 560–561
audit rules in IDS
    applying, 578
    configuring, 576–578
    defined, **574**
AUI (Attached Unit Interface) cable drops, 36
AURP (AppleTalk Update Routing Protocol), **299–300**,
    302–304. *See also* AppleTalk protocols
    appletalk protocol aurp command, 303
    and configuring AppleTalk, 299–300, 302–303
    defined, **299–300**, **302–303**
    interface tunnel command, 303

tunnel mode aurp command, 303
tunnel source and tunnel destination commands, 303
tunneling AppleTalk, 302–304
authentication. *See also* passwords; security
    authentication proxy feature in CBAC, 573
Authorization Failure Traps in HSRP protocol, **555**
Autonomous System Boundary Routers (ASBRs), **177,**
    179–180
autonomous systems (ASs)
    defined, **145–146**
    EIGRP protocol and, 195
    IGRP protocol and, 156
    OSPF protocol and, 175, 179
AutoSummarize routes feature, 95, 98, 154

B

B channels, 319, 320, 332–333
backing up. *See also* dial backup; replacing
    backup delay command, 335–336
    backup interface command, 335–336
    backup load command, 335–336
    Internetwork Operating System, 231–232
    router configurations, 224–225, **528–530**
    router images with copy flash tftp command, 526–
        528
    routes with static routing, 264–265, *264*
Backup Designated Routers (BDRs), **110, 171, 172–173**
backup routes, **194**
Backward-Explicit Congestion Notification (BECN),
    360, 362–363
bandwidth requirements for LANs, 103–105
banners for Telnet access, 386–387
Banyan Vines networks, 554
Basic Rate Interface (BRI), **319–320**. *See also* ISDN
    configuring, 319–320
    configuring SPIDs (Service Provider IDs), 320
    defined, **319**
    Dial-on-Demand Routing (DDR) and, 320
    establishing a call, 320
    identifying ISDN switch types, 319–320
    isdn spid1 and isdn spid2 commands, 320
    isdn switch-type command, 320
    Link Access Procedure on the D-Channel (LAPD)
        frame format, 319
BDRs (Backup Designated Routers), **110, 171, 172–173**
BECN (Backward-Explicit Congestion Notification),
    360, 362–363
BGP (Border Gateway Protocol), **146, 559–564**
    as an exterior gateway protocol, 146
    BGP communities, **559–564**
    defined, **559**
BIAs (Burned In Addresses), **553**

big endian data storage, **6**
binary equivalents of IP addresses, 69–73
blocking
    data with standard access lists, 403–405, *404*
    Java applets in CBAC, 570–571
    traceroute command, 417
boot sequence for routers, **216,** *217*
boot system commands for configuring routers, 226–
    227
Border Gateway Protocol. *See* BGP
BRI. *See* Basic Rate Interface
bridges
    bridge-group command, 41
    IEEE 802.3 Ethernet standard and, 39–41, *39*
    Source Route Bridging (SRB), 48, 49–52, *50, 51*
    transparent bridges
        Cisco routers as, 40–41
        IEEE 802.3 Ethernet standard and, 39–40, *39*
broadcasts
    broadcast multi-access networks, 172–173
    broadcast storm case study, 521–522
    directed broadcasts, 398–400, *399*
    enabling UDP broadcast forwarding, 266
buffered system logging, **452–455, 456–457**
Burned In Addresses (BIAs), **553**
bytes in IP addresses, 69

C

cable range settings in AppleTalk networks, 297, 298,
    299
cabling. *See also* connectors
    Attached Unit Interface (AUI) cable drops, 36
    cable pinouts, **589–592**
    coaxial cables, 37, *37*
    troubleshooting, 505, *506*
    unshielded twisted-pair (UTP) cables, 38
calculating
    composite metrics
        defined, **202**
        for EIGRP protocol, 192, 202
        for IGRP protocol, 157–158
        load for IGRP protocol, 158
        reliability for IGRP protocol, 158
CAR (Committed Access Rate) features, 359
Carrier Sense Multiple Access with Collision Detection
    (CSMA/CD), **31–32**
case studies
    classless routing with RIPv2, 167–168
    configuring dial backup for Frame Relay, 337–338
    migrating IPX to Ethernet 802.2, 292–293
    network design, 117–119, *118*
    router security, 445–449, *445*

SNMP (Simple Network Management Protocol), 483–484
spare router configuration, 543–546
TCP/IP case studies, **267–270**
traffic prioritization case studies
    queuing algorithms, 378–379, *378*
    SAP filtering, 380–381, *380*
troubleshooting case studies, **519–522**
Catalyst 6509 switch, 93
CBAC (Context-Based Access Control), **565–573**. *See also* firewalls
    applying inspection rules to interfaces, 569–570
    authentication proxy feature, 573
    configuring, 566–567
    configuring IP access lists at the interface, 568
    defined, **565–566**, *566*
    defining inspection rules, 569
    Denial of Service (DoS) attack detection and prevention, 571
    dynamic port mapping feature, 572
    extended access lists and, 568
    ip inspect command, 568–571, 573
    Java blocking feature, 570–571
    Microsoft NetShow support, 573
    no ip inspect trafficlist in command, 570
    real-time alerts, 571–572
    selecting interfaces for inspecting packets, 567, *567*
    SMTP attack detection and prevention, 572–573
    timeout and threshold settings, 568–569
CDP (Cisco Discovery Protocol), **246**, **394–395**, **497–499**
    defined, **246**
    security problems, 394–395
    show cdp neighbors command, 498–499
    troubleshooting with, 497–499
changing
    IP addressing schemes, **260–262**
    metric variance in IGRP protocol, 160
    value of RIP default timers, 150–151
channel service units. *See* CSU/DSUs
CHAP (Challenge Handshake Authentication Protocol), **58–59**, *59*
Chargen (character generator) service, 395–398
charts of TCP/IP networks, **244**
cheater charts of TCP/IP networks, **244**
checking version of Internetwork Operating System, 233–234
CIR (committed information rate), **361**, 362, 363, 427
circuit-switched circuits, **55–56**
Cisco Discovery Protocol (CDP), **246**, **394–395**, **497–499**
    defined, **246**
    security problems, 394–395

show cdp neighbors command, 498–499
    troubleshooting with, 497–499
Cisco null modem cable connections
    9-pin to 9-pin connections, 590
    9-pin to 25-pin connections, 591
Cisco routers, **121–142**. *See also* routers
    800/900 ISDN routers, 129, *130*
    1000 series routers, 94, 583–584
    1400 DSL routers, 130, *130*
    1600 modular data routers, 131, *131*, 140–141, *141*
    1700 modular access routers, 131–132, *132*
    2000 series routers, 581–583
    2500 fixed configuration data routers, 94, 133, *134*, 141–142, 581–583
    2600 modular voice/data routers, 94, 105, 134–135, *134*, 583–584
    3000 series routers, 581–583
    3600 modular voice/data routers, 93, 106, 135–136, *136*, 141, 583–584
    MC3800 multiservice routers, 136–137, *137*
    4000 modular data routers, 93, 137–139, *138*, 141, 581–584
    7000 series routers, **93**, **105**, **122–128**, **581–583**
    12000 series routers
        12000 GSR series, 122
        12000 Terabit System, 122
        12012 GSR switch router, 122, *123*
        hardware redundancy in, 525–526
        network design and, 93
    address overloading, 80–81, 440, 443, 444
    AGS series routers, 581–583
    Cisco Catalyst 6509 switch, 93
    FastEthernet support, 43
    high-end or core routers, **91–93**, *92*, **121–128**
    IEEE 802.3 Ethernet support, 38
    NPMs (Network Processor Modules), 138
    ping command on, 489–492
    small/medium business routers, **129–139**
    Token Ring support, 49
    traceroute command on, 495–496
    as transparent bridges, 40–41
    when to use which models, **139–142**, *140*, *141*, *142*
Cisco Technical Assistance Center (TAC), **537–542**. *See also* disaster recovery
    customer support product groups, 541
    escalating calls, 542
    gathering information before contacting, 537
    how TAC works, 540–542
    opening a case, 540–541
    priority levels, 541–542
    sending e-mail, 538
    telephone numbers, 538–540
    Web support, 537–538

CiscoView software, 473–475
CiscoWorks 2000 CWSI Campus, **475–480**. *See also*
  network management
    CDP (Cisco Discovery Protocol) and, 476, 479, 480
    enabling RCP, 479–480
    network discovery process, 475–476
    Resource Manager Essentials, 478–480
    seed devices and, 475–476
    setting up routers for, 479–480
    topology maps, 477–478
CiscoWorks software, 473
classes of IP addresses, 74–75
classfull versus classless routing protocols, **146–147,**
  147
classless routing with RIPv2 case study, **167–168**
clear counters command, 461–462
clear ipx route command, 288, 289, 291
clear snapshot quiet-time command, 335
CLI (command-line interface). *See* commands
clients, snapshot client command, 333–334
CMIP over TCP/IP (Common Management Information
  Protocol over TCP/IP), 464
coaxial cables, 37, *37*
collisions
    collision domains, 38–39
    IEEE 802.3 Ethernet standard and, 31–32
    late collisions, 45
    troubleshooting, 45
commands. *See also* Internetwork Operating System;
  prompts; utilities
    aaa accounting, 389–390
    aaa new-model, 389
    abbreviating, 222
    access-list, 80, 278–279, 326, 372
    appletalk commands. *See also* debug commands
      appletalk bandwidth-percent eigrp, 209
      appletalk cable-range, 297, 298, 299
      appletalk discovery, 299
      appletalk domain, 301–302
      appletalk domain hop-reduction, 301–302
      appletalk domain remap-range, 301–302, 303–
        304
      appletalk domain-group, 301–302, 303
      appletalk eigrp, 208
      appletalk eigrp active-time, 209
      appletalk eigrp-timers, 209
      appletalk protocol, 300
      appletalk protocol aurp, 303
      appletalk protocol eigrp, 208
      appletalk routing, 87–88, 296–297
      appletalk zone, 297
      no appletalk protocol, 300
      no appletalk protocol eigrp, 208–209

no appletalk protocol rtmp, 300
no appletalk route-redistribution, 209
show appletalk ?, 304–305
show appletalk domain, 311
show appletalk globals, 308
show appletalk interface, 307
show appletalk route, 305–306
show appletalk traffic, 308–310
show appletalk zone, 306–307
area-address, 184
backup delay, 335–336
backup interface, 335–336
backup load, 335–336
bridge-group, 41
clear counters, 461–462
clear ipx route, 288, 289, 291
clear snapshot quiet-time, 335
configuring routers 225–227
conform, 359–360
copy commands
    copy flash tftp, 231–232, 526–528
    copy run tftp, 530
    copy running-config startup-config, 221
    copy tftp flash, 237–238, 530–531
    copy tftp run and copy tftp start, 536–537
crypto, 430–431
crypto ipsec, 431–433
crypto map, 434–435
debug commands
    debug all, 152, 219
    debug dialer, 333
    debug frame-relay lmi interface, 245–246
    debug ip igrp transaction, 158–159
    debug ip rip, 151–152, 153–154
    debug ipx routing activity, 288–291
    debug ipx sap activity, 288
    debug isdn-q921 and debug isdn-q931, 333
    debug priority, 350–351
    limitations of, 152, 313
    no debug all, 219
    troubleshooting with, 499–502
debug commands for AppleTalk networks, **312–314**
debug commands for TCP/IP networks, **255–260**
default-information originate always, 180
deny any any, 421
description, 246–247
Dial-on-Demand Routing commands, **323–327**
    debug dialer, 333
    dialer map snapshot, 333–334
    dialer pool-member, 327, 336
    dialer string, 327, 336
    dialer-group, 323, 327, 328
    show dialer, 329–330

show interface, 331–332
show interfaces, 332–333
show isdn active, 330
show isdn status, 330–331
early-token-release, 49
eigrp log-neighbor-changes, 196
encapsulation, 57
encapsulation ppp, 58, 59, 60
exceed, 359–360
fair-queue, 347
frame-relay commands, 360–364, 514–518
interface commands. *See also* show commands
    backup interface, 335–336
    debug frame-relay lmi interface, 245–246
    interface dialer, 326
    interface fastethernet, 43, 44
    interface tokenring, 49
    interface tunnel, 303
    passive-interface, 155
    show appletalk interface, 307
    show ip eigrp interfaces, 202–203
    show ip interface, 163–164
    show ip ospf interface, 176–177
    show ipx interface, 281–282
ip commands. *See also* show commands
    ip access-group, 424
    ip access-list extended, 422–424
    ip audit, 574–578
    ip bandwidth-percent eigrp, 196
    ip community-list, 560
    ip domain-lookup, 79
    ip forward-protocol udp, 266
    ip hello-interval eigrp, 196
    ip helper-address, 266
    ip hold-time eigrp, 196
    ip hosts, 79
    ip http, 390–391
    ip inspect, 568–571, 573
    ip irdp, 557–558
    ip nat inside destination, 81–82
    ip nat inside source, 80, 81
    ip nat inside source static, 442
    ip nat pool, 80, 81–82, 443
    ip nat translation, 442–443
    ip ospf cost, 176
    ip ospf hello-interval, 189
    ip route, 263, 264, 265
    ip subnet-zero, 77
    ip summary-address eigrp, 196
ipx commands. *See also* show commands
    ipx access-list, 425–426
    ipx bandwidth-percent eigrp, 207
    ipx default-route, 277

ipx delay, 277
ipx down, 276
ipx gns-reply-disable, 374
ipx gns-response-delay, 373–374
ipx gns-round-robin, 277, 374–375, *375*
ipx hello-interval eigrp, 207
ipx hold-time eigrp, 207
ipx input-sap-filter and ipx output-sap-filter, 373
ipx internal-network, 184, 276
ipx ipxwan, 185, 272, 276
ipx link-delay, 185
ipx maximum-hops, 185, 207
ipx maximum-paths, 276–277
ipx nlsp enable, 184–185
ipx nlsp metric, 185
ipx output-gns-filter, 376–377, *376*
ipx rip-multiplier, 369
ipx route, 277
ipx router eigrp, 204
ipx router nlsp, 184
ipx router rip, 370
ipx routing, 85, 86, 275–276, 292–293
ipx routing activity, 370
ipx sap-incremental eigrp, 206–207, 371–372
ipx sap-multiplier, 367–368
ipx throughput, 185
ipx update interval rip, 369
ipx update interval sap, 367
ipx update sap-after-rip, 369
IRDP protocol commands, 557–558
is-type, 188
isdn spid1 and isdn spid2, 320
isdn switch-type, 320, 321, 323
logging buffered, 452–453
map-class frame-relay, 361, 363–364
media-type 10baset, 38
metric maximum-hops, 159
metric weights, 158, 196
neighbor, 164–165, *165*
net, 187–188
network, 204
no access-list, 419
no appletalk protocol, 300
no appletalk protocol eigrp, 208–209
no appletalk protocol rtmp, 300
no appletalk route-redistribution, 209
no auto-summary, 196
no cdp enable, 395
no cdp run, 395
no ip directed-broadcast, 399–400
no ip domain-lookup, 79
no ip http server, 390
no ip inspect trafficlist in, 570

no ip irdp, 557
no ip routing, 41
no ip source-route, 400
no ip split-horizon, 164
no ipx down, 276
no ipx router rip, 205–206, 369
no login, 230
no network 9F, 205
no ntp, 394
no redistribute, 207
no service finger, 394
no service tcp-small-servers, 395–396
no service udp-small-servers, 395–396
no shutdown, 276
passive-interface, 155
permit any any, 414, 418
ping command troubleshooting, **488–492**
    IPX ping case study, 519–520
ping commands
    advanced ping techniques, 250–251
    and classless routing with RIPv2, 167–168
    extended ping command, 251–252, 267–268,
        489–490
    IP name resolution and, 78
    ping apple, 310–311
    ping and ICMP (Internetwork Control Message
        Protocol), 248–250
    ping ipx, 186, 286–287, 490–492, 519–520
priority group, 349
question mark (?) command, 221–222, 304–305,
    312–313
queue-limit, 349
queue-list, 353–354
random-detect, 358–359
rate-limit, 359
redistribute, 179–180
rmon, 481–482
route-map com_attrib_access-list, 561
router commands
    copy running-config startup-config, 221
    router bgp, 561
    router eigrp, 195
    router igrp, 156
    router isis, 187, 188
    router ospf, 175
    router rip, 149
router management commands, **457–463**
service config, 226–227
service password-encrypt, 230
service timestamps log uptime, 454
show commands
    show appletalk ?, 304–305
    show appletalk arp, 308

show appletalk domain, 311
show appletalk globals, 308
show appletalk interface, 307
show appletalk route, 305–306
show appletalk traffic, 308–310
show appletalk zone, 306–307
show arp, 496–497
show cdp neighbors, 498–499
show controllers, 509–510
show crypto ipsec, 434
show crypto map, 434
show dialer, 329–330
show environment, 462–463
show frame-relay lmi, 514–515
show frame-relay map, 515–516
show frame-relay pvc, 516–518
show ip access-lists, 413–414, 417–418
show ip eigrp interfaces, 202–203
show ip eigrp routing, 199–201
show ip eigrp topology summary, 203–204
show ip eigrp traffic, 203
show ip interface, 163–164
show ip irdp, 558
show ip ospf, 181–182
show ip ospf database, 171, 182–183
show ip ospf interface, 176–177
show ip ospf neighbor, 183
show ip route, 160–161
show ipx access-list, 285
show ipx commands listed, 286
show ipx interface, 281–282
show ipx route, 186, 280–281
show ipx servers, 284–285, 365
show ipx servers unfiltered, 373
show ipx traffic, 283–284
show isdn active, 330
show isdn status, 330–331
show logging, 453–454, 455
show processes, 458–459
show processes cpu, 459–460
show processes memory, 459
show queue, 346–347
show queuing custom, 354
show run, 528–529, 535
show start, 528–529
show version, 233–234, 527
show interface
    in FDDI networks, 53–54
    for monitoring routers, 460–461
    troubleshooting network physical layer problems
        with, 506–507
    troubleshooting telecommunication lines with,
        510–511

verifying Dial-on-Demand Routing, 331–332
viewing traffic queuing algorithms, 355–356
show interfaces
    for Dial-on-Demand Routing (DDR), 332–333
    for IGRP protocol, 158
show ip protocols
    for EIGRP protocol, 197–199
    for IGRP protocol, 161–162
    for RIP protocol, 149–150
shutdown, 276
snapshot client and snapshot server, 333–334
snmp server enable traps, 465–466
snmp-server community, 391–392
snmpwalk, 466–468, 469
tacacs-server, 388–389
telnet monitor, 502
tftp-server flash, 239–240
timers basic, 150–151
trace
    extended trace command, 254–255
    testing IP connectivity with, 252–254
    trace ipx, 287–288
traceroute, **417, 492–496**
    TTL (Time to Live) values and, 492–494, *493,*
    494
traffic prioritization commands
    conform, 359–360
    debug priority, 350–351
    exceed, 359–360
    fair-queue, 347
    priority group, 349
    queue-limit, 349
    queue-list, 353–354
    random-detect, 358–359
    rate-limit, 359
    show interface, 355–356
    show queue, 346–347
    show queuing custom, 354
tunnel commands
    tunnel, 102
    tunnel mode aurp, 303
    tunnel source and tunnel destination, 303
undebug all, 152
variance, 160
version 2, 153
xmodem, 532–533
Committed Access Rate (CAR) features, 359
committed information rate (CIR), **361**, 362, 363, 427
common cable pinouts. *See* cabling, cable pinouts
Common Management Information Protocol over TCP/
    IP (CMIP over TCP/IP), 464
communities. *See* BGP (Border Gateway Protocol), BGP
    communities

composite metric calculation
    defined, **202**
    for EIGRP protocol, 192, 202
    for IGRP protocol, 157–158
compression, **6**
Config Maker utility, 225
Config mode, **220–221**
configuring. *See also* setting; setting up
    AppleTalk, **87–88, 295–304**
    AppleTalk domains, 300–302
    Basic Rate Interface (BRI), 319–320
    CBAC (Context-Based Access Control), 566–567
    dial backup, 335–336
    dial backup for Frame Relay case study, 337–338
    Dial-on-Demand Routing (DDR), **321–326, 328**
    dialer profiles, 327
    discard eligibility for Frame Relay traffic shaping,
        364
    EIGRP routing for AppleTalk networks, 208–209
    EIGRP routing for IP networks, 195–197
    EIGRP routing for IPX networks, **111, 112, 204–**
        207, 370–372
        and disabling IPX RIP, 112, 205–206
        incremental SAPs (Service Advertising Protocols),
            111, *111,* 206–207, 370–372, *371*
        overview of, 111, *111,* 204
    ELMI (Enhanced Local Management Interface) for
        Frame Relay traffic shaping, 363
    encryption in Virtual Private Networks, 430–432
    HSRP (Hot Standby Router Protocol), 550–553, *550*
    IDS audit rules, 574, 576–578
    IDS (Intrusion Detection System), 574
    IGRP (Interior Gateway Routing Protocol), 156–160
    IP access lists, 568
    IP routing, 78
    IPX (Internet Packet Exchange) protocol, **85–86,**
        274–278, *274*
    IPX RIP update interval, 369–370
    IS-IS (Intermediate System to Intermediate System)
        protocol, 187–188
    Network Address Translation, 80–82
    NLSP (NetWare Link Services Protocol), 184–185
    OSPF (Open Shortest Path First) protocol, 174–180,
        174, 179, 180
    Primary Rate Interface (PRI), 321
    RIP (Routing Information Protocol), 149–152, *149*
    RIPv2 protocol, 153–155
    routers, **220–221, 223–227, 543–546**
        in Virtual Private Networks, 435–440
    SAP update interval, 367–368, *368*
    snapshot routing, 333–335
    SNMP (Simple Network Management Protocol),
        391–394, *393*

spare routers, 543–546
SPIDs (Service Provider IDs), 320
transparent bridging on Cisco routers, 40–41
Virtual Private Networks (VPNs), **429–440**, *433*
    overview of, 429, *430*
conform command, 359–360
congestion. *See also* traffic prioritization
    defined, **11–12**
    pinhole congestion, 211
connection-oriented versus non-connection-oriented
    protocols, **10–12**, *11*, *12*
connectivity, managing, 95
connectors. *See also* cabling
    FDDI connectors, 53–54
    Vampire Taps, 36
console
    console cable pinouts, 590
    console logging in IDS, 576
    console password, 228–229
    copying Internetwork Operating System image from
        console, 531–533
    requirements, 532
contacting Technical Assistance Center, 537
contention domains, 39
Context-Based Access Control. *See* CBAC
context-sensitive Help in router modes, 221–222
convergence, 191, 193
copy commands
    copy flash tftp, 231–232, 526–528
    copy run tftp, 530
    copy running-config startup-config, 221
    copy tftp flash, 237–238, 530–531
    copy tftp run and copy tftp start, 536–537
copying Internetwork Operating System image from
    console, 531–533
copying and pasting router configurations, 533–535,
    534, *535*
core routers, **91–93**, *92*, **121–128**
cost metric value settings
    for IS-IS (Intermediate System to Intermediate
        System) protocol, 187
    for NLSP (NetWare Link Services Protocol), 185
    for OSPF (Open Shortest Path First) protocol, 176–
        177
costs
    of fault tolerance, 115–116, *116*
    of system downtime, 524
counters
    clear counters command, 461–462
    error counters, 507–509
    in IP access lists, 417–418
Coup messages in HSRP protocol, **549**

CPSWInst utility (Router Software Loader), 234–237
CRC (cyclic redundancy checking) errors, 45
creating. *See also* defining
    BGP community lists, 560
    dialer profiles, 326
    map classes for Frame Relay traffic shaping, 361–
        364
    Network Address Translation pools, 443–444
    SAP filters, 278–279
Critical level in system logging, 452
crypto command, 430–431
crypto ipsec command, 431–433
crypto map command, 434–435
CSMA/CD (Carrier Sense Multiple Access with
    Collision Detection), **31–32**
CSU/DSUs (channel service units/digital service units)
    CSU/DSU to CSU/DSU crossover cable pinouts, 592
    CSU/DSU to telecom demarcation point cable
        pinouts, 592
    and troubleshooting broadcast storms, 521
    and troubleshooting serial line problems, 511–513,
        512
custom queuing algorithm, **351–356**, *351*
customer support. *See* Cisco Technical Assistance
    Center
cutting and pasting router configurations, 528–529, *529*
cyclic redundancy checking (CRC) errors, 45

D

D channels, 319, 331–332
DACs (Dual Attached Concentrators), **52**
DASs (dual-attached stations), **52**
data center integration feature, 126
data compression, **6**
Data Link Connection Identifiers (DLCIs), **61**, *61*, *62*,
    364, 514
Data Link layer of OSI model, **20–23**, *20*, *21*, *22*
Data Terminal Equipment (DTE) devices, **317–318**
DDR. *See* Dial-on-Demand Routing
debug commands
    for AppleTalk networks, **312–314**
    debug all, 152, 219
    debug dialer, 333
    debug frame-relay lmi interface, 245–246
    debug ip igrp transaction, 158–159
    debug ip rip, 151–152, 153–154
    debug ipx routing activity, 288–291
    debug ipx sap activity, 288
    debug isdn-q921 and debug isdn-q931, 333
    debug priority, 350–351
    limitations of, 152, 313
    no debug all, 219

for TCP/IP networks, **255–260**
troubleshooting with, 499–502
Debugging level in system logging, 453
DECnet protocol, 554
dedicated circuits, 55
default route settings for OSPF protocol, 179–180
default timers in RIP protocol, 150–151
default-information originate always command, 180
defining. *See also* creating
    CBAC inspection rules, 569
    hosts to be translated in Network Address
      Translation, 442
    transform sets in Virtual Private Networks, 432–
      435, *433*
delay values for IGRP protocol, 157–158
Denial of Service (DoS) attacks, 571
deny any any command, 421
description command, 246–247
Designated Routers (DRs), **110, 171, 172–173**
designing networks. *See* network design
Destination SAPs (DSAPs), **33–34,** *34*
detecting
    Denial of Service (DoS) attacks, 571
    SMTP (Simple Mail Transfer Protocol) attacks, 572–
      573
DHCP (Dynamic Host Configuration Protocol)
    defined, **266**
    versus HSRP (Hot Standby Router Protocol), 548
diagramming TCP/IP networks, **241–244**
    advantages of, 241–242
    at-a-glance cheater charts, 244
    by hand, 242
    with NetSuite software, 242, *243*
    with Visio software, 242, *243*
dial backup, **335–338.** *See also* ISDN
    backup delay command, 335–336
    backup interface command, 335–336
    backup load command, 335–336
    configuring, 335–336
    configuring dial backup for Frame Relay case study,
      337–338
    defined, **335**
    dialer pool-member command and, 336
    dialer string command and, 336
Dial-on-Demand Routing (DDR), **56, 104, 298, 321–**
    333
    on AppleTalk networks, 298
    Basic Rate Interface (BRI) and, 320
    circuit-switched circuits and, 56
    configuring, **321–326,** 327–328, *322*
      dialer idle-timeout command, 324, *325*
    debug dialer command, 333
    defined, **321**

dialer map snapshot command, 333–334
dialer profiles, **326–328,** 336
    network design and, 104
    verifying, **329–333**
diconfig files, 224
Diffusing Update Algorithm (DUAL), **110–111, 193–**
    194, *194*
Digital Network Architecture, Session Control Protocol
    (DNA SCP), 7
digital service units. *See* CSU/DSUs
Dijkstra's algorithm, 170, 174, 179, 182
directed broadcasts, 398–400, *399*
disabling. *See also* enabling
    CDP (Cisco Discovery Protocol), 395
    console logging in IDS, 576
    IP source routing, 400
    IPX RIP for EIGRP routing on IPX networks, 112
    IRDP (ICMP Router Discovery Protocol), 557
    passwords, 230
    RTMP (Routing Table Maintenance Protocol) or
      Apple RIP, 300
    services, 394–398
    split horizon, 164
disaster recovery, **523–546, 581–584**
    Cisco Technical Assistance Center (TAC), **537–542**
    costs of system downtime, 524
    hardware redundancy, **525–526**
      redundant power supplies, 525
    planning, 523–524
    recovering and resetting passwords, **581–584**
      in 1003, 4500, 3600, and 2600 series routers,
        583–584
      in 2000, 2500, 3000, 4000, 7000, and AGS series
        routers, 481–483
    router configuration backup, **528–530,** *529*
    router configuration replacement, **533–537,** *534,*
      535, 537
    router image
      backing up with copy flash tftp command, 526–
        528
      replacing with copy tftp flash command, 530–
        531
    router software failure, **531–533**
    spare router configuration case study, **543–546**
    swapping out routers, 530
discard eligibility configuration for Frame Relay traffic
    shaping, 364
discard service, 395–398
discovery mode in AppleTalk networks, 299
distance-vector routing protocols, **145–168.** *See also*
    link-state routing protocols; protocols
    administrative distance, 148
    autonomous systems (ASs), 145–146, 156

classfull versus classless routing protocols, 146–147, *147*
classless routing with RIPv2 case study, 167–168
defined, **145**, **165–166**
IGRP (Interior Gateway Routing Protocol), **146**, **155–162**, *156*
  administrative distance and, 148
  AutoSummarize routes feature, *95*
  as a classfull protocol, 147
interior versus exterior gateway routing protocols, 146
IPX RIP protocol, **271–272**, **369–370**
  disabling for EIGRP routing, 112, 205–206
RIP (Routing Information Protocol), **98–101**, **106–108**, 146, **148–155**, *99, 100, 107, 108, 149*
  AutoSummarize routes feature, 95, 154
  classfull versus classless protocols and, 147
  classless routing with RIPv2 case study, 167–168
  versus EIGRP protocol, 110–111
  versus IGRP (Interior Gateway Routing Protocol), 158–160
  RIPv2 (RIP version 2), 147, 152–155, 167–168
RTMP (Routing Table Maintenance Protocol) or Apple RIP
  and configuring AppleTalk, 87, 88, 297, 299–300
  disabling, 300
  no appletalk protocol rtmp command, 300
split horizon technique, 148, **162–165**, *163, 165,* 195
distribution routers, **93**
DLCIs (Data Link Connection Identifiers), **61**, *61, 62,* 364, 514
DNA SCP (Digital Network Architecture, Session Control Protocol), 7
domains
  AppleTalk domains, **300–304**, 311
  collision domains, 38–39
  contention domains, 39
  Domain Name Services (DNS), **78–79**
  ip domain-lookup and no ip domain-lookup commands, 79
DoS (Denial of Service) attacks, 571
downtime costs, 524
DRs (Designated Routers), **110**, 171, **172–173**
DSAPs (Destination SAPs), **33–34**, *34*
DSL routers, 130, *130*
DSUs (digital service units). *See* CSU/DSUs
DTE (Data Terminal Equipment) devices, **317–318**
Dual Attached Concentrators (DACs), 52
DUAL (Diffusing Update Algorithm), **110–111**, **193–194**, *194*
dual-attached stations (DASs), **52**

duplex mismatches, **45**
Duplicate IP Address messages in HSRP protocol, *555*
dynamic address translation, **440**
Dynamic Host Configuration Protocol (DHCP)
  defined, **266**
  versus HSRP (Hot Standby Router Protocol), 548
dynamic node discovery in AppleTalk networks, 298
dynamic packet filtering, **413–414**
dynamic port mapping feature in CBAC, 572

E

e-mail
  SMTP (Simple Mail Transfer Protocol) attack detection and prevention, 572–573
  Technical Assistance Center e-mail address, 538
early-token-release command, 49
Easy IP protocol, **82**
EBCDIC character set, *5*
echo service, **395–398**
editing. *See* changing
EGP (Exterior Gateway Protocol), 146
800 ISDN routers, 129, *130*
802.3 Ethernet standard, **30–41**. *See also* Ethernet networks
  5-4-3 rule, 37
  10Base2 (Thinnet) standard, 36, 37, *37*
  10Base5 (Thicknet) standard, 36, *37*
  10BaseT standard, 36, 38
  Attached Unit Interface (AUI) cable drops, 36
  bridges and, 39–41, *39*
  Carrier Sense Multiple Access with Collision Detection (CSMA/CD), 31–32
  Cisco routers support for, 38
  Cisco routers as transparent bridges, 40–41
  collision domains and, 38–39
  collisions and, 31–32
  contention domains and, 39
  defined, **30**
  Destination SAPs (DSAPs) and, 33–34, *34*
  Ethernet 802.3 frames, 33–34, *33, 34, 85*
  Ethernet II frames, 32, *33, 85*
  extending Ethernet segments, 38–40, *39*
  how 802.3 Ethernet works, 30–31, *31*
  jam signals, 31
  Logical Link Control headers in Ethernet 802.3 frames, 33–34, *34*
  Organizational Unit Identifiers (OUIs) and, 34–35
  Physical layer specifications, 35–36
  repeaters and, 37, 38–39
  SAPs (Service Access Points) and, 33–34
  segmentation devices, 39

SNAP (Sub-Network Access Protocol) frames, 34–35, *35*, 85
Source SAPs (SSAPs) and, 33–34, *34*
transparent bridges and, 39–41, *39*
Vampire Taps, 36
EIGRP (Enhanced Internet Gateway Routing Protocol), 110–112, 191–211. *See also* IGRP; protocols
  administrative distance and, 148
  advertised versus feasible distances and, 194
  as an interior gateway routing protocol, 146
  appletalk bandwidth-percent eigrp command, 209
  appletalk eigrp active-time command, 209
  appletalk eigrp command, 208
  appletalk eigrp-timers command, 209
  appletalk protocol eigrp command, 208
  autonomous systems (ASs) and, 195
  AutoSummarize routes feature, 95
  as a classless protocol, 147
  composite metric calculation, 192, 202
  configuring EIGRP routing for AppleTalk networks, **208–209**
  configuring EIGRP routing for IP networks, **195–197**
  configuring EIGRP routing for IPX networks, **111, 112, 204–207, 370–372,** *111, 371*
  convergence and, 191, 193
  defined, **110–112,** *111,* **191–192**
  Diffusing Update Algorithm (DUAL), 110–111, 193–194, *194*
  eigrp log-neighbor-changes command, 196
  enabling, 195
  features, 191–192
  Hello packets and, 193–194
  ip bandwidth-percent eigrp command, 196
  ip hello-interval eigrp command, 196
  ip hold-time eigrp command, 196
  ip summary-address eigrp command, 196
  load sharing with EIGRP case study, **210–211**
  metric weights command, 196
  MTUs (Maximum Transmit Units) and, 111
  multicast updates, 192
  neighbors tables, 193–194, *194*
  network design and, 192
  no appletalk protocol eigrp command, 208–209
  no appletalk route-redistribution command, 209
  no auto-summary command, 196
  versus RIP (Routing Information Protocol), 110–111
  route redistribution and, 101, 192, 207, 209
  router eigrp command, 195
  specifying interfaces, 195
  split horizon and, 195
  subnet masks and, 192

  successors (primary routes) and feasible successors (backup routes), 194
  updates, 192
  verifying IP EIGRP, show ip route command, 201–202
  verifying IP EIGRP routing, **197–204,** *197*
ELMI (Enhanced Local Management Interface), **363**
Emergencies level in system logging, 452
enable password, **230, 231**
enable secret password, **230–231**
enabling. *See also* disabling
  AppleTalk discovery mode, 299
  AppleTalk domains, 301
  AppleTalk routing, 87–88, 297
  console logging in IDS, 576
  EIGRP for AppleTalk, 208
  EIGRP (Enhanced Internet Gateway Routing Protocol), 195
  IDS (Intrusion Detection System), 574–575
  IDS post office system, 575–576
  IGRP (Interior Gateway Routing Protocol), 156
  IPX routing, 85, 86, 275–276, 292–293
  IS-IS (Intermediate System to Intermediate System) protocol, 187
  NLSP (NetWare Link Services Protocol), 184
  OSPF (Open Shortest Path First) protocol, 175
  Remote Network Monitor (RMON), 481
  RIP (Routing Information Protocol), 149
  SNMP (Simple Network Management Protocol), 391–392
  UDP broadcast forwarding, 266
encapsulation
  and configuring IPX protocol configuration, 275
  encapsulation command, 57
  encapsulation ppp command, 58, 59, 60
  HDLC encapsulation, 57
  in IPX addressing, 84–85
  OSI model and, 23–24, *24*
  tunneling and, 101
encryption
  configuring in Virtual Private Networks, 430–432
  crypto command, 430–431
  crypto ipsec command, 431–433
  crypto map command, 434–435
  defined, **7**
  encrypting passwords, 230
  show crypto ipsec command, 434
  show crypto map command, 434
Ending Delimiter field in tokens, 47–48, *47*
Enhanced Internet Gateway Routing Protocol. *See* EIGRP
Enhanced Local Management Interface (ELMI), **363**
error counters, 507–509

Errors level in system logging, 453
escalating Technical Assistance Center calls, 542
establishing static routes for Dial-on-Demand Routing, 322
Ethernet networks, **30–46, 55, 292–293, 589**. *See also* local area network (LAN) technologies
    Ethernet crossover cable pinouts, *589*
    Ethernet encapsulation and configuring IPX protocol, 275
    Fast EtherChannel standard, **46**
    FastEthernet standard, **41–45**
        full-duplex operation, 44–45, *44*
        half-duplex operation, 43, *43*
    Gigabit Ethernet standard, **55,** 125–126
    IEEE 802.3 standard, **30–41**
        5-4-3 rule, 37
        10Base2 (Thinnet) standard, 36, 37, *37*
        10Base5 (Thicknet) standard, 36, *37*
        10BaseT standard, 36, 38
        Destination SAPs (DSAPs) and, 33–34, *34*
        Ethernet 802.3 frames, 33–34, *33, 34,* 48, 85
        extending Ethernet segments, 38–40, *39*
        how 802.3 Ethernet works, 30–31, *31*
        Logical Link Control headers in Ethernet 802.3 frames, 33–34, *34*
        SNAP (Sub-Network Access Protocol) frames, 34–35, *35,* 85
        Source SAPs (SSAPs) and, 33–34, *34*
        transparent bridges and, 39–41, *39*
        Vampire Taps, 36
    IPX addressing and Ethernet frames, 84–85
    migrating IPX to Ethernet 802.2 case study, 292–293
examples. *See* case studies
exceed command, 359–360
extended access lists, **401–402, 405–414**. *See also* access lists
    access list numbers and, 402
    CBAC (Context-Based Access Control) and, 568
    defined, **401, 405**
    with dynamic packet filtering, 413–414
    ICMP (Internetwork Control Message Protocol) redirects and, 411–412, *412,* 416
    show ip access-lists command, 413–414, 417–418
    with static packet filtering, 406–410, *407, 408, 410*
    TCP three-way handshake and, 406–409, *407, 408*
    UDP packets and, 409–410, *410*
extended ping command, 251–252, 267–268, 489–490
extended TACACS (Terminal Access Controller Access Control System), 388, 389
extended trace command, 254–255
extending Ethernet segments, 38–40, *39*
Exterior Gateway Protocol (EGP), 146
exterior gateway routing protocols, **146**

F

fair-queue command, 347
Fast EtherChannel standard, **46**
FastEthernet standard, **41–45**. *See also* Ethernet networks
    100BaseFX standard, 42–43
    100BaseT4 standard, 42–43
    100BaseTX standard, 41–43
    Cisco router support for, 43
    defined, **41**
    full-duplex operation, 44–45, *44*
    half-duplex operation, 43, *43*
fault tolerance, **52–53, 91–93, 112–116**. *See also* network design
    cost of, 115–116, *116*
    example, 91–93, *91, 92*
    FDDI features, 52–53, 113–114, *113*
    Frame Relay networks and, 115
    ISDN and, 115
    redundant paths, 114, 115
    on wide area networks, 115
FCS (frame check sequence) errors, 45
FDDI (Fiber Distributed Data Interface) networks, **52–54**. *See also* local area network (LAN) technologies
    connectors, 53–54
    defined, **52**
    Dual Attached Concentrators (DACs), 52
    dual-attached stations (DASs), 52
    fault tolerance features, 52–53, 113–114, *113*
    frame structure, 54, *54*
    Multi-Mode Fiber, Single-Mode Fiber and, 52
    optical bypass switches, 53, *53*
    single-attached stations (SASs), 52
    wrapping feature, 52–53
feasible distances, **194**
feasible successors, **194**
FECN (Forward-Explicit Congestion Notification), **360**
Fiber Distributed Data Interface. *See* FDDI
fields
    in IP packets, 67–69, *68*
    in IPX packets, 83–84, *83*
    in TCP segment headers, 65–66, *65*
    in UDP (User Datagram Protocol) headers, 67, *67*
FIFO (first-in first-out) queuing, 342
File Transfer Protocol (FTP), 343
files, diconfig files, 224
filters
    BGP community filtering, 561
    dynamic packet filtering, 413–414
    filtering SAPs, **278–280, 372–373, 380–381**
    GNS filters, 376–377, *376*
    static packet filtering, 406–410, *407, 408, 410*

Index

FIN flag in TCP headers, 406
Finger service, 394
firewalls, **415–417, 421–425, 564–578**
    CBAC (Context-Based Access Control), **565–573,** *566, 567*
    IDS (Intrusion Detection System), **574–578**
    IP access lists and, 415–417, *415*
    Phase I and Phase II Firewall feature set versions, 564–565
    protecting networks without, 421–425, *422*
5-4-3 rule, 37
flags in TCP headers, 406–408, *407, 408*
flash memory
    copy flash tftp command, 231–232, 526–528
    copy tftp flash command, 237–238, 530–531
    requirements, 105–106
    tftp-server flash command, 239–240
flash updates in IGRP protocol, 158–159
flow control
    at the Data Link layer, 21
    at the Network layer, 19–20, *19*
    at the Transport layer, 12, *12*
forklift upgrades, **139**
Forward-Explicit Congestion Notification (FECN), **360**
1400 DSL routers, 130, *130*
4000 modular data routers, 93, 137–139, *138*, 141, 581–584
Frame Relay networks, **61–62, 115, 117, 162–163**. *See also* wide area network (WAN) technologies
    BECN (Backward-Explicit Congestion Notification), 360, 362–363
    committed information rate (CIR), 361, 362, 363, 427
    configuring dial backup for Frame Relay case study, 337–338
    defined, **61**
    Enhanced Local Management Interface (ELMI), 363
    fault tolerance and, 115
    FECN (Forward-Explicit Congestion Notification), 360
    Frame Relay traffic shaping (FRTS), **360–364**
    Local Management Interface (LMI), 61, *62*, 245–246
    in network design case study, 117
    port speed and, 361
    split horizon technique and, 162–163
    testing Frame Relay environments, 245–246
    troubleshooting, **513–518**
        example, 513–514, *513*
    virtual circuits, 61, *61*
    Virtual Private Networks and, 427
Frame Status Field in Information/Control frame, 48, *48*
frames. *See also* packets

Ethernet frames
    Ethernet 802.3 frames, 33–34, *33, 34*, 48, 85
    Ethernet II frames, 32, *33*, 85
    IPX addressing and, 84–85
    SNAP (Sub-Network Access Protocol) frames, 34–35, *35*, 85
    FDDI frame format, 54, *54*
    frame check sequence (FCS) errors, 45
    HDLC frame format, 56–57, *57*
    Information/Control frame, 48, *48*
    Link Access Procedure on the D-Channel (LAPD) frame format, 319
    PPP frame format, 57–58, *58*
    Token Ring frame format, 47–48, *47, 48*
    Token Ring frames versus Ethernet frames, 48
FRTS. *See* Frame Relay networks, Frame Relay traffic shaping
FTP (File Transfer Protocol), 343
full-duplex FastEthernet operation, **44–45**, *44*

G

gathering information before contacting Technical Assistance Center, 537
Get and Get Next commands in SNMP, 464, 465, 466–469, *467, 468*
Get Nearest Server (GNS) requests. *See also* IPX (Internet Packet Exchange) protocol
    defined, **273–274, 373–377**
    GNS filters, 376–377, *376*
    ipx gns-reply-disable command, 374
    ipx gns-response-delay command, 373–374
    ipx gns-round-robin command, 277, 374–375, *375*
    ipx output-gns-filter command, 376–377, *376*
    sending, 373–377, *375, 376*
    show ipx servers unfiltered command, 373
Gigabit Ethernet standard, **55**, 125–126
Global Configuration mode, 348, 349, 353
GNS. *See* Get Nearest Server (GNS) requests

H

half-duplex FastEthernet operation, **43**, *43*
hand diagramming TCP/IP networks, 242
hardware redundancy, **525–526**. *See also* disaster recovery
    in Cisco 7000 series routers, 525
    in Cisco 12000 series routers, 525–526
    redundant power supplies, 525
HDLC (High-Level Data Link Control) protocol, **56–57**, *57*
headers in TCP protocol, 65–66, *65*, 406–408, *407*
Hello messages in HSRP protocol, 549

Hello packets
  defined, **171–172**
  EIGRP protocol and, 193–194
  Hello interval case study, 189–190
Help in router modes, 221–222
HEMS (High Level Entity Management System), 464
High Level Entity Management System (HEMS), 464
high-end routers, **121–128**
High-Level Data Link Control (HDLC) protocol, **56–
    57**, *57*
hop count
  IGRP settings, 159
  reducing in AppleTalk domains, 301–302
  RIP protocol and, 99–101, 148
host tables, **79**
Hot Standby Router Protocol. *See* HSRP
HP OpenView
  HSRP (Hot Standby Router Protocol) and, 555
  Network Node Manager (NNM), 471–472, *473*
  Web site, 555
HSRP (Hot Standby Router Protocol), **547–555**
  active-forwarder routers, 549
  Authorization Failure Traps, 555
  in Banyan Vines networks, 554
  BIAs (Burned In Addresses), 553
  configuring, 550–553, *550*
  Coup messages, 549
  DECnet protocol and, 554
  defined, **547**
  versus DHCP protocol, 548
  Duplicate IP Address messages, 555
  Hello messages, 549
  how HSRP works, 548–550, *550*
  HP OpenView and, 555
  ICMP protocol and, 555
  IPX protocol and, 555
  versus IRDP (ICMP Router Discovery Protocol), 548
  listening state, 549–550, 553–554
  MAC addresses and, 548, 553–554
  versus ProxyARP (Address Resolution Protocol),
    548
  Resign messages, 549
  versus RIP (Routing Information Protocol), 548
  speaking-and-listening state, 549–550
  standby command, 553
  standby-routers, 549
  in Token Ring networks, 554
  uses for, 548
  XNS protocol and, 554
HTTP servers, 390–391
hubs, replacing with switches, 507–508
hybrid routing protocols. *See* EIGRP

HyperTerminal
  router configuration backup and, 529, *529*
  router configuration replacement and, 534–535,
    534, 535

I

ICMP (Internetwork Control Message Protocol)
  debug ip icmp command, 259
  HSRP (Hot Standby Router Protocol) and, 555
  ICMP redirects, 411–412, *412*, 416
  ICMP types and codes, 585–588
  IRDP (ICMP Router Discovery Protocol), **548, 556–
    558**
  network management and, 463
  ping command and, 248–250
identifying
  interesting traffic for Dial-on-Demand Routing, 322
  ISDN switch types, 319–320
IDS (Intrusion Detection System), **574–578**. *See also*
    firewalls
  applying audit rules, 574, 578
  configuring, 574
  configuring audit rules, 574, 576–578
  defined, **574**
  enabling, 574–575
  enabling or disabling console logging, 576
  enabling post office system, 575–576
  ip audit commands, 574–578
IEEE 802.3 Ethernet standard, **30–41**. *See also* Ethernet
    networks
  5-4-3 rule, 37
  10Base2 (Thinnet) standard, 36, 37, *37*
  10Base5 (Thicknet) standard, 36, *37*
  10BaseT standard, 36, 38
  Attached Unit Interface (AUI) cable drops, 36
  bridges and, 39–41, *39*
  Carrier Sense Multiple Access with Collision
    Detection (CSMA/CD), 31–32
  Cisco routers support for, 38
  Cisco routers as transparent bridges, 40–41
  collision domains and, 38–39
  collisions and, 31–32
  contention domains and, 39
  defined, **30**
  Destination SAPs (DSAPs) and, 33–34, *34*
  Ethernet 802.3 frames, 33–34, *33, 34, 85*
  Ethernet II frames, 32, *33, 85*
  extending Ethernet segments, 38–40, *39*
  how 802.3 Ethernet works, 30–31, *31*
  jam signals, 31
  Logical Link Control headers in Ethernet 802.3
    frames, 33–34, *34*

Organizational Unit Identifiers (OUIs) and, 34–35
Physical layer specifications, 35–36
repeaters and, 37, 38–39
SAPs (Service Access Points) and, 33–34
segmentation devices, 39
SNAP (Sub-Network Access Protocol) frames, 34–35, *35*, 85
Source SAPs (SSAPs) and, 33–34, *34*
transparent bridges and, 39–41, *39*
Vampire Taps, 36
IGRP (Interior Gateway Routing Protocol), **146**, **155–162**. *See also* distance-vector routing protocols; EIGRP
administrative distance and, 148
autonomous systems (ASs) and, 156
AutoSummarize routes feature, 95
changing metric variance, 160
as a classfull protocol, 147
composite metric calculation, 157–158
configuring, 156–160
debug ip igrp transaction command, 158–159
defined, **146**, **155–156**, *156*
delay values, 157–158
enabling, 156
hop count settings, 159
load calculations, 158
load sharing, 159–160
metric maximum-hops command, 159
metric weights command, 158
reliability calculations, 158
versus RIP protocol, 158–160
router igrp command and, 156
show interfaces command and, 158
show ip protocols command and, 161–162
show ip route command and, 160–161
troubleshooting update problems, 158–159
updates and flash updates, 158–159
variance command, 160
incremental SAPs (Service Advertising Protocols), 111, *111*, 206–207, 370–372, *371*
information gathering before contacting Technical Assistance Center, 537
Information/Control frame, 48, *48*
Informational level in system logging, 453
input SAPs, 279–280
inside local and inside global addresses, **79**
inside and outside interfaces, 441–442
inspection rules in CBAC, 569–570
integrated IS-IS (Intermediate System to Intermediate System) protocol, **187**
interesting traffic identification for Dial-on-Demand Routing, 322
interface commands

backup interface, 335–336
debug frame-relay lmi interface, 245–246
interface dialer, 326
interface fastethernet, 43, 44
interface tokenring, 49
interface tunnel, 303
passive-interface, 155
show appletalk interface, 307
show interface, *53–54*
show interface command
    in FDDI networks, 53–54
    for monitoring routers, 460–461
    troubleshooting network physical layer problems with, 506–507
    troubleshooting telecommunication lines with, 510–511
    verifying Dial-on-Demand Routing, 331–332
    viewing traffic queuing algorithms, 355–356
show interfaces command
    for Dial-on-Demand Routing (DDR), 332–333
    for IGRP protocol, 158
show ip eigrp interfaces, 202–203
show ip interface, 163–164
show ip ospf interface, 176–177
show ipx interface, 281–282
interfaces
adding interface descriptions, 246–247
applying SAP filters to, 279–280
in EIGRP configuration, 195
interface problems in router configuration replacement, 535
in OSPF configuration, 175–176
in RIP configuration, 149, *149*
routing data to null interfaces, 405
interior gateway routing protocols, **146**
Intermediate System to Intermediate System protocol. *See* IS-IS
internal network addresses for NetWare servers, 276
INTERNET BGP community, **559**
Internet Packet Exchange protocol. *See* IPX
Internet Protocol. *See* IP access lists; IP addresses; ip commands; IP (Internet Protocol)
Internetwork Control Message Protocol. *See* ICMP
Internetwork Operating System (IOS), **105–106**, **215**, **231–240**. *See also* commands; prompts
backing up, 231–232
Committed Access Rate (CAR) features, 359
copy flash tftp command and, 231–232, 526–528
copy tftp flash command and, 237–238, 530–531
copying IOS image from console, 531–533
defined, **215**
dial backup feature, **335–338**
Global Configuration mode, 348, 349, 353

Map Class Configuration mode, 361
memory requirements, 105–106
tftp-server flash command and, 239–240
updating, **232–240**, *239*
Intrusion Detection System. *See* IDS
IOS. *See* Internetwork Operating System
IP access lists, **414–425, 568**. *See also* access lists
    adding to firewall security with, 415–417, *415*
    blocking traceroute probes, 417
    configuring, 568
    counters, 417–418
    deny any any command, 421
    ip access-group command, 424
    ip access-list extended command, 422–424
    logging, 418–421, *420*
    no access-list command, 419
    permit any any command and, 414, 418
    and protecting networks without firewalls, 421–425, *422*
IP addresses, **69–82, 269–270**. *See also* TCP/IP protocol suite
    access-list command, 80
    address overloading, 80–81, 440, 443, 444
    binary equivalents of, 69–73
    bytes, 69
    changing IP addressing schemes, **260–262**, *261*
    classes of, 74–75
    configuring IP routing, 78
    defined, **69**
    DNS (Domain Name Services) and, 78–79
    Duplicate IP Address messages in HSRP protocol, 555
    host tables and, 79
    implementation case study, 269–270
    inside local and inside global addresses, 79
    ip domain-lookup and no ip domain-lookup commands and, 79
    ip hosts command and, 79
    ip nat inside destination command, 81–82
    ip nat inside source command, 80, 81
    ip nat pool command, 80
    ip subnet-zero command, 77
    IP subnetting, 75–77
    name resolution and, 78–79
    Network Address Translation (NAT) protocol and, 77, 79–82
    octets, **69**
    outside local and outside global addresses, 79–80
    Port Address Translation (PAT), 81
    private IP addresses, 77
    subnet masks, **73–75**
        EIGRP protocol and, 192
        in router configuration setup, 223

ip commands
    ip access-group, 424
    ip access-list extended, 422–424
    ip audit, 574–578
    ip bandwidth-percent eigrp, 196
    ip community-list, 560
    ip domain-lookup, 79
    ip forward-protocol udp, 266
    ip hello-interval eigrp, 196
    ip helper-address, 266
    ip hold-time eigrp, 196
    ip hosts, 79
    ip http, 390–391
    ip inspect, 568–571, 573
    ip irdp, 557–558
    ip nat inside destination, 81–82
    ip nat inside source, 80, 81
    ip nat inside source static, 442
    ip nat pool, 80, 81–82, 443
    ip nat translation, 442–443
    ip ospf cost, 176
    ip ospf hello-interval, 189
    ip route, 263, 264, 265
    ip subnet-zero, 77
    ip summary-address eigrp, 196
    show ip access-lists command, 413–414, 417–418
    show ip eigrp interfaces command, 202–203
    show ip eigrp routing command, 199–201
    show ip eigrp topology summary command, 203–204
    show ip eigrp traffic command, 203
    show ip interface command, 163–164
    show ip irdp command, 558
    show ip ospf command, 181–182
    show ip ospf database command, 171, 182–183
    show ip ospf interface command, 176–177
    show ip ospf neighbor command, 183
    show ip protocols command
        for EIGRP protocol, 197–199
        for IGRP protocol, 161–162
        for RIP protocol, 149–150
    show ip route command, 160–161, 181
IP (Internet Protocol), **67–69, 82, 195–197**. *See also* TCP/IP protocol suite
    configuring EIGRP routing for IP networks, 195–197
    defined, **67**
    Easy IP, 82
    IP packets, 67–69, *68*
    IP ping response symbols, 490–492
    IP source routing, 400
    testing IP connectivity, **248–255**, 489–490
    verifying IP EIGRP routing, **197–204**, *197*

IPX (Internet Packet Exchange) protocol, **82–86**, **111**, **112**, **204–207**, **271–293**, **425–426**, **519–520**. *See also* protocols

configuring, **85–86**, **184–185**, **274–278**, *274*, 292–293, 374–375, *375*

configuring EIGRP routing for IPX networks, **111**, **112**, **204–207**, 370–372

incremental SAPs (Service Advertising Protocols), 111, *111*, 206–207, 370–372, *371*

defined, **82**

Get Nearest Server (GNS) requests

defined, **273–274**, 373–377, *375*, *376*

GNS filters, 376–377, *376*

ipx gns-round-robin command, 277, 374–375, *375*

ipx output-gns-filter command, 376–377, *376*

HSRP (Hot Standby Router Protocol) and, *555*

IPX access lists, **425–426**

IPX addresses, **84–85**

and configuring IPX, 275

ipx link-delay command, 185

ipx maximum-hops command, 185

ipx nlsp enable command, 184–185

ipx nlsp metric command, 185

IPX RIP protocol, **271–272**, **369–370**

disabling for EIGRP routing, 112, 205–206

ipx router nlsp command, 184

IPX socket numbers, 425–426

ipx throughput command, 185

IPX troubleshooting case study, **519–520**

migrating to Ethernet 802.2 case study, 292–293

network management and, 95

packet structure, 83–84, *83*

SAP filters, **278–280**, **372–373**, **380–381**

case study, 380–381, *380*

SAP (Service Advertising Protocol), **272–273**, **365–369**, **370–373**, **380–381**

access-list command and, 278–279

configuring SAP update interval, 367–368, *368*

debug ipx sap activity command, 288

ipx sap-incremental eigrp command, 206–207, 371–372

SAP broadcast problems, 365–367, *366*

sending incremental SAP updates with EIGRP protocol, 111, *111*, 206–207, 370–372, *371*

traffic considerations, **365–377**, **380–381**

configuring SAP update interval, 367–368, *368*

GNS filters, 376–377, *376*

ipx gns-round-robin command, 374–375, *375*

ipx output-gns-filter command, 376–377, *376*

ipx sap-incremental eigrp command, 206–207, 371–372

SAP broadcast problems, 365–367, *366*

SAP filtering case study, **380–381**, *380*

sending Get Nearest Service (GNS) requests, 373–377, *375*, *376*

sending incremental SAP updates with EIGRP protocol, 111, *111*, 206–207, 370–372, *371*

verifying IPX operation, **280–291**

ping ipx command, 186, 286–287, 490–492, 519–520

show ipx route command, 186, 280–281

show ipx servers command, 284–285, 365

IRDP (ICMP Router Discovery Protocol), 548, 556–558. *See also* ICMP (Internetwork Control Message Protocol)

IS-IS (Intermediate System to Intermediate System) protocol, **187–188**. *See also* link-state routing protocols

ISDN (Integrated Services Digital Network), **55**, **60**, **115**, **117–119**, **317–338**. *See also* Dial-on-Demand Routing (DDR); wide area network (WAN) technologies

800/900 ISDN routers, 129, *130*

Basic Rate Interface (BRI), **319–320**

isdn switch-type command, 320, 321, 323

as a circuit-switched technology, 55

D channels and, 319, 331–332

Data Terminal Equipment (DTE) devices, 317–318

debug isdn-q921 and debug isdn-q931 commands, 333

defined, **60**

dial backup, **335–338**

fault tolerance and, 115

ISDN components, 317–318

in network design case study, 117–119, *118*

network termination devices (NT1 and NT2), 318

Primary Rate Interface (PRI), **320–321**

reference points, 318

show isdn active command, 330

show isdn status command, 330–331

and sizing networks, 104

snapshot routing, **333–335**

terminal adapters, 318

terminal equipment devices (TE1 and TE2), 317–318

troubleshooting, 333

J

jam signals, **31**

Java blocking feature in CBAC, 570–571

L

LANs. *See* local area network (LAN) technologies

LAPD (Link Access Procedure on the D-Channel) frame format, **319**

late collisions, **45**
Layer 2 devices, 26
Layer 3 addresses, mapping to phone numbers in Dial-on-Demand Routing, 322–323, *322*
Layer 3 devices, 26
Layer 3 switching, **26–27**
LCP structure in PPP protocol, *57–58, 58*
leased lines, **55**, 104
level 1 and level 2 routers, **187**
levels of priority in Technical Assistance Center, 541–542
Link Access Procedure on the D-Channel (LAPD) frame format, 319
link saturation, 366–367
Link State Advertisements (LSAs), **170, 179**
Link State Updates (LSUs), **172**
link-state routing protocols, **169–190.** *See also* distance-vector routing protocols; protocols
    defined, **169**
    IS-IS (Intermediate System to Intermediate System), **187–188**
    NLSP (NetWare Link Services Protocol), **183–186**
    OSPF (Open Shortest Path First) protocol, **108–110**, *109,* **170–183**, *189–190*
        administrative distance and, 148
        as an interior gateway routing protocol, 146
        AutoSummarize routes feature, *95*
        as a classless protocol, 147
        configuring, 174–180, *174, 179, 180*
        route redistribution and, 98–101, *99, 100*
        summarization settings, 174, 178–179, *179*
listening state in HSRP protocol, 549–550, 553–554
little endian data storage, **6**
LLC (Logical Link Control) headers in Ethernet 802.3 frames, 33–34, *34*
LLC (Logical Link Control) layer in OSI model, **20**, *20*
LMI (Local Management Interface)
    defined, **61**, *62*
    Enhanced Local Management Interface (ELMI), 363
    router setup and, 245–246
    and troubleshooting Frame Relay networks, 514–515
load calculations for IGRP protocol, 158
load sharing
    with EIGRP protocol case study, 210–211
    in IGRP protocol, 159–160
local area network (LAN) technologies, **30–55.** *See also* Ethernet networks; wide area network (WAN) technologies
    FDDI (Fiber Distributed Data Interface) networks, **52–54**
        fault tolerance features, *52–53,* 113–114, *113*

LAN bandwidth requirements, 103
Token Ring networks, **46–52**, **554**
    Information/Control frame, 48, *48*
    Source Route Bridging (SRB), 48, 49–52, *50, 51*
    Token Ring frame structure, 47–48, *47, 48*
    tokens, **46–47,** *47*
local loopback mode of CSU/DSUs, **512–513**, *512*
Local Management Interface (LMI)
    defined, **61**, *62*
    Enhanced Local Management Interface (ELMI), 363
    router setup and, 245–246
    and troubleshooting Frame Relay networks, 514–515
logging
    console logging in IDS, 576
    IP access lists, 418–421, *420*
    IPX access lists, 426
    system logging (syslog), **452–457**
Logical Link Control headers in Ethernet 802.3 frames, 33–34, *34*
Logical Link Control (LLC) layer in OSI model, **20**, *20*
loopback interfaces, **174–175**
lower layers of OSI model, **8**
LSAs (Link State Advertisements), **170, 179**
LSUs (Link State Updates), **172**

M

MAC. *See* Media Access Control (MAC) layer
maintaining adjacencies in OSPF protocol, 171–173
manageability of networks, **94–103.** *See also* network design
    connectivity and, 95
    defined, **94**
    IPX protocol and, 95
    modems and, 94–95
    out-of-band management, 94–95
    Remote Authentication Dial-In User Service (RADIUS) and, 94–95
    route redistribution, 98–101, *99, 100*
    route summarization, 95–98, *96, 97*
    Telnet and, 95
    tunneling, 101–103, *102,* 302
Management Information Bases. *See* MIBs
management. *See* network management; router management
Management Stations versus Management Agents, **464**
manually diagramming TCP/IP networks, 242
Map Class Configuration mode, 361
map classes for Frame Relay traffic shaping, 361–364
map-class frame-relay command, 361, 363–364
mapping Layer 3 addresses to phone numbers in Dial-on-Demand Routing, 322–323, *322*

masks
    access list masks, 403
    subnet masks, **73–75**
        EIGRP protocol and, 192
        in router configuration setup, 223
MC3800 multiservice routers, 136–137, *137*
Media Access Control (MAC) layer. *See also* OSI
    defined, **20**, *20*
    MAC addresses, **22–23**
        bridges and, 39–40, *39*
        HSRP (Hot Standby Router Protocol) and, 548, 553–554
        IPX addressing and, 84
media-type 10baset command, 38
medium-sized business routers, **129–139**
memory
    flash memory
        copy flash tftp command, 231–232, 526–528
        copy tftp flash command, 237–238, 530–531
        requirements, 105–106
        tftp-server flash command, 239–240
    NVRAM (non-volatile RAM), 220
    router RAM requirements, 105–106
messages in HSRP protocol, 549, 555
metrics
    changing metric variance in IGRP protocol, 160
    composite metric calculation, **202**
        for EIGRP protocol, 192, 202
        for IGRP protocol, 157–158
    cost metric value settings
        for IS-IS (Intermediate System to Intermediate System) protocol, 187
        for NLSP (NetWare Link Services Protocol), 185
        for OSPF (Open Shortest Path First) protocol, 176–177
    ipx nlsp metric command, 185
    metric maximum-hops command, 159
    metric weights command, 158, 196
    SNMP system uptime metric, 468–469
MIBs (Management Information Bases)
    Remote Network Monitor (RMON) and, 480, 481–482
    in SNMP protocol, 466, 467, 471, 472
Microsoft HyperTerminal
    router configuration backup and, 529, *529*
    router configuration replacement and, 534–535, *534, 535*
Microsoft NetShow, 573
migrating IPX to Ethernet 802.2 case study, 292–293
MIX (multiservice interchange) feature, 126
modems
    1-1 modem cable 9-pin to 25-pin connections, 591

Cisco null modem cable 9-pin to 9-pin connections, 590
Cisco null modem cable 9-pin to 25-pin connections, 591
    network management and, 94–95
modifying. *See* changing
MSFC (Multi Switch Feature Card), 93
Multi Switch Feature Card (MSFC), 93
Multi-Mode Fiber, 52, 55
multicast updates in EIGRP protocol, 192
multiplexing, **16–18**, *17*
multiservice interchange (MIX) feature, 126

N

N-RESETS, 9–10
name resolution, **78–79**
named access lists, 402
NAT. *See* Network Address Translation
native mode in Remote Network Monitor, 481
NBMA (non-broadcast multi-access) networks, 162–163, 172–173
neighbor command, 164–165, *165*
neighbors tables in EIGRP protocol, 193–194, *194*
net command, 187–188
NetShow software, 573
NetSuite software, 242, *243*
NetWare. *See* IPX (Internet Packet Exchange) protocol; NLSP (NetWare Link Services Protocol)
Network Address Translation (NAT), 77, **79–82**, **440–444**
    access lists and, 442
    address overloading, 80–81, 440, 443, 444
    advantages of, 81–82
    configuration examples, 80–82
    creating NAT pools, 443–444
    defined, **79**, **440**
    defining hosts to be translated, 442
    dynamic address translation, 440
    features, 440
    inside local and inside global addresses, 79
    ip nat inside destination command, 81–82
    ip nat inside source command, 80, 81
    ip nat inside source static command, 442
    ip nat pool command, 80, 81–82, 443
    ip nat translation command, 442–443
    outside global and outside local addresses, 79–80
    private IP addresses and, 77
    setting inside and outside interfaces, 441–442
    setting up translation parameters, 442–443
    static address translation, 440, 441–443, 444
network addresses, internal network addresses for NetWare servers, 276

network command, 204
network design, **89–119, 523–524**
    case study, 117–119, *118*
    disaster recovery planning, 523–524
    EIGRP protocol and, 192
    fault tolerance, **52–53, 91–93, 112–116**
        cost of, 115–116, *116*
        example, 91–93, *91, 92*
        FDDI features, *52–53,* 113–114, *113*
    manageability, **94–103**
        route redistribution, 98–101, *99, 100*
        route summarization, 95–98, *96, 97*
        tunneling, 101–103, *102,* 302
    overview of, 89–90
    scalability, **90–94,** *91–92*
    sizing, **103–112**
        EIGRP (Enhanced Internet Gateway Routing
            Protocol), 110–112, *111*
        OSPF (Open Shortest Path First) protocol, 108–
            110, *109*
        RIP (Routing Information Protocol), 106–108,
            107, 108
Network File System (NFS) protocol, 7
Network layer of OSI model, **18–20,** *19*
network management, **94–103, 463–482.** *See also*
    router management
    CiscoView, 473–475
    CiscoWorks 2000 CWSI Campus, **475–480**
        CDP (Cisco Discovery Protocol) and, 476, 479,
            480
    CiscoWorks, 473
    CMIP over TCP/IP (Common Management
        Information Protocol over TCP/IP), 464
    HEMS (High Level Entity Management System), 464
    HP OpenView Network Node Manager (NNM),
        471–472, *473*
    ICMP (Internetwork Control Message Protocol)
        and, 463
    and network design, **94–103**
        route redistribution, 98–101, *99, 100*
        route summarization, 95–98, *96, 97*
        tunneling, 101–103, *102,* 302
    network management systems, **469–471,** *470*
    outsourcing of, 470
    Remote Network Monitoring (RMON), 480–482
    SGMP (Simple Gateway Management Protocol),
        463–464
    SNMP (Simple Network Management Protocol),
        391–394, 464–469, 483–484
        case study, 483–484
        Get and Get Next commands, 464, 465, 466–
            469, *467, 468*
        HP OpenView Network Node Manager (NNM)
            and, 471–472, *473*
        MIBs (Management Information Bases) and MIB
            trees, 466, *467,* 471, 472
        security issues, 391–394, *393*
    Network Node Manager (NNM), **471–472,** *473*
    network numbers, remapping in AppleTalk domains,
        301
    Network Processor Modules (NPMs), **138**
    network termination devices (NT1 and NT2), **318**
    Network Time Protocol (NTP), 394
    networks. *See also* local area network (LAN)
        technologies; wide area network (WAN)
        technologies
        Banyan Vines networks, 554
        broadcast multi-access networks, 172–173
        non-broadcast multi-access (NBMA) networks,
            162–163, 172–173
        physical layer problems, **505–510.** *See also*
            troubleshooting
            cables, **505,** *506*
        point-to-point networks, 172–173
    NFS (Network File System) protocol, 7
    9-pin to 9-pin null modem cable connections, 590
    9-pin to 25-pin 1-1 modem cable connections, 591
    9-pin to 25-pin null modem cable connections, 591
    900 ISDN routers, 129, *130*
    NLSP (NetWare Link Services Protocol), **183–186.** *See
        also* link-state routing protocols
        area-address command, 184
        configuring, 184–185
        cost metric value settings, 185
        defined, **183–184**
        enabling, 184
        ipx internal-network command, 184
        ipx ipxwan command and, 185
        ipx link-delay command, 185
        ipx maximum-hops command, 185
        ipx nlsp enable command, 184–185
        ipx nlsp metric command, 185
        ipx router nlsp command, 184
        ipx throughput command, 185
        ping ipx command and, 186
        show ipx route command and, 186
        updates, 183–184
        verifying NLSP operation, 186
    NNM (Network Node Manager), **471–472,** *473*
    no access-list command, 419
    no appletalk protocol command, 300
    no appletalk protocol eigrp command, 208–209
    no appletalk protocol rtmp command, 300
    no appletalk route-redistribution command, 209
    no auto-summary command, 196

no cdp enable command, 395
no cdp run command, 395
no debug all command, 219
no ip directed-broadcast command, 399–400
no ip domain-lookup command, 79
no ip http server command, 390
no ip inspect trafficlist in command, 570
no ip irdp command, 557
no ip routing command, 41
no ip source-route command, 400
no ip split-horizon command, 164
no ipx router rip command, 205–206, 369
no login command, 230
no network 9F command, 205
no ntp command, 394
no redistribute command, 207
no service finger command, 394
no service tcp-small-servers command, 395–396
no service udp-small-servers command, 395–396
no shutdown command, 276
NO_EXPORT, NO_ADVERTISE, and NO_EXPORT_
    SUBCONFED BGP communities, **560**
non-broadcast multi-access (NBMA) networks, 162–
    163, 172–173
non-connection-oriented protocols, **10–12**, *11, 12*
non-volatile RAM (NVRAM), 220
Notifications level in system logging, 453
Novell. *See also* IPX (Internet Packet Exchange)
        protocol
    object types, 272–273
NPMs (Network Processor Modules), **138**
NT1 and NT2 (network termination) devices, **318**
NTP (Network Time Protocol), 394
null interfaces, 405
null modem cable connections
    9-pin to 9-pin connections, 590
    9-pin to 25-pin connections, 591
NVRAM (non-volatile RAM), 220

O

object types in SAP packets, **272–273**
octets, **69**
100BaseFX Ethernet standard, 42–43
100BaseT4 Ethernet standard, 42–43
100BaseTX Ethernet standard, 41–43
1000 series Cisco routers, 94
Open Shortest Path First protocol. *See* OSPF
Open Systems Interconnection model. *See* OSI
opening a case with Technical Assistance Center, 540–
    541
OpenView
    HSRP (Hot Standby Router Protocol) and, *555*

Network Node Manager (NNM), 471–472, *473*
    Web site, *555*
operating system. *See* Internetwork Operating System
optical bypass switches, **53**, *53*
Organizational Unit Identifiers (OUIs), **34–35**
OSI (Open Systems Interconnection) model, **3–24, 26–
    27**
    Application layer, 4–5
    Data Link layer, 20–23, *20, 21, 22*
    defined, **3–4**, *4*
    encapsulation and, 23–24, *24*
    Logical Link Control (LLC) layer, 20, *20*
    lower layers, 8
    Media Access Control (MAC) layer, **20**, *20*
    Media Access Control (MAC) layer addresses, **22–23**
        bridges and, 39–40, *39*
        HSRP (Hot Standby Router Protocol) and, 548,
            553–554
        IPX addressing and, 84
    Network layer, 18–20, *19*
    Physical layer, 23
    Presentation layer, **5–7**
    Session layer, 7
    and switches versus routers, 26–27
    TCP/IP protocol suite and, 64, *64*
    Transport layer, **8–18**
        connection-oriented versus non-connection-
            oriented protocols, 10–12, *11, 12*
        flow control and, 12, *12*
        multiplexing, 16–18, *17*
        positive acknowledgment with retransmission,
            14–15, *15*
        windowing, 12–14, *13, 14*
    upper layers, 4
OSPF (Open Shortest Path First) protocol, **108–110,
    170–183, 189–190.** *See also* link-state routing
        protocols
    ABRs (Area Border Routers), 174
    administrative distance and, 148
    as an interior gateway routing protocol, 146
    areas, 173–174, 177–178
    ASBRs (Autonomous System Boundary Routers),
        177, 179–180
    autonomous systems (ASs) and, 175, 179
    AutoSummarize routes feature, 95
    BDRs (Backup Designated Routers), 110, 171, 172–
        173
    broadcast multi-access networks and, 172–173
    as a classless protocol, 147
    configuring, 174–180, *174, 179, 180*
    cost metric value settings, 176–177
    default route settings, 179–180
    default-information originate always command, 180

defined, **108–110**, *109*, **170**
DRs (Designated Routers), 110, 171, 172–173
enabling, 175
Hello interval case study, 189–190
Hello packets and, 171–172
hop count and, 99–101
how OSPF works, 108–110, *109*, 170–171
ip ospf cost command, 176
ip ospf hello-interval command, 189
ip ospf network point-to-multipoint command, 189–190
loopback interfaces, 174–175
LSAs (Link State Advertisements), 170, 179
LSUs (Link State Updates), 172
maintaining adjacencies, 171–173
non-broadcast multi-access (NBMA) networks and, 172–173
overview of, 108–110, *109*
point-to-point networks and, 172–173
redistribute command and, 179–180
RFCs (Requests for Comments), 190
versus RIP (Routing Information Protocol), 108
route redistribution and, 98–101, *99*, *100*, 179–180
router identification numbers (RIDs), 174–175
router ospf command, 175
show ip ospf command, 181–182
show ip ospf database command, 171, 182–183
show ip ospf interface command, 176–177
show ip ospf neighbor command, 183
show ip route command, 181
specifying interfaces, 175–176
SPF or Dijkstra's algorithm, 170, 174, 179, 182
stub areas, 172, 177–178
summarization settings, 174, 178–179, *179*
topological databases and, 170–171, 182–183
totally stubby areas, 178
verifying OSPF operation and configuration, 181–183
virtual links and, 109–110, *109*
OUIs (Organizational Unit Identifiers), **34–35**
out-of-band management, **94–95**
output SAPs, 279–280
outside local and outside global addresses, **79–80**
outsourcing of network management, 470

P

packets. *See also* frames
CBAC (Context-Based Access Control) and, 567, *567*
debug ip packet command, 257–258
dynamic packet filtering, 413–414
Hello packets, **171–172**

EIGRP protocol and, 193–194
Hello interval case study, 189–190
IP packet structure, 67–69, *68*
IPX packet structure, 83–84, *83*
object types in SAP packets, 272–273
packet-switched circuits, 56, 162
protocol analyzers and, 503–505
RARP (Reverse Address Resolution Protocol) packets, 514
TTL (Time to Live) values, 492–494, *493*, *494*
UDP packets and extended access lists, 409–410, *410*
PAP (Password Authentication Protocol), **58**, *58*
passive-interface command, 155
passwords, **58**, **227–231**, **384–385**, **387**, **581–584**. *See also* security
console passwords, 384–385
disabling, 230
encrypting, 230
no login command and, 230
PAP (Password Authentication Protocol), 58
Privileged Exec mode and, 229–230
recovering and resetting, **581–584**
in 1003, 4500, 3600, and 2600 series routers, 583–584
in 2000, 2500, 3000, 4000, 7000, and AGS series routers, 481–483
security considerations, 229–230
service password-encrypt command, 230
setting console password, 228–229
setting enable password, 230, 231
setting enable secret password, 230–231
setting up local usernames and passwords, 387
setting vty password, 227–228, 230
User Exec mode and, 228, 229
username password command, 387
PAT (Port Address Translation), **81**
permanent virtual circuits (PVCs), **56**, **61**, **427**, 516–518
permit any any command, 414, 418
Phase 1 versus Phase 2 AppleTalk protocols, 87
Phase I and Phase II Firewall feature set versions, 564–565
phone numbers for Technical Assistance Center, 538–540
Physical layer of OSI model, **23**
physical layer problems, 505–510. *See also* troubleshooting
cables, 505, *506*
error counters and, 507–509
replacing hubs with switches, 507–508
with show controllers command, 509–510
with show interface command, 506–507
physically swapping out routers, **530**

ping commands
    advanced ping techniques, 250–251
    and classless routing with RIPv2, 167–168
    extended ping command, 251–252, 267–268, 489–
        490
    IP name resolution and, 78
    ping apple command, 310–311
    ping and ICMP (Internetwork Control Message
        Protocol), 248–250
    ping ipx command, 186, 286–287, 490–492, 519–
        520
    troubleshooting with, **488–492**
        example, 488–489
        IPX ping case study, 519–520
pinhole congestion, **211**
pinouts. *See* cabling, cable pinouts
planning. *See also* network design
    disaster recovery, 523–524
point-to-point networks, 172–173
Point-to-Point Protocol (PPP), **57–60**, *58, 59*
ports
    dynamic port mapping feature in CBAC, 572
    Port Address Translation (PAT), 81
    port monitor ports, 505
    port speed in Frame Relay networks, 361
    SPANs (switch port analyzers), 505
    telnetting to chargen port of routers, 397–398
    well-known ports, 16–18
positive acknowledgment with retransmission, **14–15,**
    15
post office system in IDS, 575–576
power outages, 220
power supply redundancy, 525
PPP (Point-to-Point Protocol), **57–60**, *58, 59*
Presentation layer of OSI model, 5–7
    data compression and, 6
    defined, **5**
    encryption and, 7
    little endian versus big endian data storage, 6
preventing
    Denial of Service (DoS) attacks, 571
    SMTP (Simple Mail Transfer Protocol) attacks, 572–
        573
Primary Rate Interface (PRI), **320–321**. *See also* ISDN
    B channels and, 320
    configuring, 321
    defined, **320**
    isdn switch-type primary command, 321
primary routes, **194**
prioritizing traffic. *See* traffic prioritization
priority group command, 349
priority levels in Technical Assistance Center, 541–542
priority queuing algorithm, **347–351**

private IP addresses, 77
Privileged Exec mode, **219–220, 229–230**
product groupings in Technical Assistance Center, 541
profiles. *See* Dial-on-Demand Routing (DDR), dialer
    profiles
promiscuous mode in Remote Network Monitor, 481
prompts. *See also* commands; Internetwork Operating
    System
    Router(config-router)# prompt, 156, 195
    Router_name# prompt, 219
    Router_name> prompt, 219
    Router(router-config)# prompt, 149
protecting networks without firewalls, 421–425, *422*
protocol analyzers, **502–505**
protocols. *See also* AppleTalk protocols; distance-vector
    routing protocols; EIGRP; HSRP; IPX; IRDP; link-
    state routing protocols; OSPF; SNMP; TCP/IP
    protocol suite
    ARP (Address Resolution Protocol, **496–497**
        ProxyARP (Address Resolution Protocol), 548
    AutoSummarize routes feature, 98
    BGP (Border Gateway Protocol), 146
    CDP (Cisco Discovery Protocol), **246, 394–395,**
        497–499
    CHAP (Challenge Handshake Authentication
        Protocol), 58–59, *59*
    classfull versus classless routing protocols, 146–147,
        147
    CMIP over TCP/IP (Common Management
        Information Protocol over TCP/IP), 464
    connection-oriented versus non-connection-oriented
        protocols, 10–12, *11, 12*
    DECnet, 554
    DHCP (Dynamic Host Configuration Protocol)
        defined, **266**
        versus HSRP (Hot Standby Router Protocol), 548
    DNA SCP (Digital Network Architecture, Session
        Control Protocol), 7
    Easy IP, 82
    EGP (Exterior Gateway Protocol), 146
    FTP (File Transfer Protocol), 343
    HDLC (High-Level Data Link Control), 56–57, *57*
    interior versus exterior gateway routing protocols,
        146
    NAT (Network Address Translation), 77, 79–82
    NFS (Network File System), 7
    NTP (Network Time Protocol), 394
    PAP (Password Authentication Protocol), 58
    PPP (Point-to-Point Protocol), 57–60, *58, 59*
    RARP (Reverse Address Resolution Protocol), 514
    selecting routing protocols, 106–112
    Session-layer protocols, 7

SMTP (Simple Mail Transfer Protocol) attacks, 572–573

SNMP (Simple Network Management Protocol), 391–394, *393*

STP (Spanning Tree Protocol), 40, 507, 521–522

traffic prioritization with, 342–343, *343*

Transport layer protocol classes, 8–10

XNS, 554

ProxyARP (Address Resolution Protocol), 548

PSH flag in TCP headers, 406

PVCs (permanent virtual circuits), **56, 61, 427,** 516–518

Q

question mark (?) command, 221–222, 304–305, 312–313

queuing algorithms, **344–356, 378–379.** *See also* traffic prioritization

case study, **378–379,** *378*

custom queuing, 351–356, *351*

priority queuing, 347–351

queue-limit command, 349

queue-list command, 353–354

selecting, 344–345, *345*

weighted fair queuing, 345–347

R

R reference point in ISDN, **318**

RADIUS (Remote Authentication Dial-In User Service), 94–95

RAM. *See* memory

random-detect command, 358–359

RARP (Reverse Address Resolution Protocol), 514

rate-limit command, 359

real-time alerts in CBAC, 571–572

recovering passwords, **581–584.** *See also* disaster recovery

in 1003, 4500, 3600, and 2600 series routers, 583–584

in 2000, 2500, 3000, 4000, 7000, and AGS series routers, 481–483

redistribution of routes

defined, **98–101,** *99, 100*

EIGRP protocol and, 101, 192, 207, 209

no redistribute command, 207

OSPF protocol and, 179–180

reducing hop count in AppleTalk domains, 301–302

redundancy

hardware redundancy, **525–526.** *See also* disaster recovery

in Cisco 7000 series routers, 525

in Cisco 12000 series routers, *525–526*

redundant power supplies, *525*

redundant links between AppleTalk domains, 302

redundant paths, 114, 115

reference points in ISDN, **318**

reliability calculations for IGRP protocol, 158

remapping network numbers in AppleTalk domains, 301

remote access VPN topology, 428–429, *428, 429*

Remote Authentication Dial-In User Service (RADIUS), 94–95

remote loopback mode of CSU/DSUs, **512–513,** *512*

Remote Network Monitoring (RMON), **480–482**

Remote Procedure Calls (RPCs), 7

repeaters, 37, 38–39

replacing. *See also* backing up

hubs with switches, 507–508

router configurations, **533–537**

with Copy and Paste commands, 533–535, *534, 535*

HyperTerminal and, 534–535, *534, 535*

router images with copy tftp flash, 530–531

Requests for Comments (RFCs)

on ICMP (Internetwork Control Message Protocol), 248

for OSPF protocol, 190

on Remote Network Monitor (RMON), 480

on SNMP (Simple Network Management Protocol), 464

resetting passwords, **581–584**

in 1003, 4500, 3600, and 2600 series routers, 583–584

in 2000, 2500, 3000, 4000, 7000, and AGS series routers, 481–483

Resign messages in HSRP protocol, 549

resolving IP addresses, **78–79**

response symbols in IP and IPX ping commands, 490–492

RFCs. *See* Requests for Comments

RIDs (router identification numbers), 174–175

RIF (Routing Information Field) in Information/Control frame, 48, *48,* 50–52, *51*

RIP (Routing Information Protocol), **98–101, 106–108, 146,** 148–155. *See also* distance-vector routing protocols

administrative distance and, 148

as an interior gateway routing protocol, 146

AutoSummarize routes feature, 95, 154

changing value of default timers, 150–151

classfull versus classless protocols and, 147

classless routing with RIPv2 case study, 167–168

configuring, 149–152, *149*

configuring RIPv2, 153–155

debug ip rip command and, 151–152, 153–154
defined, **106–108**, *107, 108,* **148**
versus EIGRP protocol, 110–111
enabling, 149
hop count and, 99–101, 148
versus HSRP (Hot Standby Router Protocol), 548
versus IGRP (Interior Gateway Routing Protocol),
    158–160
IPX RIP protocol, **271–272, 369–370**
    disabling for EIGRP routing, 112, 205–206
versus OSPF protocol, 108
passive-interface command and, 155
RIPv2 (RIP version 2), 147, 152–155, 167–168
route redistribution and, 98–101, *99, 100*
router rip command and, 149
RTMP (Routing Table Maintenance Protocol) or
    Apple RIP
    and configuring AppleTalk, 87, 88, 297, 299–
        300
    disabling, 300
    no appletalk protocol rtmp command, 300
show ip protocols command and, 149–150
specifying interfaces, 149, *149*
split horizon and, 148
timers basic command, 150–151
verifying RIP configuration, 149–150
version 2 command and, 153
RMON (Remote Network Monitoring), **480–482**
ROM Monitor mode, **218**
route backup with static routing, 264–265, *264*
route redistribution
    defined, **98–101,** *99, 100*
    EIGRP protocol and, 101, 192, 207, 209
    no redistribute command, 207
    OSPF protocol and, 179–180
route summarization
    defined, **95–98,** *96, 97*
    OSPF settings, 174, 178–179, *179*
route-map com_attrib_access-list command, 561
router commands
    copy running-config startup-config, 221
    router bgp, 561
    router eigrp, 195
    router igrp, 156
    router isis, 187, 188
    router ospf, 175
    router rip, 149
router console
    console cable pinouts, 590
    console logging in IDS, 576
    console password, 228–229
    copying Internetwork Operating System image from
        console, 531–533
    requirements, 532

router management, **453–463.** *See also* network
        management
    commands, **457–463**
    overview of, 451–452
    system logging (syslog), **452–457**
Router Software Loader (CPSWInst utility), 234–237
Router(config-router)# prompt, 156, 195
Router_name# prompt, 219
Router_name> prompt, 219
Router(router-config)# prompt, 149
routers, **216–231.** *See also* Cisco routers; Internetwork
        Operating System
    ABRs (Area Border Routers), 174
    access routers, 93–94
    active-forwarder routers, 549
    applying standard access lists to, 404
    ASBRs (Autonomous System Boundary Routers),
        177, 179–180
    BDRs (Backup Designated Routers), 110, 171, 172–
        173
    boot sequence, 216, *217*
    configuration backup, **528–530**
        with Cut and Paste commands, 528–529, *529*
        HyperTerminal and, 529, *529*
    configuration replacement, **533–537**
        with Copy and Paste commands, 533–535, *534,
            535*
        HyperTerminal and, 534–535, *534, 535*
    configuring, **220–221, 223–227, 543–546**
        in Virtual Private Networks, 435–440
    core routers, 91–93, *92,* 121–128
    Data Link layer and, 21–23, *22*
    distribution routers, 93
    DRs (Designated Routers), 110, 171, 172–173
    as Layer 3 devices, 26
    level 1 and level 2 routers, 187
    MAC addresses and, 22–23
    overview of, 215
    RAM requirements, 105–106
    router advertisements and router solicitations, 556
    router identification numbers (RIDs), 174–175
    router image
        backing up with copy flash tftp command, 526–
            528
        replacing with copy tftp flash, 530–531
    router modes, **217–222**
        Privileged Exec mode, 219–220, 229–230
        User Exec mode, 218–219, 228, 229
    router setup in TCP/IP networks, **245–248**
    security, **384–400, 445–449**
        case study, 445–449, *445*
        directed broadcasts, 398–400, *399*
        Smurf attacks, 398–400, *399*

SNMP (Simple Network Management Protocol), 391–394, *393*
seed routers, 299
selecting, 105–106
software failure, **531–533**
spare router configuration case study, **543–546**
standby-routers, 549
swapping out, **530**
versus switches, 25–27, *25*
routing. *See also* Dial-on-Demand Routing
  configuring IP routing, 78
  configuring IPX routing, 85–86, 275–276, 292–293
  IP source routing, 400
  OSI model and, 26
  Routing Information Field (RIF) in Information/
    Control frame, 48, *48*, 50–52, *51*
  RTMP (Routing Table Maintenance Protocol) or
    Apple RIP
    and configuring AppleTalk, 87, 88, 297, 299–
      300
    disabling, 300
    no appletalk protocol rtmp command, 300
  selecting routing protocols, 106–112
  snapshot routing, **333–335**
  source routing, 400
  static routing, **262–265**
    advantages of, 262–264, *263*
    establishing static routes for Dial-on-Demand
      Routing, 322
    ip route command and, 263, 264, 265
    for route backup, 264–265, *264*
  versus switching, 25–27, *25*
  to null interfaces, 405
Routing Information Protocol. *See* RIP
routing protocols. *See also* distance-vector routing
    protocols; link-state routing protocols
  classfull versus classless routing protocols, 146–147,
    147
  interior versus exterior gateway routing protocols,
    146
  selecting, 106–112
RPCs (Remote Procedure Calls), 7
RST flag in TCP headers, 406
RTMP (Routing Table Maintenance Protocol) or Apple
    RIP
  and configuring AppleTalk, 87, 88, 297, 299–300
  disabling, 300
  no appletalk protocol rtmp command, 300
rules
  5-4-3 rule in Ethernet standard, 37
  applying CBAC inspection rules to interfaces, 569–
    570
  audit rules in IDS, **574**

applying, 578
configuring, 576–578
running configurations
  diconfig files and, 224
  saving, 221
rxboot mode, **218**

S

S reference point in ISDN, **318**
SAP (Service Advertising Protocol), **272–273**, **365–369,**
  370–373, 380–381. *See also* IPX (Internet Packet
  Exchange) protocol
  access-list command and, 278–279
  configuring SAP update interval, 367–368, *368*
  debug ipx sap activity command, 288
  defined, **272–273**
  filtering SAPs, 278–280, 372–373, 380–381
  Get Nearest Server (GNS) requests, **273–274, 373–**
    377
    GNS filters, 376–377, *376*
    ipx gns-round-robin command, 277, 374–375,
      375
    ipx output-gns-filter command, 376–377, *376*
    sending, 373–377, *375*, *376*
  ipx sap-incremental eigrp command, 206–207, 371–
    372
  ipx sap-multiplier command, 367–368
  ipx update interval sap command, 367
  ipx update sap-after-rip command, 369
  object types in SAP packets, 272–273
  SAP broadcast problems, 365–367, *366*
  SAP tables, 272
  SAP updates, 272–273
  sending incremental SAP updates with EIGRP
    protocol, 111, *111*, 206–207, 370–372, *371*
SAPs (Service Access Points), **33–34**
SASs (single-attached stations), **52**
saving router configurations, 220–221
scalable networks, **90–94.** *See also* network design
  access routers and, 93–94
  core routers and, 91–93, *92*
  defined, **90**, *91*
  distribution routers and, 93
scripts, setup scripts, 223
secondary IP addresses, **261–262**, *261*
security, 58, **227–231, 383–400, 445–449.** *See also*
    access lists; Virtual Private Networks
  overview of, 383–384
  password recovery and resetting, **581–584**
    in 1003, 4500, 3600, and 2600 series routers,
      583–584
    in 2000, 2500, 3000, 4000, 7000, and AGS series
      routers, 481–483

passwords, **58**, **227–231**, **384–385**, 387, 581–584
router security, **384–400**, **445–449**
case study, 445–449, *445*
directed broadcasts, 398–400, *399*
Smurf attacks, 398–400, *399*
SNMP (Simple Network Management Protocol), 391–394, *393*
in Virtual Private Networks, 427–429, *428*, *429*
seed routers, **299**
segment headers in TCP protocol, 65–66, *65*, 406–408, *407*
segmentation devices, 39
selecting
alternate routing protocols in AppleTalk networks, 299–300
interfaces in CBAC for inspecting packets, 567, *567*
IP addresses, 260
queuing algorithms, 344–345, *345*
routers, 105–106
routing protocols, 106–112
system logging levels, 452–453
sending
e-mail to Technical Assistance Center, 538
Get Nearest Server (GNS) requests, 373–377, *375*, *376*
incremental SAP updates with EIGRP protocol, 111, *111*, 206–207, 370–372, *371*
serial line problems, 511–513, *512*
servers
Get Nearest Server (GNS) requests, **273–274**
ipx gns-round-robin command, 277
sending, 373–377, *375*, *376*
HTTP servers, 390–391
internal network addresses for NetWare servers, 276
setting up syslog servers, 455–457
show ipx servers command, 284–285, 365
snapshot server command, 333–334
Service Access Points (SAPs), **33–34**
Service Advertising Protocol. *See* SAP
service config command, 226–227
service password-encrypt command, 230
Service Provider IDs (SPIDs), **320**
service security problems, 394–398
service timestamps log uptime command, 454
Session layer of OSI model, **7**
Set commands in SNMP protocol, 464, 465
setting. *See also* configuring
BGP community attributes, 560–561
console password, 228–229
enable password, 230, 231
enable secret password, 230–231
inside and outside interfaces in Network Address Translation, 441–442
vty password, 227–228, 230

setting up. *See also* configuring
local usernames and passwords, 387
Network Address Translation parameters, 442–443
routers in TCP/IP networks, **245–248**
syslog servers, 455–457
setup scripts for configuring routers, 223
1700 modular access routers, 131–132, *132*
7000 series routers, **93**, **105**, **122–128**, **581–583**
7100 VPN router, 123–124, *124*, *125*
7200 Multifunction Platform router, 125–126, *126*
7206VXR router, 126, *126*
7500 series routers, 127–128, *128*
hardware redundancy in, *525*
network design and, 93, 105
overview of, 122
recovering and resetting passwords, 581–583
SGMP (Simple Gateway Management Protocol), **463–464**
show commands
show appletalk ?, 304–305
show appletalk arp, 308
show appletalk domain, 311
show appletalk globals, 308
show appletalk interface, 307
show appletalk route, 305–306
show appletalk traffic, 308–310
show appletalk zone, 306–307
show arp, 496–497
show cdp neighbors, 498–499
show controllers, 509–510
show crypto ipsec, 434
show crypto map, 434
show dialer, 329–330
show environment, 462–463
show frame-relay lmi, 514–515
show frame-relay map, 515–516
show frame-relay pvc, 516–518
show interface command
in FDDI networks, 53–54
for monitoring routers, 460–461
troubleshooting network physical layer problems with, 506–507
troubleshooting telecommunication lines with, 510–511
verifying Dial-on-Demand Routing, 331–332
viewing traffic queuing algorithms, 355–356
show interfaces command
for Dial-on-Demand Routing (DDR), 332–333
for IGRP protocol, 158
show ip access-lists, 413–414, 417–418
show ip eigrp interfaces, 202–203
show ip eigrp routing, 199–201
show ip eigrp topology summary, 203–204
show ip eigrp traffic, 203

show ip interface, 163–164
show ip irdp, 558
show ip ospf, 181–182
show ip ospf database, 171, 182–183
show ip ospf interface, 176–177
show ip ospf neighbor, 183
show ip protocols command
    for EIGRP protocol, 197–199
    for IGRP protocol, 161–162
    for RIP protocol, 149–150
show ip route command
    for IGRP protocol, 160–161
    for OSPF protocol, 181
show ipx access-list, 285
show ipx commands listed, 286
show ipx interface, 281–282
show ipx route, 186, 280–281
show ipx servers, 284–285, 365
show ipx servers unfiltered, 373
show ipx traffic, 283–284
show isdn active, 330
show isdn status, 330–331
show logging, 453–454, 455
show processes, 458–459
show processes cpu, 459–460
show processes memory, 459
show queue, 346–347
show queuing custom, 354
show run, 528–529, 535
show start, 528–529
show version, 233–234, 527
shutdown command, 276
Simple Gateway Management Protocol (SGMP), **463–464**
Simple Mail Transfer Protocol (SMTP) attacks, 572–573
Simple Network Management Protocol. *See* SNMP
Single Mode Fiber, 52, *55*
single-attached stations (SASs), **52**
1600 modular data routers, 131, *131*, 140–141, *141*
sizing networks, **103–112**. *See also* network design
    bandwidth requirements, 103–105
    Dial-on-Demand Routing (DDR) and, 104
    EIGRP (Enhanced Internet Gateway Routing Protocol), 110–112, *111*
    flash memory requirements, 105–106
    ISDN and, 104
    LAN bandwidth, 103
    leased lines and, 104
    OSPF (Open Shortest Path First) protocol, 108–110, *109*
    RIP (Routing Information Protocol), 106–108, *107*, *108*

router RAM requirements and, 105–106
    selecting routers, 105–106
    selecting routing protocols, 106–112
    WAN bandwidth, 103–105
small business routers, **129–139**
SMTP (Simple Mail Transfer Protocol) attack detection and prevention, 572–573
Smurf attacks, 398–400, *399*
SNAP (Sub-Network Access Protocol) frames, **34–35**, *35*, 85
snapshot routing, **333–335**. *See also* ISDN
    clear snapshot quiet-time command, 335
    configuring, 333–335
    defined, **333**
    dialer map snapshot command, 333–334
    snapshot client and snapshot server commands, 333–334
    troubleshooting, 335
SNMP (Simple Network Management Protocol), **391–394, 464–469, 483–484**. *See also* network management
    case study, 483–484
    defined, **464–465**
    Get and Get Next commands, 464, 465, 466–469, *467, 468*
    HP OpenView Network Node Manager (NNM) and, 471–472, *473*
    Management Stations versus Management Agents, 464
    MIBs (Management Information Bases) and MIB trees, 466, 467, 471, 472
    RFCs (Requests for Comments), 464
    security issues, 391–394, *393*
    Set commands, 464, 465
    snmp server enable traps command, 465–466
    snmp-server community command, 391–392, 468
    snmpwalk command, 466–468, 469
    system uptime metric, 468–469
    traps, 464–466
sockets, IPX socket numbers, 425–426
software failure, **531–533**. *See also* disaster recovery; utilities
    console requirements, 532
    copying Internetwork Operating System image from console, 531–533
    xmodem command and, 532–533
Source Route Bridging (SRB), **48**, 49–52, *50, 51*
source routing, 400
Source SAPs (SSAPs), **33–34**, *34*
Spanning Tree Protocol (STP), 40, 507, 521–522
spare router configuration case study, **543–546**
speaking-and-listening state in HSRP protocol, 549–550

specifying interfaces
    in EIGRP configuration, 195
    in OSPF configuration, 175–176
    in RIP configuration, 149, *149*
SPF algorithm, 170, 174, 179, 182
SPIDs (Service Provider IDs), **320**
split horizon technique, 148, **162–165**, *163*, *165*, 195
SQL (Structured Query Language), 7
SRB (Source Route Bridging), 48, **49–52**, *50*, *51*
SSAPs (Source SAPs), **33–34**, *34*
standard access lists, **401–405**. *See also* access lists
    access list numbers and, 402
    applying to routers, 404
    blocking data with, 403–405, *404*
    defined, **401**, 402–403, *403*
standby command in HSRP protocol, 553
standby-routers, **549**
Starting Delimiter field in tokens, 47–48, *47*
startup sequence for routers, **216**, *217*
static address translation, **440**, 441–443, **444**
static node discovery in AppleTalk networks, 298
static packet filtering, **406–410**, *407*, *408*, *410*
static routing, **262–265**
    advantages of, 262–264, *263*
    establishing static routes for Dial-on-Demand
        Routing, 322
    ip route command and, 263, 264, 265
    for route backup, 264–265, *264*
STP (Spanning Tree Protocol), 40, 507, 521–522
Structured Query Language (SQL), 7
stub areas in OSPF protocol, **172**, **177–178**
Sub-Network Access Protocol (SNAP) frames, **34–35**,
    35, 85
subnet masks
    defined, **73–75**
    EIGRP protocol and, 192
    in router configuration setup, 223
subnetting, **75–77**
successors, **194**
summarization of routes
    defined, **95–98**, *96*, *97*
    OSPF settings, 174, 178–179, *179*
support. *See* Technical Assistance Center
SVCs (switched virtual circuits), **56**, **427**
swapping out routers, **530**
switched virtual circuits (SVCs), **56**, **427**
switches
    Frame Relay switches, 513–514
    identifying ISDN switch types, 319–320
    as Layer 2 devices, 26
    Layer 3 switches, 26–27
    Multi Switch Feature Card (MSFC), 93
    port monitor ports, 505

    protocol analyzers and, 505
    replacing hubs with, 507–508
    versus routers, 25–27, *25*
    SPANs (switch port analyzers), 505
switching
    circuit-switched circuits, 55–56
    Layer 3 switching, 26–27
    OSI model and, 26–27
    packet-switched circuits, 56, 162
    versus routing, 25–27, *25*
switching between User Exec mode and Privileged Exec
    mode, 219
SYN flag in TCP headers, 406–408, *407*
system downtime costs, 524
system logging (syslog), **452–457**
    buffered logging, 452–455, 456–457
    logging buffered command, 452–453
    logging facility local6 command, 456
    selecting logging levels, 452–453
    service timestamps log uptime command, 454
    setting up syslog servers, 455–457
    show logging command, 453–454, *455*
    time stamping log messages, 453–455
system uptime in SNMP protocol, 468–469

T

T reference point in ISDN, **318**
tables. *See also* RTMP (Routing Table Maintenance
    Protocol)
    host tables, 79
    neighbors tables in EIGRP protocol, 193–194, *194*
    SAP tables, 272
TAC. *See* Technical Assistance Center
TACACS (Terminal Access Controller Access Control
    System), **387–391**
TAs (terminal adapters), **318**
TCP/IP protocol suite, **11**, **16–17**, **63–82**, **241–270**. *See
    also* IP access lists; IP addresses; ip commands; IP
    (Internet Protocol)
    case studies, **267–270**
    changing IP addressing schemes, **260–262**, *261*
    CMIP over TCP/IP (Common Management
        Information Protocol over TCP/IP), 464
    debug commands for TCP/IP networks, **255–260**
    defined, **63**
    DHCP (Dynamic Host Configuration Protocol), **266**
        versus HSRP (Hot Standby Router Protocol), 548
    diagramming TCP/IP networks, **241–244**
        with NetSuite software, 242, *243*
        with Visio software, 242, *243*
    history of, 63
    OSI model and, 64, *64*

router setup in TCP/IP networks, **245–248**
static routing, **262–265**
    advantages of, 262–264, *263*
    for route backup, 264–265, *264*
TCP (Transmission Control Protocol), **11, 16–17, 64–66, 406–408**
    as a connection-oriented protocol, 11, *11*
    multiplexing and, 16–17, *17*
    TCP segment headers, 65–66, *65*, 406–408, *407*
    three-way handshake, 11, *11*, 406–408, *407*
    testing IP connectivity, **248–255**
    with extended ping command, 251–252, 267–268, 489–490
UDP (User Datagram Protocol)
    as a connectionless protocol, 64
    debug ip udp command, 259–260
    defined, **67**, *67*
    DHCP protocol and, 266
    enabling UDP broadcast forwarding, 266
    extended access lists and, 409–410, *410*
    ip forward-protocol udp command, 266
    ip helper-address command and, 266
WRED (Weighted Random Early Detection)
    mechanism and, 356–360, *358*
TE1 and TE2 (terminal equipment) devices, **317–318**
Technical Assistance Center (TAC), **537–542**. *See also* disaster recovery
    customer support product groups, 541
    escalating calls, 542
    gathering information before contacting, 537
    how TAC works, 540–542
    opening a case, 540–541
    priority levels, 541–542
    sending e-mail, 538
    telephone numbers, 538–540
    Web support, 537–538
telecommunication line problems, **510–511**
telephone numbers for Technical Assistance Center, 538–540
Telnet
    access banners, 386–387
    access lists and, 386
    IP name resolution and, 78
    network management and, 95
    router security and, 385–387
    telnet monitor command, 502
    telnetting to chargen port of routers, 397–398
    traffic prioritization and, 343
    viewing debug output from Telnet sessions, 502
10Base2 (Thinnet) Ethernet standard, 36, 37, *37*
10Base5 (Thicknet) standard, 36, *37*
Terminal Access Controller Access Control System (TACACS), **387–391**

terminal adapters (TAs), **318**
terminal equipment devices (TE1 and TE2), **317–318**
testing
    Frame Relay environments, 245–246
    IP connectivity, **248–255**
    with extended ping command, 251–252, 267–268, 489–490
TFTP (Trivial File Transfer Protocol)
    backing up Internetwork Operating System (IOS), 231–232
    backing up router configurations, 224–225
    configuring routers, 223–224
    copy flash tftp command, 231–232, 526–528
    copy run tftp command, 530
    copy tftp flash command, 237–238, 530–531
    copy tftp run and copy tftp start commands, 536–537
    tftp-server flash command, 239–240
    updating Internetwork Operating System with TFTP commands, 237–240, *239*
Thicknet (10Base5) standard, 36, *37*
Thinnet (10Base2) Ethernet standard, 36, 37, *37*
three-way handshake using TCP protocol, 11, *11*, 406–408, *407*
3000 series routers, 581–583
3600 modular voice/data routers, 93, 106, 135–136, *136*, 141, 583–584
MC3800 multiservice routers, 136–137, *137*
threshold settings in CBAC, 568–569
time stamping system log messages, 453–455
Time to Live (TTL) values, 492–494, *493*, *494*
timeout settings in CBAC, 568–569
timers basic command, 150–151
Token Ring networks, **46–52, 554**. *See also* local area network (LAN) technologies
    Active Monitor, 47
    Cisco router support for, 49
    defined, **46**
    early-token-release command, 49
    how Token Ring works, 46
    HSRP (Hot Standby Router Protocol) and, 554
    Information/Control frame, 48, *48*
    interface tokenring command, 49
    Source Route Bridging (SRB), 48, 49–52, *50*, *51*
    token bits, **46**
    Token Ring frame structure, 47–48, *47*, *48*
    Token Ring frames versus Ethernet frames, 48
    tokens, **46–47**, *47*
topological databases in OSPF protocol, 170–171, 182–183
topology mapping in HP OpenView Network Node Manager (NNM), 472, *473*
totally stubby areas in OSPF protocol, 178

trace commands
    extended trace command, 254–255
    testing IP connectivity with, 252–254
    trace ipx command, 287–288
traceroute command, **417, 492–496**. *See also* troubleshooting
    blocking with access lists, 417
    on Cisco routers, 495–496
    defined, **492**
    TTL (Time to Live) values and, 492–494, *493, 494*
traffic
    commands
        show appletalk traffic, 308–310
        show ip eigrp traffic, 203
        show ipx traffic, 283–284
        identifying interesting traffic for Dial-on-Demand
            Routing, 322
traffic prioritization, **341–381**. *See also* congestion
    commands
        conform, 359–360
        debug priority, 350–351
        exceed, 359–360
        fair-queue, 347
        priority group, 349
        queue-limit, 349
        queue-list, 353–354
        random-detect, 358–359
        rate-limit, 359
        show interface, 355–356
        show queue, 346–347
        show queuing custom, 354
    defined, **342**
    FIFO (first-in first-out) queuing and, 342
    Frame Relay traffic shaping (FRTS), **360–364**
    FTP (File Transfer Protocol) and, 343
    IPX traffic considerations, **365–377, 380–381**
        configuring SAP update interval, 367–368, *368*
        GNS filters, 376–377, *376*
        ipx gns-round-robin command, 374–375, *375*
        ipx output-gns-filter command, 376–377, *376*
        ipx sap-incremental eigrp command, 206–207,
            371–372
        SAP broadcast problems, 365–367, *366*
        SAP filtering case study, **380–381**, *380*
        sending Get Nearest Server (GNS) requests, 373–
            377, *375, 376*
        sending incremental SAP updates with EIGRP
            protocol, 111, *111,* 206–207, 370–372, *371*
    with protocols, 342–343, *343*
    queuing algorithms, **344–356, 378–379**
        case study, **378–379**, *378*
        custom queuing, 351–356, *351*
        selecting, 344–345, *345*

    Telnet and, 343
    uses for, 341
    when to use, 344
    WRED (Weighted Random Early Detection)
        mechanism, 356–360, *358*
transform sets in Virtual Private Networks, 432–435,
    433
Transmission Control Protocol. *See* TCP/IP protocol
    suite
transparent bridges
    Cisco routers as, 40–41
    IEEE 802.3 Ethernet standard and, 39–40, *39*
Transport layer of OSI model, **8–18**
    congestion and, 11–12
    connection-oriented versus non-connection-oriented
        protocols, 10–12, *11, 12*
    defined, **8**
    flow control and, 12, *12*
    multiplexing, 16–18, *17*
    positive acknowledgment with retransmission, 14–
        15, *15*
    protocol classes, 8–10
    windowing, 12–14, *13, 14*
transport mode in Virtual Private Networks, 433, *433*
traps
    Authorization Failure Traps in HSRP protocol, *555*
    in SNMP protocol, 464–466
troubleshooting, **485–487, 505–522**
    case studies, **519–522**
        broadcast storms, 521–522
        IPX problem, 519–520
    CSU/DSUs (channel service units/digital service
        units)
        and troubleshooting broadcast storms, 521
        and troubleshooting serial line problems, 511–
            513, *512*
    duplex mismatches, 45
    Frame Relay networks, **513–518**
        example, 513–514, *513*
    IGRP update problems, 158–159
    ISDN networks, 333
    network physical layer, **505–510**
        cables, 505, *506*
    overview of, 485–486
    priority queuing and, 349
    snapshot routing, 335
    telecommunication lines, 510–511
    troubleshooting philosophies, 486–487
troubleshooting tools, **488–505**
    ARP (Address Resolution Protocol), **496–497**
        ProxyARP (Address Resolution Protocol), 548
    CDP (Cisco Discovery Protocol), 497–499
    debug commands, 499–502

ping command, **488–492**
    IPX ping case study, 519–520
protocol analyzers, 502–505
traceroute command, **417**, **492–496**
    TTL (Time to Live) values and, 492–494, *493*, *494*
TTL (Time to Live) values, 492–494, *493*, *494*
tunneling
    AppleTalk, 302–304
        tunneling AppleTalk over IP case study, 315–316
    defined, **101–103**, *102*, **302**
    interface tunnel command, 303
    tunnel mode aurp command, 303
    tunnel mode in Virtual Private Networks, 433, *433*
    tunnel source and tunnel destination commands, 303
turning off. *See* disabling
turning on. *See* enabling
25-pin to 9-pin 1-1 modem cable connections, 591
25-pin to 9-pin null modem cable connections, 591
2000 series routers, 581–583
2500 fixed configuration data routers, 94, 133, *134*, 141–142, 581–583
2600 modular voice/data routers, 94, 105, 134–135, *134*, 583–584
12000 series routers
    12000 GSR series, 122
    12000 Terabit System, 122
    12012 GSR switch router, 122, *123*
    hardware redundancy in, 525–526
    network design and, 93

U

U reference point in ISDN, **318**
UDP (User Datagram Protocol)
    as a connectionless protocol, 64
    debug ip udp command, 259–260
    defined, **67**, *67*
    DHCP protocol and, 266
    enabling UDP broadcast forwarding, 266
    extended access lists and, 409–410, *410*
    ip forward-protocol udp command, 266
    ip helper-address command and, 266
undebug all command, 152
unshielded twisted-pair (UTP) cables, 38
unsuccessful ping commands, 492
updates
    EIGRP updates, 192
    IGRP updates, 158–159
    IPX RIP updates, 272, 369–370
    LSUs (Link State Updates), 172
    NLSP updates, 183–184
    SAP updates, 272–273

updating Internetwork Operating System, **232–240**
    with TFTP commands, 237–240, *239*
upgrades, forklift upgrades, **139**
upper layers of OSI model, **4**
URG flag in TCP headers, 406
User Datagram Protocol. *See* UDP
User Exec mode, **218–219**, **228**, **229**
utilities. *See also* commands
    CiscoView software, 473–475
    CiscoWorks 2000 CWSI Campus, **475–480**. *See also* network management
    CiscoWorks software, 473
    Config Maker, 225
    CPSWInst utility (Router Software Loader), 234–237
    FTP (File Transfer Protocol), 343
    HEMS (High Level Entity Management System), 464
    HP OpenView Network Node Manager (NNM), 471–472, *473*
    Microsoft NetShow, 573
    NetSuite software, 242, *243*
    Remote Network Monitoring (RMON), 480–482
    router software failure, **531–533**
    Telnet
        access banners, 386–387
        access lists and, 386
        IP name resolution and, 78
        network management and, *95*
        router security and, 385–387
        telnet monitor command, 502
        telnetting to chargen port of routers, 397–398
        traffic prioritization and, 343
        viewing debug output from Telnet sessions, 502
    TFTP (Trivial File Transfer Protocol)
        backing up Internetwork Operating System (IOS), 231–232
        backing up router configurations, 224–225
        configuring routers, 223–224
        copy flash tftp command, 231–232, 526–528
        copy run tftp command, 530
        copy tftp flash command, 237–238, 530–531
        copy tftp run and copy tftp start commands, 536–537
        tftp-server flash command, 239–240
        updating Internetwork Operating System with TFTP commands, 237–240, *239*
    Visio software, 242, *243*
UTP (unshielded twisted-pair) cables, 38

V

Vampire Taps, **36**
variance command, 160

verifying
      AppleTalk operation, **304–311**
      Dial-on-Demand Routing (DDR), **329–333**
      IP EIGRP routing, **197–204**
            overview of, 197, *197*
      IPX operation, **280–291**
            ping ipx command, 186, 286–287, 490–492,
                  519–520
            show ipx route command, 186, 280–281
      NLSP operation, 186
      OSPF operation and configuration, 181–183
      RIP configuration, 149–150
versions
      checking version of Internetwork Operating System,
            checking, 233–234
      show version command, 233–234
      version 2 command, 153
viewing
      debug output from Telnet sessions, 502
      IRDP protocol configuration settings, 558
virtual circuits
      in Frame Relay networks, 61, *61*
      permanent virtual circuits (PVCs), 56, 61, 427, 516–
            518
      switched virtual circuits (SVCs), 56, 427
virtual links, 109–110, *109*
Virtual Private Networks (VPNs), **123–124, 426–444**
      Cisco 7100 VPN router example, 123–124, *124, 125*
      configuring, **429–440**
            defining transform sets, 432–435, *433*
            overview of, 429, *430*
            tunnel mode versus transport mode, 433, *433*
      defined, **426–429**, *427, 428, 429*
      Frame Relay networks and, 427
      Network Address Translation (NAT), 77, **79–82**,
            440–444
      remote access VPN topology, 428–429, *428, 429*
      security issues, 427–429, *428, 429*
Visio software, 242, *243*
voice/data integration services, 126
VPNs. *See* Virtual Private Networks
VTY line security, 385–386
vty password, **227–228, 230**

W

Walk command in SNMP protocol, 466–468, 469
Warnings level in system logging, 453

Web sites
      Cisco Technical Assistance Center (TAC), 537–538
      HP OpenView, 555
      NetSuite software, 242
      Novell object types, 273
weighted fair queuing algorithm, **345–347**
Weighted Random Early Detection (WRED)
      mechanism, **356–360**, *358*
well-known ports, **16–18**
wide area network (WAN) technologies, **55–62**. *See also*
      Frame Relay networks; ISDN; local area network
      (LAN) technologies
      CHAP (Challenge Handshake Authentication
            Protocol), 58–59, *59*
      circuit-switched circuits, 55–56
      Dial-on-Demand Routing (DDR), 56, 104, 298
      DLCIs (Data Link Connection Identifiers), 61, *61,
            62*, 364, 514
      fault tolerance and, 115
      HDLC (High-Level Data Link Control) protocol,
            56–57, *57*
      leased lines, 55, 104
      packet-switched circuits, 56, 162
      PAP (Password Authentication Protocol), 58
      permanent virtual circuits (PVCs), 56, 61, 427, 516–
            518
      PPP (Point-to-Point Protocol), 57–60, *58, 59*
      switched virtual circuits (SVCs), 56, 427
      WAN bandwidth requirements, 103–105
windowing, **12–14**, *13, 14*
wrapping, **52–53**
WRED (Weighted Random Early Detection)
      mechanism, **356–360**, *358*

X

X.25 networks, 162, 298
xmodem command, 532–533
XNS protocol, 554

Z

zones in AppleTalk networks
      appletalk zone command, 297
      assigning, 297
      debug apple zip command, 314
      defined, **87**
      show appletalk zone command, 306–307

TAKE YOUR CAREER TO THE NEXT LEVEL

with 24seven books from Network Press

- This new series offers the advanced information you need to keep your systems and networks running 24 hours a day, seven days a week.
- On-the-job case studies provide solutions to real-world problems.
- Maximize your system's uptime—and go home at 5!
- $34.99; 7½" x 9"; 544–704 pages; softcover

Paul Robichaux
0-7821-2531-X

Craig Hunt
0-7821-2506-9

Gary Govanus
0-7821-2509-3

Matthew Strebe
0-7821-2529-8

John Hales, Nestor Reyes
0-7821-2593-X

GET CISCO CERTIFIED WITH THE EXPERTS!

**CCNA™: Cisco®
Certified Network Associate®
Study Guide, 2nd Edition**
0-7821-2647-2

**CCDP™: Cisco® Internetwork
Design Study Guide**
0-7821-2639-1

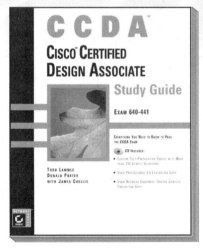

**CCDA™: Cisco® Certified Design
Associate Study Guide**
0-7821-2534-4

CISCO STUDY GUIDES FROM SYBEX

◆ Written by renowned author Todd Lammle and his team of expert authors

◆ Up-to-date, comprehensive coverage of the revised Cisco exams

◆ Hands-on and written labs, plus hundreds of sample questions

◆ Assessment tests and practice exams

◆ Two technical edits ensure accuracy and relevance of information

◆ 700-800 pp; 7.5x9; Hardcover; $49.99

CUTTING-EDGE TEST PREP SOFTWARE ON THE CD

Electronic Flashcards help reinforce key information

Custom Testing Engine simulates Cisco's test format

Bonus Exam assesses knowledge retention

Searchable Ebook allows readers to study anytime, anywhere

Bonus CD Content: *CCNA Virtual Lab e-trainer* demo, *Dictionary of Networking* Ebook, and software utilities!

Also available:

CCNP™: Support Study Guide • 0-7821-2713-4 • Summer 2000
CCNP: Remote Access Study Guide • 0-7821-2710-x • Summer 2000
CCNP: Switching Study Guide • 0-7821-2711-8 • Fall 2000
CCNP: Routing Study Guide • 0-7821-2712-6 • Fall 2000
CCIE™: Cisco® Certified Internetwork Expert Study Guide
0-7821-2657-X Summer 2000

www.sybex.com SYBEX®

Learn To...

Configure advanced IPX properties	**Chapter 11**
Configure a Service Advertisement Protocol (SAP) filter	**Chapter 11**
Configure AppleTalk cable ranges	**Chapter 12**
Configure AppleTalk zones	**Chapter 12**
Configure advance AppleTalk properties	**Chapter 12**
Configure legacy dial-on-demand routing (DDR)	**Chapter 13**
Configure dial backup with ISDN	**Chapter 13**
Configure dial backup for Frame Relay	**Chapter 13**
Choose a queuing strategy	**Chapter 14**
Configure custom queuing	**Chapter 14**
Configure priority queuing	**Chapter 14**
Configure weighted fair queuing	**Chapter 14**
Make a router a bastion host	**Chapter 15**
Create and test access lists	**Chapter 15**
Set up logging	**Chapter 15**
Set up a syslog server	**Chapter 15**
Set up a Terminal Access Controller Access Control System (TACACS) server	**Chapter 15**
Develop and implement a livable security policy	**Chapter 15**